Vatican City: Biblioteca Apostolica Vaticana, MS Vat. lat. 227, saec. XV (1444), membr., f. 4v.
©Biblioteca Apostolica Vaticana (Vatican Library).

Early Renaissance Invective
and
The Controversies of Antonio da Rho

by

David Rutherford

RENAISSANCE TEXT SERIES

VOLUME 19

THE RENAISSANCE SOCIETY OF AMERICA

Medieval and Renaissance Texts and Studies

Volume 301

© 2005 Renaissance Society of America, Inc.

Published by: Arizona Center for Medieval and Renaissance Texts and Studies,
PO Box 874402, Tempe, AZ 85287-4402.

MRTS Volume 301
Renaissance Text Series Volume 19

ISBN: 0-86698-345-7

Library of Congress Cataloging-in-Publication Data

Rutherford, David, 1952-
  Early Renaissance Invective and the Controversies of Antonio da Rho / by David Rutherford.
      p. cm. — (Renaissance text series ; v. 19) (Medieval and Renaissance texts and studies ; v. 301)
  Includes bibliographical references (p.).
  ISBN-13: 978-0-86698-345-7 (alk. paper)
  ISBN-10: 0-86698-345-7 (alk. paper)
  1. Antonio, da Rho, 15th cent.—Criticism and interpretation. 2. Invective, Latin (Roman and Renaissance)—Translations into English. 3. Antonio, da Rho, 15th cent.—Translations into English. 4. Satire, Latin (Medieval and modern)—History and criticism. 5. Invective—Italy—History—To 1500. 6. Cicero, Marcus Tullius—Influence. Jerome, Saint, Influence. 7. Invective in literature. 8. Humanists—Italy. 9. Invective—Italy. I. Antonio, da Rho, 15th cent. II. Title. III. Series. IV. Medieval & Renaissance Texts & Studies (Series) ; v. 301.

PA8450.A88Z86 2005
877'.04—dc22

2005021086

Digitally printed on acid-free paper by Yurchak Printing, Inc. of Lancaster, PA

For Susan

TABLE OF CONTENTS

I. Introduction 1

II. Editorial Procedure 41

III. Sigla 44

IV. Antonio da Rho, *Philippic against Antonio Panormita* 45
    Prologue 51
    The First Objection 61
    The Second Objection 77
    The Third Objection 105
    The Fourth Objection 125
    Peroration 187

V. Antonio da Rho, *Apology against a Certain Archdeacon and His Loathsome Sycophant Accomplices* 191

Appendix I : Antonio Panormita, *Etsi facile* (letter to Rho) 245

Appendix II : Antonio Panormita, *Litteras a te* (letter to Rho) 256

Appendix III : Antonio da Rho, *Etsi nonnullos* ("Anonymous Invective") 258

Appendix IV : Poetic Invectives (1429–33) 264

Appendix V : Pier Candido Decembrio, *Philippicam tuam* (letter to Rho) 277

Appendix VI : Pier Candido Decembrio, *Nouum profecto* (letter to Rho) 279

Appendix VII : Antonio Panormita, *De effigie Solis*
    Epistola ad Filippum Mariam Viscontem 285
    Oratio de Effigie Solis 287

Appendix VIII : Antonio da Rho, "Invectiva : Ubi 'Obloqui'"
Excerpta ex libro *Imitationum rhetoricarum* 300

Appendix IX : Antonio da Rho, "Words We Ought to Use only to Execrate Vice"
Excerpta ex libro *Imitationum rhetoricarum* 314

Bibliography 321

Index of Names and Topics 341

Index of Texts Cited 353

Index of Manuscripts 359

LIST OF ILLUSTRATIONS

Vatican City: Biblioteca Apostolica Vaticana, MS Vat. lat. 227,
  saec. XV (1444), membr., f. 4v ii
Milan: Biblioteca Ambrosiana, MS B 124 sup.,
  saec. XV^1, chart., f. 119r 48
Naples: Biblioteca Nazionale, MS VI.D.7,
  saec. XV^1, chart., f. 98r 49
Milan: Biblioteca Ambrosiana, MS M 49 sup.,
  saec. XV^1, membr., f. 16r 195

ACKNOWLEDGMENTS

Over the years many people have assisted me with this book in things great and small. I am deeply indebted and grateful to them, and not least for their encouragement, which kept me on course. Foremost among those to whom I am indebted is John Monfasani, whose generous contribution of time and effort made this book possible. Not only did he spend long hours working with me on Antonio da Rho's intractable Latin, but his humor and friendship did much to alleviate the seemingly interminable frustrations. I am also pleased to recognize the many improvements made possible by my readers for The Renaissance Society of America. Charles Fantazzi read the translations and proposed many refinements. He also saved me from some embarrassing lapses. The Introduction owes much to David Marsh for his many insightful suggestions. I am grateful to Erika Rummel and Charles Witke for reading and commenting on early drafts of the translations. And on many a pleasant summer evening Arthur Field submitted to being queried about opaque Latin phrases and other issues of humanistic culture. Silvia Fiaschi generously gave of her time and expertise to advise me on the technical aspects of the invective poetry in Appendix IV. I am most appreciative to Tim Krause, who contributed his consummate editorial skill to the whole.

At various times others have considered details or discussed aspects of this work with me and shared with me their erudition and wisdom about one matter or another. In this regard I especially thank Bob Black, Shane Butler, Charles Ebel, Riccardo Fubini, Doina Harsanyi, Anna Krzyszowska, Francisco Ortiz de La Renta, Kristen Lippincott, Roberta Morosini, Michèle Mulchahey, Bill North, John O'Malley, Pablo Ojeda O'Neill, Tom Roche, Michael Rocke, Ingrid Rowland, Tom Tentler, and Clarice Zdanski. My thanks also go to my colleagues Tom Benjamin, Eric Johnson, and Steve Scherer, who have encouraged and inspired me throughout. I acknowledge an enormous debt of gratitude to the late Rev. Edmund F. Miller, S.J. His enthusiasm for classical languages and history set me on a marvellous journey of discovery that I could never have imagined.

Several institutions and foundations have supported my research, translation, and writing. Early in the process The American Philosophical Society gave me a grant to work on the manuscripts and transcriptions. On more than one occasion I received support from my home institution, Central Michigan University, especially from the College of Humanities and Social and Behavioral Sciences and from Faculty Research and Creative Endeavors. Some work on this project was done while I was the Andrew W. Mellon Postdoctoral Fellow at the American Academy in Rome in 1996. Later years of summer residence in this *locus amoenus* proved especially useful: the Academy staff has my deepest appreciation. The Villa I Tatti, The Harvard University Center for Italian Renaissance Studies, has consistently supported and encouraged my work. I first proposed these texts for translation while I was there as the National Endowment for the Humanities Fellow in 1989–90. The staff of the Villa I Tatti has assisted me generously and graciously in ways I will never forget and could never repay, not least during the final stages of this work in my year of sabbatical (2003–04) and as Visiting Professor (2004–05).

INTRODUCTION

1. Return to Invective

Antonio da Rho (1395–1447), the author of the two works edited and translated here, acknowledged that his generation owed Francesco Petrarca "a great debt of gratitude" since they could now "follow the trail" of Ciceronian style "everywhere."[1] Rho might well have added that this stylistic debt to Petrarca included his having pointed out the trail to classical invective. For Petrarca's initial *Invective against a Physician* (1352) marked the first attempt since late antiquity to consciously employ classical rhetorical invective against an opponent. Petrarca followed with three other invectives against this physician before the exchange ended. He returned to the genre three more times in his *Invective against a Man of High Rank with No Knowledge or Virtue*, in his *On His Own Ignorance and That of Many Others*, and in his *Invective against a Detractor of Italy*.[2] Petrarca's recourse to this classical genre was unusual, but having chosen to take it up, he not surprisingly took his lead from the invectives exchanged by Cicero and Sallust and by Jerome and Rufinus. He also mentioned those exchanged by Aeschines and Demosthenes as further antecedents to the tradition, although he knew about these Greek examples only secondhand.[3]

Throughout the Middle Ages, to be sure, people did not shrink from attacking, insulting, cursing, and otherwise verbally abusing their enemies. The word "invective," coined in late antiquity, was variously used right through the Middle Ages.[4] Yet Peter Lombard's "Invective against those who say God can do nothing except what he wills"[5] indicates just how little affinity this work has with classical invective, for it is set in the scholastic *sic et non* tradition. Hence, few studies of medieval invective attempt to portray it as a continuation or revival of a classical genre, and they make virtually no references to classical authors and to surviving invective orations from antiquity, either genuine or spurious. Nor do these studies demonstrate a concern with or even an awareness of the theoretical passages on invective found in ancient rhetorical

---

[1] *Apology* §33. When not using Antonio da Rho's full name, I refer to him simply as "Rho" throughout to avoid confusing him with other Antonios, especially Antonio Panormita.

[2] Marsh 2003, viii–x; for texts and English translations, see Petrarca 2003.

[3] Petrarca *Against a Physician* 4.203; cf. Marsh 2003, xi. Scholarly debate continues, but the invectives of Cicero/Sallust are now usually regarded as spurious.

[4] See Ludwig 2001, 103; Ricci 407–08.

[5] Peter Lombard *Sentences* Book 4, Dist. 43.

manuals, such as Cicero's *On Invention*, the pseudo-Ciceronian *Rhetoric to Herennius*, and Quintilian's *The Education of the Orator*.[6]

When one reflects on the range of Renaissance literary ill humor, in both poetry and prose, that is loosely called "humanist invective," a few observations come to mind. First of all, most of it was written subsequent the two works considered here: Antonio da Rho's *Apology against a Certain Archdeacon and his Loathsome Sycophant Accomplices* (1427/28) and his *Philippic against Antonio Panormita* (1431/32). Among the antecedents that loom large, we find Petrarca's four invectives mentioned above and Lorenzo Marco de' Benvenuti's and Leonardo Bruni's invectives against Niccolò Niccoli at the beginning of the fifteenth century. Roughly contemporary with Rho's *Philippic*, Francesco Filelfo composed many of his one hundred *Satires*, some of which are in fact poetic invective and not satire.[7] These antecedents are summarized in Felice Vismara's *L'invettiva, arma preferita dagli Umanisti nelle lotte private, nelle polemiche letterarie, politiche e religiose*.[8] Vismara offers worthwhile insights into humanist invective, but his garbled information about Rho's *Apology* and *Philippic* mandates a clearly posted *caveat lector* for the whole of the book.[9] The appearance of good modern editions and translations of humanistic literature is now bringing the landscape of Renaissance invective into ever-sharper focus.

Ennio Rao, the editor of Bartolomeo Facio's *Invective against Lorenzo Valla*,[10] has raised a crucial question in a separate paper entitled "Humanistic Invective as a Literary Genre": "Is the humanistic invective to be considered a literary genre? or are we to demote the word *invective*, the sole title of so many humanistic works, to the status of an adjective, modifying (improbably) an implied noun, such as *oratio, satura, epistola*, etc.?"[11] Rao acknowledges the fifteenth-century return to the "threefold division of oratory" in the classical manuals and to the model invectives from antiquity mentioned above, as seen in Gasparino Barzizza's *On composition* (1423) and George of Trebizond's *Five Books on Rhetoric* (1435).[12] Although the most dramatic examples for the breakout of the form that Ennio Rao considers came not until the years between 1440 and 1455 in the polemics of Poggio Bracciolini and Lorenzo Valla, Rao thinks that the "treatise writers [were] not keeping pace with development in the material under their scrutiny."[13] In the end he concludes that like the "hodge-podge" called satire that the Romans claimed as uniquely theirs, "the

---

[6]See Beaumatin and Garcia. Cf. Ricci 407–08, who argues for a continuity of tradition from antiquity to the Renaissance, but does so based on continuous usage of the label "invective" and on the steady appearance of polemical literature. In his estimation, all polemical literature counts as "invective" regardless of whether it conformed in any way to classical standards of the rhetorical genre.

[7]Filelfo's *Satires* were mostly composed between 1430 and 1433, but they were not completed until 1449 (I thank Arthur Field for this information.) Filelfo wrote one of these (*Satyrae* 3.6) to Rho. See the critical edition and note by Silvia Fiaschi (Filelfo 170–76).

[8]Vismara 1900a; see also Voigt 1880, 443–52; 1888–97, 435–42.

[9]See n. 96 below.

[10]Facio 1978.

[11]Rao 1988–90, 265.

[12]Rao 1988–90, 265–66.

[13]Rao 1988–90, 266.

claim can be made for the humanists that they were the creators and practitioners of . . . a meta-genre" that included prose, verse, undelivered orations, open letters, philosophical treatises, dialogues, and commentaries.[14]

The question that Ennio Rao poses will find no definitive answer here, not least because Antonio da Rho's *Apology* and *Philippic* precede by a decade the proliferation of forms that Rao spoke of as taking place after 1440. Ennio Rao discusses how Jerome, for example, had shown the way to take invective from its judicial or deliberative setting, which at minimum imagined an oral delivery, and to give it a strictly literary form, mostly in letters.[15] But included in Jerome's invectives were quotation and commentary. Jerome had, we might say, already shown how to put "old wine in new skins." In quoting his enemies in order to demolish their thought, Jerome was often trying to establish that his enemy was a heretic. When the humanists quoted their enemies, they were not much worried about heresy.[16] They were instead pursuing the theme of *res externa* and the topic of *oratio inepta* as discussed below. Given that the humanists were driven to perfect their Latin style, with no little snobbery involved, it comes as no surprise that *oratio inepta* would loom large in their invectives. Antonio da Rho persistently turned to it in his *Philippic against Antonio Panormita*. In some instances, such as Lorenzo Valla's *Notations on the Errors of Antonio da Rho* (1447), this is the sum total of the invective.

One may ask why this specific subject, which was only one of the three themes and one of the ten or fifteen possible topics, constitutes a break with the genre or the creation of a new genre? My own inclination is to regard what the humanists were doing as a maturation of the genre of classical invective as had Jerome in shifting it from oration to letter. I also regard poetic invective as a separate tradition (and a distinct genre) going back at least to Ovid and including Claudian. When we look at the work of the Renaissance humanists and consider its deviation from the classical genres, another factor to consider is how well any given humanist understood invective and its *lex operis*. In any case, changed cultural circumstances and sensibilities can to some degree explain the variance. After all, the humanists, try as they might to refine their sensibilities for things classical, were not ancient Romans who would be instinctively put off by novelties resulting from literary ineptitude or lack of cultural refinement. Maybe Henri-Jean Martin's observation in *The History and Power of Writing* (1994) applies here. He argues that great centers of civilization have shown little need to modify a system of writing. It is instead on the edges of or during the breakdowns of these civilizations that one finds the change. As Martin puts it: "'progress' — or efficiency — was the province of newcomers and 'barbarians.'"[17] But before examining the historical milieu of the two works edited and translated here, we must first discuss invective as a genre developed in antiquity.

---

[14]Rao 1988–90, 266.

[15]Rao 1988–90, 264.

[16]A rare exception is Rho's feeble attempt to turn Panormita into another Helvidius (*Philippic* §100). Another might be found in the accusations against Lorenzo Valla in 1440–41 while he was in the employ of Alfonso V of Aragon (Valla 1970, 9).

[17]Martin 507–08.

2. Invective as a Genre

Romans largely accepted Aristotle's division of rhetoric into three genres: (1) forensic, dealing with legal prosecution and defense, (2) deliberative, arguing for or against political decisions, and (3) epideictic or declamatory, a social display of praise and blame.[18] Rhetorical invective, the blame element of epideictic oratory, was known to the Romans as *vituperatio* or (more rarely) as *invectio*.[19] (The other terms applied to it, *maledictum* and *convicium*, are discussed below.) The word *invectiva* did not come into use until late antiquity.[20] Other classifications of rhetorical genres existed in antiquity, but the influential rhetorical manuals such as Cicero's *On Invention*, the pseudo-Ciceronian *Rhetoric to Herennius*, and Quintilian's *The Education of the Orator* accepted Aristotle's division. The rationale for classifying rhetoric into these three genres was not immediately obvious to Romans. As Quintilian admitted, subsuming all of rhetoric under three headings required him to explain "the reason that led earlier writers to restrict a subject of such variety to such narrow bounds."[21] For unlike the Greeks, the Romans were not accustomed to making eulogies and instead made the greatest use of epideictic oratory in a forensic context. Cicero had earlier acknowledged this anomaly, stating that praise and blame (*laus* and *vituperatio*) could be deployed in every kind of rhetoric (*in omni genere causarum*).[22]

The use of epideictic rhetoric in Roman trials calls attention to aspects that distinguish their trials from modern courtroom practice.[23] A Roman prosecutor would argue the relevant facts of a case, introducing and explaining the evidence while attempting to establish the motives of the accused. In addition, however, the prosecutor would employ invective in an attempt to demolish the credibility and integrity of the accused. Even when the evidence was abundant, invective remained a significant part of the prosecution's case. Skilled selection of appropriate themes and topics along with the introduction of evidence and the narration of details were required to make the vilification stick. Such was Cicero's prosecution of Verres, where court proceedings were mostly used to introduce and explain the overwhelming evidence against Verres, leaving the invective (in part because Verres then fled) to circulate in written orations that imagined actual delivery.[24] Rhetorical manuals and schools of rhetoric recognized the centrality of invective in successful prosecution and sought to train advocates in the technical refinements of character

---

[18] Aristotle *Rhetoric* 1358b and 1366a–1367b; see Merrill 5; for epideictic rhetoric (*genus demonstrativum*), see O'Malley 1979, 36–42; for the relationship between form and content, see O'Malley 1979, 238–43.

[19] Merrill 5.

[20] See Ludwig 2001, 103; and Rao 1988–90, 264.

[21] Quintilian *The Education of the Orator* 3.4.4 (LCL).

[22] Cicero *On the Orator* 2.85.349. Quintilian (*The Education of the Orator* 3.4.11) says that the influential Greek rhetorician Isocrates had subscribed to this position too.

[23] On the role of advocacy, the "vicarious voice," in the Roman court system, see Crook esp. 13–29 and 146–71; see also Kennedy 1972, 7–18.

[24] See Butler 35–84.

assassination. A gifted, well-trained advocate would know both how to destroy an opponent methodically and skillfully through the use of invective and, conversely, how to defend a client with equal skill through the use of praise (*laus*), which is invective's opposite.

The themes of invective were standard and, according to the rhetorical manuals, came under three headings: external circumstance (*res externa*), physical attributes (*corpus*), and mental traits (*animus*).[25] The pseudo-Ciceronian *Rhetoric to Herennius* reduced to ten topics the fifteen found in Cicero's *On Invention*.[26]

First, the external circumstances to be exploited were birth, education, power, glory, citizenship, and friendships. If the person was from noble lineage, one could say he was a disgrace to his ancestors; if he was born to parents of low status (*turpitudo generis*), make slurs against their occupation (bakers and butchers featured prominently among these) and say that he was a shame even to them. Low humor, including puns on personal names, frequently figured in this ridicule. If the person enjoyed the advantages of excellent education, say that he used it in the basest of pursuits or neglected its advantage; if he demonstrated insufficient urbanity or had little education, ridicule his bad manners and uncouth speech (*oratio inepta*). A somber or stern expression could be sneered at as pretentious; a good reputation as hypocrisy. If his citizenship was respectable, even Roman, indicate the disgrace and threat to the city; if he was a foreigner, play to xenophobia by accentuating the supposed undesirable characteristics of his ethnicity. If he had friends who were respectable and influential, make unfavorable contrasts with them; if acquaintances were prostitutes, pimps, sycophants, or enemies of the state, emphasize these associations in lurid or stark detail. Epicureanism, lavish banquets, dancing, and drinking bouts were especially useful grist for the mill.[27]

The second category of themes, physical attributes (*corpus*), were to be exploited as indicative of bad personality traits. Fragility, poor health, and ugliness were sure signs of debauchery and immorality. Eccentricities in dress and manner demonstrated undesirable personality traits, which were often drawn from the figures and stereotypes of comedy. Wearing Greek sandals, having one's toga too long, or going about dripping with unguents were ridiculed as dandified or silly and evidence of bad personal taste.[28]

Third, the prosecution would impugn a person's mental traits (*animus*), or what we might call a person's character. In considering a person's *animus*, one looked for ways to demonstrate the absence of virtue, focusing particularly on the four cardinal virtues: prudence (wisdom), justice, fortitude (courage), and moderation (self-control). These mental traits opened the door to impugn someone's

---

[25]For a concise summary of Roman invective, see Nisbet 192–97; for a longer study of the invective tradition, see Koster; for an enumeration of the themes of invective, see Merrill, esp. 9–11. Merrill early on employs the term "satiric-invective," suggesting that invective and satire were a single continuous tradition (1–3). Because in actuality Merrill treats strictly of rhetorical invective, this confusing term has minimal consequence (cf. Coffey 6–10).

[26]*Rhetoric to Herennius* 3.13–15; Cicero *On Invention* 1.34–36, 2.177–78; see Merrill 9–11.

[27]Merrill 6.

[28]Merrill 7.

motives. The individual had not shown prudence (*prudentia, ratio*) but had engaged in mindless, heedless, unthinking, furious, insane, or self-indulgent reaction (*amentia, furor, caecitas mentis, insania, libido*). The person did not act with justice (*iustitia*) but rather showed cruel, tyrannical, rapacious behavior (*crudelitas, luxuria, avaritia*). The person did not act out of courage (*fortitudo*) but from audacity or gall (*audacia, temeritas*). The person did not show restraint or discipline (*modestia*), but shamelessness or licentiousness (*impudicitia, impudentia*).[29]

The thrust of persuasive invective was *ad hominem* attack, and its essence was malicious caricature and ridicule. The themes deployed were to be determined by exploiting an opponent's recognizable traits and circumstances. These traits could be distorted through exaggeration or denigration but their effectiveness relied on the court finding them, if not in every instance convincing, at least recognizable. Unsubstantiated rumors could be reported as fact, and casual encounters with the disreputable could be turned into perduring and intimate associations. Small details (*mendaciuncula*) could be made up, especially in the narration, in order to spice up or lend credibility to the portrayal. Effective caricature of an opponent did not require an orator to exhaust the list of themes or topics. It did require him to know how to select those external circumstances, physical characteristics, and personality traits that could be deployed with the greatest effect. Alleging the existence of these traits in an opponent was never in itself sufficient. Successful invective needed to relate the themes to the facts and charges in a particular case. All of them had to be elaborated through clever narration and amplification.

In antiquity other literary genres were closely related to rhetorical invective, most notably satire and poetic invective, which overlapped in their language and themes. These were unlike rhetorical invective in that they had distinctly different purposes. Whereas rhetorical invective was deployed for forensic or deliberative purposes, poetic invective served merely to settle a score. It was written to humiliate and embarrass an enemy or rival publicly. Wit and humor were used in poetic invective only to foster ridicule. Scurrilous and obscene language couched in brilliant verse, especially in epigram form, aided in propagating the insults to the widest possible audience.[30]

The Romans regarded satire as their only native literary form.[31] Satire, unlike poetic invective, had as its objective the correction of social practice or sometimes the improvement of a particular individual by chiding bad behavior. It could be sharp. Although it did on occasion and according to taste use an obscene word, wit was the means by which it accomplished its ends. Wit was the seasoning that abated the sharpness and alleviated the cynicism of satire. But wit carried too far degenerated into scurrility (*scurra*).[32] Good satire depended on "much use of mild jest and slight use of bitter invective."[33] Until the Roman scholar Varro introduced

---

[29]Merrill 7.

[30]See Coffey 6–8; Hollar; Koster 148–56; and Ullman 1917.

[31]Quintilian (*The Education of the Orator* 10.1.93): *satura quidem tota nostra est*. The Greeks knew satire but for them it was not an independent genre. See Coffey 3–4.

[32]Ullman 1917, 125.

[33]Ullman 1917, 128.

the Menippean tradition, which combined prose and poetry, satire had always been conceived as poetry.[34] Only in late antiquity did authors begin to acknowledge "satiric elements" in prose compositions.[35]

Although in antiquity rhetorical invective made use of many satiric and comedic elements, it was regarded as a subdivision of epideictic (that is, declamatory) rhetoric. In writing about Roman satire, Michael Coffey remarks on "the importance of the formal classification by genres in ancient literature and the existence of a hierarchy of genres." Contemporary literature, as he notes, often blurs genre distinctions "to which writers and critics in former ages would have responded instinctively."[36] Literary criticism in antiquity, developed in large part by the Alexandrians, came to recognize a variety of genres and also reached a general consensus about a hierarchy of genres. Each genre was thought to have an "archetypal master," that is, an author whose work had set the form. In the work of the master one could discern the *lex operis*, which were the rules of style thought to govern a particular form. The work of the archetypal master was not, however, regarded as flawless. Nor was it thought impossible to develop the form beyond the work of the archetypal master. A clever genius could stretch the rules of style according to taste and circumstance or even transcend the form.[37] Moreover, each form had both topics and language that were regarded as appropriate to it. Whereas some genres excluded certain topics and language, other genres could share topics and language although these were regarded as belonging mostly to one or the other form.[38] Obscene words, for instance, might appear in satire but were mostly reserved for the lower forms of epigram and poetic invective. By the early fifteenth century, humanists usually worked with a good understanding of the rules governing these genres. Some, like Antonio da Rho with rhetorical invective and Antonio Panormita with poetic invective, resorted readily to their preferred genre.

3. Antonio da Rho

The Milanese Franciscan Antonio da Rho (1395–1447) has mostly left his mark as a humanist, even though he received the traditional Franciscan theological training and consistently styled himself a theologian. Rho understood clearly that his own pursuit of "humanistic studies" (*studia humanitatis*)[39] was the result of Francesco Petrarca's having "awakened Ciceronian charm" and "chased it from its hiding place." He also recognized that his own generation owed Petrarca "a great debt of gratitude" because they were now able to "follow the trail" of Ciceronian

---

[34]For satire as a genre and its purpose, style, circulation, and methods, see Coffey; Ullman 1917; and Witke.
[35]See Wiesen 2–4.
[36]Coffey 7.
[37]Coffey 5.
[38]Coffey 7.
[39]For the phrase "humanistic studies" (*studia humanitatis*), see *Apology* §18 n. 60.

style "everywhere." But Petrarca had failed, Rho conceded, to achieve "that splendor and sweetness of speech in which many presently excel."[40] Rho could have made this remark aptly about himself. In the space of about twenty-five years he produced a substantial number of humanistic treatises, teaching aids, orations, letters, and poems. Yet these have been little studied, in large part because they lack the stylistic "splendor and sweetness" that he himself admired in the ancients and welcomed in his contemporaries, even if it can be said that his style had much improved between his early works of the late 1420s and his last in 1444. At any rate, he was a force to be reckoned with in his own day and held a number of important positions in Visconti Milan. His life and work catch our eye not least because he happened, in the words of the Chinese curse, "to live in interesting times." Not that he endured unusual personal trials: as far as we know, he suffered mostly from the gout and a bruised ego. Rather, his life and work merit attention because they reflect the political, religious, social, economic, and cultural ferment taking place on the Italian peninsula and across Europe. His polemics with colleagues and superiors, scholastics and humanists, provide us with insights into a larger milieu. In Rho's *Apology* and *Philippic* we see the dynamics of courtly politics and humanistic patronage as well as the frictions inherent in conflicting institutional claims. We also observe in these texts the tensions arising from the demands of professional responsibilities and rivalries. The *Apology* and *Philippic* indicate a decisive embracing of new cultural developments while also revealing a deep respect for tradition and a desire for continuity. Because Rho records things that he both approves and condemns, the *Apology* and *Philippic* illuminate tensions between cultural traditions and innovations.

Rho was born in 1395, the year in which Gian Galeazzo Visconti (1351–1402) paid 100,000 gold florins to the Holy Roman Emperor Wenceslaus for the hereditary title of Duke of Milan. In the opening years of the fifteenth century, as Rho was just beginning his primary education, Lombardy and much of Italy were abuzz with talk of Gian Galeazzo Visconti's wars of conquest in northern Italy. The growing wealth, power, and prestige of the Visconti family loomed ever larger at home as well. It was displayed and celebrated in the imposing presence of the family palaces, in the patronage of the Certosa of Pavia, and in the ongoing construction of the Duomo of Milan. Gian Galeazzo's conquests heralded the prospect of his becoming king of Italy. Yet in 1402, just as he prepared to move against Florence, the last major center of resistance north of Rome, he died from the plague.

During the minority of Gian Galeazzo's oldest son, Giovanni Maria (1389–1412), the territories once under Visconti control slipped away. Rho's primary and secondary education took place precisely in these years of declining Visconti fortunes. In 1412, when Rho at age seventeen left Milan for Padua to study dialectic, Gian Galeazzo's second son, Filippo Maria Visconti (1392–1447), became Duke of Milan. Although extraordinarily superstitious and reclusive, Filippo Maria managed by 1421 to recover many of his father's territories. He

---

[40] *Apology* §33.

accomplished this through a potent mix of able administration, shrewd diplomacy, ruthless intrigue, and skilled handling of his mercenary generals.

In addition to these political developments, which probably affected Rho only indirectly during his teenage years, three important religious developments must have affected him more directly. The first of these was the Great Western Schism (1379–1417), which brought the papacy near to collapse as an effective international institution. When in 1413, at age eighteen, Rho made his decision to enter the Franciscan Order, three men claimed to be pope. The allegiances divided between the claimants had ramifications well beyond the papacy itself and brought turmoil to convents, monasteries, parishes, and dioceses across Europe. Rho's earliest years as a Franciscan coincided with the attempts of the Council of Constance to respond to the institutional chaos both of the papacy and of the Church in general. Even though the Council of Constance eliminated the claimants and in 1417 succeeded in electing Pope Martin V, the success of this solution remained for some years in doubt. The participants of the council also set forth an ambitious reform proposal: the reform of the Church "in head and members" (from pope to pew) and "in faith and morals" (from thought to act). This may well constitute the most audacious reform ever proposed for any major institution. The proposal did contain a minor flaw: the council's participants had failed — for reasons easily imagined — to settle who was going to reform whom. Even so, hope ran high for new beginnings. When Martin V passed through Milan a year after his election in order to dedicate the altar of the Duomo, Rho composed a poem for him that reflects the hope which many shared for his papacy.[41] For Martin and his successors the reform of the papacy, the restoration of papal independence, and ultimately the reform of the church required freedom from economic and political interference of secular powers. This freedom could only be gained, so far as they could see, through the recovery and control of the papal territories. Yet like others, Filippo Maria Visconti, Rho's prince, had different plans for these territories, and over the years he manipulated Church councils, particularly the Council of Basel, to reform the papacy in accordance with his designs. Most notably he sought to thwart the papacy's territorial ambitions.[42] Consequently, for most of Rho's professional life he worked to negotiate a balance between the formidable triad of pope, duke, and council.

A second religious development, the quarrel between the Conventual and Observant Franciscans, more directly influenced Rho's life. The Franciscans were bitterly divided, with the Observants arguing that true apostolic poverty and the Rule of Saint Francis prohibited both institutional and individual ownership of property. This struggle had raged intermittently, sometimes violently, in the Franciscan Order ever since the death of Saint Francis in 1226. A papal decision in 1318 in favor of the Conventuals had failed to halt either the theological debate or the institutional disputes. In 1415 the Council of Constance made important

---

[41]Metrica commendatio Martini V: *Magne Ligur patrieque decus*. . . . (Milan: Biblioteca Ambrosiana, MS B 116 sup., 95r–97v).
[42]Gill 1959, 53,140; Viti 1994b, 540, 542, 544.

new concessions to the Observants, which immediately intensified the quarrel.[43] Rho must have known about this quarrel when he entered his novitiate in 1413; he certainly lived the rest of his life in its shadow. In Milan, Rho's own convent at San Francesco Grande, a Conventual house, enjoyed a decided resurgence after 1418, and it remained a significant institutional force in Franciscan politics throughout the 1430s and '40s. One of its members, Antonio Rusconi, served as Provincial Minister and eventually as Minister General of the Order (1443–49). After 1450, Sant' Angelo, the rival Observant house in Milan, took the lead under the patronage of the new Duke of Milan, Francesco Sforza.[44]

A more general religious development in this period has been described as a profound spiritual and moral crisis. Signs of a crisis began in the mid-fourteenth century. It resulted from a combination of factors, most notably the trauma of recurrent plagues, the constant economic uncertainties, the ceaseless wars of emerging territorial states, and the chronic disarray of ecclesiastical institutions. The sermons and reform agendas of the itinerant preachers, particularly the Observant Franciscans, sought in various ways to address the crisis. Such preachers, in particular San Bernardino da Siena (1380–1444), had a profound effect on Rho's life, as he himself asserts. He may have heard San Bernardino preach on several occasions, including in 1413 and 1416 in Padua and in 1418 in Milan.[45] San Bernardino traveled throughout Italy preaching penance and his version of moral reform with remarkable success. To the Franciscans he urged the strict observance of Franciscan Rule. To individual penitents he urged the veneration of the Holy Name for a renewed spirituality. To city magistrates he urged harsh sumptuary laws to regulate women's dress and adornment, the expulsion of the Jews to end usury, rigorous intervention to curb gambling, and the founding of houses of prostitution to discourage sodomy.[46] Rho's conversion to the Franciscan Order demonstrates the power of such preaching. Although he chose to become a Conventual (an Observant convent had yet to be founded in Milan), he showed certain sympathies for the Observant cause. By his later years, Rho had established friendly relations with the Observant Franciscan Alberto Sarteano.

We know little about the more private aspects of Rho's life. His name "Rho" (Latin *Raudensis* or *de Raude*) simply designated his place of origin, the village of Rho a few kilometers northwest of Milan. Even this comes to light only because his Observant friend Alberto Sarteano once paused there on a journey and used the occasion to write to Rho. Many men, Sarteano wrote, had singlehandedly made the humble place of their birth famous.[47] The humanist Lorenzo Valla,

---

[43]Moorman 441–56, 479–500.

[44]Ferrari 1979, 446–47, 451–57; Rutherford 1990, 85–87.

[45]Lombardi 13 and n. 23; for the life and preaching of San Bernardino, see Debby; Mormando.

[46]On Bernardino's preaching, see Debby 127–56: 127–36 (family), 137–46 (women), 146–48 (prostitution), 148–53 (homosexuality), and 168–95 (usury and the Jews). Cf. Rho's unidentified quotation (*Imitations* 141v–142r; Appendix IX, *Meretrix*): "Someone said that to go whoring in your youth is not a vice" (*Quidam dicit quod scortari in iuvene non est vitium*).

[47]Sarteano 400, 393, 406–08 (sequential but with confused pagination).

Rho's onetime friend and eventual antagonist, gives us one of our few glimpses of Rho's family. In his dialogue *On the True and False Good*, Valla indicated that Rho's father, younger brother, and sister had died by 1433 (perhaps this sister was the same Agata whom Rho visited in Brescia in 1425).[48] If his family's circumstances were modest, they did manage to gain him a solid Latin education by contemporary standards.

Rho entered the Franciscan Order in 1413, presumably at San Francesco Grande, which was the largest church in Milan before the building of the Duomo. He there spent most of his life.[49] But if his *Philippic* is accurate, he arrived in Padua a year before he entered the Franciscan Order. He came to Padua, perhaps as a postulant, to begin his study "of dialectic and the introduction for boys" under Giacomo della Torre da Forlì.[50] In his *Apology* Rho says that he entered the Order at eighteen and that Matteo Pritelli da Cremona and Lodovico da Pirano were his "catechists and teachers." He then spent "three whole years" studying dialectic, apparently between 1414 and 1417, before returning to Milan in 1418. The next four or five years (1418–23) must have kept him mostly in Padua at Il Santo, the great Franciscan church and convent of Sant' Antonio. There he took his masters degree in theology. By October of 1423, now about twenty-eight years old, Rho began teaching in the *studium* of San Francesco Grande as a *sacrae paginae professor*. Apart from the time in Padua pursuing his education, he is known to have left Milan only a few times. In 1425, as mentioned above, he visited his sister Agata in Brescia; and in 1436 he traveled to the Council of Basel. The reading list in his *Apology* (1427/28) leaves little doubt that he had spent some time in nearby Pavia reading in the Visconti Library.[51]

Between the mid-1420s and mid-1430s, Pavia and Milan hosted a number of celebrated lawyers and humanists who engaged in a flurry of intellectual debate and professional activity. Rho himself participated in a number of ways, not least in the writing of his *Apology* and *Philippic*. By 1431 he had translated into the vernacular the *Lives of the Caesars* of Suetonius and other authors for Duke Filippo Maria Visconti.[52] He had by this time given at least one oration for the anniversary celebration of the duke's installation.[53] For much of this period Rho served alone as the duke's official court orator, a post he would periodically occupy throughout his life. Sometime before the end of 1432 — when the ducal councilor Francesco

---

[48] Valla 1970, 133 (3.25.17); for Rho's visit to his sister, see Rutherford 1990, 82n.

[49] The church and convent were suppressed and then demolished in the early nineteenth century. The records are now at the Archivio di Stato in Milan (see Rutherford 1990, 83–98 and nn. 30–38).

[50] *Philippic* §47.

[51] Lombardi 57 n. 4.

[52] Rho's translation of *The Lives of the Caesars* from Suetonius and other authors into Italian exists in two copies (see Pellegrin 1955a, 388–89). The Vatican manuscript (BAV, MS Urb. lat. 437) is said to be the dedicatory copy made by Angelo Decembrio in 1431. It contains *Lives* through Valentinian III, but indicates (f. 138r) that its exemplar was incomplete. Many of these additional *Lives* derive from the *Scriptores historiae augustae*. Some sources are difficult to identify because most *Lives* are only extracts or summaries, perhaps from some intermediary source. Duke Filippo Maria Visconti received other translations from Milanese humanists, including some from Pier Candido Decembrio.

[53] Rutherford 1990, 88–89n.

Barbavara, the primary literary patron at the Visconti court, was disgraced — Rho wrote for him a *Genealogy of the Scipios and Catos*.[54] By 1433, Rho was completing his *Rhetorical Imitations*, the dedicatory letters of which he variously reworked during the next decade.[55]

In the decade following the first circulation of his *Rhetorical Imitations* in early 1433, friction between Rho and Lorenzo Valla grew steadily. In the controversy with Antonio Panormita, Valla switched his allegiance in 1432 to the faction of Rho and Pier Candido Decembrio. But having lost his position at the University of Pavia for which Panormita had supported him, Valla in 1433 moved to Milan, where he worked as a tutor. During this time, he and Rho appear to have gotten on well, although Rho looked condescendingly on Valla — his junior by a dozen years — whose position carried little status.

Three works are pivotal in understanding the controversy between Rho and Valla: (1) Rho's *Rhetorical Imitations* (1433), (2) Valla's similar and more successful work, *On the Elegances of the Latin Language* (1440), and (3) Valla's *Notations on the Errors of Antonio da Rho* (1443–47), in which Valla enumerated what he regarded as mistakes in Rho's *Rhetorical Imitations*. The apple of discord was grammatical usage in classical texts. At question is whether Rho plagiarized material from Valla or instead quoted Valla and pointed out a mistake, the latter being the most probable.

Tension between them surfaced with the release of Valla's *Elegances* in 1440, in which Valla recounts at length an incident with a "friend":

> There are those who, in order to appear to have discovered them first, repeated and hastened to publish some of the things I taught, which they heard either from me or from my students, for I never concealed these things. . . . When I in friendship read certain little books of one of those men in his presence, I discovered some things of my own and I recognized those things secretly stolen from me that I did not know I had let slip. I omit his name. . . . He of course handled it carelessly and unlearnedly so that you would know it to be stolen from another, not something he produced himself; something he heard and did not invent. I, however, was upset and I said to the man: "I recognize this elegance. I declare my ownership and can accuse you of plagiarism." Even though he was blushing, he still responded with humor and wit saying that it was permitted to use the things of a friend as one's own. "But this," I said, "is abuse, not use. For it happens to leave nothing for me, when you have seized the prize for that which I labored." Then he replied even more urbanely that I was a poor parent who evicted from my dwelling the sons that I fathered and brought up; he not only from mercy but for our friendship took them into his own home and reared them as his

---

[54] Vatican City: BAV, MS Ottob. lat. 1321, 1r–50r; cf. Rutherford 1990, 88n.
[55] See Monfardini.

own. I have ceased to be angry with him, understanding that a much greater fault must be attributed to me for neglecting my goods than to that man for taking goods neglected by another.[56]

Although Valla omitted specifics, he did not strive to be especially cryptic. With his phrase "certain little books of one of those men" he was unmistakably referring to Rho and his *Rhetorical Imitations*. It is not clear why Valla referred to Rho's *Imitations* as "little books" since this work now constitutes a single large volume and Valla himself later described them as "commentaries."[57] Perhaps he saw Rho's notebooks or individual quires that were yet to be bound as a codex. We also have no way to verify the claims of Valla, such as his assertion that Rho "blushed" in response to the accusation of plagiarism. In any case, Valla cleverly used it as a device to indicate Rho's admission of guilt. The same is true of Rho's alleged witty turn on the Latin word *plagiarius*, which literally means "kidnapper." Whatever uncertainty remains about Valla's reliability in reporting the details of this event, the person and work intended are obvious.

Valla repeated this accusation three years later in his first version of the *Notations on the Errors of Antonio da Rho* (1443), written, he says, when Giovanni Alzina asked him to review a copy of Rho's *Imitations* and note his objections for the private use of Alzina's son. As Valla tells the story, during this reading he came upon Rho's entry under *omnis* where Rho censures "some who believe" that *quisque* and *quique* can only follow a superlative.[58] Valla omitted Rho's conclusion to this entry: "But let these men [that is, "Valla"] resume the lowest seat in elementary school. Let them read Macrobius, who used *die quoque*, i.e., *omni*, and *homine quoque* in the

---

[56]Valla *Elegances of the Latin Language* (2, Pref. [1962, 1:412]): *Sunt enim qui nonnulla horum quae a me praecipiuntur, vel de me, vel de auditoribus meis audita (numquam enim ista suppressi) in opera sua retulerint festinantque edere, ut ipsi priores invenisse videantur. . . . Quorum unius libellos quosdam pro amicitia quum legendos eo praesente cepissem, deprehendi quaedam mea, et quae me amisisse nesciebam, furto mihi sublat cognovi. Parco illius nomini. . . . Negligenter ille quidem et inscite tractatus, ut scires aliunde decerptum, non ex se prolatum; et auditum, non excogitatum esse. Conturbatus tamen sum, et inquam homini: "Hanc ego elegantiam agnosco, et manicipium meum assero, teque plagiaria lege convenire possum." At ille erubescens, ioco tamen atque urbanitate elusit, quod diceret, uti rebus amicorum licere ut suis. "At istud," inquam, "abuti est, non uti. Nihil enim mihi reliqui sit ubi tu huius rei in qua ipse laboravi, palmam semel occupaveris." Tum ille etiam urbanius, quod malus parens essem, qui filios, quos genuissem et educassem, e contubernio eiicerem; ipse tum misericordia, tum amicitia nostra ad se domum suam colligeret atque educaret pro suis. Destiti in illum stomachari intelligens multo magis mihi bona mea negligenti quam illi bona ab aliis neglecta colligenti vitio dandum esse. Quare quis non videt non inhonestum esse ea me mandare literis ex me inuenta, quae alii ne furto quidem sublata, turpe sibi ducunt scriptis suis inserere?*

[57]See n.60 below.

[58]Valla *Notations on the Errors of Antonio da Rho* (Pref. [1962, 1:390]): *Cum autem ad vocabulum 'omnis' pervenissem, meque illic etsi non nominatim, tamen aperte reprehendi animavertissem, non exiguam sane bile, vel criminis, vel accusatoris indignitate contraxi; intellexique famae meae, quae a falsis amicis in discrimen adduceretur, esse succurrendum.* Valla goes on to say (Pref. [1962, 1:412–13]): *Cur in eo quod a me, id est ab auditoribus meis, audivisti, non fuisti gratus? Ubi de 'per' et 'quam' praecipis, observare non potes (quod summopere pudendum est) si modo recte praecipis.* Elsewhere Valla (*Elegances of the Latin Language* 2, Pref. [1962, 1:412]) identifies the material thus: *Erat autem locus de 'per' et 'quam' in compositione, de qua re proximo libro disputavi, et de 'quisquam' cum adiungitur superlativo.*

singular and not in the superlative."[59] Valla did say that when he discovered this attack by an old friend, he no longer felt compelled to restrain his criticism and composed the *Notations*. The same material that Valla had earlier accused Rho of plagiarizing, he here accuses Rho of attacking. For in response to Rho's refutation of those who believe that *quisque* and *quique* must follow a superlative, Valla writes: "Who are these, Rho, who so believe? Obviously I alone have taught this, which you have taken from my students, and which I read in your commentaries at your residence and in your presence, as I have testified in the proem of the second book of the *On the Elegances of the Latin Language*."[60] Valla circulated the first version of the *Notations* only privately. News of it reached Maffeo Vegio in Rome, who wrote to Valla seeking to dissuade him from open controversy with Rho. Vegio consistently referred to Rho's action as a "refutation" of Valla (*sensa quaedam tua reprehenderit*) and not as a "plagiarism" (*quae furto mihi sublata*) as Valla had spoken of it. Vegio continued: "This one thing I know, that it is permitted among writers to teach their own opinions in books even alongside the censure of other writers, if only the statements are rejected and refuted while having preserved modesty and the integrity of the words and of their value whose meaning is fixed."[61] Rho's only known response to Valla's attack is a single sentence in a late edition (1443?) of his *Imitations*. "A certain elementary school teacher," Rho says, in writing "a recent book on expressions" claimed as his own "many things that I said."[62] Rho appears to be speaking solely of Valla's *Elegantiae* (2, pref.) and not also of his *Notations*, since at that point he, like Valla, refrained from naming his adversary. After Rho's death in 1447, Valla revised his *Notations* making them books VII and VIII of his *Elegances*. He published them along with his invective *Antidote against Facio* in 1449. Valla continued to write disparagingly of Rho and his *Imitations* into the 1450s.

Many of Rho's early themes and controversies would reemerge in 1444 with the completion of his *Three Dialogues against Lactantius*, which he dedicated to Pope Eugenius IV. In them Rho examined the question of Lactantius' status and significance. Many readers, especially among the humanists, regarded Lactantius (ca. 250–ca. 325), the courtier of the first Christian Emperor Constantine and the "most eloquent of the Latin fathers," as a theologian. Some of them even mentioned him in company with Augustine and Jerome. But Rho rejected Lactantius

---

[59]Rho (*Imitations* 165r–165v): *Aliqui credunt quod 'quisque' et 'quique' non recte ponatur nisi post superlativum pluralem ut 'optimos quosque viros' et 'sanctissimi quique viri.' Sed recumbant in ludi novissimo loco. Legant Macrobium qui in singulari numero neque superlativo dixit 'die quoque,' id est 'omni,' et 'homine quoque.'* Valla later added Rho's insult to his *Notations* (1962, 1:412).

[60]Valla (1962, 1:412): *Qui sunt isti, Raudensis, qui ita credunt? Nempe solus ego hoc tradidi, quod tu ab auditoribus meis accepisti quodque ego apud te ac te praesente legi in commentariis istis tuis, ut testatus sum in secundi libri De elegantia linguae latinae prooemio.*

[61]Vegio (1442?) to Lorenzo Valla (Sabbadini 1891, 89): *Hoc unum scio, liberum esse scriptoribus sententias suas monumentis tradere etiam cum nota aliorum, dum modo id fiat servata modestia et honestate verborum atque eorum honore, quorum sententia stat dicta vel improbare vel refellere.*

[62]Rho *Imitations* (Padua: Biblioteca Capitolare, MS C 72, 269v): *Sic nuper, dum haec scriberem, audivi de quodam ludi magistro, qui, cum has Imitationes meas inspexisset, librum de vocabulis novum aggressus est in quo multa quae dixi sparsim digerit et sua esse testatur.* Cf. Monfardini 54.

as a "doctor" of the Church and insisted that he should be read as an author of the humanistic studies (*studia humanitatis*),[63] that is, alongside Cicero, Seneca, and Livy. Rho's *Three Dialogues against Lactantius* sought to correct what he saw as the excessive reverence for Lactantius by his contemporaries. Rho's dialogues not only directly attacked Lactantius, but also indirectly attacked some of Rho's contemporaries, whose unrestrained enthusiasm for Lactantius he mistrusted. Although the tone of these dialogues struck many of Rho's contemporaries as excessively harsh, it would not be accurate to call them invectives. Consistent with this critical but "softer" tone, the criticism of Lactantius provided cover for Rho's attempts to refute certain ideas of Lorenzo Valla without having to expose himself to the charge of ingratitude or treachery. Valla had, after all, chosen Rho for the "Christian" interlocutor in his dialogue *On the True and False Good* (1433). As Valla put it, he had accorded Rho the honor that Cicero assigned to Scipio or Plato to Socrates.[64] In fact, Rho disagreed with some concepts that his "Socratic" *persona* had articulated in Valla's dialogues, concepts which he thought derived from Lactantius or at least shared the same flawed presuppositions.[65]

Rho dedicated his *Three Dialogues against Lactantius* to Pope Eugenius IV. But did Rho perceive in Eugenius an especial interest in Lactantius? There is little direct evidence to suggest this. Besides the inventory of Eugenius' library, which records a manuscript of Lactantius, Rho's dialogue constitutes the only other clear evidence connecting Eugenius and the works of Lactantius. The dedication of the dialogues to Eugenius probably reflects the recent reconciliation between the pope and Filippo Maria Visconti, who in 1439 defended the legitimacy of Eugenius' papacy against the Council of Basel. Beyond the secular political context, Rho may have had motives that reflect Franciscan politics and the deepening rifts occasioned by their controversies. In June of 1443 the Conventual Franciscans, the wing of the Order to which Rho belonged, had rejected the Observant Alberto Sarteano, whom Eugenius had backed for Minister General of the Franciscan Order. Perhaps Rho and most of the members of the Convent of San Francesco Grande in Milan sought to signal their support of Eugenius. Since Rho lacked the personal resources to pay for parchment, a professional scribe, an illuminator, and a suitable binder, it is clear that he had the support either of the duke or of the Convent of San Francesco Grande, perhaps even both.[66] At any rate, in September

---

[63] For the phrase *studia humanitatis*, see *Apology* §18 n. 60.

[64] Valla (1962b, 390): *Etenim (ut alia necessitudinis signa praeteream) inter me et Antonium Raudensem quid magis ostendi potuit quam quod in libris De vero bono partes ei (ut sic dicam) censorias tribui defensionemque religionis, ut non plus in libris De republica tribuerit aut Scipioni Cicero aut Socrati Plato?*

[65] Rutherford 1998.

[66] The dedicatory copy of Rho's *Three Dialogues against Lactantius* is in the Vatican Library, MS Vat. lat. 227. This manuscript would have been extremely costly to produce. It consists of 199 vellum folios prepared to the highest standards and bearing Eugenius' coat of arms. It also includes a full folio illumination depicting Rho on one knee offering the manuscript to Eugenius, who is surrounded by his court (see page iv above). The manuscript was corrected by Rho himself. Rho's autograph copy of the dialogues is also in the Vatican Library, MS Ottob. lat. 1903 (see Rutherford 1990, 86–87, 93–95; 1998). For Eugenius IV's bibliophile interests, see Bignami Odier 2–3, 37–38.

of 1443 the Visconti secretary Pier Candido Decembrio carried a part of the first dialogue containing the dedication on his diplomatic mission to Eugenius, who was then in Siena — which suggests an element of ducal sponsorship or recognition. If Eugenius read the first part of the work at that time, the subsequent expansion of the work implies that Eugenius found it acceptable. Still, it is unlikely that Rho dedicated his dialogues to Eugenius as one especially interested in Lactantius, and the dedication may have been an afterthought. In other words, Rho began the dialogues moved by his perception of Lactantius' significance within broader cultural and intellectual currents; whereas his motives for dedicating the dialogues to Eugenius were grounded in the immediate political events. The change in political circumstances, both secular and religious, facilitated the circulation of his dialogues at the papal court. Perhaps they would have become known there anyway, but the presence of Rho's dialogues in Rome was to prove significant, especially after the advent of printing.[67]

Throughout his life Rho remained a regular participant in Milanese religious, political, and intellectual affairs. In July of 1436 he attended the Council of Basel as one of the theologians who were to prepare Western churchmen to discuss the "conception of Mary" with the Greeks.[68] Rho and Ludovico Strassoldo, another Franciscan in the entourage, were probably chosen because they were Franciscan theologians. For under the influence of their great theologian Duns Scotus, the Franciscans had become the major proponents of the Immaculate Conception. Although the Council of Basel did not make its pronouncement until 1439, it became the first council to affirm the validity of the doctrine.[69] Rho also served as one of three ecclesiastical judges whom Filippo Maria Visconti appointed in 1439 to hear a case against two recalcitrant members of the Order of the Humiliati.[70] Near the very end of his life Rho served on a panel of six theologians and ecclesiastics assembled to hear a case of conscience for Filippo Maria Visconti. The duke's chaplain asked them to determine whether a prince, that is, Filippo Maria, could be saved when he lacked the means to make restitution for years of oppressive loans and confiscatory taxes. The panel responded on 9 May 1446, saying that the duke would be judged by a merciful God. But, they added, without knowing the information from the duke's Secret Council on which his decisions had been made, they could not determine whether he had made these decisions in order to preserve his territory *in extremis* or if he had merely been self-serving.

---

[67]The complete text of Rho's *Three Dialogues against Lactantius* has never been printed. His list of Lactantius' philosophical, theological, and exegetical errors was printed, however, in one form or another, with almost every edition of Lactantius from the Subiaco *editio princeps* of 1465 through the Migne edition of 1844. This last contained three separate versions of Rho's list. A high number of references to Rho's list in secondary literature incorrectly identify it as being emendations of the text of Lactantius: it is not. If Rho ever emended the text of Lactantius, the manuscript has not been identified.

[68]Segovia 895–97; Sabbadini 1911, 32n; Rutherford 1990, 89n.

[69]Lamy, esp. 396–408, 591–613.

[70]Puccinelli 43–46.

INTRODUCTION   17

This hedge, uncharacteristic of Rho, be it noted, constitutes the final record of his activity. Circumstantial evidence clearly points to 1447 as the year of his death, but no document specifically confirms this.[71]

4. Cicero and Jerome

In his *Philippic against Antonio Panormita* (1431/32) Antonio da Rho stated that he had no fear of Panormita since he had Perseus and Hercules on his side. These great warrior heroes of antiquity are no doubt metaphorical references to two authors whom Rho a few lines later called his "teachers, both learned and skilled." He further clarified his metaphor by saying pointedly: "To be sure, Cicero is one, but foremost is my Jerome." Rho also specified what he had learned from these teachers. Cicero, he said, had taught him "to hammer out new *Philippics*"; from Jerome he had learned "to hammer out new *Jovinians*." These two, Rho told Panormita, "bolster me in confronting you."[72]

Cicero (106–43 BCE) was an advocate, politician, and philosopher whose life spanned the turbulent years of late Republican Rome. He rose to fame as an advocate and has since been regarded as the greatest orator Rome ever produced. In the aftermath of the assassination of Julius Caesar, Cicero delivered a series of orations against Mark Antony that he referred to as his *Philippics*. Cicero took this title from the speeches of the great Athenian orator Demosthenes (384–322 BCE) against Philip II of Macedonia (the father of Alexander the Great). Cicero's *Philippics* aroused Roman resistance to Mark Antony and prevented his move on Rome. In retaliation, Mark Antony struck a deal with Octavius Caesar at the formation of the second triumvirate to have Cicero proscribed. Cicero's severed head and hand were dumped on the Rostrum in the Roman Forum along with the heads of the others proscribed.[73] Nevertheless, on the example of these orations, a *Philippic* became synonymous with an oration publicly attacking an enemy.[74]

St. Jerome (ca. 342–420) was one of the greatest linguistic scholars of antiquity, and became famous among Christians for his Latin translations of the Old Testament and Apocrypha and his revisions of the older Latin translations of the New Testament. These translations, along with his prefaces to and commentaries on the books of the Bible, profoundly influenced Christianity in the West. Jerome, however, had received an excellent education in classical pagan literature.

---

[71]Regoliosi 1984, 561; Rutherford 1990, 90n.
[72]*Philippic* §173.
[73]Plutarch *Cicero* 48–49.
[74]Mark Antony's demand for Cicero's hand as well as his head indicates the damage caused by the circulation of Cicero's written speeches (see Butler 1–3, 103–23; cf. Richlin 1999; Conte 1843–85). Although Cicero had an important place in medieval education, for many Renaissance humanists (e.g., Rho) he came to represent the greatest achievements of Latin prose literature. Study and imitation of his orations, letters, and treatises (many recirculated after centuries of neglect) formed something like the "core curriculum" for a Renaissance humanistic education (see Black 2001, 212–15; Witt 2000, 58–60, 125–28, 274; Conte 408–24).

This training conditioned his unshakable preference for the style of Cicero over that of biblical literature. Jerome, like many educated Christians, believed devoutly in the truth of Sacred Scripture, but its lack of refinement violated his literary sensibilities. This difficulty culminated in his famous dream, in which an angel, as Jerome wrote, dragged him before the divine tribunal and accused him of being a Ciceronian and not a Christian.[75]

Jerome was also well known for his polemical works: *Against Jovinian, Against Vigilantius, Against Helvidius, Against John of Jerusalem, Against the Books of Rufinus, Against the Pelagians,* and *Against the Luciferians.* These were mostly invective letters against his opponents. From these Rho singles out Jerome's caustic attack on Jovinian, who (according to Jerome and Augustine) shared the views of Helvidius that virginity had equal status with marriage and that fasting had no more merit than thankful eating.[76]

As models for invective, Cicero and Jerome have much in common but they are also strikingly different, having been separated culturally and intellectually by some four centuries. Jerome stood near the end of an ancient rhetorical tradition heavily influenced by Cicero. New circumstances presented him with certain possibilities either not available or not acceptable to Cicero. Perhaps the most significant difference between Cicero and Jerome was the context in which they used invective. In addition, however, to their development of the themes and vocabulary of invective, they have a larger significance for Rho: Cicero dignified invective as a genre; Jerome licensed Rho to use it.

5. Cicero

Cicero would have known and practiced invective mostly in a forensic setting. It was a weapon to be used against an opponent or a weapon to be repelled when defending a client in a lawsuit or a prosecution. Cicero much less frequently, but no less famously with his *Philippics* and *Catilinaria,* used invective in his deliberative oratory, that is, as speeches to the senate or public. The purpose of forensic and deliberative invective was to discredit and vilify an opponent with the precise aim of getting a judgment against him or of turning policy and opinion against him.[77] Although some of these speeches were never delivered and circulated only as written texts, in all of them Cicero addressed his opponent as though he were confronting him in the courtroom or the senate.

---

[75]Jerome *Letter* 22. For Jerome's biography, see Kelly. In the late Middle Ages and Renaissance Jerome's cult emerged with particular strength in art and popular saints' lives. Many Renaissance humanists shared an enthusiasm for his linguistic knowledge and his literary skills, especially as seen in his letters (see Rice 1985; McManamon 1985).

[76]Most evidence about the Christian monk Jovinian (d. 405) comes from hostile witnesses: Jerome's *Against Jovinian* and Augustine's *On the Good Marriage* and *On Holy Virginity* (cf. *Invectiva: ubi "Obloqui"* §4–§10, Appendix VIII below; cf. *Philippic* §173 and *Apology* §16).

[77]Coffey 8.

Insofar as invective became a genre of writing for Cicero, it presupposed, if only in an imaginary context, that the oration had actually been delivered. This would also be the case with some pseudonymous classroom works from antiquity like the invectives of Cicero and Sallust, which also became important models for Renaissance invective.[78]

The extent to which Cicero bolstered Rho in his confrontation with Panormita becomes apparent not only in the choice of genre and language of Rho's *Philippic* but also from the selections he quoted in his *Rhetorical Imitations* under the heading of "Vilifying" (Appendix VIII below). There, "for those who have been provoked," Rho laid out "the vocabulary of invectives" (*invectivarum vocabula*) and recommended reading Cicero's speeches against Verres, Catiline, and Mark Antony (that is, his *Philippics*), and his invectives against other individuals. Rho quoted passages from Cicero's Verrine orations and from his oration *In Defense of Caelius*. Rho did quote from Cicero's *Philippics* too but only indirectly through Quintilian (4.2.124). To these Rho added lengthy selections from Cicero's oration against Piso. These are the most important examples of rhetorical invective in Cicero's *oeuvre*. Rho did not quote from the invectives of Cicero and Sallust, even though he was familiar with them. In his *Apology* (§18), for instance, he writes: "I frequently held in my hands [Cicero's] *Philippics* or *Speeches against Mark Antony* and those cynical invectives, so to speak, which he vehemently thundered against Verres, against Catiline, against Sallust, and against many other people." Rho obviously took all of these as equally authentic, as had Petrarca earlier and as did other Renaissance humanists.

Surprisingly, Rho took only two excerpts from the first of Cicero's four authentic speeches against Catiline but took twenty-one from the rare pseudo-Ciceronian *Declamation against Lucius Sergius Catilina*, a spurious work attributed to Cicero in nearly all of the manuscripts.[79] Rho quoted it as a work of Cicero and showed no hesitation in accepting this faulty ascription. His excerpts in the *Rhetorical Imitations* (early 1433) make his the earliest known use of the *Declamation* (Appendix VIII, §3)[80] although it must have had some circulation

---

[78]For Cicero, see Butler; for Pseudo-Cicero and the Cicero/Sallust material, see De Marco 1991; Osmond and Ulery 187, 196–201, 220–21, 321–26; see also Schindel; Seel 1966a and 1966b.

[79]By its second printing (Venice, 1491), the editors, doubting the attribution to Cicero, attributed it to Ovid's teacher, M. Porcius Latro, a name found in only one manuscript. After this too was recognized as incorrect, it circulated as the work of "pseudo-M. Porcius Latro." Recent editions make no attempt to name the author and simply refer to it as the *Declamation against Lucius Sergius Catilina*. Scholars have also reached no agreement about its provenance, either when it was written or when it began circulating. All extant manuscripts date from the fifteenth century, most from the latter half of the fifteenth century (see Kristoferson 5–57). For a critical edition (with an introduction in Swedish), see Kristoferson; for Kristoferson's text with an Italian translation and introduction, see De Marco 1991; for a critical text based on fewer manuscripts but with a good introduction in German, see Zimmerer. While this book was in proofs, I learned of, but have not seen, Katrin Schurgacz's new edition (Trier: WVT, 2004).

[80]The first dedication of the *Imitations* is to Archbishop Bartolomeo Capra, who died in 1433.

earlier simply as one of Cicero's orations against Catiline.[81] The first clear reaction against Ciceronian authorship came in 1451 when Poggio expressed surprise to hear of a "fifth" Catilinarian. He rightly doubted its authenticity but still wanted to acquire a copy.[82] Others also held the *Declamation* suspect. Cardinal Bessarion, for example, made a note in his manuscript indicating he had no idea who wrote it.[83] In any case, Rho must have come across the *Declamation* in a manuscript containing orations ascribed to Cicero, some or most of which were probably genuine. As seen earlier, Rho in his *Apology* (§18) named the invectives of Cicero he had read by 1427/28, but his statement is too imprecise to determine whether he was referring only to the *Declamation* or to some or all of the four genuine *Catilinaria*.[84]

6. St. Jerome

The two longest series of excerpts on "Vilifying" to appear in Rho's *Rhetorical Imitations* are quotations from Jerome[85] and from Rho's own *Philippic*.[86] Jerome, in contrast to Cicero, practiced invective not as a deliberative or forensic activity but as a strictly literary exercise. While Cicero had partially affected this transition from oration to literature by circulating orations that he never actually delivered, Jerome's invectives never feign to have been delivered orally. This transition has other precedents as well, but Jerome would merit serious consideration as the "archetypal master" of the strictly literary, epistolary invective adopted by the

---

[81] Since no manuscript antedates the fifteenth century, Schanz (154) has suggested that it was a fifteenth-century forgery; Castiglioni (1929, 268) has made the case directly. By contrast, in favor of its origin in antiquity, perhaps late antiquity, is its resemblance to the Cicero/Sallust invectives, which are usually thought to have originated in ancient classrooms (see De Marco 1991, 89–91).

[82] Poggio (*Lettere* 3.10, 31.XI.1451) recognized that the incipit ("*Si quid precibus apud deos immortales . . .*") did not match the four accepted *Catilinaria*, and he knew that Cicero himself had only mentioned four (see Zimmerer 31–34, 45–46; Voigt 1880, 1:246, 2:265). Because Poggio referred to it as a "fifth Catilinarian" (but gave the incipit of the *Declamation*), care must be taken to distinguish it from another pseudonymous text that is known as the "Fifth Catilinarian," the incipit of which is: "*Non amplius tempus otii, patres conscripti . . .*" (see De Marco 1960a, 1960b, 1961/64, and 1991).

[83] "*Declamatoris nescio cuius in Catilinam oratio*" (see Kristoferson, 18–19, on Venice: Biblioteca Marciana, MS Marc. lat. Z 427). Remigio Sabbadini said the work was discovered not later than 1439 (Sabbadini 1996, 1:127, n. 6). The *Declamation* first went to print (Rome, 1490) in Pomponius Laetus' edition of Sallust's *Opera* along with his *spuria* (Kristoferson 29–30). For this edition Sabbadini (1996, 2:214) has both the publication date ("1471") and the publisher ("Bussi") incorrect. This is the date for the second printing of Sallust by Windelin of Speyer but not of the first printing of the *Declamatio* under the name of M. Porcius Latro (see Osmond and Ulery 199, 220).

[84] *Apology* §18. The Visconti Library had several manuscripts inventoried in 1426 simply as "Orations of Cicero," but Elisabeth Pellegrin (1955a and 1955b) could not locate the extant copies of these manuscripts. Perhaps they no longer exist, but the imprecise description in the inventory makes them difficult to identify.

[85] Appendix VIII, §4–§10 below.

[86] Appendix VIII, §14–§17 below.

Renaissance humanists.[87] The complete transition is dramatically represented in his invectives, which are either letters addressed to some individual sympathetic to his cause or letters written directly to the individuals being attacked. In addition to setting an example for epistolary invective, Jerome also legitimized elements of invective that certain cultural assumptions and the requirements of effective prosecution had earlier held in check. In the Roman court, an invective that went too far would be regarded not as legitimate invective (*accusatio*) but malediction (*maledictum* or *convicium*), that is, as mere insulting or cursing one's opponent.[88]

Whatever practical difficulties may have obscured the line between invective and malediction in its judicial context, Jerome effectively erased the theoretical distinction by importing language from the Imprecatory Psalms and by resorting to the Christian practice of cursing or anathematizing heretics. The Imprecatory Psalms, or, as they are sometimes called, the Vindictive Psalms, were formal curses of an enemy.[89] The strict meaning of the Greek word "anathematize" (*anathematizo*) is "make accursed" or "bind by a curse." In Christian usage it came ordinarily to mean "damn" or "excommunicate," as in St. Paul's expression "Let them be anathema."[90] Jerome's invectives were penned not with a judicial context in mind but were instead intended to vilify his opponents to the widest possible (mostly Christian) audience. Extreme though they might be, some of his most measured invectives were against his personal critics. In these he often tempered his invective with argument and evidence. Utterly extreme are some of his invectives against bishops, monks, women, and Jews.

According to David Wiesen, Jerome was "the author of the final chapter in the brilliant volume of ancient satire. . . ."[91] Wiesen correctly points out the enormous range of satiric elements in Jerome's writings. Wiesen is also right in seeing Jerome as someone who loved to turn a satiric phrase and did so frequently, even in his commentaries on scripture. Jerome on a few occasions even spoke of himself as imitating Horace and Juvenal.[92] Antonio da Rho, however, situated Jerome not in the satirical but in the invective tradition, and convincingly so, as had Petrarca

---

[87]Cf. Rao 1988–90, 264: "The late classical and early Christian periods abound with writings which bore the title of *invectiva*, or which were referred to as such. Even in such an age of common polemics, one man stood above all others, St. Jerome. He had a real talent for the invective. . . . Besides his own powerful rhetorical arsenal, Jerome, a great admirer of the classical pagan authors, deployed their satiric material; in addition he quarried the vast invective elements from the Bible. . . . This peculiar combination of pagan and Christian elements is the trademark of Jerome's invectives. Other noteworthy examples of invectives are Julian the Apostate's orations against Constantius and two poetic invectives by Claudian, not to mention several writings of Arnobius, Tertullian, and Paulus Orosius."

[88]See Merrill 35–36.

[89]Those referred to as the "Imprecatory Psalms" are Psalms 35, 58, 59, 69, 83, 94, 109, 137, and 140. Other Psalms also contain imprecations: 5.10, 10.15, 28.4, 31.17–18, and 40.14–15.

[90]For Jerome, see Wiesen 90–112, 167–88; for the New Testament precedents see I Corinthians 16.22, Romans 9.3, and Galatians 1.9; cf. also I Timothy 1.20 and I Corinthians 5.5. For Rho's attempt at making Panormita a heretic, see *Philippic* §100.

[91]Wiesen 264.

[92]Wiesen 2 and n. 5.

before him.[93] As Rho saw it, Jerome, in addition to being one of the greatest scholars of antiquity, was a prolific writer of invective. Not only did Jerome write invective, but, as noted above, he can be said to have developed the genre into an epistolary form. As had always been the case with invective, he included many satiric and comedic elements. That being said, when Jerome penned his letters (which amounted to short treatises) *Against Jovinian*, *Against Vigilantius*, *Against Helvidius*, *Against John of Jerusalem*, *Against the Books of Rufinus*, *Against the Pelagians*, and *Against the Luciferians*, he was not writing satire but invective.

While Antonio da Rho valued Jerome as a writer of invective, he was troubled by the unrestrained nature of some of Jerome's scurrility. Rho, whose admiration glows in his frequent reference to "my Jerome," recognized that the saint at times appeared to have completely lost self-control.[94] If Rho did not doubt the ethics of following Jerome in his more extreme passages, he at least hesitated about the efficacy of doing so. To be sure, Rho could in his own way be extreme, even cruel, as is evident in his less-than-subtle threats to Panormita about having him hauled before an inquisition. But Rho could not easily reconcile Jerome's vicious and abusive language with his own Christian ethics and Franciscan profession, especially with the ideals articulated in the Sermon on the Mount and the Rule of Saint Francis. Rho, in short, took precautions to be more restrained in his invective than Jerome. That Jerome had penned invectives of such a caustic nature gave Rho ample cover, or so he thought, in going the distance he did.[95] Many humanists, when writing their own invectives, did not share Rho's scruple.

7. The *Apology*

Antonio da Rho wrote his *Apology against a Certain Archdeacon and his Loathsome Sycophant Accomplices* to the Minister General of the Franciscan Order, Antonio da Massa Marittima (d. 1435). Although the external evidence discussed below indicates the event to which the *Apology* responds, the internal evidence standing alone fixes the date of its composition between 1426 and 1428. Giuseppe Lombardi has fixed the *terminus a quo* as 1426, the year of the appearance in Milan of Antonio Panormita's *Hermaphrodite*, and the *terminus ad quem* as 1430, when Antonio da Massa was replaced as Minister General of the Franciscans. Rho's remarks about Panormita's *Hermaphrodite* (§31) and his statement that he often met Bartolomeo Capra outside the convent of San Francesco Grande (§53)

---

[93]Cf. Coffey 8, who would agree that Jerome was not a writer of satire. In speaking of the genre of Roman satire, Coffey states emphatically that "the line of verse satire ended with Juvenal, and satire in a mixture of prose and verse with Petronius." He goes on to say that "the case for the continuity of the classical tradition of satire [in late antiquity and through the Middle Ages] cannot be made good."

[94]*Philippic* §177.

[95]*Philippic* §177 and *Apology* §16. The closest Rho comes to hesitation about Cicero is a statement regarding Cicero's *Against Piso*: "Was Cicero a bit angry at the time? Yes, but he was fulfilling the responsibilities of an orator" (*Philippic* §108).

led Lombardi to conclude further that the *Apology* must have been written before Panormita came to Milan in 1429, and, more precisely, before Bartolomeo Capra left Milan to become the governor of Genoa in late February of 1428.[96]

Further external evidence establishes the "precise incident" which triggered the *Apology*. If Rho was appealing a decision already made (as it appears), then the *Apology* was written after June of 1427 and before late February of 1428 when Capra left for Genoa. Although Rho nowhere named the "certain archdeacon," the evidence points securely to Manfredo Gambaloita, the archdeacon of the Cathedral Chapter in Milan, who remained in his post until 1435. Moreover, little doubt remains that the "loathsome sycophant accomplices" were some, or all, of the cathedral canons.[97] Six years earlier, on 21 July 1421, the archdeacon and canons met and chose the Dominican Pietro Alzate to fill the chair of theology vacated at the death of the Franciscan Francesco Crivelli. The record of this meeting survives and it lists those in attendance.[98] Some turnover among the canons may have taken place in the intervening six years, but most surely still held their positions. The action taken at the chapter meeting in 1427 would have closely mirrored that taken at the previous appointment of 21 July 1421. For the appointment in 1427, the only witness is a document that either ratifies or predisposes the chapter proceedings: most probably but not certainly the former. This document was drawn up in Milan authorizing the appointment of the Dominican Marco da Vimercato "to lecture on theology in the major church of this our city of Milan."[99]

Although Rho's disappointment might seem to explain his motives, the depth of his indignation and his sense of injustice suggests that something more was involved. Rho's reaction to the archdeacon and canons becomes understandable

---

[96]See Lombardi's (42) analysis of the internal evidence regarding the time frame of the *Apology*. Vismara (1900a, 201–09) earlier made complete hash of the historical context of Rho's *Apology* and *Philippic*, thinking the *Philippic* was written *before* the *Apology*. Vismara concluded that various ecclesiastics had been deeply offended that in writing his *Philippic* Rho had "adopted the style of the humanists to defend morality" (*avesse adottato lo stile degli umanisti per difendere la morale*). So many complaints reached Antonio da Massa that "Rho was forced to write an apology" (*tanto che il Raudense fu obbligato a stendere una apologia*). Vismara was also shocked that "this friar had married his religion to humanism!" (*che questo frate ha sposato la sua religione all' umanesimo!*). Vismara made this remark in reaction to an unsourced quotation, which by its arrangement suggests that it came from the *Philippic*. It does not, and I have not found the quotation in any of the related documents: the *Philippic*, Rho's correspondence, or the *Anonymous Invective* (which Vismara thought not to be by Rho).

[97]Probably most, possibly all, of the same Canons at the Chapter Meeting on 21 July 1421 (see n. 98 below).

[98]Manfredo Gambaloita was archdeacon from 1413 to 1435 (Castiglioni 1954, 33). He presided in 1421 accompanied by Paganino Besozzi, Giovanni Grassi, Dionigi Brivio, Pietro Cotta, Maffiolo Brivio, Luigi La Strata, and Ambrogio Bossi, "*omnes canonici sive ordinarii prefate Mediolanensis ecclesie*" (Milan: ASM, fondo Notai, R.C., busta 202). I am indebted to Dottore Grazioso Sironi for directing me to this document.

[99]The document (Maiocchi 2/1:236; see also Corradi 186–87) records the appointment of Stefano Bandello da Tortona to the post in Pavia formerly held by Marco da Vimercato and Marco's transfer to Milan (*loco magistri Marci de Vicomercato, ab ea lectura ad lecturam theologie, in Ecclesia Maiori huius nostre civitatis Mediolani, nuper translati*).

(though not necessarily defensible) if we examine the history of the appointments to the chair of theology at the Duomo and consider the appointment for which Rho was passed over in June of 1427. We find a clue in the rotational patterns for appointments of the religious orders, both in Milan and in Pavia. These rotations clearly show that at the end of the Dominican Pietro Alzate's tenure the Franciscans expected to hold the next appointment and thus nominated Rho for the position.

At this point we should review what little is known of the Dominican Marco da Vimercato and make some comparisons between Vimercato and Rho. They were about the same age (Rho was thirty-two) and at similar stages in their careers. Vimercato took his degree in Pavia in 1423 in the same year that Rho had earned his degree in Padua.[100] The *rotuli* of the University of Pavia show that Vimercato, even as a simple friar (with a bachelors degree?), had been lecturing on metaphysics and Aristotle's *Parva naturalia* in Pavia since 1419 and that he held a joint appointment in theology and logic in the academic year 1425–26 and again in 1426–27.[101] Rho had been listed since 1423 in the minutes of the chapter meetings at San Francesco Grande in Milan as "professor of the sacred page" ("professor of theology" in Franciscan parlance) and had from that time consistently styled himself a theologian.[102] What theological topics he lectured on during these years remains unknown, but he must also at that time have pursued humanistic studies and even taught them occasionally.[103]

The reader has ample opportunity in the *Apology* itself to peruse Rho's own view of the matter, but it is worth noting what he regarded as the principal charge brought against him: namely, ignorance.[104] He further explained this charge when he took up the question of reading the poets, which he feared would "aggravate the wound my adversaries have inflicted."[105] A few years later in the prologue to his *Rhetorical Imitations* he wrote that "some people" (presumably, the archdeacon and his sycophants) have attacked him because they thought it improper for a theologian to teach pagan literature.[106] This points to what, in the view of the archdeacon and canons, must have constituted a significant difference in the education and teaching experience of Rho and Vimercato. Although we know little about Vimercato's education or interests beyond his university experience, some reasonable guesses can be made from these hints. As a Dominican lecturing on theology, metaphysics, and Aristotle's *Parva naturalia*, Vimercato probably struck

---

[100]For Vimercato, see Maiocchi 2/1:199 (*bachalarius*), 2/1:210 (*magistratus seu doctoratus*); for Rho, see *Apology* §49 n. 186.

[101]Maiocchi 2/1:185, 198, 199, 220, 226, 227.

[102]Rutherford 1990, 82–88.

[103]See nn. 106 and 108 below.

[104]*Apology* §2.

[105]*Apology* §29.

[106]Rho (*Imitations* 4v): "For they say that a theologian should not pass on knowledge about the literature and sayings of the pagans and disclose certain unknown and hidden rites" (*Dicunt enim haud licere theologum litterarum harum verborumque gentilium notitiam tradere, ignotos et occultos quosdam ritus in lucem afferre*). For Rho's reworking of this passage, see Monfardini xlx.

the archdeacon and canons as a "real" theologian. Even though Rho clearly had similar university training and solid scholastic credentials, Rho's statement suggests that the archdeacon and canons were not prepared to concede Rho's humanistic notion of what a theologian should know and when he should know it.

When Rho sought the intervention of the Franciscan Minister General, Antonio da Massa, he expected the Minister General to pressure the proper Milanese authorities, presumably both ecclesiastical and secular, to remedy the situation. Rho claimed that he was on familiar terms with both the Archbishop of Milan and the Bishop of Bergamo, the latter also a Conventual Franciscan. The powers and the prerogatives of the archdeacon and canons could be substantial,[107] even sufficient to circumvent the will of Rho's Order locally and ignore the archbishop's support, which Rho implied that he had. But in late 1427 or early 1428, while Rho was struggling through the twists and turns of Milanese ecclesiastical politics, Antonio da Massa found himself in his own political imbroglio that required papal intervention. No evidence indicates that Antonio da Massa ever received the *Apology*, and it looks even less probable that he ever made a response. For in 1429, Pope Martin V sacked him for his inability to manage the bitter quarrel between the Conventual and Observant wings of the Franciscan Order. The removal of Antonio da Massa as Minister General in 1429 and the election of Guglielmo da Casale Monferrato in 1430 almost certainly mean that no one at that level of the Franciscan Order ever intervened in this Milanese "quarrel among the monks."

His failed candidacy for the chair of theology at the Duomo of Milan did not actually harm Rho's career. Inasmuch as he styled himself a theologian, it may have tarnished his dignity; but inasmuch as humanistic studies made him their captive, it must have furthered these studies, which were, after all, his long suit. When the famed humanist educator Gasparino Barzizza died in 1430, Rho assumed his position in the *studium* of Milan and taught there for many years.[108]

Rho's *Apology* recounts the course of his education, including which authors he has read, arranged according to categories. It also reveals his devotion to and affection for various authors and subjects. As Giuseppe Lombardi has observed, his references to works and their titles closely corresponds to the inventory of the Visconti Library in Pavia, which was one of the largest libraries in Europe. Elizabeth Pellegrin's study of the Visconti Library and its inventories identifies many manuscripts from the Visconti Library which are now scattered across Europe, and makes it possible to see Rho's sources. When

---

[107] For the institutional structure of the archdiocese, and specifically on the duties and powers of the archdeacon, see Cattaneo, esp. 661–63.

[108] Barzizza is known to have suffered poor health leading up to his death, now securely dated at the end of June 1430 (Mercer 135–36). One of Rho's inaugural orations (presumably the first one) for this position in the *studium* of Milan is extant, and he there speaks of the recent death of Barzizza (Lombardi 25, 119, 126). Bertola Visconti, in a letter dated 7 August 1432, speaks of the death of Barzizza and of *sacer theologus Raudensis noster successor in palestra* (Milan: Biblioteca Ambrosiana, MS H 48 inf., 108r-v; Fossati 355). This implies that Rho held the position at least during the previous academic year (1431–32).

Rho speaks of books as his "internal friends," it becomes clear that he is mostly working from memory or perhaps occasionally from notes. Rarely could he pull a book off the shelf to refresh his memory. His blunders, in fact, often prove to be accurate recollections of mistakes found in manuscripts from the Visconti Library. When he was "an old man" (about fifty), he tells us how age had broken his body and weakened his mind, forcing him to sit and read his oration. Whereas formerly, he said, "whatever I wrote or read, I so committed to memory, as if it were impressed and stamped there, that at the time I thought libraries and books were for me superfluous."[109]

Although he followed the advice of Antonio Loschi and abandoned his childhood ambition to become a poet in order to pursue philosophy,[110] his ardor for the pursuit of eloquence never waned. He also carried throughout his life the interest in natural philosophy that is evident in his *Apology*. But by professional choice he remained fundamentally devoted to theology, that is, to his Franciscan vocation as a "professor of the sacred page." This reflects his adherence to the traditional view that all knowledge and all other disciplines had value insofar as they served theology. Rho, in many respects like the Franciscans generally, valued rhetoric in large part because it served preaching.[111] Throughout his life Rho held that rhetoric, philosophy, and theology should be regarded in an ascending order of importance.[112]

8. The *Philippic*

When in late 1427 or early 1428 Rho wrote the *Apology* to his Minister General, Antonio da Massa, he expressed his reluctance to speak about the poets, since doing so would "aggravate the wound" that his adversaries had opened. He explained that whenever these "severe men" saw anyone handle the poets, they would "bite and rend with censorious words . . . as if to know the poets were a sin."[113] He urged his adversaries to read "Augustine, Jerome, Basil the Great, the Apostle Paul, and finally Moses and Canon Law." They would learn from these "that to have once studied the poets is in no way a sacrilege," but rather that "to know them [was] very worthwhile."[114]

Rho enumerated the poets whom he had read and gave a brief description of them and their merits. Virgil's serious works, not surprisingly, Rho thought were unsurpassed. Even Virgil's "lascivious and obscene verse," supposedly written in

---

[109] *Funeral Oration for Niccolò Piccinino*, 1444: *Quicquid semel scripseram aut legeram, ita ipsi memoriae impressum et sigillatum commendaram, ut bibliothecas iam mihi et libros supervacuos esse putarem* (Milan: Biblioteca Ambrosiana, MS B 124 sup., 143r–148v; Fossati 350).

[110] *Philippic* §47.

[111] For Franciscan preaching and rhetoric, see O'Malley 1986.

[112] Rutherford 1998, esp. 178–85.

[113] Rho speaks derisively of a group of "severe men" (*Apology* §24), who are doubtlessly the same men who attacked him for studying the poets (*Apology* §29).

[114] *Apology* §29.

his youth, Rho admitted to having read. He remarked further that he knew well Ovid, Lucan, Statius, Juvenal, Persius, and Horace.[115] He lamented not having found copies of comic poets Caecilius and Ennius, but he had read Plautus and Terence with enthusiasm and pleasure.[116] Before Rho turned his pen to the authors of "the age preceding and extending into our own,"[117] he said that for the present he would omit "a dense mob of . . . glory seekers": Catullus, Tibullus, Propertius, and the obscene Martial.

Along with these he named "our contemporary, a certain Antonio Panormita, whose genius will not be condemned but his life someday will be unless he writes serious verse subsequent to his filthy ones (as Virgil did)." Concerning these lascivious poets, Rho remarked, "it more than sufficed me to have read them once, and perfunctorily at that."[118] Without having named the work, Rho was clearly referring to *The Hermaphrodite*, a book of skillfully crafted verse that Antonio Beccadelli, usually called "Panormita," published in late 1425.[119] Panormita's friends had actively disseminated the book, and it quickly received high praise. In a letter to Panormita, Guarino Veronese lauded him for having matched the verse of Catullus and Ovid but expressed some reservations about *The Hermaphrodite*. Panormita suppressed Guarino's criticisms and attached the letter as introductory material to the work.[120] Panormita also used a letter from Poggio in the same way but left intact Poggio's expressed (but possibly disingenuous) misgivings about writing such material.[121]

Panormita dedicated the work to Cosimo de' Medici. He later sent a copy to the Marchese Gian Francesco Gonzaga of Mantua, who was reported to have read it with enthusiasm. In neither instance, however, did Panormita find the patronage for which he hoped. He eventually completed his law degree at Pavia on the advice of the Archbishop of Milan, Bartolomeo Capra, and in December of 1429 he became the handsomely paid aulic poet of Filippo Maria Visconti, the Duke of Milan. To Panormita's great satisfaction, Emperor Sigismund, on the merits of *The Hermaphrodite*, crowned him poet laureate in 1432 at Parma.[122]

Many Observant Franciscans — including Roberto da Lecce, Alberto Sarteano, and San Bernardino da Siena — soon denounced *The Hermaphrodite* in their sermons. For Panormita had not only imitated the style of Catullus, Ovid,

---

[115]*Apology* §30.
[116]*Apology* §31.
[117]*Apology* §32.
[118]*Apology* §31.
[119]The nickname "Panormita" derives from his hometown, the Sicilian city Palermo (Latin *Panormus*). For the recent critical text of *The Hermaphrodite* by Coppini, see Beccadelli 1990a; for an English translation based on the older Latin text by Forberg, see Beccadelli 2001; and Cossart.
[120]Cinquini and Valentini 55–56.
[121]Poggio's *Facetiae* are notable for the racy stories circulating at the Papal Court. It is not easy to reconcile Poggio's authorship of the *Facetiae* with his remarks to Panormita about the impropriety of now writing something like *The Hermaphrodite*.
[122]For Panormita, see Corbellini 1–291; Resta 1954 and 1965; Sabbadini 1891, 1–47; 1916, 5–28; Cinquini and Valentini.

and Martial, but he also rivaled them in sexually graphic content. According to his morally indignant contemporaries, it was nothing but filth and obscenity. His *Hermaphrodite* lampooned and vilified friends and foes alike in their public and private life. It engendered considerable hostility for its representation of various sexual taboos and because it with some regularity resorts to material that is transparently autobiographical.

A series of events between 1427/28, when Rho wrote the *Apology*, and 1431/32, when he wrote the *Philippic*, clearly changed the way Rho felt about the author of *The Hermaphrodite*. He remarked in the *Apology* (§31) that Panormita's life might come under censure but his genius would not. This in no way detracted from Panormita's prized self-image as a poet and did no more harm to Panormita's reputation than his Epicurean *persona dramatis* in Valla's *On Pleasure*. Panormita had even expressed satisfaction for that recognition. For that matter, Rho's remark says nothing that Panormita did not say in his *Hermaphrodite*. But it is a near certainty that Panormita encountered Rho's remarks about him in the *Apology* only after moving to Pavia in 1429, that is, as he was confronting increasing condemnation as the author of *The Hermaphrodite*. As a result, he probably interpreted Rho's statement in the most sinister light. Panormita would also have encountered the remark in the context of various professional rivalries for the chair of rhetoric held by the ailing Gasparino Barzizza (who died at the end of June 1430). Panormita would not himself have been interested in this position, which paid at best forty florins per year, since he was retained as aulic poet at ten times that figure. Panormita did back Lorenzo Valla for the position, and Rho probably sought the position either for himself or for some member of his circle. Barzizza's chair in Pavia remained open in 1430–31. Rho did, however, take over his position in Milan perhaps as early as 1430–31 but at least by 1431–32,[123] the year that Lorenzo Valla filled the position in Pavia.

But just as this game of musical chairs was getting underway in late 1429, a series of literary attacks commenced that became increasingly vicious with each exchange. Although we do not know the names of all the participants in the controversies, we do know the names of the major figures. In one camp, Antonio da Rho and Pier Candido Decembrio, the ducal secretary and ambassador, worked steadily against Panormita. Initially, Panormita's circle included Niccolò Piccinino, Cambio Zambeccari, Antonio Cremona, Giovanni Feruffino, Catone Sacco, and Lorenzo Valla. Others, like Maffeo Vegio, appear to have remained on friendly terms with both sides.[124]

It is unclear who started the dispute. The earliest statement we have from Rho about Panormita is the one discussed earlier from the *Apology* of 1427/28. If Panormita first saw this remark in 1429, that may have set things in motion. In any case, the controversy became public when someone began circulating Latin verses attacking Panormita in mid-1429.

---

[123]See n. 108 above.
[124]This assumes that Vegio did not write *Prostitutes of Pavia* (see n. 141 below).

In August of that year Panormita wrote a letter to Cambio Zambeccari in which he said: "I learned about that poetry published against me not so long ago and its author — who was as uneducated as he was filthy — and I was full of pain for him and for his profession. For no particular reason except that he was induced by envy and singular irrationality, he provoked and tore into me, a foreigner and fellow poet who was conducting his life modestly."[125] Panormita obviously meant but did not name Rho. His reference to "the poetry published against me" and his description of it as "filthy" strongly suggest that Panormita had in mind the *Prostitutes of Pavia* (Appendix IV/1 below).

By September of 1429, some Latin poetry attacking Rho had begun to circulate. Antonio Cremona wrote to Panormita asking if he had written this verse against Rho. Panormita responded: "I certainly didn't compose that poetry, and, I'd say (*pace* the author), they're not like mine at all. You venture this presumptuously, as I would say, who never had an adequate grasp of the elegaic style or of the Sicilian Muses. But I've written more verbosely about this to him. I'm extremely delighted if he wasn't the instigator of that effrontery against me, as only you affirm, and restore and confirm my goodwill toward him. Nevertheless, should he turn out to be the author of that poem, I'll let him know that I'm no eunuch. Meanwhile I offend no one, since I've yet to make up my mind."[126] At almost the same time Panormita was writing to Cambio Zambeccari saying: "On the Rho matter you want to know what I myself have decided to do. Listen to this: I've resolved to compose another *Priapeia* to insult him.[127] And I've already completed many epigrams in which I've greatly surpassed, if not Virgil, at least myself. . . . These things are laid out so that if Antonio da Rho turns out to be the author of the blasphemy against me, as almost everyone recognizes, [I would say to him], 'you should pay a fine and undergo punishment'; if however he was not

---

[125]Panormita (VIII.1429) to Cambio Zambeccari (Sabbadini 1910a, 99–100): *Versus illos in me dudum editos iam et auctorem non minus indoctum quam impurum cognoveram eique satis abunde indolui et professioni suae, qui me advenam et compoetam et modeste vitam agentem lacessiverit laniaveritque nullam praesertim ob causam nisi adductus invidia et iniquitate singulari.*

[126]Panormita (IX.1429) to Antonio Cremona (Sabbadini 1910a, 81–82): *Cupis abs me scire an versus in Raudensem editos nuper ipse confecerim. Non composui equidem versus illos, neque (auctoris pace dixerim) meis similes vel minima sunt ex parte; facis arroganter, ut dicam, qui nundum satis intelligas filum elegiae et Musae Sicilienses. Sed hac de re ad eum verbosius scripsi, qui si non fuerit magister illius impudientiae contra me, ut solus affirmas, permaxime gaudeo et meam in se benivolentiam instauro ac confirmo; qui tandem, num versus auctor extiterit inveniatur, faxo me virum sentiat non spadonem, interea incertus neminem offendam.* Panormita's statement that he has "written more verbosely about this to him" may refer to the letter *Etsi facile* (Appendix I below). Sabbadini doubted that the timing would allow this identification. Rho does say that *Etsi facile* had circulated at court "a few days before he delivered it to me" (*Philippic* §3). One would have to assume that it had circulated since late 1429 without Rho's knowledge.

[127]By naming them his *Priapeia* Panormita indicated that these were obscene poems, imitating the so-called *Appendix Vergiliana*, a disparate collection of sexually explicit poems that circulated as the work of Virgil's youth. These poems were known to the humanists as Virgil's *Priapeia*. Modern scholars agree that, with the possible exception of *Catalepton* 5 and 8, Virgil did not write them (Conte 430–33; cf. *Apology* §30).

the author, it's only just that an innocent man should not suffer punishment."[128] Panormita made a similar assertion in a letter of March or April of 1430 to Sancio Balbo: "We've published a certain little book of epigrams on this topic against Rodent, the theologian. And we've greatly surpassed *The Hermaphrodite* in both acrimony and elegance, and (you may also add) in lewdness. I'm not sending it to you before you yourself demand it and before you, Sweetie, give me some little gift."[129] Clearly somewhere between September 1429 and April 1430 Panormita had lost all his inhibitions about circulating the *Priapeia* or about naming Rho as their intended target.

To these *Priapeia* someone responded with an invective against Panormita that laid out many of the themes Rho would later develop in his *Philippic*. Although this response is usually designated the *Anonymous Invective* (Appendix III below), Rho is most likely its author. Its present fragmentary state is an untitled and anonymous piece due to the loss of the end of the work. Remigio Sabbadini rejected Felice Ramorino's earlier attribution of the *Anonymous Invective* to Rho,[130] arguing against Rho's authorship on a single piece of evidence, namely, that the name "Rho" (*Raudensis*) appears there in the third person.[131] Yet third person references to himself are characteristic of Rho.[132] Even Sabbadini observed that Rho's *Philippic* follows or repeats the *Anonymous Invective* in important ways and that its author was probably a friar.[133] Furthermore, the defense of Jerome found in the *Anonymous Invective* is as consistent with Rho's pen as with that of any of his contemporaries.[134] And finally, the *Anonymous Invective* can with reasonable certainty be identified as the work Rho referred to in his *Philippic* when he wrote: "I recall having previously responded to him . . . basically blasting him then just as now."[135] Rho went on to say that his *Philippic* was more drawn out due to the growing body of material on Panormita. He further surmised that Panormita had either chopped the earlier work to pieces or had thrown it into the fire.

Whatever doubts may linger about the authorship of the *Anonymous Invective*, we can date it from the end of 1429 or early 1430. Panormita wrote in March or April of 1430 that he had finished his *Priapeia* against Rho. Then in

---

[128]Panormita (1429) to Cambio Zambeccari (Sabbadini 1910a, 101–02): *In re Raudensia cupis scire quid ipse statuerim. Ita accipe. Priapeiam alteram in eius ignominiam componere consilium ceperam, et feceram iam plurima epigrammata in quibus, si non Virgilium, longe me tamen exsuperaveram. . . . Haec eo tendunt ut, si Antonius Raudensis in me maledicentiae auctor extiterit, ut iuxta omnes sentiunt, 'tu patiare mulctem'; si vero minus fuerit, aequum est innocens ne plectatur.*

[129]Panormita (III/IV.1430) to Sancio Balbo (Sabbadini 1910a, 142–43): *Libellum quendam epigrammatum edidimus hoc loci in Rodium theologum; longe Hermaphroditum exsuperavimus et acrimonia et elegantia et, tu etiam adicias, petulantia; eum ad te non dimittam prius quam tute illum expostulaveris quamque me affeceris aliquo, Zucare, munusculo.*

[130]Ramorino 1880, 10.

[131]Sabbadini and Barozzi 2.

[132]See *Apology* §66 and *Philippic* §101, §145, §159, §178, §179.

[133]Sabbadini and Barozzi 3.

[134]See Introduction 39 n. 173 below.

[135]*Philippic* §189.

1431 Panormita openly circulated his letter to Rho, *Etsi facile* (Appendix I below), to intimidate him into silence.[136] Rho responded with his *Philippic*, which he must have passed around only in a limited circle in early 1432.

Contemporary statements about the invective poetry being circulated at that time were often shrouded in cryptic references. This has left the sequence of the extant poems and the reactions to them uncertain. Enough of the verse has survived, however, to give us the tone and character of the insults. One poem of seventy-two lines, *Prostitutes of Pavia* (Appendix IV/1 below), vilified Panormita with a no-holds-barred character assassination.[137] It purported to be a message from the prostitutes and pimps of Pavia, who tell the city of Milan to applaud the arrival of the "very well-hung Hermaphrodite who wiggles his ass like a woman." After this delicate beginning, the language gets coarse. Sometime later, a poem attacking Rho appeared that feigned to be a letter from Joan of Arc to the Senators of Milan (Appendix IV/3 below). In it "Joan" protested that the Milanese had sent this stupid, filthy, demonic, monstrous priest to her masquerading as a human. In early 1432 Panormita wrote to Maffeo Muzano with hackles raised: "I hear that some poetry was just recently published against Antonio da Rho and that he mistakenly thinks that I've turned out to be the author of this effrontery. He acts as boys usually do who begin to cry whenever they're caught stealing."[138] Panormita may have meant by "some poetry" the pseudo-Joan of Arc poem, but since he makes this remark in 1432 he must have been referring to his own *Priapeia*. Whatever poetry against Rho he meant, Panormita continued to snarl: "And people say that long ago Rho himself composed some extremely filthy poetry [*Prostitutes of Pavia?*] against me and my purity. I confess that I've not responded to this poetry until now for good reason. But when I decide to retaliate I'll enter combat with him not secretly as a thief but with a trumpet call, so that if some score must be settled, let it rather be for the person who stated his cause in a proclamation."[139] In his *Philippic*, Rho convincingly denied having written any such poetry and went on to assert (not altogether implausibly) that Panormita wrote it himself. He correctly pointed out that Panormita had in his *Hermaphrodite* said similar things about himself and that such writing was consistent with poetry and language of a kind Panormita had already circulated.[140]

In accordance with his own stated values, however, Rho might in this context have approved such language, written either by himself or by a friend, say Maffeo

---

[136]Rho (*Philippic* §3) says that he received Panormita's letter "last year from Pavia," probably 1431.

[137]Rho (see below) says that Panormita wrote it, which, if true, puts a completely different spin on the question.

[138]Panormita (early 1432) to Maffeo Muzano (Sabbadini 1910a, 145–46): *Audio quosdam versus nuperrime editos in Antonium Raudensem atque eum falso putare me illius impudentiae auctorem extitisse. Facit ut pueri solent qui percussores dum sint flere incipient.*

[139]Panormita (early 1432) to Maffeo Muzano (Sabbadini 1910a 145–46): *Et eum quidem Raudensem aiunt fecisse iamdudum contra me meamque puritatem foedissima quaedam carmina, quibus adhuc fateor me non respondisse bonam ob causam. Cum vero vicem reddere animo instituero, non clam more latronum sed signo dato secum confligam, ut si quid imputandum sit, sibi sit potius qui edicto causam dederit.*

[140]*Philippic* §36–§46.

Vegio (to whom it is ascribed in two manuscripts).[141] For in his *Rhetorical Imitations* he presented something close to an exhaustive list of Latin sexual terms — some medical, most obscene — and summed up with an explanation that such words ought to be used "only to execrate vice" (Appendix IX). He continued: "Some shameless men in our time not only play with such words and strew their verse with them, but, what is most shocking, they do not so much demand the execrated practice of bisexual cohabitation and promiscuous obscenities from literature as teach and glorify these things."[142] This leaves the question unresolved, however. Would Rho have considered writing something like *Prostitutes of Pavia* against Panormita as "execrating vice"? Probably not, if he were thinking of himself as the author. But if Rho suspected that one of his friends wrote it, he might have simply shrugged it off as falling under that rubric.

The details of Panormita's life as Rho recounted them in the *Philippic* cannot always be corroborated. Such, for instance, is the case with Rho's statement about Panormita having to flee Siena and another remark about one of Panormita's companions having to flee Bologna (§132). Furthermore, a number of the details that Rho related can now be refuted. Evidence suggests, for instance, that Rho asserted wrongly that Panormita had married before leaving Sicily (§132). Consequently, his other allegations regarding the wife's stolen dowry and its having been squandered on whores and sodomites cannot stand. Rho was also wrong when he related the rumor that Panormita had plagiarized his commentary on Plautus from Guarino Veronese (§120). And Cosimo de' Medici, contrary to Rho's claim, did not throw the dedicatory copy of Panormita's *Hermaphrodite* into the fire (§132). Rho's rhetorical restraint, atypical of much humanist invective, makes his work deceptively persuasive. He may not have possessed evidence contrary to the ugly rumors floating about, but his willingness to propagate any vicious gossip about Panormita requires us to examine his assertions carefully.

This raises the question of Rho's citation of evidence, especially his quotations from the letters of various contemporaries, including the letters of Panormita himself. Constant checks can be made on the accuracy of Rho's reading and reporting by following up his references to Panormita's letter *Etsi facile*, since the *Philippic* was a direct response to that letter (Appendix I below). In order to corroborate or discredit his vilification of Panormita we must consider his quotations from other letters, only some of which are known to have survived. One such letter came from the hand of Poggio and circulated widely, not least because Panormita affixed it to his *Hermaphrodite* as introductory material.[143] In this case we are able compare Rho's summary and "quotations" with the letter itself. Rho acknowledged Poggio's praise of "Panormita's talents" but downplayed them as "trivial and perfunctory compliments." In this passage Rho appears to quote Poggio, but what follows in fact is a paraphrase of Poggio's statement. Rho may have simply

---

[141]No attribution is secure: three manuscripts attribute it to Rho, two others to Maffeo Vegio, but others give no attribution (Rutherford 1990, 104).

[142]Rho *Imitations* 133v–135r: *Luxuria* (Appendix IX below).

[143]*Philippic* §76–§77.

quoted the passage from memory, bungling it just enough to produce a paraphrase. To his credit Rho represented Poggio's central idea fairly. At various times in the *Philippic* Rho quoted statements of Panormita. For instance, we encounter a summary of a poem in *The Hermaphrodite* that gives directions to a brothel in Florence and the names of the prostitutes who worked there.[144] Rho's summary is misleading neither in detail nor in tone, the latter being what he most sought to exploit.

When we consider Rho's use of evidence from Panormita's correspondence, the surprise is that he did not quote from it more frequently, especially if he was more or less honest when he said that "Practically every day [Panormita's] puny letters, poetry, and sundry lucubrations are left with me. . . ."[145] Panormita himself boasted that his letters "number[ed] about a thousand" and were even at that time circulating widely in northern Italy.[146] Two instances of the use of Panormita's letters will suffice for illustration. In one passage Rho "anticipated" a response to his criticism of Panormita for careless composition in his letters. Rho opened this passage with "But Panormita will immediately recover and say. . . ." In actuality Rho summarized a letter of Panormita to Francesco Barbavara, even quoting various phrases from it.[147] In another passage, Rho directly acknowledges the letter that he was quoting and paraphrasing by remarking parenthetically to Panormita "as you wrote to Cambio da Bologna, your Maecenas." Again Rho has reported the statement with reasonable accuracy. But what one might regard more generously as an expression of exuberant gratitude on the part of Panormita, Rho took as an expression of insufferable arrogance and malicious intent.[148] It is by no means obvious that Rho was wrong.

From such passages we may judge others which do not survive. I mention two examples in particular because Rho included them for their obvious shock value. The first of these were "some laws which the infernal man sought to get enacted on behalf of his whores, catamites, and sodomites." According to Rho, Panormita had called these laws his "Futuarian Laws," meaning literally "Fuckers' Laws." Rho went on to say that Panormita had "broadcast these laws practically throughout the whole world using the associations of pimps and whores. . . ." Beyond giving the title of these laws, speculating about how they circulated, and trusting to his readers' imagination, Rho provided little information about them except a sneering criticism of Panormita's amateurish attempt to imitate archaic legalese.[149]

Another example that we must judge without benefit of the originals is a series of quotations ostensibly from the correspondence of Giovanni Aurispa, an admired

---

[144]*Philippic* §74; Panormita's poem is in *Hermaphrodite* 2.37.

[145]*Philippic* §117.

[146]See *Philippic* §118 n. 292. Panormita went on to say that he did not want his letters "to be numbered among my works or to be pulled together into a collection." Contrary to this assertion, Panormita did pull together a collection of his letters, leaving them in his own hand (Vatican City: Biblioteca Apostolica Vaticana, MS. Vat. lat. 3371).

[147]*Philippic* §118 and n. 292.

[148]*Philippic* §178 and n. 512.

[149]*Philippic* §137.

Sicilian humanist with whom Rho unfavorably contrasts Panormita.[150] These quotations allude to a certain "Adonis," a name that Aurispa in all probability did not use. If the passages from Aurispa's letters are read substituting some other name for "Adonis," Rho's interpretation becomes suspect as tendentious, even wildly tendentious. Regardless of the name that Aurispa used, Rho still may have been correct about the situation Aurispa was discussing. For although Rho may have distorted or exaggerated some of the details and evidence, his report does not conflict with Panormita's notoriety for having male lovers.[151] Two were known by their Greek literary nicknames. One was called "Ergoteles" after an immigrant to Himera from Crete whose Olympic victory Pindar celebrated in *Olympic Ode* 12. The other was called "Hylas" after the young, beautiful companion of Hercules, who had been stolen by the Nymphs and was long sought by Hercules thereafter. Ergoteles has been identified as a young Bolognese, Tomaso Tebaldi, whom Panormita met in Bologna and took with him to Rome and then to Lombardy.[152] Hylas has been identified as Enrico da Napoli, whom Panormita had with him only in Naples.[153] When Rho made references to or changed the name in Aurispa's letter to "Adonis," he was almost certainly speaking of Ergoteles. Similarly, when Lorenzo Valla related his story about "Hylas" in his invective *Antidote against Facio*, he doubtless was speaking of Ergoteles as well.[154] Rho and Valla must have switched nicknames, because the significance of "Ergoteles" was by no means clear, whereas the significance of "Adonis" and "Hylas" was unmistakable. Not only do we have statements from other contemporaries, such as Valla, but we have Panormita's own statements in his *Hermaphrodite* and correspondence.[155] Near the end of the *Philippic*, Rho states that his best evidence against Panormita was that "wretched little book, [*The Hermaphrodite*, which] will never be read without declaring your indecency, how filthily, recklessly, lustfully, and barbarously you've lived your life. The same witness will always be at hand."[156]

---

[150] *Philippic* §94–§99.

[151] This assumption, as Rho points out, mostly derived from things Panormita said about himself in *The Hermaphrodite* and from letters and poems (see n. 155 below).

[152] See *Philippic* §132 n. 338.

[153] Enrico da Napoli, nicknamed "Hylas," who was Panormita's lover in Naples, must be distinguished from Enrico Hylas da Prato, who was hanged and quartered for trying to poison Filippo Maria Visconti (Sabbadini 1910b). See also Regoliosi 1981, 266–67; Sabbadini 1910a, 144, n. 1; Sabbadini and Barozzi 15; Cinquini and Valentini 32.

[154] See *Philippic* §132 n. 338.

[155] Panormita dedicated a poem to Ergoteles (Natale 130): "Since the poet is unable to send you money, he sends you poems. But you value poems more than money. Verse [after all] will snatch anyone from the jaws of Death: Itys and Hylas live on in song. O fortunate boy, whom the poets love, O boy, grateful to the poet that you are not to die a boy. Yes, the holy poet loves you, and he struggles in order to keep you alive too. You alone study how he loves you. Be well, therefore, Ergoteles, lone hope of a dear parent, the ancestral hope, by god, a boy but old in seriousness" (*Cum nequeat nummos, mittit tibi carmina vates, / Tu tamen argento carmina pluris habe. / Eripiunt quemvis a mortis dente camoenae. / Carmine vivit Itys, carmine vivit Hylas. / Fortunate puer, quem dilexere poetae. / Grate puer vati, non moriere puer. / Et te sanctus amat vates, ut teque perennet / Conatur, modo tu cur amet ille stude. / Ergo vale, Ergoteles, cari spes una parentis, / Spes patria hercle puer, sed gravitate senex*).

[156] *Philippic* §182.

Even if Rho sounds convinced of everything he alleged against Panormita, his occasional forays as a preacher of repentance against Panormita sound disingenuous. It is not when Rho condemned pederasty, sodomy, adultery, and other sexual activity on his list of moral transgressions: about these he spoke with sufficient sincerity. Rather, it is his calculated threats to expose Panormita to public shame and humiliation, even raising the specter of an inquisition, instead of attempting to lead Panormita to private guilt and contrition that give pause about Rho's candor in his preaching, or, more accurately, in his sermonizing.[157]

While the exchange between Panormita and Rho was underway, Pier Candido Decembrio and Panormita carried on their own campaign of insults and reprisals. In one instance Decembrio ridiculed Panormita's first major attempt to earn his annual 400 florins from Duke Filippo Maria Visconti. Panormita had composed an oration that lionized Filippo Maria Visconti as the Sun. This "Oration on the Imagery of the Sun" (Appendix VII below) was read publicly on more than one occasion. In late 1431 Decembrio wrote a dialogue (now lost) with himself, Rho, and possibly others as interlocutors. As Rho described it, Decembrio's dialogue was "filled with open ridicule and jokes" about Panormita's "Sun."[158]

Regarding a more serious matter, Guarino Veronese in early 1429 wrote in praise of Francesco Bussone, "il Carmagnola" (ca. 1380–1432), formerly a Milanese *condottiere* and member of Filippo Maria Visconti's Secret Council. In 1426 Carmagnola had defected to the Venetians, who had formed a coalition with Florence and Savoy to block Milanese expansion. Decembrio, a secretary and ambassador of Filippo Maria Visconti, responded to Guarino. Panormita's rebuttal of Decembrio seems not to have survived; indeed he himself probably tried to suppress it. For Panormita to praise the Venetians and Carmagnola while pursuing a career at the court of Filippo Maria Visconti was singularly imprudent. Decembrio seized this opportunity to attack Panormita and Guarino as well. Decembrio continued to use Panormita's political gaffe against him, but especially so when at the end of 1432 Panormita's most important patron, Francesco Barbavara, another member of the duke's Secret Council, fell into disfavor and went into exile.[159] In 1433 Panormita unhappily found himself demoted from aulic poet to lecturer of rhetoric, with his salary reduced from 400 to thirty florins per year. His days as a courtier of Filippo Maria Visconti were over.

Much of the political undertow in Rho's *Philippic* derives from the precarious situation in which Antonio Panormita found himself as a result of the Carmagnola debacle. Consequently, toward the end of the controversy, members of Panormita's circle began to align themselves with Rho and Decembrio. The humanist professor

---

[157] *Philippic* §173–§174.

[158] See *Philippic* §125–§131.

[159] Sabbadini and Barozzi 43–47. Decembrio's letter to Rho against Panormita (Appendix VI below) was written subsequent to the execution of Carmagnola (5 May 1432). Nothing in Rho's *Philippic* shows any awareness of this event, which makes it nearly certain that the *Philippic* was written before Decembrio's letter.

of rhetoric, Lorenzo Valla, and the distinguished jurist, Catone Sacco, both turned against Panormita and moved into the circle of Rho and Decembrio. Antonio Cremona, one of Panormita's friends and Barbavara's close associate, within a few years of Barbavara's exile had become an Observant Franciscan. If Panormita was not completely isolated, he must have felt increasingly abandoned in Milanese circles. After finding employment in Naples with Alfonso V of Aragon, Panormita went on to an illustrious and lucrative career in the southern kingdom. When Lorenzo Valla also took a position with Alfonso V, he and Panormita renewed their enmity and continued their mutual recriminations and invectives.

The chorus of condemnation that rose against *The Hermaphrodite*, especially from Franciscan quarters, has led some to see Rho's *Philippic* simply as one more, and perhaps the most forceful, Franciscan attack on *The Hermaphrodite*. This interpretation misses the mark in that Rho's *Philippic* attacked Panormita and not *The Hermaphrodite*. To the extent that Rho made *The Hermaphrodite* an issue, it was for the purpose of vilifying Panormita himself. At every twist and turn in the *Philippic*, Rho sought to refute Panormita's letter *Etsi facile* (Appendix I below) and to respond to its charges. Although *prima facie* Rho might seem to be (as he said of himself) "a respectable and modest man"[160] who was shocked by *The Hermaphrodite*, he frequently gives us reason to doubt that he was shocked and occasionally gives us evidence to refute such an assertion. In his attempt to discredit and vilify Panormita personally and professionally, he resorts to any piece of gossip. He exploits allegations about sexual taboos and plays to Lombard xenophobia with his slurs against Sicilians. He even denounced Panormita as a heretic, a veritable Helvidius, for insulting the Virgin.

On some level, no doubt, Rho thought all these things true, and perhaps convinced himself that they were simply and profoundly true. The reader, on the other hand, has to grapple with things that are profoundly complex. Rho further compounds this complexity through the use of the genre of rhetorical invective and by his recourse to its standard themes and topics. The *Philippic* responded to specific charges in Panormita's *Etsi facile*, it attacked Panormita himself, and it exploited a variety of highly charged issues. The reader should bear in mind that the *Philippic* only circulated in an extremely narrow circle, for it is doubtful that more than four or five copies ever existed: the manuscript *stemma* posits the existence of four. Rho himself only spoke of three: his own, Panormita's, and Decembrio's. Most of the pieces written by the various factions in this literary exchange circulated more widely and some were even posted publicly. Why not the *Philippic*? Because — as indicated in Panormita's offer of peace (Appendix II below) — Rho almost certainly suppressed it as a tradeoff for Panormita's suppression of his *Priapeia*. This collection of obscene verse vilifying and ridiculing Rho survives only in few fragments and most of those are quotations found in other authors. Through the assistance of the lawyers Catone Sacco (by this time Rho's confidant) and Domenico Feruffino (Panormita's friend) the open hostilities were finally ended. When Panormita agreed to "break his pen" and "abstain from

---

[160] *Philippic* §23.

invectives" as Rho had asked, both men must have agreed to suppress these works as well as to abstain from circulating future attacks.[161] They were undoubtedly expected to restrain members of their respective circles as well, although Valla had only just begun his attacks on Panormita. In later years, as discussed above, Valla would write against Rho also. As noted earlier, Rho reproduced long extracts from his own *Philippic* in his *Rhetorical Imitations* under the heading "Vilifying."[162] Indeed, these excerpts amount to an epitome of the *Philippic*, which indicates that Rho himself regarded his *Philippic* as an invective. Yet in his excerpts, he did not name Panormita as the target of his invective, but merely said that he had written these things "against a certain sycophant." In Milanese circles and probably elsewhere this would not have proved an especially cryptic reference.

Apart from the titillating aspects of this controversy with Panormita, it involved Rho once more with the broader issue of the utility of the poets and poetry that frequently engaged the early humanists.[163] For in condemning Panormita's *Hermaphrodite*, Rho would appear to have sided with those "severe men" denounced in his *Apology* who had disapproved his reading the poets.[164] Panormita's verse, after all, differed little, if at all — as Rho himself acknowledged — from those ancient poets whose literary value Rho had earlier defended or whose poetry he at least thought should be tolerated. But even in this controversy Rho never rejected the utility of ancient poetry, even though he deplored much of its content and valued more highly the disciplines of philosophy and theology. In the prologue to his *Rhetorical Imitations*, on which he must have been working while writing the *Apology* and *Philippic*, Rho invoked patristic example not only for reading the poets, but also for the manner in which they were to be handled. Most particularly he relied on the authority of Jerome, who had advanced the metaphor of "shaving the head of the woman captive," an allegorical application of Deuteronomy 21.11–13. This passage enjoins an Israelite to shave the head and pare the nails of any woman captive before he took her as a wife.[165] Rho explained: "Jerome here seemed to construe or understand such a woman as nothing but the obscene and libidinous teaching of pagans, from which God said all filth and smut ought to be removed. And finally Jerome meant that it is permitted to adapt this teaching to sacred literature when it has been washed, dried, and polished."[166] Panormita, in his letter *Etsi facile*, attempted to defend himself by appealing to Rho's humanist sensibilities and by invoking

---

[161]Catone Sacco must have already moved into Rho's circle by the time of this meeting.

[162]Appendix VIII, §14–§17 below.

[163]See Aguzzi-Barbagli; Esposito Frank; Greenfield; Sabbadini 1896a, 78–83; 1885, 93–99; Trinkaus 1970, 2:683–721; 1983b.

[164]*Apology* §24 and §29.

[165]Jerome *Letter* 21.13. For this metaphor (shave the head of the captive woman) as "appropriation" and the other common metaphor (plunder the Egyptians) as "reappropriation," see Camporeale 1976, 66–79.

[166]Rho (*Imitations* 5r): *Ubi Hieronymus ipse de muliere tali nihil quicquam aliud interpretari aut intellegere videbatur quam obscenam eorum gentilium luxuriantemque doctrinam, cuius omnem illuviem spurcitiamque dicebat ipse deus tolli oportere, et tandem illam perlutam, tersam expolitamque sacris litteris accommodari licere.*

Catullus' statement that the poetry may be impure but the poet himself is chaste.[167] Rho faulted Panormita for having chosen the poet Catullus for his primary defense. For if Panormita had read the Fathers, or at least Aristotle, he would have known that you are what you produce, or, in biblical language, you know the tree by its fruit.[168] Rho then paraphrases Poggio's letter to Panormita in which Poggio warned Panormita away "from this wanton genre of writing." Following what Rho described as "some trivial and perfunctory compliments of Panormita's talent," Poggio had said that "one could legitimately put in writing — indeed properly, gravely, and soberly — some things before Christ and other things after Christ. . . ." Poggio correctly argued, Rho believed, that "Virgil, Homer, and that whole host of poets and philosophers were of one era . . . but we are living in another."[169] In short, Rho thought that one could now usefully *read* those ancient poets who had laced their poetry with obscenities, but that one should not now *write* such poetry. He, however, would admit to having read these poets "only once, and perfunctorily at that."[170]

Rho on several occasions in the *Philippic* criticizes Panormita's vaunted identity as a poet ("a bad poet" according to Rho), and then denounces Panormita as a liar. Patristic and clerical attacks against poets as liars had created longstanding animosity in certain circles that the humanists occasionally took pains to dispel. The word "poet" comes from the Greek word *poiein*, meaning, "to make" or "to fabricate." It carried with it much of our sense of "fiction," which derives from the Latin word *fingere*, meaning "to make, devise, or imagine." To have merely asserted that Panormita was a poet and therefore a liar would have aligned Rho with the "severe men" who were his enemies. But when he said that Panormita had not learned "to create appropriate fictions but rather to tell manifest lies," Rho at one stroke attacked bad poetry and defended good poetry.[171] The imagination of a good poet should veil truth with apposite, attractive tropes; the imagination of a bad poet would veil lies with inappropriate, beguiling images.[172]

9. Continuities

A survey of Rho's life and work reveals a number of pervasive themes. The passion for knowledge in every human science that he manifested in his *Apology* remained strikingly evident in his *Three Dialogues against Lactantius,* written toward the end

---

[167] Panormita *Etsi facile* §1 (Appendix I below); cf. Martial 1.4.8.
[168] *Philippic* §69.
[169] *Philippic* §77; Coppini 148–49.
[170] *Apology* §31.
[171] *Philippic* §156; see also §150 and §191.
[172] Rho's position closely follows Lactantius (*Divine Institutes* 1.11.24–25): "They [the poets] do not know the limits of poetical licence and how far one may go in a fiction, since a poet's business lies in transposing reality into something else with metaphor and allusion and in covering up the misrepresentation with charm. To misrepresent the whole of one's subject matter is merely inept, however; to do that argues a liar, not a poet" (trans. Bowen and Garnsey). Cf. Petrarca 1975, 842, and n. 29.

of his life. His personal devotion to humanistic studies, to philosophy, and to theology governed not only his intellectual diversions but also his sustained and diligent professional commitment. It remained a sore point with him that the archdeacon and canons (and perhaps others) had criticized him for attempting to unite in his person and profession elements that they considered fundamentally incongruous, namely his simultaneous pursuit of theology and humanistic studies. He, however, persisted in his pursuit of both, arguing that his choice rested on an example both ancient and venerable: Saint Jerome.

In this regard, no phrase better encapsulates Rho's self-perception than his oft-used expression "my Jerome" (*Hieronymus meus*). Nor did his contemporaries fail to notice his admiration for Jerome, and in their writings references appear to "his Jerome" and "your Jerome."[173] Rho invoked Jerome's example to defend the utility of all human knowledge. More significantly, Jerome's example justified and explained Rho's *Apology*, *Philippic*, and *Three Dialogues against Lactantius*. Rho said in his *Apology* that he would not be bashful about singing his own praises, since Jerome had catalogued his own life and works without embarrassment at the end of his book *On Illustrious Men*.[174] Nor, he said, would he hesitate to write a *Philippic* against Panormita lest he appear to acquiesce in Panormita's charges; he followed, after all, in the path Jerome had marked out with his *Apology against Rufinus*.[175] And finally, with the release of his *Three Dialogues against Lactantius* in 1444, which constituted both the apex and conclusion of his literary career, Rho imagined that he brought to his contemporaries the same assistance that Jerome had offered fifth-century Christians with his censure and refutation of Origen. However incompletely he may have imitated the full scholarly and literary range of his model Jerome, Rho at least achieved notable proficiency in following him as a polemicist.

10. Style

Some remarks are in order regarding the style of Rho's *Philippic* and *Apology*, focusing on Rho's own notions of what constituted good Latin style. His statements and criticisms give the reader critical insights about his stylistic choices, however skillfully or poorly he carried them through.

One criticism that Rho brought against Panormita's epistolary style was his "paucity of words," that is, his limited vocabulary. According to Rho this was a failing of Panormita's style. Accurate or not, this criticism of Panormita points to one aspect of Rho's own style. In contradistinction to his disdain for "paucity" in Panormita's writing, Rho valued "copiousness" and sought in his own writing to

---

[173]*Philippic* §35. Decembrio to Rho (Milan: Bibl. Naz. Braid., MS AH.XII.16, 91v): *ut Hieronymus tuus inquit*. Valla 1962b, 396: *Et Hieronymus (quem suum Raudensis appellat)*.

[174]*Apology* §4.

[175]*Philippic* §35.

demonstrate a mastery of Latin vocabulary. Although Rho would not complete his *Rhetorical Imitations* until 1433, he must have had this material largely in hand by late 1431 or early 1432 when he was writing his *Philippic*. His impressive range of vocabulary, not least in the use of obscure words and phrases (classical and medieval) and his ability to cite authors with a high degree of accuracy, points to habits of methodical collection and organization such as we find in his *Imitations*. His preoccupation with copiousness is also reflected in his Latin style. It shows up in the duplication or even multiplication of words, often through the use of synonyms or near synonyms. Following a practice that became common in late antiquity, Rho rarely chose between "gloats" or "brags," preferring instead to write "gloats and brags" (*gloriatur et iactat*).[176] Why should he write either "famous" or "illustrious" when he could write "famous and illustrious" (*clarus et illustris*)?[177] Examples of this "copia" are legion. Readers will decide for themselves to what extent Rho's penchant for copiousness as reflected in this practice marred or graced his style.

Another stylistic feature of Rho's work is his frequent recourse to parenthetical elements and subordinate clauses in long periodic sentences, which reflects his attempt to imitate classical Latin. In addition to Rho's stylistic pursuit of these parenthetical and subordinated elements, he strives to weave into his own prose numerous words, phrases, and sentences of other authors, sometimes with admirable effect. Whatever one concludes about Rho's prose style, he deserves credit for rarely making grammatical mistakes. But often he expresses himself so awkwardly that the grammar and syntax become obscure. Some sentences contain ambiguities that can only be resolved by checking Rho's use of a word or phrase in his other writings or by locating his classical and patristic models. For this reason I cite his *Rhetorical Imitations* (1433), his *Three Dialogues against Lactantius* (1444), and the vocabulary of his other surviving works and correspondence in my notes.[178]

Finally, I should note that Rho's *Philippic*, although a letter addressed to Pier Candido Decembrio, switches in several instances to direct address with Antonio Panormita. I have signaled this in the translation by the use of quotation marks. Moreover, since Rho describes these direct exchanges with Panormita as using "familiar and colloquial language,"[179] the translation of these passages includes contractions in order to indicate this variation in style.

---

[176] *Philippic* §109.

[177] *Philippic* §160.

[178] The Avignon manuscript of the *Imitations* (Bibliothèque Municipale, MS 1054) has an extensive index. A similar, perhaps identical, index also accompanies the copy in Padua (Biblioteca Capitolare, MS C 72). Rho's *Three Dialogues* and his surviving correspondence I consulted through a computer search of my transcriptions. For a list of manuscripts and publications of Rho's surviving works, see Rutherford 1990.

[179] *Philippic* §157.

EDITORIAL PROCEDURE

1. Appendices

For all the Latin texts included in the Appendices, classical orthography has been adopted without any indication in the apparatus unless word choice was involved. To have done otherwise would have complicated the apparatus with minutiae of scribal training and preferences not related to establishing the text.

2. The *Philippic*

The title of the *Philippic* is clearly attested with only minor variants in the manuscripts. Both of the surviving exemplars are undated fifteenth-century manuscripts, made at the time of the controversy or shortly thereafter. Manuscript A (Milan: Biblioteca Ambrosiana, MS B 124 sup., saec. XV^1, ff. 112r–142r) is the more carefully copied of the two exemplars. It bears the title in a colophon in the hand of the scribe: *The Philippic against* (in) *Antonio Panormita felicitously ends*. Some near contemporary added a title at the beginning in the margin: *The Fourth Philippic of Antonio da Rho against* (in) *Antonio Panormita addressed to Pier Candido* [*Decembrio*], *Ducal Secretary and Most Eloquent Man, Felicitously* [*Begins*]. The "Fourth Philippic" (*Philippica quarta*) must have been a slip for "Four Philippics" (*Philippicae Quattuor*), taking each of the four "Objections" as individual *Philippics*. These four divisions of the text are designated in the margins in what appears to be the same hand that added the title. To these I have added the "Prologue" and "Peroration" subdivisions. Manuscript N (Naples: Biblioteca Nazionale, MS VI D 7, saec. XV^1, ff. 98r–113r), bearing the colophon of the scribe, Rolandus Scibbeke de Alamania, gives a more simple title with minor variations at the opening and at the closing: *The Philippic of Friar Antonio da Rho against* (contra) *Antonio Panormita*; colophon: *The Philippic against* (in) *Antonio Panormita*.

In editing the manuscripts of the *Philippic*, I have made no attempt to preserve the idiosyncratic orthography of the individual scribes. I have separated without indication a few words frequently or always compounded in the manuscripts and preferred "mq" instead of "nq," since scribal usage is inconsistent or indistinguishable because of abbreviations. Throughout the *Philippic*, I have chosen to respect classical orthography without further indication, except in matters that affect word choice.

3. The *Apology*

Although for the *Apology* it is possible that a lost manuscript stands between the autograph M (Milan: Biblioteca Ambrosiana, MS M 49 sup., saec. XV[1], I+42+II ff.) and V (Vatican City: Biblioteca Apostolica Vaticana, MS Ottob. lat. 1321, saec. XV[1], ff. 52r–91v), nothing in the variants would require it. Readings in M omitted from V suggest that V has been copied directly from M. The many instances in V of letters dropped from or added to words (M = caementariorum / V = -tarium; M = insulsis / V = insulis; M = uideantur / V = uideatur) result from careless copying but are also consistent with V having been copied from M.

On the basis of the "corrections" regarding Decembrio (§54) and the deletions regarding Panormita (§31), we can be certain that V belonged to some contemporary who both despised Decembrio and who either belonged to Panormita's circle or at least did not want to offend members of that circle.

Orthographic Changes for the *Apology*

(Parentheses indicates reading in M)

Since the original orthography of the autograph of the *Apology* is of interest to some specialists, I have chosen to respect classical orthography in the text but to preserve the original orthography and my changes in the list below. Mostly this is a matter of diphthongs "e" or "æ" for "ae" or "oe," switching of "c" and "t," "i" and "y," "t" and "th," or the doubling or singling of consonants. I have only noted the orthographic changes in the critical apparatus when it affects word choice (e.g., *molis* / *mollis*).

General Vocabulary:

academia (acha-), accepi (accaepi), aegritudo (aegre-), aemulos (æmulos), aequare (æquare), amicitia (-cia), bellus/a/um (belus/a/um), caementarius (cemen-), ceterus/a/um (caete-), coaequare (coæquare), coepi (caepi), colaphus (colla-), contio (-cio), debacchatus (debacha-), dumtaxat (dun-), e (ae), e uestigio (æuestigio), edissero (ædis-), egregius/a/um (aegre-), eliminare (æli-), eloquentia (ælo-), emineo (æmineo), enixior (æni-), enodare (æno-), epitoma (-thoma), erigere (aeri-), erubescere (æru-), erudire (æru-), essentia (-cia), euadere (æua-), euoluere (æuo-), faex (fex), femella/rius (foemel-), fescennina (-cenina), fretus (fraetus), hinnulus (innu-), historia (hys-), hymenaeum (-neum), hypostasis (ipos-), ilicet (illicet), inconexe (inconne-/incone-), istaec (istec), laetor (letor), loedoria (ledo-), maeror (moeror/me-), mellitula (meli-), mustiones (musci-), namque (nan-), nefas (nephas), negotio (-cio), numquam (nun-/non-), operae pretium (opereprecium), otium (ocium), paelex (pelex), palinodia (paly-), parallela (paralella), penthemimeris (pentimemeris), percepi (-caepi), pilas (pylas), procedere (-cædere), rhythmos (rithimos/rithmos), scommata (scomata), seria (saeria), sesquipedalis (sexqui-), setius (secius), summae meritae (summe merite), symposium (simpho-), tinniens (tiniens), uolup (uolupe)

Proper Nouns:

Antonius (Antho-), Apollonius (Apolo-), Apuleius (Apulleius/Apulleus), Arache (Aragne), Blaesilla (Ble-), Boethius (Boetius), Bonifatius (Bonifacius), Coluccius (Collucius), Curtius (Curcius), Cyllenius (Cille-), Domitianus (Domici-), Gaius (Caius), Graecus (Grae-/Græ-), Gratianus (Graci-/Grati-), Hebraeus (-reus), Herodotus (Ero-), Hieronymus (Hierony-/Hyeroni-/Hieroni-), Lucilius (Lucillius), Martialis (Marci-), Martianus (Marci-), Mercurius (Merchu-), Philippica (Fi-), Philippus (Fi-), Polybius (Poli-), Propertius (-cius), Plutarchus (-cus), Pythagoras (Pitha-), Sallustius (Salus-), Saraceni (Sarra-/Sara-), Thersites (Ter-), Varro (Varo), Vergilius (Virgilius).

SIGLA

AL	=	*Aristoteles Latinus*. Corpus Philosophorum Medii Aevi Academiarum Consociatarum Auspiciis et Consilio Editum. Editioni curandae praesidet L. Minio-Paluello. Brussels: de Brouwer / Leiden: Brill, 1953–.
ETR	=	*Encyclopedia of the Renaissance*. Ed. Paul F. Grendler et al. 6 vols. New York: Charles Scribner's Sons, 1999.
GDLI	=	*Grande dizionario della lingua italiana*. Ed. Salvatore Battaglia and Giorgio Bàrberi Squarotti. 21 vols. Turin: Unione Tipografico-Editrice Torinese, 1961–2002.
GRBM	=	*A Dictionary of Greek and Roman Biography and Mythology*. Ed. William Smith. 3 vols. London: John Murray, 1890.
KJV	=	Bible, King James Version.
LCL	=	The Loeb Classical Library. Cambridge, MA: Harvard University Press.
OCD	=	*The Oxford Classical Dictionary*. Ed. N. G. L. Hammond and H. H. Scullard. 3rd ed. Oxford: Clarendon Press, 1996.
ODB	=	*The Oxford Dictionary of Byzantium*. Ed. A. P. Kazhdan et al. 3 vols. Oxford and New York: Oxford University Press, 1991.
ODCC	=	*The Oxford Dictionary of the Christian Church*. Ed. F. L. Cross and E. A. Livingstone. 3rd ed. Oxford: Oxford University Press, 1997.
PL	=	*Patrologia Latina*. Paris: Migne, 1855–.
PW	=	A. Pauly, G. Wissowa, and W. Kroll. *Real-Encyclopädie der klassichen Altertumswissenschaft*. 24 vols. in 49. Stuttgart: A. Druckenmüller, 1893–1963.
TLL	=	*Thesaurus linguae Latinae*. Leipzig-Stuttgart, Tuebner, 1900–91.

ANTONIO DA RHO

PHILIPPICA IN ANTONIVM PANORMITAM

PHILIPPIC AGAINST

ANTONIO PANORMITA

MANUSCRIPTS

A = Milan: Biblioteca Ambrosiana, MS B 124 sup., s. XV[1], ff. 112r–142r.
N = Naples: Biblioteca Nazionale, MS VI D 7, s. XV[1], ff. 98r–113r.

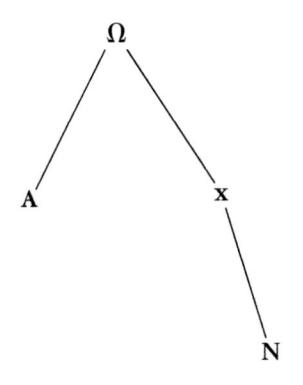

```
        Ω
       / \
      /   \
     A     x
            \
             \
              N
```

Milan: Biblioteca Ambrosiana, MS B 124 sup., saec. XV[1], chart., f. 119r.
©Biblioteca Ambrosiana (Auth. No. F 34/05).

Naples: Biblioteca Nazionale, MS VI.D.7, saec. XV[1], chart., f. 98r.
With permission of the Ministero per i Beni e le Attivitià Culturali.

ANTONII RAVDENSIS

PHILIPPICA IN ANTONIVM PANORMITAM[1]

1 [A112r/N98r] Cum nihil quicquam haberem rebus de his nostris publicis aut priuatis quod ad te, Candide, uir ornatissime, ut saepe alias in praesentia scriberem, conducere tamen uisum est mihi pro mutuo fere ab incunabulis[2] inter nos[3] amore studio et fide Ioannem
5 famulum tuum, quem ad me hesterna die dimisisti, ⟨PROLOGVS⟩ haud uacuis manibus ad te hac ex urbe rediturum.
Obsignaui itaque illi[4] has litteras quas tibi meo nomine hortatus sum reddere prope tempus deberet; tibi uel obsequio meo salutem multam ascriberet. Scio equidem tuis illae in manibus nihil senescent, quippe qui
10 cum familiarem tibi calamum meum apicesque dignoueris, statim — sic mihi persuadeo — illas exsolues,[5] ubi, nihilo setius non modo te rogatum ceterum et adiuratum uelim, iterum atque iterum euoluas eas, lectites, scruteris, animaduertas. Intelleges enimuero his ex ipsis nouum e Sicilia[6] insula monstrum nouumque portentum quoddam istac aetate
15 nostra exortum esse, magnum, ut aiunt, *horrendum ingens*, cui uidelicet non torui non truces desint oculi; non rabies non pestis absit.
2 Quid inquam? Spumat enim, stridet, bacchatur, insanit. Alios quidem territat; alios premit; et incautos occupat. Alios non dicam lacessere proritareque, uerum extinguere aut exorbere[7] omnino con-
20 tendit. Neminem splendidum opinatumque uirum a morsibus suis immunem habet; singulis — modo sibi[8] praestitum esset — incognita scelera, inaudita flagitia, labes notasque taeterrimas, ne solus unus ipse spretae honestatis laesaeque pudicitiae insimularetur, ultro et libenter inscribit. Crederes illum inhumanum alterum Cacum aut Geryonem
25 esse, seu uerius dixerim, Nemeum prae ferocia leonem aut aprum illum Erymanthium urbes, nationes, prouincias dentibus suis depopulaturum,

---

[1]Antonii . . . Panormitam *scripsi* : Antonii Raudensis ad Petrum Candidum ducalem secretarium uirum eloquentissimum Philippica in Antonium Panormitam quarta feliciter ⟨incipit⟩. *mg. suppl.* A^1 : Filipica fratris Antonii Raudensis contra Antonium Panormitam *N*
[2]incunabulis] -bilis *N*
[3]inter nos] *tr.* N : ᵇnos ᵃinter *corr. A*
[4]itaque illi *tr. N*
[5]exsol-] exol- *A*
[6]Sic-] Sec- *N*
[7]exor-] esor- *N*
[8]sibi *in ras. N*

[50]

THE PHILIPPIC OF ANTONIO DA RHO AGAINST ANTONIO PANORMITA[1]

Prologue

1 Although, illustrious Candido, I had absolutely nothing to write you this time about our public or private affairs as I have often done before, nonetheless because of the mutual love, devotion, and trust that we have shared almost from the cradle, I thought it good to engage your servant Giovanni, whom you sent to me yesterday, so that he not return to you from the city empty-handed.[2] I have accordingly sealed for him this letter, which I insisted he should quickly deliver to you in my name. At my request he is also to add my best wishes. I know, of course, that the letter will in no way go unread in your hands. For when you recognize my familiar pen and script, you will, I am convinced, open it instantly. Then I would like you to pore over, peruse, scrutinize, and ponder it again and again not merely as if you were asked, but even as if you were sworn to do so. You will clearly understand from it that some new monster has arisen from the island of Sicily, a new portent for our time, "horrifying," as they say, "in his great size."[3] He glares with savage and ferocious eyes; he comes with fury and death.[4]

2 What am I talking about? He froths. He hisses. He fumes. He rages. Indeed, he terrifies some people, others he corners, and the unwary he seizes. Still others he endeavors not just to challenge and provoke, but even, I would say, to kill and devour completely. He considers no one of distinction or fame to be exempt from his bite. He wantonly and willfully attributes unparalleled atrocities, shocking indecencies, hideous stigmas and ignominies to each of them — provided that the person is his better — lest he be the only one accused of having spurned decency and betrayed modesty. You might believe that he is another inhuman Cacus or Geryon or, I might say more accurately, the Nemean lion because of his ferocity or the Erymanthian boar bent on depopulating cites, nations, and provinces by fang

---

[1] For the title, see Editorial Procedure 41 above.

[2] For Pier Candido Decembrio, see especially Borsa; Ditt; Ferrari 1984; Gabotto; Simonetta 42–53; and Viti 1987. In an undated letter, Decembrio wrote to Rho about the death of one of his retainers, Giovanni di Grado, who is, with high probability, our present Giovanni (Florence: Biblioteca Riccardiana, MS Ricc. 827, 125r–v).

[3] Jerome *Letter* 106.57; cf. Virgil *Aeneid* 4.181.

[4] Sicily, as far back as the Homeric epic cycles, had a reputation for terrifying monsters, the most famous being Scylla and Charybdis and the Cyclops, Polyphemus.

[51]

cui occurrere et reluctari atque illo cum decertare — sic enim belua gloriatur — nemo uelit, nemo fidat, nemo possit. Nam quanto errore ignorationeque sui is omnium insolentissimus [A112v] corripiatur atque frustretur, dum sese praeter reliquos ad sidera subducere et attollere connititur, tunc plane percipiet, ne intempest⟨iu⟩e quidem, cum non unum aut alterum at complures quaqua uersum — Hercules quibus clauam extorquere ipse nequeat — aduersus eum dimicaturos intelleget.

3 Ex illo siquidem anno superiore litterulam quandam, ubi mihi salutem multam de more impertit qui nullam cupit, ex Ticino nomine suo dimissam accepi; esurie quadam ieiunitateque uerborum frigescentem, amplitudine uero mortiferi ueneni et copia redundantem, ubi quid nebulo ille dementissimus in me falso[9] obganniat quidue sycophanta mentiatur, tu, qui a puero uirtutibus doctrinisque optimis innutritus es, rogo iudex, rogo censor accesseris. Visa itaque huiusce monstri litterula ipsa perlectaque dumtaxat semel praetereuntibus, ut ita dixerim, ocellis (dixi "monstri," sed uerius quod de se credit "sapientissimi et humanissimi uiri") animaduerti statim et intellexi plane animi uehementiam illam suam, qua ultro citroque et in diuersum, ut assolet, amens et insanus agitabatur. Quippe qui more suopte, suopte ingenio illatrans semper insultansque honestissimorum uirorum existimationi,[10] dignitati, et gloriae, praesertim famae ac nomini meo, per praeuios dies aliquot, anteaquam illam[11] manu sua caelibe conscriptam obsignatamque mihi redderet, apud primarios summique ordinis [N98v] huiusce ciuitatis uiros exemplaria ipse praemiserat. Quae uel ego ipse alienis in manibus primum inspexi, postume uero in meis nouissimus omnium quidem et tenui et legi. Quod calliditatis et astutiae genus Pyrrhique nouum stra⟨te⟩gema de[12] industria, sed temere quidem, ex[13] portentuoso Panormita illo commentum atque conflatum esse, neque a turpibus sibi similibus neque ab integris sanctisque uiris, qui eius modestiae immo impudentiae suae iam pridem conscii sunt, ambigitur. Verum hanc fabricam ludumque Punicum, id est exemplaria seminare prius quam reddere mihi litteras primarias, uideas percuncterisque et oro et obsecro.

4 Quid istuc? Verebatur enim pro sua [A113r] impuritate, pro integritate mea, si huiuscemodi litterula sua uni mihi soli et ante alios,

---

[9]falso *om. A*
[10]existi-] exti-*N*
[11]eam] *mg. suppl. N*
[12]de] *s.l. suppl. A*
[13]ex] et *N*

[5]This list of monsters is taken from Jerome *Against Vigilantius* 1 (cf. Wiesen 222). *Cacus* was Vulcan's giant son whom Hercules killed for the theft of Geryon's cattle left in Hercules' charge (Ovid *Fasti* 1.543–74). *Geryon* was a legendary monster with three bodies who lived in Erythea, a place later identified with one of the islands off Gades (Cadiz, Spain). The *Nemean lion* preyed on the inhabitants

or tusk.[5] No one would wish, no one would dare, no one would be able — or so the beast brags — to oppose, to resist, or to fight with him.[6] But now he will see that not one person or another but many people, from whom Hercules himself could not wrest the club,[7] are set to fight him from every side. At this, even he, the most arrogant of all people, will — in the nick of time — comprehend clearly the extent to which he had been taken in and deceived by his own error and ignorance when trying to exalt himself and rise above everyone to the stars.

3 Last year I received a wretched little letter from him, sent under his name from Pavia.[8] In it, in his usual manner, he wishes me good health but desires the opposite. This letter suffers from a hunger and emptiness of words but overflows with a profusion and abundance of deadly poison. What faults that completely demented wretch wrongly denounces in me there! What lies that slanderer tells about me there! I ask you, Candido, who from a boy have been nourished in virtue and the best teaching, to serve as judge. I ask you to serve as censor.[9] Upon seeing this monster's wretched little letter, I perused it only with a quick glance. (I call him a "monster," but he regards himself as "the wisest and most humane of men.") I immediately recognized and understood clearly that violent temperament of his. As usual, this crazed, insane fellow is driven in every direction. In keeping with his custom and nature to always bark at and attack the reputation, dignity, and glory of honorable men, and especially my fame and name, a few days before he delivered the letter to me, written and sealed by his celibate hand,[10] he himself had distributed advance copies among the city's leaders and highest ranking men. I myself first saw the letter in someone else's copy, but afterwards I, the very last of all, handled and read my own copy. Neither shameful men such as he nor upright and holy men already privy to his modesty, or rather effrontery, doubt what sort of shrewdness and cunning or new Pyrrhic stratagem[11] the monstrous Panormita has deliberately but rashly devised and executed. Still, I plead and beseech that you, Candido, mark and investigate this Punic trick and sport:[12] namely, his distribution of copies before he sends me the original letter.

4 Why did he do this? In the face of his perversity and my integrity, he feared that if a wretched little letter such as his were delivered to me alone, as was right, and before it was delivered to others, many people throughout the court

---

of the Valley of Nemea. Hercules killed the lion with his bare hands, and representations of Hercules showed the lion's skin draped over his arm. The *Erymanthian boar* was killed by Hercules in the Erymanthian Mountains of Arcadia.

[6] Cf. Jerome *Against Vigilantius* 1.2.

[7] The club was Hercules' preferred weapon, Hercules usually being represented with his club and the skin of the Nemean lion (n. 5 above).

[8] For the text and translation of the letter, see Panormita *Etsi facile* (Appendix I below).

[9] A Roman official charged with (among other things) the supervision of public morals.

[10] For Rho's sarcastic use of *caelebs*, see *Philippic* §36.

[11] Pyrrhus (319–272 BCE), King of Epirus (now northwestern Greece), was famous for his dazzling tactics. He defeated the Romans at Asculum (279 BCE) at costs so dear to himself that his victory was reckoned a defeat.

[12] Phoenicians, whom the Romans called "Punics," were regarded by the Romans as deceitful; hence "Punic" came to mean "treacherous" (cf. Livy 21.4.9–10).

uti par erat, traderetur, iam nequaquam illa quemadmodum expetebat per subsellia transcriberetur a plurimis neque plateis compitisque, uti cupiebat, quasi fabula cantaretur. Duxit idcirco pro nominis sui dissipatione et gloria ⟨ut⟩ exemplaria illa uulgo decantanda seminaret, denique me ad Kalendas Graecas participem communicatumque faceret. Sed a sententia cessit et reddenda tandem reddidit, astute quidem et probe. Putaui tum non deesse me mihi neque oculos aut frontem credidi diutius (quasi oscitabundum quempiam) perfricari oportere ceterum euigilantem insomnemque prodire,[14] teque penes has conquestiones meas, tamquam ad me alterum exponere necesse esse, linguae deinde illi[15] Socraticae occurrere quidem et uicem reddere.

5 Quid ni? Minabatur enim interitum nisi tacerem. Ideo responderem — omnino me impulit — recte quidem, ne uiderer tacendo crimen obiectum agnoscere lenitatemque meam signum quoddam malae conscientiae interpretaretur. Verum uel Salomoni morem gerere et inniti operae pretium existimaui. Ex litteris enim sacris aiebat: *Responde stulto iuxta stultitiam suam, ne sibi ipsi sapiens esse uideatur*. Quid ergo?

Semper ego auditor tantum? numquamne reponam,
uexatus totiens

ab hac obscena et immani belua? Legisti apud Ciceronem, certo scio, Crassum illum eloquentiae principem *in illius orationis suae principio, quam contra collegam censor habuit*, dixisse *quae natura aut fortuna darentur hominibus in his rebus uinci posse se aequo animo*[16] *pati; quae sibi ipsi homines parare possent, in his rebus se uinci pati non posse*. Numquid ego hanc lubricam procacemque linguam subsurdaster et infans praeteriero? Num pro falsis quae uera sunt ea illi non meminero?

6 Nolo tamen[17] putes, mi Candide, me faecibus sordibusque suis diutius immoraturum. Quid hoc est? Non equidem quo sperem olim quasi nouus pugil pro maledictis iterum responsurus insurgere, aut quo timeam ex illo pollui aut deturpari me quoquo pacto posse, seu in mores illius suillos ulla e regione commigrare, uerum potius quod ab huiuscemodi [A113v] corruptissimo inquinatissimoque hominum genere meapte natura longe abhorream; animus uel ipse meus non modo ab illo ceterum et a commilitonibus suis quanto absentior atque distractior eo amplius frugi et incolumis esse uideatur. Futurus sum igitur qui non turpibus petulantibusque[18] uerbis eius singulis — non enim omnes actus decantandi neque tota fabula conficienda est — sed capitibus et partibus haud nullis, ne absolute quidem illis omnibus, responsum dedam. Animum quoque sic belle institui meque omnem

---

[14]insomnemque prodire] insomnemque curam prodire *N*
[15]illi *om. N*
[16]aequo animo *tr. N*
[17]tamen] tantum *N*
[18]petulantibus-] -tissimis- *A*

would simply fail to transcribe it as he hoped and it would not be chanted like a play in the piazzas and at the crossroads as he desired. So for the diffusion and glory of his name he decided to distribute copies for public recitation and finally to make me a participant and recipient of it on the Greek Kalends.[13] But he backed off from that idea, and in the end shrewdly, and indeed properly, he delivered to me what he had to deliver. I took thought at the time not to neglect my own advantage nor did I believe thereafter that I should shamefully cover my eyes or face (like someone yawning) but that I ought to appear fully awake and alert. I also believed it was necessary to explain my complaint to you, Candido, as my alter ego, and then in fact to counter that Socratic tongue of his[14] and repay him in kind.

5 And why not? He threatened my ruin unless I remained silent. Therefore I responded — he absolutely drove me to it — and I did so rightly lest in being silent I seem to admit the alleged crime and lest he interpret my gentleness as a sign of a bad conscience. Still, I considered it particularly advantageous to observe and trust the custom of Solomon. For in the Bible Solomon says: "Answer a fool according to his folly, lest he imagine himself to be wise."[15] So why "must I always be the listener, and constantly vexed never respond"[16] to this obscene and monstrous beast? I know you have read in Cicero that Crassus, that prince of eloquence, "in the opening of the oration that he delivered as censor against a colleague," said that "while he could bear with equanimity to be beaten at those things that nature or fortune granted to men, he could not suffer to be beaten at those things that men were able to accomplish for themselves."[17] Was I to have ignored his slick and overbearing tongue by remaining deaf and dumb? Was I not to remind him of the truth in place of his lies?

6 But I do not want you to think, my Candido, that I am going to tarry long in his scum and slime. Why? No, not because I expect one day to rise like a young boxer ready to answer the taunts anew, nor because I fear that he can somehow pollute or disfigure me or that I can engage directly in his swinish way of life, but rather because I recoil instinctively from a debauched and filthy person like him. Even my mind seems more fit and sound the greater its distance and dissociation not only from him but even from his comrades. Consequently, I am not going to respond to each one of his foul and abusive words (for every act need not be recited, nor need the whole story be rehearsed). I shall respond only to the principal points and to some parts, and not fully even to them. In addition, I have trained my mind and defined my whole character so well that in the respected and sacred practice of a Christian I would rather aid and defend myself than

---

[13]That is, "never": the Greeks did not give dates according to "Kalends" (cf. Suetonius *Augustus* 87.1 for the original jest by Augustus).

[14]That is, "that sarcastic tongue of his" (cf. *Philippic* §25).

[15]Proverbs 26.5.

[16]Juvenal 1.1–2.

[17]Cicero *On the Orator* 2.11.45.

ita perscripsi, ut Christiani spectato more et sancto[19] potius opem mihi ferrem defensitaremque — scutum tenerem, gladium reiicerem — quam illius exquisita elaborataque flagitia insimularem, honeste quidem. [N99r] Non enim considero quid ipse mereatur, sed quid me deceat.

7 Cui tamen ad confutandas refellendasque fabulas illas suas et cantilenas, quin immo ad retorquenda eius in faciem singula quaeque uenenata tela — iugulum enim uideo — uberrima mihi ac[20] locuples et succurrebat et nunc succurrit oratio. Sustuli certe perlectis litterulis suis calamum et excussi; atque bilem, si quae tamen illa fuit praesto quidem, repressi Chrysippi philosophi more ac tenui stomachum, ut non minus me sacerdotem temperantem praestarem quam ipse poetam nescio quem saeuientem praestitisset.

8 Declararem nunc tibi, ni[21] fortasse arrogans dicerer, modestiae meae signa nonnulla. Quot enimuero scelera numero atque flagitia pectore huius sancti nostri Panormitae uersantur, quae plane ut stellae caelo[22] ita extant — plurima, horrida, taeterrima, perobscena — quibus ita immiscetur, confunditur, illabitur, ut ambiguum nouumque[23] animal quoddam, cui multum bestiae innote⟨sc⟩at nihil hominis inesse, uideatur; tot numero profecto quaqua uersum patebant aditus, unde caput in suum commenta illa sua meras et absolutas nugas tota[24] reiicerem.

9 Quid admiramur? Plenus undique uir iste rimarum erat e quibus sanctissimi illi mores sui ipsis in recessibus mentis atque animae latebris clare quidem et luculente introspicerentur. Sese omnem uulgo aperuerat, prodiderat pectus, chlamydem quoque gymnasia quaeque aliquando sulcantem more philosophi atque crepidulas ipsas exuerat, ut paene inconsideratus ipse homo gymnosophista philosophus [A114r] quispiam nudus deuorato pudore uideretur[25] occurrere. Verum enimuero religioni addictus [prouinciam tam grandem et inextricabilem] expaui ne forte introgressus scaenam illam uirtutum suarum, immo petulantiarum labyrinthum, inde me expedire more Thesei aut eliminare sine subtegmine et globo[26] possem.

---

[19]more et sancto] et sancto more *N*
[20]ac] et *A*
[21]ni] ne *N*
[22]stellae caelo *tr. N*
[23]nouumque] non numque *N*
[24]tota] totas *A*
[25]uideretur] uidetur *N*
[26]et globo] *mg. suppl.*, aut filo *in ras. A*

---

[18]Chrysippus of Soli (ca. 280–207 BCE) was a Greek Stoic philosopher whose defense of Stoicism against the skepticism of the New Academy (Platonic) came to represent something close to a Stoic orthodoxy, in this case, that the wise man is not moved by passion but controlled by reason.

denounce, honorably to be sure, his exquisitely elaborate crimes. I retain the shield and cast away the sword. For I do not consider what he deserves, but what is appropriate for me.

7 Even so, I had then and still have at hand a full and rich harangue to confute and repudiate those tales and gossips or rather to fling back every single poisoned spear into his face (I even see his jugular). After perusing his wretched little letter, I certainly picked up my pen and hammered out this harangue. And yet like the philosopher Chrysippus,[18] I repressed my anger (if it was in fact present) and restrained my disgust so that I might show myself no less a patient priest than he has shown himself to be some raving poet.

8 Lest perhaps I be called arrogant, let me now recount to you some signs of my modesty. For however many enormities and crimes reside in the breast of this holy Panormitan of ours — crimes as plain as the stars in the sky (legion, horrid, loathsome, and obscene), crimes in which he is so embroiled, stuck, and immersed that he looks like some strange new animal, lacking all human attributes but having much of the bestial — just as many openings are available on all sides, through which I might throw his fabrications back in his face as pure and absolute nonsense.

9 Why do we marvel? The man was full of fissures through which those sanctimonious morals of his could be seen and far too well in the very recesses of his mind and secret places of his soul. He entirely opened himself to the public; he bared his chest; he also stripped off, along with his very sandals, his Greek robe, which as the sign of a philosopher would once upon a time cut a swath through any school.[19] Consequently, this virtually senseless man swallowed his shame and was seen to go about like some nude gymnosophist philosopher.[20] But as a man consecrated to religion, I feared that by some chance once I walked onto the scene of his virtues, or rather, into the labyrinth of his lewdness,[21] I could not extricate myself or withdraw from it without a ball of thread like Theseus.[22]

---

[19]It is not altogether clear what Rho means by *chlamys sulcans more philosophi*. The difficulty results from his use of *sulco, -are* (plow, furrow, cleave; when with water or air: sail, swim, fly). Rho modelled this statement on Livy's description of Scipio (29.19.11–12): *cum pallio crepidisque inambulare in gymnasio*. Neo-Latin usage often failed to distinguish between the *chlamys* (Greek military cloak) and the *pallium* (an outer garment, often considered Greek and the attire of a philosopher). A similar usage is found in Decembrio (1432, 126r), who wrote about Panormita in Bologna, *nondum chlamys diffluebat*, presumably meaning that Panormita had not yet taken his degree (cf. *Philippic* §53).

[20]This plays on the stereotypical image of a guru. From antiquity onward the gymnosophists were usually reckoned to be from India, but sometimes from Egypt. Rho (*Imitations* 173v: *Pauper*) wrote: "Gymnosophists are said to philosophize in loincloths alone." He almost certainly took this and a shared emphasis on nudity and shame from Augustine (*City of God* 14.17): ". . . certain men who practice philosophy in the nude (and hence are called gymnosophists) nevertheless use coverings for their genitals, though they have none for the other parts of the body" (LCL). Rho later summarized this passage of his *Philippic* (*Imitations* 161v; Appendix VIII §14 below): "I called him [i.e., "a certain sycophant"] some gymnosophist philosopher, who having swallowed his shame, appeared before me as if nude."

[21]Rho (*Imitations* 115v: *Lascivius*; Appendix IX below): "Likewise *lascivia, libido,* and *importunitas* are *petulantia*."

[22]Theseus was the Athenian hero who used a thread given him by Ariadne to find his way out of the Labyrinth after killing the Minotaur.

10 Post deinde accuratior rem meam atque consultior inspexi: qui qualisue ipse forem, quae consuetudinis meae ratio, qui religionis cultus, quae professionis dignitas, haud inscius intellexi; atque contra, quanti homuncio Siculus is ille insurgeret, quantique ultimae faecis Pyrrhia quidam aut Geta reluctaretur, in ipsum figens oculos obtuitu primo ad obolum usque quidem et[27] assem, pulchre animaduerti. Quippe qui nec uiribus ullis, nulla arte, nullo ingenio exuperare me uel imbecillum posset, sin contra ego illum perturbassem — quod etiam sublanguidis quam facillimum esset — non minor mihi ob degenerem pugnam ignominia quam gloria collata uideretur; non minorem ignominiam,[28] certo dixerim, quam si Thersitem ex equo, ut aiunt, Hector praecipitem fecisset, aut si Alexandri canes, qui generositate[29] quadam nullum animal praeter leones aggrediebantur, in damas formidolososque lepusculos impetum fecissent.

11 Existimaui itaque, ut Plauti sui sententia utar, floret enim aliquando *plus scire satius* esse *quam loqui*. Neque huiusce Siculi mores sequi oportere ratus sum, qui aut alienae uitae aut linguae suae parcere necdum didicisset, qui ueluti rabula quidam circumforaneus, immo utpote saeuiens fera canisque alter ille Cerberus, honestissimis quibusque uiris illatrat semper. Verum potius Flaccum meum, Dauid, quem is subulcus lyricum esse nescit, aemulandum esse constitui, qui cum Saulem Regem sui inimicissimum in spelunca seorsum delitescentem offendisset illumque necare sine arbitris et impune potuisset, utique noluit sed pepercit, eumque quam clementer pristinae libertati condonauit. Vlcisci quidem hominis est, praesertim iniuria lacessiti, uerum parcere id plane Christianum decet.

12 Quid me existimas[30] dicere? Alii enimuero oculos eius foderent, linguam conuellerent, pollices praeciderent, regiones corporis [A114v] ceteras[31] Volcano suo, ut ita dixerim, consecrarent.

---

[27]et] ad *N*
[28]ignominiam] *mg. suppl.*, pugnam *in ras. A*
[29]generosi-] granosi- *N*
[30]existi-] exti- *N*
[31]regiones corporis ceteras] regiones ceteras corporis ceteras *N*

---

[23]Pyrrhia is a drunken, thieving slave girl in a lost play of Titinius (Horace *Epistle* 1.13.14); Geta is a Greek slave in Terence's comedy *Phormio*.

[24]Hector was the greatest of the Trojan warriors. He was the eldest son of the King of Troy, Priam, and of his chief wife, Hecuba.

10 Thereafter, I considered my advantage more carefully and deliberately. I understood, quite consciously, who and what sort of person I was, what rules governed my behavior, what worship in my religion involved, and what dignity my profession demanded. On the other hand, I was fully aware of how this Sicilian runt would rise to the occasion and to what extent some Pyrrhia or a Geta[23] would fight for the last dregs, fixing his or her eye on the last miserable little coin at the first glint of money. He could not overpower me, weak as I am, by any force, art, or talent. By contrast, if I had unnerved him (which would be very easy even for those somewhat frail), clearly the amount of ignominy brought on me because of the degenerate quarrel would match any glory I would gain. Indeed, I could say that it would be no less ignominy than if Hector[24] had knocked Thersites[25] headlong from his horse, or if Alexander's dogs, which because of their high breeding attacked nothing but lions, hurled themselves upon deer and terrified little hares.[26]

11 I thought, therefore, (to use a saying of his favorite author Plautus[27]) that one stands out who "knows too much rather than says too much."[28] Nor did I think that I ought to follow the customs of this Sicilian, who has not yet learned to spare us either his foreign ways or his foreign tongue. He continually barks at all honorable men like some shyster going about the town, or rather like a raging wild animal and another Cerberus.[29] I determined, however, that I had to emulate David,[30] who is my Horace,[31] though unrecognized as a lyric poet by that swineherd. For when David had stumbled on King Saul, his greatest enemy, hiding alone in a cave and had the opportunity to kill him with impunity since there were no witnesses, nonetheless he chose not to do so, but spared him and restored him ever so kindly to his former liberty.[32] Yes, to avenge is human, especially if one has suffered an injury, but it clearly behooves a Christian to refrain from vengeance.

12 What do you think I am saying? Surely other people would gouge out his eyes, rip out his tongue, cut off his thumbs, or sacrifice other parts of his body

---

[25]Thersites — the loud, foul, and rude Homeric Greek warrior — became the archetype of those engaging in offensive behavior or using repulsive language. Odysseus beat him into a cowed silence for railing at King Agamemnon (Homer *Iliad* 2.211–77).

[26]Cf. Curtius 9.1.31–33.

[27]Panormita took great pride in his *Commentary on Plautus* (see *Philippic* §120; cf. also §27), a Roman comic poet/playwright (ca. 250–184 BCE). Twenty-one plays have survived, one in fragmentary state, and they are generally conceded to be genuine. Plautus was read much less during the Middle Ages than his near-contemporary Terence. Twelve of the plays were discovered and brought to Italy only in 1429 (Sabbadini 1914, 238–59; 1996, 1:11–12 and 2:240–42; Conte 49–63; cf. *Apology* §31 and §39).

[28]Plautus *Epidicus* 60a.

[29]Cerberus was the monstrous dog guarding the entrance to the underworld. He was said to have three heads and the tail of a snake (Virgil *Aeneid* 6.417–23).

[30]David (d. ca. 970 BCE) was a shepherd boy who became the second king of Israel and was the reputed author of many of the Psalms.

[31]Quintus Horatius Flaccus (65–8 BCE) was an Augustan Roman poet whose *Art of Poetry* was a fundamental text for humanistic views of poetry (Conte 292–320).

[32]Cf. I Samuel 24.1–23.

Ego uero deo meo permonitus immo iussus, qui ut inimicos diligamus, oremus quoque pro persequentibus et calumniantibus nos imperat, illi ueniam dedo; illi ignosco, nulla in me illius sollicitudo.

13 Quid ergo? Panormitam sane quidem in ipsum Panormitam reiicio, ut qui uulgo uir corruptissimus est non ignotus, tandem sese introspiciat scruteturque; et qualis pro studiorum suorum exercitatione Cato aut Laelius hactenus euaserit intellegat. Non defuerit unum tamen quod, modo uelit, haud mediocre suae salutis futurum medicamentum esse uideatur: id uidelicet, dum probe loqui [N99v] unus e numero brutorum nescit, uel obmutescat omnino uel iterum atque iterum conticescat. Quod si secus, ut insolentissimus est, urgebit ac perget. Videto ille, quandoquidem[32] promiscue singulos carpere dilacerareque semper accinctus est, ne amens inopsque consilii sibi ipsi[33] manum inferat nomenque suum sanctum exulceret atque antiquae notae notas recentes maculae quoque senescenti nouas maculas insuat, quasdam ex integro nulla tempestate, nulla aetate mortalium dissuendas.

14 Nunc quando, mi Candide, uerba quae in illum sum facturus expectas furoreque illo poetico iuxta Democriti Platonisque sententiam eum iam exalbescere, immo excandescere uideo; quando mea quoque iam e portu tuta et felix enauigauit oratio, uela siquidem pandenda sunt, quo facilius eius insidiis possim per pelagi terrores et minas, donec deferbuerit aestus, securus occurrere.

15 Primum itaque et inter cetera quod mihi obiiciat praecipuum, ubi Siculus iste, *homo — ut de Antonio ait Cicero — humanitatis expers et uitae communis ignarus*, se quam sapientem me uero insanum arbitratur, id unum est quidem. Non solum enim[34] castigat, ceterum

PRIMA OBJECTIO

---

[32]quando- *om. N*
[33]ipsi] ipse *N*
[34]enim] *s.l. suppl. A*

---

[33]The phrase "to his Vulcan" refers to the location of Vulcan's forge, which was said to be located under Mount Etna in Panormita's native Sicily. Rho allusion contains a threat of punishment either by branding or, more likely, by ripping off the flesh with red hot tongs: that is, Rho threatens an inquisitorial process (cf. *Philippic* §23 and §134).

[34]Cf. Matthew 5.44.

[35]Marcus Porcius Cato (234–149 BCE) was known as "Censorius" for his stern traditional morality. C. Laelius (Cons. 140 BCE), a pupil of Diogenes the Stoic, was celebrated by Cicero for knowing how "to dine well" without making pleasure the Supreme Good (Cicero *About the Ends of Goods and Evils* 2.8.24). According to Petrarca (*Letters on Familiar Matters* 6.3.42): "Certainly Solomon is held wise among the Hebrews, as is Lycurgus among the Spartans, Solon among the Athenians, and Cato or Laelius among us [Latins]."

(so to speak) to his Vulcan.[33] But having been warned — rather ordered — by my God, who decrees that we love our enemies as well as pray for our persecutors and those who speak evil against us,[34] I grant Panormita pardon; free of anxiety about him, I forgive him.

13 Why so? Because I am simply remanding Panormita to Panormita himself so that he who is known to the public as an utterly debauched man may at last take a good look at and examine himself and may now recognize what sort of Cato or Laelius he has turned out to be for all his studies.[35] He did not lack, however, for an effective medical remedy if only he wanted to use it. Namely, since one who is a brute does not know how to speak properly, let him just shut up or time and again bite his tongue. But if, since he is irrepressibly arrogant, he behaves otherwise, he will persistently press on. Then, inasmuch as he always stands ready to tear into and to rip apart everyone indiscriminately, let him learn, as he must, not to do violence insanely and helplessly to himself and further damage his own holy name. Let him learn, as he must, not to sew fresh marks of disgrace onto an old one and new stigmas to an aging one since certain marks of disgrace and stigmas should not be ripped open anew in any age or human epoch.

14 Now, my Candido, I see that you are awaiting the speech which I am about to make against him and that he is now blanching, or rather is incandescent with that poetic fury described by Democritus and Plato.[36] My oration too has now navigated safely and happily out of port[37] and only the sails need now be unfurled in order for me to meet securely and more easily his ambush amid the terrors and threats of the sea provided the breakers cease to roll.[38]

THE FIRST OBJECTION

15 First, then, among his other cavils, he in fact especially criticizes me for one particular thing. On this point, this Sicilian — "a human devoid of humanity and ignorant of civility," as Cicero said of Mark Antony[39] — thinks himself so wise and me on the other hand insane. For he not only castigates but he also denounces

---

[36]Rho alludes to Cicero's statement (*On the Orator* 2.46.194): "For I have often heard that — as they say Democritus and Plato have left on record — no man can be a good poet who is not on fire with passion and inspired by something very like frenzy" (LCL). (*Saepe enim audivi poetam bonum neminem — id quod Democrito et Platone in scriptis relictum esse dicunt — sine inflammatione animorum exsistere posse et sine quodam afflatu quasi furoris*). Plato, in his dialogue *Phaedrus* (245A), has Socrates explain the concept of "divine mania" (*mania Mouson*), "fury," or "madness": "A third kind of possession and madness comes from the Muses. This takes hold upon a gentle and pure soul, arouses it and inspires it to songs and other poetry. . . . But he who without the divine madness comes to the doors of the Muses, confident that he will be a good poet by art, meets with no success, and the poetry of the sane man vanishes into nothingness before that of the inspired madmen"(LCL). Cf. also Cicero *On Divination* 1.37.80; and *Philippic* §62, §96, §161, §178; for "divine mania," see Dalfen 77–137.

[37]Cf. Cicero *Tusculan Disputations* 4.14.33.

[38]Cf. Varro *On Agriculture* 2.2.11.

[39]Cicero *Philippics* 2.4.7.

195 insimulatur et damnat quod Suetonium Tranquillum ad clarissimum Principem Filippum Mariam maternam in linguam traduxerim. Adiicit quoque statim nouus iste noster e Sicilia censor me — temere prorsus et inconsulto — id traductionis munus obeundum inuasisse. Subinde temeritatem ipsam meam acriter et acerbe castigasse se putat,
200 quando scilicet fanda atque nefanda quae ipso Suetonio habentur eum Principem docere ultro et insinuare perrexerim.

16 Hei paene occidi! Nam siquidem peracutum hunc hominem[35] cernimus [A115r] et argutum.

17 Attende, rogo, quam instructus nouus hic Achilles descendat
205 in aciem. Quid Achilles? Verius illum simiam quandam[36] litterariam dixerim. Putatne[37] igitur sapiens simia haec? Putatne rugatis labiis curuisque naribus persuadere posse uirtutes et uitia ita confundi commiscerique, ut seorsum haec illa Princeps noster minime percipiat? Et quasi rosas uernas, ut ait, quae sine spinis excerpi nequaquam pos-
210 sunt, ita uirtutes a uitiis putat sine labe secerni aut seligi nulla arte, nullo ingenio posse?

18 Videsne hunc primum impetum? Haec sunt profecto uerba — quid rides, Candide? — quae interloquendum me persaepe ut paene obmutescam terrent, perinde quidem atque
215 elephantos porcina uoce deterreri testamur. O ineruditum hominem insularem uixdum primis elementis imbutum! Suntne istaec illius aduersum me[38] quae infringi nequeant argumenta? Excrea pulmonem, Panormita, quod si minus, saltem caenosam illam aestuantemque linguam comprimere mordicus malis quam
220 eiusce Suetonii traductionem ob historias quae ibi lectitantur mihi uitio dare.

19 Videtne quorsum excors et inconsideratus homo iste erumpat? Videtne dum gladiator inermis me uulnerare satagit, quot clarissimis ornatissimisque uiris insultet atque uno male-
225 dicto suo plerosque omnes inuoluat? Ita enimuero Herodotum, Aristonem Chium, Thucydidem, Theopompum inuadit; Liuio detrahit; Iosephum lacerat; Sallustium carpit; Trogum incusat; Q. Curtium, Cornelium Tacitum, Florum, Iustinum, Lampridium, Orosium, Eusebium, et huiusce generis multos, qui rerum ante-
230 cessiones et historias conscripsere, temere quidem lacessit ac mordet.

---

[35]hunc hominem *tr. N*
[36]quandam] quadam *N*
[37]-ne] *s.l. suppl. N*
[38]me *om. N*

---

[40]Gaius Suetonius Tranquillus (ca. 70–after 122) was a Roman advocate, bureaucrat, and scholar of equestrian rank. His *Lives of the Caesars* include twelve biographies from Julius through Domitian. Suetonius had a significant place in the Carolingian Renaissance, and *florilegia* of his work continued

and condemns the fact that I have translated Suetonius[40] into the vernacular for the distinguished prince, Filippo Maria.[41] Our new censor from Sicily also adds immediately that I rashly and unadvisedly rushed to undertake this work of translation. Next, he thinks that he has sharply and severely censured my temerity, when, of course, I proceeded spontaneously to teach and recommend to the prince both the mentionable and the unmentionable things that Suetonius records.

16 Oh, I am nearly ruined! Right. But only if we judge the man to be acute and clever.

17 Notice, please, how well equipped this new Achilles charges into battle. Did I say Achilles? I might more truly have called him some literate ape. Does this ape, then, think himself wise? Does he think that through wrinkled lips and crooked nose he can persuade us that virtues and vices are so confused and intermingled that our prince can scarcely distinguish one from the other? And does he think that the virtues cannot be separated or picked out unsullied from the vices by any art or skill, as if they are spring roses (as he said), which somehow cannot be picked without the thorns?[42]

18 Do you see this first assault? These are in fact the very words (why do you laugh, Candido?) that in conversations frequently terrify me into silence as the proverbial squeal of a pig scares away elephants. What an uneducated islander this man is, barely initiated in the rudiments![43] Are his arguments against me beyond refutation? "Cough up your lungs, Panormita. If, however, that proves too much, you should at least prefer to bite down on your putrid, inflamed tongue rather than to charge me with vice for having translated our Suetonius because of the stories that one often reads there."

19 Does this senseless and thoughtless man see where his outburst is leading? Does this unarmed gladiator see how many splendid and well equipped men he insults while he is busy wounding me? And does he see that with his one curse he damns almost all of them? For he thus assails Herodotus, Ariston of Chios,[44] Thucydides, and Theopompus; he drags down Livy, lacerates Josephus, nips at Sallust, and finds fault with Trogus. He rashly provokes and rends Quintus Curtius, Cornelius Tacitus, Florus, Justinus, Lampridius, Orosius, Eusebius, and many like them, who have recorded the background and history of events.

---

to be used, especially in France, during the Middle Ages. Petrarca and Boccaccio greatly admired his work, and he was increasingly read throughout the Renaissance. His *Lives of the Caesars* set the form of the biographical genre until well into the eighteenth century (Conte 546–50).

[41] For Panormita's statement, see *Etsi facile* §4 (Appendix I below). For Rho's translation of *The Lives of the Caesars* from Suetonius and other authors into Italian, see Introduction n. 52 above.

[42] Panormita *Etsi facile* §4 (Appendix I below).

[43] For the significance of this slur against "islanders," see *Philippic* §166–§167; cf. also *Philippic* §1 and §33.

[44] Actually, Ariston *of Ceos* (fl. ca. 225 BCE), not *of Chios*. Rho confounded the two Aristons. The "historian" meant here, a Peripatetic philosopher and writer of *Lives of the Philosophers*, was from Ceos (*Ceus* or *Cius*). The other, Ariston *of Chios*, i.e., *Chius*, (fl. ca. 250 BCE), was a Stoic philosopher who wrote virtually nothing.

20 Num idcirco hi uiri, quod multorum flagitia multorum sanctissimos mores litteris mandauere, damnandi aut accusandi sunt? Numquid rem gestam narrare docere est? Numquid singula, quae libris magno studio maioreque negotio lucubrata et tradita sunt, tametsi optimis mixta sint[39] pessima, non identidem lectitanda sunt? Ineptit siquidem aut saltem delirat Beccadellus noster, suo quoque pro more a ueritate longe omnino abhorret. Genus enim hoc hominum ad conflandas historias, quod magno usui omni posteritati futurum esset, caelitus indultum esse non ambigitur, [A115v] qui licet saepenumero rebus fandis atque nefandis uariisque annotamentis, modo illa uera sint, libros insperserint et ut saepe confuderint, non [N100r] eo fit tamen quo ea ipsa confusa confuse atque promiscue et sine electione recipiantur, ceterum potius quo quaeque taeterrima sunt fugiamus, quae uero splendida et optima se tribuunt complectamur; denique, ut priorum regum philosophorumque monimenta atque praecepta, quorum memoria alioquin cum asinis sepulta esset; monimenta, dico, quae a nobis pro fuga, pro lapsu[40] temporum recesserunt, quasi instituendae exornandaeque futurae uitae, consilia et argumenta quaedam atque exemplaria omni posteritati omni saeculo in commune et ob oculos statuant.

21 Miror, modo locus iocandi detur, hunc pantomimum, qui comediarum lectionibus dumtaxat quotidie totus sudat atque uersatur — haec est enim sua sancta et sola religio, neque philosophiae aut alteri doctrinae afficitur — Demeam saltem Terentianum illum suum nequaquam lectitasse. Eius enim quemadmodum commonefaceret filium extant haec uerba: *Inspicere, tamquam in speculo uitas omnium iubeo.* (Audisne Panormita?) *Atque ex aliis sumere exemplum sibi:* "*hoc facito,*" "*hoc fugito,*" "*hoc laudi est,*" "*hoc uitio datur.*"

---

[39]sint] sunt *N*
[40]pro lapsu] prolapsu *A*

---

[45]Although Panormita was from a distinguished Bolognese family that had gone into exile in Palermo, Rho occasionally (*cf. Philippic* §76, §132, §133, and §174) mocks Panormita's family name "Beccadelli," the literal meaning of which in archaic Italian is "butcher" (see GDLI 2: 138 *Beccheria*). Decembrio (1432, 81v; cf. Sabbadini 1891, 16) also wrote to Panormita: ". . . a man whose father is a butcher and . . . his mother a baker? Who does not laugh . . .?" (*An veritus es, ne tibi macellum et pistrinum obiectarem? . . . Quid enim plenius, quid uberius accedebat quod petulantiae tuae obicerem quam id ipsum hominem lanista patre et, eo quidem pauperrimo genitum, matre pistrinaria? Quis non ridet genus et stemmati nobis obiectare?*).
[46]For *obiter dicta* of other humanists on history and the later development of an *ars historica*, see Black 1987b; and Ianziti 1988.
[47]Jerome (*Letter* 84.7.1–2) articulated this principle on the authority of St. Paul (I Thess. 5.21): "Prove all things; hold fast that which is good" (KJV).

20 Are these men, then, to be condemned or accused because they have committed to writing both the hideous acts and the saintly practice of many people? Is to narrate an activity the same as to teach it? Ought we not to read over and over again all the details that historians with great study and with even greater labor have vigilantly written in books and passed on to us even if the worst acts are intermingled with the best? Since in fact our Beccadelli[45] acts the fool or is at least crazy, he is also remaining true to himself when he completely recoils from the truth. For there is no doubt that heaven has blessed us with the sort of men who can write history, because they are of great service to all posterity. Granted that they frequently interspersed and as often infused their books with things mentionable and unmentionable and with sundry annotations (provided that they are true), nonetheless, it does not follow that people receive this jumble confusedly, indiscriminately, and without choice.[46] Rather, let us flee whatever is loathsome; let us embrace what shows itself splendid and best.[47] Then, before our eyes as a common possession of all will stand the records and precepts of former kings and philosophers, whose memory otherwise would have been buried with asses[48] — records, I say, which would have slipped away from us with the flight and lapse of time. As if to instruct and to embellish the life of those in the future, these records and precepts constitute advice and a host of arguments and examples for all posterity in every age.

21 Grant me space for a jest here. This pantomime astounds me.[49] Every day he sweats over and is completely engaged in reading comedies — for this is his holy religion, and his only one; for he has no interest in philosophy or other learning — yet he has never so much as read his own Terentian Demea.[50] For we have at our disposal this piece of advice from Demea when he is admonishing his son: "I order you to contemplate the lives of everyone as if you are looking into a mirror." (Are you listening, Panormita?) "And let others serve as an example to you: 'Do this,' 'Avoid that,' 'This is commendable,' 'That's considered a vice.'"[51]

---

[48]The Prophet Jeremiah (22.19) cursed Jehoakim, condemning him to be buried like an ass, i.e., to be dragged outside the city and left to rot (*Sepultura asini sepelietur, putrefactus et proiectus extra portas Ierusalem*).

[49]Mimes and pantomimes (and other references to dancers) are euphemisms for *cinaedi* or *catamiti*, that is, for "sodomites" (see Rho *Imitations* 144v–145r: *Mimus*, Appendix IX below; see also Merrill 84).

[50]Demea is an upperclass character in the comedy *The Brothers*, written by Publius Terentius Afer (ca. 190–159 BCE), an early Roman playwright (comic poet), who came to Rome as a slave from North Africa. When he was manumitted, he took the name *Terentius* (Terence) from the senator who had owned him. His plays were imitations or adaptations of Greek plays, but he was much admired by Cicero and others. His plays are central to the development of literary Latin right through the Middle Ages and Renaissance (Conte 92–103; and Black 2001, 144–45, 178–80, and 254–56).

[51]Terence *The Brothers* 415–18.

22 Verum hic noster archimagirus, cocorum antistes, ea ipsa eadem in scaena non Demeam, quia uirtutes seorsum a uitiis prosequendas praecipit, uirum quidem grauem et honestum exaudit, uerum statim cum Syro illo Epicureo *luxuriae popinali, scortis,* exoletisque deditus, uel utique caupo quispiam temulentus glutones, helluones, ambrones, gurdos, lurcones, decoctores, nepotes, popinones, parasitos amplectitur; et in *pridiana semesaque obsonia* atque fragmenta pingui iure natantia secum transit; ipsique Syro, quasi nactus nouam academiam, usque adeo se totum dedicauit, ut recte Zethus alter Pacuuianus optimis sanctisque moribus immo *philosophiae bellum indixerit,* flagitia uel simul horrenda perhorrendaque non re minus quam sermone ligurire uideatur.

23 Pro sceleratum! Stipulam enim et ignem apponendum illi, non nobis, at[41] alteri professioni solutiori relinquamus. Quid ni? Absolutior enim atque liberior, quantum ad me attinet, uir iste redditur quod ea flagitia factitarit quae a uerecundo et modesto uiro [A116r] audire non possit.

24 Sed accipe tandem quos peragrantis gulae monitus ex Syro illo sortitus est:

> *Pisces ex sententia* (ait),
> *nactus sum: hi mihi ne corrumpantur cautio est.*
> *Nam id nobis tam flagitium est quam illa, Demea,*[42]
> *non facere uobis quae modo dixti; et quod queo*
> *conseruis ad eundem istunc praecipio modum:"hoc sal*[43]
> *salsum est, hoc adustum est, hoc lautum est parum:*
> *illud recte: iterum sic mementote." Sedulo*
> *moneo quae possum pro mea sententia:*
> *postremo, tamquam in speculum, in patinas, Demea,*[44]
> *inspicere iubeo.*

[41]at] et *N*
[42]Demea *hic N, post* est *A*
[43]sal *om.* N
[44]Demea *Ter.* : *om. AN*

---

[52]*Archimagirus* (head-chef/head-butcher) is a rare Latin word (Septuagint Greek *archimagieros*) found in Jerome (*Hebraic Questions on Genesis* 37.36) and Augustine (*Questions on the Heptateuch* 1.127 and 1.136). Rho uses various "cooking" metaphors (e.g., *Philippic* §40 and *Apology* §47), all of which allude to "Martial the Cook," which is the expurgated version of the Roman poet Martial, ca. 40–104 (Conte 505–11). In the Middle Ages, someone purged Martial's text of the heterosexual obscenities but left the homosexual ones. John of Salisbury, Walter Map, Vincent of Beauvais, and others attributed this expurgated version to "Martial the Cook" (Conte 509). Rho's use of these cooking metaphors follows, no doubt, Jerome (*Letter* 54.10): "nothing inflames the body and titillates the genitals more than undigested food and convulsive belching" (*nihil sic inflammat corpora et titillat membra genitalia nisi indigestus cibus ructusque convulsus*). Other Roman satirists as well as medieval and Renaissance moralists routinely associated gluttony with sexual excess, often specifically with sodomy (see Wiesen 77–79, 134–35, 182–83; Rocke 21–22, 107; Jordan; and Corbellini 1930, 52).

22 But our head-chef here, the high-priest of cooks,[52] fails to heed Demea's admonition in this scene. For Demea, a truly grave and honorable man, teaches that virtues must be pursued by distinguishing them from vices. But Panormita, who is addicted like the Epicurean Syrus[53] "to gourmet delicacies, whores,"[54] and sodomites,[55] regularly embraces, like some drunken innkeeper, gluttons, gourmands, lechers, idiots, overeaters, spendthrifts, prodigals, cookshop habitués, and parasites. He returns by himself "to yesterday's half-eaten leftovers"[56] and to chunks of food swimming in a greasy broth. He has so totally dedicated himself to Syrus, as if he had stumbled on a new academy, that rightly like another Pacuvian Zethus he has declared war on good and holy customs, in fact "he has declared war directly on philosophy."[57] He even seems to lust after shameful acts that are at the same time shocking and terrifying no less in the doing than in the telling.

23 What a wretch! Let us leave him to be piled with straw and set on fire, not by us, but by another less fettered profession.[58] Why not do it? Well, as far as I am concerned, the man becomes more dissolute and unrestrained because he practices those shameful acts that he cannot hear spoken of by a respectable and modest man.

24 But listen, then, to the recommendations he gets for an aberrant appetite from Syrus, who said: "I've found the fish I wanted. I have to watch out that they're not spoiled. For among us servants that's as much a disgrace as for you masters not to do the things that you, Demea, were just talking about. And insofar as I'm able, I teach my fellow slaves the same way: 'That's too salty,' 'That's burned,' 'That's not cleaned right,' 'That's just right,' 'Remember to do it like that next time.' I do my best to teach what I can from what I know. Finally, Demea, I order them to look into the dishes as if into a mirror."[59]

---

[53]Syrus is a slave in Terence's comedy *The Brothers*.

[54]Apuleius *Metamorphoses* (*The Golden Ass*) 8.1.

[55]Rho glosses the classical Latin word *exoletus* as being synonymous with the medieval Latin word 'sodomite' (*Imitations* 134r: *Luxuria*; Appendix IX below): "Lampridius [*Alexander Severus* 39.2] . . . said about Alexander: 'He had no association with male prostitutes (*exoleti*), so that he wanted to outlaw them,' namely sodomites." Rho also uses the term more loosely (cf. *Apology* §47 n. 169) and glosses it less precisely (*Imitations* 134r: *Luxuria*; Appendix IX below): "*Absoleti* and *exoleti* are impure and foul in lust" (*sunt immundi et foetidi in luxuria*). For the medieval theological invention of the word "sodomy" and "sodomite," see Jordan; see also Hergemöller esp. 27–38, and 144–62.

[56]Suetonius *Tiberius* 34.

[57]Zethus preferred hunting to his brother Amphion's music. The tragedian Pacuvius (220–130 BCE) adapted a play about this rivalry from the *Antiope* of Euripides (ca. 480–ca. 406 BCE), the Athenian tragic playwright (cf. *Philippic* §159). In the passage quoted here, Cicero (*On the Orator* 2.37.155) applied this metaphor to Mark Antony's grandfather.

[58]With this statement Rho again raises the spectre of an inquisition, where Panormita would be "relaxed to the secular arm" for punishment (cf. *Philippic* §12 and §134).

[59]Terence *The Brothers* 420–29.

290 **25** Videsne, Candide, quibus speculis mores Siculus immo Suculus iste componat? quae uitia declinet? quas uirtutes prosequatur? Siquidem Demeam uir iste Socraticus fugit, Syrum uero concelebrat. Rosas putat legere; spinas colligit: et quod mihi dat uitio de se periculum facit. Virtutum enim uitiorumque discrimen percipit nullum. 295 Syrum ipsum quod Demea sit arbitratur, nam caecus utrumque confundit ac miscet. Quod si non est — uidelicet, quod non ista misceat et confundat ceterum rerum distantias et discretiones recte dignoscat — tunc turpius id quidem et inconsultius, dum ultro et conscius in uoluptatum officinam quandam, immo extremam latri- 300 nam ⟨init⟩, sese dealbare ac procurare contendit. Cuperem aures iam suas coram accommodaret: putatne quemadmodum ad rerum uarietates praecipiendas ipse quasi talpa captus est oculis, ceteros uel hac turpi caecitate damnatum iri, ut quae fugienda sunt illi amplectantur; quae uero amplectenda sunt ea fugi oportere arbitrentur?

305 **26** In hoc plane uidemus Suetonium sibi prorsus incognitum esse, qui, dum inter alios Caesares Neronis uitam describeret, ut doceret uirtutes prosequendas, uitia uero declinanda esse, quodam loco de ipso Nerone[45] in hanc sententiam, inquit, usque nunc de Nerone tamquam de homine locuti sumus; nunc de ipso [N100v] 310 tamquam de monstro dicemus.

27 Cernimus itaque[46] hunc grammaticulum, purum, ut ita dixerim, onagrum, nondum ludi puerilis subsellia aut paedagogium exuisse. Quid sibi uelit historiarum notitia, quid usus afferant, quid habeant condimenti nihil callet; sonos illarum et antiquas tubas[47] — 315 auritus ut est — exaudit quidem; quorsum erumpant nihil exaudit. Fabulas femineas inter colos et fusos ad lucernas aut cantilenas Ka[A116v]roli[48] Regis et Arturi[49] compitis et plateis uulgo decantatas[50] planius intelligit. Qui utique tamen sese tanti facit, ut illis Plautinis interiectionibus suis priscoque illo, ut ita dixerim, Euandri 320 genere scribendi[51] — uidelicet *apludam edit et flocces bibit* — diphthongis quoque alphabetis insuetis,[52] quibus epistolae suae omnes[53] scatent, se Varronem alterum linguae Latinae facile principem

---

[45]in hanc . . . de Nerone *om. N*
[46]itaque] -a- *s.l. suppl. A*
[47]antiquas tubas] ᵇtubas ᵃantiquas *corr. A*
[48]Karoli *A* : -ruli *N*
[49]Arturii] Arcturi, -c- *s.l. suppl. A*
[50]decantatas] -tatis *A*
[51]genere scribendi *tr. N*
[52]insuetis] inconsuetis *N*
[53]omnes] *s.l. suppl. A*

---

[60]Rho's pun on *siculus / suculus* only works in Latin.
[61]Some verb with the sense of *init*, that is, "going into," has been dropped (conjecture of John Monfasani).

25 Do you see, Candido, what virtuous habits this native of Sicily, or rather of Swinery,[60] practices in front of the mirror? What vices he shuns? What virtues he pursues? If this devotee of Socrates shuns Demea, he certainly consorts with Syrus. He thinks he is picking roses; he collects thorns. And what he considers a vice in me he tries for himself. For he recognizes no distinction between virtue and vice. He thinks that Syrus is the same as Demea. For he blindly confuses and mixes them up. But if this is not the case, namely, that he does not mix them up and confuse them, but correctly recognizes their distinctions and differences, then it is all the more shameful and foolish for him to try to clean and groom himself while willfully and knowingly [frequenting][61] a workshop of pleasures, or rather an utterly filthy latrine. I would now like him to lend me an ear. Does he think that just as he has been blinded like a mole in distinguishing the varieties of things, so others through this wretched blindness should be condemned to embrace what ought to be shunned and shun what ought to be embraced?

26 In this we clearly see that Panormita is thoroughly unacquainted with Suetonius, who, in order to teach that virtues must be pursued and vices rejected, says at one point in his description of Nero: "In the same general sense we have until now spoken about Nero as if about a man; now we shall speak about him as if about a monster."[62]

27 And so we discern that this measly teacher of ABCs is, as I would put it, a pure ass,[63] who has not yet quit the benches of primary school or ceased to be a schoolmaster. He understands nothing about what a knowledge of the sundry histories means, what usefulness they impart, or what kind of flavor they possess. Long-eared animal that he is, Panormita certainly hears the sounds of these histories and the ancient trumpets; for what purpose they blast he hears nothing. He more clearly understands the old wives' tales recounted among the distaffs and spindles at lamplight or the old songs of Charlemagne and Arthur commonly chanted at the crossroads and in the piazzas.[64] In spite of that he is enormously pleased with himself because of his quotations from Plautus and his archaic style of writing. He is, as I would put it, extremely smug in his Evanderesque style, for example, "he eats the chaff and drinks the lees."[65] He also has a fondness for unusual diphthongs and spellings, which abound in all his letters. Based on this, he boasts of having become another Varro,[66] indisputably the prince and most authoritative teacher of the Latin

---

[62]Suetonius, in his *Lives of the Caesars*, said this about Caligula (*Caligula* 22.1), not about Nero.

[63]This is a scholastic proverb (Fumagalli 2118; for the low status of the grammarian, see Black 2001, 31–33; cf. also *Philippic* §79, §135, §145 and *Apology* §6).

[64]The legend of Roland (Orlando), the Knight of Charlemagne killed at Roncesvalles on 15 August 778, and the legend of King Arthur (sixth century) had circulated in Italy since the twelfth century (Grendler 290–91). For chanting "at the crossroads and in the piazzas," cf. Jerome *Letter* 57.13.

[65]Aulus Gellius (11.7.3) cited Evander's phrase as an example of archaic language that he once heard a pretentious lawyer use supposing it to be a moving expression. Neither judge nor jury knew what the words meant, looked at one another with some consternation, and then all burst into laughter.

[66]Marcus Terentius Varro (116–27 BCE), who was famed in his own day as a scholar, was generally recognized thereafter as the greatest scholar ancient Rome ever produced. His work *On the Latin Language* was of profound authority for Renaissance humanists in their philological pursuits (Conte 210–20; cf. *Apology* §47 n. 168).

praeceptoremque grauissimum euasisse glorietur; quippe ita ut *e bibliothecis* nos omnis *eiicere* atque philosophos quosque *censoria uirgula* suoque iure quodam eliminare posse se solum arbitretur.

28 Pro ridiculum caput! Cum ex his quae statim attigimus, tum imprimis quod Caesarum antecessiones et gesta censet, si morum incolumitas si integritas uitae seruanda est, neque a principibus legi neque a me traduci ulla ratione oportere. Verum enimuero nisi, omnino ferreus ut assolet, rigeat et[54] obstupe(sc)at atque indomitus calcitret, Ciceroni suo familiari ac[55] socio (sic enim arroganter illum appellat) cedat — uelit, nolit — oportebit: *Historia*, inquit, *testis* est *temporum, lux ueritatis, uita memoriae, magistra uitae, nuntia uetustatis.*

29 "Quo abis, inuicte? Quid tergiuersaris, grauissime censor? Qui nobis historias auferre et illas oblitterare conaris? Quibus utique sublatis, cum de futuris rebus nihil certum, de praesentibus nisi pauca et illa paene incognita teneamus,[56] quid aliud restat, nisi ut maiorum gesta, monimenta, exempla, quae animos maxime et a uitiis auocare[57] et ad uirtutes impellere solent, nulla apud reges, nulla apud principes, nulla apud nationes et populos habeamus?[58] Deleantur iam omnes libri; oblitterentur singula quae mandata litteris, quae sempiternae memoriae consecrata sunt, ita ut anteaquam nati essemus quid acciderit, quae sors mortalibus rebusque ceteris fuerit, omnino nesciamus. Non pueri semper, non muta quaedam[59] animalia uiueremus?"

30 Bacchatur exinde et quasi cynocephaleus Mercurius uidetur oblatrare: non honestati, non religioni meae conduxisse Suetonium ipsum et imprimis ad Principem traducerem. Esto ut cupit et quod falsum est: id uerum esse sibi nihil[60] diffiteamur, uidelicet huiuscemodi scriptionem honestati et religioni meae fore dissentaneam. Quid idcirco me solum unum toto orbe uerba pro uerbis reddentem lacessit? [A117r] Quid Augustinum, Hieronymum, Orosium, Eusebium, et huius loci ac ordinis clarissimos uiros sanctissimosque, qui ab ipsius mundi incunabulis gesta conscripsere, intactos praetermittit? Sed numquid legibus honestatis soli sacerdotes obstringuntur; ceteri hominum uagi sunt, et ita soluti palabundique, ut quacumque de re turpi data[61] uel honesta, libere, impune, sine reprehensione dissertare possint? Quo ex Solone aut Lycurgo seu Numa Pompilio hae de sacerdotibus leges honestatis emanarunt atque rogatae sunt? Num

---

[54]et] atque *N*
[55]ac] at *N*
[56]teneamus] tenamus *N*
[57]auocare] euo- *N*
[58]habeamus] habemus *N*
[59]quaedam] quo- *A*
[60]sibi nihil *tr. N*
[61]turpi data *tr. N*

language and, of course, presumes that he can single-handedly "expel all of us from the libraries" and in his own right "blacklist" every philosopher.[67]

28 What a ridiculous individual! First because of the traits that we have just touched upon. Second and most especially because he thinks that under no circumstance should princes read nor should I translate the background and deeds of the Caesars if princes are safely to preserve their morals and their integrity of life. But, in fact, unless, inflexible as he is, he remains unmoved, becomes senseless, and fiercely resists, he will have to yield willy-nilly to Cicero, his "friend and companion" (as he arrogantly refers to him). For Cicero says: "History is the witness of the times, the light of truth, the life of memory, the teacher of life, and the herald of antiquity."[68]

29 "Where, invincible one, do you retreat? Why, austere censor, do you waver? Why do you attempt to take the histories away from us and obliterate them? Since concerning the future nothing is certain; concerning the present we hold only a few things certain and even those barely known, if even histories are taken from us, what else remains? Nothing would be left for kings, princes, nations, and peoples of the deeds, records, and examples of our ancestors. And these things reckon most in recalling minds from vice and in impelling them to virtue. All right. Let all books be destroyed; let everything entrusted to writing and consecrated to everlasting memory be obliterated so that we are completely ignorant of what happened and of the lot of mortals and of other things before we were born. Would we not live forever like children or dumb animals?"

30 He then flies into a rage and seems to bark like a dog-headed Mercury[69] saying that it is contrary to my honor and religious profession to have translated Suetonius, and especially to have done so for the prince. Even though it is false, let us assume what he wants. Let us not deny for a moment what is intrinsically false, namely, that this kind of literature would be contrary to decency and to my religious profession. Why, then, does he attack me alone in the whole world when I am only making a literal translation? Why does he exempt from scandal Augustine, Jerome, Orosius, Eusebius, and the brilliant and holy men of that rank and order, who have delineated events from the beginning of the world itself? But can it be that laws of decency constrain only priests, while other people are exempt and can thus wander about unfettered and discourse freely, safely, and blamelessly about anything whatever, disgraceful or honorable? From what Solon or Lycurgus or Numa Pompilius did these laws of decency concerning priests originate or were they approved?[70] Suetonius was a most eloquent

---

[67] Jerome *Letter* 61.2 (to Vigilantius).

[68] Cicero *On the Orator* 2.9.36.

[69] The Egyptian god Thoth became associated with the Greek god Hermes or the Roman god Mercury. He was often depicted as "dog-headed," that is, having the face of a baboon (see Lactantius *Divine Institutes* 1.6.2–5; Roeder 859–63; cf. *Philippic* §140 n. 376). Rho also alludes to Augustine's statement (*City of God* 16.8) about the Cynocephali (Dog-heads), "whose dogs' heads and actual barking are evidence that they are rather beasts than men" (LCL).

[70] These are the legendary lawgivers: Solon to Athens, Lycurgus to Sparta, and Numa Pompilius to Rome.

360 Suetonius, uir eloquentissimus, idemque Panormitae nusquam agnitus, qui primus, ut aiunt, Neruae Imperatori, sanctissimo principi, De uita Caesarum librum eum ipsum inscripsit, quem legi debere a principibus nostris — Siculus iste religionem esse ducit![62] — optimorum e coetu uirorum quia sacerdotio caruit nequaquam explodetur? Nos
365 autem qui sacerdotes initiati sumus, si Caesares ipsos exarauerimus, digni euadimus qui inde explodamur exibilemurque?

31 At si perinde res habet ac ille existimat, sacerdotes uidelicet solos honestatis esse debitores, honestas ipsa quidem Gades Herculis iam nihil attingit. Breuiore enim ambitu contractioreque sese con-
370 tinet. Reges nescit; philosophos reiicit: qui tamen philosophi, plebis ac populi exemplaria quaedam ac[63] specula caelo delapsa esse creduntur. Denique intra ipsa ciuitatum pomeria nulli theatro nulli regioni se exibet aut sui copiam facit, uerum solis templis, solis diuinis [N101r] aedibus honestas ipsa uersatur ac splendet.

375 **32** Nunc iam urinam huius quam honestissimi uiri oportet speculemur. Quid sabulosa est? Codrus hic noster profecto torsionem iliacam patitur. Procuret itaque se ne crepuerit. Quod tamen si crepuerit, ex liuore magis quam ualitudine illa crepuisse uidebitur. Non est id praeterea turpissimum argumentum, mi Candide, quod
380 aeque amicum et inimicum laedit?

33 En is erratum suum nihil aduertit aut quo imprudens collabatur nihil agnoscit, qui eodem sermone, dum me insectatur premitque, principem uel mecum pertrahit et inuoluit. Qui rosas credit, quasi sit oculis captus, non sine laesione decerpere ne [A117v]
385 illas attingere quidem possit, cum et puellae uirgines ludibundae certatim ex illis serta componant, calathos oppleant, sinusque distendant? Hocine diuino ingenio scriptisque suis illustrare se ipsum putat, et propediem suaemet uiuens interesse posteritati? Sunt istaec poemata illa insignia Vergilium, ut ait, obscuratura quae Principe de illo nostro
390 perillustri singulos ac perpetuos annos pollicetur? Nulla tamen ad aures suas quae loqueretur[64] in hunc diem uisa Calliope. Sed afferat, rogo, quo sub Graeculo haec, quae tam argute molitur, inscitiae meae

---

[62]esse ducit] [b]ducit [a]esse *corr. A*
[63]ac] et *N*
[64]loqueretur] -quetur *N*

---

[71]Suetonius dedicated (ca. 120 CE) his *Lives* to the Praetorian Septicius Clarus. The Emperor Trajan (98–117) put Suetonius in charge of Roman public libraries, and he served in the imperial archives during the reign of Hadrian (117–38). Perhaps Rho took Pliny the Younger's *Letter* (5.10) urging Suetonius to write as referring to the release of the *Lives* (which it does not). If Pliny's letter dates from the time of Nerva's reign (96–98), Suetonius would have been at best in his late teens, having been born ca. 70 CE (Conte 546–50; cf. *Philippic* §15 nn. 40–41 above).
[72]The Pillars of Hercules are now called the Straits of Gibraltar, and at that time represented "the ends of the earth."

man — and an author whom Panormita has never understood. He, so they say, first dedicated his book *On the Lives of the Caesars* to the most August prince, Emperor Nerva,[71] a book that our princes ought to read (but which this Sicilian considers a religious offense!). Just because Suetonius was not a priest, he is never to be ejected from the company of virtuous men? Or conversely, do those of us who have been consecrated priests deserve then to be hissed off stage and expelled from this company if we have written about the Caesars?

31 But if the matter really stands as he supposes, specifically, that only priests are bound to Decency, then even Decency herself no longer reaches the Pillars of Hercules.[72] For she confines herself within a smaller and tighter circle. She does not know kings; she rejects philosophers — philosophers, nevertheless, who are believed to have descended from heaven to be examples and mirrors for the masses and the people. In sum, Decency does not show or grant access to herself in any theater or quarter within the city but instead dwells and shines in lonely precincts and solitary temples.

32 Now is the time to examine the urine of this most honorable of men. Why is it gravelly? This Codrus[73] of ours is certainly suffering from colic cramps. Let him take care not to fart.[74] But nonetheless, if he does fart, he will seem to have done so more from spite than from ill health. Besides, my dear Candido, is it not disgraceful that he offends friend and foe alike?

33 Look. He does not notice his mistake or recognize what he is unknowingly falling into. For while he attacks and presses me, in the same speech he also draws in and entangles the prince with me.[75] Now who is so blind as to believe that roses cannot be picked or even be touched without injury[76] when even playful girls eagerly braid garlands, fill baskets, and stuff their gathered skirts with them? Does he think that this divine genius of his and his writings distinguish him and that while still alive he is shortly to be present at his own immortality? Are these the brilliant poems that he promises year in and year out about our most illustrious prince that are going to put, as he says, Virgil in the shade?[77] Yet no Calliope[78] has been seen to this day speaking into his ear. But let him produce, please, the Greekling[79] under whose tutelage he nightly composed such subtly belabored

---

[73]Codrus was a poet jealous of Virgil (cf. *Eclogue* 7.21–28).

[74]Farting is a trope for offensive speech (cf. *Philippic* §183 and Martial 12.77).

[75]That is, Filippo Maria Visconti, Duke of Milan, for whom Rho translated the *Lives of the Caesars* (see *Philippic* §15 n. 41 and Introduction n. 52 above).

[76]Panormita *Etsi facile* §4 (Appendix I below).

[77]Publius Vergilius Maro (70–19 BCE) was the most celebrated of the Augustan Roman poets and the author of the *Aeneid, Eclogues*, and *Georgics*. His close friend and patron, Maecenas, introduced him to Octavius Caesar's circle. In part because of this close connection with Caesar Augustus, ancient grammarians thought that his great epic poem *Aeneid* was written "to imitate Homer and to praise Augustus" (Conte 276). Virgil was later associated (incorrectly) with some sexually explicit verse known to the humanists as the *Priapeia*, presumably written in his youth. From antiquity into the modern period, Virgil was far and away the most influential of all Roman poets. In the Middle Ages and Renaissance he was frequently called "Maro" (Conte 262–91; cf. *Philippic* §145–§149; and *Apology* §22).

[78]Calliope (meaning "beautiful voice") is the Muse of epic poetry.

[79]That is, "let him produce, please, the child's grammar book in sing-songy verse. . . ." *Graecismus*, written in 1212 by Evrard de Béthune, was a widely used grammar book which employed verse to help pupils remember the grammatical rules of Latin (see Black 2001, 76–83).

argumenta lucubrarit. Dicetne academiae[65] has strophas atque nodosa theoremata sub ullo nouo Mnesarcho aut Carneada nuper percalluisse? Logi sunt et nugae. Quorsum igitur tam insolens sui aestimatio? Quid de se[66] sibi tam magnifice persuadet, ut *caprearum oculos* ipse *talpa* glebosa *contemnat*? Non tibi inter sanos furere et prope inter sobrios bacchari istic uinolentus insularis uidetur? Plutarchus enim — quo plures in eum reiiciam — uir doctissimus idemque philosophus, Latinis uiris Graecos contendens, non Porcii Catonis non Aristidis, immo non Caesaris non Alexandri et insolentias et uirtutes, quae in medium et passim legerentur, exarauit?[67] Quid ergo rei est ut non illi sub Traiano aequissimo Imperatore diem dicat? Mihi uero se diem dicturum nisi taceam minitetur!

34 Leonardus uero noster Aretinus, "uir Atticus" et omnium iudicio alter paene Cicero, cum multa penes nos Graeca eiusce Plutarchi pro linguae imperitia nequaquam tenerentur ⟨nisi⟩ nobis ipse Latina reddidisset, quid illum non incusat?[68] Quid uenenum inglutit?[69] Quid non euomit? Quid singulos clanculum et in angulis mordet, me uero palam? Extingueturne umquam haec febris? Vmquamne cerebri uitio sanus emerserit?

35 Sic et ille Hieronymus meus, uir, uel si sanctissimis comparetur, sanctitate conspicuus idemque sacerdos lectissimus, dum muliercularum monachorumque uarios mores et plurimis et grauibus epistolis depinxisset, cum a plerisque delatoribus tum imprimis ab Rufino, Aquileiensi presbytero, uiro uel ipso eloquentissimo, insimulatus est. Aeque cum Origenis Periarchon e Graeco Latinum fecisset, [A118r] in canum morsus a quibus diriperetur concidisse se statim intellexit. In illum enim e uestigio collatrantes

---

[65]academiae] -damiae *A*
[66]se] *s.l. suppl. A*
[67]exarauit] -uint *N*
[68]incusat] -satur *N*
[69]inglutit] non inglutit *A*

---

[80]That is, Panormita's *Priapeia* (cf. *Philippic* §178–§181).
[81]Mnesarchus was an Athenian Stoic philosopher who flourished between 110 and 103 BCE; Carneades was known for founding the New Academy, or Sceptical Academy, in the early second century BCE.
[82]Jerome *Letter* 70.6.
[83]For the significance of this slur against "islanders," see *Philippic* §166–§167; cf. also *Philippic* §1, §18.
[84]Cato and Aristides were paired in Plutarch's *Lives*. Marcus Porcius Cato (234–149 BCE) was known as "Censorius" for his stern traditional morality. Aristides (d. after 467 BCE) was an Athenian statesman known for his honesty (cf. *Philippic* §143 and *Apology* §25).
[85]For the translations of Plutarch available, see n. 87 below.
[86]Panormita *Etsi facile* §5 (Appendix I below).
[87]Leonardo Bruni da Arezzo (1370–1444) was a humanist disciple of Coluccio Salutati. Rho would have known Bruni mostly as a Greek scholar (cf. *Apology* §25, §34, and §37) and possibly as the Chancellor of Florence (1427). Prior to 1431/32, when Rho wrote this *Philippic*, Bruni had translated

arguments concerning my ignorance.[80] Will he claim to have recently become skilled in these strophes and intricate theorems of the Academy under some new Mnesarchus or Carneades?[81] These poems are empty words and trifles. So where, then, does he get such an inflated opinion of himself? Why does he have such a grandiose view of himself that he has become a cloddy "mole despising the eyes of gazelles"?[82] Does that wine-sodden island yokel[83] not seem to you to rave among the sane and to be pretty much a drunkard among the sober? For did not Plutarch — from whom I could cite many examples to him — who was both a scholar and a philosopher, in comparing the Greeks with the Latins, describe both the excesses and virtues of Porcius Cato and Aristides,[84] and especially of Caesar and of Alexander?[85] And these accounts of excesses and virtues were read to audiences far and wide. Why then does Panormita not bring him to trial under the most equitable Emperor Trajan? Yet he threatens that he is going to prosecute me if I do not shut up![86]

34 But as for our Leonardo Aretino — an Atticus[87] and in everyone's judgment almost another Cicero — who for our benefit has rendered into Latin the many Greek works of the aforementioned Plutarch that would have remained completely inaccessible to us given our ignorance of the language, why does Panormita not accuse him? Why does he swallow poison? Why does he not vomit it up? Why does he slander everyone else privately and secretly, but me publicly? Will his fever ever be extinguished? Will he ever recover sanity after his mental defect?

35 Take the case even of my Jerome, a man of conspicuous sanctity even when compared to the most saintly people and likewise a most exceptional priest. Many accusers and especially Rufinus, Bishop of Aquileia, an eloquent man in his own right, denounced him for depicting the inconstant behavior of maidens and monks in his numerous, weighty letters.[88] Similarly, when he had translated Origen's *On First Things* from Greek into Latin, he understood at once that he had fallen into the jaws of dogs that would tear him asunder.[89] The whole

---

Aristotle's *Nicomachean Ethics* and *Politics*, and Ps.-Aristotle's *Economics*; St. Basil's *Homily to Youth on Reading the Books of the Pagans*; Xenophon's *On Tyranny*; Demosthenes' *In Defense of Diopithes* and *In Defense of Ctesiphon*; selections of Homer's *Iliad*; Plato's *Phaedo, Gorgias, Phaedrus, Apology of Socrates, Crito*, and *Letters*. Leonardo Bruni translated into Latin a number of Plutarch's *Lives*: Mark Antony, Cato, the Gracchi, Aemilius Paulus, Demosthenes, Sertorius, and Pyrrhus (Plutarch's *Moralia* were available in a medieval Latin translation). Bruni's contemporaries complimented him as a "close friend of Cicero" (i.e., very eloquent) with the name "Atticus," alluding both to his knowledge of Greek and to the Atticus of Cicero's *Letters to Atticus* (see Field 1998; Hankins 1997, and Witt 2000, 392–442).

[88]See Jerome's *Letters* 22 and 125 (cf. Wiesen 70–73, 119–27, and 155–60).

[89]Jerome translated Origen's *On First Things* and wrote glowingly of Origen (Jerome *Against the Books of Rufinus* 1.6). Jerome's admiration for Origen and his accurate rendering of Origen's *On First Things* became the subject of a bitter controversy after a certain Atarbius demanded repudiation of Origenism. In defense of Origen, Rufinus produced a bowdlerized translation of *On First Things*, claiming the suspect passages were interpolations. Origen's original Greek text is now lost, leaving Rufinus' bowdlerized translation and fragments of Jerome's more faithful rendering as the only surviving witnesses to Origen's work (see Kelly 203 and 234–42).

420 omnes insurrexere quod haereses innumeras, quae ipso Origenis in libro Graeco sermone tegebantur, in Latinos Christi tirones et ipsos rudes transfundere ac seminare conaretur.

36 Atque hoc de congressu primo iam satis. In quo tamen non putet uelim sacra haec incepta ita cito confectum iri. Permoleste qui-
425 dem alio eiusce litterulae suae loco ferre uidetur Orpheus iste noster nescio quos uersiculos perobscenos aduersus nomen suum celebre, famam quoque illam eius **SECVNDA OBJECTIO** sanctam et caelibem editos esse; cumue ipse solus, ut ait, e pectore meo emanauisse ad credendum adduci nequeat et
430 addubitare uideatur, facile tamen cum a multis tum imprimis a nonnullis consacerdotibus meis suaderi id ipsum sibi et astipulari dicit.

37 Loquiturne ioco an serio? Non quidem sic facile — non sic facile, ut hic circulator facile blaterat — de aetate perfecta uitaeque integritate uirorum illustrium falsa creduntur, eorum praecipue qui ea
435 uirtutum morumque iecere fundamenta ut uel a maximis uentis euelli immo ne labefactari quidem ullo pacto possint. Quis umquam hominum per exacta illius aetatis meae curricula me in faecibus suis aut suo in illo uolutabro more suillo deprehendit, ut petulantia caenosaque uerba in quemquam effudisse digito consignarer? Quis
440 [N101v] umquam uersus tam impudentes ex ore aut calamo meo profectos esse censuerit, cum suo numquam in ludo uersatus sim, numquam ephebiam illam suam — O tempora fulminibus digna! — ubi suilla uocabula ipsa colleguntur,[70] ubi Beelphegor ille suus perpetuo adoratur, introii?

445 **38** Atqui commodum ad id quod de consacerdotibus meis me accusantibus homo — ut est uafer! — adducit redeundum est, ubi primum nequeo non admirari unde haec sartago sua tanta uerborum taeterrima colluuione ebulliat ac semper exaestuet; unde tot impurissimis sermonibus tot impudentissimis uerbis redundet et effluat.
450 Non illi, ut ignis ipse subsidat, fomenta aliquando defuerint? *Apelles* pictor, ut aiunt, *dicebat pi*[A118v]*ctores illos peccare qui non sentirent quid esset satis.* At huic sartagini nihil nimis immo ne satis quidem.

---

[70]colle-] col- *s.l. suppl. A* : colli- *N*

---

[90]Orpheus, founder of the religious movement of Orphism, was famed as a singer and mythological poet. Augustine described him as one of the "theological poets" (*City of God* 18.14). Ovid says that Orpheus, upon the death of his betrothed Eurydice, repulsed the advances of women and became in Thrace "the originator of pederasty" (*Metamorphoses* 10.79–85 and 10.152–54; for Orpheus and institutionalized pederasty, see Percy 48, 55–56, 139).

[91]In the same sense that Orpheus was "holy and celibate" (see n. 90 above).

[92]Panormita *Etsi facile* §1 (Appendix I below).

[93]Panormita *Etsi facile* §5 (Appendix I below).

[94]Cf. Proverbs 26.11; II Peter 2.22; and Jerome *Hebraic Questions* praef.

[95]Rho explains (*Imitations* 132v: *Lupanar*; Appendix IX below): "An *ephebia* is a place of prostitution for boys."

snarling pack rose against him instantly for trying to introduce and disseminate among Christ's simple Latin novices the innumerable heresies that lay concealed in Origen's book under the veil of its Greek.

THE SECOND OBJECTION

36 But enough now about this first encounter. Nevertheless, let him not think as a consequence that I am going to want these sacred undertakings to be concluded so swiftly. Indeed, our Orpheus[90] seems at great pains to report elsewhere in his wretched little letter that some extremely obscene little poem has been published against his celebrated name, even against his very reputation for holiness and celibacy.[91] Whereas he alone, so he says, cannot be led to believe and expresses open doubt that this poetry had emanated from my heart,[92] nevertheless he asserts that many people and especially some of my fellow priests easily persuade him and get him to agree that it is mine.[93]

37 Is he joking or serious when he says this? Lies about the professional accomplishments and the personal integrity of illustrious men are not in fact so readily believed — not so readily as this charlatan easily blathers — especially about those who have so laid the foundations of their virtues and morals that even the strongest gales cannot blow them down or destroy them in any way. Throughout the entire span of my life, what man ever caught me in Panormita's filth or in his hog wallow[94] so that I could be identified as a person who would spew out nasty and vile words against anyone? Who would ever think that such lewd poetry could proceed from my mouth or pen when I have never attended his school for vice or entered his brothel for boys[95] where one acquires this swinish language, where his Beelphegor[96] is adored in perpetuity? What a generation, deserving to be struck down by lightning!

38 But I must return for the moment to what the man (conniver that he is!) alleged about my fellow priests accusing me.[97] Let me say first, I cannot help but wonder what makes that pot of his bubble and boil with such a lurid mishmash of words; what makes it surge and overflow with such vile language and shameful expressions. Will he never run out of wood so the fire can die down? According to legend, the painter Apelles "used to say that those painters err who do not sense what is sufficient."[98] But nothing is too much for this pot of his; indeed nothing is ever enough.

---

[96]Beelphegor was a Moabite god (Numbers 25.1–3) described by Origen (*Homiles on Numbers* 20.1) as an "indecent idol" (*idolum turpitudinis*). Jerome (*Commentary on Isaiah* 8.25.9 and elsewhere) gives the specific explanation that Rho has in mind: "*Beelphegor*, who in Latin is known as *Priapus*." Priapus was the fertility god sporting an enormous erection, whose image was commonly found in Roman gardens (see Richlin 1983, 9, 66, and 121–24). Panormita was at this time composing scurrilous poetry against Rho which he referred to as his *Priapeia* (Sabbadini 1910a, 101–02; cf. *Philippic* §178–§181).

[97]Panormita *Etsi facile* §5 (Appendix I below).

[98]Cicero *The Orator* 22.73.

39 Creditur quidem iamque trito[71] sermone diffamatum est hanc suam fuisse a pueris Mineruam suumque genium,[72] ut si uel belle loqui niteretur, ob cicatricem uulneri superinductam iam omnino nesciret. Quid istuc miramur? Vulgo enim, ut nunc attigi, peruagatur opinio illum hosce perditissimos mores simul cum lacte ab nutricis uberibus puerulum combibisse. Quando igitur commenticia uerba; quando nouas inexauditasque fabricas in dies excitat, quis, iterum dicam, locus admirationi,[73] potissimum quando huiuscemodi doctrinis et artibus, quasi quodam in ludo innutritus,[74] studium operamque ipse nauauerit? Sed ad illum iam aliquantisper si libet sermonem uertam.

40 "Heus! Tu cedo, sodes. Qui sunt hi consacerdotes mei qui me tuae laesae maiestatis eximiae tam impudenter tam falso accusant? Numquid — pro pudor! — flagitiosi aut sacrilegi uiri contubernales mei sunt, aut me pro foribus exoletorum examina ad auroram consalutant? Numquid inter phialas et phasides aues parasitaster quispiam aut ganeo mecum ligurit aut symbolum ponit? Videto, rogo, ne mustiones, immo combibones, tui potius illi sint, quos consacerdotes meos post cenam dubiam aut somniaris aut finxeris. Quis enim nunc Propertius aut Tibullus, immo Martialis Coquus uersus tam petulantes et spurcos euomeret, nisi sub te praeceptore foedissimos[75] illos lucubrasset percalluissetque aut ab illa tua impuritatum officina illos secum attulisset? Quid ad haec iam pallore iam rubore suffunderis? Vnde tibi hi uesani flagrant uultus? Vnde oculi torui atque ora furentia? Numquid Mithridatis celebratam antidotum, qua caput tuum exanclatum[76] et inane sanaretur, amisisti? Didicimus sub Zenone aut Antisthene neminem Epicurum seu Peripateticum euasisse; sub Aristotele et Theophrasto Stoicus inuentus est nullus. Quales enim praeceptores sunt, pares discipulos, pares uel doctrinas et artes nasci quidem oportere atque in commune prodire necesse est.

---

[71]trito] tuto *N*
[72]genium *N* : ingenium *A*
[73]locus admirationi] ᵇadmirationi ᵃlocus *corr. A* : admirationi locus *N*
[74]innutritus] immitatus *N*
[75]foedissimos] -simo *N*
[76]exanclatum] exaudatum *N*

---

[99]Panormita *Etsi facile* §5 (Appendix I below).

[100]In ancient Rome, important politicians were escorted to the forum by their hangers-on in what was known as the morning "greeting" or *salutatio*. (I thank Charles Fantazzi for this information.) On Rho's use of *exoletus* (sodomite), see Philippic §22 n. 55.

[101]Rho (*Imitations* 132v: *Lupanar*, and 141v–142r: *Meretrix*; Appendix IX below) closely associates *ganeum* (house of gluttony) and *lupanar* (brothel). Medieval and Renaissance moralists routinely

39 People believe, in fact — and by now it is thoroughly noised about — that this has been his genius and talent from childhood, so that even if he tries to speak beautifully, he now has absolutely no idea how to go about it because of the scar that has grown over. Why do we marvel at this? For the common rumor going around, which I just mentioned, is that as a little boy he imbibed these utterly dissolute morals with the milk of his nurse's breasts. When, therefore, he concocts neologisms and daily contrives new and unheard-of shenanigans, what room, I ask, is there for surprise, especially since he has made a study and career of such arts and sciences as if he were trained in some school? But if I may, let me address him directly for a moment.

40 "Hey, you there! Tell me something if you would. Who are these fellow priests of mine who so brazenly and falsely accuse me of having wounded your supreme majesty?[99] Are my comrades hideous and sacrilegious men? For shame! Or come morning, do swarms of sodomites greet me at the door?[100] Can it be said that some lowly parasite or glutton licks his fingers or leaves his token with me among the saucers and pheasants?[101] Look, if you would, Panormita, those gnats, or rather barflies,[102] whom after a dubious dinner[103] you either dreamed or imagined to be my fellow priests, are instead your own cronies. Well now, what Propertius or Tibullus, or even 'Martial the Cook'[104] would vomit up poetry so ugly and filthy unless he'd labored long nights under your tutelage and had become well practiced in those perversions or had produced them alongside you in your workshop of obscenities? Why do you first blanch, then blush at this?[105] Why this rage that inflames your countenance? Why the wild eyes and furious expressions? Did you omit Mithridates' celebrated antidote, which, if you endured it, would restore even your empty head?[106] We learn that no Epicurean or Peripatetic ever emerged under the tutelage of Zeno or Antisthenes; that no Stoic was ever found under the tutelage of Aristotle and Theophrastus. For as the teachers, so the disciples; indeed even their tenets and methods rightly originated from equal effort and ought to circulate as their common product.

---

associated gluttony with sexual excess, often specifically with sodomy (see Rocke 21–22, 107; *Philippic* §22 n. 52, *Apology* §31 n. 108 and §47).

[102]Rho plays on the words *mustiones* and *bibiones* (wine or vinegar gnats), and *combibones* (drinking-buddies or "barflies"). Rho (*Imitations* 25r: *Bibere*): "*Mustiones* and *bibiones* are the same thing [Isidore *Etymologies* 12.8.16]." Cf. *Apology* §47.

[103]Rho (*Imitations* 41r: *Convivium*): "A *cena dubia* is one in which so many courses are offered, that 'you are uncertain what you should take first' [Terence *Phormio* 343]."

[104]See *Philippic* §22 n. 52.

[105]Cf. Jerome *Commentary on Titus* 1.7 and *Letter* 130.5; cf. also Wiesen 224.

[106]That is, Mithridates "the Great," King of Pontus (120–63 BCE), who lived in fear of assassination and consequently stayed on a steady diet of antidotes. Martial (5.76) refers to a certain Cinna, who in dining so poorly had fortified himself against hunger just as Mithridates had made himself immune to poison by eating small bits of it regularly.

485 **41** "Fit itaque ex his plana coniectio, ut aut tute aduersum [A119r] te ipsum uersus illos edideris, aut unus quippe ipsis ex commilitonibus tuis, qui nobilitandi ingenii causa nomini tuo illuderet, eos illos excuderit. Neque admirationi fuerit aut insaniae tuae dabitur, te aduersum te id scribendi genus obisse: nulla enim de te,
490 nouo poeta, erat opinio, nulla existimatio, nullus rumor; non aderant quae te splendidum praestarent ullae uirtutes. Quod igitur bonis doctrinis et artibus ac uitae integritate praestare nequiuisti, optimorum uirorum incusatione — si illis connumerari debes! — tibi famam et gloriam nouo aucupio comparare studuisti. Pro
495 nequam! Et gentium minime. Si tute[77] tibi ipsi manum iniecisti, quid alios iniuriarum arcessis? Quid tua in culpa alienum scutum quo tutus euadas assumis?

42 "Exemplo non omnino dissimili uideris usus illius qui, cum uulgo esset ignotus nihilque boni posset facinoris excogitare
500 quo nobilis fieret, Dianae templum incendit; et nullo prodente sacrilegium ipsum, in medium processit clamitans sese incendium subiecisse. Sciscitantibus Ephesi principibus quam ob causam hoc fecisset, respondit ut 'Quod bene non poteram, male omnibus innotescerem.'"

505 **43** Ita enim pila luditur, mi Candide: ita in alterutrum sarcinulae reiiciuntur. Vidi ego nonnullos saepenumero tam scelestae tam percorruptae naturae [N102r] uiros, qui lutum sordesque ceteras e domo sua eliminarent eiicerentque, atque in limen pro foribus uicini quam proximi clam illo tamen ac nihil
510 aduertente accumularent, quo mundiores illi ipsi nitidioresque praeter ceteros praedicarentur. Quod sane quidem officii, immo flagitii genus perinhonestum est, a bonis sanctisque moribus prorsum abhorrens. Quid enim scelestius perditiusque fieri potest quam uirum quemlibet, bonum aut malum, clanculum occidere,
515 statimque post facinus, alterum nemini nocentem ac cuiusuis criminis omnino nescium et ignarum insimulare?

44 Verum quo hi ferantur probe intellego. Rentur enim huiuscemodi obtrectatores quin — uerius dixerim incentores et *phagoloidoroi*, ut aiunt, *id est comedentes senecias* — sese crimen
520 euasuros et ab sceleribus absolutum iri, si Catonem quempiam [A119v] aut unum ex primoribus utpote socios complicesque secum dolo malo inuexerint. Pro sanctorum atque[78] hominum fidem! Persuadent hi namque sibi: "peccantium multi-

---

[77]tute] tu *N*
[78]atque] *s.l. suppl. A*

[107]On Herostratus and his burning of the Temple of Diana, see Valerius Maximus 8.14 ext. 5 and Aulus Gellius 2.6.18.

41 "This, then, obviously leads us to suppose either that you, Panormita, published this poetry against yourself or that in fact one of your own cronies hammered it out, one who mocked your name in order to tout your 'genius.' It will either occasion no surprise or will be chalked up to your insanity that you took to writing against yourself in this genre. For no expectation, no esteem, no reputation existed about you, a poet-come-lately; you possessed no virtues that could make you resplendent. Therefore, because you couldn't excel with good arts and sciences and in wholesomeness of life, you strove through the novel snare of denouncing distinguished men to obtain fame and glory for yourself — as if you ought to be numbered among them! What rubbish! Not on your life. If you've laid a hand on your own person, why do you indict other people for the injury? If you're at fault, why do you take someone else's shield to get off unscathed?

42 "You look a lot like the fellow who, since he was a nobody and incapable of a good deed that would bring him renown, burned the Temple of Diana. With no one to betray his sacrilege, he ran into the crowd shouting that he'd flung the torch. When the rulers of Ephesus asked why he'd done it, he responded: 'Since I was incapable of good, I might become famous through evil.'"[107]

43 Well, my Candido, that is how the game is played: do not get left holding the bag. I have often seen men of such a wicked and debauched nature that they cleaned and rid their own house of garbage and other filth, secretly dumping it in the doorway of the nearest inattentive neighbor in order to be declared cleaner and neater than others. This kind of conduct,[108] or rather misconduct, is scandalous and directly at odds with good and holy customs. What, in fact, can one do that is more wicked and wretched than to ruin secretly any man you will, good or evil, and immediately after the deed, blame another who is harmless, unsuspecting, and ignorant of any crime?

44 But I understand perfectly well where these people are headed. For such detractors — I would say more accurately, instigators and so-called "*phagoloidoroi*,[109] that is, those who gobble up slander"[110] — suppose that they are going to escape indictment and be absolved from their atrocities if they have fraudulently implicated

---

[108]Rho (*Imitations* 114v: *Officium*): "*Officium* is the behavior proper to any person as defined by the status and customs of his city. Hence we speak generally of *officium* as what man owes to man and creation to the Creator, but we speak specifically of what children owe their parents, a free man owes his patron, and a friend owes a friend." ("*Officium*" *est congruus actus alicuius personae secundum status et mores suae civitatis. Unde generaliter "officium" dicitur quod homo homini debet et creatura creatori, sed specialiter dicitur quod filii debent parentibus, libertas patrono, amicus amico*).

[109]Rho (*Imitations* 54v: *Detrahere*): "*Phagoloidori* are devourers (*comedentes*) or embodiers (*incorporantes*) of curses (*maledicta*); these are for us devourers of *senecias*. . . . *Senecia*, as some think, is a filthy (*immundum*) animal. Other people think that it is the hair (*pilatura*) from an old man's lips or his drool, which are all foul (*immunda*), or the gills (*chules*; ms. = *ibules*) of fish, which rot immediately. . . ." Cf. Iohannes de Ianua's *Catholicon* (almost certainly Rho's authority for this information about *senecia*) which gives a circumlocution for "gills": "the red area that is beneath the ear of a fish whereby one discerns whether it is fresh or not" (*Illud rubrum quod est sub aure piscis per quod discernitur an sit recens an non*). Cf. also Pliny the Elder *Natural Histories* 9.69.

[110]Jerome *Commentary on Ezekiel* prol.

tudine culpam seu maculam minui peccatorum." Verum enimuero falluntur totaque aberrant uia, cum ueritas inter plagas
nitere uulnerandamque[79] pro tempore labefactari et opprimi possit; necari uero numquam.

45 Sed telam inceptam percurramus.

46 Miratur admodum[80] uir iste sagax et industrius, ut ait, uersiculos hos turpes in se editos esse, qui paulo ante de laudibus
suis haud nullos ex me acceperit pulcherrimos honestissimosque.
Deliratne an[81] insanit uir iste? Neque apud se est, qui uersus honestis-
simos suis de laudibus aut ex me aut quouis alio graui uiro sibi conscriptos esse subblanditur? Inflaturne ita homo — ut est insolentissimi
spiritus — supinus et ceruicosus,[82] ut se diuum quempiam aut saltem
uirum clarum et illustrem caelo datum arbitretur, ad quem
exornandum efferendumque huiuscemodi insignia[83] aut oratorum aut
poetarum uerba debeantur?

47 Quid inquam? Potuit nimirum uersus conspicuos
illos meos uidisse, uerum quid sibi uellent hominem brutum
delinitumque haud intellexisse. Tu uero coniecturas, mi Candide,
inspicito; tempora et aetates quibus primum ipsi editi sunt suppu-
tato. Iam annus plane circumuoluitur undeuicesimus quo uersus
eos, quibus Panormita hic noster falso gloriatur, ad Antonium
Luscum, uirum eloquentissimum, me scripsisse commemini.
Adulescentiae tunc[84] fines necdum transmiseram; non sacerdos id
temporis initiatus eram; nondum philosophias aut sacras litteras
percallueram; dialecticen dumtaxat puerilesque Isagogas ex
praeceptore meo eodemque[85] philosopho celebratissimo, Iacobo
Forliuiensi, ea ipsa aetate tenera accipiebam. Ipsum itaque
Antonium Luscum, ex millibus unum, illis in uersibus poeticene
prius an philosophiae operam nauarem consulebam. Respondit
operae pretium esse maius philosophias primum; reliquas quoque
doctrinas occultioris et artes assequi studerem; mox uero, quando

---

[79]uulnerandam- *scripsi* : -dum- *AN*
[80]exinde *post* admodum *N*
[81]an] aut *N*
[82]ceruico-] ceruco- *N*
[83]insignia] -ni- *s.l. suppl. A*
[84]tunc *s.l. suppl. A*
[85]-que *s.l. suppl. N*

---

[111]Marcus Porcius Cato (234–149 BCE) was known as "Censorius" for his stern traditional morality. Rho probably has in mind a passage from Panormita's letter (1.XII.1426) to Archbishop Bartolomeo Capra (Beccadelli 1746, 108 [2.23]): "I am therefore sending my *Hermaphrodite* to you, indeed a lewd little book, but the greatest orators, the most holy poets, the gravest philosophers, the most restrained men, and finally Christians have all flirted with this lewdness. And certainly 'it is

as their accessory and accomplice a Cato or some dignitary.[111] Oh faith of saints and men! They really convince themselves by thinking, "I've diminished the fault and stain of my sins by hiding in a crowd of sinners." But without a doubt they fool themselves and get it completely wrong, for truth can shine even in adversity, and even when wounded it can only for a time be shaken and oppressed. But killed? Never.

45 But let us pick up where we left off.

46 This laborious sage is rather surprised, he says, that this filthy little poem got published against him, since a short time earlier he received from me some really beautiful and honorable lines praising him.[112] Is the man delirious or insane? He has lost his grip on reality, flattering himself that either I or any other serious person wrote highly respectful poetry praising him. Is this haughty and stubborn man so inflated — what an arrogant disposition! — that he thinks of himself as someone divine or at least as a man sent from heaven, both brilliant and illustrious, to whom orators or poets owe such notable expressions of praise and adulation?

47 What am I talking about? He doubtlessly could have seen my well-known poetry, but the misguided simpleton never understood what it meant. So, my Candido, examine his assumptions. Calculate when and at what age I first composed this poetry. As I recall, I wrote these lines that our Panormita wrongly gloats over nineteen years ago to Antonio Loschi, a most eloquent man.[113] I had yet to pass from the age of adolescence; I had yet to be consecrated a priest; and I had yet to become versed in philosophy and sacred literature. At that tender age, I had only learned dialectic and the *Isagoge*[114] for boys from my teacher, the celebrated philosopher, Giacomo da Forlì.[115] And so I consulted by means of this poetry the incomparable Antonio Loschi on whether I should devote effort first to poetry or to philosophy. He responded that philosophy was more worthwhile initially and that I should also strive to acquire the remaining arts and the more recondite sciences, but that I should

---

fitting that the poet himself be chaste and pious; his little poems require nothing of the kind' [Catullus 16.5–6], which you know full well given your erudition." (*Mitto igitur tibi meum Hermaphroditum, libellum quidem lascivum, sed ea lascivia, qua summi oratores, sanctissimi poetae, gravissimi philosophi, viri continentes, et Christiani denique praelusere. Et sane "castum esse decet pium poetam / ipsum versiculos nihil necesse est," quod tu pro tua eruditione plenissime nosti*).

[112]Rho refers to the lines "Now, my Antonio, honor and light of the Latin language, pray help me . . ." (*Antoni mi, nunc decus et lux una Latini / eloquii succurre precor* . . .) cited by Panormita *Etsi facile* §1 (Appendix I below).

[113]Antonio Loschi (ca. 1365–1441), whom Rho here implies was his teacher (cf. *Philippic* §63 n. 151 and *Apology* §38), became Chancellor for the Visconti Dukes of Milan in 1387 and Apostolic Secretary in 1404 (see Witt 2000, 388–90 and 463–66). Nineteen years prior to the writing this *Philippic* would have been 1413, when at eighteen years old Rho went into the Franciscan Order. This places Rho's birth in 1395 (cf. *Apology* §6).

[114]Rho refers almost certainly to the *Summulae logicales* of Peter of Spain (ca. 1205–77), which became the standard introductory text for teaching logic (De Rijk 1970 and 1972; and Van Steenberghen 138–40).

[115]Giacomo della Torre da Forlì (d. 1414) was a teacher in Padua about whom we know little. Rho would have studied under him around 1412, that is, when Rho was about seventeen years old, and perhaps the year before Rho entered the Franciscan Order (see Sabbadini and Barozzi 11, where Rho's age is conjectured incorrectly; see also Monfardini 7–8; and Lombardi 8–10; and *Apology* §6).

555 gratum esset, poeticen ipsam attingerem. Placuit uti foro atque consilio, ubi cum plane philosophias ipsas sacrasque litteras [A120r] non sine negotio essem assecutus. Visa est mihi deinceps iam natu grandi poesis ipsa prae suauitate et gloria ceterarum artium quam excolerem inanis quidem et uacua.

560 **48** Sed ecce baburrum! Opinione enimuero hac una illuditur homo dementissimus: uidelicet quod illum nunc nuper, qui aetate iam edita sum, consuluerim discipulus ne[86] philosophiae fierem. Neque percipit aut supputat exactis iam[87] superioribus annis, cum nondum Siciliam insulam aut Panormum exisset suum, me iam 565 huiuscemodi doctrinas et artes publicitus praecepisse atque uersus illos quibus gloriatur excudisse.

49 Vis errorem hunc suum dissoluamus explicemusque? Gloriatur siquidem uecors iste et insulsus homo quoniam uocitatur Antonius, eosce uersus ad sese impraesentiarum, quasi solus ipse, 570 uti phoenix, et nemo alter toto orbe uiuat Antonius, dimissos esse. Sed emungat purgetque nasum suum: praestiterit, ut qui aures indociles habet, naribus saltem expiatis[88] intellegat.[89] Nomina enim et Lusci et Panormitae uno Antonii nomine proprio perstringuntur, idque ipsum nomen eisdem alphabetis et characteribus exaratur.

575 Inde fortasse se Luscum Antonium esse persuasum habet, atque in illum — Pythagoreus enim est — transmi[N102v]grasse gloriatur: immo neque Pythagoreus est, ut recte intellego, neque animorum ubi sint[90] sedes nouit. Qui non igitur demiretur unde sibi haec tanta orta est[91] socordia? Nonne animaduertit[92] sese diuerso caelo 580 diuersa Olympiade longe ab illo natum esse? Musis quoque non illustribus, ut ille est, ceterum agrestibus innutritum?[93]

50 Quod si fortasse inter eos[94] haud nullam similitudinem est inuenire aut communem ideam accipere, nullam aliam profecto eam esse censuerim[95] praeterquam quod ille e Luscorum non

---

[86]discipulus ne *tr. N*
[87]iam *om. N*
[88]expiatis] *mg. suppl. A*
[89]intellegat] intellegat uti piscis *N*
[90]sint] sunt *A*
[91]est *om. N*
[92]animaduertit *scripsi* : animo uertit *AN*
[93]innutritum] innututum *N*
[94]inter eos *tr. A*
[95]censuerim] scen- *N*

[116]Rho would have been thirty-seven years old.
[117]That is, "with an official appointment."
[118]Panormita left Sicily in 1419. Rho probably wrote the poetry in question shortly before 1413 when he entered the Franciscan Order. No certain date can be fixed for when Rho began teaching "such arts and sciences publicly." Assuming he knew when Panormita left Sicily, Rho must mean that

afterwards pursue poetry when it was convenient. This was perfectly acceptable to me since it served my self-interests and plans, inasmuch as I had already pursued philosophy and sacred literature earnestly. Afterwards, however, when I had grown older, poetry itself seemed to me truly inane and vacuous compared to the sweetness and glory of the other arts that I have cultivated.

48 But look at the idiot! Indeed this utterly demented man suffers from the delusion that I, who am now a mature adult,[116] would have just of late consulted him about whether I should become a disciple of philosophy! Nor did he take note of or count the years gone by — when he had not yet left the island of Sicily or his hometown of Palermo — that I had already taught such arts and sciences publicly[117] and had already composed the poetry about which he gloats.[118]

49 Would you like us to analyze and explain his error? Since he is called Antonio, the silly, insipid man gloats that these lines were just now sent to him as if (like a Phoenix)[119] he were the only Antonio in the whole world. But let him blow and pick his nose: he will show that he at least learns with purged nostrils, like those who have nonfunctional ears.[120] Yes, the common personal name "Antonio" yokes together the last names "Loschi" and "Panormita," and both of them use the same spelling to write it. Perhaps from this Panormita has persuaded himself that he is Antonio Loschi and congratulates himself that he — a Pythagorean — has transmigrated into Loschi. But in fact he is no Pythagorean, as I know perfectly well, nor does he recognize where souls reside.[121] Who then would not wonder where he got this enormously stupid idea? Did he not notice that he was born far away from Loschi under a different sky and in a different Olympiad?[122] Did he fail to see that he was not nurtured like Loschi among the respectable epic Muses but rather amid the coarse rustic ones?

50 But if it is possible to find some semblance between them or to acknowledge a commonality, I would judge that it extends to absolutely nothing else except that the former arose from the noble family of the *Lusci* (Loschi),

---

he assumed some instructional role after taking his bachelors degree in December of 1418. He must otherwise be referring less precisely to when he became "professor of the sacred page" at San Francesco Grande in 1423, that is, seven or eight years before the present controversy erupted (see Rutherford 1990, 83).

[119] The phoenix was a fabulous, solitary bird said to live for five centuries before setting itself on fire and rising anew from its ashes (cf. Lactantius *On the Phoenix*).

[120] An additional phrase "like fish"(*uti piscis*) appears in manuscript N. Rho must have written the phrase and either (1) indicated that it should be dropped but the scribe of N missed the deletion marks or (2) indicated that it should be inserted but the scribe of A missed the insertion mark. The scribe of A consistently worked more carefully than the scribe of N, so A has been followed here. The phrase, nonetheless, gives some clarification about the idea expressed.

[121] Cf. Iamblichus *On Pythagoras* 14.63; and Porphyry *On Pythagoras* 26, 27, 45.

[122] "A different sky" (*diverso caelo*) imitates Macrobius (*Saturnalia* praef. 11), who writes *nos sub alio natos caelo*, meaning in a different land. "A different Olympiad" (*diversa Olypiade*), meaning "at a different time," trades on the Greek method of giving dates according to an Olympiad, that is, the four-year span between the start of the Olympic Games.

585 ignobili familia exortus, hic uero re ipsa quidem est luscus. Aut si fortasse, quod liquet, repuerescit rhetorumque coniecturas oblitus est, dignus iam fit, qui obolum accipiat, ad emendas nuces et migret. Audiat tamen prius epilogum oportet. Quemadmodum enim hisce uersibus meis honestissimis sese falso effert et exuscitat,
590 ita illis turpissimis, quibus mihi si perinde est ut[96] loquitur, succenset. Iactat se quidem et falsus est. Puto tamen propediem fore ut multam, [A120v] immo et uersuram, ipse dissoluat atque in illius frontem huiuscemodi faba cudatur,[97] didiceritque denique antiquius esse uirtutem uirtute suscitare quam turpi cote alienae
595 tonstrinae nouaculas exacuere.

51 Scriberem de his plura, uerum qui me admonet alius locus commodum adeundus est. Tene, rogo, quae dixerim; tantisper uersipellem hunc uirum conuenturus sum.

52 "Queso itaque, heus tu homo prudens, quo tela quae mihi
600 obiicis in te uertam et *clauum clauo* eiiciam? Quid sibi uolebant uersus illi,[98] quos tu ad patres conscriptos[99] sine tabellario aut nuntio, sine arbitris, sine anulo, et ne cognoscerere, qui tamen auctor extitisti sine ullo nomine, aut tuo aut alieno, aduersum me dimisisti, inelegantes illos quidem inconnexos, percorruptos, tuopte[100]
605 uel more dicendi spurcissimos? Num tu, qui et nomine et re infamis es, nomen meum tollere moliebare meque sempiternis tenebris et umbris numquam in lucem olim proditurum inuoluere? Canas receptui oportet. Altiore enim Musa, acriore ingenio, exactiore doctrina et arte, immo et grauiore imprimis uiro opus
610 erat, quando ita facile e coetu conuentuque hominum iri me oblitteratum arbitrabare. At quid illos palam ad me non dabas? Quid enim, si Achilles ille ineluctabilis[101] es omnisque deturbas et (uti iactas), nulli cedis, me rusticanum militem quem inuaderes extimescebas? Quo abiit sella nitens? Vbi nobile frenum? Vbi illa
615 uerborum tam insolens ostentatio? Plane uirum alterum interiorem alterum exteriorem te declaras.

53 "Quid istuc? Chlamydem quidem et crepidulas uideo; non poetam, non philosophum uideo. Non enim illa[102] tui animi magnitudine aut tristitia aut seueritate, quam oculis, oratione, gestu coram
620 polliceris, in rostra descendisti, qui tam impudenter uersus illos locis

---

[96]ut *scripsi* : ac *AN*
[97]faba cudatur] cucadtur faba, -d- *in ras. N*
[98]illi *om. N*
[99]*prae* con-, c. *N*
[100]tuopte] tuope *N*
[101]ineluc-] me luc- *N*
[102]illa *N* : tua illa *A*

while the latter is in fact *luscus* (half-blind).[123] Or if he proves to be entering his second childhood (which looks obvious) and has forgotten that rhetoricians elaborate inferences from the facts, it now becomes a guy like him to take a small coin, buy his nuts and move on. It would do him good, however, to hear beforehand the epilogue. For just as he mistakenly flatters and inspires himself with this honorable poem of mine, so he becomes enraged at that foul one, if it is in fact mine as he says. He boasts and is deceived. Nevertheless, I think that he will soon pay a fine, or rather even a debt, and this will recoil against him.[124] He will have finally learned that it is better to arouse virtue with virtue than to sharpen his razors with another barbershop's filthy stone.

51 I could write more about this, Candido, but another issue comes to mind that must now be addressed. Please keep my remarks in mind. Meanwhile, I am going to talk directly to this shifty fellow.[125]

52 "Hey, Panormita! I ask you, wiseguy, where should I fling back the shafts that you hurl at me and drive out 'one nail with another'?[126] What was the meaning of that poetry against me? How should I take those inelegant, disjointed, debauched, and utterly filthy lines typical of the way you speak, which you sent to the Senators without a courier, messenger, witness, or seal so you wouldn't be recognized? (You nonetheless are obviously their author, whether they carry no name, your name, or someone else's name.) Were you, who are infamous in name and deed, attempting to obliterate my name and to envelop me in shadows and eternal darkness never again to see the light? You're best advised to sound a retreat. For when you decided that I would be easily obliterated from the company and assembly of men, it required a higher Muse, a sharper genius, a clearer art and science, or rather a much more respected man than you. But why didn't you openly present this poetry to me? For if you're some invincible Achilles and bring down everyone and yield to none (as you boast), why did you stand in fear of me, a rustic soldier facing your onslaught? Where's the glittery saddle gone? Where's the noble steed? What's become of all that insolent blustering? Clearly you show yourself to be one man internally and another externally.

53 "What's this? I see a Greek cloak and sandals; but not a poet, not a philosopher.[127] For you haven't ascended the rostrum with your greatness of soul, seriousness, or severity, which you announced openly with your eyes,

---

[123]The Latin form of the name "Loschi" (*Lusci, -orum*) means "one-eyed" or "half-blind." The Italian word *losco, -chi*, has the sense of the Latin word *strabo, -onis*, i.e., having a squint.

[124]Cf. Erasmus *Adagia* I.i.84 for speculation about the origins of the expression *in me faba cudetur*.

[125]Plautus *Bacchides* 651–60: "Not a soul can be worth anything, unless he knows how to be good and bad both. He must be a rascal among rascals, rob robbers, steal what he can. A chap that's worth anything, a chap with a fine intellect, has to be able to change his skin (*vorsipellis*). He must be good with the good, bad with the bad; whatever the situation calls for, that he's got to be" (LCL).

[126] Cicero *Tusculan Disputations* 4.35.74.

[127]Rho appropriated an expression of contempt that originated in the Roman sense of disdain for the Greek *chlamys* and *crepidulae*. Romans usually regarded their fellow countrymen who wore these Greek items as at best putting on airs and at worst as being effeminate (see Richlin 1983, 92–93; cf. *Philippic* §9).

publicis, pro foribus Senatus templorumque, compitis ac plateis noctu[103] — ut es *trium litterarum homo* — uilissimorum latronum more suspendi iussisti.

54 "Quo abis,[104] inuicte? Quid faciem claudis? Quid, luride uir, cadauerose, iam tandem erubescis, qui numquam erubescere consuesti? Nihil est ut infitias[105] eas; nihil ut purges? Visus enim est palam idemque agnitus in[A121r]tempesta nocte plenilunio e specula e loco edito, ille ille (nostin?) qui schedulas eas apponebat, unus quidem ex catamitis tuis tui facinoris quam doctissimus occultissimusque. Quin immo et confabulantes haud nulli commilitones tui ipso sermone temere quidem, ut saepe uerba effluunt, deprehensi atque conuicti sunt. Vis pro re hac omne flagitium tuum clare, luculente, ac quasi sub diuo aperuerim? Ille ille (nostin?) qui ceteris locis uersiculos illos tuos infames suspenderat, cum Maecenatem ex tuis unum ea nocte repeteret domumque eius requieturus — sic illum commonefeceras — reuertisset, foribus uel eiusce Maecenatis tui illos implicuit.

55 "Quid id? Callide quidem astute, ut si Forte Fortuna ad opinionem huiusce criminis alius quispiam collaberetur — poena enim capitis plectitur — ipse ille tuus praestigiator nullo pacto artifex aut auctor doli mali esse[106] crederetur. Tu tamen euasisti non indignus, qui capite plectereris. [N103r] Atqui tecum bene actum est quidem, ne hoc sordido supplicii, immo perhonesto genere mortem oppeteres, quippe qui alio loco, ut uulgo aiunt, futurus es, ubi quid sibi uelit Lex Iulia, immo quidem Scantinia, nisi dii tui bene uortant, periculum facies."

56 Animaduertisne, optime Candide, quatenus[107] uir iste et mihi et sibi ipsi succenset stomachaturque? Putasne in Stoicum uirum, quem se esse mentitur, bilem surrepere aut incendi choleram ita ullo pacto posse? Plane professionis huiuscemodi oblitus est nec

---

[103]noctu] nocte noctu *N*
[104]abis] abiis *N*
[105]infitias *scripsi* : -cias *AN*
[106]esse *om. A*
[107]quatenus] quatenus *ut uid.*, idest 'quo' *s.l. suppl. N*

---

[128]This is a joke (from Plautus' *The Pot of Gold* 325–26) that works only in Latin. As Rho (*Imitations* 95v) explains it: "Plautus said of a servant: 'He is a man of three letters,' i.e., a *fur* (thief). . . ."

[129]That is, Panormita's reputed young male lover, Tomaso Tebaldi of Bologna, usually called "Ergoteles," but Rho calls him "Adonis" (see *Philippic* §90–§104).

[130]The "Maecenas" meant here is Francesco Barbavara (exiled, December 1432), who was still at this time chancellor and a member of Filippo Maria Visconti's Secret Council. Among Panormita's patrons or "Maecenases" (cf. *Philippic* §33 n. 77) were Zanino Ricci (d. early 1428), whose brother was the Abbot of Sant' Ambrogio; Cambio Zambeccari, an official at the Visconti court (d. June 1431); Bartolomeo Capra, Archbishop of Milan and Govenor of Genoa (d. 1433); and Luigi Crotto, an official at the Visconti court (d. after 1447). Cf. *Philippic* §80, §121, §131, §143, §170, §175, and §178; for Panormita's relationship with these men, see Sabbadini 1910a and 1916.

speech, and gesture. No, like the vilest of thieves and 'being a man of three letters,'[128] you've shamelessly ordered that poem to be posted by night in public places, on the doors of the senate and churches, and at the crossroads and in the piazzas.

54 "Where are you going, invincible one? Why do you hide your face? Why do you, a sallow, cadaverous man blush now, one who never used to blush? Is there nothing you can deny; nothing you can disprove? What about the man who in the dead of night with a full moon was publicly seen and even recognized from an elevated watchtower? The one who posted these placards? Did you know him? He was one of those catamites[129] of yours who's most practiced in and secretive about your crime. And sure enough, even some of your comrades-in-arms, while conversing with each other, exposed and convicted themselves by their reckless talk as secrets often leaked out. Would you like me to disclose clearly, in detail, and as if in broad daylight your entire disgraceful act? That catamite (did you know him?), who posted your infamous poem in other places, when that night, per your instructions, he was headed for the house of one of your Maecenases in order to rest there, even fastened them to your Maecenas' doors.[130]

55 "Why did he do this? It was shrewdly cunning, as if someone else collaborated with Lady Luck in thinking up this crime — for it's punishable by death — that your trickster in no way be thought the perpetrator or author of this malicious deed.[131] You, however, managed to escape although you were not unworthy of capital punishment. But things went well for you so that you didn't meet death by this sordid, or rather, by this honorable form of punishment, since you're destined for another place, as they say, where you'll experience the penalties of the Julian or even the Scantinian Law unless your gods make things turn out better."[132]

56 Do you notice, my good Candido, how angry and irritated that man gets both with me and with himself? Do you think that bile can somehow imperceptibly seize or cholera so inflame a Stoic man such as Panormita pretends to be? Clearly, this shifty fellow has forgotten about his claim to Stoicism or doesn't know where to plant his feet. For he expelled from his company every Zeno,

---

[131]Rho is referring to Cicero's statement (*The Republic* 4.10.12) that the Twelve Tables, the earliest Roman Law code (451–450 BCE), made it a capital crime to defame anyone with poetry (*Nostrae . . . contra duodecim tabulae cum perpaucas res capite sanxissent, in his hanc quoque sanciendam putaverunt, si quis occentavisset sive carmen condidisset, quod infamiam faceret flagitiumve alteri* [fragment preserved in Augustine *City of God* 2.9]). However this law might have been applied at the time the Twelve Tables were written, Roman courts clearly did not enforce it in later times (see *Philippic* §61 n. 143; cf. also §138 and §140).

[132]Rho refers to the section of the Julian Law against adultery and to the Scantinian Law against sexual taboos (*nefandam Venerem*), here specifically against pederasty (see Hergemöller 26–27). Rho is also alluding to a passage of Juvenal (2.36–50) in which one Laronia denounced men who displayed statues of moral philosophers and harangued other people about morals, yet were themselves routine violators of the Julian and Scantinian Laws (cf. *Philippic* §137).

650 quo pedes sistat uir lubricus agnouit. Zenonem enim, Cleanthem, Chrysippumque et simile philosophorum agmen, quorum necessitudine aliquando subgloriari uidebatur, e[108] contubernio suo omnis eiecit. Alium quidem hominem[109] indutus est quando optimos quosque carpere, mordere, labefactare; a nemine rem ipsam[110]
655 seriam omnino audire[111] uelit.

57 Tritum enim elogium[112] est quod uiso fure canes illatrant. Quid ergo? Solusne iste uociferabitur et linguam exacuet; nos muti et infantes praeterierimus? Dicam iam sibi illud Philoctetis: *turpe est mihi tacere cum barbaris.* Quid istuc? Reticentiis enim illustrium uirorum ii semper abutuntur. Aut si tacendum est, audiat oportet quod ad
660 Philip[A121v]pum Crassus: *Si Crassum uis coercere; haec tibi lingua excidenda est.*

58 Aeque nunc tu, si lubet, quantum ad nos attinet, *par pari referto,* uel si excisionem timet, deponat ipse gladium; ego scutum
665 abiiciam.

59 Atqui inter stomachandum admodum, aegre permolesteque ferre uidetur, ut est homo eneruis et mollis,[113] non tam mulierosus quam flagitiosus, quod uel in libellum illum suum, quem monstruoso nomine Hermaphroditum appellat, inuectum est.

670 **60** Quid ni? Aegre eo loci nimirum honori suo, dignitati, existimationi, et gloriae detractum uir iste delirus arbitratur, quasi libello illo sublato fama intereat tanti uiri. Ridiculum profecto excordemque hominem! Cuius adhuc praeter sordidam nulla opinio, nullus rumor inualuit. At si aliquando resipiscat
675 bonamque in mentem futurus sit, neque animi uitio ad aetatem usque confectam et fractam laboret, fateatur plane[114] necesse erit. Nos quoque ceterique, qui[115] rem suam pulchre nouimus, declarabimus in huiuscemodi Hermaphroditum uersus illos, immo in ipsum Panormitam peropportune quidem decantatos esse; illi,
680 illi *patellae dignum* definitumque *operculum* ad amussim et unguem, ut aiunt, dicemus accessisse; talibusque labiis, ut ita dixerim, tales lactucas recte appositas esse indicabimus. Praestabat tamen ut ille ipse libellus cum auctore,[116] aut si minus, saltem cum libello auctor in insulas terrasque ultimas perdi-
685 tissimorum hominum more deportaretur, quin ad extremos inferos sempiterno aeuo sepeliretur, quam penes nos senescens

---

[108]e] et *N*
[109]quidem hominem *tr. N*
[110]ipsam *scripsi* : ipse *A* : ipsam *corr.* ipse *N*
[111]omnino audire *tr. N*
[112]elogium] -gum *N*
[113]mollis] molis *A*
[114]plane] alias 'sane' *s.l. suppl. A* : sane *N*
[115]qui] quis *A*
[116]libellus *post* auctore *N*

Cleanthes, Chrysippus, and like band of philosophers, in whose friendship he once seemed to take some pride. Indeed, he turned into a different man when he chose to denigrate, criticize, and destroy every person of note and completely refused to listen to anyone about this serious matter.

57 Well, it is a trite maxim that dogs bark when they see a thief. What? Will he alone shout and sharpen his tongue, while we walk by mute and speechless? Let me quote here what Philoctetes said in his own behalf: "It is a disgrace for me to keep silent in the face of barbarians."[133] What does this mean? That barbarians always abuse the reticence of illustrious men. Or if silence is required of us, let Panormita hear what Crassus said to Philip: "If you want to restrain Crassus, you must cut out his tongue."[134]

58 It is time for you, Candido, if you want, to give Panormita "tit for tat,"[135] inasmuch as this affair affects you and me both, or if he fears having his tongue cut out, let him put down his sword, and I shall lay aside my shield.

59 Yet while working himself into a complete tantrum, he has the appearance of someone being put upon and harassed. This comes from his being a soft and weak man who is not so much a womanizer as a pervert. That was even the charge brought against that wretched little book of his, which he calls by the monstrous name *The Hermaphrodite*.[136]

60 Why not say he is a pervert? On this subject, the deranged man actually thinks that he will suffer a loss of honor, dignity, esteem, and glory, as if the fame of such a great man would perish were that wretched little book to disappear. What an absolutely ridiculous and senseless man! Up till now he has earned no esteem or reputation except a sordid one. But if he is ever to come to his senses and to regain his sanity, and not slip because of mental impairment into complete dotage, he obviously must confess this. We and others who know well his ways shall pronounce the following jingle against a hermaphrodite like him, indeed a jingle which is most appositely recited against Panormita. As the line goes: "We say that the lid matched and fit the dish to a tee."[137] Or as I would put it, such lettuce goes perfectly with such lips. Nevertheless, one would prefer that the wretched little book along with its author, or failing that, that in any case the author along with the wretched little

---

[133]Cicero *On the Orator* 3.35.141.

[134]Cicero *On the Orator* 3.1.4.

[135]Terence *The Eunuch* 445; cf. Cicero *Letters to Friends* 20.19 (1.9.19).

[136]Panormita (*Hermaphrodite* 1.42.3–4) wrote to Cosimo de' Medici: "I have composed the booklet in two parts, Cosimo, because the Hermaphrodite has the same number of parts. This was the first part, the second then follows: the first was the cock, the next will be the cunt" (*In binas partes diduxi, Cosme, libellum: / nam totidem partis Hermpahroditus habet. / Haec pars prima fuit, sequitur quae deinde secunda est: / haec pro pene fuit, proxima cunnus erit*). Hermaphrodite was the offspring of Hermes (messenger of the gods) and Aphrodite (goddess of love). In the mythographers, Hermaphrodite came to represent "inappropriate lascivious speech." Boccaccio (*Genealogies of the Gods* 3.21): "[The mythographer] Albericus claims that Hermaphrodite, who was born of Mercury [Greek: Hermes] and Venus [Greek: Aphrodite], signifies inappropriate lascivious speech, which appears too effeminate in tender expressions when it ought to be virile. (*Hermaphroditum ex Mercurio et Venere genitum vult Albericus lascivientem preter opportunitatem esse sermonem, qui, cum virilis esse debeat, nimia verborum mollicie videtur effeminatus*)." Cf. *Philippic* §74 and Panormita *Hermaphrodite* 1.3.1–4, 1.13, and 2.20; cf. also Coppini 1997.

[137]Jerome *Letter* 7.5; cf. Wiesen 68–69.

atque ob oculos adulescentium[117] certatim deuolans ab castis sanctisque moribus, illos in eam impuritatem Sicelidam, officinam suam, pelliceret, taetroque obscenitatis[118] genere imperitorum gregem pollueret labefactaretque.

61 Vbi nunc Iuuenalis, quem is ludi magister secum damnare cupit, non ille his uerbis parentes alloquitur? *Exigite* ab ipsis praeceptoribus, *ut* quisque

> *mores teneros ceu pollice ducat,*
> *ut si quis cera uultum facit; exigite, ut sit*
> *et pater ipsius*[119] *coetus,*[120] *ne turpia ludant,*
> *ne faciant uicibus.*

Verum is corruptus et elegus uolupe [A122r] quidem flagitia palpat, non exulcerat. Non etiam *libros Archilochi e ciuitate Lacedaemonii exportari iusserunt, quia eorum parum uerecundam ac pudicam lectionem arbitrabantur?* Non Plato, *cum ratione formaret qualis*[121] esse res publica deberet, *tamquam aduersarios* ciuitatis, *poetas* — credo de turpibus dixerit — *censuit urbe pellendos?* Non apud Romanos *Duodecim Tabularum lege poetae, fabularum compositores, laedere ciuium famam* sub capitis poena *prohibentur?*

62 Purgat se statim spiritus iste immundissimus, et ait *aetate tenera* imbecillique, lasciuiente uel natura prima, iocari quidem licuisse[122] et fingere turpia; datumque caelitus ut aliquando sine uitio pulchre peropportuneque insaniretur atque in quaeque flagitia decantanda passim et impune locus haberetur, quippe qui flagitia illa in praesentia iam natu grandis Panormita ipse ac moribus tristior reprehendit omnino ac damnat. Quis fidei locus? Numquid nudis his uerbis et tibi et mihi et ceteris, qui praestigias illius offuciasque[123] plane[124] cernimus, facere satis pro sceleribus suis arbitratur? [N103v] Id licere fortasse sibi plerique existimarent concedi oportere, nisi reliquam insequentem aetatem turpioribus

---

[117]adulescentium] -tum *N*
[118]obsceni-] osceni- *N*
[119]ipsius] illius *N*
[120]coetus *om. A*
[121]qualis] -les *N*
[122]licuisse] licucisse *N*
[123]offucias- *scripsi* : offi- *AN*
[124]plane] *s.l. suppl. A*

[138]Accretions to the *Lex Iulia*, in particular the *Lex Romana Visigothorum*, had by the third century stipulated that anyone seducing a boy or girl or molesting a married woman should be deported to an island (see Hergemöller 26–27).

[139]Juvenal 7.237–40.

book, should be deported as are the worst criminals to the most remote islands and distant territories.[138] Indeed, he should be buried for eternity in the lowest hell. That would be better than having him seduce youngsters into his Sicilian cesspool, which he calls his workshop; better also than having him pollute and destroy with such disgusting filth the simple-minded youths that follow him, while he grows old among us and strives to abandon chaste and holy practices in full view of the youngsters.

61 Now does not Juvenal, whom this elementary school teacher desires to damn along with himself, take up this issue with parents? "Demand," he says, from these teachers "that each of them form youthful morals, just as anyone creates a face in wax with his thumb. Demand from the teacher that he be a father to his class and not have them play disgraceful games or pull dirty tricks on each other."[139] But this debauched, elegiac poet even lustfully indulges shameful acts; he does not excoriate them. Besides, "did not the Spartans order the books of Archilochus[140] to be banned from their city because they thought reading them was too immodest and indecent"?[141] Did not Plato, "when setting out the rational principles" of a republic, "think that poets" — I believe he spoke about the filthy ones — "must be run out of town as enemies of the city"?[142] Among the Romans, "did not a law of the Twelve Tables," under pain of death, "prohibit poets, the fabricators of tales, from injuring the fame of citizens"?[143]

62 This utterly foul sprite promptly excuses himself and says that it was certainly permissible to jest and feign shameful acts in weak and "tender years,"[144] which are, as it were, innately lascivious. He continues to excuse himself by saying that through no personal fault, a divine fury[145] seized him from time to time in an attractive and most fitting way and that he found the opportunity to sing each indecency far and wide with impunity. Indeed, at present Panormita himself says that since he is now much older and of more stern morals he completely censures and condemns those indecencies.[146] On what grounds are we to trust him? Surely he does not think he is going to make amends for his enormities to me, to you,

---

[140]That is, Archilochus of Paros (late eighth to early seventh century BCE), who composed in several meters, but whose fame in part derived from his "aggressive, antagonistic, often coarse, vulgar, obscene, and vituperative" iambic verse (Henderson 17–23).

[141]Valerius Maximus 6.12.ext.1; cf. also Walter Burley *On the Lives and Customs of the Philosophers* 21.

[142]Cf. Plato *Republic* 10.607a–d; cf. also Cicero *Republic* 4.10.12, *Tusculan Disputations* 2.11.27, and Horace *Epistle* 2.1.152-155.

[143]Augustine *The City of God* 2.14; cf. also *The City of God* 2.9. For the Twelve Tables, see *Philippic* §55 n. 131; cf. also *Philippic* §138 and §140.

[144]Panormita *Etsi facile* §2 (Appendix I below).

[145]Cf. *Philippic* §14 n. 36, §96, §161, and §178.

[146]Panormita (*Etsi facile* §2; Appendix I below): "Nor does anyone hate *The Hermaphrodite* more than I. The author is disgusted and revolted by reading or circulating it. . . ." (*Neque Hermaphroditus cuipiam magis quam mihi ipsi odio est, et editionis simul et lectionis auctorem in primis taedet pigetque.* . . .) Panormita made a similar statement earlier in a letter to Giovanni Lamola (20.IX.1427; Sabbadini and Barozzi 36): "To me *The Hermaphrodite* seems to be a thing too obscene, which I would send to serious men, but its release shames and revolts the author" (*Hermaphroditus res nimis obscena mihi visa est, quam viris gravissimis mitterem, sed auctorem pudet pigetque editionis*).

sceleratioribusque rebus accumulatam esse conspicarentur. Ego uero nulli aetati, nulli professioni, nulli ordini turpitudinem uel minimam puto concessum iri.

63 Neque satis teneo quid certum aut constans mihi hoc de uiro spondere possim. *Tenera aetate*, ut ait, libellum illum molitus est; nunc *grandior natu* illum utpote[125] infamem habet. Si perinde res habet atque dicit, quid illum se penes quasi deliciolum fouet? Quid illum dies noctesque interbibendum euoluit et lectitat, uersus quoque prioribus turpiores nunc nuper componit et abiicit? Quid infamia illa sua fruitur?[126] Quid illum, quando[127] grauitati ac nomini suo tam egregie consulit, in fragmenta ac frusta non concidit? Quid non *lignorum* petit *aliquid*[128] ocius et *marito Veneris* — ut Iuuenalis ait — illum quam familiariter consecrat? Quid illum his superioribus exactis pauculis annis Veronam, Bononiam, Romam — non infans, non puer, ut ait, non adulescens, [A122v] ceterum editae iam aetatis — per tabellarios deferendum dimisit? Quid Mediolanum urbem splendidissimam purissimamque spurcitiis ipsis nunc nuper oppleuit? Quid imperitis scholaribus nouo dicendi genere, ut fit, pellectis transcribendum per subsellia accommodat et dietim exponit?

64 Video iam quorsum erumpat, quidue comminiscatur intellego. *Ad excusandas* enim *excusationes in peccatis* uersiculum illum Catulli, dei sui, quem in buccam ex industria semper comparatum habet, statim decantabit:

castum decet esse poetam ipsum
pium, uerisculos nihil necesse est.

65 Pro bellicosum uirum! Hic nisi firmiore pede in insidias perstiterimus, uideo plane rem nostram *a prima acie*, ut aiunt, *ad triarios* redire oportere.

---

[125]illum utpote] ^butpote ^aillum *corr. A*
[126]fruitur] finitur *A*
[127]quando] quia *N*
[128]petit aliquid *tr. N*

---

[147]Panormita *Etsi facile* §2 (Appendix I below). Panormita also made this claim in a letter (1.XII.1426) to Archbishop Bartolomeo Capra, in response to Capra's desire to read *The Hermaphrodite* (Beccadelli 1746, 108 [2.23]): ". . . if indeed the thing is in fact lewd, but it is a work of my youth. . . ." (. . . *siquidem res admodum laciva est, at adolescentis opus.* . . .).
[148]Panormita *Etsi facile* §3 (Appendix I below).
[149]Juvenal 7.24–25. That is, "burn it" by using it for kindling: Venus, goddess of love, was married to Vulcan, the god of fire and forge.
[150]This is how Panormita described himself (*Etsi facile* §2–§3; Appendix I below). He would have been thirty-two years old when the book circulated in 1426 and thirty-eight years old at the time Rho was writing this *Philippic*.

and to others, with these simple words? We see right through his chicaneries and lies. Perhaps many people would consider the young entitled to such licence if they did not perceive that even more loathsome and atrocious things would pile up throughout the remainder of life. I, however, think that to no age, to no profession, or to no rank is even the least indecency going to be conceded.

63 Nor do I have adequate grounds that would enable me to vouch for anything certain or constant about this man. "In my tender years,"[147] as he says, he composed that wretched little book. But now being "older,"[148] he naturally holds it in disrepute. If things do stand as he says, why does he coddle that book at home as though it were his darling? Why does he peruse and pore over it to its last dregs day and night? And why is he even now drafting and dashing off new poetry dirtier than the former? Why does he take pleasure in that shameful reputation of his? Inasmuch as he is so terribly concerned about his reputation for seriousness, why does he not chop the book up into bits and pieces? Why does he not seek "something quicker than firewood," as Juvenal says, and consecrate it completely "to the husband of Venus"?[149] Why did he, just a few years ago — when he was not a toddler, a boy, or a youth, as he claimed, but was already at an advanced age[150] — dispatch the book by courier to Verona, Bologna, and Rome?[151] Why did he just recently blanket the gleaming and unsullied city of Milan with this filth? Why, to transcribe the book, does he provide benches for ignorant students, who have been seduced (as commonly happens) by a new kind of speech? Why does he lecture to them on it daily?[152]

64 I already envision him blurting out his response, or rather I know what story he will concoct. For "in order to excuse his sins,"[153] he will promptly chant that little poem of his god Catullus, which he always keeps purposely on the tip of his tongue: "It is fitting that the poet himself be chaste and pious; his little poems require nothing of the kind."[154]

65 Ooooh, what a warrior! Unless we hole up in a fortified position, we could get ambushed here. I see clearly that our line "has to fall back from the front," as they say, "to join forces with the reserves."[155]

---

[151]Rho refers to the earliest circulation of *The Hermaphrodite* among Panormita's friends in 1426 when Panormita had Giovanni Lamola carry it from Bologna and deliver it to Guarino Veronese in Verona and to Poggio and Antonio Loschi in Rome. Guarino and Poggio's letters of reaction (2.II.1426 and 3.IV.1426 respectively) appeared as prefatory material to the subsequent release of *The Hermaphrodite* (see Coppini LXXIII–LXXXVI, and Sabbadini and Barozzi 19–25; for the texts of the letters, see Beccadelli 1990a, 144–59; for Loschi see *Philippic* §47 n. 113, §47–§50, and *Apology* §38).

[152]These allegations concerning its recent release in Milan, if true, make a lie of Panormita's claim that "the author is disgusted and revolted by reading or circulating it" (see Panormita *Etsi facile* §2, Appendix I below; and *Philippic* §62 n. 146).

[153]Psalms 140/141.4.

[154]Catullus 16.5–6; and Panormita *Etsi facile* §1 (Appendix I below). See Gaisser 21–23 and 286–87 nn. 91–97; see also Ludwig 1990, esp. 188–91, who argues that apart from Panormita citing the example of Catullus to defend his use of *lascivia*, *The Hermaphrodite* itself shows "very few borrowings from Catullus."

[155]Livy 8.8.11.

66 At quem imperatorem aut ducem in medium profert? Cuius momenti? Cuius prudentiae aut maiestatis? Catullum poetamne?

67 Abunde quidem ab gentibus spectatus est collaudatusque. Quid non Hieronymum aut Augustinum aut ex prophetis unum suae causae patronos exhibuit?[129] Quid saltem Aristotelem,[130] philosophorum facile principem, suae tutelae non asciuit? Is enim ex similibus actibus eosdem habitus fieri tradit: *Itaque uidendum esse*, ait, *quales actus edamus, nam quales illi sunt tales habitus sequi necesse est*. Concluditque non parum ad rem nostram, sed plurimum immo totum pertinere, hoc uel illo modo ab adulescentia insuescere.

68 "Sentisne, ueterane Panormita? Sentisne?"

69 Et alio loco inquit uoces esse *earum quae sunt in anima passionum* notas. At quoniam fortasse, immo certo[131] scio, nulla sibi cum Aristotele necessitudo, nulla familiaritas est, deum ipsum nostrum[132] saltem exaudiat oportebit: *Vnaquaeque arbor*, ait,[133] *de fructu suo cognoscitur. Neque enim de spinis colligunt ficus: neque de rubo uindemiant uuam. Bonus homo de bono thesauro cordis sui profert bonum: et malus homo de malo*[134] *thesauro cordis sui profert malum. Ex abundantia enim*[135] *cordis os loquitur*. Ab Ioanne uero dictum est: *Qui de terra est, ⟨. . .⟩ de terra loquitur*.[136] Tum qui flagitiosus est[137] et spurcus, de flagitiis et spurcitiis loqui oportere necesse est. Non et Iudaei ad Petrum dixerunt: *Vere et tu ex illis es: nam et*[138] *loquela tua ma*[A123r]*nifestum te facit*. Recte quidem. *Prudentia* enim *hominibus*, aiunt, *grata est, lingua uero plerumque suspecta*. Non ex linguarum diuersitate, alios Germanos, alios Pannonios, alios Graecos, alios Latinos, alios Panormitas, alios

---

[129]exhi-] -h- *s.l. suppl.* A
[130]Aristotelem] *mg. suppl.* A
[131]certo] -te A
[132]nostrum *om.* A
[133]ait] *s.l. suppl.* A
[134]malo *om.* N
[135]enim] *s.l. suppl.* A
[136]ita aeque de caelo de caelo loquitur *marg. gl.* A
[137]est *post* spurcus N
[138]et *om.* N

---

[156]"Jerome, Augustine, or one of the Prophets" alludes to a series of patristic and biblical texts found in Canon Law, that is, Gratian's *Decretum* (D.36–38). In the scholastic tradition of arranging texts pro and con (*sic et non*), some quotations support, others attack the study of poetry and secular literature. Gratian's rubrics and later humanist argument reconciled the apparent contradiction in order to support the study of poetry and secular literature (Rutherford 1997; cf. *Apology* §17 and §29). The author (Antonio da Rho?) of the "Anonymous Invective" (Appendix III §15 below) blamed Panormita for inducing Guarino Veronese to assert that Jerome agreed with the sentiments of

66 But who is this general or commander whom he is throwing against our center? What is the strength of his forces? In which campaigns has he served? What insignia does he wear? Surely not Catullus, a poet!

67 To be sure, pagans have heaped honors and commendations on Catullus. But why has Panormita not paraded Jerome, Augustine, or one of the Prophets as defenders of his cause?[156] Why has he not at least enlisted Aristotle, who is easily the prince of philosophers, to protect him? For Aristotle teaches that one's habits derive from corresponding actions. "Therefore," Aristotle says, "we must observe how we act, for our habits follow necessarily from our actions."[157] Aristotle also concludes that during our youth habits become ingrained in exactly that way, which is a point that relates not just a little, but a lot, or rather completely to our subject.

68 "Do you hear, Panormita, you old warhorse? Do you hear?"

69 And elsewhere Aristotle says that speech is a sign "of the passions that are in the soul."[158] But perhaps, or rather since I know for a fact that Panormita has no close bond or acquaintance with Aristotle, he ought at least to listen to our God himself. "Every tree," [Jesus] said, "is known by its own fruit. For from thorns men do not gather figs, nor from a bramble bush do they gather grapes. A good man out of the good treasure of his heart brings forth that which is good; and an evil man out of the evil treasure of his heart brings forth that which is evil. For from the abundance of the heart the mouth speaks."[159] Moreover, John said: "He that is of the earth [. . .] speaks of the earth."[160] He, then, who is shameful and filthy must from necessity speak of the shameful and filthy. Did not the Jews say to Peter: "Surely you also are one of them, for your speech betrays you."[161] Justly so.

Catullus 16.5–9 and that he even used language like that found in *The Hermaphrodite*. "Anonymous" is referring to Guarino's statement to Giovanni Lamola (Coppini 1990, 146): "Indeed even our Jerome, a man who was especially outstanding for his chastity and integrity, did not find this opinion [of Catullus (16.5–9)] repugnant. He gave enormous licence to his pen in lusting and open whoring when he struck up a discussion about prostitutes, [saying]: 'Therefore, when everyone had gone away, a very attractive whore arrived, began to caress his neck in a delicate embrace, and, what is also shocking to say, to stroke his manhood, so that, when his body had been aroused with lust, this shameless victor could lay down on top of him' [Jerome *Life of St. Paul, the First Hermit* 3]." (*A qua quidem sententia et noster Hieronymus non abhorret, homo castimonia et integritate praeditus in primis, qui, cum in meretricis sermonem incidisset, quantam lascivienti ac vere scortanti calamo permisit usurpare licentiam!:* "*Quo cum, recedentibus cunctis, meretrix speciosa venisset, coepit delicatis stringere colla complexibus, et, quod dictu quoque scelus est, manibus attrectare virilia, ut, corpore in libidinem concitato, se victrix impudica superiaceret.*")

[157]Cf. Aristotle *Nicomachean Ethics* (trans. Lincolniensis) 54b20.

[158]Aristotle *On Interpretation* (trans. Boethius) 16a3–4.

[159]Luke 6.44–45.

[160]John 3.31. John was one of the original Twelve Apostles and said to be the author of the Fourth Gospel, the Book of Revelation, and three of the Catholic Epistles.

[161]Matthew 26.73. Peter was one of the original Twelve Apostles and said to be the first Bishop of Rome and the author of two of the Catholic Epistles. According to Matthew's Gospel (cited here), while Jesus was on trial in the Sanhedrin, Peter's accent or dialect identified him as a fellow Nazarene, which led to Peter's "three denials of Christ."

Syracusanos iudicamus? Quid itaque quando oratio omnino non conuenit, sese *castum pium*que *poetam* pollicetur? *Quod medicorum enim est*, ut apud Flaccum,

> *promittunt medici, tractant fabrilia fabri.*

Ita quae spurca sunt, spurci litteris mandant.

70 Heus tu, Panormita, sentisne?[139] Qualem itaque orationem et linguam habes qualesque res moliris et scriptitas, talem te intus animum tenere necesse est. Ait enim ille ipse idem Aristoteles perfecti consummatique habitus esse facile ac delectabiliter operari. Quis autem praeter te lenones et lupas et exoletos et fornices et ephebias depicturus iucundior inuenietur atque facilior? Ita enimuero primis in labiis has faeces obscenitatesque usu quodam comparasti ut non tam facile spuere quam illas eructare et euomere posse uideare. Ne[140] tibi quidem, tametsi[141] ille bene tu male uersificaturus, Sidonius cedit [N104r] Antipater. Solebat enim, ut aiunt, *uersus hexametros aliosque uariis modis atque numeris fundere ex tempore*, apud quem *tantum hominis ingeniosi et memoris ualuit exercitatio ut, cum se mente et uoluptate erexisset in uersum, uerba sequerentur*. Tu quoque benedicendo nullus es, maledicendo uero malus[142] et praesto.

71 Legimus saepenumero, Candide, dum in ludo pueri uersaremur, Phormionem, illum Peripateticum Ephesi,[143] praesente Hannibale *aliquot horas* locutum esse *copiosius de imperatoris officio deque omni re militari. At cum ceteri, qui illum*[144] *adierant,*[145] *uehementer delectati essent, sciscitabantur*[146] *ab Hannibale, quidnam ille*[147] *ipse de illo philosopho iudicaret, qui Punicus non tam bene Graece quam libere*[148] *respondisse fertur multos se deliros senes saepe uidisse. sed qui magis quam Phormio deliraret uidisse neminem.*

72 Id mirumne? Experientia enim gignit, ut aiunt, artem. Alios etenim natura, alios doctrina, alios multa periclitatio, usus, et exercitatio quaedam claros et illustres reddit; uerum imprimis exercitatio ipsa et iuge periculum, due res extant quidem, [A123v] quae ipsi naturae atque doctrinae magno adiumento fiant quaedamque ornamenta illis adiecta esse[149] uideantur.

---

[139]sentisne] satisne *A*
[140]Ne *scripsi* : Nec *AN*
[141]tam-] *s.l. suppl. N*
[142]malus] multus *N*
[143]Ephesi] -siae *N*
[144]illum] *N, Cic.* : eum *A*
[145]adierant] audi- *Cic.*
[146]sciscitabantur] quaerebant *Cic.*
[147]ille] illa *N*
[148]qui Punicus . . . libere] hic Poenus non optime Graece, sed tamen libere *Cic.*
[149]esse *om. N*

For "men appreciate prudence," they say, "but the tongue they mostly hold suspect."[162] Do we not determine from differences in language that some people are Germans, others Pannonians, Greeks, Latins, Palermitans, and Syracusans? Why, then, does he swear that he is a "chaste and pious poet" when his speech completely belies this claim?[163] For "doctors undertake what appertains to doctors," as Horace puts it, "craftsmen handle tools."[164] Hence, the filthy commit filthy things to literature.

70 "Hey, Panormita, did you hear that? This is why of necessity the words you use, the way you talk, what you compose, and what you habitually write reflects your inner thoughts. For Aristotle himself says the same thing: that we do easily and delectably what stems from deeply ingrained habit.[165] Yet who is found to be more prone than you to depict with verve and gusto pimps, whores, sodomites, brothels, and child prostitutes? For with a measure of practice you have these perversions and obscenities so ready on the tip of your tongue that you seem able not so much to spit them out as to heave and vomit them up.[166] Not even Antipater of Sidon[167] yields to you, although he would versify well and you badly. For he was wont, as they say, 'to pour out extemporaneously hexameter verse and other kinds of poetry in various meters. In his case, practice so served the man's talent and memory that, when he made up his mind to speak in verse, the words simply followed.'[168] Similarly, you, who bless nobody, because you're evil, excel when it comes to cursing."

71 We as schoolboys, Candido, often read about Phormio, the Peripatetic from Ephesus, who in the presence of Hannibal[169] spoke "profusely for several hours about a general's duty and about every military topic. But whereas the others present were greatly thrilled, when they asked Hannibal what he thought about the philosopher, he, being Punic, is said to have responded in Greek more frank than elegant that he had seen many an old lunatic, but none who ranted more than Phormio."[170]

72 It is no wonder, because experience, as they say, begets art. For nature makes some people famous and distinguished, for others education does this, and for others still extensive experience, performance, and practice accomplish it. But primarily practice and dogged determination achieve this. These two attributes greatly augment nature and education and are in some way seen to be ornaments enhancing them.

---

[162]Cicero *The Orator* 42.145.
[163]Catullus 16.5.
[164]Horace *Epistle* 2.1.115–116, who is probably quoted from Jerome *Letter* 53.7 (cf. Wiesen 37).
[165]Cf. Aristotle *Praedicamenta* 2.4.2 and *Eudemian Ethics* 1220b.
[166]Cf. Cicero *Philippic* 5.7.20.
[167]Antipater of Sidon was a Greek epigrammatist who flourished ca. 125 BCE.
[168]Cicero *On the Orator* 3.50.194.
[169]Hannibal was the General of the Carthaginian (Punic) forces during the Second Punic War (218–201 BCE). Punics spoke a Semitic language, i.e., Phoenician (which the Romans called "Punic").
[170]Cicero *On the Orator* 2.18.75.

73 Sed quorsum haec? Male enim omnino[150] res habet cum naturae improbae disciplina et usus accessit. Redeant itaque iam in lucem uelim Sardanapalus et Heliogabalus, Nero quoque ipse cum Sporo, et huius palaestrae plerique omnes; audiant uelim Panormitam, philosophum Hermaphroditi sui, promiscuae quoque luxuriae monitus ac praecepta, immo stercora et faeces, e suggestu celebrantem. Tametsi hi singuli ita spurci ante hac uulgo habiti sint ut nihil supra, fatebuntur nihilo setius Panormitam ipsum nequaquam delirare ut Phormio ille aut somniare, quin immo ex illius praeceptione multa ipsi didicisse fatebuntur admirabunturque, quae hactenus illis incognita inauditaque, nunc uero nuper lucubrata et inuenta esse uideantur. Quibus his ex omnibus fit, ut sentinas,[151] latrinas quoque, cetera uel flagitia quae in hanc aetatem feliciter cecinerit delectabiliterque, e spurco intus et immundo spiritu suo, ueluti diutino ex habitu, esse profecta sine controuersia iudicentur.

74 Qua ratione igitur? quo argumento? quibus fretus[152] caelicolis sanctum piumque poetam sese praedicat, qui sexus utriusque uersiculos taetros, perhorrendos, Hermaphroditum uidelicet ipsum suum?[153] O perditam mentem profanamque! Scortis et exoletis Florentiam ipso in lupanari quasi academiae bibliothecis delegauit consecrauitque. Hocine est casti et pii poetae iter? haec ad superos uia illa lactea[154] stellarum, *ipso candore nobilis* atque conspicua? haec illa studiorum suorum negotiosa peregrinatio, qua sese *tollere humo* ostentat ac iactat *uictorque uirum* gestit *uolitare per ora*? qui ad Florentiae uisenda scorta et exoletos, ita quaeque diuersoria nescientibus iter adulescentibus ita Maeandros declarauit, ut perlecto libello suo sanctissimo, iam nemo quisquam delirare, nemo deuiare debeat? Ita meretrices illas catamitosque quam sibi familiares comparauit, ut quasi nomenculator quidam, quasi leno domesticus, quasi sordidae pecuniae campsor et trapezita facilius singulatimque suo nomine eas

---

[150]omnino] *s.l. suppl. A*
[151]senti-] centi- *N*
[152]fretus] fictus *N*
[153]ipsum suum] ᵇsuum ᵃipsum *corr. A*
[154]lactea] lacertea *N*

---

[171]Assur-danin-pal (ca. ninth century BCE), known to the Greeks and Romans as Sardanapalus, was a king of Assyria who was fabled for his wealth and hedonism; Heliogabalus was a Roman Emperor (218–22 CE) legendary for his good looks, extravagance, cruelty, and debauchery.

[172]Nero, Roman Emperor from 54 to 68 CE, was the last of the Julio-Claudian line. His name became synonymous with debauchery, cruelty, and lechery. Sporus was a youth whom Nero ordered to be castrated before taking him in marriage as his wife (Suetonius *Nero* 28).

[173]See *Philippic* §59 n. 136 and Panormita *Hermaphrodite* 1.3.1–4.

[174]Rho used "libraries" (plural) because according to Roman custom an academy was expected to have a Greek library and a Latin library, housed in separate but adjacent locations (Casson 80–85). Renaissance libraries tried to reinstitute this ancient institutional practice. For instance, when the

73 But why am I saying this? Because things take a decided turn towards evil when discipline and practice combine with an wicked nature. I would like Sardanapalus and Heliogabalus,[171] even Nero along with Sporus,[172] and nearly all of this school now to return life. I would like them to hear Panormita, the philosopher of his *Hermaphrodite*, at the rostrum declaiming advice and precepts of unrestrained promiscuity, or rather, declaiming on shit and utter garbage. Even though previously every single one of these men had a reputation for being so filthy that nothing was beyond him, all of them will nonetheless acknowledge that Panormita is not at all ranting or hallucinating like Phormio, but instead, even they will admit with amazement that they have learned many things from his instruction. These are things which previously they knew nothing about and had never heard of, but which now loom like recent inventions and elaborations. For all these reasons, the cesspools and latrines or other lewd acts that he has recounted with verve and gusto to people of today remove all doubt but that they spring from his filthy, polluted inner self, stemming, as it were, from longstanding habit.

74 For what reason, then, and by what proof, or with trust in what gods does he proclaim himself to be a holy and pious poet, since that vile, revolting collection of bisexual poetry, *The Hermaphrodite*, is his very own?[173] What a depraved and impious mind! He dedicated and consecrated Florence to whores and sodomites in that brothel [described in *The Hermaphrodite*] as if he were in the libraries of an academy.[174] Is this the path of a chaste and pious poet? Is this the Milky Way, the starry road to the gods, visible and "majestic by its very whiteness"?[175] Is this the laborious pilgrimage of his studies through which he pretentiously boasts that he "lifted himself from the ground" and as "as victor of men he brags that his name flies from mouth to mouth"?[176] Is this the man who described the meandering path to young people unfamiliar with the inns when coming to see the whores and sodomites of Florence so that once they had studied his saintly little book, none of them ought to get lost or stray off course?[177] So this is how he procured the courtesans and Ganymedes so familiar to him. Consequently, like some nomenclator,[178] pimp, hustler, or loan shark, he knows how to call them all

---

Library of San Marco in Florence was repaired at Medici expense in 1453, a new addition was dubbed the "Greek Library" and was used to house all "oriental" manuscripts: *quorum etsi aliqui Indica, Arabica, Chaldaica, Hebraicaque litteris scripta, maior tamen pars Graeci habentur* (Ullman and Stadter 25 and n. 3; inventory 248–67). For the founding of the Vatican Library and its division into Greek and Latin libraries, see Boyle xi–xiii; Lee 118–19; Müntz 3:121–35; and Müntz and Fabre 148–58.

[175]Cf. Ovid *Metamorphoses* 1.169, whose expression is *candore notabilis ipso*.

[176]Virgil *Georgics* 3.9.

[177]Panormita gives directions for finding the brothel in Florence in *Hermaphrodite* 2.37. A reference to the Meander River, however, does not appear there, so the simile must be Rho's own.

[178]A nomenclator was a type of Roman slave whose duty was to inform his master of the names of everyone he met. An interlinear gloss in manuscript N adds "that is, 'a boy'" (*idest, puellus*). Elsewhere, Rho himself glosses this term (*Imitations* 155r): "*Nomenculator*, a 'name-servant' (i.e., *nomen-kalator*), as it were, who calls everyone by his own name. It is believed to be the kind of service rendered by a herald (*genus officii creditur quasi bidellus*)."

omnes compellare norit quam quot numero ipse oculis uideat aut pedibus [A124r] inambulet supputare didicerit, quin immo quam uxoris suae permolestum sibi nomen ipse meminerit.

75 Vrgebit statim et saepe alias sordibusque suis non modo Nasonem aut Vergilium, ceterum Senecam Socratemque[155] ipsum, uiros continentissimos, secum inuoluet. Quin et apostolos homo impudentissimus[156] atque prophetas aliquando aberrasse — uerbis modo fides ⟨non⟩ adhibeatur — libenter mentietur. O foeditatem hominis flagitiosam! O impudentiam, nequitiam, libidinem non ferendam! An idcirco se existimat innocentem si quicquid suum est in alios transferat, uulneribusque suis mederine putat dum alios ipse maledictis oppresserit uulnerauentque?

76 Poggii quidem Florentini, quem ut ipsius dignitas poscit honoris gratia nomino, uiri cum eloquentissimi tum modestissimi, epistolam quandam lectitasse commemini, qua Panormitam, Beccadellum istum, commonefaciens ab huiuscemodi petulantissimo [N104v] scribendi genere auocare nitebatur, ubi post haud nullas minutas perfunctoriasque ingenii sui laudationes,[157] statim infert alia ante Christum, alia post Christum litteris mandari licuisse probe quidem, grauiter, sancte. Non, ea nocte qua uirgo caelestis dei filium enixa est, omnes in orbe natura et ipso sexu abutentes (ut ex sanctorum litteris habetur) una hora mortem obiere, quo posteros omnis, si non pudor aut horror, si non leges aut decreta, saltem timor ipse diuinus coerceret?

77 Pulchre itaque ipse Poggius "Alia," inquit, "fuere Vergilii et Homeri tempora omnisque illius siluae poetarum philosophorumque," quos in testes hic poeta raucus asciuit, "alia nos uero tempora percurrimus." Id enim temporis Apollo, Sibylla, sancta Themis, ipse Iupiter, et multa huiuscemodi, non minus daemonum portenta quam deorum simulacra, toti propemodum orbi oracula et fata quaedam, immo plane fatua multa praedicebant.[158] Poterant tunc

---

[155]Socratem-] -rantem- *N*
[156]impudentissimus] *mg. suppl. sed* incontinentissimus *non in ras. A*
[157]sui laudationes *tr. N*
[158]praedi-] prodi- *N*

---

[179]Panormita (*Hermaphrodite* 2.37) names the prostitutes: Elena, Matilda, Gianetta, Clodia, Galla, Anna, Ursa, Pitonessa, and Thais (cf. *Prostitutes of Pavia* 49–51, Appendix IV/1 below).

[180]An allusion to the rumor reported in the "Anonymous Invective" (Appendix III §3 below) and later by Decembrio (1432, 127v) that Panomita abandoned a wife in Sicily after squandering her dowry. All known evidence indicates that this rumor is false. Panormita (first?) married in late 1433 or early 1434 to one Filippa, a neighbor of Giovanni Feruffino. She died in 1444, and he remarried in 1447 (see Besomi and Regoliosi 227; and Sabbadini 1891, 16–17; and 1910a, 158–59; cf. also *Philippic* §132).

[181]Seneca the Younger (ca. 4 BCE–65 CE) was a Roman Stoic moral philosopher, whom Christians later elevated in moral authority through the circulation of a spurious correspondence

by name[179] more easily and singly than he has learned to count what he sees with his eyes or paces off with his feet, yes even more easily than he remembers the name, so obnoxious to him, of his own wife.[180]

75 He will immediately begin protesting and implicate in his own sordid affairs not only Ovid and Virgil, but the most self-restrained of men, Seneca and Socrates himself.[181] Moreover, this absolutely shameless man will lie with no qualms and say — give no credence to these words — that the apostles and prophets sometimes strayed. What a shockingly repulsive man! Such effrontery, depravity, and unbearable lust! Does he really consider himself innocent if he attributes to someone else all his personal failings? And does he think that he has cured his own wounds when he is crushing and wounding others with his blasphemies?

76 I recall, in fact, having read a certain letter of Poggio Fiorentino, an eloquent and modest man, whom I name here out of the respect his dignity requires,[182] in which he tried to dissuade Panormita, this Beccadelli,[183] and turn him away from such a wanton genre of writing. After some trivial and perfunctory compliments of Panormita's talents, Poggio immediately postulates that one could legitimately put in writing — indeed properly, gravely, and solemnly — some things before Christ and other things after Christ. Did not (as we gather from the writings of the saints) everyone in the world who was abusing nature and sex in particular die within the hour on the night that the Blessed Virgin gave birth to the Son of God, so that if shame or revulsion and laws or decrees did not restrain all future generations, fear of God in and of itself would do so?[184]

77 Poggio has it right when he says "Virgil, Homer, and that whole host of poets and philosophers were of one era," whom this raucous poet employed as witnesses, "but we are living in another."[185] For in those days Apollo, the Sibyl, sacred Themis, Jupiter himself, and many like them,[186] who were portents of demons as much as idols of gods,[187] uttered sundry oracles and prophecies, or

---

between him and the Apostle Paul. Socrates (469–399 BCE) was an Athenian philosopher who turned philosophy to the investigation of human conduct, especially as he is represented in the dialogues of his most famous disciple Plato (cf. *Apology* §25).

[182]Poggio's letter (3.IV.1426) circulated with Panormita's *Hermaphrodite* (see *Philippic* §63 n. 151; for the text of the letter see Poggio *Letter* 2.5 and Beccadelli 1990a, 144–59).

[183]See *Philippic* §20 n. 45; cf. §132, §133, and §174.

[184]Cf. Jacobus de Voragine *Golden Legend*, "The Nativity of Our Lord" (written in 1275). He probably took his lead from the *Rhymed Life of the Blessed Virgin and the Savior*, an anonymous work composed ca. 1200 (see Hergemöller 148–49 and 152–53).

[185]This is Rho's paraphrase, not a direct quotation from Poggio's letter of 3.IV.1426 (*Letter* 2.5).

[186]These are ancient divinities associated with prophetic utterances: *Apollo*'s shrine at Delphi, where the Oracle of Apollo was located, became the most important religious site in the Greek world; the *Sibyl* (later twelve in number) was a female prophet who uttered ecstatic, enigmatic oracles; *Sacred Themis* was a prophetic earth goddess, who later became associated with Justice and Righteousness; *Jupiter*, the chief god of the Romans, was a weather god whose temple on the capital (the highest structure in ancient Rome) was frequently struck by lightning, which the Romans thought portentous.

[187]Cf. Jerome *Letter* 75.3; and *Philippic* §112.

liberius uates illi maledicere quam tempestate hac ipsi Panormitae
870 iam benedicere liceat. Nunc etenim diebus nostris his deus uerus et
omnipotens dominus alloquitur nos in filio suo. Qui, cum morum
integritatem, uirtutum praestantiam, sensuum castimoniam complectatur prosequaturque ad discipulos in monte, ait: *Beati mundo
corde: quoniam ipsi deum uidebunt.*

875   **78** Quid ergo ad caelestis clangorem tubae nihil exaudit? Quid
scurrilia illa et[159] informia [A124v] eloquia, quae uel ex Pauli iudicio
atque sententia *bonos mores corrumpunt,* minus missa facit? Quid ad
crucis uexillum gemebundus haud euolat? Quid non una cum meretrice illa euangelica domini pedes complexatur ac[160] tenet? Quid cum
880 sanctissimo illo latrone atque sicario, accepta cruce errata sua, non
deflet? Aut si crucem, uti diabolus, cominus adire reformidat, quid
non cum publicano illo stans eminus percutit pectus suum et ait,
"*Deus, propitius esto mihi peccatori*"? Ita enim fortasse aliquando
obtingeret — sed horam nescio — ut quo abundasset iniquitas
885 superabundaret et gratia, et e Saulo sanctorum insecutore adulescen-
tulo, Paulus *apostolorum minimus* prorsus euaderet, clausulam huic
orationi iam libenter obsignarem, et cum Maria Magdalene ac cruce
quam gratissimum esset iucundissimumque obire sermones meos.

    79 Verum ipse me alio trahit ubi ego ex illo "sacerdos sanctis-
890 simus" appellor. Pro! Habetne ultra aliquid quo neruos suae
loquacitatis extendat? Vellem equidem paululum humani si non
Christiani pudoris saltem assumeret, ne despecta
calcataque conscientia sua uerbis se purgatum **Tertia Objectio**
existimaret, qui rebus urgetur. Iterum dicam, me
895 sacerdotem sanctissimum appellat. Putatne iste litterator et paeda-
gogus, dum puellus in ludo uersarer nequaquam didicisse qui post
hominum terga linguae canum aestuantes[161] protendantur,[162] aut
asini exagitentur[163] auriculae, aut qui ciconiarum colla curuentur?
Numquid gloriatur quasi cachinnos[164] illius cauillosque, immo iro-
900 nias, ipse nihil intellegam, qui primis in[165] labiis cor ipsum intueor et

[159]et] atque *N*
[160]ac] et *N*
[161]aestu- *scripsi* : extu- *AN*
[162]protendantur] -end *litterae ultimae deletae sunt N*
[163]exagi-] ex- *s.l. suppl. A*
[164]cachin-] cathin- *N*
[165]in] *s.l. suppl. A*

[188]Matthew 5.8.
[189]I Corinthians 15.33.
[190]That is, the "woman sinner"(Luke 7:36–50), who was commonly identified as Mary Magdalen (see n. 196 below).
[191]According to Luke's Gospel (23.39–43), Jesus, being crucified between two thieves, when reviled by one and defended by the other, granted the latter entrance into Paradise.

rather many manifest lunacies, to virtually the whole world. These prophets were then more at liberty to curse than Panormita is now to bless. And indeed now in our own day, the true God and omnipotent Lord speaks to us in his Son. When he, the Son, summarized and described the integrity of morals, the excellence of the virtues, and the chastity of the senses to his disciples on the Mount, he said: "Blessed are the pure of heart, for they shall see God."[188]

78 Why then does Panormita not hear the celestial trumpet's blast? Why does he not abandon those scurrilous and degrading expressions, which in Paul's judgment and opinion "corrupt good morals"?[189] Why does he not fly groaning to the standard of the Cross? Why does he not, in the company of that evangelical courtesan, embrace and even cling to the feet of the Lord?[190] Why does he not weep bitterly with that saintly thief and murderer who recognized his mistakes while on the cross?[191] Or if, like the Devil, he dreads to go near the Cross, why does he not, "standing afar off" with the Publican,[192] strike his breast and say: "God, have mercy on me a sinner"?[193] For if perhaps at some point — but do not ask me when — it were ever to happen that "where sin abounded, grace did much more abound,"[194] and from the young man Saul, the persecutor of the saints, Paul, "the least of the apostles," would emerge,[195] I would instantly and freely signal the close of this oration, and I would be most gratified and agreeable to have my sermonizing end with Mary Magdalen and the Cross.[196]

The Third Objection

79 But he draws me to another passage, where I am called "a most holy priest."[197] Well! Has he no other way to strain his verbal power? I certainly wish that he would at least acquire a modicum of human if not of Christian modesty so that after having disdained and trampled his conscience, he would not think he has cleared himself with mere words when he is threatened by the facts. Let me say again, he calls me "a most holy priest." Does this teacher of children's

---

[192]Luke's Gospel (18.10–14) portrays the Publican (a Jewish tax collector for the Romans) as a guilt-ridden sinner in contrast to the Pharisee, who is represented as self-righteous and hypocritical.

[193]Luke 18.13.

[194]Romans 5.20.

[195]I Corinthians 15.9; cf. Acts 7.57–8.3, 9.1–2. Saul of Tarsus (d. ca. 65 CE) was a Hellenistic Jew, a Pharisee, and Roman citizen, who took the name Paul and styled himself "Apostle" after becoming a Christian.

[196]Mary Magdalen was said to have become a follower of Jesus after he cast demons out of her. According to Mark's Gospel, she was at the crucifixion (15.40), a witness to the empty tomb (16.1), and the first to whom the Risen Christ appeared (16.9): thus her epithet "The Apostle to the Apostles." She was commonly identified with the "woman sinner" (of Luke 7.36–50), who washed Jesus' feet with her tears and dried them with her hair, and therefore came to represent the penitent prostitute. In the Middle Ages and Renaissance mendicants preached her example as that of the perfect penitent (see Jansen 5 and 212–28).

[197]Panormita *Etsi facile* §3 (Appendix I below).

quorsum erupturus sit primis ipsis in uerbis agnosco? Me itaque sacerdotem sanctissimum appellat, qui plane peccator sum. Quis enim a peccato immunis est? Infansne unius diei? Minime quidem. *Si dixerimus*, ut sacrae litterae[166] testantur, *quod peccatum non habemus,*
905 *nos ipsos seducimus, et ueritas in nobis non est.* Et in Psalmo dicitur: *Omnes declinauerunt, simul inutiles facti sunt; non est qui faciat bonum,*[167] *non est usque ad unum.* Diuinum enim est quod labe uacat. Quis itaque ille fuerit qui sese peccati expertem uindicet? Qui dicat "non erraui," "nihil admisi," "frontem sine nota et macula profero,"
910 quando ne ipsi *caeli* quidem *mundi sunt in conspectu eius*?

80 Nescio uir iste mollis quem [A125r] se intus intueatur; scio quem se foris iactabundus ostentet. Puto tamen, intus animo exilium eo esse ducit ubi turpitudini locus desit, ut recte Clodius ille Pulcher censeatur aut Hortensius Corbio, quorum absentia[168] noctu
915 et interdiu lupanaria ingemiscebant; foris autem se tertium Catonem e caelo lapsum bene moratum, frugi, temperantem[169] pollicetur. Ita quippe *ut ex contrariis diuersisque naturis nouam beluam, nonnumquam monstrum* sibimet repugnantem, *esse compactam*[170] qui secum uersantur praedicent *iuxta poeticum illud*:

920 *prima leo, postrema draco, media* [N105r] *ipsa, Chimaera.*

Recte mihi iste uel uisus est, qui, si libidini dominandi libido abutendae naturae conferenda est, Catilinae quidem conferri possit. Iste etenim multa habet — ut de Catilina ipso ait Cicero — *non expressa signa, sed adumbrata uirtutum.* Utitur *hominibus improbis*: eis impro-
925 bis, dico, officinae suae, quibus tamen utpote *uiris optimis* — scio non sunt quos nunc laetus Maecenates, nunc subirascens[171] Mercenates appellat suos — *se deditum esse* dissimulat. *Cum tristibus* quasi nouus Catilina *seuere, cum remissis iucunde, cum senibus*[172] *grauiter, cum iuuentute non comiter* quidem — ut de Catilina Cicero
930 ait — ceterum petulanter et spurce, in alium et alium quasi alter Achelous ad pugnam Herculis uicissim se deformat immutatque.

[166]litterae] scripturae *N*

[167]non est . . . bonum *om. N*

[168]absentia *AN* : idest 'morte' *s.l. suppl. N*

[169]temperantem *N* : -ratum *corr. mg.* -rantem *A*

[170]ut ex contrariis . . . poeticum illud *AN* : ut ex contrariis diuersisque naturis unum monstrum nouamque bestiam diceres esse compactam iuxta illud poeticum *Hier.*

[171]subirascens] -irapus *N*

[172]senibus] saeui- *A*

[198]See *Philippic* §27 n. 63; cf. *Philippic* §135 and §145.

[199]I John 1.8.

[200]Psalms 52/53.4.

[201]Job 15.15.

[202]Cf. Valerius Maximus 3.5.4–5, who gives brief descriptions (under the subheading "Degenerate Descendants of Illustrious Parents") of these two little-known late republican, early imperial Romans.

ABCs[198] think that I as a small schoolboy never learned how panting dogs loll their tongues behind the backs of men? or how an ass wiggles its ears? or how storks bend their necks? Does he gloat as if I failed to understand his guffaws and gibes, or rather his sarcastic remarks? For on the tips of his lips I see into his very heart and at his first words I intuit where he is headed. I then who am clearly a sinner, he calls a most holy priest. For who is free from sin? A day-old baby? Hardly. As Holy Writ testifies, "If we say that we have no sin, we deceive ourselves, and the truth is not in us."[199] And in the Psalms it is said: "All have turned aside and together become corrupt; there is no one who does good, no not one."[200] For what lacks defect is divine. Who, then, would claim that he is free from sin? Who would say "I have not sinned," "I yielded to nothing sinful," or "I show my face free of mark or stain," when not even the "heavens themselves are clean in God's sight"?[201]

80 I do not know this sensitive man he sees within himself, but I do know the bragging outward man who struts around. Nevertheless, I think, in his heart he considers himself to be in exile in any place that lacks opportunity for indecency. So he could justly be considered another Clodius Pulcher or Hortensius Corbio, whose absence made the brothels groan day and night.[202] Outwardly, however, he assures us that he is the third Cato,[203] sent from heaven, well-mannered, honest, and temperate. Consequently, those who spend time with him say that "he is a new beast concocted out of contrary and diverse natures, a monster, as the poet puts it,"[204] sometimes fighting with itself: "the front a lion, the back a dragon, the middle itself the Chimera."[205] Indeed I think he can rightly be compared to Catiline,[206] since his lust for sexual perversion can be compared to Catiline's lust for absolute power. For as Cicero says about Catiline, Panormita has many "indistinct but shadowy signs of virtues"; he associates with "villainous men," I mean those villains in his workshop, but "he pretends to be devoted" to these men as if they are in fact "virtuous men."[207] I know they are not those whom he calls his Maecenases[208] when he is in a good mood, and his Money-bags when he is in a bad one. And like a new Catiline, "he comports himself severely with the austere, pleasantly with the relaxed, and gravely with the aged," but "with the young" not even "sociably," as Cicero said about Catiline,[209] but insolently and lewdly. He alternately transforms and changes himself from one thing to another as though he were another Achelous in a fight with Hercules.[210]

---

[203]See Juvenal 2.40 where he says of someone "He fell from heaven a Cato III" (*tertius e caelo cecidit Cato*). That is, he was of the same stature as (1) Marcus Porcius Cato (234–149 BCE), known as "Censorius" for his stern traditional morality, and (2) his great-grandson, Marcus Porcius Cato Uticensis (95–46 BCE), whose opposition to Caesar came to represent a principled stand for republican ideals.

[204]Jerome *Letter* 125.18 (cf. Cicero *In Defense of Caelius* 5.12 and Wiesen 229–30).

[205]Lucretius 5.905 (quoted here from Jerome *Letter* 125.18).

[206]Catiline led a conspiracy to take over Rome. Cicero exposed the plans and convinced the Senate to send an army against Catiline, defeating and killing him in 62 BCE.

[207]Cicero *In Defense of Caelius* 5.12.

[208]See *Philippic* §54 n. 130; cf. also §121, §131, §143, §170, §175, and §178.

[209]Cicero *In Defense of Caelius* 6.13.

[210]Achelous, when fighting with Hercules, took the form of a man, a snake, and a bull (Ovid *Metamorphoses* 9.1–88).

81 Ecce nunc igitur nostrum sanctissimum[173] poetam! (Paene, ut de me ait, dixi "sacerdotem.") Quid miratur? Quid stupet? De rebusne notissimis me dicere addubitat? Qui Gnathone ac Milite Glorioso uulgo sit notior?[174]

82 Sed ad priora redeamus. Ego uero etsi uermis et non homo, etsi non "sanctissimus" ut ille illudit et ringit⟨ur⟩, immo peccator sum, caelicolas omnes nihilo setius quos ille aut abiicit aut nescit obseruantia quadam atque religione reuereor, summumque illum totius orbis architectum supplex et pauimento stratus deum uidelicet meum quidem adoro, diuinisque suis nominibus uel numine uero[175] inspecto semper obseruantissimus assurgo.

83 At subnectit statim et inuehitur:

En animam et mentem cum qua dii nocte loquuntur.

84 Pro perii! Conuiciatur iam quidem! Verum ille aut ledorias aut scommata aut Sphingis dicat aenigmata, satis atque super illum intellegimus. Facetus enim esse cupit, sed friget: mentiendi quidem habet facultatem, fingendi uero artem uir ineptus et bardus nullam habet. Sic Granius et Vargula, ut aiunt, uolebant [A125v] esse faceti et salsi et erant scurrae. Verum enimuero quando uir iste plenus inuolucris hos logos ac somnia comminiscitur atque ex illa commentationum suarum taberna pro ueris falsa seminare contendit, miseret me sane quidem delictorum suorum simul et errata[176] sua paene ego ipse defleo.

85 Nequeo tamen mihi ipsi non gratulari, quippe qui istac aetate nostra antiqua ex integro miracula quae sacris leguntur litteris instaurari et exoriri uideo. Tradunt enim asinam illam Balaam locutam esse et articulata uerba quae illa nihil intellegeret[177] quasi humana uoce edidisse. Sic asinus hic noster ad me (ut est auritus!) uerba quae nihil intellegat profert:

En animam et mentem (ait) *cum qua dii nocte loquuntur.*

86 Credidit baburrus sacrilegium dixisse; ueritatem dixit. Alloquitur plane deus ipse meus non modo noctes, ut ait, ceterum singulos dies, omnes[178] horas, quaeque momenta quos sui cultus religionisque obseruantissimos esse[179] conspicatur, meique loci uiros commonefacere his uerbis exhortarique uidetur: *Beati estis cum*

---

[173]nostrum sanctissimum *tr. N*

[174]uulgo sit notior] notior uulgo sit *N*

[175]uero] non *N*

[176]errata] peccata *N*

[177]nihil intellegeret] nihil ᵘᵃintellegat profert: En animam et mentem . . . dii nocte loquuntur^cat intellegeret *corr. A*

[178]omnes] -nis *N*

[179]esse] e caelo *N*

81 Look at our most holy poet now! (I almost said "priest," as he said of me.) Why is he amazed? Why is he shocked? Is he bewildered that I talk about well-known things? Who could be more widely known than Gnatho or the Bragging Soldier?[211]

82 But let us return to his earlier assertions. Even if I am in fact a worm and not a man, even if I am not "most holy" as he mocks and smirks but instead a sinner, nonetheless I venerate with a certain observance and piety all the saints whom he either abandons or does not know. And indeed, suppliant and prostrate on the ground, I adore that Supreme Architect of the whole world, that is, my God, and I always rise dutifully when his divine names or true divinity appear.

83 But Panormita promptly throws in this snide remark: "Look at the heart and mind the gods talk to at night."[212]

84 Oh, I am ruined! Now he really taunts me! But let him make insults, sarcastic remarks, or riddles of the Sphinx, we understand him only too well. For he wants to be clever, but he falls flat. He indeed has the talent for lying, but the clumsy, stupid man lacks the finesse for tongue-in-cheek. Thus Granius and Vargula wanted to be clever and witty but were, as they say, buffoons instead.[213] When, however, this man, who brims with intrigues, fabricates these yarns and fantasies, and strives to distribute falsehoods as verities from the tavern of his ruminations, I admit to feeling sorry for his faults and at that moment I myself nearly weep for his blunders.

85 Yet I cannot keep from congratulating myself, because I see in our own time that the miracles of old, read about in Holy Writ, are being performed and are reappearing. For the Bible says that Balaam's ass spoke and that the ass articulated almost in a human voice words that it did not understand.[214] So our ass here (My! What ears he has!) quoted words to me that he could not understand: "Look at the heart and mind," he says, "the gods talk to at night."[215]

86 The blockhead believed that he had uttered a sacrilege, but instead he spoke the truth. My God himself speaks plainly to those whom he sees as most attentive to his worship and religion, and he does so not only at night, as Panormita says, but every single day, at all hours, and at any moment. God seems to remind and exhort men in my circumstances with the following words: "Blessed are you when men speak evil against you, and when they

---

[211]Gnatho is a parasite in Terence's *Eunuch*; the "Braggart Soldier" is the central character in Plautus' *Miles Gloriosus*.

[212]Juvenal 6.531; cf. Panormita *Etsi facile* §1 (Appendix I below).

[213]See Cicero *On the Orator* 2.60.244. Granius was a famous herald of the late Republic; Vargula was a friend of Julius Caesar.

[214]The ass, as the story goes, spoke to Balaam when he rode out to curse the Israelites at the Moabite King's request (Numbers 22.21–31).

[215]Juvenal 6.531; cf. Panormita *Etsi facile* §1 (Appendix I below).

maledixerint uobis homines, ac[180] *persecuti uos fuerint, et dixerint omne malum aduersum uos mentientes,*[181] *propter me: gaudete, et exultate, quoniam merces uestra copiosa est in caelis.*

970 **87** Subsurdasterne est an obstupescit? Et huiuscemodi sermones qui illi — modo audire uelit — qui mihi, qui mortalibus cunctis totiue[182] terrarum orbi ex deo dicuntur nihil intellegit? Numquid uelut illa Balaam asella quid ipse idem aut ceteri loquantur nihil agnoscit? Sed id certo unum habeat exploratum uelim: nisi aliquando
975 homo ipse profligatissimus resipiscat, ni in dies doleat, ni cito paeniteat, ni singulas noctes lectum suum lauerit lacrimisque stratum suum rigauerit, publicitus sibi suisque catamitis commilitonibusque deus ipse noster, aequissimus iudex, diem dicet. Clamabit enim uoce ualidissima: *Discedite a me, maledicti, in aeternum* et benemeritum
980 *ignem, paratum diabolo et* Panormitae et *angelis eius.*

88 Contremiscitne et horret?[183]

Steteruntne comae aut uox[184] *faucibus haesit?*

Haurit uerba quidem, qui tametsi est *homo trium litterarum*, non tamen auribus adhuc deminutus est. Quid ergo [A126r] frustra itaque,
985 ut aiunt, asello lyra sonat? Idcirco eius in aures non est tam lyra quam bucina aut sistro concrepandum. Non enim terrores, non minas, non iudicem illum ubi Crassus et Antonius muti futuri sunt magni pendit.

89 Quid miramur? Abduxit enimuero ab sacris litteris, *sibi soli* — paene Adonidi suo dixi — *sciolus*, prurientes illas aures suas.
990 Hieronymo, Augustino, Christianoque nomini [N105v] bellum indixit ab illorumque praeceptione, studio, doctrina prorsus abhorret; cui neque delicias huiuscemodi pro illius impuritate[185] delibare tributum est. Totus nimirum languet et euanescit in poesim. Quam poesim! Ad obscenos utique sermones ut agapeta quidam cum
995 Valerio Martiali natus est, Propertium atque Tibullum et huiusce factionis pompam infamem studio, fide, et amore lucubratiunculis chameuniisque[186] prosequitur, postume uero sancti Hermaphroditi libelli sui ita adulteriis stuprisque — turpiora enim missa facio sceleratioraque — detinetur, irretitur, eneruatur, ut omni tempore
1000 alienus suus numquam olim futurus esse uideatur.

[180]ac] et *N*
[181]metientes] -ense *N*
[182]totiue] toti uel *A*
[183]-ne et horret? *scripsi* : -ne exhorret? *AN*
[184]-runtque comae et uox *Verg.*
[185]impuritate] utilitate *N*
[186]chameuniis- *scripsi* : caumenis- *AN*

[216]Matthew 5.11–12.
[217]This is a direct quotation of Matthew 25.41 except for the addition of "Panormita."
[218]Virgil *Aeneid* 3.48.

persecute you and say all manner of evil against you for my sake: rejoice and be glad, because your reward is in heaven."[216]

87 Is Panormita going deaf or is he struck dumb? And does he not understand statements of this kind that God spoke to him (if he would but listen), to me, to all mortals, or to the whole world? Does he, like Balaam's ass, understand nothing of what either he himself or others are saying? But I would like him to hold one thing as absolutely certain, namely that, as a most depraved man, unless he come to his senses, unless he grieve, unless he repent, and unless he bathe his bed and moisten his blanket each night with tears, our God himself, the most equitable of judges, will publicly indict him, his catamites, and his comrades-in-arms. For he will cry with a loud voice: "Depart from me, you accursed, into the deserved eternal fire, prepared for the Devil, Panormita, and his angels."[217]

88 Does he tremble and shudder? "Did his hair stand up or his voice stick in his throat"?[218] He certainly absorbs the words since his ears have not yet shrunk, even though he is "a man of three letters."[219] So why then, as they say, does the lyre sound in vain for the ass?[220] Because one must not so much sound a lyre as blast a horn or clang a cymbal in his ears. For he pays little heed to terrors or to threats or to that Judge before whom even Crassus and Antonius are going to stand mute.[221]

89 Why do we marvel? Sure enough, he withdrew his itching ears from sacred letters,[222] "being a literary aesthete in his eyes only"[223] — I almost said in the eyes of his Adonis.[224] He declared war on Jerome, Augustine, and the Christian name and he completely recoiled from their precept, study, and teaching; and because of his impurity he is not allowed to taste such delicacies. Without a doubt he utterly languishes and becomes completely dissipated in writing poetry. And what poetry! As something of a panderer[225] along with Valerius Martial, he was born especially to write obscenities. And he studiously, faithfully, and lovingly pursues Propertius and Tibullus and the infamous procession of this faction, working long hours by lamplight and sleeping catch-as-catch-can.[226] But in the end he is so delayed, entangled, and enervated by the adulteries and illicit sex acts — I omit the more filthy and perverted aspects — of that wretched little book of his, the *Saint Hermaphrodite*, that it appears he will never again be estranged from it through all time.

---

[219]That is, *fur*, a thief or robber (see *Philippic* §53 n. 128).

[220]Jerome *Letter* 27.1.2 (cf. Wiesen 201).

[221]Crassus and Antonius were two Roman lawyers who became models of eloquence in Cicero's dialogues the *Brutus* and *The Orator*.

[222]Cf. II Timothy 4.3.

[223]Jerome *Letter* 50.22; *Against Helvidius* 1.17; and *Commentary on Ezechiel* 2.12 (cf. Wiesen 185).

[224]Adonis was Venus' handsome young lover, whom jealous Mars had killed by a wild boar. Here Rho uses the name for one of Panormita's young male lovers, Tomaso Tebaldi of Bologna, usually called by the nickname "Ergoteles" (see Introduction 33–34; cf. *Philippic* §54, §132).

[225]Rho (*Imitations* 127r: *Leno et Lena*, Appendix IX below): "An *agapeta* is an agent of lusts" (*Agapeta est conciliator libidinum*). Rho also gives another gloss (*Imitations* 133v–135r: *Luxuria*, Appendix IX below): "An *agapeta* is one who keeps company with women unlawfully" (*Agapeta qui cum mulieribus illicite conversatur*).

[226]*Chameunia* (χαμευνία) is a rare word that Rho would have found in Jerome (*Letter* 52.3) meaning literally "sleeping on the ground" (*super pavimentum dormitio*).

90 Ex his nunc familiaribus uerbis quo tela eius in frontem quae mihi statim iaciebat retorqueri sentiat. Versum in me decantatum in se decantari exaudiat: haud erit iniurium.

En animam (uidelicet) *et mentem cum qua dii nocte*
1005 *loquuntur.*

91 Sed num plures dei sui[187] extant numero aut dumtaxat unus est qui Panormitam hunc admittunt, ut mensis illorum accumbat quam familiariter epuleturque?[188] Vtrum noctu solum (uti de me mentitur) non autem interdiu illum e somno excitant conueniuntque?
1010 Expediat iam mihi deos ipsos, rogo. Etenim qui qualesue sint? Quo caelo inhabitent? An apud Perseum in septentrione, an apud Orionem in meridie, an in Zodiaco suo apud Virginem aut Aquarium suum Ganymedem edat uehementer expeto.[189] O iterum dixerim:[190]

animam et mentem cum qua dii nocte loquuntur!

1015 **92** Taceat tamen interloquendum; taceat e[191] cubili et contubernio suo diuam eiectam Pudicitiam collateraleque semper sibi infamiae suae sigillum illud, si sapit, aut celet aut mores, si queat, immutet.

93 Quid ut taceat persuadeo? In se quidem mutus[192] est; in
1020 alios, uelit nolit, dicacissimus uerbosissimusque. Atque cupisne declarem ita rem [A126v] suam ut quos sepultos et ignotos in hunc diem deos suos arbitratur in lucem coram prodire sentiat, siquidem dum famae ac nomini suo ut nunc et alias inimicus esset, honori quoque et integritati suae uir ipse perditus suo pro more, immo
1025 infelice natura, nihil inseruire seu consulere uideretur?

[187]dei sui *tr. N*
[188]epu-] expu- *N*
[189]expeto] expecto *N*
[190]iterum dixerim *tr. N*
[191]e *om. N*
[192]mutus] muta *N*

---

[227]Juvenal 6.531.
[228]Panormita writes (1429) to a certain Marcettus (Beccadelli 1746, 163–64 [3.25/i.e., 35]): "But if I have prevailed upon you on account of that kindness of yours in which you excel among mortals, I would believe myself to be have attained the life of the immortal gods: and that line of our poet I will often chant to you: 'You grant me a couch at the feasts of the gods' [Virgil *Aeneid* 1.79; LCL]. . . ." (*Quod si pro tua illa benignitate, qua inter mortales excellis, a te exoravero, vitam deorum immortalium adeptum me esse crediderim: illudque poetae nostri ad te saepius decantabo: "Tu das epulis accumbere divum. . . ."*). Cf. *Philippic* §93, §109, and §171.
[229]This allusion is remarkably cryptic, but Rho must have believed that those familiar with Panormita would catch the drift of his sarcastic remark. In this context "Ganymede" appears to be a sobriquet for someone (or someones), namely, Panormita's putative lovers: Ergoteles, that is, Tomaso Tebaldi da Bologna (Perseus?) and Hylas, that is, Enrico da Napoli (Orion?). If, on the other

PHILIPPIC AGAINST ANTONIO PANORMITA   113

90 From these familiar words let him now guess where into his line the spears that he just hurled at me are being thrown back. Let him hear the poetry that he chanted against me chanted against himself (it will not be unjust). That is to say, "Look at the heart and mind the gods talk to at night."[227]

91 But does Panormita have many gods who receive him, so that he reclines and feasts at their table so familiarly, or has he only one?[228] Do they rouse him from sleep and visit him only at night (as he says falsely about me) but not by day? Now let him explain those gods to me, please. Who or what, in fact, might they be? In what heaven might they dwell? I really want to know whether he produces his Ganymede with Perseus in the North, or with Orion in the South,[229] or in his Zodiac in the house of Virgo or Aquarius.[230] Well, I should say again: "Look at the heart and mind the gods talk to at night!"[231]

92 But let Panormita stop interrupting. Let him stop talking about the goddess Chastity whom he has evicted from his couch and tent. And if he has any sense, let him conceal the symbol of his infamy that is ever at his side,[232] or, if he can, let him change his behavior.

93 Why do I argue that he should be silent? To be sure, with himself he is mute, but with other people he is, willy-nilly, extremely talkative and verbose. And in fact, Candido, do you want me to reveal his affairs in a way that he will see those gods of his conjured up in broad daylight whom he supposes to be buried and unknown to this day?[233] I can do so, since — having both now and in times past been an enemy to his own fame and reputation — this debauched man, out of habit or rather out of his wretched nature, also seemed to care nothing for or to take any interest in his morality and integrity.

---

hand, "Ganymede" is a synonym for *The Hermaphrodite*, then Rho must be referring to the belief, expressed later by Lorenzo Valla (*Antidote against Facio* 4.14.2), that Panormita wrote the first book of his *Hermaphrodite* in Siena (Orion?), the second book in Bologna (Perseus?). The word *edat* (produces) is often — but not exclusively — used of literary production. The *arcana* behind these references can be found in the mythographer Hyginus, a copy of which was available in the Visconti library (Pellegrin 1955a, A 204). According to Hyginus (*Poetic Astronomy* 2.12), Perseus received the gifts of *talaria* and *petasus* (winged shoes and hat) from Mercury "who is thought to have loved him" (trans. Grant). Hyginus also reports (*Poetic Astronomy* 2.34) that "some say that Orion lived with Oenopion in too close intimacy" (trans. Grant). It seems nonsensical, however, that Rho would make a coded insult so arcanely cryptic.

[230]This allusion is even more cryptic than the former. It must be some inside joke for which critical information is now lacking. The *arcana* for this reference would seem to reveal nothing at all: the mythographers (following Ovid *Metamorphoses* 1.150) say that Aquarius is Ganymede; Virgo is Astraea, or Justice, the last immortal to leave earth.

[231]Juvenal 6.531.

[232]Rho is alluding to Panormita's young male lover, Ergoteles (see Introduction 33–34 above; *Philippic* §89 n. 224 and §132 n. 338). In referring to him as a "symbol" (*sigillum*) always at Panormita's side, Rho alludes to Zeus' abduction of Ganymede. Cf., for example, Prudentius (*Crowns of Martyrdom* 10.233–34): "What does the symbol of the attendant bird mean that is always attached to Jupiter?" (*Quid vult sigillum semper adfixum Iovi / avis ministrae?*) These symbols become part of the standard artistic representation of gods and legendary heros (for representations of Ganymede in Renaissance art, see Saslow; in Greek art, see Kempter).

[233]Cf. *Philippic* §91, §109, and §171.

94 Aurispa, uir utriusque linguae perbelle imbutus; uir, inquam, haud minus eloquens quam modestus et frugi, cui uel grauitas comitasque sine discrimine[193] ab Cicerone indultae esse uideantur, hunc Panormitam[194] quadam epistola uerbis non mediocribus alloquebatur dicens: *Vale, mi Panormita, et Adonidem carum habe. Sed ita carum tamen ut neque amori tuo erga amicos tuos*[195] *officiat nec dignitati. Quod utinam*, ait, *fieri possit.*

95 Egregie quidem, mi Candide, probe, sancte. Item idem Aurispa ad eundem Siculum, post Adonidis conciliatos non sine negotio parentes — optimi enim cuiusque uiri est lites pro uirili componere — ita inquit:[196] *Tuum ergo officium, Panormita, erit ita puerum Adonidem docere ut pater uult, immo ut facis. Plura enim facis quam pater ipse postulet, immo multo magis tu Adonidem tuum amas quam aut parentes aut germani.*

96 Ridesne an horres Candide? Coniecta, nunc Aurispam audisti, quem deum amicus noster exardeat. Item alia[197] epistola ita scribit: *Aurispa Antonio Panormitae suauissimo poetae et fatuo uiro, immo stulto et furioso, salutem plurimam cupit et fortunam felicem. Cogita tute tecum, Panormita, an ueris nominibus te appellem.* Et infra: *Feci Adonidis patrem ex atroci et infensissimo tibi mitem*[198] *et amicissimum; feci Adonidis auiam*[199] *ex tristi et lacrimosa iucundam et laetam. Esto igitur securus Adonidis.*

97 Putabam, mi Candide, exactis iam prioribus saeculis istunc Adonidem fato suo functum esse. Hieronymus enim meus, quo non minus ac Cicerone quam familiariter utor, ad Paulinum in haec uerba scribit: *Ab Adriani temporibus usque ad imperium Constantini per annos circiter centum octuaginta in loco resurrectionis*[200] *simulacrum Iouis, in crucis rupe statua ex marmore Veneris a gentilibus posita colebatur, existimantibus persecutionis auctoribus quod tollerent nobis fidem resurrectionis et crucis, si loca sancta per idola polluissent. Bethleem nunc nostram, et augustissimum orbis locum de quo Dauid canit:* [A127r] *"ueritas de terra orta est,"*[201] *lucus inumbrabat* ⟨. . .⟩ *Adonidis, et in specu ubi quondam Christus paruulus* natus est, *Veneris amasius plangebatur.*

---

[193]discrimine] -minatione *N*
[194]Panormitam] -mita *N*
[195]tuos *om. N*
[196]ita inquit *om. N*
[197]Item alia *Sabb.* : Ita alia *AN*
[198]mitem] mittem *A*
[199]auiam] auam *N*
[200]resurrecti-] -rexi-*N*
[201]est *Hier.* : *om. AN*

94 Aurispa[234] is a man with excellent training in both languages[235] and a man, I say, who is no less eloquent than restrained and earnest, and who is endowed with a gravity and courteousness akin to that of Cicero's. In one of his letters he addressed Panormita in the following extraordinary terms, to wit: "Farewell to my Panormita, and hold Adonis dear.[236] But hold him dear in such a way that he does not become an obstacle either to your love for your friends or to your dignity." He added, "Would that it could be done."[237]

95 Aurispa spoke remarkably well, my Candido: properly and virtuously too. Likewise, after Aurispa had won over Adonis' parents with some difficulty (for to the best of their ability virtuous men compose quarrels), Aurispa said the following to the same Sicilian: "Therefore your duty, Panormita, shall be to teach the boy Adonis in the way his father wishes, in fact as you are doing. For you do many more things than his father demands; indeed, you love your Adonis much more than either his parents or siblings do."[238]

96 Do you laugh or shudder, Candido? Now that you have heard Aurispa, guess what god our friend carries a torch for. Again in another letter Aurispa writes this: "Aurispa wishes well-being and good fortune to Antonio Panormita, the sweetest poet and fatuous man, indeed, a foolish and mad one. Consider for yourself, Panormita, whether I could call you truer names."[239] And later he added: "I have turned Adonis' father from a man furious and bitterly hostile into one gentle and most friendly; I have turned Adonis' grandmother from a woman sad and crying into one delightful and cheerful. Therefore, rest assured about Adonis."[240]

97 I used to think, my Candido, that this Adonis had already met his fate many centuries ago. For my Jerome, with whom I am on no less familiar terms than with Cicero, makes this statement when writing to Paulinus: "From Hadrian's time right up to the reign of Constantine,[241] or for about a hundred and eighty years, an image of Jove was worshiped on the location of the resurrection, while the pagans placed a marble statue of Venus on the promontory of the crucifixion. The instigators of the persecution thought that they would take away our faith in the crucifixion and resurrection if they polluted the holy sites with idols. At that same time a grove of Adonis shaded our Bethlehem, even the world's most sacred place, about which David chanted: 'Truth has risen from the earth,' and Venus' lover, Adonis, was mourned in the cave where the infant Christ was once born."[242]

---

[234]Giovanni Aurispa (ca. 1372–1460) was another Sicilian expatriate, a teacher of Greek, and translator of Lucian (Marsh 1998a; and Sabbadini 1890). Although some letters of Aurispa do survive (Sabbadini 1931), those cited here seem not to be extant.

[235]That is, Latin and Greek.

[236]See Introduction 33–34 above; and *Philippic* §132 n. 338.

[237]Aurispa's lost letter?

[238]Aurispa's lost letter?

[239]Aurispa's lost letter? Rho takes the term *furiosus* as emphasizing Panormita's madness, ridiculing Panormita supposed "inspired mania." Cf. *Philippic* §14 n. 36, §62, §161, and §178.

[240]Aurispa's lost letter?

[241]The Roman Emperor Hadrian died in 138 CE; Constantine became Emperor in 306 CE.

[242]Jerome *Letter* 58.3; cf. Psalms 84/85.12.

98 Putabam, iterum inquam, fato suo functum esse. [N106r] Sed ecce, a morte suscitatus est neque posthac est mortem oppetiturus! Sit itaque — ut Aurispa ait — *securus Adonidis*. Pro immundissimum, inquinatissimum, spurcissimum hominem!

99 Sed iterum atque iterum Aurispam exaudias uelim: subblandiri Panormitae ipse uidetur, quem tamen et mordet et damnat. Eum enim ita alloquitur: *Verum illud scio, Panormita, Musas scilicet elegorum fautrices odio uirgines habere. Pontanus uero non modo uirgo est, sed ab omni Venere abhorret. Tu, Panormita, qui in ea re palmam habes, rescribe an Pontanus admitti debeat in numero[202] eorum qui elegos faciunt Musis gratos.*

100 Ex his, mi Candide, cumulus sanctitatis hauriendus est. Palmam enim elegorum Aurispa docente Panormita noster habet. Consequens fit ut uirginitatis omnisque[203] castimoniae insidiator sit: Adonidis sui quoque[204] elegos decantarit, quin immo, quasi alter Heluidius, templum domini, sacrarium Spiritus Sancti, uidelicet Virginem Matrem cognitam a sponso Ioseph[205] esse contendat.[206]

101 Pro sordidum elegum plagiariumque! Quo se uertat nescit. Vndique in angustias truditur. Video iam quemadmodum obstupe⟨sc⟩at, occidat, pereat, dicatque gemebundus: "Hem, istuc unde ut in me tam scite tu, Raudensis, irrepas illabarisque, animum uel meum intus unus scruteris, uiscera penitissima intellegas? Quis me tibi tam apertum et notum praestitit? tam familiarem, tam meimet copiosum fecit, ut aeque luculente[207] Raudensi e specula tua scelera mea conspicarere[208] atque ipse conspicor? Vtrum clanculo[209] cubiculum meum[210] irrupisti? Vtrum clitellas in Helicone meas aut cassidiles et sitarchias euoluisti? Et, ut apertius dixerim, numquid manticas meas — ubi infamis Hermaphroditus meus lugebat — atque sarcinulas meas excussisti?"

102 Quid enim demiratur se sciri, se[211] palpari, Siculus iste, qui in commune et sub diuo undique effluit et Italiae angulis

---

[202]numero] -rum *A*
[203]omnis] hominis *A*
[204]quoque] *s.l. suppl. A*
[205]sponso Ioseph *tr. N*
[206]contendat] -tendebat *N*
[207]luculente] -lent *N*
[208]conspicarere] -care *N*
[209]clanculo] -cule *N*
[210]meum *om. N*
[211]se *N* : si *A*

---

[243]Aurispa's lost letter?
[244]Probably Francesco Pontano, who, along with his brother Lodovico, was a friend and sometime correspondent with Panormita (Sabbadini 1890, 155, 205–06; Cinquini and Valentini 49–50).

98 I used to think, I repeat, that Adonis had met his fate. But look how he has returned from the dead and will never again face death! Let Panormita then, as Aurispa said, "rest assured about Adonis."[243] What an utterly foul, filthy, and nasty man!

99 But, Candido, I want you to hear Aurispa say this over and over. He appears to flatter Panormita, whom he still both criticizes and condemns. In fact, Aurispa said this to him: "I know it to be true, Panormita, that the Muses — namely, the patrons of elegiac verse — hold virgins in contempt. Yet Pontano[244] is not only a virgin but also recoils from all sexual activity. You, Panormita, who hold the prize in this, write back to me whether Pontano ought to be admitted into the circle of those who compose elegiac verse, favored by the Muses."[245]

100 From these letters, my Candido, we must draw out the full measure of his virtue. For as Aurispa informs us, our Panormita holds the prize in elegiac poetry. Consequently, Panormita is someone who lies in wait to ambush virginity and every sort of chastity. He also recites the elegiac poetry of his Adonis, or even worse, he contends, like another Helvidius, that the temple of the Lord, the sanctuary of the Holy Spirit, that is, the Virgin Mother, was known by her husband Joseph.[246]

101 What a sordid elegiac poet and child abductor! He does not know where to turn. He is forced from all sides into a corner. Now I see how he becomes befuddled, collapses, withers, and groans aloud: "Where did you get this ability, Rho, that you so cleverly and stealthily slip inside of me or are the only one to probe deep into my mind and understand my innermost heart? Who rendered me such an open book to you? Who made me such a confidant of yours and who made me spill so much about myself to you that from your luminous Rhodense lookout you observe my perversions as well as I observe them myself? Have you secretly broken into my bedroom? Have you rifled through my packsaddle or game and bread bags on Mount Helicon?[247] And finally, to speak more plainly, have you shaken out my packs and bags on the site where my infamous *Hermaphrodite* grieved?"[248]

102 Well, why is this Sicilian astonished that he is known and flattered considering that he is publicly gossiped about everywhere and in broad daylight and

---

In a letter to Sancio Balbo, Panormita described Francesco as "mad now for a year from a love potion" (Sabbadini 1910a, 142).

[245] Aurispa's lost letter?

[246] Helvidius was a fourth-century Latin theologian, who defended marriage and refused to recognize virginity as a more virtuous state. He also denied the perpetual virginity of Mary, the mother of Jesus (Kelly 104–07). We know his thought almost exclusively from his adversaries, Jerome (*Against Helvidius*) and Augustine (*On Heretics* 84). If Rho has a specific statement of Panormita in mind, it seems forever lost to us. Rho may have simply extrapolated from Panormita's "contempt for virginity," perhaps as expressed by Panormita's *persona dramatis* in Lorenzo Valla's *On Pleasure* (see *Philippic* §132 n. 346), that Panormita believed (like Helvidius) that Mary did not remain a virgin.

[247] Mount Helicon was the haunt of the Muses.

[248] Rho (using *luget* instead of Panormita's *taedet*, *pudet*, and *piget*) must be alluding to Panormita's statement (*Etsi facile* §2, Appendix I below) and to a similar one in a letter to Giovanni Lamola (see *Philippic* §62 n. 146; cf. also *Philippic* §119).

omnibus[212] quam Ciceroni Antonius aut Catilina sit notior. Nonne nomen ex Romanis illis antiquis sortitus est ut iam dicatur *Publius Antonius Panormita* (paene dixi [A127v] *Publicus*)? Haec ipsa tamen, suauissime Candide, quae hoc loco attigimus sunt ex densissima flagitiorum suorum silua decisi infirmiores ramusculi haud nulli ac pauculi quidem.

103 Sed ad sigillum unde digressi sumus redeundum arbitror. Vbi tamen, quo iam intellegar nihilo luculentius, dixerim oportet[213] satis ac super res innotescit, et quid sibi sigillum hoc[214] ipsum[215] uelit, tametsi Aurispa sileat, nemo non intellegit. Illud enimuero quasi diuinum quiddam homo is petulans et eneruis in deliciis habet, quo uelut ultimo fine et[216] bono fruitur, quoue ne hora Chaldaica quidem quominus lateri suo inhaereat carere potest. O mores taetros! O tempora non indigna fulminibus! Atque audi ridiculum, immo impudentiam inauditam intuearis, rogo. Deierat enim se, hercle, admodum timere (idcirco collaterale semper habet) ne noctu clanculo a plagiariis sibi aut abigeis auferatur quo sublato prae Venere ipse tum pereat. O iterum dixerim impudentiam inauditam! Cicero in oratione Pro Caelio excusationes has et apologias non nescisse uidetur. *Propter nescio quam, credo* — inquit — *timiditatem et nocturnos quosdam inanes metus tecum semper pusio cubitauit.* Sed uel Iunius tametsi mordeat subblandiri creditur[217] dum ait:

Nonne putas melius, quod tecum pusio dormit?

104 Recte iam teneo quos angulos, quos recessus petiturus sit. Quid recessus? Sane quidem quorsum exeat quorsumue palam uir prodigus et infrenis prodeat. Fortasse intimius atque ipse uellet illum[218] intellego. Non enim dicet:

"*Formosum pastor Corydon ardebat Alexin*"?

Inuolucris enim integumentisque sermo bucolicus scatet sine

---

[212]angulis omnibus *A* : undique angulis omnibus *N*
[213]oportet] -or- *s.l. suppl. A*
[214]hoc] *s.l. suppl. N*
[215]ipsum] ipsi *N*
[216]et] ac *N*
[217]tametsi . . . creditur] subblaniri creditur tum etsi mordeat *N*
[218]uellet illum *tr. N*

---

[249]I have found no information corroborating Rho's statement that Panormita took the ancient Roman name "Publio." Nor is it readily apparent why Panormita would have styled himself this way, unless perhaps in imitation of Virgil's praenomen. Rho's pun, however, twists the respectability of an old Roman name into ridicule of Panormita's notoriety.

[250]Cf. *Philippic* §92.

may be better known in every corner of Italy than Mark Antony or Catiline was to Cicero. He chose, did he not, from the ancient Romans the name he is now called by, "Publio Antonio Panormita"? (I almost said "Publico.")[249] Yet, dearest Candido, the things that we have touched on here are some, indeed only a few, of the punier twigs cut from the dense forest of his indecencies.

103 But I am resolved to return to the symbol whence we digressed.[250] To be understood now as clearly as possible on this matter, I must say, nevertheless, that it is known well enough and more than well enough, and everyone understands what the symbol itself stands for even if Aurispa remains silent. Indeed, wanton and weak, Panormita is enraptured with that symbol as if it were something divine, so that he enjoys it as the supreme end and good or so that he cannot suffer it to leave his side even for a Chaldean Hour.[251] What foul ways! What an age! Worthy of being struck by lightning![252] And so listen to the absurd man, or rather, please, mark his shocking effrontery. He keeps Adonis constantly by his side because he swears that he is, by god, in absolute fear that kidnappers or cattle rustlers will secretly steal Adonis from him during the night and with him taken away he would himself die as did Venus.[253] Again I say, what shocking effrontery! Cicero in his oration *In Defense of Caelius* seems aware of these excuses and apologies. "I believe," he said, "on account of some cowardice and certain fatuous nocturnal fears, a small boy always slept with you."[254] But even though Juvenal makes cutting remarks,[255] he too is believed to be pandering when he says: "Do you not think it better that a little boy sleep with you?"[256]

104 I now rightly grasp what nooks and crannies he is going to seek out. What nooks am I alluding to? Certainly, the very ones from which the extravagant and unrestrained man may come out or openly reveal himself. Perhaps I understand him more profoundly than he would like. Will he not of course say: "'The shepherd Corydon burned for the handsome Alex'"?[257] He will reiterate, as he often does elsewhere, "For under its covers and wrappings, bucolic language gushes forth without deceit and riddles."[258] Indeed, he wrote

---

[251]There were some twenty different methods of dividing the hours in the Renaissance. The Chaldean hour was the shortest method of calculating an individual hour. The Chaldean system divided the night and the day into twelve equal segments that varied in length throughout the year as days and nights grew shorter or longer. Minutes and seconds existed as theoretical concepts but were not a measurable unit of time until mechanical clocks became common. (I thank Kristen Lippincott for this information.)

[252]Cf. Martial 9.70.1 and 9.70.5.

[253]For Adonis see n. 224 above. Rho probably confuses the story (perhaps intentionally) with that of Hylas, the young, beautiful companion of Hercules. Hylas was stolen by the Nymphs, and Hercules thereafter long sought for him. Both nicknames were used for one of Panormita's young male lovers, Tomaso Tebaldi of Bologna, usually called by the nickname "Ergoteles" (see Introduction 33–34 above; cf. *Philippic* §54, §132 n. 338).

[254]Cicero *In Defense of Caelius* 15.36.

[255]"Makes cutting remarks": that is, Juvenal wrote satire attacking Roman society and customs.

[256]Juvenal 6.34.

[257]Virgil *Eclogues* 2.1.

[258]Rho is almost certainly quoting from a lost letter or letters of Panormita (see Introduction 32–33 above).

1120 fuco, sine[219] aenigmate," ut saepe alias iterum loquetur. Platonem enimuero, quasi aliena macula sine uitio maculam suam diluere credat, sibi assimilem scrib⟨eb⟩at. Atque ob id istuc quidem quod in huiuscemodi sermonem aliquando ceciderit:

> *dum semihiulco suauio*
> 1125 *puellum meum suauior,*
> *dulcemque florem spiritus*
> *duco, et aperto tramite*
> *anima aegra saucia*
> *cucurrit ad labias mihi,*

1130 et huiusce impudentiae obscenitatisque multa quae sequuntur. Fatebor nimirum iam pridem quae Plato scribit mihi haud incognita, quandoquidem et Noctes Atticas Satur[A128r]naliaque, ubi aeque istaec habentur, me praetextatum et a puero lectitasse commemini.

105 Atqui audiat uelim quid ad Theodo[N106v]sium clarissi-
1135 mum Imperatorem Mediolanensis noster Ambrosius, uir utique omni sanctitate praeditus, doctrina conspicuus, seueritate rigidus responderit. Cum enim Imperator ille, uti scelus suum alieni sceleris purgaret, exemplo Dauid Regis adulterium simul et homicidium interexcusandum obiecisset, inquiens quod nihilo setius propheta
1140 summus[220] euasisset, "Quid excusas aut purgas te?" inquit Ambrosius. "*Secutusne es errantem? Sequere paenitentem.*"[221]

106 Aeque et huic Platonis abortiuo discipulo dicamus licebit: "Si Platonem errantem illum lasciuientemque ad hunc diem prosecutus es, ipsum nunc aemulare philosophantem." Sed Panormita homo
1145 istic ambagiosus[222] est et nihili. Quid enim Platonis uulnera, si quae[223] tamen illa fuere, impudens tam temere tam fidenter exulcerat? Non tibi uisum est latrantem hanc lyciscam procacem quidem, in[224] iniurias et conuicia semper armatam, modo linguam, modo dentes passim exacuere? Pro mulierosum et quasi longaeuae meretricis attrita
1150 fronte inconsideratum hominem. Non pudet per os foetidum suum

---

[219]sine . . . sine] siue . . . siue *N*
[220]summus *scripsi* : sumus *AN*
[221]paenitentem *AN* : corrigentem *Ambr.*
[222]amba-] ambi- *N*
[223]quae] qua *N*
[224]in *om. N*

[259]Cf. Panormita *Etsi facile* §1 (Appendix I below). In a letter to Poggio, Panormita (*Epistolae tuae* 30–46) explained the poetic tradition of *lascivia* at length and enumerated the authors who used this language.
[260]This quotation of Pseudo-Plato comes from Aulus Gellius 19.11; cf. Macrobius *Saturnalia* 2.2.15. For Ps.-Plato and the use of this verse, see Gaisser 249. See Panormita 1990b, 39–46 for the statement to which Rho is referring.

that Plato was similar to him, as if he believes another's stain cleanses his own without a trace.[259] And this explains why, of course, Plato on occasion lapsed into speech like this: "While I kiss my boy with half-parted kiss and inhale the sweet flower of his breath, my anxious, stricken heart runs to my lips on an open path."[260] Then many things follow of a shameless and obscene nature. To be sure, I will confess that I have for a long time now been aware of what Plato wrote inasmuch as I remember that as a boy and as a youth I read the *Attic Nights*[261] and the *Saturnalia*,[262] both of which include these verses.

105 All the same, I wish he would listen to what our Ambrose of Milan, a man especially endowed with every sanctity, eminent in teaching, and unwavering in austerity, responded to the celebrated Emperor Theodosius.[263] For when the emperor, to justify his own crime with that of another, brought up as an excuse the example of King David's adultery and homicide saying that nonetheless he had ended up a great prophet. Ambrose responded: "Why do you excuse or justify yourself?[264] Have you followed the sinner? Follow the penitent."[265]

106 Likewise, we too will be at liberty to say to this aborted disciple of Plato: "If to this day you have followed the Plato who sins and lusts, imitate now the Plato who philosophizes." But this man Panormita is ever evasive and worthless. For why does this shameless man so recklessly, so boldly exacerbate Plato's wounds, if they really existed?[266] Does it not seem to you, Candido, that this uncontrolled, barking wolf-dog, is relentlessly on the prowl snapping and snarling, at one moment growling ferociously, at another flashing his fangs at everything? What a womanizer and witless human being with a furrowed brow like an aged

---

[261]Aulus Gellius (fl. ca. 170), the author of the *Attic Nights*, quotes and comments on history, law, poetry, philosophy, grammar, literary criticism, and textual questions. For many authors or works (Latin and Greek) we have only the fragments that are preserved in his quotations, including this passage from Ps.-Plato (Conte 583–84; see *Apology* §22).

[262]Ambrosius Theodosius Macrobius, the author of the *Saturnalia*, is variously identified as the Macrobius serving as Prefect of Spain in 399 or the Theodosius serving as Praetorian Prefect of Italy in 430. Following one hypothesis or the other, his *Saturnalia* are dated 330–40 or 384–95. The difference in the dating of the *Saturnalia* allow it to be interpreted "as one of the last cries of a paganism that is embattled in defense of its values" or alternatively "as the idealized representation . . . of an epoch now closed, whose cultural it wishes to preserve for posterity" (Conte 629–32, quotation 630; cf. *Apology* §18 and §22).

[263]In addition to Ambrose's statement, Rho echoes the language of Paul of Milan (*Life of St. Ambrose* 14.24).

[264]Ambrose *Apology for the Prophet David* 1.4.15; cf. also Ambrose *Letter* 51.

[265]Ambrose *On the Education of a Virgin* 4.31. That is, "You have imitated David in his sinning, now imitate him in his penance."

[266]Rho suggests that this erotic homosexual verse attributed to Plato may be apocryphal, which in fact it is (see Gaisser 249). Rho's observation is perhaps astute, but since he nowhere else demonstrates special insight into Plato's *corpus*, one suspects that he doubted its authenticity simply as a matter distaste for its content.

spurcumque philosophum tam illustrem et sputo et spuma sui oris inuoluere?

107 Quid non me ut iam taceam dimittit? Ex his certo, mihi crede, unus est quos in Epidico Plautus suus reprehendit:

1155   *Plerique omnes sunt* (ait), *quos cum nihil refert pudet;*
       ubi pudendum est, ibi eos deserit pudor.

Cicero namque, Augustinus imprimis, Hieronymus uel ipse meus tametsi Aristotelem, facile omnium principem, efferant, Platonem unum tamen[225] semper excerpunt. Hic uero, quasi Areopagita nouus, sententia sua atque iudicio tanti philosophi nomen et gloriam deformabit atque uelut infamem ex academia sua, homo ut est masculini generis non communis, illum eiiciet?

108 Ah, ueniae quidem locus his pro rebus inuentus est. Quorsum? Errorem enim priuati hominis ipse homo petulans libidinosusque non philosophi sanctam professionem, non maiestatem[226] amplectitur, uitium quoque ipsum, non doctrinam, non immutatos castigatosque mores aemulatur. Ex quibus oritur ut haud minus in Panormitae pudicitiam ipse Cicero uideatur inuehi quam in Pisonem inuectus est. [A128v] Stomachatus tunc estne Cicero minime? Sed oratoris officio defunctus est. *Admissarius iste,* Piso uidelicet — sic[227] enim aiebat Cicero — *simulatque audiuit uoluptatem a philosopho tantopere laudari* (Audisne, Panormita?), *nihil expiscatus est, sed sic*[228] *suos uoluptarios*[229] *sensus omnis incitauit, sed ad illius orationem adhinniit, ut non magistrum uirtutis, sed auctorem libidinis a se illum inuentum arbitraretur.*

109 Quo feror? Non tamen ita omnino cum pudicitia, ut uulgo de se dicitur, pudorem aut ueram religionem abiecit; non ita superstitione ulla noua distrahitur afficiturque, quin, praeter Iouis Catamitum illum (paene dixi Veneris Adonidem) alios quoque deos, nihili tamen sunt, uano et inani cultu reuereatur. Musas etenim Sicelidas, tametsi agrestes et impudicas, et Panormitam Apollinem quendam, Hermaphroditum imprimis uel ipsum suum, quod sibi[230] honores olim amplissimos immortalemque sui nominis famam polliceantur, deos suos esse gloriatur et iactat. O fortunatum poetam, melioribus quidem annis exortum! Numquamne — modo dii illi sui aliquid possint ac bene uortant[231] — ex hominum memoria oblitterandum?

---

[225] unum tamen] ᵇtamen ᵃunum *corr. A*
[226] maiestatem *N* : mages- *A*
[227] sic] sicut *N*
[228] sic] hic *N*
[229] uoluptarios] -tua- *A*
[230] sibi] si *N*
[231] uortant] uomitat *N*

courtesan!²⁶⁷ Is he not ashamed to involve such an illustrious philosopher with the spit and drool of his fetid, filthy mouth?²⁶⁸

107 Why does he not leave me alone so that I can finally keep quiet? Believe me, he is without a doubt one of those people whom his Plautus censures in *Epidicus:* "Most people," Plautus says, "feel shame about insignificant things; but where shame is necessary, there shame deserts them."²⁶⁹ For although Cicero, Augustine above all, and even my own Jerome praise Aristotle, who is easily the prince of all [philosophers], they nonetheless always make an exception of Plato alone. But will Panormita, as if a new member of the Areopagus,²⁷⁰ dishonor the name and fame of such a great philosopher by issuing a sentence and judgment, and will this man, as an exceptional example of manliness, eject Plato, from his own Academy disgraced?

108 Ah, to be sure, there was a certain tolerance of such behavior. So what? Our man Panormita, of course, being lewd and lecherous, embraces the error of the private man rather than the sacred profession and majesty of the philosopher; he imitates his vice, not his teaching, not his strict and unwavering character. The result is that Cicero himself seems to rail no less against Panormita's chastity than he does against Piso. Was Cicero a bit angry at the time? Yes, but he was fulfilling the responsibilities of an orator. For as Cicero said: "This stud (namely Piso), as soon as he heard that a philosopher had praised pleasure so much" (are you listening, Panormita?), "did no research, but instead so stimulated all his sensations of pleasure and whinnied so much at the philosopher's discourse, that he thought he had discovered in him not a master of virtue but an expert on lust."²⁷¹

109 Where am I headed? I am saying that he has not, however, so completely cast off shame and true religion along with chastity, as is commonly said about him, and he is not so distracted or influenced by any new superstition, that he does not also with a vain and empty admiration revere other gods — though they are worthless — in addition to Jove's Catamite (I almost said Venus' Adonis).²⁷² In fact, he gloats and brags that his gods are the Sicilian Muses, rustic and shameless though they be, and a certain Apollo of Palermo,²⁷³ and most especially even his very own *Hermaphrodite*, because they promise him a great multitude of honors some day and the immortal fame of his name. What a fortunate poet, to have been born in these better times! Will his name never — provided that those gods of his can do anything and be of any use — be obliterated from human memory?

---

²⁶⁷The image of the "furrowed," "worn," or "hardened brow" (*frons attrita*) is Jerome's Vulgate rendering of Ezekiel 3:7–9; which indicates obstinacy or stubbornness (cf. Jerome *Commentary on Ezekiel* 3:7–9; *Commentary on Zacharia* 3; and Wiesen 211).

²⁶⁸Cf. Jerome *Letter* 109.1 (against Vigilantius). For references to the "impure mouth" (*os impurum*) in Roman invectives as allusions to fellatio, cunnilingus, or anilingus, see Richlin 1983, 26–29, and index; cf. also *Philippic* §137. Both manuscripts A and N mark this as a question, not a statement. The question mark was used as a sign of wonderment, so perhaps this statement should be regarded as an exclamation.

²⁶⁹Plautus *Epidicus* 166a–166b.

²⁷⁰The Areopagus was the highest Athenian judicial court, which met on the Hill of Ares (Mars' Hill).

²⁷¹Cicero *Against Piso* 69. The philosopher in question is Epicurus.

²⁷²Cf. *Philippic* §91, §93, and §171.

²⁷³This sarcastic reference is perhaps to Panormita himself. Cf. *Philippic* §110 below, where Rho makes a similar sarcastic remark about "the Apollo of Sicily."

110 Sed quos cachinnos et plausus audio? Aha, aha, hehe! Musae ab Helicone profecto et Apollo Delphicus sacro suo risere sacello aiuntque: "Videat hic *mutus Quintilianus*, immo raucus Vergilius, ne huiuscemodi expectatione[232] frustretur, ne Musas, immo picas illas elegiacas, et Apollinem illum Siculum, Hermaphroditum[233] quoque, ac sempiternam illam famam in sempiternum fumum infensus sibi deus aliquando reiiciat, mittaturque postume cum libellis obscenis ac futilibus epistolis

> *in uicum* (ut Flaccus ait) *uendentem thus et odores*
> *et piper et quicquid cartis amicitur ineptis.*"

111 *En* (iam itaque) *animam et mentem cum qua dii nocte loquuntur!*

112 Sed uenio nunc ad illum litterulae suae laborem ultimum[234] ubi inuidiam sibi tantopere molestam esse conqueritur; qua se morderi et angi tam aegre fert.[235] Verum si illis in suis quas ad me [N107r] dedit litterulis non me haesitabundus ast alios criminatur, ipsi uiderint. Sin uero me sibi inuidere posse persuasum habet, dicat rogo, cum nequeam ipse utique non admirari, dicat rogo qui fieri possit. Quae enim conuentio lucis ad tenebras, Christi ad Belial esse potest? Quale fuerit commercium Christi ipsius ad Herculem [A129r] aut Francisci mei ad Apollinem, quae *magis portenta* — ut Hieronymus ait — *quam nomina* esse uidentur?

Qvarta Objectio

113 At quorsum uir iste insaniat qui sibi inuideri posse arbitratur, iam satis luculenteque aucupari uideor. *Quomodo* enim *Euphorbus in Pythagora renatus esse* uulgo dicitur. Sic iste se Hippiam Eleum Stoicum esse quidem arbitratur; animum uel ipsius[236] ac mentem cum doctrinis uniuersis et artibus in ipsum transmigrasse credit. Qui *cum Olympiam uenisset* — ut ait Cicero — *illa quinquennali celebritate ludorum, omni paene Graecia audiente gloriatus est nihil quicquam esse ulla in arte rerum omnium quod ipse nesciret, nec solum has artes quibus liberales doctrinae atque ingenue continerentur, geometriam, musicam, litterarum cognitionem et poetarum, atque illa quae de naturis rerum, quae de hominum moribus, quae de rebus publicis dicerentur, sed anulum quem haberet, palliastrum quo amictus, soccos quibus indutus esset, se sua manu confecisse.*

---

[232]expecta-] expta- *N*
[233]Hermaphroditum *om. N*
[234]laborem ultimum] ᵇultimum ᵃlaborem *corr. A*
[235]fert] *corr. A*
[236]ipsius] illius *N*

110 But what is all this laughter and applause that I hear? "Ha, Ha, Ha! Whooee!" Undoubtedly it is the Muses from Helicon and Apollo of Delphi in his sacred shrine laughing and saying: "Let this 'tongue-tied Quintilian,'[274] or rather this croaking Virgil, beware that he not delude himself with such expectations. Let him beware lest God being furious with him one day consign to eternal flames the Muses (or rather those elegiac magpies), the Apollo of Sicily, *The Hermaphrodite* also, and his eternal fame. And finally let him be sent along with his obscene books and futile letters 'into the street' — as Horace said — 'where they sell frankincense, aromatic spices, and pepper and wrap it all with pages of hapless literature.'"[275]

111 Now "look at the heart and mind the gods talk to at night!"[276]

The Fourth Objection

112 But I come now to the last labor of his wretched little letter, where he complains bitterly that envy so annoys him and where he reports that he is so painfully stung and tormented. But if in that wretched little letter sent to me, he in fits and starts accuses others as well as me, they themselves will see it.[277] If, however, he is persuaded that I can envy him, please let him, yes, please let him tell us how, since I myself at least cannot help but wonder at it. For what association has light with darkness, Christ with Belial?[278] What fellowship has Christ with Hercules or my Francis with Apollo,[279] who seem to be, as Jerome says, "portents rather than names."[280]

113 But now I think I grasp clearly enough why this man raves and supposes that he can be envied. For the story is commonly told "how Euphorbus was reborn in Pythagoras."[281] So Panormita supposes that he is the Stoic Hippias of Elis[282] and even believes that Hippias' soul and mind along with all his tenets and methods have transmigrated into him. As Cicero says: "When Hippias had come to Olympia for the five-year gathering of the games, he gloated with almost all of Greece listening that there was nothing in any universal art that he did not know. For he had mastered not only those arts that constitute learning for the genteel and free-born — geometry, music, knowledge of literature and poetry — as well as those that pronounce on the nature of things, on human customs, and on public affairs, but also that he himself had made with his own hands the ring he had on, the cloak he was dressed in, and the shoes he wore."[283]

---

[274]Jerome *Against Vigilantius* 1 (cf. Wiesen 222–23).

[275]Horace *Epistle* 2.1.269–70.

[276]Juvenal 6.531.

[277]Panormita *Etsi facile* §2 (Appendix I below).

[278]Belial was an ancient Semitic name for "the chief of evil spirits" (Deuteronomy 13.13), which in later times came to mean "Satan."

[279]Cf. Jerome *Letter* 22.29; and II Corinthians 6.14–15.

[280]Jerome *Letter* 75.3; cf. *Philippic* §77.

[281]Jerome *Against Vigilantius* 1.15; cf. Iamblichus *On Pythagoras* 14.63 and Porphyry *On Pythagoras* 26, 27, and 45.

[282]Hippias of Elis (ca. 485–415 BCE), a Sophist (not a Stoic), is mostly known from Plato's dialogues *Hippias maior* and *Hippias minor*.

[283]Cicero *On the Orator* 3.32.127.

114 Quis igitur huic nouo et Virbio Hippiae non inuideat? Ne sibi id satis est quidem. Sese enim post deinde Gorgiam Leontinum, Thrasymachum, Protagoram, Prodicum, Euathlium,[237] qui omnes *arrogantibus uerbis profitebantur se docere quemadmodum causa quaeque inferior dicendo fieri superior posset*, aut superaturum aut saltem aequaturum illos existimat. Quis itaque liuore non exarserit?

115 Sed cedo nunc tu, optime Candide, quem esse illum arbitrere. Video quid aias:

"*Grammaticus, rhetor, geometres, pictor, aliptes,
augur, schenobates, medicus, magus: omnia nouit.*"

Inquies:

"*Ille per extentum funem iam posse uidetur ire poeta.*

Quid funem?

Sicelis infamis *in caelum iusseris ibit.*"

116 Hic iam argumentari licet estque plane percipere, Candide, tot enumeratis artibus atque doctrinis hominum in orbe diuersa exoriri ingenia, dissimilis quoque naturas et mores nasci. Videmus animos nunc hebetes obtususque, nunc peracutos et acres, immo diuinos, mirabile dictu, in medium prodire; alios re quidem, alios opinione magis atque magis laborare. Sic itaque — ut unde discessimus[238] redeamus — Panormita noster, quando sese uirum esse eum[239] magni pendit cuius inuidia quisque excandeat corrodaturque, non re utique ceterum sua tamen quippe deprauata opinione negotiatur ac tota ad nundinas errat uia.

117 [A129v] Cupisne rem seriam tibi quam multi nascentes hac tempestate suae factionis oratores minime percipiunt dixerim? Deponuntur ferme singulos dies penes me litterulae suae, sui uersus, suae quaeque lucubratiunculae, quas, ut euoluam lectitemque, rogant multi, premunt, urgent. Verum paene in singulis quae manus ad meas hactenus conuolarunt aut uerborum in sensu aut in syllabis aut in ipsis minutis elementis minusque rotundis perihodis, insigne[240] certe illius[241] aliquod peccatum offendi, qui sese tamen earum rerum antiquissimarum quam doctissimum peritissimumque

---

[237]Euathlium] Hippiam Elium *Cic.*
[238]dis-] re- *N*
[239]esse eum *tr. N*
[240]insigne] in signum *N*
[241]certe illius *tr. N*

114 Who, therefore, does not envy this new Virbius Hippias?[284] But even that does not satisfy him. For he thinks that in time he is going to surpass or at least equal Gorgias of Leontini, Thrasymachus, Protagoras, Prodicus, and Euathlius, all of whom "professed in arrogant language that they taught how every inferior cause could be made the superior through oratory."[285] Well, who will fail to burn with envy?

115 But now you, my good Candido, tell me who you think Panormita is. I see what you are going to say: "'A grammarian, rhetorician, geometrician, painter, trainer, prophet, tightrope-walker, medical doctor, sorcerer; he knows how to do it all.'"[286] You will say, "'To me that poet now seems to be able to dance on a tightrope.'[287] Why a rope? 'Were you to order him on it,' the infamous Sicilian 'will go to his Maker.'"[288]

116 Now at this point, Candido, one may draw the obvious conclusion that the world produces people of diverse talents as well as begets different natures and customs for the long list of arts and branches of learning. We see in our midst minds now dull and dim, now sharp and bright, indeed, to our amazement, divine. Some labor ever harder in fact, others by reputation. Thus — that we may return to where we left off — when our Panormita fancies himself a man towards whom everyone should burn and be consumed with envy, he is not dealing with fact at all but rather with his own twisted opinion, and he completely loses his bearings.

117 Do you want me to relate to you a serious fact that many of the orators from his faction who are just now starting their careers scarcely perceive? Practically every day his wretched little letters, poetry, and various lucubrations are left with me, which many people beg, press, and urge me to peruse and pore over. But to date, in almost everything that has strayed into my hands, I have hit upon some glaring blunder of his, either in the meaning of words and in syllabification or in errors ranging from the very letters of the alphabet to imperfectly formed

---

[284]A sneer mocking Panormita as the reincarnation of both Hippias of Elis (see n. 282 above) and Virbius, who was said to be a reincarnation of Hippolytus, the mythological son of Theseus and Hippolyte, Queen of the Amazons (Virgil *Aeneid* 7.765 ff. and Ovid *Metamorphoses* 15.544 ff.).

[285]This quotation is from Cicero *Brutus* 8.30 as is the list of Sophists: *Gorgias of Leontini* (ca. 483–376 BCE) was an influential Sophist and teacher of rhetoric who came to Athens as an ambassador in 427 BCE and is best known from Plato's dialogue bearing his name; *Thrasymachus of Chalcedon* (fl. ca. 430–400 BCE) was a Sophist known mostly from his role in Plato's *Republic*, where he articulated the idea that "might is right"; *Protagoras of Abdera* (fl. ca. 460–445 BCE) was an early Sophist, who mostly taught in Athens and is famous from Plato's dialogue *Protagoras* and for his dictum "Man is the measure of all things"; *Prodicus of Ceos* (fl. late fifth century BCE) was a Sophist who appeared in Athens on diplomatic missions and is represented in Plato's dialogues as on friendly terms with Socrates; *Euathlius* must be a corrupt reading from Rho's manuscript of Cicero's *Brutus*, because the manuscript should have read *Hippias Eleus*, that is, Hippias of Elis (see *Philippic* §113 and n. 282 above).

[286]Juvenal 3.76–77.

[287]Horace *Epistle* 2.1.210–11.

[288]Juvenal 3.78.

e caelo delapsum antistitem gloriatur et iactat. Grammaticum enim se dicit qui barbare loquitur et in officio cuius magister esse uult labitur. At secum bene actum est quidem, qui magniloquentiae suae censores haud nullos et iudices agrestes maternam paene linguam expedientes inuenit. Quicquid ille crocitauerit, coaxauerit, seu amore seu errore, utpote Vergilio dulcius quiddam atque concinnius laudibus ad Iouem extollitur.

118 O caecitate summa damnatum hunc gregem! *"Felices," inquit Fabius, "essent artes si de illis soli artifices iudicarent."* Qui philosophos intelleget nisi qui dogmatum uarietates percalluerit? Qui poetam agnoscet nisi qui uersus cudere ac[242] numeros supputare[243] didicerit? Multo itaque consultius et antiquius, *C. Lucilius homo doctus* — ut apud Ciceronem est — *et perurbanus, dicere enim solebat ea quae scriberet neque ab indoctissimis se*[244] *neque ab doctissimis legi uelle, quod alteri nihil intellegerent, alteri plus fortasse quam ipse de se percontari*[245] *uiderentur.* Numquid cerdo tonsoriam aut sutor [N107v] unguentariam recte iudicauerit? Verum statim sese recipiet ac dicet res se pueriles, epistolas uidelicet quotidianas, sine studio et cura, sine cultu et ornatu transigere, dum uero subuolat per apices iuris et summa sequitur fastigia rerum aut caelum ingreditur; se ipsum cum elaboratum id temporis tum[246] diuinum esse. Egregie[247] quidem uerum diuus ille Hieronymus setius atque[248] ipse sentit rem hanc et monet et docet. *Non sunt contemnenda*, ait, *quasi parua sint, sine quibus magna*[249] *constare non possunt. Ipse elementorum ordo et parua institutio praeceptoris, aliter de erudito, aliter de rustico ore profertur.* [A130r] Turpe quidem qui magna profiteatur, minuta suae professionis ignoret. Seruius Sulpicius, par Ciceroni[250] aut primus

---

[242]ac] et *N*
[243]supputare] -portare *N*
[244]se *Cic.* : *om. AN*
[245]percontari] -cunctari *N*
[246]tum] tamen *N*
[247]Egregie] -gio *N*
[248]setius atque *tr. N*
[249]magna] magni *N*
[250]Ciceroni] -ronis *N*

---

[289]Rho is presumably speaking about autographs of Panormita's writings and the newly fashionable *littera antiqua*, which the humanists developed in imitation of Carolingian script. The humanists preferred it to Gothic script, which they referred to as *littera moderna* (see De la Mare 1973, Ferrari 1988, and Ullman 1960; cf. *Philippic* §147).

[290]Jerome *Letter* 66.9. Fabius Pictor (fl. late third century BCE) was the first Roman senator to write a history of Rome in Greek.

periodic sentences.[289] He, nevertheless, gloats and brags that he himself is the most learned, skilled, and heaven-sent master of these ancient matters. Indeed, he calls himself a grammarian, he who himself speaks barbarously and who commits errors in the very obligations he wants to teach. But, to be sure, things have turned out well for him, since he has discovered some rustic censors and judges of his grandiloquence who can barely decipher the vernacular. Anything he creaked or croaked, inspired either by the erotic or by the erratic, is praised to the high heavens as if it were more delightful and elegant than a line from Virgil.

118 What a rabble they are, cursed by total blindness! "'The arts would be blessed,' said Fabius, 'if the practitioners alone were to judge them.' Who understands philosophers except he who" has thoroughly mastered "their various teachings?"[290] Who can appreciate a poet except he who has learned to hammer out lines and to compute meter as well? Therefore, more deliberately and venerably, according to Cicero, "Gaius Lucilius, a learned and highly urbane man, used to say that he did not want either the very ignorant or the very learned to read the things he wrote, because the former would understand nothing and the latter perhaps" would seem to question him more closely "than he would himself."[291] Could a tanner judge the cutting of hair or a cobbler the making of ointments? But Panormita will immediately recover and say that while he soars through the greatest matters of law and engages in high-level affairs or reaches the summit of success, he dispatches puerile matters, that is his daily correspondence, without study or care and without refinement and ornamentation; but all the while, he himself is not only polished but even divine.[292] Quite otherwise than Panormita sees it, Saint Jerome admonishes and teaches admirably on this matter. "One must not shun," Saint Jerome says, "on the pretext that they are small, those elements that make great things possible. The very order of the alphabet and the first

---

[291] Cicero *On the Orator* 2.6.25. Gaius Lucilius (d. 102 BCE) was a Roman poet whose poetry dealt with his personal reflections.

[292] Rho did not simply anticipate Panormita's response but took it from Panormita's letter (mid-1432) to Francesco Barbavara (Sabbadini 1910a, 134), in which he defended himself against his detractors. They ask, Panormita says: "'What has Panormita written in a long while?' 'Nothing,' they say, 'except some tiny letters.' Even I confess that my kind of letter writing is not elaborate and that it is not at all carefully considered. Nor do I want my letters to be numbered among my works or to be pulled together into a collection, although they number about a thousand. Nevertheless, they are carried around, read, and copied out even beyond Cisalpine Gall [i.e., "Lombardy"] not without glorifying our prince. And unless certain *cognoscenti* of eloquence are deceiving me, they tell me that young people take great delight in and benefit enormously from these tiny letters and compete strenuously to seek them out and even to emulate them. I have met some people who inform me that neither my letters nor my precepts are at all harmful but are thus in fact a benefit, so that for reasons of style these letters are readily esteemed as if they were the offspring of princes" (*"Quid legitur ex Panormita tam diu?" "Nihil," inquiunt, "praeter quasdam epistulucias." Fateor et ego meum hoc genus epistulandi non elaboratum, non magni admodum aestimandum, neque id ego dinumerari volo in operibus meis aut in corpus redigi, quamvis numero sint circiter mille. Circumferuntur tamen, leguntur, exscribuntur etiam extra hanc Galliam non sine laudatione principis nostri. Et nisi me fallunt studiosi quidam eloquentiae, adulescentes magnam percipere voluptatem atque utilitatem aiunt ex hisce epistuluciis atque sedulo quaeritare atque etiam aemulari contendere. Novi quosdam quibus scio nihil obfuisse vel epistulas vel praecepta mea, sed ita demum profuisse ut in dicendo iuventutis universae facile principes habeantur.*).

post illum, consuluit de re amici Quintum Mucium. Cumque semel et iterum responsum accepisset ab illo neque intellegeret, ait Quintus: *Turpe est patricio et nobili ad*[251] *causas oranti ius in quo uersaretur ignorare.*

119 Vrgebit statim acclamabitque:[252] "Proferam epistolas has meas,[253] hos uersus, exercitationesque meas[254] quae — quandoquidem Hermaphroditus cum fama eius luget — ego cupio[255] ut illae saltem a doctis iudicentur."

120 Fatebor primum equidem, mi Candide, Commentaria eius in Plautum, ex illis sudoribus suis omnibus opus unum perlucubratum, nequaquam me uidisse, quae tamen (nisi fama mentiatur) a Guarino, uiro pererudito, ut aiunt, furatus est. Plautum etenim eum, dico, qui a nobis nouiciis nisi se auctore, ne ab ipso Plauto quidem (modo in lucem redeat), intellegi aut sciri posse gloriatur. Pro arrogantiam inauditam! Nos omnes sues, se solum Mineruam esse, qui comicum illum recte calleat, arbitratur. Totum orbem hac ipsa expectatione obsessum tenet. Vota ad deos thurificationesque, ne inter commentandum Panormita uir tantus intereat, emittuntur. Ambrosia quoque illum nutriendum quo diuturnius uiuat atque margaritis putant. Sed iam, ueluti ad sanctorum reliquias fieri assolet, cerei et faces comparandae sunt, ut, cum proferri coram debuerit, non sine lampadibus et sacro igne succinctisque ritu Gabino sacerdotibus Plautus ipse in medium genibus inflexis uideatur adoreturque. Ex his itaque gloriosis sese colit, sese momento habet, se obseruat, se sibi totum uindicat, et Plautino contubernio praeter Catamitum et Adonidem suum aut elegum quempiam impudicum lasciuientemque ipse totius elegiae pater et princeps admittit nullum.

---

[251]ad] et *A*
[252]acclamabit-] -mabitur- *N*
[253]meas *scripsi* : suas *AN*
[254]meas *scripsi* : suas *AN*
[255]ego cupio *scripsi* : ille cupit *AN*

---

[293]Jerome *Letter* 107.4.

[294]Servius Sulpicius Galba (consul 108 BCE) and Quintus Mucius Scaevola (consul 95 BCE) were famous jurists whose *personae dramatis* appear in Cicero's *On Friendship*, Cicero having studied law under Scaevola.

[295]Justinian *Digest* 1.2.2.45.

[296]This passage contains gross slippage between direct and indirect discourse. It must originally have been written as either one or the other and now suffers from incomplete revision. I have emended it to direct discourse in conformity with its lead-in phrase (cf. *Philippic* §101 n. 248).

[297]Rho has this wrong. Guarino Veronese, known for his teaching of Plautus, wrote to Giovanni Spilimbergo in August of 1432 saying he had only a few scattered notes on Plautus. He may have given Panormita some advice on Plautus (Colombo 223–25; cf. *Philippic* §11 n. 27, §27; and *Apology* §31; for Guarino, cf. *Apology* §39).

lessons of the teacher are uttered one way by an educated mouth and another way by a rustic one."[293] It is disgraceful that he who pronounces on the great things of a profession should not know the small things of that profession. Servius Sulpicius, who was equal or second only to Cicero, consulted Quintus Mucius concerning friendship.[294] And when Sulpicius had several times received Quintus' response and did not understand it, Quintus said: "It is disgraceful for a patrician and nobleman who is pleading a case to be ignorant of the law with which he is concerned."[295]

119 Panormita will immediately retort and protest: "I produced my letters, poems, and exercises, which I desire to be judged at least by learned men, since *The Hermaphrodite* grieves along with its fame."[296]

120 In fact I will first of all confess, my Candido, that I have never seen his *Commentary on Plautus*, the only work from all those labors of his that he produced by burning the midnight oil. These, however, (unless rumor lies) he purloined from Guarino,[297] who is, so they say, an extremely erudite man. And indeed, I am telling you, Panormita gloats that without him as our guide neither we novices nor even Plautus himself, were he to return to life, could understand and know Plautus. What unheard-of arrogance! He imagines that we are all swine and that he alone is Minerva, who knows how to explain this comic poet correctly.[298] He holds the whole world hostage with this suspense. Vows and offerings of incense are dispatched to the gods lest so great a man as Panormita should die while composing his commentary. It is also thought necessary to nourish him with ambrosia and even with pearls in order to prolong his life.[299] But now, as customarily occurs at the site of the reliquaries of the saints, candles and torches must be procured so that when Plautus himself has to be brought forward,[300] he will be viewed and venerated publicly on bent knees, with lamps and sacred fire and priests girt according to the Gabine rite.[301] In this fashion Panormita worships, aggrandizes, and honors himself with these vainglories and claims everything as his own. And as the very father and prince of all elegiac poetry, he admits no one to his Plautine tent except his Catamite and Adonis or some shameless and lascivious love poet.

---

[298]This plays on the image of the proverbial pig who lectured Minerva, goddess of wisdom and the arts, that is, the unlearned individual who attempts to teach the expert.

[299]Ambrosia is the "food of the gods." The eating of pearls refers to legends of ostentatious consumption, most particularly to stories about Cleopatra eating them as a show of indifference to their cost (Pliny the Elder *Natural Histories* 9.121–22).

[300]That is, when the text of Plautus with Panormita's *Commentary* is going to be read publicly.

[301]The Romans adopted the *cinctus Gabinus*, a ceremonial way of wearing the toga, from the Gabii, the inhabitants of an ancient city in Latium near Rome (Isidore *Etymologies* 19.24.7).

121 Verum spero fore quo propediem risum inuitis nobis nouus hic commentator, Auerrois aut[256] Victorinus, excutiat, dicamusque uersiculum quam notissimum:

*Amphora coepit
institui, currente rota cur urceus exit?*

Ceteras uero eius Maecenaticas et quotidianas epistolas, ratus nouum Lysiam aut Isocratem offendisse adusque stomachum et nauseam, inspexi et legi. Visa una, [A130v] uisae sunt[257] omnes. Eadem omnibus facies suppellexque;[258] cantilena est eadem. Sed et ieiunus ubique fame⟨sc⟩et, nudus, mendicabundus. Palliastro tamen illo pertrito quoad potest sese attollit et effert, semicinctiisque illis suis omnis affatur et conuenit: "Pauper quidem est Hypocras, ut eisdem saepe fomentis atque collyriis — neque illis permutatis — oculis aeque et[259] calcaneis medeatur, singulosque huiuscemodi unguento conciliatos habere cupit."

122 Quid singulos? Non sic Aurispam, uirum humanissimum eloquentissimumque, suae dignitatis, sui nominis perpetuum — ut ita dixerim — bucinatorem, amplectitur? Modici[260] enim aeris alieni, uidelicet tribus ex aureis, ipsum lacessit[261] et damnat, atque ut est omnium inimicorum amicus, immo omnium amicorum inimicus — illum miror maledicendi ornatum — his uerbis alloquitur: *Antonius Panormita salutem dicit Aurispae suo. Non putabam ad te fore scripturum per haec tempora.* Et infra: *Circumspicias te, fidem tuam, facinora; quem parui facias etiam cogita, qui, tametsi minimus*

---

[256]aut *om. N*
[257]sunt] *s.l. suppl. A*
[258]suppel*l*ex-] -l- *s.l. suppl. A* : -plex- *N*
[259]et] *corr. N*
[260]modici *Sabb.* : modi *AN*
[261]lacessit] lacescit *N*

---

[302]Ibn Rushd (1126–98) was an Islamic Aristotelian scholar from Cordoba known to the Latin West as Averroës or simply as "The Commentator." His commentaries on Aristotle, once translated into Latin, shaped Aristotelian thought in the West for centuries (Curtis 111–14).

[303]Victorinus of Pettau (d. ca. 304) wrote the first Latin commentaries on Sacred Scripture. Almost all of his writings are lost, probably abandoned for their millenarian views that fell into disfavor in the Latin church after Augustine (ODCC).

[304]Horace *The Art of Poetry* 21–22.

[305]That is, Panormita's letters to his patrons or "Maecenases" (see *Philippic* §54 n. 130; cf. also §80, §131, §143, §170, §175, and §178; for an index to Panormita's letters, see Sabbadini 1910a).

[306]Lysias of Syracuse (ca. 459–ca. 380 BCE), a supporter of Pericles and Athenian democracy, gained recognition as an orator through his ability to take everyday language and elevate it to a forceful literary style (OCD).

[307]Isocrates (436–338 BCE) was a tremendously influential Athenian teacher of oratory who became famous for his written speeches, being too shy to deliver them himself (OCD).

[308]*Hypocras* is a medieval spelling for *Hippocrates* (469–399 BCE), the influential Greek physician famed for the "Hippocratic Oath" (see Siraisi 1–10). This spelling probably resulted from the medieval

121 But I look forward to the time soon when this new commentator, surely another Averroës[302] or a Victorinus,[303] will provoke us to laughter against our will, and we will recite the famous jingle: "Why does what started out a great double-handled storage jar turn out to be a tiny pitcher as the wheel keeps turning?"[304] I have certainly seen and read his Maecenatic letters[305] and daily correspondence, imagining that I had stumbled upon a new Lysias[306] or Isocrates[307] until the disgust and nausea set in. If you have seen one of his letters, you have seen them all. The same form and style appear in all of them, and their refrain never varies. But in fact, he is everywhere gaunt with hunger, naked and a beggar. Nevertheless, in his poor tattered cloak he rises and puffs himself up as much as he can, and when he wears those aprons of his, everyone nods and says: "Hypocras[308] is certainly poor. Hence with the same poultices and salves he often medicates the eyes and the heels alike without differentiation, and he wants to prescribe such an unguent for every single individual."[309]

122 What do I mean by everyone? Does he not embrace Aurispa this way, though Aurispa is a most humane and eloquent man, the continual trumpeter, as I would say, of Panormita's dignity and name? For because of a modest debt,[310] namely for three gold coins, Panormita harassed and condemned him. And since Panormita is a friend of all enemies, or rather an enemy of all friends — I marvel at how smoothly he curses someone — he addresses Aurispa in these words: "Antonio Panormita sends greetings to his Aurispa. I did not think that I would be writing to you at this time." And further down Panormita says: "You had better watch out for yourself, your good name, and your actions. You should consider the person whom you even now despise, since he, although he be tiny, carries a sting. If you postpone the least thing, a space for repentance will not remain. I shall not deal further with you but with your prince, d'Este,[311] or with

---

misunderstanding (followed by Rho) that the name derived from *hypo* (under) and *krasis* (mixture). *Hippocrates* actually derives from *hippo* (horse) and *krator* (power). See *Webster's Unabridged Dictionary*. "hippocras."

[309]This parodies the medical aphorism "contraries cure contraries" (*contraria contrariis curantur*), e.g., cold cures hot (see Siraisi 143–44).

[310]Sabbadini corrects this (Sabbadini and Barozzi 15) to a better reading (*modici*), but both manuscript A and N have (*modi*). *Modici* means "for a modest debt"; *modi* means "for the amount of a debt." Sabbadini is correct that "for a modest debt" improves both the Latin and the logic, since Rho further devalued the "three gold coins" — roughly a month's salary for a professor of rhetoric — to "the meanest coin" (§123). Sabbadini was only looking at the Ambrosiana manuscript and he does not indicate, as he often does, that his improvement was an intentional break with the exemplar. In such instances where Sabbadini does indicate an intentional break, it is noted here in the critical apparatus as a "conjecture."

[311]Niccolò d'Este III (1393–1441), Duke of Ferrara, brought Aurispa to his court in 1427 and Guarino Veronese in 1429 as tutors to his adult sons. That Niccolò's sons were in their early twenties when these tutors were brought in clearly reverses the usual educational order of *Ars et Mars* (see Gundersheimer 85–87), but it would eventually give high visibility to the belief of humanists that a humanistic education particularly suited the governing class and that it was requisite to the right use of power (see Grafton and Jardine, esp. 1–29; and Grendler 1989, 128). Panormita's resentment resulted from Aurispa having gotten the position at Ferrara in late 1427 that Panormita had come there hoping to secure (see Sabbadini 1891, 28).

sit,[262] gerit[263] *aculeum. Minimam si rem distuleris, locus paenitentiae non relinquetur. Amplius tecum non agam, sed cum Estensi Principe tuo, cum Italia:*

"*Flectere si nequeo*[264] *superos, Acheronta mouebo.*"

Tu si sapis, ne expecta sagittas meas; te paeniteat errati; pete ueniam; restituas mutuum: alioquin senties quod Socraticus deus iste tuus non praeuiderat. De his hactenus et quidem satis. Nam certo scio facies officium tuum ne euomam ego bilem, ne sentiant gentes sentinae tuae putorem.

123 Pro puerilem hominem, qui gratius supputet obolum quam amicum! Quid plura? Illas itaque eius epistolas [N108r] sputo conspersas in extrema munera, immo in Gemonias ipsas abiiciendas existimaui.

124 Sentisne Panormita?

125 Vnam ex illis tamen, quam ad illustrissimum Principem nostrum superioribus Kalendis habuit, non probare non possum. Solem enim epistolam illam appellat, ubi quid Phoebus, quid illius equi, quid currus, quid radii sibi uelint mirandum in modum nescientibus nobis aperit; ibi se ipsum superasse et ostentat et gaudet: omnis scholas,[265] quaeque gymnasia puerorumque subsellia, Italiam denique omnem, quasi in tenebris sine Sole reliqui essemus, oppleuit.

126 [A131r] O glebosum hominem, rusticanum montanumque! Solem credit excudisse, lunam declarauit taetris utique maculis quaqua uersum inspersam. Vidistine, Candide, in aede[266] Virginis dum Sol ille apud astrologos eosdemque philosophos exactis pauculis[267] diebus coram legeretur, quae ludificationes, qui risus, qui ioci applausu[268] omnium habiti sint? Ludibrio statim prae ignoratione philosophiae astrologiaeque et in sibilum omnibus haberi coepit.

---

[262]sit] est *N*
[263]gerit *coniec. Sabb.* : -runt *AN*
[264]nequeo] nequeam *N*
[265]scho-] -h- *s.l. suppl. A*
[266]aede *scripsi* : aedem *AN*
[267]pauculis] paucis *N*
[268]applausu] a plausus, -s- *s.l. suppl. N*

---

[312]Virgil *Aeneid* 7.312.
[313]Panormita's lost letter?
[314]In ancient Rome, the corpses of executed criminals were ceremonially dumped or dragged down the Gemonian Steps ("Steps of Sighs") leading from the Aventine Hill to the Tiber River (Suetonius *Tiberius* 53.2).

all of Italy: 'If I cannot influence the gods, I will move Hell.'³¹² If you have any sense, do not await my arrows. Rue your mistake. Seek forgiveness and restore the loan. Otherwise, you will experience what that Socratic god of yours had not foreseen. I have now said more than enough about these things. For I know for sure that you will do your duty so that I do not vomit my bile upon you and people do not smell the putrescence of your cesspool."³¹³

123 What a childish man! He reckons the meanest coin more desirable than a friend! Why say more? Accordingly, I have determined that those letters of his must be thrown away showered with spit as a last offering to the dead, or rather, dumped on the Gemonian Steps.³¹⁴

124 "Do you hear, Panormita?"

125 I cannot resist, however, examining one of these letters, the one he delivered to our most illustrious prince some months ago.³¹⁵ For he named that letter "The Sun," and in it he marvelously explains to us ignoramuses the meaning of Phoebus, his horses, his chariot, and the spokes of its wheels.³¹⁶ He brags and revels there that he has outdone himself and that he has flooded with light every learned discussion, every grammar school, every schoolboy's bench, and finally all of Italy, as though we would remain in darkness without "The Sun."

126 What a clodhopper! A bumpkin fresh from the hills! He thinks that he has fashioned the Sun but he has described the Moon, speckled in every direction with vile stains.³¹⁷ Did you notice, Candido, that while "The Sun" was read publicly to the astrologer-philosophers in the Church of the Virgin a few days ago, everyone made sport, smiled, and joked about it? Everyone immediately began to make him a laughing stock, and he was hissed off stage for his ignorance of philosophy and astrology.³¹⁸

---

³¹⁵This cover letter and the *Oration on the Imagery of the Sun* (Appendix VII below) were apparently read publicly in Pavia in (late?) 1431. The letter circulated earlier, perhaps in another version, because Francesco Piccinino first mentions it with a secure date on 8 November 1430 (Sabbadini 1891, 13; 1910a, 59 n. 6). In letters between Rho and Gervaso da Piacenza (*artistarum et medicinae rector*), Rho requests a copy be sent from Pavia of "the Panormitan Sun that has newly shone in the darkness" (*Solem Panormitanum quem noviter in tenebris illuxisse . . . ex Ticino ad me mitteres* [Vatican City: Biblioteca Apostolica Vaticana, MS Pal. lat. 1592, 127v-128v]). These letters between Rho and Gervaso could only have been written in late 1431, because Gervaso only held the position of Rector in late 1431. The plague broke out in the early summer of 1431 and the University did not reopen until 29 November. By January 1432 Antonio da Novi was the *de facto* Rector (Maiocchi 21: 430, 431, 442, 445, 446; and Corradi 8).

³¹⁶Phoebus Apollo was believed to be the Sun since at least the fifth century BCE, a view which came to prevail in the Hellenistic and Imperial periods (OCD).

³¹⁷Cf. Panormita *Oration on the Imagery of the Sun* §18 (Appendix VII/2 below).

³¹⁸Panormita's *Oration of the Imagery of the Sun* (Appendix VII/2 below) was perhaps delivered on 16 June 1432, the anniversary of Filippo Maria Visconti's installation as duke. Rho's description of the reaction, however, (if in any way true) is strangely incongruous with such a solemn ceremony (cf. *Philippic* §175). Presumably it was read at the Duomo of Milan, Santa Maria Nascente ("the Church of the Virgin"?), which had been under construction since 1386 with the special patronage of the Visconti, the main altar having been dedicated in 1418 by Pope Martin V.

127 Quid iam inquam? *Poetam*ne hunc cuius *liuore*, ut ait, rumpimur adorabimus? Hui! Sese quidem nescit ac sibi ipsi alienus est. Cognosce enimuero quando poeticen profiteatur, compluria debuit quae non *in bicipiti Parnaso*, certo scio, tam repente somniauit: singulas uidelicet artes, quasque doctrinas, hominum mores, rerum[269] ingenia, totius orbis regiones et situs, antecessiones et gesta, leges et plebiscita, humana diuinaque iura; quid caelo, quid mari, quid terra[270] ageretur. Denique *philosophari sibi necesse* est, non *paucis* tamen, ut Neoptolemus aiebat. Quem tandem posthabitis his oratoris[271] ac poetae principiis necessariis, id unum solum summatim didicisse percipimus, uidelicet nihil scire. Praestabat itaque Charmandrum aut Epigenem, Ptolomeum aut Alfonsum astrologos adisset illosque quid de sole dicendum esset[272] consuluisset, quam quae statim uel a semidoctis refelli quirent temere quidem in commune largiretur. Sic enim consulto Aratum poetam, *astrologiae ignarum, inter doctos homines ornatissimis atque optimis uersibus de caelo stellisque*[273] dixisse pueri audiuimus. *Nicandrum Colophonium* quoque *poetica quadam facultate, ab agro tamen remotissimum, de rebus rusticis scripsisse praeclare*[274] intelleximus. Sed id egregie dictum quod ab Hesiodo usurpauit Aristoteles, ab Aristotele Cicero, ab Cicerone Liuius[275] experimur identidem[276] euenire solere, *eum* uidelicet *primum uirum esse*[277] *qui ipse consulat qui in re*[278] *sit; secundum eum qui bene monenti oboediat; qui nec ipse consulere nec alteri parere sciat, eum extremi ingenii esse.*

128 Surdescisne, Panormita?

---

[269]rerum] rerium *N*

[270]quid mari, quid terra *tr. N*

[271]oratoris *N* : -riis *A*

[272]esset] est *N*

[273]stellis-] stelis- *A*

[274]scripsisse praeclare *tr. N*

[275]Ab Hesiodo poeta [*Opera et dies* 293] accepit Aristoteles hos uersus primo *Ethicorum: Optimus ille quidem qui per sese omnia noscens / Praeceptor suus ipse sibi meliora peregit / Ille bonus rursum monitus qui recta sequetur / Qui nec ipse uidet, neque credit recta monenti / Hic nulla parte est utilis*, etcetera [95ᵇ5–95ᵇ10 (trans. Robert Grosseteste, AL 26.3)]. Post Aristotelem dixit Cicero in oratione *Pro Aulo Cluentio* [84] ferme sententiam eadem: *Sapientissimum eum esse dicunt, cui quando opus sit ipsi ueniat in mentem: proxime accedere illum, qui alterius bene inuentis obtemperet.* Post Ciceronem, Titus Liuius *De bello punico* hanc eandem, ut mihi textu patet, dixit sententiam.] *in mg. in manu scribae N*

[276]identidem] iten- *A*

[277]uirum esse *tr. N*

[278]qui in re] quid in rem *Cic.*

---

[319]Panormita *Etsi facile* §2 (Appendix I below).

[320]Mount Parnasus was the haunt of the Muses, who inspired art, music, and literature. Ennius, whom the Romans regarded as their most notable ancient poet, was said to have dreamed that "the soul of Homer took possession of him"; Persius (pr.2) says this happened "on Parnassus," but Propertius (3.3) gives the location as "on Helicon" (Witke 81–82 and 81n).

127 What am I saying now? Shall we adore "this poet, who," as he says, "has us bursting with envy"?[319] Ha! He does not know himself and is a stranger to himself. Indeed, take note that when he lectures on poetry, he should have learned many things which he did not, I am sure, suddenly dream up "on twin-peaked Mount Parnassus."[320] To be specific, he should have learned each and every art and branch of learning, human customs, the nature of things, the geography and topography of the whole world, historical events and their antecedents, statutes and popular ordinances, and human and divine laws; what was happening in heaven, on the sea, and on earth. Finally, "it is necessary for him to philosophize" but not "on just a few points," as Neoptolemus advised.[321] In short, we see that since he disregarded the necessary rudiments of the orator and poet, he superficially learned this one thing only, namely, to know nothing. Consequently, he would have done better to have gone to the astrologers Charmander and Epigenes or Ptolemy and Alfonso[322] and to have consulted them about what to say concerning the Sun, rather than to have rashly taught in public things that even the semi-educated could immediately refute. For likewise as schoolboys we ourselves heard that the poet Aratus "spoke by design about heaven and the stars among learned men in well polished and excellent poetry, although he had no expertise in astrology."[323] We also observed "that Nicander of Colophon, although well removed from the farm, wrote brilliantly about rural matters with a measure of poetic skill."[324] But we ourselves have often experienced as true the astute maxim which Aristotle repeated from Hesiod, and Cicero from Aristotle, and Livy from Cicero,[325] namely, "The best man is he who advises from experience; the second best is he who follows one who gives him good advice; the worst is he who knows neither how to advise nor how to take advice from others."[326]

128 "Are you going deaf, Panormita?"

---

[321]Cicero *Tusculan Disputations* 2.1.1.

[322]Charmander and Epigenes of Byzantium were astronomers of uncertain date mentioned here to represent esoteric knowledge (cf. Seneca *Natural Questions* 7.5.2, 7.4.1, 7.6.1; and Pliny the Elder *Natural Histories* 7.160 and 193); Ptolemy and Alfonso represent standard astronomical authorities (cf. *Apology* §8, §11, and §55).

[323]Cicero *On the Orator* 1.16.69-70.

[324]Cicero *On the Orator* 1.16.69-70.

[325]The scribe of the Naples manuscript, Rolandus Scibbeke de Alamania, copied Rho's gloss into the margin (108r): "Aristotle, in Book I of his *[Nicomachean] Ethics* [95^{b}5-95^{b}10], took these lines from the poet Hesiod [*Works and Days* 293]: 'He is indeed best who, familiarizing himself with everything, has as his own teacher achieved something better for himself. He is good who, besides having been advised, follows what is right. He is completely useless who neither sees what is right nor believes one who advises what is right.' After Aristotle, Cicero expressed almost the same idea in his oration *In Defense of Aulus Cluentius* [84]: 'They say that he is wisest whose own mind arrives at what is essential; that he comes next who obeys what another man has well conceived.' After Cicero, Titus Livy expressed the same idea in *On the Punic War* as I [Rho] have shown in the text."

[326]Livy 22.29.8.

129 Sed hoc de Sole abunde[279] alio libello lusimus. Credo illum lectitasti ubi Panormitae nostri ineptias atque quisquilias, quae a plerisque adulescentulis[280] medio[A131v]criter sciolis in deliciis habentur, explicauimus. Vnum tamen sua poesi ac mathematica re dignum uisus sum praeterierim. Quando enim multa praeclare de curru, de Phoebi equis perorasset, percunctarer ex illo[281] (non intempestum uideretur) an uanescente aurora prius temo, deinde rotarum axes exorirentur, seu primum ipsae rotae posteriores et extremae, demum aureus ipse temo ordine perturbato sequeretur. Dicam quod intellectu sit commodius et apertius. Caudaene prius equorum quam capita apud Parthos et Assyrios nasci uiderentur, an e regione capita prius quam caudae cernerentur? Vtrumuis dixerit, declarandum restabat, ex poetarum uerbis atque sententiis praesertim eorum quos sibi tantos auctores ac testes asciuit. Nunc temonem, nunc rotas praeire, nunc capita equorum nunc caudas quidem anteferri oportere, ita ut non modo confusa — ex poetis enim hic Siculus nihil agi confuse hercle iurat — ceterum uel repugnantia carminibus suis ipsi poetae ludere persaepe uideantur.

130 Sed quid solis effigiem perillustri Principi nostro utpote rem quandam, cui non anteferri non aequari res ulla altera possit ascribit? Qui sol ipse tamen a cursu[282] detinetur suo ac retro flectitur uelit nolitque cum Saturno et Luna, cum Libra et Ariete ceterisque signis et erronibus per uim, tametsi nitatur in aduersum quasi mancipium[283] quoddam non sui imperii, non sui iuris, ab cursu proprio eo semper reiicitur retorqueturque, unde se asserere nullo pacto possit? Quid non potius sidus aliquod nouum futurum quod esset sole ipso splendidius, extra octauum caelum, extra Bootem et Hydram *geminosque Triones* commentus est? Quid non illi caelo inuisibili quod stellas omnis statim et proxime supereminet, quod omnia inuoluit[284] sidera, quod ipsis sideribus caret, quod non a motu suo [N108v] omnium uelocissimo retardatur, pro ipso Principe nostro ut[285] eum super solem altius digniusue collocaret nouum sidus ipsum imposuit?

---

[279]abunde *hic A, post* libello *N*
[280]adulescentulis] -tibus *N*
[281]ex illo] ab ex illo *N*
[282]cursu] curso *N*
[283]principium *ante* manicipium *ut uid. delere N*
[284]inuoluit *N* : inno- *A*
[285]ut *N* : et *A*

---

[327]Although Rho here (late 1431 or early 1432) writes as if this booklet were a joint composition (and it may have been), he clearly speaks ironically when he says "I believe, Candido, you carefully read the passage." For in writing to Gervaso da Piacenza in late 1431 (see *Philippic* §125 n. 315), Rho indicated that Gervaso would soon receive "a dialogue of this Palermian Sun that Candido Decembrio

129 But we ridiculed "The Sun" enough in another little book. I believe, Candido, you carefully read the passage where we explained the absurdities and rubbish of our Panormita, things which many young dilettantes cherish as their favorites.[327] I think, however, I omitted there one thing worthy of his poetry and astrological concerns. For when he expounded in dazzling fashion many things about the chariot and the horses of Phoebus, I should have asked him (it would not have been out of place) whether first the tongue of the chariot and then the axles with the wheels appeared over the horizon with the fading dawn, or if in reverse order, first the back wheels appeared and eventually the golden tongue of the chariot followed. Let me talk about something more easily and clearly understandable. Among the Parthians and Assyrians were the horses' tails seen to rise earlier than their heads, or conversely, did these peoples make out the horses' heads earlier than their tails? Whichever of the two he said, it remained to be attested from the words and opinions of the poets, especially of those whom he took as his great authorities and witnesses. Now the tongue, now the wheels had to come first; now the horses' heads, now their tails had to face forward. In this way, consequently, the poets themselves seem often in their poems to be playing not only with confusions — for this Sicilian swears, honest to god, that the poets do nothing confusedly — but even with contradictions.

130 But why does he ascribe to our most illustrious prince the symbol of the Sun as something that has no better or equal? Yet why is the Sun kept forcibly from its course and made to double back willy-nilly along with Saturn and the Moon, with Libra and Aries, and with the other constellations and planets, and even though the Sun struggles forward like some slave (not under its own authority and not under its own right), it is always rejected and turned back from its own course and has no way to liberate itself from this condition?[328] Why did he not rather contrive the fiction that some new star will emerge more splendid than the Sun itself, beyond the Eighth Heaven, beyond Boötes and Hydra, and beyond the "Twin Carts"?[329] Why did he not place this new star as a symbol of our prince in the invisible heaven that immediately thereafter stands above all stars, that envelops all stars, and that is itself devoid of stars? Why not a new star that is unrestricted in its motion, which is the swiftest of all? Would he not in this way have set up this new star as a symbol of our prince inasmuch as he located the new star above the Sun in a more lofty and dignified position?

---

published, filled with open ridicule and jokes. . . ." (*dialogum eiusce Panormitani Solis, quem Candidus Decembris . . . edidit, loedoriis refertum atque facetiis accipias. . . .*). Rho may have meant by the phrases "we joked" and "we explained" that his *persona dramatis* was one of the interlocutors in a dialogue (now lost). The clause "that Decembrio published" could mean either "written by Decembrio" or "circulated by Decembrio," leaving open the possibility that Rho was its author.

[328]The motion of the heavens was variously explained in geocentric science. Rho seems here to have lumped together all motion contrary to diurnal rotation: the retrograde motion of the planets; the oblique reverse motion of the Sun, Moon, and planets; and the precession of the equinoxes. (I thank Kristen Lippincott for this information.)

[329]Jerome *Commentary on Amos* 2.5; cf. Virgil *Aeneid* 3.516. At least since Homer's time, "Twin Carts" were the usual designation of Ursa Maior and Ursa Minor (the Big and Little Dipper).

131 Quid imposuit? Caelos stellarumque exortus et obitus ignorat Panormita noster. Terrenus est omnis et cum iumentis deorsum fertur, neque motus sursum metiri nouit, qui, ueluti sus, in luto uersatur, neque caelum in terram proiectus suspicere potest, cui neque cerebrum succurrit ad uulgares lunas designandas. [A132r] Haec estne fortasse inuidia illa (quia de caelis ita scite loquitur) ob quam succensere sibi digladiarique oporteat? Vellem iam coram exponeret recenseretque — quando ipsi haud nouimus — mores, uirtutes, doctrinas, artes quibus se perbelle[286] imbutum in auribus illustrium Maecenatum ostentat et praedicat, inuidiamque hanc, quam uti scutum extremum ubique recipit in medium, ut ipse saltem ad horam aliquando intellegeretur, enarraret.

132 Num inuidemus (non de Panormita dixerim quoniam sanctus est, at de synonymo sibi) Beccadello? Num inuidemus quod Senis interueniente Antonio Pratensi, uiro honestissimo, Florentiae operam nauante Aurispa suo, plurimum apud Martinum Papam pro illo curiosissimus salarium impetrare nequiuerit? Num inuidemus? Pro impudentissimum hominem perditissimumque! Num inuidemus quod ad Cosmum Medicum, Florentiae florentissimum ciuem atque grauissimum, Hermaphroditum inscripsit libellum utique ubi ars abutendi sexus atque naturae impudentissime[287] traditur, quo inspecto, honestatis amantissimus Cosmus statim ipse in ignem abiecerit? Num inuidemus quod Romae crumena uanescente (pro scelus!) ab se Beccadello *puer* suus (intellegitne?) *ad merendum* uulgo artabatur? Num inuidemus quod e[288] ciuitate Senis, acclamante populo ob suarum uirtutum praestantiam, numquam rediturus exactus sit? Num inuidemus quod ex factiosis commilitonibus suis unus, pro sordidissimo delicto Iudaeorum more, ciuitate Bononia, legum nutrice, circumsectus abscesserit, sibi uero, ut impunem se plagiarium[289] eriperet e Bononia ipsa? *Pedibus* enim *timor addidit*

---

[286]perbelle] -bellum *N*
[287]naturae impudentissime *tr. N*
[288]inuidemus quod e] inuidemus ᵘᵃquod ex factiosis commilitonibus suis^cat quod e *corr. A*
[289]ut impunem se plagiarium *AN* : ut poenae se plagarum *coniec. Sa*

[330]Cf. Proverbs 26.11; II Peter 2.22; and Jerome *Hebraic Questions* praef.
[331]Lactantius (*On the Wrath of God* 20.10–11) writes: "And though God their designer made them with elevated faces and upright stance and raised them to the contemplation of the heaven and the knowledge of God (*illos . . . ore sublimi, statu recto figuratos ad contemplationem caeli et notitiam dei excitauerit*), they preferred to bend down to the earth like cattle (*curvare se ad terram maluerunt et pecudum modo humi repere*). For having turned away from the sight of heaven and of God . . . a person is low, stooped, and crawling who worships the earth . . . which he ought to have trodden underfoot." Cf. also Lactantius *Divine Institutes* 3.20.11–12.

131 Why did he place the symbol in the heavens? Our Panormita knows nothing about the heavens and the rising and setting of the stars. He is entirely earthly and is carried downwards with the beasts. He knows nothing about measuring upward motion, since he returns to the wallow like a hog.[330] Neither can he look up toward heaven while grovelling on earth, nor does he have a brain capable of designating the ordinary phases of the Moon.[331] Is this — the fact that he speaks so expertly about the heavens — perhaps that envy which gives him every right to get enraged and into vicious fights? I would now like him to lay out and review publicly (since we ourselves do not know them) the customs, virtues, sciences, and arts in which he is so expertly trained as he boastfully asserts while chewing the ears off his illustrious Maecenases.[332] I would also like him to describe this envy, which he adopts everywhere in public as his ultimate shield, so that he may at least be understood at some specific time.

132 Are we really envious of Beccadelli? (I do not speak about Panormita since he is a saint, but about his synonym.)[333] Are we really envious that many an enthusiastic supporter of his at the court of Pope Martin V[334] could not obtain a salary for him, despite the intervention in Siena of the highly respected Antonio da Prato[335] and the exertions in Florence on his behalf by his friend Aurispa?[336] Are we really envious of that? What an absolutely impudent and desperate man! Are we really envious that he dedicated his wretched little book *The Hermaphrodite* to Cosimo de' Medici, Florence's most prosperous and important citizen, a book, to be sure, in which the art of abusing sex and nature is brazenly taught? and that, as a man deeply committed to decency, Cosimo examined it and promptly threw it into the fire?[337] Are we really envious that when he found himself in Rome with a shrinking purse (how wicked!), Beccadelli regularly

---

[332]See *Philippic* §54 n. 130; cf. also §80, §121, §143, §170, §175, and §178.

[333]See *Philippic* §20 n. 45; cf. §76, §133, and §174.

[334]Oddo Colonna (1368–1431), who, after his election at the Council of Constance in 1417, stayed in Florence from February 1419 to September of 1420 before finally going to Rome (see Introduction 9 above). Panormita left Sicily for the continent (Florence) in 1419 (Catalano-Tirrito 170; Sabbadini 1891, 17).

[335]Although both manuscripts A and N read *da Prato*, the person in question must be Antonio Roselli *da Pratovecchio* (ca. 1380–1466), who was a famous teacher of Civil and Canon Law in Florence and Siena. He came to hold a high position in the papal curia and later (1438) quarrelled with Pope Eugenius IV before moving to a position at the University of Padua (see Black 1985, 221–22; and Coppini lxxvi–lxxviii).

[336]That is, Giovanni Aurispa (ca. 1372–1460): see *Philippic* §94 n. 234 and §122.

[337]Cosimo, "il Vecchio," de' Medici (1389–1464) may have staged some act of burning *The Hermaphrodite*, but for this there is no evidence (unless one takes Rho's statement as evidence). He certainly did not burn the dedicatory copy, which still exists (Florence: Biblioteca Laurenziana, MS Plut. 34, cod. 54, 1r–34v; cf. Coppini, 1990 xviii–xix). It is now bound with another work, but the wormholes (which penetrate only one of the two works, the other being pristine) indicate that it was at one time bound separately.

alas, remigium ipsarum *alarum* adiumento fuerit. Num inuidemus quod patrimonii sui nepos, immo gurges et uorago, heres ipse successerit atque uxoris suae, castissimae Penelopes, inter exoletos et scorta amplissimam dotem absumpserit, ⟨di⟩lapidauerit, ligurieritque? soceros optimos spe fraudauerit? totam denique insulam Siciliam²⁹⁰ suo nomine perinfami deturpauerit obscuraueritque? Num inuidemus quod aduersus Leonardum Aretinum, uirum utique omni nostrate laude superiorem, [A132v] partes Epicuri, quem minime intellegit, quodam dialogo defendendas acceperit, ubi ebrietatem non fastiditam uirtutem esse dicat sed dulcem semper et gratam, pateras redundantes et coronata uina prae omnibus cibis in deliciis habeat,²⁹¹ matrimonium deinde damnet, uirginitatem impugnet?²⁹² Num inuidemus quod Caucasum et Olympum, profundissimos montes, excitaturum se in dies polliceatur, deinde statim coaxantes ranas aut ridiculos mures ipse parturiat?

---

²⁹⁰Siciliam] -liae *N*
²⁹¹habeat *coniec. Sabb.* : habeantur *AN*
²⁹²impugnet] -nat *N*

---

³³⁸This phrase is from Aulus Gellius 2.18.3. The rumor about Panormita (cf. Introduction 32–34 above) gets reported in several versions. Decembrio (1432, 127v) says that Panormita, having fled his wife, joined up with the "unwarlike Ergoteles" (*Ergotulo sociatus inermi, uxorem credo fugitabas*), who sang to the accompaniment of the lyre and begged for money "in the Forum, in the Amphitheater, and in every celebrated place and crossroads in Rome" (*in foro, in amphiteatro, in celeberrimis denique Romae vicis et compitis, praecinente puero, vulgo stipem porrigente, facetissimos versus lyra modulatus es*). According to Remigio Sabbadini (1891, 39–40), the story that is most believable comes from the monk Giacomo, who said that he remembered Lucano Miniato (already dead by that time) and Panormita's young Ergoteles, "adorned no less by the nobility of his talent than by the form of his body" (*Venit . . . mihi in memoriam Miniatis Lucani . . . atque item Ergotelis illius tui adolescentuli, qui non minori ingenii nobilitate quam forma corporis erat ornatus*). Giacomo recalled that Ergoteles walked around singing among Panormita's guests while they were eating and drinking (*quo versus poeticos ad mensam inter prandendum blande suaviterque cantante*). Lorenzo Valla (*In Facium* 3.8.34) tells a similar story with the significant additions that Panormita, with the help of *Hylas* (not Ergoteles), poisoned and robbed their guest, Lucano Miniato, a papal secretary who had a reputation as a gambler, and they immediately fled Rome. (*Venit mihi . . . in mentem Miniati cuiusdam qui fuisse dicebatur insignis aleator . . . veneno sustulit et bonam partem ex mortui [immo necdum mortui] censu compilavit, adiutus Hyla suo, per quem ut alios multos ita miserum Miniatum illexerat atque inescaverat. Rem loquor minime obscuram.*) See Regoliosi 1981, 266–67.

³³⁹Rho's vague statement trades on a rumor that circulated at least as early as the so-called "Anonymous Invective" (Appendix III below), almost certainly written by Rho himself (see Introduction 30 above), namely, that Panormita had to flee Siena because his passion became so uncontrollable after he had bitten a boy's lips that he could not restrain himself from "the most sordid and foul sex act" (Appendix III §6 below; cf. Sabbadini 1910a, 33; 1891, 19).

³⁴⁰I have found no other reference to this episode apart from this account by Rho. Perhaps Rho confounds, intentionally or unintentionally, some story about the exile of the Beccadelli family from Bologna two generations earlier (cf. Colangelo 1–15).

³⁴¹Virgil *Aeneid* 8.224.

constrained "his boy" (does he understand me?) "to earn money by prostitution?"[338] Are we really envious that he was driven out of the city of Siena by popular demand because of the outstanding nature of his virtues and forbidden ever to return?[339] Are we really envious that one of the comrades-in-arms from his gang fled Bologna, the nurse of the law, for the utterly sordid offense of having in this city been circumcised according to the Jewish custom? Are we really envious that he kidnapped himself, as it were, unscathed from Bologna?[340] For "fear gave wings to his feet"[341] and "those flapping wings"[342] delivered him. Are we really envious that on the heels of becoming an heir he became a prodigal, indeed a squanderer and devourer of his own patrimony? that he has frittered away, destroyed, and consumed amid sodomites and whores the very substantial dowry of his wife, a most chaste Penelope?[343] that he has defrauded his noble in-laws of their hope? and finally that he has disfigured and darkened the whole island of Sicily with the infamy of his name? Are we really envious that in a certain dialogue he agreed to be the champion of Epicurus,[344] whom he scarcely understood, against Leonardo Aretino,[345] a man more than worthy of the whole nation's praise? Are we really envious that in this dialogue he said that drunkenness was not averse to virtue but sweet and pleasing? that he there considered the overflowing bowls and garlanded wine jars more delectable than any food? and that he then condemned marriage and attacked virginity?[346] Are we really envious that he promises daily to be on the verge of generating the highest mountains, Caucasus and Olympus, and then straightway gives birth to croaking frogs or funny little mice?[347]

[342]Virgil *Aeneid* 6.19.

[343]This sobriquet is taken from Odysseus' Penelope, who became the archetype of chastity and fidelity in the face of abandonment. Rho refers to a rumor (almost certainly false) reported earlier (by himself?) in the so-called "Anonymous Invective" (Appendix III §3 below) and later by Decembrio (1432, 127v) that Panomita abandoned a wife in Sicily after squandering her dowry (see *Philippic* §74 n. 180).

[344]Panormita's *persona dramatis* spoke for the Epicurean position in the first version of Lorenzo Valla's dialogue *On Pleasure* (see n. 346 below; cf. *Philippic* §100 n. 246).

[345]Leonardo Bruni da Arezzo's (1370–1444) *persona dramatis* spoke for the Stoic position in the first version of Lorenzo Valla's dialogue *On Pleasure* (see n. 346 below; for Bruni, see *Philippic* §34 n. 87 and *Apology* §25, §34, and §37).

[346]Rho speaks as though statements made by Panormita's *persona dramatis* were made by Panormita himself. Lorenzo Valla, because of an unspecified insult and perhaps also because of Panormita's growing notoriety, wrote Panormita out of the second version (1433), giving the Epicurean position to the *persona* of the respectable Maffeo Vegio, the Stoic position to the *persona* of Catone Sacco, and the Christian position to the *persona* of Antonio da Rho. The first version of Valla's dialogue (which Rho would be quoting or paraphrasing in here) is apparently lost, but the following examples from Valla's rewrite give the drift of what Panormita's Epicurean *persona* would have said [Panormita]: "Wine is, therefore, something proper and natural to man alone, like language. What praise would really be worthy of such a good? O Wine, author of delight, master of joys, companion of happy times, solace in adversity!" (Valla *On Pleasure* 1.24.3–4; trans. Hieatt and Lorch). [Panormita]: "I take this position: whoever originated sacred virgins introduced into the state an abominable custom that ought to be extirpated everywhere, even though people attached to it the name of religion (it is rather a superstition). . . . Courtesans and whores deserve better of the human race than do sanctified and chaste virgins" (Valla *On Pleasure* 1.43.2; trans. Hieatt and Lorch).

[347]This derives from Horace's pun (*The Art of Poetry* 139) on *mons* (mountain) and *mus* (mouse).

133 Scitne me Beccadellus iste (paene dixi Leccadellus) de rebus cum uerissimis tum notissimis dicere? Hui! Animaduertitne quorsum[293] fune aut camo uilissimum mancipium pertrahatur? *Vita hominum*, ait Plinius, *altos recessus magnasque habet latebras.* At[294] contra uir iste effluit et undique rimas declarat suas; sese omnem exhibet; nudus quidem, uti *mulus* uenalis aut asinus, *quibus non est intellectus*, sine fuco et lenocinio uideri et palpari[295] potest. Ad obolum et assem quanti sit cuius praestantiae aut maiestatis, tametsi neminem impudicum id lateat, nos praecipue tamen, alterius palaestrae uiri *pauci* quidem sed *quos aequus amauit* ipse deus, nescituri esse non possumus.

134 Verum uirtutum morumque suorum naturam uel stultis non ignotam missam faciamus. Dicat dumtaxat ille ipse, qui omnem Italiam, uniuersa studia singula, quaeque famosissimarum urbium gymnasia non minus incestauit et polluit quam contriuit, quas Pandectas aperuit, quae Digesta, quos Codices hactenus lucubrauerit. Accepitne ab Authenticis ipsis crimine ex illo quod utique nominare, ne et dicentis os et aures audientium[296] polluantur, turpissimum est, *fames, pestilentias, terrae motus* accidere solere? Legitne Codicibus Publicis ad Legem Iuliam quid imperator adiecerit? *Cum uir nubit in feminam*, ait (audisne Panormita?) [N109r] et *ubi sexus perdit locum, ubi scelus est quod non proficit scire, ubi Venus mutatur in alteram formam, ubi amor quaeritur et non inuenitur: iubemus insurgere leges, armari iura gladio, ultore, ut exquisitis poenis subdantur infames qui sunt uel futuri sunt, rei*. Nouitne saltem ex Plautino suo Curculione *fumo comburi*[297] *nihil posse, flamma posse?* Mirabile auditu quidem: his minis, his terroribus nihil contremiscat, [A133r] nihil immutetur, nihil egregii facinoris quicquam aggrediatur, denique, iureconsultorum auditione perpetua mores uiro graui dignos nihil aliquando componat.

---

[293]Animaduertitne quorsum] Animaduertitne quorum quorsum *N*
[294]At] Ac *N*
[295]uideri et palpari] ᵇpalpari et ᵃuideri *corr. A*
[296]aures audientium *tr. N*
[297]comburi] cumburri *A*

[348]"Leccadelli" puns on various forms of *leccator*, a glutton or lecher (cf. *Philippic* §22 n. 52 and §40 n. 101; for the mockery of "Beccadelli," see *Philippic* §20 n. 45; cf. §76, §132, and §174).
[349]Pliny the Younger *Letter* 3.3.6; cf. Cicero *In Defense of Marcellus* 22.
[350]Psalms 30/31.9; cf. Jerome *Against Vigilantius* 1.2.
[351]Virgil *Aeneid* 6.129.
[352]The *Body of Civil Law* (*Corpus Iuris Civilis*), compiled and organized under the Emperor Justinian (d. 565), was divided into three parts: (1) the Code (*Codex*), comprised of the imperial *constitutiones*; (2) the Pandects (*Pandectae*) or Digests (*Digesta*), case summaries in appeals from lower to higher courts; and (3) the Novels (*Novellae*), the new laws of Justinian, which were also called *Authentics* because they were translations of the Greek originals.

133 Does that Beccadelli of yours (I almost said Lecherelli)[348] know that I speak of things not only true but also well known? Whew! Does that wretched slave notice where the rope or collar drags him? "Human life," Pliny says, "has the most remote hideaways and strongest refuges."[349] But this man, on the contrary, pours out his secrets and declares them everywhere; he reveals himself completely; and what is more, stripped bare, he can be viewed and stroked without disguise and flattery as if he were on the block like an ass or "mule which has no intelligence."[350] Even though every scoundrel knows this, we especially, however, as men of the opposing camp, "few in number," to be sure, "but under the loving protection"[351] of God himself, cannot but come to know down to the last farthing what his excellence or grandeur amounts to.

134 But let us set aside the nature of his virtues and morals, which is known even to fools. Let this man, who has worn out as much as defiled and polluted all of Italy, every single university, and every school of the most famous cities, tell us just what *Pandects* he has cracked the covers of, what *Digests* or *Law Codes* he has so far labored over late into the night.[352] Has he not learned from the *Authentics* that "famines, plagues, and earthquakes"[353] usually happen on account of that crime that is too foul to say aloud lest both the speaker's mouth and the hearers' ears should be polluted? Has he read in the *Civil Codes*[354] what the Emperor added to the Julian Law? The Emperor says (are you listening, Panormita?): "When a man marries in the role of a woman,[355] and where gender loses its identity, where an enormity exists that is harmful to know about, where Venus changes into another form, and where love is sought and is not found:[356] in such instances, We order that the laws rise up and that rights be armed with the sword of vengeance so that present and future those guilty of such offense undergo carefully chosen penalties."[357] Does he know at least from his Plautine *Curculio* that "smoke can burn nothing, but flames can"?[358] It is truly amazing to hear, but at these threats and intimidations he never trembles, he never changes, he never attempts anything of distinction, and ultimately, even though listening constantly to jurists, he never develops morals worthy of a serious man.

---

[353]*Novella Justiniani* 77.1. The Emperor Justinian in 538 issued a law against "all who sinned against nature, who swore by their hair, and blasphemed against God in other ways." He intensified the penalties (*acerbiores poenas*) after the so-called "Justinian Plague" or 542–44 (see Hergemöller 28–29; for *Authentics* see n. 352 above).

[354]This law was introduced by the first Christian Emperor Constantine's sons, Constans and Constantius, on 4 December 342 (see Hergemöller 27; for *Civil Law*, see n. 352 above).

[355]On the use of *in* with the accusative in the sense of *velut* (as if), see McKibben, esp. 168–69.

[356]These euphemisms could refer to almost any sexual taboo, apparently not least the male in a passive role (e.g., "where gender loses it identity") whether in a hetero- or homosexual act (see Boswell 50n, 122n; Richlin 1983, 87–98, 136–39, 220–22; and Rocke 233–34; for Venus changing "into another form," see Dalla; and Hergemöller 27–28). Writers of confessional manuals regarded these taboos as even worse if they occurred between a married couple because such acts violated the sacrament of marriage (Tentler 186–208).

[357]*Codex Justiniani* 9.9.31; cf. John of Salisbury *Policraticus* 3.13.

[358]Plautus (*Curculio* 54) makes this statement in reference to the escalating danger of romantic involvement: what starts with kisses ends with sex. Rho certainly has escalating danger in mind, but refers rather to the threat of inquisition: what starts with accusation ends with burning at the stake (see Hergemöller 30–33; cf. *Philippic* §12 and §23).

135 Cupisne hanc tibi tam crassae socordiae fenestram aperiri? Plane singulos ex assuetudine magis quam[298] discendi cura aut uoto auditus[299] quidem,[300] *senex elementarius* non intellecturus scholas ingreditur. Subsellium habet. Locum occupat. Vmbram efficit. Codicem prae se tenet, quem etsi aperit, fortuito aperit: ne legit quidem. Apertum esse id satis sibi esse uidetur, tametsi legem aut parafum praeceptoris nesciat. Quid ergo? Leges quae coram leguntur aures attingunt quidem non complent, quas his[301] uerbis alloquitur: "Qui tantus est strepitus? Qui clamor? Quae quotidiana uociferatio elegiacis nostris studiis aliena?" Ad leges itaque aures eius exurdescunt; succi introrsum stilla non tollitur. Quid mirum dum Hermaphroditum suum animo intus molitur, corpore quidem praesentem scholis sese praestat, mente uero ac cerebro extra peruagatur; et cum histrionibus Atellanis scurris et pantomimis, sui impos sibique[302] ipsi absens abducitur? Itaque saepenumero sub praeceptore aut oscitare quidem aut frontem auresque perfricare conspicitur.

136 Suntne pluria quae[303] hoc ex labyrintho inextricabili dici queant? Pluria? Plane cum quas res cumque enumerasse putauerimus (flagitiorum enim suorum tantus est ambitus), ampliora et pluria restant quae nullis amplexibus obiri aut astringi possint. Quid possint? Magno enim cerebro opus esset.

137 Non sum tamen tam abrasae aut oblitteratae memoriae,[304] quin tot inter nefandissima[305] scelera iam pridem tecum legisse teneam ex studiis sudoribusque suis (O scelus inauditum! flagitium inexcogitatum!) leges haud nullas, quas homo Tartareus ipse rogauerat, easque contra Iuliam, Scantiniam, Voconiam, Liciniam ipse Panormita, daemon alter, pro lupis, catamitis, et cinaedis suis "Futuarias" uocitabat. Quas uel[306] pro sui nominis, credo, aeterna et indelebili gloria per lenonum scortorumque conuentus et conciliabula toto paene orbe dissipauerat. O mores taetros! O tempora digna[307]

---

[298]quam *om. N*
[299]auditus] -turus *N*
[300]quidem] quidam *N*
[301]his] is *A*
[302]sibique] suique *N*
[303]pluria quae] pluria ᵘᵃplane cum quas res cumque enumerasse putauerimusᶜᵃᵗ quae *corr. N*
[304]aut oblitteratae memoriae] ᵇmemoriae ᵃaut ᵃoblitteratae *corr. A*
[305]nefan-] *corr. A*
[306]uel *om. A*
[307]tempora digna] *corr. A*

[359]Seneca the Younger *Letter* 36.4; see *Philippic* §27 n. 63; cf. *Philippic* §79 and §145.
[360]In primary and secondary education, most students studied under private teachers with whom parents signed individual contracts, not unlike the way someone might now learn music, art, or dance (see Grendler 29; and Witt 2000, 193–97). *Parafum* is a medieval vernacularism deriving from the late Latin *paragraphus*, a "sign of separation" (see Dizionario Garzanti, *parafa*).

135 Do you, Candido, want me to open a window for you onto such crass indifference? Clearly more from habit than from an interest in learning or a wish even to listen, Panormita enters the schools "as an old man learning his ABCs"[359] who will never understand anything. He takes his seat on a bench. He fills a space. He casts a shadow. He holds a book in front of him, and even though he opens it, he opens it at random: he does not even read. It seems enough for him that the book is open, although he does not even recognize his teacher's contract or the signature on it.[360] What is the result? The laws that are read aloud go in one ear and directly out the other. And he addresses them with these words: "Why so much noise? Why all the shouting? What is this daily clamor alien to our elegiac studies?" Panormita's ears, then, grow deaf to the law, but not a drop of the wax clogging them gets removed. What wonder is it that while he labors mentally to produce his *Hermaphrodite*, bodily he is present in school, but his thoughts and imaginings wander outside? What wonder is it that Atellan actors, jesters, and pantomimes[361] seduce him when he himself lacks self-control and self-awareness? Hence, one often sees him yawning or rubbing his brow and ears when the instructor is teaching.

136 Out of this inextricable labyrinth is there more that we can say? More? Clearly when we start to think that we have counted everything, many more things remain that no boundaries can delimit and accommodate. Such is the extent of his indecencies. How could they be enumerated? I must say, it would take a great brain to do so.

137 I, however, am not such an amnesiac or so forgetful that I do not recall having read long ago with you, Candido, among the many abominable perversions coming out of his studies and labors, some laws which the infernal man sought to get enacted on behalf of his whores, catamites, and sodomites. Panormita, this new demon, called them the "Futuarian Laws"[362] in opposition to the Julian, Scantinian, Voconian, and Licinian Laws.[363] What shocking wickedness! An unthinkable outrage! He broadcast these laws practically throughout the whole world through the associations of pimps and whores for the everlasting and indelible glory, I believe, of his name. What foul morals! May lightning strike this age! What a demented person, or rather, what a terrible monster and "aberration that ought to be deported to the ends of the earth"[364] and "to be plunged into the depth of the sea" either in a parricide's leather sack or "tied to a donkey's

---

[361]"Atellan" refers to a type of vulgar farce known for using course, obscene language. It originated in the Oscan towns of Italy, but it became closely associated with the particular Oscan town of Atella, near Naples (Quintilian *The Education of the Orator* 6.3.47). For the significance of pantomimes, see *Philippic* §21 n. 49.

[362]Literally: "The Fuckers' Laws."

[363]Each of these laws (cf. *Philippic* §55) regulated specific concerns: Julian (adultery), Scantinian (sexual taboos), Voconian (dowries and women's inheritance), and Licinian (illegal aliens).

[364]Jerome *Against Vigilantius* 1.8; cf. Wiesen 220–21.

fulminibus! O insanum caput, immo monstrum horrendum *portentum*que *in terras ultimas deportandum* [A133v] aut culeo seu
1530 *mola asinaria in profundum maris* demergendum! *O praecidendam linguam et in frusta* secandam! Suntne haec somnia aut Sibyllae[308] ambages? Quem[309] enim homini huic impudentissimo, pro hisce legibus turpissimis, foedissimis, immundissimis, non dicam Christum, deum et dominum meum, iam designatum ultorem, sed, ut aliquando sane-
1535 tur resipiscatque, Hippocratem aut Asclepiadem dabimus? aut ex qua pyxide leporino illi, ut ita dixerim, cerebro antidotum inueniemus? Actum est, ilicet. Scelerum enim sepulcro immobilis flagitiorum uinculis colligatus iacet. Nulla postliminii spes *ad*[310] *intimum iam cerebrum ipsum sentinae putredo peruenit*. Nam interloquendum os
1540 hermaphroditicum foetet, et dum animam e pulmone spirat atque respirat, putorem elegiacum a quo uirgines abhorrent profert.

138 Quid inquam? Inferendis tamen his Futuariis Legibus, eloquentiam priscam effingere et mentiri admodum conatus est. Imperatiuis enim latores ipsi legum ut saepe utebantur, uerbi causa:
1545 *Iusta imperia sunto, hisque ciues modeste ac sine recusatione parento*, et huius generis alia. Ita iterum dixerim eloquentiam priscam effingere et mentiri conatus est ut, nisi illarum legum hic Panormita, *bipedum omnium*[311] *nequissimus* bipes, auctor et lator rogatorque certo sciretur, ex Duodecim Tabulis hae ipsae suae leges decisae ali-
1550 quando ab honestissimis uiris esse uideantur.

139 "Sed quae[312] huiusce foedissimae rogationis causa, sanctissime Panormita? Qui stimulus? Quis incentor? Quo daemone percitus?" Respondeat, rogo.

140 Videlicet audiuerat ad corrigendas, modificandas,
1555 digerendas, ampliandas[313] [N109v] eas illas Tabularum Leges decemuiros e sapientioribus, grauioribus Romanis — Appium quidem Claudium, Genuicium, Vetium, Iulium, Manlium, Sulpicium, Sextum, Curiatium, Romedium, Postumium — delectos esse. Legerat Moysem Hebraeis Leges digito dei conscriptas attulisse; Phoroneum
1560 Regem primum Graecis leges et iudicia constituisse, Mercurium

---

[308]Sibyllae] -biblee *N*
[309]Quem *N*: Quae *A*
[310]ad *N*: ab *A*
[311]omnium *N, Plin., Apul.* : hominum *A*
[312]quae *N*: quem *A*
[313]digerendas, ampliandas] ampliandas, di*rig*endas *N*

[365]Matthew 18.6.
[366]Jerome *Letter* 61.4 (to Vigilantius); cf. Jerome *Letter* 109.3 (against Vigilantius) and Wiesen 220–21.

millstone."³⁶⁵ "That tongue of his! It ought to be cut out and chopped to pieces!"³⁶⁶ Are these the visions or enigmas of the Sibyl? Whom, therefore, shall we provide for this impudent man, so that he eventually be cured of these wicked, foul, and impure laws, and recover his sanity? Surely not Christ, I would say, my God and Lord, whom I already called my Avenger, but rather some Hippocrates or Asclepiades?³⁶⁷ Or in what container shall we find the antidote, as I would say, for this harebrain? He is done for. It is all up for him. For bound in permanent shackles of indecency, he lies entombed in his atrocities. No hope of recovery "now penetrates through that putrid cesspool to the innermost core of his brain."³⁶⁸ For when his hermaphroditic mouth opens, it reeks;³⁶⁹ and when he inhales and exhales breath from his lungs, he utters elegiac rottenness that makes virgins recoil.

138 What am I saying? Despite all of this, he tried hard to imitate and feign an archaic literary style when proposing his Futuarian Laws. For the proposers of laws often used imperatives, as for example in this statement: "Commands shall be just, and citizens shall submit to them temperately and without objection,"³⁷⁰ and other injunctions of this kind. So, I would reiterate, he tried to imitate and feign an archaic literary style to make it seem that honorable men had at some point extracted these laws of his from the *Twelve Tables*,³⁷¹ when in fact we knew for sure that Panormita, "the most depraved biped of all bipedal beasts,"³⁷² was the author, introducer, and proposer of those laws.

139 "But what is the cause of this foul proposal, most saintly Panormita? What motivates it? Who incites it? What demon impels it?" Please, let him respond.

140 No doubt he heard that the Decemviri — Appius Claudius, Genucius, Vetius, Julius, Manlius, Sulpicius, Sextus, Curiatius, Romedius, and Postumius³⁷³ — were selected from the wiser, more virtuous Romans to reform, limit, organize, and augment the laws of the *Tables*. He read that Moses carried to the Hebrews the Law written by the finger of God;³⁷⁴ that King Phoroneus established laws and courts for the Greeks;³⁷⁵ that Mercury Trismegistus did the same for the

---

³⁶⁷Asclepiades (d. ca. 40 BCE) was a famous doctor from Bythinia who practiced in Rome. For Hippocrates, see *Philippic* §121 n. 308.

³⁶⁸Jerome *Letter* 61.3 (to Vigilanius).

³⁶⁹Cf. Jerome *Letter* 109.1 (against Vigilantius); for "impure mouth" (*os impurum*), see *Philippic* §106 n. 268.

³⁷⁰Cicero *Laws* 3.3.6.

³⁷¹For the Twelve Tables, the earliest Roman Law code, see *Philippic* §55 n. 131 and §61 n. 143; cf. also *Philippic* §140.

³⁷²Pliny the Younger *Letter* 1.5.14; cf. Apuleius *Metamorphoses* (*The Golden Ass*) 4.10.

³⁷³Rho takes this list of the Decemviri (the Ten Men) from Livy (3.33.3), who also gives their praenomen. But Rho's manuscript of Livy must have been corrupt: for "Vetius" read "Veturius"; for "Sextus" read "Sestius"; for "Romedius" read "Romilius" (cf. Rho *Imitations* 55v–56v: *Decemviris*).

³⁷⁴The Tables of the Torah (Law) were said to have been "the work of God, and the writing was the writing of God" (Exodus 32.15–16; KJV).

³⁷⁵Phoroneus is known from Argive legend, which represents him as having lived before Deucalion's flood and states that he was one of the judges between Hera and Poseidon (OCD).

Trismegistum Aegyptiis, Solonem Atheniensibus, Lycurgum Apollinis auctoritate Lacedaemonibus, Numam Pompilium Romanis, quos omnis immortalitatem assecutos[314] [A134r] honestissimam non iniuria[315] arbitrabatur.

141 Quid honestissimam? *Ex lege enim*, aiunt, *humana*[316] *coercetur audacia; tuta inter improbos uersatur innocentia*. Improbis uero, formidato supplicio, impetus et nocendi facultas tollitur. Praeclare uero Cicero in his De legibus, *Cum dico "legem,"* ait, *nihil aliud intellegi uolo*,[317] *quam "imperium," sine quo nec domus ulla nec ciuitas nec gens nec hominum uniuersum genus stare nec rerum natura omnis nec ipse mundus*[318] *potest*. Dum itaque uetus prouerbium inualuisset — *leges* bonas, uidelicet, *malis ex moribus* procreari — ratus est Panormita, hic noster legislator, se immortalitati omnibusque saeculis consecratum iri, si, commutato prouerbio, bonis ex moribus leges illas Futuarias inquinatissimas ipse porcorum omnium inquinatissimus[319] largiretur.

142 Videtne iam tandem se laqueis et quasi oestrum quoddam aranearum cassibus deprehensum e quibus, nisi pro maledictis multam talionemque meritam[320] dissoluat, nisi et *fustibus caesus in metallum* exigatur, enodari ullo pacto nequeat? Euanescetne aut, uelut anguis lubricus, migrabit e manibus? Instat tamen et urget, seque excutit quoad potest, atque poetam se non tam feliciter quam arroganter profitetur: *Musas* ait sibi[321] quam familiares easque — quod peculiare, quod suum est — *Sicelidas* esse. Credo equidem illas et sibi et[322] Theocrito necessitudine quadam una uel ex familia deuinctas, idcirco insolentius gloriae cupidis[323] compluribus et inflatis hominibus blandiri caelumque polliceri. Mihi uero acerbe (nisi terga[324] maturauerim) uidetur minitari, quem tamen eadem litterula — facete (modo sciret) interloqui uoluit[325] — me "compoetam" appellat suum.

---

[314]assecutos] assuetos assecutos *N*
[315]iniuria] -riam *N*
[316]aiunt humana] ᵇhumana ᵃaiunt *corr. A*
[317]aliud intellegi uolo *N, Cic.* : aliud intellegi aliud uolo *A*
[318]ipse mundus *N, Cic.* : *tr. A*
[319]ipse porcorum omnium inquinatissimus *om. N*
[320]meritam] -ta *N*
[321]ait sibi *tr. N*
[322]et *om. N*
[323]cupidis] -dos *N*
[324]terga] a terga *N*
[325]uoluit] noluit *N*

Egyptians,[376] Solon for the Athenians, Lycurgus by Apollo's authority for the Spartans, and Numa Pompilius for the Romans.[377] All of them, Panormita observed, attained, not without just cause, a most honorable immortality.

141 Why most honorable? "For," they say, "it is by law that human audacity is restrained and innocence lives securely among the unprincipled. Fear of punishment, in fact," removes "from the unprincipled" the impulse and licence to injure.[378] Moreover, Cicero in *On Laws* stated clearly, "When I say 'law' I want understood nothing but 'governing authority,' without which no home, no city, no people, no humanity, no system of nature or the universe itself can stand."[379] Consequently, as long as the old proverb held, namely, that "bad practice begets good laws,"[380] our legislator Panormita imagined that he was going to be solemnly immortalized for all time, if he, the filthiest of all pigs — in altering the proverb — out of good practice gave us those filthy Futuarian Laws.

142 Does he now finally realize that like a fly in a spider's web he is caught in a trap from which he cannot extricate himself unless he pays a just fine and talion for his insults and unless he is "flogged and condemned to the mines."[381] Will he disappear or slither out of our hands like a slimy snake? He urgently insists, nevertheless, that he is a poet and shakes himself and professes himself to be such more with arrogance than with effect. "The Muses," he says, "are Sicilian"[382] and are on intimate terms with him, since it is something that belongs to him. Indeed, I concede that a certain affinity binds the Muses to him and to Theocritus as though they were from a single family.[383] This explains why the Muses flatter and promise the skies to many who are more brazenly vainglorious and puffed up with their self-importance. But he seems to threaten me harshly unless I quickly retreat. Yet in this same wretched little letter he called me his "fellow poet."[384] He wanted to speak wittily — if he only knew how!

---

[376]Hermes Trismegistus (that is, "Thrice-Great Hermes" or "Great Great Great Thoth"), known from a collection of Greek texts called the *Hermetica*, was mistakenly identified as the ancient Egyptian god of letters (see *Philippic* §30 n. 69; see also Copenhaver 1992; and Copenhaver and Schmitt 146–47).

[377]Cf. *Philippic* §30.

[378]Augustine *Letter* 153.6.16; cf. Isidore *Etymologies* 5.20.1 and Peter Abelard *Sic et Non* Quaest. 156.

[379]Cicero *Laws* 3.1.3.

[380]Macrobius *Saturnalia* 3.17.10.

[381]Pliny the Younger *Letter* 2.11.9.

[382]Panormita *Etsi facile* §5 (Appendix I below).

[383]Theocritus, a native Sicilian from Syracuse, was described by Quintilian (*The Education of the Orator* 10.1.55) as having "a rustic and pastoral muse." Aulus Gellius (9.9.4–11) compared Theocritus unfavorably to Virgil (cf. *Philippic* §33 n. 77), who had modelled his *Eclogues* on the idyllic poetry of Theocritus. Guarino Veronese, in his letter (*Posteaquam alteras* 147) to Panormita which circulated with *The Hermaphrodite*, wrote to Panormita that: "You imitate Theocritus, the ancient alumnus of Sicilian soil, evoking the poet with primeval sweetness" (*Theocriton, antiquum Siculae telluris alumnum, / effingis, prisca revocans dulcedine vatem*). Cf. *Philippic* §109–§110; for Theocritus, see Witke 32–34.

[384]Panormita *Etsi facile* §1 (Appendix I below).

143 Hem! Asciscantur iam canes! Hic iacet lepus. Hoc loco plane (quia "poeta est") "inuideri sibi" aperte declarauit. Recte quidem. Enimuero si uocem eius, si faciem, si liniamenta, si gestus, si ingressum, si inflexiones ceteras, et motus intuebimur, poetam esse grauissimum lepidissimumque nequaquam[326] diffiteamur oportebit. *Gradu* enim ita[327] *suspenso, summis*que inambulat *digitis; sublatis* quoque *umeris*[328] ita pedetentim procedit *in publicum,* ut testudo Ferrariensis quaedam esse omnino[329] uideatur: optimum plane [A134v] poetae signum. *Verba* deinde *uix pauca ac per interualla* capit, eaque *sesquipedalia* in digitos digerit, *ut potius illum singultire* quam *proloqui* uelit arbitrere. Se totum, ut saepe recipit *aduersante natura* componitque, timet effluere, tamen *ampullas proiicit* semiadopertulisque[330] oculis quam caste conspicatur, ut magis Catonem[331] ex uano et ficto homine se aut Aristidem quam Roscium aut Hylam et Pyladem agnoscas. Adducit deinde intuentibus eum Maecenatibus supercilia, contrahit nares, frontem rugat, labia sugit,[332] caput non sine reliquo corpore inflectit: quae singula extant, ut nosti, tristioris consideratiorisque poetae ornamenta.

144 Verum si ex poetis quempiam ipse nobis reddit, Appuleium quidem effingere, referre, exprimere illum credas. Sunt tamen inter illos quae distent haud nulla.[333] Appulei⟨i⟩ namque lucubratiunculae[334] et studia plus olei, Hermphroditi[335] uero sui uigiliae et chameuniae[336] plus Veneris et Bacchi sapiunt. Ille quadrupes,

---

[326]nequaquam *om. N*
[327]ita] *mg. suppl. N*
[328]umeris] *mg. suppl. A*
[329]omnino] *s.l. suppl. A*
[330]semiadopertulisque] -adopor- *N* : -que *s.l. suppl. A*
[331]Catonem *om. N*
[332]labia sugit *hic A, post* inflectit *N*
[333]nulla] *corr. A*
[334]lucubratiun-] -bratun- *N*
[335]Hermaphroditi *N* : -phrodi *A*
[336]chameuniae *scripsi* : caumeniae *AN*

---

[385]Panormita *Etsi facile* §2 (Appendix I below).
[386]Terence *Phormio* 867; Seneca the Elder *Suasoriae* 2.17.
[387]Jerome *Letter* 125.16 (to Rusticus); cf. Wiesen 178–79, 230–31.
[388]Jerome *Letter* 125.18 (to Rusticus); cf. Wiesen 229.
[389]That is, "foot-and-a-half-long words," which comes from Horace *The Art of Poetry* 97. Remembering the points one is to make in an oration by ticking them off on the fingers comes from Quintilian *The Education of the Orator* 11.3.114. The image here is of Panormita having to count on his fingers just to get through the syllables of his pretentious phrases.
[390]Jerome *Letter* 125.18 (to Rusticus); cf. Wiesen 229.

143 Ho! Now sic the dogs! Here lies a hare. In this place he openly declared that he is obviously envied because "he is a poet."[385] Right he is. For, if we examine his voice, face, features, posture, gait, and other mannerisms and movements, we should not deny at all that he is a serious and charming poet. For a certainty, he "minces around on tip-toes."[386] He also "makes his public entrance slowly with shoulders held high"[387] so that he looks exactly like some Ferrarese turtle: this is clearly the best sign of a poet. Then "he seizes upon just a few words with pauses in between"[388] and counts off these "sesquepedalian words" on his fingers[389] so that you would think he wants "to hiccough rather than to speak."[390] He is afraid to divulge himself completely, with the result that he frequently pulls back and composes "against his inclinations."[391] Yet he "blurts out inflated expressions"[392] and with half-closed eyes peeks about chastely[393] in order that you may recognize in this fatuous and deceitful man a Cato or an Aristides instead of a Roscius, Hylas, or Pylades.[394] Then with his Maecenases looking on,[395] he knits his brows, contracts his nostrils, wrinkles his face, purses his lips, and turns his head and body simultaneously. Each of these, as you know, stands out as the accoutrements of a more melancholic and thoughtful poet.[396]

144 But if he does remind us of any one the poets, you might think that he is impersonating, echoing, and imitating Apuleius.[397] There are, however, some differences between them. For the late night studies of Apuleius smell more of the lamp, but the vigils and sleeping catch-as-catch-can that produced Panormita's *Hermaphrodite* smell more of Venus and Bacchus.[398] In addition, Apuleius presented himself as a four-footed ass, Panormita as a two-footed ass; the former as an

---

[391]According to Cicero (*On Duties* 1.31.110), to possess an "unwilling Minerva" (Minerva being the goddess of wisdom and the arts) is to attempt something "with nature opposing or fighting" (*invita Minerva, ut aiunt, id est adversante et repugnante natura*), that is, without any natural ability (cf. Horace *The Art of Poetry* 385).

[392]Horace *The Art of Poetry* 97.

[393]Cf. Apuleius *Metamorphoses* (*The Golden Ass*) 3.14.

[394]For Cato and Aristides, see *Philippic* §33 n. 84. Roscius (d. 62 BCE) was a famous actor whose eyes were crossed (Cicero *On the Nature of the Gods* 1.79). Suetonius describes Hylas and Pylades and their punishment by Caesar Augustus: "Hylas, a pantomimic actor, was publicly scourged in the atrium of his own house . . . and Pylades was expelled from the city and from Italy as well. . . ." (*Augustus* 45.4; LCL).

[395]See *Philippic* §54 n. 130; cf. also §80, §121, §131, §170, §175, and §178.

[396]"Knitted" or "lowered brows" (*adductum* or *demissum supercilium*) and "wrinkled face" (*rugata fronte*) are expressions from Jerome (*Letters* 53.7, 125.18, and *Against Jovinian* 1.34), which were used "to portray hypocritical solemnity" and "are standard details of Jerome's portraits of haughtiness" (Wiesen 91, 98, 212, and 229–30). Rho combines these attributes with the characteristics of an ape (cf. *Philippic* §17).

[397]That is, Apuleius of Madaura (ca. 125–ca. 170) who in his work *Metamorphoses* (*The Golden Ass*) told of his misadventures after a sorceress smeared him with an unguent and turned him into an ass. Much of what is known about Apuleius comes from his *Apology*, in which he defends himself against a charge of magical practices. He was born to a prosperous North African family of Madaura and studied at Carthage and Athens. He travelled and gave lectures in Rome and several places in the East. His other surviving works are *A Selection of Oratorical Flowers*, *On Plato and his Teaching*, *On the God of Socrates*, and *On the World* (Conte 553–70; cf. *Apology* §24).

[398]Venus was the goddess of love; Bacchus, the god of wine (cf. Panormita *Hermaphrodite* 1.4.4).

iste bipes; ille foris, iste intus asinus esse plane perhibetur; ille rerum omnium scientissimus, hic ignorantissimus quidem. En iam itaque poetam gloriosum, cui iam nemo non inuidere debeat!

145 Sed ut orationem iterum atque iterum ad se uertam linguacem quidem hominem locutuleiumque:[337] "Quid in ostentationibus pollicitationibusque tam prodigus et infrenis es? Quid ineptiarum tuarum tot uolumina passim tot turbas fundis? Quid *umidis lapsantibus*que *uerbis* tot de te futuras expectationes, quasi nesciaris, effutis et blateras? Putasne, pure grammaticule et litterator, pro arbitratu tuo quos destinaueris scriptis tuis illustrare celebrareque, quibus afficiaris immortales efficere, quos oderis, uti Rhodum illum[338] [N110r] clarissimum uirum honestissimumque odis, quasi perpetuo extinctos sepeliri oportere? Hae sunt quidem e tonstrinis pertritae fabulae. Necdum enim[339] eo doctrinae aut artis inscendisti[340] ut Homerum seu Vergilium aequare possis; quibus quidem aspirare tibi remotius est difficiliusque quam te, iam pridem asinum, in hominem ex integro iterum uerti. Vnde hanc igitur ingenii felicitatem tibi uindicas tuis ut uersibus alios deos, alios semideos *uictosque Penates* quando collibuerit caelo consecraturum te pollicearis? Te tibi plane, ut uideo, nimium credis et altius quam Minerua tua aut genium patiatur eniteris.

146 "Ani[A135r]maduertimus Vergilium, ut est apud Macrobium, *doctissime ius pontificium*[341] *tamquam* id unum profiteretur[342] *in multa et uaria operis sui parte* seruasse, ut non iniuria pontifex maximus ab omnibus credi posset; ita *iuris auguralis*[343] *scientiam* quae summo honori habebatur percalluisse, *ut, si aliarum disciplinarum* — ut Flauianus ait — *doctrina destitueretur, haec illum uel sola professio sublimaret.* Eustathius uero de illo sic: *Maxime praedicarem quanta de Graecis cautus et tamquam aliud agens modo*

---

[337]locutu-] *corr. A*
[338]Rhodum illum *tr. N*
[339]enim *om. A*
[340]inscen-] incen- *N*
[341]pontificium *Macr.* : -cum *AN*
[342]profiteretur] -tetur *N*
[343]auguralis] angularis *N*

---

[399]"The Braggart Poet" (*poeta gloriosus*) is a turn on Plautus' "The Braggart Soldier" (*miles gloriosus*).
[400]Aulus Gellius 1.15.1.
[401]See *Philippic* §27 n. 63; cf. *Philippic* §79 and §135.
[402]Panormita in his letters and poems used "Rhodes" to refer sarcastically to Rho (see Sabbadini 1891, 2–5). Rho obviously resented the remarks but used the third person here presumably in order that he not verify the identification or provide opportunity for the rejoinder "if the shoe fits. . . ." (cf. *Philippic* §178).
[403]Regarding transformation from an ass to a man, see n. 397 above.

ass outwardly, the latter as an ass inwardly; the former as thoroughly knowledgeable, the latter as thoroughly ignorant. Well now, look at the braggart poet whom everyone nowadays is supposed to envy![399]

145 But let me keep on directing my harangue at this loquacious chatterbox of a man: "Why are you, Panormita, so extravagant and unrestrained in your boasts and promises? Why do you indiscriminately pour out so many volumes and such a mass of absurdities? Why do you babble and blather 'with sodden and stumbling words'[400] about so many imminent prospects for yourself, as if you didn't know what their real likelihood was? Do you, who are nothing more than a measly teacher of children's ABCs,[401] think that those whom you've decided to glorify and celebrate in your writings should become immortal at your discretion? and that those whom you hate, just as you hate Rhodes,[402] that well-known and respectable man, ought to be obliterated as if snuffed out forever? All this, to be sure, is tired gossip from the barbershop. For you've not yet attained a level of learning and art whereby you can equal Homer or Virgil. Indeed, the chances of you equaling them are far more remote and difficult than for you, who have been an ass now for a long time, being turned back once more into a man.[403] On what basis, therefore, do you claim this blessed talent of yours which allows you to promise that when heaven pleases you're going to hallow in verse other gods, demigods, and 'the conquered Penates'?[404] It's obvious, at least to me, that you're inordinately self-confident and reach beyond what your Minerva or talent permits.[405]

146 "According to Macrobius,[406] we see 'the great learning with which Virgil has observed the rules of the pontifical law in many different parts of his work'[407] as if it were his only profession, so that everyone could with justification believe him to have been the Pontifex Maximus.[408] Virgil became so thoroughly conversant with 'the knowledge of the augural law,' which was held in highest honor, 'that even if he were unskilled in all other branches of learning,' as Flavianus said, 'the exhibition of this knowledge alone would win him high esteem.'[409] Eustathius, moreover, said this about him: 'I should give the highest praise to his use of Greek models — a cautious use and one which may even have the appearance of being accidental, since he sometimes skillfully conceals the debt, although at other times he imitates openly — did I not admire even more his knowledge of astronomy and of the whole field of philosophy, and the sparing and

---

[404]Virgil *Aeneid* 1.68. The Penates are the tutelary gods of the Roman state, thought to have been brought from Troy by Aeneas. In other words, Panormita promises to write poetry equal to Virgil's *Aeneid* (see *Philippic* §33 n. 77).

[405]For the significance of "an unwilling Minerva," see n. 391 above.

[406]For Macrobius, see *Philippic* §104 n. 262.

[407]Macrobius *Saturnalia* 1.24.16 (trans. Davies 157).

[408]The *Pontifex Maximus* was the head of the College of Priests and therefore of the state religion of Rome. *Pontifex Maximus* means literally, "the chief bridge maker," a skill that early Romans apparently regarded as a form of magic somehow belonging to the realm of the sacred.

[409]Macrobius *Saturnalia* 1.24.17 (trans. Davies 157). Virius Nicomachus Flavianus, a Roman aristocrat whose *Annales* are now lost, and Eustathius (of Cappadocia?), a contemporary philosopher, are interlocutors in the dialogue of the *Saturnalia*.

artificis[344] *dissimulatione, modo professa imitatione transtulerit, ni*[345] *me maior admiratio de astrologia totaque philosophia teneret, quam parcus et sobrius operi suo nusquam reprehendendus aspersit.*

147 "Tu uero, nouelle Poeta, nouis alphabetis dumtaxat imbutus atque diphthongis, audesne tam temere caelos et aeternitatem spondere et astipulari? Vergilius idem (ut loco allegato[346] lectitamus) omnia *dicendi genera* complexus est:[347] cum Cicerone *copiosum*, cum Sallustio *breue*, cum Frontone *siccum*, cum Plinio Secundo *pingue et floridum*. Cedo tu nunc sodes rogo, quando non omnia uti Vergilius ea genera amplecteris — cedo rogo — quo uno saltem in horum genere uerseris? Quid erubescis? Libere dixerim te diuinis his mensis non — siquidem licet — accumbere. Quid ergo? Habe iam tu solus pro palma quintum genus, uidelicet ut spurce semper ac petulanter colloquare.

148 "Quatuor tamen his generibus Vergilius[348] aliisque studiis plurimis mirandum in modum praeditus, dum Aeneam suum scribit, non mediocriter frigere, immo quasi paeniteat[349] suscepti operis, apparet. Extat enim eius ad Augustum breuis sed insignis epistolae frustum[350] quoddam: '*Ego uero,*' ait, '*frequentes a te litteras accipio*'; *et infra:* '*De Aenea quidem meo, si mehercle iam dignum auribus haberem tuis, libenter mitterem,*[351] *sed tanta inchoata res est ut paene uitio mentis tantum opus ingressus mihi uidear, cum praesertim, ut scis, alia quoque studia ad id opus multoque potiora impertiar.*'

149 "Quo nunc te proripis, hominum insulsissime? Qua caeli regione tu, noctua implumis,[352] uolaturus es quando ipse Vergilius pro se laborat ac uitio mentis Aeneam ipsum[353] suum inchoauisse paenitere propemodum uideatur? Num tu sic facile sine Athenis aut academia ulla, sine sudore et [A135v] negotio aliquo, uno dumtaxat anseris calamo quos uelis caelo deos pingis,[354] quos uelis expingis,[355] sic alter ille poeta Graecus leuitate quadam temere atque promiscue Periclem, Atheniensium ducem, *spectatae uirtutis uirum*, perinde atque *Cleonem, Cleophontem, et Hyperbolum*, ciues *improbos seditiosos*que, pro arbitratu sepelire arbitrabatur?

---

[344]artificis] -ci *Macr.*
[345]ni] in *N*
[346]allegato] memorato *N*
[347]est *om. A*
[348]Vergilius *om. A*
[349]paeniteat] -niat *N*
[350]frustum] *corr. A*
[351]mitterem] -tere *N*
[352]implumis *N* : in plumis *A*
[353]ipsum] *mg. suppl. A*
[354]pingis *hic A, post* calamo quos *N*
[355]quos uelis expingis *om. N*

restrained way in which he makes occasional, and everywhere praiseworthy, use of this knowledge in his poems.'[410]

147 "But do you, poet-come-lately, who are imbued only with new Latin characters and diphthongs,[411] so brazenly dare to promise with assurance the heavens and eternity? Virgil himself (as we read in the above mentioned source) encompassed every 'style.'[412] Along with Cicero he was 'copious,' along with Sallust he was 'concise,' along with Fronto he was 'dry,' and along with Pliny the Younger he was 'rich and ornate.'[413] Come now, if you would, since you don't embrace, like Virgil, all of these styles, please tell us which of these styles you've cultivated? Why do you blush? I'd say frankly that you don't recline at these divine tables, if such were permitted. What's the result? You alone now are preeminent in a fifth style,[414] namely, always talking filthily and rudely.

148 "Virgil was wonderfully skilled in these four styles and many other studies. Yet while writing his *Aeneid*, he appeared in no small way paralyzed, or rather, he seemed to have regretted having taken up the task. For a fragment of his brief but famous letter to Augustus exists in which Virgil said: 'I am getting many letters from you.' And he continues later: 'As for my Aeneas, if I now had anything worthy of your attention, I should gladly send it. But the subject on which I have embarked is so vast that I think I must have been almost mad to have entered upon it, all the more so since, as you know, there are other, much more important studies which claim from me a share in the work.'[415]

149 "Where are you flitting off to now, Panormita, you ignoramus? To what celestial region are you going to fly, you unfledged owl,[416] when even Virgil struggled with self-doubt and apparently came to regret that from a mad impulse he undertook his *Aeneid*, of all things? Do you really have the power to paint in or out of the heavens any god you want without consulting the Athenians or any academy, without any sweat and bother, or with a solitary goose quill? Are you not instead like that other poet, the foolish Greek, who brashly and indiscriminately thought he could bury at his own discretion Pericles, the leader of the Athenians and 'a man of outstanding virtue,'[417] just as he had buried 'the unprincipled and seditious citizens, Cleon, Cleophon, and Hyperbolus'?[418]

---

[410] Macrobius *Saturnalia* 1.24.18 (trans. Davies 157); for Eustathius see n. 409 above.

[411] Rho is referring to the newly fashionable *littera antiqua* and of the growing awareness that "ae" or "oe" in classical orthography had become simply "e" in what we now call "medieval" Latin (see *Philippic* §117 n. 289).

[412] Macrobius *Saturnalia* 5.1.7 (trans. Davies 283).

[413] Macrobius *Saturnalia* 5.1.7 (trans. Davies 283).

[414] Macrobius *Saturnalia* 5.1.7. As Rho makes clear, Macrobius delineated what became recognized as "the four styles."

[415] Macrobius *Saturnalia* 1.24.11 (trans. Davies 155–56; minor punctuation changes mine).

[416] The owl is the symbol of Minerva, the goddess of wisdom and the arts. Note in this regard Rho's reference three lines later to "a solitary goose quill."

[417] Orosius *Histories against the Pagans* 1.21.

[418] Cicero *Republic* 4.10.11; cf. Augustine *The City of God* 2.9. Aristophanes (d. ca. 385 BCE), an Athenian comic playwright, attacked the members of the Athenian war party and, by implication, the Athenian politician Pericles.

150 "Venio nunc ad Ciceronem quo de lis extat[356] immortalis: ipsene eloquentia an Caesar armis praeualuerit? Num is diuino paene illi ingenio suo (modo serio, non ioco loqueretur) uisus est[357] omnino diffidisse, cum rerum gestarum suarum immortalitatem a poeta lucrio tantopere tamquam *impudenter — epistola* enim *non erubescit*, ait — exposceret, ut uel eas res ornari roget[358] *etiam uehementius quam* poeta ipse *fortasse* sentiret? *in eo* quoque *leges historiae* neglegat dicat? *amorique* suo denique *plusculum etiam quam concedat ueritas* largiatur persuadeat?

151 "De te ipso tute nunc uide, qui credis uno epigrammate et elogio seu tribus dactylis et spondeis rumores optimos et tibi et aliis in omnem posteritatem elargiri. *Non te plus sapere* iam *quam oportet sapere* declarasti, dum quod alieni muneris est occupare praesumis, et caelos caelicolis ipsis polliceri uidearis, praesertim quando Maronem ipsum operis incepti prope paeniteat, Cicero uero facere sibi satis nisi ope aliena adiutus nihil arbitretur? Vtrum aliquotiens didicisti qui qualisue deesse non debeat, qui scriptis suis aliorum uitam celebrare et illustrare uelit: eum illum quidem non illustrem aut incelebrem non esse[359] oportere? Lectitastine satyricum[360] illud?

> Sed tamen est operae pretium cognoscere, quales
> aedituos habeat belli spectata domique
> uirtus, indigno non committenda poetae.

Legisti apud Naeuium poetam etiam,[361] Hectora nequaquam satis laetari si dumtaxat laudaretur, sed addebat uel *ab laudato uiro* id fieri oportere? Sic Naeuius ergo Hectorem ipsum, sic Homerus Achillem, sic Vergilius Aeneam, sic Xenophon Agesilaum,[362] sic Herodotus Themistoclem, sic Curtius Alexandrum, sic quisque non indoctus Caesarem: Liuius, Plutarchus, Suetonius, Lucanus, clarissimi omnes et honestissimi uiri. Non sic uel *Alexander* — ut ait Cicero — *ab Apelle* [A136r] *potissimum pingi et*[363] *a Lysippo fingi uoluit, quod*

---

[356]extat] *corr. A*
[357]est] et *N*
[358]roget *om. N*
[359]non esse] non *s.l. suppl. A*
[360]Lectitastine satyricum [*l.* 1694] . . . [*l.* 1744] hoc saeculo *om. N*
[361]etiam *scripsi* : esse *A*
[362]Xenophon Agesilaum *scripsi*, *tr. A*
[363]et *Cic.* : *om. AN*

---

[419]Reflected in the aphorism: "Which is mightier, the pen or the sword?"
[420]Cicero *Letters to Friends* 22.1–2 (5.12.1–2).

150 "I come now to Cicero, the object of the endless dispute about whether he accomplished more with eloquence than Caesar with arms?[419] Provided that he spoke seriously and not jokingly, are we to take Cicero as distrusting his nearly divine talent when he 'impudently,' as it were, ('for,' as he said, 'a letter does not blush')[420] demanded immortality for his accomplishments from a money-grubbing poet?[421] and 'even requested that his accomplishments be represented more sensationally than' the poet himself 'would perhaps have intended'? and that the poet 'should ignore the laws of history'? and finally that the poet, 'out of his love of Cicero, should grant a little more than the truth allows'?[422]

151 "Now look at yourself, Panormita. For you believe that a single inscription and epitaph or three dactyls and spondees from you will leave to all posterity the most favorable reports of you and others. Haven't you declared that you now 'think more highly of yourself than you ought to think,'[423] when you presume to fill an office that's not your own[424] and appear to promise apotheosis to the gods themselves, especially when Virgil himself nearly regretted having started his work,[425] and even Cicero imagined that his aspirations wouldn't be fulfilled without assistance from someone else?[426] Haven't you heard more than once who or what sort of person one must be who wants to celebrate and glorify in his writings the life of other people? Haven't you heard, in fact, that he who himself lacks prestige or acclaim ought not to do it? Haven't you read the Satirist repeatedly where he says: 'But at any rate it is worth knowing what sort of temple-keepers attend Virtue, for having been looked after in war and peace, she must not be entrusted to an unworthy poet'?[427] Haven't you also read in the poet Naevius that Hector was never fully pleased by praise alone, but as Naevius added, that it should be done 'by a man who had himself been praised'?[428] Thus Naevius praised Hector, Homer praised Achilles, Virgil praised Aeneas, Xenophon praised Agesilaus, Herodotus praised Themistocles, and Curtius praised Alexander. And thus only someone learned — Livy, Plutarch, Suetonius, and Lucan, all famous and respectable men — praised Caesar. Likewise, as Cicero said, didn't even 'Alexander

---

[421] Lucius Lucceius, an ally of Cicero, was a historian — not a poet — who wrote a history of the period from 90–81 BCE. Cicero's letter, cited here, makes perfectly clear that Lucceius was writing a history. But insofar as Lucceius might have agreed to stretch the truth or "fictionalize" Cicero's role in stopping the Catiline Conspiracy (and we have no evidence that Lucceius in fact did so), Rho must have thought Lucceius had crossed the line between history and poetry, presumably into epic or Rho must have confused him with the poet Lucilius (see n. 291 above). Cicero obviously did not share Rho's scruple about embellishing a historical account, at least in any instance where it made him look better. On poetry and history; lies and truth, see Introduction 38 above; cf. also *Philippic* §156 and §185.

[422] Cicero *Letters to Friends* 22.3 (5.12.3).

[423] Romans 12.3.

[424] Cf. Augustine *Against the Letter of Parmenianus* 2.29.

[425] See *Philippic* §148 above.

[426] Cf. Cicero *Letters to Friends* 22.1 (5.12.1).

[427] Horace *Epistle* 2.1.229–231.

[428] Gnaeus Naevius (d. 201 or 204 BCE) was an early Roman writer of tragedies and comedies. His play *Hector proficiscens*, cited here through Cicero (*Letters to Friends* 22.7–8 [5.12.7–8]), does not survive (cf. also Cicero *Tusculan Disputations* 4.31.67).

illorum artem cum ipsis tum etiam sibi ob artificum praestantiam excellentiamque *gloriae fore* arbitrabatur?

152 "Verum si ita magnifice, immo arroganter, de te sentis, uir ceruicose, et tanto cerebro gloriaris, ut his cum illustribus uiris aeque accumbere queas existimes, timeo magnopere ne eo insaniae uenias ⟨aut⟩ aliquando pertrahare, ut *trabe ex alta*[364] cum Latini uxore — tuae necis tute auctor (nisi taurus ille Siculus, te maiora supplicia luiturum, maneat) denique toti mundo futurus infamis — aut cum Iuda pendeas.

153 "Sed uideorne tibi iam[365] de inuidia quam mihi obiectas fecisse satis uberiusque, immo uerius, atque ipse fortasse uoluisses disseruisse?[366] Hac de re, itaque, tametsi non ad cumulum, abundiuscule tamen.

154 "Nunc ad id sermonem uerto quo me *compoetam*[367] appellas tuum. Hem? Putasne te intus teneam qui mihi foris per ironias subblandiris? Non enimuero inter nugandum aut per interualla quaedam, uerum statim et primis in labiis quos sermones sis habiturus quorsumue sis erupturus ipse praeuideo, neque longius abire aut occulere te potes quin e uestigio ob oculos meos nudus omnino deuerseris.

155 "At te maiorem in modum oratum, Panormita sanctissime, immo per id quod tibi iucundius in uita semper astitit[368] obsecratum, uelim ne me poetam dixeris. Professionem enim eiuscemodi (modo Vergilii bona uenia dicere possim) haud mediocriter exhorreo, neque Sophocleos cothurnos aut hircum tuum foetidum a poetis pro praemio decertatum tanti facio, ut tuum nomen ipse profitear. Quippe qui longe antiquius existimaui cum Francisco et apostolis, immo cum ipso omnium principum principe, domino Iesu Christo, domino quidem et deo meo, non cothurnatis sed nudis pedibus ingredi; cum Lazaro quoque illo mendico et inope,

---

[364]ex alta] ab alta *Liv.*
[365]iam] *s.l. suppl. A*
[366]disser- *scripsi* : deser- *A*
[367]compoetam *scripsi* : cum poetam *A*
[368]astitit *scripsi* : astititit *A*

---

[429]Cicero *Letters to Friends* 22.7 (5.12.7).

[430]Virgil *Aeneid* 12.603. Amata was Aeneas' mother-in-law. She hanged herself thinking that Aeneas had killed her husband Latinus and slaughtered his army (Virgil *Aeneid* 12.593–611).

[431]That is, Judas Iscariot, who, according to the Gospels, betrayed Jesus of Nazareth. Matthew (27.5) states that Judas "went and hanged himself" (KJV). Acts (1.18–19) states that "falling headlong, he burst asunder in the midst, and all his bowels gushed out" (KJV). Reconciling these accounts, Augustine (*On Acts with Felix the Manichaean* 1.4) concluded that Judas had botched the attempt to hang himself but had met a suitable end for an apostate anyway.

want Apelles in particular to portray him and Lysippus to sculpt him, such was their artistic superiority and excellence, because he thought their art was going to bring as much glory upon themselves as it would upon him'?[429]

152 "But, you obstinate man, do you feel so proud, indeed so arrogant and boastful about having such a great mind that you think you can recline at table as an equal of these illustrious men? If so, I very much fear that you're going so insane or will be driven sooner or later to the point of insanity that you'll hang 'from a high beam' with the wife of Latinus[430] or with Judas.[431] If only that Sicilian Bull were around today then you'd be paying a greater penalty![432] Yet since you serve as your own executioner, you're finally going to become universally notorious.

153 "But, in your view, have I now dealt adequately with the envy that you accuse me of harboring against you? And have I discussed it more copiously, or rather, more truthfully than you yourself would perhaps have wished? Well then, although I've not reached the worst of it, I've nevertheless gone on at some length.

154 "Now I turn to that statement where you call me your 'fellow poet.'[433] Oh? Do you think that I should be deeply attached to you when you're only being ironic in your public flattery of me? But I myself instantly intuit the words on the tip of your tongue (when, of course, you're not driveling or stuttering) or anticipate what tack your outburst is going to take. Nor can you drift into the distance or conceal yourself when I see right through you in a flash.

155 "But, my saintly Panormita, I implore you with even greater fervor, indeed I beg you for the sake of that [profession of poet] which has always been rather agreeable to you in this life: would you please not speak of me as a poet. For (*pace* Virgil) I in no small degree abhor such a profession. Nor, in order to profess your title myself, would I hold in great esteem the Sophoclean buskins or your stinking billy-goat that poets compete for as a prize.[434] In fact, I've long preferred to walk not buskined but barefoot with Francis and the apostles,[435] or rather with the prince of all princes, the Lord Jesus Christ, yes my Lord and my God. And I've long preferred to beg with Lazarus[436] — that destitute mendicant infested with

---

[432]Phalaris (ca. 570–554 BCE), the tyrant of Acragas (Agrigento), commissioned a bronze bull in which he roasted his victims alive, including the bull's maker, Perillus (Pliny the Elder *Natural Histories* 34.19.89; cf. *Philippic* §166).

[433]Panormita *Etsi facile* §1 (Appendix I below).

[434]Buskins are a heavy soled, high-laced sandal worn by tragic actors. The word "tragedy" derives certainly but inexplicably from the Greek word for "billy-goat" (*tragos*).

[435]St. Francis of Assisi (1181–1226) was the founder of the Franciscan Order to which Rho belonged. It was an order of begging friars commonly referred to as a "mendicant" order. Going barefoot or with sandals ("discalced") represented for some religious, and St. Francis in particular, a central component of genuine apostolic poverty (Matthew 10.10). The Franciscans usually understood this to mean *completely* barefoot.

[436]Although Lazarus is not further identified and the rich man not named, the story (Luke 16.19–31) becomes known as "Lazarus and Dives," simply making a proper noun of the Latin common noun *dives* (rich man).

ulceribus pleno, penes illum instratum ostro pictisque tapetis, lautius epulantem, stipem et eleemosynam canibus e mensa deiectam et excussam exposcere, quam cum Plauto illo tuo urbe Roma ob annonae caritatem ad molas in pistrino collo circumferendas locari, aut cum Naeuio a triumuiris, quod in urbis primarios sed imprimis in superiorem Africanum maledicta inspersisset, carceribus non sine maledictorum [A136v] retractatione infamis intrudi.[369]

156 "Quid enim unus tu hoc saeculo[370] iactabundus poeticen aut oratoriam tibi uindicas — [N110v] nec uindicas sed usurpas, quandoquidem unus poeta tantum, unus orator tantum toto orbe, qui nasci debeat, iam natus est, neque *alterum expectamus*? Sitque iudicare perdifficile et[371] supra utrum facilius quis Vergilio an Ciceroni dicendo possit aspirare, numquid te oratorem illum, quem Cicero ipse sua mente et idea, ut ait, effingere poterat, inuenire non poterat, caelitus datum esse polliceris? Perabsurdum quidem! Non enim quantula uel ex parte orator sed arator (intellegin?) nominandus es quippe qui malus uir, immo sceleratus, atque dicendi imperitus es; non itidem poeta quod neque opportune fingere ceterum mentiri aperte didicisti. Antiquius itaque atque consultius (tu utramque profiteris; ego neutram) artes, quibus aspirare *inuita*, ut aiunt, *Minerua* ipsi nequimus, inuiolatas omitteremus quam illas quodam temere uindicato iure polluere atque deturpare diceremur. *Vergilium illa felicitas ingenii*, ut aiunt, *in*[372] *oratione soluta* quidem defecit, cessit, tacuit; *Ciceronem — fortunatam* dicentem *natam* se *consule Romam — eloquentia sua in carminibus destituit*, ammouit pedem subraxitque; *Pylades in tragoedia* Bathyllum, *Bathyllus* Pyladem *in comedia* superare non potuit.

157 "Videto nunc tu dum caelos ambire et amplecti suspiras, ipse iam nullus sis uirque insolens, arrogans, ceruicosus, qui neque calcaribus ne freno quidem uti scias, passim et uulgo decanteris. Verum ad hoc, omnia quae hactenus una familiari ac domestico sermone collocuti[373] ⟨sumus⟩, eo illo[374] uno uerbo dumtaxat, quod me tibi compoetam uocitas, apprime uri et paene me

---

[369]intrudi] *corr. A*
[370]Lectitastine satyricum [*l*. 1694] . . . [*l*. 1744] hoc saeculo *om. N*
[371]et *om. N*
[372]in *Sen* : *om. AN*
[373]collo-] *corr. A*
[374]illo] ipso *N*

---

[437]This story, related by Aulus Gellius (3.3.14), is generally thought to be a fabrication, though probably not a fabrication of Gellius.

[438]The legend of the poet Naevius (see n. 428 above) and his attack on Scipio Africanus is reported by Aulus Gellius (3.3.15).

sores, a beggar at the house of the man draped in purple cloth, who idled on embroidered tapestries and feasted ever more sumptuously — for the scraps and handouts knocked off the table for the dogs. I've long preferred to go barefoot and beg rather than to be harnessed with your Plautus to a flourmill that serves Rome's bread dole,[437] or to be disgraced with Naevius, who was thrown into prison by the triumvirate and forced to retract the slurs with which he bespattered the city's leaders and above all the elder Africanus.[438]

156 "Why indeed do you boastfully claim for yourself alone in this age — nor just claim but usurp — the arts of poetry and oratory, since in the whole world the one such poet and the one such orator who ought to be born has each already been born, nor 'do we expect another'?[439] And granted that it's extraordinarily difficult to judge whether one can aspire more easily to Virgil than to Cicero in speech, do you really hold forth the promise that you're that heaven-sent orator, whom Cicero himself only managed to construct in his mind and — as he said — as an ideal he could not find?[440] Absolutely absurd! For you must not be called an orator at all but rather a churl[441] (do you understand?), since you're an evil man, indeed a criminal and unskilled in speaking.[442] You must not be called a poet either, because you've learned not to create appropriate fictions but rather to tell manifest lies.[443] So, we would have been better advised and more respectful of tradition to have left untarnished the arts of oratory and poetry (you profess both, I neither) — in which we ourselves could not aspire because, as the saying goes, our 'Minerva was unwilling'[444] — than to have been said to pollute and defile them on the basis of some rashly usurped claim to these arts. Indeed, as they say, 'the felicity of his genius' deserted, failed, and silenced 'Virgil in prose.' 'The eloquence of Cicero abandoned him in poetry'[445] and he merely added and subtracted meter when he said: 'fortunate Rome, born with him a consul.'[446] Pylades could not surpass Bathyllus 'in tragedy,' and Bathyllus could not surpass Pylades 'in comedy.'[447]

157 "Take care, while you aspire to reach and embrace the heavens, that you may just be a nobody, and people high and low everywhere consider you an insolent, arrogant, and stubborn man, who doesn't know how to use either spurs or bridle. Moreover, of all the things that we've conversed about until now in

---

[439] Rho's question sarcastically echoes the question that messengers from John the Baptist asked Jesus of Nazareth to find out if he was the Messiah (Matthew 11.3; cf. Luke 7.19–21).

[440] Cf. Cicero *The Orator* 2.7.

[441] The Latin pun (Cicero *Philippics* 3.9.22), "not an *orator* but an *arator* (plougher)," cannot be easily rendered in English. Humanists frequently hurled this insult at each other.

[442] According to Quintilian (*The Education of the Orator* 12.1.23–32), only a good man could be a true orator; the man's character made him persuasive: "a good man skilled in speaking" (*vir bonus dicendi peritus*). Cf. Monfasani 1992.

[443] For "poets as liars," see Introduction 38 above; cf. also *Philippic* §150 and §185.

[444] For the significance of "an unwilling Minerva," see *Philippic* §143 n. 391.

[445] Seneca the Elder *Controversiae* 3.pr.8.

[446] Juvenal 10.122; cf. Quintilian *The Education of the Orator* 9.4.41 and 11.1.24.

[447] Seneca the Elder *Controversiae* 3.pr.10. In the time of Augustus, Bathyllus was a famous comic dancer and Pylades was a famous tragic actor.

1770 impotem fieri sentio. Poetae etenim[375] gloriola minuta quadam affici, fortasse multi putant, possem; compoetae uero nullo pacto, nulla ratione possem. Quo ex te audito perii quidem. Quid aliud est tibi compoetam esse quam tibi consocium, contubernalem, collateralem, commilitonem, conscelestum,[376] conflagitiosum esse?
1775 Habeant id nomen qui domum tuam incolunt: molles illi cinaedi tui. Ego uero totum angiportum, immo sentinam et oletum tuum,[377] quo spurcus utpote sus in luto grunnis, ex industria [A137r] consultoque prae putore naribus abstrusis praetereo declinoque,

1780 *nulli* (enim) *fas casto sceleratum insistere limen.*

158 "Quid ergo? Non sum sane quidem is qui hac uitae nostrae breuitate, qua tu et ego ceterique mortales deuersamur quaue singulos dies non modo hominum genus ceterum ciuitates, montes, flumina, elementa ipsa, ipsum mundum pro oculis
1785 euanescere uidemus et interire, tibi compoetam fieri efflagitem. Verum caelo, ubi[378] scelera tua tute ultro[379] fateare aeuoque sempiterno, igne purgatorio defaecatus, cum beatissimis spiritibus illis perfruare, conciuem non compoetam nominari concupisco.

159 "Parce igitur. Parce si potes — poteris enim si uolue-
1790 ris — ut me huius uanissimi nominis professorem asciscas;[380] meque, si sapis, tacere permittas rogo. Iterum dixerim me tacere permittas. Raudensis iam uel tandem obliuiscaris quando morum tuorum, immo scelerum, obliuisci nequis et oro et obsecro. Aut si tantopere huiuscemodi professione gloriaris, neque me ullo pacto ab
1795 Helicone eximendum putas — utique iam falsus es — neque de musis conuenit. Ego enim quid in rem meam si et sedulo inspexerim, mihi uel deo meo fretus ipse consuluerim. Tu uero, qui Phoebum Cirrha aut Bacchum auertere Nysa tantopere niteris, caue sis alter Alcestis non ne Vergili. Euripides[381] enimuero, ut
1800 aiunt, *tris uersus triduo* edidit et in Alcestidem pro mora quasi ingenii tarditatem incusans conquerebatur. Cui Alcestis triduo *centum perfacile* cudisse dixit. Tum Euripides: Hoc ipso uno discernimur siquidem *quod tui centum post triduum* prorsus auolabunt et euanescent, mei in omnem posteritatem immortales
1805 commigrabunt.

[375]etenim] et- *s.l. suppl. A*
[376]conscelestum *N* : conceles- *A*
[377]tuum] tum *A*
[378]caelo ubi *om. N*
[379]tute ultro *tr. N*
[380]asciscas] assis- *N*
[381]Euripides] *corr. A*

familiar and colloquial language, one single expression especially inflames me and nearly makes me lose control, namely, that you refer to me as your 'fellow poet.' Perhaps many people do in fact think that some meager glory of a 'poet' can influence me, but being described as a 'fellow poet' can't influence me at all. When I heard you call me this, I absolutely died. What else does it mean to be your fellow poet than to be your bedfellow, your fellow traveller, your fellow conspirator, your fellow soldier, your fellow crook, and your fellow debauchee? Let those who reside in your house have that name: that is, your own effeminate sodomites. I, however, with nose covered against the stench, resolutely and deliberately duck past that entire alley, or rather past that open, shit-filled sewer of yours where you grunt like a filthy hog in a wallow,[448] for 'it is never proper for the pure to set foot in the realm of the damned.'[449]

158 "Why's that? Because I'm the last person who would seek to become your fellow poet in this our brief life in which you, I, and other mortals sojourn or in which every single day we see not only the human race but also cities, mountains, rivers, the very elements, and the world itself vanish and perish before our eyes. I don't want to be called your fellow poet, but I desire instead to be called your fellow citizen in heaven, where you would confess your enormities voluntarily and where, cleansed by the purgatorial fire, you would enjoy eternity with the blessed.

159 "Spare me then. Spare me if you can — for you could if you would — your claim that I profess this utterly vain title. And please, if you have any sense, let me be silent. I repeat: let me be silent. I ask and beg that you now finally forget about Rho, since you can't forget about your ways, or rather, about your debaucheries. Or if you are going to glory so much in professing such a title, do not imagine that you'll somehow remove me from Mount Helicon. You're in any case now sadly mistaken to think you could do so. Nor is there unanimity concerning our respective Muses. For even if I should sedulously look to my best interest, I would make my deliberations while trusting especially in my God. You, however, who endeavor to banish Phoebus from Cirrha or Bacchus from Nysa,[450] take care lest you be another Alcestis and not a Virgil![451] Euripides, as they say, produced 'three lines of poetry in three days,' and he complained to Alcestis, blaming the delay on his wit being somewhat slow. Alcestis said to him that he 'easily pounded out a hundred lines in three days.' Euripides responded: 'We differ from each other in this one respect: your hundred lines will fly off and vanish after three days; my immortal lines will be passed down to all posterity.'[452]

---

[448]Cf. Proverbs 26.11; II Peter 2.22; and Jerome *Hebraic Questions* praef.

[449]Virgil *Aeneid* 6.563.

[450]*Cirrha* is the port nearest to Delphi, the most famous shrine of Phoebus Apollo; *Nysa* is the mountain in India where Bacchus (the god of wine) was said to have been born.

[451]Nothing more is known of the poet Alcestis, an alleged contemporary of the Athenian tragic playwright Euripides (ca. 480–ca. 406 BCE), other than what Rho repeats in the following lines from Valerius Maximus.

[452]Valerius Maximus 3.7.11.ext.1.

160 "Quid dixi 'caue'? Video plane illi iam assimilis es dum gloriaris et iactas te effundere passim et ex tempore, immo stans pede in uno,

>compluria *nec scombros metuentia carmina nec thus.*

Non deest tamen uulgus imperitorum et examen, qui te huiusce aetatis et saeculi quasi delicias caelo datas esse congratulentur, quibus, si ab sententia[382] mea abeundum est, si non leuitate damnarer illis, profecto quam uehementer assentiar. Etenim quando ab ueritate abhorrere, ut aiunt, nequaquam decet, quaeue poetarum extet [A137v] condicio atque natura altius repetimus percunctamurque, uannum quoque recte excutimus et cribrum. Te, poetam clarum et illustrem, diluxisse [N111r] aetate hac nostra — uelimus nolimus — nulli diffiteamur oportebit, aemulique succumbamus in acie, immo et de te sentire setius atque hactenus sentierimus, necesse erit.

161 "Quid istuc? Iucunditate sane quidem et animi quadam effusione insanis perbaccharisque recte, probe, egregie. *Iucundum* etenim, ut apud poetam Graecum, *aliquando est insanire.* Platoni quoque et Aristoteli, cuiusuis artis aut[383] doctrinae totiusque philosophiae principibus, libenter quidem inniteris, neque ab eorum institutis longius abis:[384] ille Plato compotem *sui*[385] quemquam *poeticas fores*[386] ait[387] *frustra* pepulisse; hic uero *nullum magnum ingenium* extare *sine mixtura dementiae* arbitratus est. Tu itaque, poeta insignis et inclite (neque hoc fateri non possumus), ita haec es feliciter assecutus, ut impos tui iamque tibi non constans Musas pro arbitratu tuo liberius adeas alloquarisque; ingenio quoque immixto dementiae plurimum et uales et polles. Quae duo tamen non ita permisces, non ita confundis, quin dementia ipsa tua longe amplior exuperantiorque quam ingenium poeticum ipsum tuum esse uideatur.

162 "Sed ad Musas Sicelidas tuas, quas me pro ingenii imbecillitate non nosc⟨er⟩e dicis, oportet redeamus, quae quandoquidem

>*non omnes arbusta iuuant humilesque myricae,*

paulo maiora canere, ut ais,[388] doctissimae sunt.

---

[382]ab sententia] absentia *N*
[383]aut] *corr. A*
[384]abis] *corr. N*
[385]sui] *om.*, sibi *in ras. N*
[386]fores] *corr. N*
[387]ait] aut *N*
[388]ais *N* : ait *A*

160 "Why did I say 'take care'? I see clearly that you're now like Alcestis as long as you gloat and brag that extemporaneously, or rather, 'standing on one foot,'[453] you pour out hither and yon many 'poems that fear neither mackerel nor frankincense.'[454] Yet, there's a multitude — even a horde — of incompetent people who celebrate you as if you were heaven's gift to this time and age. If I were forced to abandon my own view and if I wouldn't be condemned by those same people for fickleness, I'd even strongly agree with them. In fact, as the saying goes, we should never hide from the truth.[455] And since we're reassessing and investigating more deeply the distinctive character and nature of poets, we're also justified in separating the wheat from the chaff. None of us ought to deny, willy-nilly, that you've dawned on this our age as a famous and illustrious poet. And necessity requires that we rivals give way in combat, or rather, that we feel differently about you than we've felt so far.

161 "What's my point? That you with delightful exuberance go mad and that it's right and proper that you carouse so extravagantly. For as one Greek poet says, 'it is fun at times to go mad.'[456] And indeed you rely heavily on Plato and Aristotle, the princes of every art or science and of all philosophy, and you do not stray far from their precepts. Plato, on the one hand, said that anyone 'who is in full control of his faculties has knocked in vain at the poetic gates.'[457] Aristotle, on the other, supposed that 'no great genius exists without a mixture of madness.'[458] Accordingly, O distinguished and celebrated poet (we have to admit this), you're so successful in attaining this madness that now at will and without any hesitation you approach and speak with the Muses as someone who's lost control of his faculties and become unstable. By mixing genius with madness you furthermore arrive at the height of your vigor and strength. You so fail, however, in mixing or uniting these two that your madness strikes people as far more impressive and preeminent than your poetic genius.

162 "But we ought to return to your Sicilian Muses, whom you say I don't know given the weakness of my genius. They are, as you say, deeply learned, inasmuch as 'not all groves and lowly tamarisks aid in singing loftier themes.'[459]

---

[453] Horace *Satire* 1.4.10; cf. Panormita *Against Valla* 1 (Appendix IV/10 below).

[454] Persius 1.43. That is, Panormita fails to be intimidated by the fact that the pages containing his poetry are only going to be used to wrap fish and spices in the market (cf. Catullus 95.6–7 and Horace *Epistle* 2.1.269–70).

[455] Cf. Augustine *On the Sermon on the Mount* 2.5.24.

[456] That is, Anacreon (b. ca. 570 BCE), who is cited here through Seneca the Younger (*Dialogues* 9.17.10). Seneca, like Rho, does not report the poet's name, and there is no evidence that Rho could have identified him independently.

[457] Seneca the Younger *Dialogues* 9.17.10; cf. *Philippic* §14 n. 36, §62, §96, and §178.

[458] Seneca the Younger *Dialogues* 9.17.10. Seneca misrepresents Aristotle (*Problemata* 30.1), who speaks not about *dementia* but about *melancholia* (depression? irascibility?), a condition caused by too much black bile. (I thank John Monfasani for this information.)

[459] Virgil (*Eclogues* 4.1–2) used "groves" and "tamarisks" to typify subjects of pastoral poetry. The pastoral Muses are said to be Sicilian since Theocritus, the model for Virgil's *Eclogues*, was from Sicily (see *Philippic* §142 n. 383; cf. also *Philippic* §104 and §109–§110).

163 "Hem? Iam paene inclinata acies est.[389] Sed doceas rogo: quid certaminis aut pugnae aduersum me hae picae tuae habeant? Quid putem? Comtemptumne nisi me inflectam et illas adorauero? Quid habent in uita aut hac ingenii mediocritate mea (non enim poeticen aut oratoriam uti tu profiteor), nisi, ut adhuc insueuere, mentiri pergant quod damnare possint?

164 "Non et ego, litterario in ludo uersabundus, litteras et uidi et didici? Non assidue tunc calamarias et graph⟨iar⟩ias thecas lateri meo habui quo doctorum praecepta perscriberem? Non *ferulae* saepe subduxi *manum*? Non et uersiculos pusio ipse saepe[390] confeci? Non poetas[391] paene singulos, quorum uersibus sonus[392] inanis [A138r] dumtaxat — ut ait Hieronymus — uerborumque strepitus, ueri fames, uirtutum penuria reperitur, sed Vergilium ipsum imprimis iterum atque iterum lectitaui, scrutatus sum, intellexi abunde?

165 "Enimuero nisi quod arrogantiae uerbum proloqui modestiae meae nihil conducit, qui me semper his litteris honestare non in te inuehere, me tueri non te accusare[393] constitui, iam tibi musulisque tuis poeticum neque iniuria illud decantassem:

quantoque animalia cedunt cuncta
deo tanto minor est tua gloria nostra.

166 "Sed num fortasse Siciliam insulam patriam tuam obiectaueris, quasi toto orbe poeta uel minimus qui reges illustret exoriri nequeat, nisi ea ipsa insula poetarum, quasi praegnans, illum nobis fecundissima parturiat? Pro! Idem ille ipse Panormita noster es plane, qui prius et cerebro[394] illo tuo inani te peroblectas persaepe, ut uideo. Quam enim insulam omni mari pererrato non dicam poetis, ceterum monstris atque portentis celebriorem insignioremque, nisi ueritate abutaris, tu poeta, eiusce patriae faex quaedam et abiectus indigena, declaraueris? Ibi Phalaris Zenonem occidit; ibi Dionysius, non minus deorum expilator quam contemptor, optimos quosque aut[395] affecit aut extinxit; ibi tyranni alii — qui paene numerari nequeant — ceteris immaniores crudelioresque, principatum, immo tyrannidem tremendam tenuere; ibi taurus aeneus, inauditum saeculis crudelitatis genus, inuentus est; ibi Cyclopes, ibi Gigantes, ibi Lygdamus ille

---

[389]acies est *tr. N*
[390]uersiculos pusio ipse saepe] uersiculos saepe pusio ipse *N*
[391]Non poetas] *corr. A*
[392]sonus] somnus *N*
[393]accusare] declinare *N*
[394]cerebro] cele- *N*
[395]aut] ut *N*

163 "What's that? Your front line has now almost collapsed. But explain, please. What sort of quarrel or dispute do these magpies of yours have with me?[460] What am I to think? That I'll be despised if I don't bow and worship them? What do these magpies find to complain about in my life or mediocre talent (for I don't profess, as you do, to be either a poet or an orator), unless, as hitherto has been their wont, they proceed to fabricate something that they can then condemn?

164 "Didn't I too see and learn literature while attending a beginning school for Latin? Didn't I at that time constantly hold at my side 'pen and style cases' so that I could transcribe the lessons of the teachers?[461] Didn't I often 'pull back my hand from the cane'?[462] Didn't I too as a boy frequently compose little poems? Didn't I time and again read almost every single poet in whose empty verses one finds only sound — as Jerome said — a din of words, a hunger for truth, and a dearth of virtues?[463] Didn't I minutely examine them and Virgil in particular? And didn't I thoroughly master them?

165 "Indeed, were it not that making an arrogant remark runs contrary to my modesty — since I resolve in this letter always to take the high road rather than to inveigh against you, to defend myself rather than to accuse you — I would've already recited (and not unjustly) to you and your little Muses the following bit of poetry: 'And by the amount that all animals yield to god, by just as much is your glory less than ours.'[464]

166 "But you're not by some chance about to bring up your home island of Sicily, as if a court poet (however third-rate) couldn't arise anywhere in the world unless this island, extraordinarily prolific and, as it were, pregnant with poets, gave birth to him for us? Good Lord! As I see it, you, our very own man from Palermo, are clearly one and the same person who earlier found his own empty-headedness a constant source of delight. For which island in the entire navigable sea is more celebrated and distinguished, not, I say, for its poets, but for its monsters and portents? Indeed, would you, a poet, who are an example of the flotsam and jetsam indigenous to your native island, care to answer this without perverting the truth? There Phalaris killed Zeno.[465] There Dionysius, no less a despoiler than a despiser of gods, persecuted or annihilated all the best citizens.[466] There other tyrants — they can scarcely be numbered — some more brutal and cruel than others, held fast their

---

[460]Pierius had nine daughters, who were turned into magpies for competing with the Muses (cf. *Philippic* §110).

[461]Suetonius *Claudius* 35.2.

[462]Juvenal 1.15.

[463]Cf. Jerome *Letter* 21.13.

[464]Ovid *Metamorphoses* 1.463–64.

[465]Valerius Maximus (3.2.ext.3) reports confusedly the story of Zeno of Citium (335–263 BCE) and the tyrant Nearchus by following it up with the account (3.2.ext.2) of Zeno of Elea (born ca. 490 BCE) and Phalaris, tyrant of Acragas (see *Philippic* §152 n. 432). Rho further confuses Valerius Maximus' account by making Phalaris, instead of Nearchus, the villain of the Zeno of Citium story.

[466]Dionysius II, tyrant of Syracuse (367–344 BCE), regarded himself a tragic poet and did win the Athenian Dionysiac competitions. Plato, who was disappointed in his attempt to make Dionysius into a philosopher-king, circulated a report (*Letter* 7) that defamed Dionysius for oppressive rule.

Syracusanus fuisse memoratur, homo quidem — mirabile dictu — qui numquam sudauerit neque sitierit, qui sine medullis ossibus extiterit. (Intellegin de qua logici certant, addubitantes an[396] nihilne et Chimaera sint fratres?) Ibi sulphur et ignis aeternus opportune quidem neque ab re[397] esse perhibe⟨n⟩tur; ibi Scylla, ibi Charybdis, monstra uidelicet perhorrenda, timentur a nautis; ibi Typhoeus, maximus Gigas, tota ab insula opprimitur.

Nititur ille quidem pugnatque resurgere saepe,
dextra sed Ausonio manus est subiecta Peloro,
laeua, Pachyne, tibi, Lilybaeo crura premuntur;
degrauat Aetna caput.

Inde terrae motus magnos fieri credunt; inde ipsa insula ab Italiae deliciis seu motu ipso Gigantis, seu, quod uerius est, natura operante, quasi eiusce Italiae faex quaedam membrumque putridum paruo mari [A138v] seiuncta est; inde diabolus, ut poetae aiunt, nactus uxorem.

167 "Quid me existimas dicere? Auctor extat Gregorius ille sanctissimus [N111v] *omnis insulares quidem malos esse, Siculos uero scelestissimos perditissimosque.* De poetis autem praeter te unum, quem, quasi e poetis — ueluti[398] e philosophis Cicero Platonem excipit — semper excipio, aut nulla aut exilis est mentio, maxime quando mediocres, ut aiunt,[399] *esse* poetas *non* fuit *in pretio* ne posthac erit quidem.

168 "Nunc iam tandem, Antoni, *postquam epulis* paululum *fames exempta* est, bellaria utique, quae secundae mensae nominantur, restant apponenda.[400] Verum clarius hoc loco dixerim ac uerbis paene euangelicis tecum utar: *iam ad radices* itaque huiusce tuae

---

[396]an *om. A*
[397]ab re] *corr. N*
[398]ueluti] *corr. A*
[399]ut aiunt] aut aiunt *N*
[400]apponenda] *corr. A*

---

[467]For Phalaris and the bronze bull, see *Philippic* §152 n. 432.
[468]The Cyclops were an atheistic, cannibalistic, lawless race of pastoral giants, having a single central eye. The most famous of these is Polyphemus, who captured Odysseus and his men and ate two of them before the others blinded him and escaped by clinging to the underside of his large woolly sheep (Homer *Odyssey* 9.152–566).
[469]The existence of the Giants appears to have been derived (or "confirmed") from discoveries of large bones of prehistoric animals (cf. Pliny the Elder *Natural Histories* 7.73). They were said to be a race of monstrous humans who attacked the gods and were defeated only with the help of Hercules, a mortal. Thereafter buried under various volcanoes, the attempts of the Giants to escape were the cause of earthquakes.
[470]Lygdamus won the Pancratium (combined boxing/wrestling event) at the thirty-third Olympiad (see Solinus 1.74). He was also said to be equal in size to the Theban Hercules, whose foot measured the Olympic stadium at 600 instead of the usual 625 (Forcellini; GRBM; PW). In the extant manuscripts of Solinus (Rho's source), *Lygdamis* is the better reading, *Lygdamus* the more common.

principate, or rather their horrible tyranny. There was found the Bronze Bull,[467] a sort of cruelty unheard of throughout the ages. There lived the Cyclops[468] and the Giants.[469] There Lygdamus the Syracusan is remembered as a man, amazing to say, who never sweated nor thirsted and who turned out not to have marrow in his bones.[470] (Do you understand what the logicians are arguing about when they debate whether nothing and the Chimera are brothers?)[471] There eternal fire and brimstone are thought to exist as appropriate and natural.[472] There sailors fear Scylla and Charybdis, who are dreadful monsters.[473] There Typhon, the greatest of the Giants, lies buried under the entire island.[474] 'Indeed he often struggles and fights to rise, but Ausonian Pelorus pins his right hand, Pachynum his left; Lilybaeum crushes his legs, and Etna weighs down his head.'[475] This is why, they believe, great earthquakes occur. This is why, either through the stirring of the Giant, or more accurately, through the working of nature, a narrow sea separates the delights of Italy from this island, as though it were Italy's useless and rotten limb. And this is where, as the poets say, the Devil got his wife.[476]

167 "What do you suppose I'm talking about? The authority of most holy Gregory confirms that 'all islanders, in fact, are evil, but Sicilians are the most wicked and corrupt of all.'[477] I have, however, made little or no mention of poets here beyond you alone, whom, insofar as you are a poet, I always single out, just as Cicero singled out Plato from the philosophers. But that's precisely because mediocre poets 'have never had any value,'[478] as they say, nor indeed will they ever.

168 "Now at last, Antonio, 'after the feast has banished hunger a little while,'[479] only the dessert, which is called the second course, remains to be served. But on this topic let me speak more clearly and use almost evangelical

---

[471] The Chimera was a fabled fire-breathing monster with a lion's head, goat's body (represented in art with a goat's head growing out of its back), and serpent for a tail. Rho inserts this parenthetical question to deny the actual existence of all these legendary monsters.

[472] Mt. Etna is an active volcano on the eastern end of Sicily.

[473] Scylla, a half-human monster that devoured six men at a time, lived in a cave opposite Charybdis, a maelstrom that three times a day swallowed and disgorged passing ships (Homer *Odyssey* 12.234–59). In later times they were thought to have been in the Straits of Messina.

[474] Typhon was a monster having a hundred heads, originally distinct from but often taken (as here) as one of the Giants. Zeus attacked him with thunderbolts and confined him to the underworld, igniting Mt. Etna in the process.

[475] Ovid *Metamorphoses* 5.349–52. Mount Etna is an active volcano on the eastern end of Sicily. The other references are the promontories of Sicily: Pelorus (the northeastern), Pachynum (the southeastern), Lilybaeum (the western).

[476] Cf. Plautus *The Comedy of Asses* 751–54.

[477] It remains unclear why Rho ascribed this statement to St. Gregory. If Gregory made any statement about "islanders," he must have been speaking about pagan temple keepers or about inhabitants of Roman apartment buildings (*insulae*). Peter of Blois (*Letter* 46), the apparent source of Rho's quotation, is the earliest example I find of this slur against Sicilians, but he does not ascribe it to Gregory (cf. *Philippic* §1, §18, and §33).

[478] Horace *The Art of Poetry* 372–73.

[479] Virgil *Aeneid* 1.216.

infructuosae arboris *securis* est admouenda, quam pro foliorum
1900 infecunditate radicitus exustum iri pretium operae non mediocre qui
recte sentiunt arbitrantur. Ita enim futurum est ut ediscas, immo
compellaris, aliquando reticere, qui numquam loqui didicisti.

169 "Aperi iam tandem ad digressum hunc nostrum officinam
et tabernam illam tuam. Profer ex hippoperis et sarcinulis[401] tuis
1905 thesaurum pretiosum, omnemque diuinam, immo poeticam illam
suppellectilem necdum expositam, quam intus clitella pectoris tui
copiosissimam, ut ais, celas, expone. Dic. Vbi locus inuidiae? Dic.
Qua spe ductus, qua fretus ope, quo Marte fidens, quibus felicibus
auspiciis, bellum abs te publicitus[402] mihi minitaris indictum iri?
1910 **170** "Hui!

Sic certent cygnis ululae; sic Tityrus Orpheus.

Id unum tibi tamen persuasum esto: calamum illum (intellegin?),
calamum illum e curia a Maecenatibus tuis, quos inani in dies
expectatione deludis, tibi missum, auro quidem et margaritis
1915 intextum, Vergilio aut Homero olim non indignum, nequaquam
aestimari,[403] uerum potius derideri atque uili[404] pendi.

171 "Sed num aliud quam calamum quicquam[405] ad con-
serendas[406] manus habes? Cedo, rogo, qua ex legione ueteranos
uulneribus innutritos asciueris, qui mollibus et ephebis tironibus
1920 dumtaxat hactenus ac[407] nouiciis imbellibus scates? Marcus
Antoniusne in lucem rediit ut iterum pro ueris sibi obiectis flagitiis Ciceronem occidat? Arbitrarisne me columbarum more
hortorum erectas imagines, deos quidem tuos, et inuolucra[408]
suspensa perhorrescere, qui a puero laruas et *lemures* [A139r] non
1925 exhorrui, qui *terrores magicos* ⟨. . .⟩ *portentaque Thessala* numquam
expaui? Quid ergo? Num Gorgoneos uultus extimescemus, aut
Hydram renascentem formidabimus, quippe qui contra portenta
haec ipsi nos Perseum et Alcidem retinemus.

---

[401]sarcinulis] sacirnu- *N*

[402]abs te publicitus] publicitus abs te *N*

[403]aestimari *scripsi* : extimeri *AN*

[404]uili] uile *N*

[405]calamum quicquam] calamum ᵘᵃillum e curia a Maecenatibus tuisᶜᵃᵗ quicquam *corr. N*

[406]conse-] confe- *N*

[407]ac] et *N*

[408]inuolucra] -lurci *N*

---

[480]Matthew 3.10; cf. Luke 3.9 and Jude 12.

[481]Virgil *Eclogues* 8.55. In other words, "let hoots be swan-songs; let any crooning bumpkin be the greatest of singer-composers."

[482]See *Philippic* §54 n. 130; cf. also §80, §121, §131, §143, §175, and §178.

[483]For the proscription of Cicero, see Introduction 17 above.

words with you. Accordingly, 'now the axe must be laid to the roots' of your 'unfruitful tree.'[480] People of good sense think it would be highly beneficial to burn your unfruitful tree root and branch because of its barren foliage. For thus it'll come about that you'll learn finally to keep silent, or rather will be compelled to do so, since you've never learned to speak.

169 "Now, as we part, open up at last your workshop and tavern. Fetch out from your saddlebags and backpacks your precious treasure. Reveal all of your as yet unexposed divine, or more precisely your unexposed poetic, paraphernalia, which you conceal, as you say, inside the completely stuffed packsaddle of your breast. Speak up. What's there for me to envy? Speak up. Why do you publicly threaten that you're going to declare war on me? By what hope are you led? On what help are you relying? In what Mars are you trusting? Which lucky omens do you believe?

170 "Ah yes! 'So let owls compete with swans, and let Tityrus be Orpheus.'[481] But you'd better get this one thing straight: that pen inlaid with gold and pearls (do you know the one I'm talking about?), that pen which your Maecenases,[482] because you delude them daily with false prospects, sent to you from the Senate and which once upon a time would've been worthy of Virgil and Homer, is in no way to be prized but is instead to be treated as an object of ridicule and contempt.

171 "But surely you have something besides a pen for hand-to-hand combat? Please, tell us from what legion you've called up battle-hardened veterans. For to date you surround yourself with only soft, peachy recruits and rear-echelon virgins. Has Mark Antony returned to life to kill Cicero again for accusing him of real crimes?[483] Do you suppose that I'll be frightened like a terrified dove at raised scarecrows, that is to say, at your gods,[484] and at suspended masks, I who from boyhood have neither feared evil spirits and specters nor ever dreaded 'magical terrors . . . and Thessalian portents'?[485] What's next? Shall we grow alarmed at Gorgonian faces[486] or be afraid of the 'death-defying Hydra,'[487] when we ourselves have Perseus and the son of Alceus on our side against these portents?[488]

---

[484]That is, Priapic gods which were used in Roman gardens to scare off intruders (see Richlin 1983, 9, 66, and 121–24; cf. Ovid *Fasti* 1.400 and *Philippic* §33, §37, and §181; on Panormita's "gods" cf. *Philippic* §91, §93, and §109).

[485]Horace *Epistle* 2.2.208–09. Among Greek authors (e.g., Homer, Menander, Lucian, and Aristophanes) Thessaly was famous for its witches and necromancy. Horace, like other Roman authors, made several references to Thessalian witchcraft besides the one which Rho quotes here.

[486]Gorgo (or Medusa) had two sisters, Sthenno and Euryale, who were also called Gorgons. They were represented with snakes for hair and said to be so horrifyingly ugly that all who looked at them turned to stone.

[487]*Elegy on Maecenas* (in *Appendix Vergiliana*) 83. The Hydra was a many-headed serpent, which grew two heads for every one cut off unless the wound was cauterized.

[488]Perseus, the son of Zeus and Danae, managed to kill Gorgo by looking at her only in a mirror. Hercules, the son of Alceus, defeated the Hydra (cf. *Philippic* §178). Perseus and Hercules are metaphorical references to Cicero and Jerome, whose *Philippics* and *Jovinians* Rho claimed as his models in *Philippic* §173 (see Introduction 17–18 above).

172 "Verum Plautum tuum, Plautine Panormita, nihil exaudis?

Noli, amabo (inquit), *uerberare lapidem, ne perdas manum.*

Sile itaque et obmutesce. Lingua ne prodiga nimium effluat mordicus comprime. **173** "Sunt etenim mihi (quando acerbius uiolentiusque aut respondere aut inuehi sententia esset); sunt mihi, inquam, praeceptores cum doctissimi tum peritissimi — Cicero quidem unus, uerum imprimis diuus ille Hieronymus meus — alter qui Philippicas ex integro, alter Iouinianas, quae in faciem tuam opem mihi ferant, cudere perfacile doceant. Hic nunc, si tibi constas, *dignas* mihi persoluas *grates* licebit, quod tecum non uehementi, sed amica et pedestri, ut ita dixerim, oratione sim usus. Quod si reluctaberis ueluti que *iratus Chremes tumido* iterum *ore* desaeuies, *homo ut es turbulentus, et solus in uniuerso mundo* poeta simul et belua, (*qui, ut ille ait, loquacitatem facundiam* existimas *et maledicere, omnibus, bonae conscientiae signum* abitraris), dicam tunc cum Dauid lyrico: *Pone domine custodiam ori meo: et hostium circumstantiae labris meis.* Scio pro me tibi ipse ultor dominus respondebit, qui per prophetam ait: *Mihi uindicta*[409] *et ego retribuam.* Et alio in loco inquiet: *Sedens, aduersus fratrem tuum* — tu, Panormita — *loquebaris, et aduersus filium matris tuae ponebas scandalum. Hoc*[410] *fecisti, et tacui. Existimasti inique quod ero tui similis: arguam nunc te, et statuam contra faciem tuam, et in frontem tuam sermones tuos.*
174 "Sentisne Panormita?

Steteruntne comae aut uox faucibus haesit?

Id fiet, ut cum[411] maledicta illa tua quo errore, quo spiritu immundo, quo daemone percitus[412] effuderis, arbitris et angelis et daemonibus propitius ipse mihi deus deducat in medium. Quis tum Beccadellus Siculus aut Antonius Panormita mecum conflixisse gloriabitur? *Dominus* enim *illuminatio mea est et salus mea; quem timebo? Dominus protector uitae meae; a quo trepidabo?* [A139v] *Ipse firmamentum meum est, et refugium*[413] *meum, et liberator meus. Si consistant itaque aduersum me castra, non timebit cor meum. Si exurgat aduersum me proelium, in hoc ego sperabo, quoniam faciet iudicium meum et causam meam; sedebit super thronum, qui iudicat iustitiam.*

---

[409]uindicta *Rom.* : -tam *AN*
[410]Hoc *AN* : Haec *Psa.*
[411]cum] tum *N*
[412]percitus] par- *N*
[413]refugium *Psa.N* : est add. *A*

172 "But, Plautine Panormita, don't you heed your own Plautus, who said 'Please don't hit a rock, lest you maim your hand'?[489] Therefore, shut up and be still. Bite your tongue, lest its wagging divulge too much.

173 "Indeed, if I decide to respond or attack more bitterly and violently, I have teachers. I say, I have teachers, both learned and skilled. To be sure, Cicero is one, but foremost is my Jerome. The former readily teaches me to hammer out new *Philippics*,[490] the latter to hammer out new *Jovinians*,[491] which bolster me in confronting you. You may 'render suitable thanks'[492] here and now if you're self-consistent, because I didn't use forceful language with you, but as I would say, friendly and ordinary language. But since you're 'a turbulent man and the only person in the whole world' who's simultaneously a poet and a beast, and 'since,' as Jerome put it, 'you think that loquacity is eloquence and reckon that to curse everyone is a sign of a good conscience,'[493] if you resist and vent your rage again in 'inflated utterances like the furious Chremes,'[494] then let me say with the lyric poet David: 'Place a guard, Lord, in front of my mouth; and make my lips a surrounding force.'[495] I know that the Lord, the Avenger himself, will respond to you for me, who through the Prophet said: 'Vengeance is mine; I will repay.'[496] And the Lord will say as he does elsewhere: 'Taking a seat' — you, Panormita — 'spoke against your own brother and slandered your mother's son. You have done these things, and I have remained silent. You have thought unfairly that I would be like you: now I shall censure you and condemn you to your face' and condemn your very words in your mouth.[497]

174 "Are you listening, Panormita? 'Did your hair stand on end or did your voice catch in your throat'?[498] It'll come about that when you — moved by some error or unclean spirit or demon — have poured out your insults, God himself, because he's well-disposed toward me, will unmask them publicly with the angels and demons as witnesses. Then who'll it be, a Sicilian butcher, Beccadelli,[499] or Antonio Panormita, who gloats about having clashed with me? For 'the Lord is my light and my salvation; whom shall I fear? The Lord is the guardian of my life; at whom shall I tremble?'[500] He is 'my stronghold, my refuge,

---

[489] Plautus *Curculio* 197.

[490] For Cicero, see Introduction 17–20 above.

[491] For Jerome, see Introduction 17–18 and 20–22 above.

[492] Virgil *Aeneid* 1.600.

[493] Jerome (*Against Helvidius* 1) is actually quoting Helvidius, but the antecedent of *ille* in Rho's text can only be Jerome (for Helvidius, see *Philippic* §100 n. 246).

[494] Horace *The Art of Poetry* 94. Chremes is a character in Terence's *The Lady of Andros* (*Andria*).

[495] Psalms 140/141.3. David (d. ca. 970 BCE), the second king of Israel, is the reputed author of many of the Psalms (cf. *Philippic* §11 n. 30).

[496] Moses ("the Prophet") is quoted here through St. Paul (Romans 12.19; cf. Deuteronomy 32.35).

[497] Psalms 49/50.20–21.

[498] Virgil *Aeneid* 3.48.

[499] See *Philippic* §20 n. 45; cf. §76, §132, and §133.

[500] Psalms 26/27.1.

[N112r] Et quoniam *dilexisti*[414] *omnia uerba praecipitationis, lingua dolosa, propterea deus destruet te in finem; euellet te, et migrabit te de tabernaculo tuo, et radicem tuam de terra uiuentium.*

175 "Quo abis, Inuicte? Siste pedem paululum! Exhibe te ipsum. Quo cessit amabo illa inanis, immo arrogans sesquipedalium uerborum tuorum ostentatio tua, qua[415] saepe iactabundus asserebas Romanorum Regem Serenissimum, Sigismundum, Ambrosiana aede coronari haud posse nisi inter coronandum tu, poeta insignis, esses orationem habiturus? Quid Panormum ciuitatem tuam iam pridem et ante horam per obsignatas litteras his gloriolis, immo nugis, immo fumis implesti? Quid rem tam conspicuam et illustrem teque omnino indignam, quasi nos Insubres muti et infantes essemus, tam arroganter animo praeoccupasti? Pro! Quas tum irrisiones, quos sibilos, quas linguas post terga tua exagitatas, dum Abbas eiusce aedis,[416] uir utique disertissimus, orationem habuisset, inspeximus? Suntne istaec somnia apud Ticinum et Insubres meos iam ex te pridem decantata? Minime quidem, uerum,[417] ut tute nosti, cum notissima tum uerissima[418] sunt.

176 "Quid, luride uir, in haec uerba rubore suffunderis, qui semper spurcis et flagitiosis officiis erubescere pertimescis?[419] Video iam tibi ista lectitanti rugari frontem, deflagrare oculos, tremere labia, dentes comprimi; non articulate loqui, implicari digitos, duci suspiria, capillos subrigi, aestuantemque ab imis praecordiis sanguinem commoueri, capite deprauato minitari; denique meum — si fieri posset — *os digito uelle comprimere ne audeam* uera[420] excoriare[421] quae tu, omnium hominum perditissimorum spurcissimus spurcissimorumque perditissimus, facere nihil erubescis.

---

[414]dilexisti . . . praecipitationis] omnia uerba praecipitationis dilexisti *N*
[415]qua] qui *N*
[416]aedis] *corr. N*
[417]uerum *om. A*
[418]tum] cum *N*
[419]pertimescis] -tumescis *N*
[420]uera *scripsi* : uere *AN*
[421]excoriare *scripsi* : excuiare *corr.* excusare *A* : excusare *N*

[501]Psalms 17/18.3.
[502]Psalms 26/27.3.
[503]Psalms 9(A).5.
[504]Psalms 51/52.6-7.
[505]Horace *The Art of Poetry* 97.
[506]Sigismund, King of Hungary, was elected King of the Romans in 1411, received the Iron Crown of the Lombards on 25 November 1431 (the ceremony referred to here), and was crowned Holy Roman Emperor in 1433.

my liberator.'[501] Consequently, 'if an army forms against me, my heart will not fear. If the battle surges against me, enduring this I shall still hope,' 'since he will maintain my right and my cause,[502] and he who judges righteously will sit on the throne.'[503] And since 'you have loved all slippery words, you treacherous tongue, therefore God will destroy you completely, he will uproot you, and drive you from your tent and your family from the land of the living.'[504]

175 "Why do you retreat, O invincible one? Plant your feet awhile! Show yourself. I would surely like to know where that empty, or rather, arrogant ostentation of your 'sesquepedalian words' has gone?[505] Didn't you allege in your frequent boasting that the most serene King of the Romans, Sigismund, couldn't be crowned in the Church of Sant' Ambrogio unless during the coronation you, the distinguished poet, were to give the oration?[506] Why, even before the event, did you, by means of sealed letters, fill your hometown of Palermo with news of these modest glories, or rather these trifles or these vapors? Why with such arrogance did you anticipate others in something so remarkable and illustrious and entirely beyond the likes of you, as if we Milanese[507] were tongue-tied and inarticulate? Ah! And what did we see then? I mean the snickers, the hisses, and the tongues wagging behind your back up to the time when the abbot of Sant' Ambrogio, an exceptionally skilled speaker, delivered his oration.[508] Were these the imagined glories with which you regaled people in Pavia and Milan beforehand?[509] I think not. But as you yourself recognize, what we saw is well known and completely true.

176 "Why are you red-faced at these words, you sallow man, when you're always anxious not to blush at filthy and debauched undertakings? I can see you now studying these words and wrinkling your brow: your eyes grow lackluster, your lips tremble, your teeth clench. I see you slurring your words, fidgeting with your fingers, and breathing in gasps. I see your hair standing on end, your blood boiling and your heart pounding in your chest. In your twisted mind these words threaten you. Finally, I see that you want — if it were possible — 'to seal my mouth with a finger, so that I dare not' excoriate actual deeds that you don't blush at all to perform, you the filthiest of the depraved and the most depraved of the filthy.[510]

---

[507] Rho actually says "Insubrians," Insubria being the ancient name of the territory around Milan, nearly synonymous with Lombardy (cf. *Apology* §43). The Insubres, according to unreliable accounts in Livy (5.34) and Strabo (5.213), migrated (ca. 400 BCE) from around Lyon, France, into the area around Milan (OCD).

[508] That is, Antonio Ricci, who was Abbot of Sant' Ambrogio from 1425. The church and monastery of Sant' Ambrogio was a short stone's throw from Rho's residence in San Francesco Grande. A few years earlier (1428), Rho delivered a funeral oration for the Abbot's brother, Zanino Ricci, who had been one of Panormita's Maecenases (see *Philippic* §54 n. 130; cf. also §80, §121, §131, §143, §170, and §178). Rho's depiction of Panormita's oration being ridiculed at a solemn occasion closely resembles his description of Panormita delivering his oration "On the Sun" (cf. *Philippic* §126).

[509] Rho's literal statements are "on the Ticino," that is, on the Ticino River which flows by Pavia, where Panormita resided and held a position at the University; and "among my Insubrians," that is, among the inhabitants of Lombardy (see n. 507 above).

[510] Rho picks up not only the quotation but also these other expressions of Panormita's physical reaction to reading his words from Jerome (*Letter* 27.2), who used them against his enemies to indicate their stubbornness and incorrigibility (cf. Wiesen 37n and 128).

177 "At de his iam satis. Fortasse paucioribus quam aut[422] necesse esset aut pluribus quam tu uelles quamue angustia epistolaris exigeret: illam equidem excessi; materiam [A140r] non excessi. Vtrum ipse Hieronymo temperantior aut sanctior extiterim? Quippe qui non tam inuehit quam in aduersarios ipsum eum mordentes lacessentesque[423] fulminat ac[424] paene uidetur debacchari.

178 "Garri itaque quoad uehementia et insania agitabere: oblatra, perstrepe, fulmina, et ex monte illo altissimo, quo ebrius cuiusdam numinis beneficio inscendisti, uti ad Maecenatem tuum Cambium Bononiensem scribis, pro arbitratu tuo aliis margaritas et gemmas *aliis nimbos et grandines* (ut uerbis tuis loquar), plue et ninge. Immo schedulas detractorias more latronum noctu sed locis celebratis appende, quibus, uti insuesti, me monstrum, me daemonem[425] blateres. Aut si memoriae tuae monstra nequaquam succurrunt me Centaurum, me — ut de Rhodo, honestissimo uiro, ais — Sirena[426] aut Onocrotalum, me Cerberum, Chimaeram, et Hydram, seu unam ex Stymphalidis, me Behemoth et Leuiatham dicito. Et cum omnia quaecumque monstra percurreris, te ceteris monstruosiorem cognoscito.

179 "In hisce tamen schedulis[427] tuis et uersibus aduersum Raudensem ac libellis infamibus dei filium dominum et deum meum, Christum Iesum, prosequar reuerear adorauerim. Si illum iam, qui pater est orbis, *Beelzebub uocauerunt, quanto magis* me, seruum tametsi indignum, Beelzebub esse dixeris? Et si illi dictum est quod seductor esset ac seduceret turbas, ego cur indignor si audiam ex te turbulentus aut seditiosus acclamari? Et si quod *homo* sit *uorax, et uini potator, publicanorum amicus peccatorumque* sibi

---

[422]quam aut] *corr. A*
[423]lacessentes-] lacesce- *N*
[424]ac] et *N*
[425]daemonem] -nere *N*
[426]Sirena] -nam *N*
[427]sche-] ce- *N*

---

[511]Cf. *Philippic* §14 n. 36, §62, §96, and §161.
[512]Rho is here paraphrasing and quoting from a passage of Panormita's letter (1429/30) to Cambio Zambeccari, an official at the Visconti court who died in June 1431 (Sabbadini 1896: 358–59). Panormita's own words are (Beccadelli 1746, 144 [3.18]): "But listen now, [Cambio], to what I in turn imagine and dream like the poets: that I, obviously at the favor of some god, have ascended the loftiest mountain — for it is a sacrilege to mingle heaven into jests — and there I was granted the ability to rain and shower cloudbursts and hailstorms at one moment on fields and on other men, but on you and your household to snow pearls. Therefore if you are by chance desirous of these gems, see to it, as you do, that we occasionally share our leisure time" (*Sed audi nunc, [Cambi], quid ego vicissim more poetarum fingo ac somnio: ascendisse me, scilicet dei cuiuspiam beneficio, montem altissimum — nam caelum iocis immiscere nefas est — atque inde mihi concessum ut pluere possem ac spargere tum campis*

177 "But enough about these things. Perhaps they were said either with fewer words than were necessary or with more words than you wanted or than epistolary brevity required. Epistolary brevity I've certainly exceeded; the material I've not exceeded. Did I prove myself to be more moderate or more holy than Jerome? He, of course, doesn't so much inveigh against as thunder at his adversaries, who bite and rend him. Indeed he seems almost to have lost his self control in raging against them.

178 "Jabber away, then, to the degree that vehemence and mania agitate you.[511] Crack. Rumble. Thunder. And 'drunk with the favor of some divinity,' rain and snow at will 'from that lofty mountain upon which you have climbed' — as you wrote to Cambio da Bologna, your Maecenas — showering pearls and gems on some people and unleashing 'cloud-bursts and hailstorms' (to use your own words) on others.[512] Rather, like a thief, hang by night your disparaging placards in crowded places, and blather in them, as you've become accustomed, about me being a monster and a demon. Or if you can't remember any monsters, say that I'm a Centaur, that I'm a Siren — as you say about that honorable man Rhodes[513] — or that I'm a Pelican.[514] Say that I'm a Cerberus, a Hydra, or one of the Stymphalians,[515] and say that I'm a Behemoth and a Leviathan.[516] And when you've run through every kind of monster, you'll recognize that you yourself are the most monstrous of them all.

179 "But I entreat you to show in your placards and poems against Rho and even in your ill-famed and wretched little books that I follow and revere the Son of God, my Lord and God, Jesus Christ. If they've already called him who's Father of the world 'Beelzebub, how much more'[517] should you have said that I, even though his unworthy servant, am Beelzebub? And if Jesus was said to be a demagogue who misled the masses, why should I be indignant if I hear from you that I'm declared obstreperous and factious? And if it's considered a vice in Jesus that 'he is a gluttonous man and drinker of wine and a friend

---

atque aliis hominibus nimbos et grandines; tibi vero tuisque penetralibus ningere margaritas. Harum igitur gemmarum si fortasse cupidus existis, cura, ut facis, ut otium aliquando nanciscamur). See *Philippic* §54 n. 130; cf. also §80, §121, §131, §143, §170, and §175).

[513]See *Philippic* §145 n. 402.

[514]According to Jerome (*Against Vigilantius* 1), Isaiah mentioned these monsters (known best from classical sources): Centaur (man/horse), Siren (woman/bird), and Pelican (bird/donkey). Rho says of the Pelican (*Imitations* 297r): "*Onocrotalus* or *onocrotalon*: A certain bird wearing the face of an ass and is similar in color to the swan, having a long beak." Rho thought that words with the prefix *ono-* derive etymologically from *onos, -i* (donkey).

[515]Jerome (*Against Vigilantius* 1) named other monsters known from poetic fables: Cerberus (a three-headed dog with mane and tail of snakes, that guarded the entrance to the underworld), Hydra (a many-headed serpent, which grew two heads for every one cut off unless the wound was cauterized), and the Stymphalians (man-eating birds with iron beaks).

[516]Jerome (*Against Vigilantius* 1) wrote that Job spoke of others monsters "in mystic language." There is some likelihood, however, that the Behemoth was a hippopotamus (Job 40.15–24) and the Leviathan a crocodile (Job 41.1–34).

[517]Matthew 10.24–25.

uitio datur, quid ipse bile aut stomacho commouebor si me incestum omnisque foeditatis tuae complicem decantaueris?

180 "*Sentisne quid taceam* honestatis causa et *aestuanti pectori* quae *uerba non* praestem? Verum quando summum maledicentiae[428] genus notamque taeterrimam e pectore illo tuo euomere collibuerit, me alterum esse Panormitam (Pro nomen infamiae!)[429] quam familiarem tibi atque intimum necessarium tuum, immo partem animae tuae uulgo et praedica et canta.

181 "Vis liberius dixerim? In omnem Italiam de tuis in me maledicentiis alium Hermaphroditum turpiorem iuxta genium tuum obscenioremque aliosque[430] dialogos seu nouas fabricas nouosque uersus, ut illa edicta [A140v] ostiaria foedissima, quae nuper ex me edita tuo pro more mentiris, tu uero illorum inuentor quam notus et auctor — nam lingua et calamus tuus ubique gentium putet[431] — excita si libet[432] ac semina. Neque nomen tuum inscribi libello illi oportere, quasi sit inauditum, curato aut magnificato. Lingua enim illa tua ita ueneno turget, ita spurcitiis[433] exundat, calamusque [N112v] tuus eo usque innotuit, ut tametsi nomen ipsum tuum nihil edideris, non dicam hominum uoces, ceterum ipsa gymnasia, suggestus, subsellia, parietes — medius fidius![434] — et pauimenta, non minus quam si te inscripseris, maledicentiae et falso dati sceleris te auctorem praedicabunt.

182 "Gratulor inde tamen mihi quam plurimum qui tutorem dignitatis meae ac nominis defensorem quempiam argutum et acrem inuenerim. Quid istuc? Siquidem Hermaphroditus ipse tuus aduersum te semper Achilles meus erit, et alter Alcides ipse libellus, uel si Crassus et Antonius urgeant aduersenturque, facile causam meam ubique superiorem efficiet. Ille ipse nusquam legetur quin turpitudo declaretur tua: quam spurce aut quam petulanter, quam libidinose, quam barbare uitam degeris; ille idem testis semper affuerit.

---

[428]maledicentiae] -tis *N*
[429]infamiae] -me *N*
[430]aliosque] -que *om. N*
[431]gentium putet] ᵇputet ᵃgentium *corr. A*
[432]libet] lu- *N*
[433]spurci-] -ci- *s.l. suppl. A*
[434]fidius *N* : foedius *A*

[518]Matthew 11.19; cf. *Philippic* §78 n. 192 for "publicans," that is, Roman tax collectors.
[519]Jerome *Against Rufinus* 1.31.
[520]That is, the scurrilous poetry against Rho and his circle, which Panormita called his *Priapeia* after what is now known as the *Appendix Vergiliana* (see Introduction 29–30 above; for fragments of Panormita's *Priapeia*, see Appendix IV/8 and IV/9 below; cf. also *Philippic* §33, §37, §171 and *Apology* §30).

of publicans and sinners,'[518] why will I get angry or disgusted if you scribble jingles about me being polluted and mixed up in all your loathsome activities?

180 "'Do you understand the things I don't say' for the sake of decency and what 'remarks I won't make in the heat of anger'?[519] But since you enjoy spewing out the most extreme kinds of abuse and the most hideous libel, call me another Panormita. (What a disreputable name to have!) Proclaim and sing far and wide that I'm as close to you as your intimate friend, or rather soul mate.

181 "Would you like me to speak more freely? Bring forth, if you like, and disseminate throughout all Italy another even more foul and obscene *Hermaphrodite* (which is your *forte*), compiled from your insults against me.[520] Disseminate other dialogues or new productions and poetry like that foul placard that you posted around town. Yes, I mean the one that you falsely claim in your usual lying way I recently published, when in fact it's well known that you thought it up and wrote it (for your tongue and especially your pen leave their stench everywhere).[521] Don't fuss or worry about your name being properly inscribed in that book as if it would be a surprise. For your tongue so swells with venom, so gushes with filth, and by now your pen has become so well known that even if you didn't put your name on it, not only gossip among men, but, I'd say, even schools, podiums, benches, walls, and floors — so help me god! — will declare you to be the author of the insults and of the false attribution of the crime no less than if you had signed it yourself.

182 "Just the same, I am therefore forever congratulating myself since I've discovered a sharp and shrewd protector of my dignity and a defender of my reputation. How so? That *Hermaphrodite* of yours will always be my Achilles against you, and the wretched little book will be another Hercules, always making my cause easily prevail even if a Crassus and an Antonius were urgently to oppose it.[522] The wretched little book will never be read without declaring your indecency, how filthily, recklessly, lustfully, and barbarously you've lived your life. The same witness will always be at hand.

---

[521]Rho is either referring to the *Prostitutes of Pavia* (see Introduction 31–32 above; and Appendix IV/1 below) or something very like it. He writes at some length about "some extremely obscene little verses" being published against Panormita (*Philippic* §36–§43). Panormita accused Rho of having written them (*Etsi facile* §5; Appendix I below), but Rho speculates that either Panormita published them himself or that one of his cronies wrote them "in order to tout [his] genius" (*Philippic* §41). Rho also writes about a "placards incident" (*Philippic* §52–§55), which is presumably the same one mentioned here. He there says (*Philippic* §52) that the poem was written "to the Senators" (*ad patres conscriptos*) and "against me" (*adversum me*), things which better describes the poem by Ps.-Joan of Arc against Rho (Appendix IV/3 below). But Rho goes on to say that the verse was "extremely filthy" (*spurcissimus*), which does not fit the Ps.-Joan of Arc piece at all. "Extremely filthy" unquestionably describes the *Prostitutes of Pavia*, but it was ostensibly written against Panormita, not Rho. It is possible that Rho means by "against me" (*Philippic* §52) that this obscene poetry was circulated under his name with the purpose of tarring him with the same brush as Panormita.

[522]Crassus and Antonius were two Roman orators who became models of eloquence in Cicero's dialogues the *Brutus* and *The Orator*.

183 "Quo abis, Inuicte? Quos recessus, quas latebras petis? Qua insula extrema, qua *ultima Thule* caput tuum oc⟨c⟩ulis frustra quidem? Etenim Hermaphroditus ipse te uel sepultum deducet in lucem, tuarumque cicatricum exulcerator et gladius in tuum nomen aeternus et immortalis nulla tempestate defuerit. Quis admirationi locus? Propter enim uitae tuae[435] turpitudinem sordesque domesticas de te rumor ubique gentium foetet. Et ut quanti te habeam quotidianasque tragoedias et uociferationes illas tuas quantopere perhorrescam aliquotiens intellegas, nolo equidem ex me audias, sed ab Demetrio, uiro ornatissimo, id eleganter ab eo dici solitum accipies. Eo loco aiebat: Mihi sunt *uoces imperitorum, quo crepitus uentre* redditi. *Quid enim mea refert sursum isti an deorusm sonent?* Ita aeque: *Quanta dementia est uereri, ne infamer ab infamibus!*

184 "Fatebor enimuero, si me ornasses, Panormita sanctissime, laudibusque tuis cumulatius expollisses, tuae palaestrae, tuae factionis et scholae, immo tuae ephebiae dicerer; cinaedus unus ex tuis et tecum infamis sine controuersia ab optimis quibusque tunc [A141r] digito Socratico designarer. Nunc quando me carpis dilacerasque inexauditaque flagitia de me pro more tuo libellis infamibus et uersibus mandas, signum hoc unum est et tuba quaedam clamitans: me tibi moribusque tuis omnino dissentire, in quem desaeuisti[436] dum corrigi noluisti.

185 "Quid amplius? Ego tandem,[437] mi Antoni, satis mihi fecisse morem uel mihi gessisse et his quoque qui mecum recte, modeste, honeste sentiunt teque quam notissimum habent arbitrabor, si tibi olim nullum responsum dedam, qui mentiri semper, fingere nequaquam didicisti. Te tamen obtestor per crucem domini et passionem eius, per uinculum nostrae fidei[438] ac necessitudinem intimam ne animam tuam, pro qua Christus in ipsa cruce ut illam[439] redimeret mortem obiuit, neglegas flocci pendasque. Ceterum illam sacerdotibus — leprosa enim est — aperias et ostendas, atque in

---

[435]tuae *N* : tuei *A*
[436]desaeuisti] disse- *N*
[437]tandem] quidem *N*
[438]et passionem . . . fidei] et per passionem eius et per fidei nostrae uinculum *N*
[439]ipsam *prae* illam *N*

---

[523]*Ultima Thule* (farthest Thule) was some island beyond Britain, sometimes surmised to be Iceland. Statements about it, however, are so imprecise as to make identification impossible (see Romm 121–71; cf. Virgil *Georgics* 1.30 and Pliny the Elder *Natural Histories* 6.220). *Ultima Thule* became proverbial in many European languages as the most remote, unfrequented place.

183 "Why do you retreat, invincible one? What hideaway or refuge do you seek? On what remote island or *Ultima Thule*[523] do you hide your head in vain? For *The Hermaphrodite* itself will expose you even after you're buried. You'll never be without an abscess on your scars nor ever lack for an eternal and immortal sword set against your name. Where is there room for admiration? Thanks to the indecency and private sordidness of your life, the gossip about you spreads its stink everywhere. And in order that you may sooner or later grasp what I think of you and to what extent I dread your daily histrionics and tirades, I actually don't want you to hear from me. But you will hear it from the distinguished gentleman, Demetrius,[524] who as usual put it so elegantly: 'To me the voices of the ignorant are like noisy farts. For what difference does it make to me whether these people sound off from above or below?' And likewise he said: 'What a great madness it would be for me to fear being defamed by the infamous!'[525]

184 "And I'll in fact confess, most saintly Panormita, that if you'd honored and glorified me more liberally with your praises, I'd now be spoken of as being from your training ground, from your faction, and from your school, or rather from your brothel for boys.[526] Every single person of note would without controversy then point me out with a Socratic finger as one of your sodomites and as notorious as you. Now when you rend and tear me to pieces, as is your wont, and when you report unheard-of villainies about me in your ill-famed and wretched little books and poems, one tell-tale sign blares like a clarion call. It's that I, on whom you vented your rage while refusing to reform your own self, completely differ from you and your ways.

185 "What's left? I'll think finally, my Antonio, that I've satisfied myself and my obligation to those who rightly, modestly, and respectably agree with me and who know you only too well, if I never again respond to you, a man who learned to lie constantly, but never to write imaginatively.[527] Nevertheless, I implore you for the sake of the Cross of the Lord and of his Passion and for the sake of the bond and intimate affinity of our faith that you not ignore and take lightly your soul, which Christ died on the Cross to redeem. But I ask and beg you to show your soul — leprous though it is — openly to the priests,[528] and now in your dotage[529] resume the role of a honorable man, who understands that it's his

---

[524]That is, Demetrius of Sunion, a Cynic philosopher and companion of the Roman Stoic philosopher Seneca the Younger (*Letters* 20.9, 62.3, 91.19). He taught in Rome during the reign of Caligula, was banished to Greece by Nero, and returned to Rome in the reign of Vespasian.

[525]Seneca the Younger *Letter* 91.19.

[526]See *Philippic* §37 n. 95.

[527]That is, a poet who has abused poetic licence (see Introduction 38 above; also cf. *Philippic* §150 and §156).

[528]According to the Gospels (Matthew 8.1–4, Mark 1.40–44, Luke 5.12–14), Jesus ordered the lepers he healed to comply with the Torah (Leviticus 14.2–4) in showing themselves to the priests, who were to certify that the leprosy was cured.

[529]Panormita is at this time about thirty-eight years old, one year older than Rho, who is ridiculing Panormita's statement that he "is now at a mature age" (cf. *Philippic* §63).

2080 partes honesti uiri aetate iam fracta te recipias et oro et obsecro. Cuius est — ut Pericles aiebat — et oculos et manus et linguam castigatos continere, neque tela in lapidem intorqueas, quae retrouersa plerumque uulnerant uulnerantem.

186 "Dices iam, si recte coniicio, hos monitus uacuos et 2085 inanes esse quandoquidem iam ad aerarium res tua deuoluta sit. Sed non sic, mi Panormita, non sic derepente a bona mente occidendum est. Etenim si de te excursis superioribus annis fama oblocuta est, medicamentum habes: cesset uitium, cessabit et rumor. Proiice abs te, rogo, Catullum, Propertium, Tibullum, et 2090 huiusce latrinae insequentem foedissimam turbam apud gentiles qui deum ignorabant concelebratam. Et nunc litteras sacras, nunc Hieronymum, nunc Augustinum ceterosque ad bene beateque uiuendum caelitus datos antistites, si potes — poteris enim si uolueris — quam tibi familiares efficias. Plura monerem quidem: at 2095 quoniam te surdum et oculis omnino captum esse[440] percipio, fit quod neque monitus diuinos exaudis neque de caeli pulchritudine aut stellarum mira uarietate his obuolutus in tenebris iudicium ullum ferre potes.

187 "Adeas igitur eam lucem, consulo, quae sanat et 2100 *illuminat omnem hominem uenientem in hunc mundum*. Nam quandoquidem ad haec uulnera quae infliguntur ex lingua illa tua paene medicus est nullus. Lingua uel ipsa atque oculis abutuntur [A141v] ceterisque sensibus, dum deum ipsum non laudare, non audire,[441] non intueri uolumus. Absterget dominus et deus meus 2105 linguam ipsam ponetque *digitos in auriculas* tuas, et conualesces. [N113r] *Lutum* quoque *ex sputo* pius et misericors ipse conficiet linietque oculos tuos, quos cum ad fontem Siloe laueris uisum actutum accipies. Neque ex oraculo illo Delphico ceterum ex Christo eo ipso audies *cognosce te ipsum*, euadesque iam tui censor 2110 et[442] iudex, qui mei et aliorum in hunc diem caecus insimulator accessisti.[443]

188 "Nunc utcumque sacris expletis uale, Panormita sanctissime, et si potes, me ama; si minus, saltem dilige; si minus, uel ipsum fac ut lubet. Ego uero diuina ex lege te diligere uel 2115 persequentem compellor. Nam et *qui proximum diligit, legem impleuit.*"

---

[440]esse] *mg. suppl. N*
[441]non audire *om. N*
[442]et] ac *N*
[443]accessisti] -s- *s.l. suppl. A*

duty, as Pericles said, to keep his eyes, hands, and tongue under control.[530] Neither should you hurl spears into a stone, which when they ricochet often wound the person trying to wound the other.[531]

186 "You'll now say, if I guess correctly, that these warnings are empty and futile, since your past has already been buried away in the archive. But it shouldn't, my Panormita, no, it must not fade that quickly from a good conscience. Indeed, if your notoriety from years gone by has testified against you, you have a remedy: if the vice will cease, the gossip will also cease. Please, rid yourself of Catullus, Propertius, and Tibullus. Rid yourself of that disgusting pack of authors from this latrine, much celebrated among the pagans who had no knowledge of God. And you should become just as familiar, if you can — for you could if you would — now with sacred literature, now with Jerome, now with Augustine and with other teachers bestowed by heaven for living well and happily. I could in fact recommend more things: but since I perceive that you're completely deaf and blind, the reality is that you don't heed divine warnings or, because you're shrouded in this state of darkness, you're in no position to make any judgment about the beauty of the heavens or about the astonishing variety of the stars.

187 "My advice is, therefore, approach the light which restores reason and 'illuminates every man coming into the world.'[532] For there's practically no physician who can treat the wounds which are inflicted by that tongue of yours. Your wounds damage the tongue as well as the eyes and other senses, as long as we refuse to praise, hear, or contemplate God himself. My Lord and my God will wipe clean your tongue and 'place his fingers in your ears' and you'll be healed.[533] Because he's faithful and merciful, he'll also make 'clay from spittle' and smear it on your eyes. When you've washed them at the pool of Siloam, you'll have clear sight.[534] Nor will you hear 'Know thyself' from the Delphic oracle but from Christ himself,[535] and you, who came forward until today as a blind accuser of me and others, will then become your own censor and judge.

188 "Goodbye, most saintly Panormita, now that I've done my sacred duty toward you as best I can. And love me, if you can. If you can't, at least like me. If not, do what you wish. I'm, however, compelled by divine law to love you, even though you're my persecutor.[536] For surely 'he who loves his neighbour fulfills the law.'"[537]

---

[530]Cf. Cicero *On Duties* 1.40.144.
[531]Cf. Jerome *Letter* 52.14 and Plutarch *Moralia* 810.E–F.
[532]John 1.9.
[533]Mark 7.33.
[534]Cf. John 9.6–7.
[535]Cf. Origen *Commentary on the Song of Songs* 2; cf. also Ambrose *Hexameron* 6.6.39 and *Expositions on the Psalms* 19.2.
[536]Cf. Matthew 5.43–44.
[537]Romans 13.8.

189 At quoniam loco cedit et in mores suos utpote *canis ad uomitum* quemadmodum et prius abit, ego iam sermonis in calce, quasi postliminii iure ad te, Candide optime, me recipio. Neque admirabere has me litteras nunc nuper ad te dedisse, quae ad Panormitam ipsum — paene dixi "Gomorritam" — reddendae primum uidebantur. In sententiam enim hanc nescio an eadem tuba ad eum alias me scripsisse et respondisse commemini. ⟨Peroratio⟩ Credo illas, timens ne a plurimis transcriberentur, in frusta[444] concidisse aut in ignem concremandas[445] iniecisse. Duxi itaque ab integro illas ad te scribi ne iterum euanescerent impraesentiarum oportere, quae, si Panormitae — aut illi "Gomorritae"[446] — prolixiores uehementioresque fortasse uidebuntur, certe tute et ego pro eiusce uiri flagitiis perhorrendis, pro materia turpitudini nulla ex regione defutura perbreues illas nobis[447] esse iudicauerimus.

190 Testor tamen deum meum ac[448] dominum, Iesum Christum, quem una cum caelicolis omnibus meae conscientiae arbitrum inuoco, qui et has litteras et Panormitae epistolam — illam quam ad me tandem dedit — extremo mundo Kalendisque mortalium ultimis iudicaturus est: me nihil ista scriptitasse, quasi accusationis suae gladios pertimescerem, quippe qui semper et malim accusari quam accusare patique iniuriam quam facere. At quoniam — quemadmodum a principio attigi — nisi conticerem minabatur interitum, ut responderem impulit ne tacendo fortasse commentum falso in me crimen cognoscere diceret lenitatemque[449] meam taciturnitatemque damnatae conscientiae [A142r] signum interpretaretur.

191 Sum tamen haud nescius ab luto quotidianisque faecibus illis suis minime[450] sibi temperauerit, quippe qui monstruosissimus monstra horrenda taeterrimaque non tam molietur[451] quam mentietur. Verum haec una responsio pro futuris quibusque maledicentiis suis faciat sibi satis peruelim, sitque trabes infixa oculis eius,

---

[444]frusta] -stra *N*
[445]concreman-] -men- *N*
[446]aut illi Gomorritae] ᵇilli ᵃaut Gomorritae *corr. A* : aut Gomorritae illi *N*
[447]illas nobis *tr. N*
[448]ac] *bis, semel in ras. N*
[449]lenitatem-] leui- *N*
[450]minime] *corr. N*
[451]moli-] molli- *N*

---

[538]Rho borrows the satirical usage of this image from Jerome (*Against Jovinian* 1.40), but it ultimately derives from Proverbs 26.11 (cf. II Peter 2.22; Wiesen 213).

Peroration

189 But now at the end of my harangue, since Panormita is giving up the fight and is returning to his former ways like "a dog to its vomit,"[538] I am restored to you, my good Candido, as if by the Law of the Returning Exile.[539] Nor will you marvel that I have just now sent you this letter, which seemed right to be delivered first to Panormita himself (I almost said "to Gomorrita").[540] For I recall having previously responded to him and having made this case in writing, basically blasting him then just as now.[541] I believe that he ripped it to shreds or threw it into the fire to incinerate it for fear that many people would transcribe it. I therefore concluded that it ought to be copied out anew and sent to you lest it vanish once more. If perhaps it appears to Panormita — or to that "Gomorrita" — more protracted and forceful than the former, certainly, for our part, you and I have determined that it is very brief, given the man's horrid indecencies and a subject matter that will not lack for debauchery in every detail.

190 Nevertheless, Jesus Christ, my Lord and my God, whom I invoke along with all the heavenly host as the judge of my conscience, is going to judge at the end of the world and on the final Kalends of mankind both this missive and Panormita's letter — the one that he finally delivered to me.[542] I call them all to be my witnesses that I have never made a practice of writing such things, as if I were in fear of the sword of Panormita's accusation, since I am a person who always prefers to be blamed rather than to blame and to be injured rather than to injure. But as I noted at the outset,[543] he threatened my ruin unless I kept silent. Consequently he forced me to respond so that he might not have the possibility to detect in my silence the crime of which he falsely accused me and that he might not interpret my gentleness and reticence as a sign of a guilty conscience.

191 Yet I am well aware from experience of his muck and daily scum that he has not restrained himself at all. He, after all, who is the most monstrous of men, will not so much create as counterfeit horrific and hideous monsters. But I very much wish that this one defense will satisfactorily answer him for any future calumnies. And may the beam that is planted in his eye,[544] or rather the indelible

---

[539]Roman law stipulated that citizens taken captive in war or exiled through civil disorder could reclaim their property and civil rights upon their release or return (Gaius *Institutiones* 1.129; Ulpianus *Digesta* 49.15.21.1; Iulius Paulus *Digesta* 49.15.19; see also Watson 20–21).

[540]Just as the name *Panormita* designates someone from Palermo (*Panormus*), so *Gomorrita* would designate someone from the city of Gomorrah, the ancient Near-Eastern city that God was said to have destroyed along with Sodom because no righteous person could be found in them (Genesis 18.1–19.29). According to later embellishment (which Rho accepts here), these cities were destroyed for the sin of sodomy (see Hergemöller; and Jordan).

[541]Rho is almost certainly referring to the so-called "Anonymous Invective" (Appendix III below; see Introduction 30–31 above).

[542]Panormita's letter *Etsi facile* (Appendix I below).

[543]See *Philippic* §3 and Panormita *Etsi facile* §5 (Appendix I below).

[544]This is an allusion to Jesus' statement that a person should not complain about the mote (i.e., speck) in someone else's eye when he has a beam in his own (Matthew 7.4–5; Luke 6.41–42).

immo ex cauterio[452] ignito suae fronti infamiae nota quaedam[453] immortalis nulla tempestate nulla aetate mortalium eximenda. Neque illo cum posthac decertaturus sum. Etenim uti apud familiarem mihi philosophum repperi: *Cum inquinatissimis hominibus non est conuicio decertandum neque maledictis apud impudentes et improbos uelitandum, ne tantisper similis et compar eorum fias, dum paria et consimilia*[454] *dicas atque audias.* Cum enim Metellus Numidicus, uir[455] utique sapientissimus, a C. Manlio, tribuno plebis,[456] apud populum in contione[457] lacesseretur *dictis petulantibus* iactareturque, ait: "*Nunc quod ad*[458] *illum attinet, Quirites, quoniam se ampliorem putat esse, si se inimicum mihi dictitauerit, quem ego mihi neque amicum neque inimicum recipio, de eo non sum ego plura dicturus. Nam cum indignissimum arbitror cui a uiris bonis benedicatur, tum ne idoneum quidem cui a probis maledicatur. Nunc si in eo tempore huiuscemodi homunculum nominem, in quo punire non possim,*[459] *maiore honore quam contumelia afficiam.*" [460]

192 Quid ergo, mi Candide, optimi ac sancti cuiusque uiri id esse imprimis unum arbitror? Errata castigare debeat; litigare non debeat.

193 Tu uero uale. Panormitam quoque — ut amplius ualeas — similemque palaestram — quod et facis — fuge. Deum cole et time. Te uel aeque mihi atque te tibi omnino crede.[461]

---

[452]cauterio *scripsi* : canterio *AN*
[453]nota quaedam] ᵇquaedam ᵃnota *corr. A*
[454]et consimilia] atque similia *N*
[455]uir *om. A*
[456]plebis] plus *N*
[457]contione] cen- *N*
[458]ad *om. N*
[459]possim *N* : -sum *A*
[460]afficiam *hic N, post* honore *A*
[461]*post* crede.] Deo gratias. Philippica in Antonium Panormitam explicit feliciter. *suppl. A* : Deo gratias. Philippica in Antonium Panormitam explicit feliciter per me, Rolandum Scibbeke de Alamania. *suppl. N*

mark of infamy branded on his forehead by the cautery never be removed at any time or in any age of mortals. Nor am I going to fight with him after this. For as I found one of my favorite philosophers saying: "You must not fight utterly scurrilous men by resorting to insults nor skirmish with the shameless and unprincipled by resorting to curses, lest you become exactly like them, saying and hearing equal and similar things."[545] For when Gaius Manlius, Tribune of the Commons, attacked Metellus Numidicus, who was an especially wise man, "in a speech before the people and provoked him with scurrilous statements," Metellus said: "Now, citizens of Rome, as far as that man is concerned, I am not going to say any more about him since he, whom I count neither as a friend nor as an enemy, thinks himself more eminent if he persistently claims that he is my enemy. For I not only think him absolutely unworthy to be commended by good men, but I also think him not even fit to be insulted by the virtuous. Now if I name a wretched little man like this at a moment when I cannot punish him, I bring upon him greater honor than indignity."[546]

192 What then, my Candido, do I believe is the single most important duty of every virtuous and saintly man? That he ought to correct mistakes, but he ought not to dispute them.

193 But fare well. Also flee Panormita (so that you may fare even better) and similar schools (as you also do). Worship and fear God. Wholly entrust yourself to me as you would to yourself.

---

[545] Aulus Gellius 7.11.1.
[546] Aulus Gellius 7.11.1-3.

ANTONIO DA RHO

APOLOGIA ADVERSVS ARCHIDIACONVM QVEMPIAM
COMPLICESQVE SYCOPHANTAS TAETERRIMOS

APOLOGY AGAINST A CERTAIN ARCHDEACON
AND HIS LOATHSOME SYCOPHANT ACCOMPLICES

MANUSCRIPTS

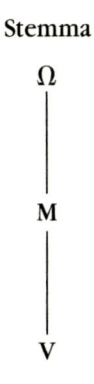

M = Milan: Biblioteca Ambrosiana, MS M 49 sup., s.XV[1], I + 42 + II ff. [Autograph]

V = Vatican City: Biblioteca Apostolica Vaticana, MS Ottob. lat. 1321, s.XV[1], ff. 52r–91v.

Stemma

$$\Omega$$
$$|$$
$$M$$
$$|$$
$$V$$

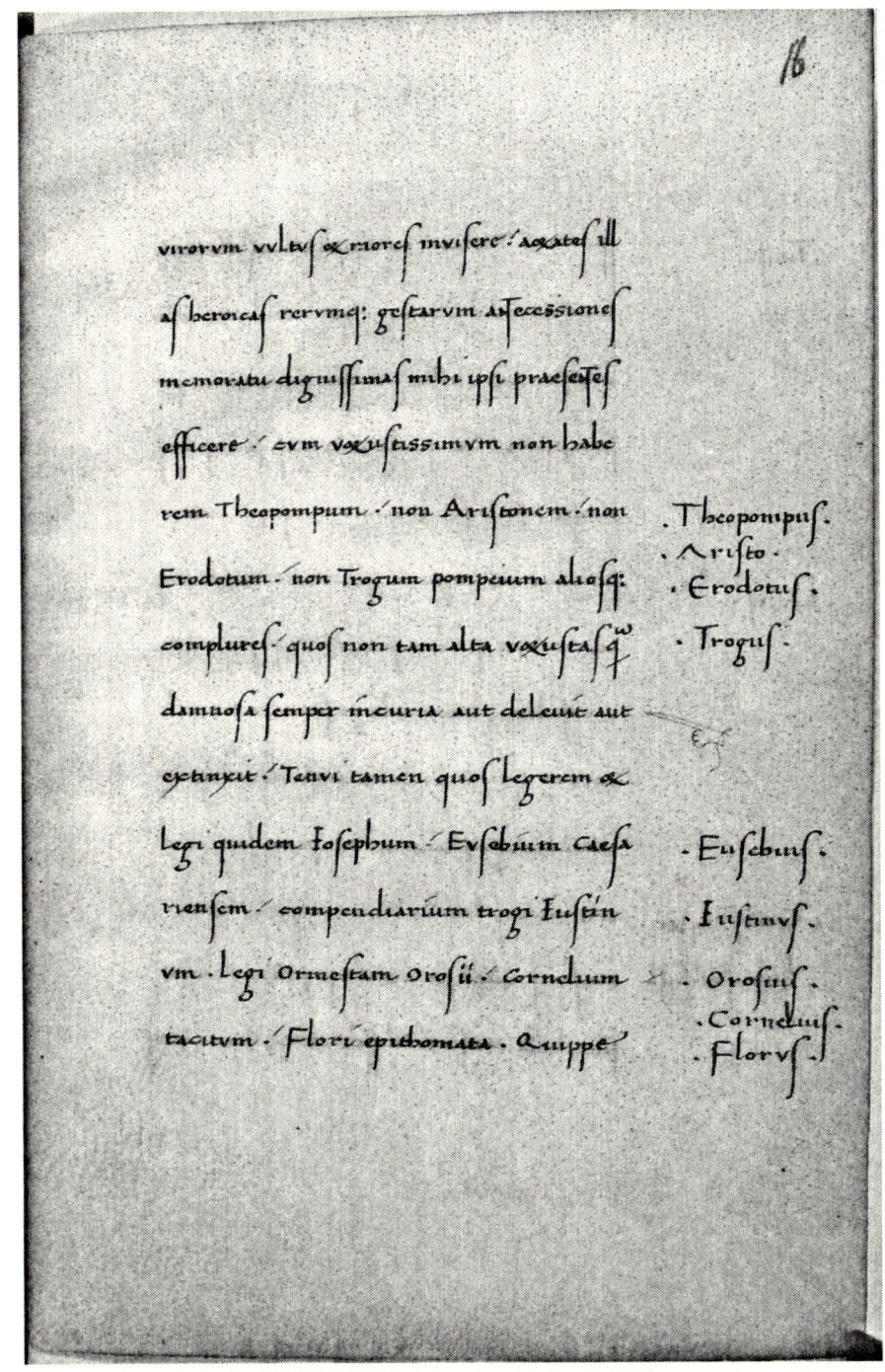

virorum vultus & mores invisere, aetates illas heroicas rerumque gestarum successiones
memoratu dignissimas mihi ipsi praesentes
efficere, cum vetustissimum non habe-
rem Theopompum, non Aristonem, non   · Theopompus ·
                                       · Aristo ·
Erodotum, non Trogum pompeium aliosque · Erodotus ·
complures, quos non tam alta vetustas q^{uam} · Trogus ·
damnosa semper incuria aut delevit aut
extinxit. Tenui tamen quos legerem &
legi quidem Iosephum, Eusebium caesa- · Eusebius ·
riensem, compendiarium trogi Iustin-   · Iustinus ·
um, legi Ormestam Orosii, Cornelium   · Orosius ·
                                       · Cornelius ·
tacitum, Flori epithomata. Quippe   · Florus ·

APOLOGIA ANTONII RAVDENSIS EX PROFESSIONE MINORVM ADVERSVS ARCHIDIACONVM QVEMPIAM COMPLICESQVE SYCOPHANTAS TAETERRIMOS SCRIPTA AD ANTONIVM MASSAM MINORVM GENERALEM

1 [1r] Etsi non nesciam, reuerendissime Generalis, ad alienam aucupandam beneuolentiam necessitudinemque qua dicundi arte quibusue principiis coram uti oporteat, ubi tamen te mihi patrem intellego, me tibi filium certo scio, ea ipsa (ut ita dixerim) rhetorum[1]
5   lenocinia,[2] quae de industria missa facio, nihil est et praesertim te penes, qui primis in labiis quid quisque pergat dicere plane dignosti, ut ducam in medium. Veniam itaque ad nudam officii uoluntatem, posthabitaque uerborum compositione affectum dumtaxat expediam.

2 Extant quidem [1v] haud nulli, lectissime praesul,[3] quibus
10 dum extinguere me nulla uis, nulla auctoritas pedem facit, obiiciunt tamen ulla ne parte colluceam quas ipsi possunt in me tenebras, atque meme sub modio, undique rodentes lacerantesque, moliuntur occulere. Qui ipsi supinae crassaeque ruditatis informes, me illiteratum prorsus, me imperitum, me ignarum omnium rerum, me
15 infantissimum, denique et extremi ingenii uirum, ubique gentium praedicant. At quoniam — ut Plautino uerbo utar —

miserorum est, ut maleuolentes sint atque inuideant bonis,

[2r] eos ipsos perinde atque impurissimos sycophantas neglectu quodam paruicuro. Nollem tamen ex huiuscemodi obtrectatorum
20 meorum latratibus (uulnerant enim semper dolosius prima tela[4]) apud te talem fieri qualem ipsi me pingere enixiore studio litigant atque contendunt. Idcirco operae pretium duxi et in rem meam fieri existimaui, pace tua ac bona uenia fretus, pro commentis in me criminosis insimulationibus palinodia contra quaedam et ex
25 aduerso laudes proprias — non sine rubore — in angustiis trusus personarem.

Semper ego auditor tantum? numquamue[5] [2v] *reponam uexatus totiens?*

---

[1] rhe-] *corr. M*
[2] leno-] *corr. M*
[3] praesul] -suli *Lomb.*
[4] tela] *corr. M*
[5] numquamue *M* : -ne *Juv.*

THE APOLOGY OF ANTONIO DA RHO, FROM THE ORDER OF THE FRIARS MINOR, AGAINST A CERTAIN ARCHDEACON AND HIS LOATHSOME SYCOPHANT ACCOMPLICES ADDRESSED TO ANTONIO DA MASSA, GENERAL OF THE FRIARS MINOR

1 Although I do know, Very Reverend General, something of the art or principles of speech one should use in public to gain another's goodwill or friendship, nevertheless when I realize that you are my father and when I know for certain that I am your son, no reason exists for me to employ what I would call the rhetoricians' charms — which I purposely omit — and especially with you, who clearly discern what each one is leading up to before it slips off the tip of the tongue. And so let me come to the undisguised purpose of my mission, and having put aside stylistic elaboration, let me simply speak my mind.

2 There are in fact some people, most worthy prelate, who, though no external force or legal authority has instigated[1] them to destroy me, still cast what darkness they can over me lest I somehow shine. And while harassing and tormenting me at every turn, they strive to hide me under a bushel.[2] These same people, deformed by torpid and coarse boorishness, announce to the whole world that I am altogether illiterate, that I am without experience, that I am utterly ignorant, that I am extremely inarticulate, and finally that I am a man of the meanest ability. But since — to borrow a phrase from Plautus — "it is characteristic of the wretched that they resent and envy the prosperous,"[3] I, with a certain insouciance, take as little notice of them as I do of their vile sycophants. Yet from this baying of my detractors (for the first cut is always the deepest) I do not want to become in your eyes such as these men with increasingly fanatic zeal strive and strain to depict me. For that reason, confident of your leave and indulgence, I thought it worthwhile and considered it to my advantage — being faced with their maliciously fabricated accusations against me — to sing "palinodes"[4] against certain statements. And having been forced into a tight spot, I thought it to my advantage on the contrary to sing (not without a blush) my own praises. "Am I always to be just a listener?" [as Juvenal says], "or may I never reply though so persistently harassed?"[5]

---

[1] The nautical metaphor *pedem facit* means literally "to set a sail" (cf. Virgil *Aeneid* 5.830).
[2] For the expression *sub modio*, cf. Matthew 5.15; Mark 4.21; and Luke 11.33.
[3] Plautus *The Captives* 583.
[4] Rho misunderstood the meaning of "palinode," thinking it to mean the repetition of earlier stated praise rather than a recantation. He also erred concerning its Latin gender, taking *palinodia* as a neuter accusative plural, instead of a feminine accusative singular that lacks the terminal "m." He wrote (*Imitations* 116v: *Laudare*): "A palinode (*palinodium*) is later praise, spoken against previously experienced insults."
[5] Juvenal 1.1–2.

3 Cicero namque — scrutemur illum — sub aemulorum suorum frequentia totus est in laudibus suis: nunc se *patrem patriae*, nunc *fortunatam* se *consule Romam*, nunc Graecorum studia in melius traduxisse gloriatur. Et ne sese dumtaxat quasi uenale mancipium quoddam gloriae audientibus traderet, ea ipsa gloria mortales ferme singulos quosque cum multis in libris tum praesertim ubi Pro Archia suauissimam illam orationem habuit pellectos declarauit. *Trahimur*, aiebat, *omnes studio laudis, et optumus quisque maxime gloria* [3r] *ducitur. Ipsi illi philosophi etiam illis in libellis, quos de gloria contemnenda scribunt, nomen suum inscribunt; in eo ipso, in quo praedicationem nobilitatemque despiciunt, praedicari de se ac nominari uolunt.* Quae sententia — etsi non eloquentius, apertius tamen exarata, non opinata[6] — apud Persium uisa est:

Scire tuum (ait) *nihil est, nisi te scire hoc sciat alter?*
At pulchrum est digito monstrari et dicier "hic est."

4 Sed quid alienae factionis rem in istam testes ascisco, cum ille nullius sanctitatis expers Hieronymus noster — secutus, inquit, *Tranquillum* et [3v] *Apollonium Graecum ab Apostolis ad aetatem* suam uirorum illustrium catalogum[7] intexens — non sese illustrem ast *in calce* libelli *quasi abortiuum minimumque Christianorum omnium* et tamen superioribus connumerandum se exararit? Altius itaque et ab incunabulis repetens cum et apostolus Paulus ueritatem, ut ait, dicens glorietur, de me uel quippiam praedicabo.

5 Puellus namque uixdum uerba formare sciens in ludo uersabundus, elementa per quae Latine[8] scribimus didici. Opuscula uaria tam iocosa quam seria et ingeniis nascentibus accommodata [4r] syllabarum numerationem, uerborum diligentiam, fabellarum memoriam, uersuum legem modificationemque ex ipsis ludi magistris excepi. Quorum etsi aliquando ambagiosa puerorum more dicacitate, numquam tamen per indocilitatem, aut colaphos aut ferulas sensi.

6 Exactis compluribus porro temporum uoluminibus post saeculi non imbibitas at delibatas illecebras, cum essem annorum duodeuiginti, opitulante mihi in naufragium periclitationemque uoto, religionem hanc tuam, qua te primorem nemo non huiusce professionis filius et

---

[6]exarata non opinata] *s.l. suppl. M*
[7]catalogum] *s.l. suppl. M*
[8]Latine *coniec. Lomb.* : -ni *M*

[6]Cicero *In Defense of Sestius* 57.121.
[7]Juvenal 10.122; cf. Quintilian *The Education of the Orator* 9.4.41 and 11.1.24.
[8]Cf. Cicero *Tusculan Disputations* 1.1.1–3.
[9]Cicero *In Defense of Archia* 11.26.
[10]Persius 1.27–28.

3 Cicero, for instance — let us read him carefully — is full of his own praises in response to his hoard of rivals: at one time he glories that he is "the father of his country,"[6] at another that Rome was "fortunate" to have him "as consul,"[7] at still another that he had translated the literature of the Greeks into something finer.[8] And in order that he not betray himself to his audience as some venal slave of glory, he declared in his many books, and particularly when delivering that charming oration *In Defense of Archia*, that this same glory attracted almost every single mortal. "The desire for praise," he said, "draws us all, and inasmuch as a person is noble, glory especially lures him. Philosophers themselves inscribe their names even on those books they write about scorning glory; in the very same place where they express contempt for publicity and recognition, they want to be publicized and recognized themselves."[9] This sentiment appears in Persius (even if not more eloquently, he nevertheless spelled it out more clearly): "Does your knowing mean nothing," he said, "unless another knows that you know? But it is charming to be pointed out and to hear it said 'Here he is.'"[10]

4 But why do I cite authorities from pagan sources on this point, when our own Jerome, though he lacked for no sanctity, followed, as he said, "Suetonius and the Greek Apollonius" in compiling a catalogue *On Illustrious Men* "from the Apostle's to his own time,"[11] and though he described himself at the end of his booklet[12] not as illustrious but "as if born prematurely and the least of all Christians,"[13] nonetheless he numbered himself among the aforementioned? Thus going back further, to my very infancy, I too shall declare something about myself, since the Apostle Paul, as he himself said, boasts while speaking the truth.[14]

5 For as a boy attending elementary school and scarcely yet knowing how to form words, I learned the Latin alphabet. I got from my elementary teachers diverse little works both humorous and serious and adapted to incipient talents "on the metric quantity of syllables, carefulness in words, the memorization of stories, and the rules for scansion of verse."[15] Although I sometimes felt either my masters' cuffs or canes for boyish smart-aleck remarks, yet never for my unteachableness.

6 By and by, after the world's allurements had been sipped but not quaffed and when I had reached my eighteenth year, a vow saved me from shipwreck and crisis, and I was transformed into a new man. I myself invaded your religious order in which every son of this profession both admires and cherishes you as head.[16]

---

[11] Jerome *Letter* 47.3.

[12] Cf. Jerome *On Illustrious Men* 135. Rho wrote as though the phrase that follows comes from *On Illustrious Men* (and perhaps that is how Rho recalled it), but it is in fact from *Letter* 47.3.

[13] Jerome *Letter* 47.3; I Corinthians 15:8–9; cf. *Apology* §65.

[14] Cf. II Corinthians 12.6.

[15] Seneca the Younger *Letter* 88.3.

[16] Rho entered the Franciscan Order in 1413 (see *Philippic* §47).

[4v] admiratur et colit, in alterum iam ipse conflatus uirum irrupi. Vbi Matthaeum quempiam Cremonensem Ludouicumque Piranensem *humanarum diuinarumque rerum* peritissimos homines, qui me perbelle instituerent,⁹ catechistas¹⁰ praeceptoresque scientiae percupidus offendi. Audiueram equidem puros elementares, puros asellos esse. Fit eo uti perpetuos tris annos dialecticae, quam pugnis similem Cicero in Finibus suis tradit, etsi in uerbis magis quam in rebus litigare uideatur, me discipulum constituerim. Neque in illa, etsi ceteras scientias sola polliceatur,¹¹ pro[5r]missior esse decreui.

7 Quinimmo rhetoricorum libros (Ciceronis enim extant bina uolumina, Aristotelis unum, Martiani unum) Victorinique commentarios, Alani, Aegidii, Petrique Blesensis, aliorumque complurium spiritu deflagrante lectitaui. Quorum doctrina usqueadeo pellectus sum, ut, cum reliquis in scientiis quadam ingenuitate animi adhuc liber peruagatus sim, ex illa nullo me pacto ueluti captiuum quempiam aut enodare aut diuellere hactenus potuerim. Circuit enim singula quaeque gymnasia, et cum ceterae sorores maiestate sua quadam gloriabundae subla[5v]tisque humeris procedant, sola eloquentia ea est quae linguam omnem exornet, quae residuis uenustatem dignitatemque formosissima impertiat. Putaui tamen detractorum meorum linguas non euasurum nisi et inde alio concessissem.

8 Proxime itaque, qui *me latifundia metiri*, qui corporum magnitudines altitudinesque, qui normam porrigere, circinum ducere, qui lapides ad filum caementariorum more redigere doceret, Euclidem praeceptorem "Inueni!" Quem profecto si quis nesciat, plane intellego concaua conuexaque perspecti[6r]uorum specula pilasque uitreas atque Ptolomei uolumen quod Almagesti nominant, diuinum magis quam humanum opus, eum ignorare oportere.

---

⁹instituerent] -runt *Lomb.*
¹⁰catechistas *scripsi* : cathetis- *M*
¹¹pollice-] *corr. M*

---

[17]Matteo Pritelli da Cremona was a little known Franciscan theologian, who studied in Bologna and received his bachelor's in 1408 and his master's in 1416 (Piana 65; Lombardi 55n).

[18]Lodovico da Pirano was a Franciscan theologian (ca. 1383–ca. 1450) known for a work on mnemonics. He later became Bishop of Forlì and attended the Councils of Basel and Ferrara-Florence (Cenci 1976, 265–71; Piana 24*–25*; Lombardi 55n).

[19]Cicero *On Duties* 1.43.153. This Stoic notion of wisdom — "the knowledge of things human and divine" — was adopted by Latin Christianity on the authority of Augustine (see Rice 1973, esp. 2–13).

[20]This is a scholastic proverb, see *Philippic* §27 n. 63.

[21]Cicero *About the Ends of Goods and Evils* 3.12.41.

[22]These must be the "Old Rhetoric," Cicero's *On Invention*, and the "New Rhetoric," the anonymous *Rhetoric to Herennius*, which Rho and his contemporaries regarded as a work of Cicero (cf. Pellegrin 1955a, A 221, 612, and 613; Lombardi 57n).

[23]Aristotle *Rhetoric* (cf. Pellegrin 1955a, A 221).

[24]Martianus Capella *On the Marriage of Philology and Mercury* (cf. Pellegrin 1955a, A 221; and *Apology* §23).

Hungry for knowledge, I there met my catechists and teachers, a certain Matteo da Cremona[17] and Lodovico da Pirano,[18] men most proficient in "things human and divine,"[19] who gave me a thorough education. I had in fact heard that "complete beginners were complete asses."[20] As a result, for three whole years I gave myself over completely to dialectic, which Cicero in his *About the Ends of Goods and Evils* confided resembles boxing,[21] although in dialectics the fighting may seem to be more verbal than real. But I decided not to tarry longer in dialectics even if it alone promised access to the other sciences.

7 Rather, with great enthusiasm I pored over the books of the rhetoricians (for Cicero has two such works,[22] Aristotle one,[23] Martianus one[24]) as well as the commentaries of Victorinus,[25] Alanus,[26] Giles,[27] Peter of Blois,[28] and the commentaries of a good many others. Their teaching so enthralled me that, like some captive, I have not yet managed in any way either to untie or to extricate myself from it, although up until then I had wandered freely in the other sciences with a certain spontaneity of spirit. For only Eloquence encompasses every single school. Although her other sisters go forth with a certain pretentious majesty and with shoulders held high, Eloquence alone adorns all language and is the lovely Lady who imparts charm and dignity to the rest.[29] Yet, I thought that I could not escape the tongues of my detractors unless I withdrew from Eloquence to another discipline.

8 And then *Eureka!* the teacher Euclid, who taught "me to measure estates,"[30] to measure the volume and height of bodies, to lay out a square, to draw an arc, and to lay stones by string like cement workers.[31] I clearly understood that if anyone did not know Euclid, of necessity he would not understand the concave and convex mirrors and glass spheres as well as Ptolemy's volume that they call the *Almagest*,[32] a work more divine than human.

---

[25] Gaius Marius Victorinus (fl. 350s CE), from North Africa, wrote two books of commentaries on Cicero's *On Invention* (cf. Pellegrin 1955a, A 614).

[26] An unidentified Alanus who wrote a commentary on the *Rhetoric to Herennius* and "enjoyed considerable authority in Italy into the fifteenth century" (Monfasani 1976, 263). He has been doubtfully identified as Alain of Lille, a twelfth-century poet, logician, and theologian (see Monfasani 1976, 262–64; and Lombardi 57n).

[27] Giles of Rome (ca. 1245–1316) *On Aristotle's Rhetoric*. The Visconti library inventory misidentifies this work as a commentary on the works of Cicero (see Pellegrin 1955a, A 626; Lombardi 57n).

[28] Peter of Blois (ca. 1135–1211) is no longer considered the author of *On the Rhetorical Art of Speaking* once attributed to him (cf. Pellegrin 1955a, A 78; Lombardi 57–59n).

[29] Cf. Martianus Capella *On the Marriage of Philology and Mercury* 5.425-38; and Black 2001, 336–37.

[30] This is Seneca's phrase from *Letter* 88.10. Euclid (fl. ca. 300 BCE) was a mathematician who taught at Alexandria. He was especially famed for his book of geometry, *Elements*.

[31] This presumes Roman construction techniques for building a wall. The exterior stone or brickwork (*opus incertum* or *opus reticulatum*) served as forms for the concrete. Both Euclid's *Geometry*, that is his *Elements*, and Campanus de Novara's commentary on it were in the Visconti Library (cf. Pellegrin 1955a, A 256 and A 255 respectively).

[32] Claudius Ptolemaeus (fl. 127–147 CE) was an Alexandrian Greek whose work as a geographer, astronomer, and mathematician transmitted much of ancient science to later generations. His *Almagest* and *Geography* were particularly important. They represented the earth as a globe (two-thirds its actual size) and the universe as geocentric. His map of the earth and his miscalculation of the earth's size figured significantly in early European "voyages of discovery." Gerardo da Cremona translated the *Almagest* from Greek to Latin ca. 1180 (cf. Pellegrin 1955a, A 292).

9 Post geometriam, non dicam pauper ceterum egenus, manus ad calculos applicui. Quid sibi uellet articulus quidue digitus didici; denique, quod in arithmetica negotiosissimum semper habitum est, non modo e quadratis (sic enim aiunt), uerum et e numeris cubicis radices exhausi. At cum praeter lupinos aut lapillos ad supputandum haberem nihil, timens eo ne ridiculus aemulis fierem, in [6v] musicam migro.

10 Ibi quid diatesaron, quid diapente diapasonque consonarent facillime tenui. Quin potius mirandum in modum, seu natura suppeditante seu (si diuinum illum Platona sequor) caelorum accentu unde ipsa anima pullulat suffragante, modo gerularum et obstetricum[12] nenias, modo exodia, modo procacia fescennina, aliquando epithalamium[13] et hymenaeum celeumataque uarios modos uariosque numeros, laxamentum requietemque in lassitudine quaeritans (*Pythagoras enim perturbationes animi lyra componebat*), nullo me instituente personui.

11 Inde ad superos transeo [7r] liberalesque inter artes astrorum situ gloriari coepi: signorum caelestium ortus et obitus; corporum propinquitates, recessus, altitudinesque;

frigida Saturni sese quo stella receptet,
quos signis[14] caeli Cyllenius erret in orbes;

qua lege tandem quaue anni tempestate sol deficeret, et pernox luna laboraret, aliaque complurima e regis Alfonsi Tabulis non sine supputationibus identidem reuolutis intellexi.

12 Tandem permulta lectitans euoluensque offendi has superiores artes, quas liberales appellamus, ab Seneca protracto sermone etsi non pror[7v]sus exibilari aut explodi, non tamen satis praesertim[15] apud spectatos, graues, seuerosque uiros extolli aut approbari. Quo fit ut eo praeuio *in* philosophiae *castra* (uerbis enim eiusce utar) *non transfuga*, uerum speculator commigrarem. Aristoteles ibi, quae rerum principia quotue forent edisserens; quid caelum, quid elementa, quid

---

[12]obstetricum] *corr. M*
[13]epitha-] -h- *s.l. suppl. M*
[14]signis *M* : ignis *Verg.*
[15]prae-] -e- *s.l. suppl. M*

---

[33]This is terminology from Boethius' *Geometric Art* (1): *On Computation with the Abacus.* Accordingly, "digits" are the numbers one through ten; "articles" are all numbers above ten to infinity (cf. Pellegrin 1955a, A 556 and A 557; Lombardi 59n).

[34]Cf. Boethius *Fundamentals of Arithmetic* 2.4.

[35]The ancients, presumably following Pythagoras, turned the study of Music into an intellectual pursuit by making it part of the study of Number, noting the ratios of the Fourth (4:3), the Fifth (3:2), and the Octave (2:1). Music also included mathematical astronomy, which studied the "harmony of the spheres." Rho probably means by this statement that he had read Boethius' *Fundamentals of Music* (cf. Pellegrin 1955a, A 555).

[36]Cf. Plato *Timaeus* 36–37.

[37]Seneca the Younger *Dialogues* 5.9.2; Iamblichus *The Life of Pythagoras* 64.114, 9.4.

9 After geometry, I applied my hand to the abacus, not, I would say, as a poor man but as a complete beggar. I learned what an "article" or a "digit" signifies;[33] and finally I learned what must always be considered most laborious in arithmetic: to determine the roots not only of squared but also of the so-called "cubed" numbers.[34] But fearing that I would become a laughingstock to my rivals since I had nothing to count besides beans or pebbles, I therefore moved on to music.

10 There I easily grasped how the intervals of the Fourth, Fifth, and Octave sounded.[35] Furthermore, I sang wonderfully either with nature sufficing or (if I follow the divine Plato) with the sound of the heavens accompanying, whence the soul itself springs.[36] And with no one instructing me I sang now the songs of nurses and midwives, now comic exodes, now licentious charivaris. Sometimes, seeking relaxation and repose in my weariness (for "Pythagoras soothed the disturbances of his soul with a lyre"),[37] I sang bridal and marriage songs and boatswains' chants, in various rhythms and melodies.

11 From there I passed on to celestial things, and among the liberal arts I began to glory in the location of the stars:[38] I understood the risings and settings of the constellations; the approaches, retreats, and altitudes of bodies; "where the cold star of Saturn recedes, into what orbits Mercury wanders through the constellations."[39] Finally, I understood by what law or season of the year the sun sets and the moon toils throughout the night and many other things from King Alfonso's *Tables*,[40] not without having frequently reworked their calculations.

12 At length, after reading and perusing a great many things, I encountered those higher arts, which we term liberal. And even if in his lengthy speech Seneca does not completely hiss at or hoot them off stage, nevertheless they are not particularly extolled and approved, especially among distinguished, weighty, and serious men.[41] So taking Seneca as my guide, I crossed over "into the camp" of philosophy "not as a defector" (to use his words), but as a scout.[42] There Aristotle, when expounding what or how the origins of things might be; when relating what heaven, the elements, and the soul could be, and how Nature could be the mother of all things permanent; when teaching what practices or methods might promote the best and worst customs,

---

[38] Cf. Seneca the Younger *Letter* 88.14.

[39] Virgil *Georgics* 1.336–37; cf. Seneca the Younger *Letter* 88.14. Rho (*Imitations* 17r–18v: *Astrologia*) lists and gives poetic references for the planets and constellations.

[40] These tables, drawn up ca. 1275 at the Court of Alfonso X of Castile, were the authority for mathematical astronomy until the sixteenth century (Lindberg 272–73).

[41] Seneca the Younger (ca. 4 BCE–65 CE) was a Roman, Stoic, moral philosopher (cf. *Philippic* 75 n. 181). In *Letter* 88, he refused to call any study "good" that results in moneymaking. Seneca also approved of "liberal studies" (those studies worthy of free people: poetry, grammar, history, mathematics, music, astronomy) only insofar as they were preparation to the study of philosophy, which teaches virtue. All studies except philosophy he characterized as "feeble and puerile."

[42] Seneca the Younger *Letter* 2.5. On the importance of this simile for Renaissance readers, see Ullman 1923, 21–38; and Ullman 1973, 113–33.

anima, quid constantium omnium natura mater posset tradens; quibus exercitationibus quoue pacto mores optumi pessumique nascerentur, quae qualisue censeretur felicitas [8r] in hominum genere, quibus institutis res publica familiarisque seruaretur erudiens; etsi non armatum Achillem me fecerit, e castris tamen suis non degenerem, non ignauum Thersitem eliminauit.

13 Vidi de Ideis eiusce Aristotelis Platonisque uerbale magis quam reale certamen. Vidi Bonettum quempiam ex Galliis Transalpinis hac tantorum philosophorum in lucta perbelle disceptantem. Vidi et Senecam ea epistula cuius initium est *Hesternam diem diuisi cum mala ualitudine* hac in re Platonem his uerbis explicare: *Haec exempla*[8v]*ria omnium rerum deus intra se habet numerosque uniuersorum quae agenda sunt et modos mente complexus est; plenus his figuris est quas Plato "ideas" appellat — immortales, immutabiles, infatigabiles. Itaque homines quidem pereunt, ipsa autem humanitas ad quam homo effingitur permanet, et hominibus laborantibus intereuntibusque*[16] *illa nihil patitur.*

14 Inde me sacrarum litterarum pelago, quas liuentes mei utpote glires altissime somniantes delirant, et qui me somniare delirareque passim garriunt, instituendum dedi. Vbi theologorum [9r] admodum lucubrata, non tamen quouis gentium harum prae rerum magnitudine satis intellecta, uocabula et legi et intellexi. Accepi plane diuinam essentiam communicari, Trinitatis hypostases non confundi; Scoti formalitates quiditatesque, Francisci relationes terminos et fundamenta, nomina essentialia personalia notionaliaque, atque attributa diuina non intacta posthabui. Quo pacto illae ipsae hypostases se ipsis relationibusne aut absolutis constituerentur; quae naturae rei distinctio, quae rationis, quae realis; quae originis signa atque naturae forent, etsi non [9v] praeter omnes doctus, non tamen cum iis insulsis insulsus euasi. Vidi quemadmodum ille sator omnium, deus huiusce machinae, quam suspicimus fundamenta iecerit molemque[17] tantam *sine follibus et incudibus* cunctipotens excitarit. Vidi qua uia

---

[16]-que] *M* : *om. Sen.*
[17]molem- *scripsi* : mollem- *M*

[43]Achilles was the heroic warrior from Thessaly who fought alongside the Greeks against the Trojans; for Thersites see *Philippic* §10 n. 25.

[44]Nicolas Bonet (ca. 1280–ca. 1343) was a Franciscan theologian and missionary who taught at the University of Paris. For his service as papal legate to the court of Kublai Kahn in Peking, he was made Bishop of Malta.

[45]Seneca the Younger *Letter* 65.1.

[46]Seneca the Younger *Letter* 65.7.

which or what sort of happiness might befit the human race, and what teachings might preserve the public good and private property; yes, there Aristotle, even if he did not make me a warrior like Achilles, still did not drive me from his camp like a dishonorable, cowardly Thersites.[43]

13 I saw that Aristotle and Plato's dispute about the Ideas was more verbal than real. I saw that a certain Bonet[44] from Transalpine Gaul arbitrated charmingly in this wrestling match between such great philosophers. I even saw that Seneca, in his letter that begins "I split the day yesterday between ill health,"[45] explained Plato on this topic with these words: "God has within himself these patterns of all things, and he holds in his mind the measures and rhythms of all things universally that are to be brought about; he is filled with the forms, which Plato calls 'Ideas' — imperishable, immutable, inexhaustible. Accordingly, humans certainly perish, but humanity itself, after which an individual is fashioned, endures and suffers nothing from individuals laboring and dying."[46]

14 Then I devoted myself to being taught the sea of sacred literature, about which my enviers talk deliriously like dormice in deepest sleep, and even babble all over the place that I am dreaming and talking deliriously. In this subject I both read and understood the words of the theologians, which have been painstakingly elaborated though insufficiently understood among the pagans because of the subject's magnitude. I distinctly comprehended that the divine essence was shared and that the Hypostases of the Trinity were not to be confused.[47] I did not leave untried Scotus' formalities and quiddities[48] or Francis' relations, terms, and foundations; his essential, personal, and notional names, as well as his divine attributes.[49] Even if I did not turn out as learned beyond all others, nevertheless I did not emerge a nitwit in the company of these nitwits. I comprehended how these Hypostases were constituted either through their very relationships or through absolutes; what was the distinction of a thing by nature, what was the distinction by reason, or what was the real distinction; or what were the markers of origin and nature.[50] I saw how the founder of all things, God, laid the foundations of this cosmic machine that we admire and, because he is all-powerful, erected so

---

[47]Early Christians struggled to preserve Hebrew monotheism in the face of their belief that the New Testament texts referred to God the Father, his Son Jesus, and the Holy Spirit as equally divine. The Trinitarian formula, adopted at the Council of Nicaea (325), settled on the "mystery" of three persons in one substance or being (Greek: *treis hypostaseis, mia ousia*; Latin: *tres personae, una substantia*).

[48]Duns Scotus (ca. 1265–1308), the preeminent Franciscan scholastic philosopher and theologian, taught at Oxford and Paris. He tried with his *formalities* to distinguish between that which was less than real (having a separate existence) but more than simply logical (being only a mental distinction). With his *quiddities* he examined the "whatness" or essence of a thing.

[49]Francis of Meyronnes (d. 1327), a Franciscan and disciple of Duns Scotus, sought in his *Explanations of Divine Terms* and *Tract on Formalities* to clarify the language used in theological propositions about the Trinity.

[50]According to Peter Lombard (d. 1160), a sacrament is "a visible form of invisible grace" (4.1.4). Following Peter Lombard, the Catholic Church holds the number of sacraments to be seven: Baptism, Confirmation, the Eucharist, Penance, Extreme Unction, Orders, and Matrimony.

ille ipse deus hominum generi misceri potuerit atque in cruce moribundus, fuso antidoto e uulneribus suauissimo, naturam lapsam erexerit.

15 Transeo hinc in ecclesiae propugnatorem egregium Augustinum a quo quis abhorreat,[18] cum quem sequatur tutiorem non offendat ducem, aut [10r] deuiare aut perire necesse est. Qui tamen dum Ciuitatem dei molitur, Lactantium in multis non erubescit imitari;[19] dum Confessiones suas dicit, Plutarchum Suetoniumque Tranquillum illustrissimorum uirorum mores ab incunabulis tradentes uidetur exprimere; dum Verum cultum definit, Officia Ciceronis insequitur. Academiam et Diuinationem suam etsi ab eo ipso Cicerone mutuauit,[20] in melius tamen redegit.

16 Praetereo nunc reliquam librorum uoluminumque suorum condensissimam siluam, quam non tam sileo quam numerare ne[10v]queo, et Augustino eloquentiorem sanctioremque Hieronymum tota mente complector. Legi quo pacto uirgines caelibesque uiduas et monachos nunc moneat, nunc laudibus efferat. Vidi pro maledictis (neque enim ipse morsus alienos euasit) quam mordicus — nescio ne dicam uehementer — usque respondeat. Legi in Iouinianum aliosque palestrae consimilis quasi ex illo missa caelitus fulmina. Legi eum in Origenis Periarchon, percepique quanta eloquentia et exactissima dicundi arte se purget. Hic est plane pro altari lampas ecclesiae quam, post sacrarum litte[11r]rarum tot e Graeco et Hebraeo cum traducta tum commentata uolumina, non Auster non ipse Boreas extinguere ualeat.

17 Dicerem quas uidi Gratiani Distinctiones, Causas, Consecrationesque; dicerem summorum pontificum Decretales epistulas, Bonifatium atque Clementem, glosulasque etsi non excussas saltem uisas Iohannis Andreae; dicerem quemadmodum imperatorum leges ab Iustiniano conflatae sint, quibus titulis proferantur in medium, et si iocari in aemulos licet, titulus is suus erit: *ff.* De Vernaciis, £. Bibe, §. Bonum Vinum.

---

[18]abhor-] -h- *s.l. suppl. M*
[19]imi-] *corr. M*
[20]Mutuo et mutuor idem signant antique (Papias). *mg. glos. M*

[51]Cicero *On the Nature of the Gods* 1.54.
[52]On Augustine's *City of God* and his use of Lactantius' *Divine Institutes*, see Garnsey; and O'Daly 40–52. The title *On True Worship* (*De vero cultu*) is the title of Book VI of Lactantius' *Divine Institutes*, which Rho probably just confused with *On True Religion* (*De vera religione*), a work of Augustine. Lactantius' *On True Worship*, however, did circulate independently (and mistakenly) as a work of Augustine.
[53]See, for example, his *Letters* 22 and 125.
[54]For Jerome's polemical writings, see Introduction 18 and 20–22 above.
[55]*Distinctiones*, *Causae*, and *Consecrationes* were the major divisions of Gratian's *Decretum* (ca. 1140). See *Philippic* §67 n. 156; cf. *Apology* §29.

great a colossus "without bellows and anvils."[51] I saw in what way God himself could be united with the human race and how, dying on the cross, he restored fallen nature by that sweetest of antidotes pouring from his wounds.

15 Next I moved on to Augustine, the preeminent defender of the church, since anyone who follows him will not find a safer leader, and anyone who deviates from him must either stray or perish. Nevertheless, while building his *City of God*, he does not blush to imitate Lactantius in many things; while making his *Confessions*, he seems to reproduce Plutarch and Suetonius, who related the habits of the most illustrious men from their youth; and while defining *True Worship*,[52] he followed closely the *On Duties* of Cicero. Even if Augustine borrowed his *Academy* and *Divination* also from Cicero, he returned them in better condition.

16 I pass over for the moment the rest of the dense forest of Augustine's books and volumes, which I am not so much reticent about as unable to count, and give my full attention to Jerome, who was more eloquent and holier than Augustine. I read how Jerome would at one moment remonstrate with and at another praise highly virgins, unmarried widows, and monks.[53] I saw how mordantly — perhaps I should say vehemently — he would respond to insults (for he himself did not escape the backbiting of other people). I read the thunderbolts that he hurled as if from heaven against Jovinian and others of a similar school.[54] I read him attacking Origen's *On First Things*, and I perceived how much eloquence and artfully crafted speech he used to defend himself. After having translated and expounded so many volumes of sacred literature from Greek and Hebrew, he is clearly the lamp before the church's altar that neither the South Wind nor the North Wind has the force to extinguish.

17 I could say which *Distinctiones*, *Causae*, and *Consecrationes* of Gratian I know;[55] I could say that I know the *Papal Decretals* — "Boniface" and "Clement"[56] — and even if I have not closely examined, I at least know the glosses of Giovanni d'Andrea;[57] I could say how Justinian assembled the laws of the emperors and published them by headings;[58] and, if it is permissible to tease my rivals, I could say that their headings will be: *ff*. From Vernaccia, £. Drink, §. Good Wine.[59]

---

[56]*Decretals* are papal letters that respond to a particular question and have the force of law. Subsequent to Gratian's *Decretum*, authoritative collections were compiled of the decretals of Gregory IX, 1234; Boniface VIII, 1298; and Clement V, 1317.

[57]Giovanni d'Andrea (ca. 1270–1348) was the most famous ecclesiastical jurist ("the fount and trumpet of Canon Law") in years leading up to the Great Western Schism (1378–1417). Teaching at the Universities of Padua and Bologna, he argued strongly for absolute papal authority over church and council (see Tierney 18 and 259–60).

[58]Justinian was the Byzantine Emperor from 527–65. He, with substantial assistance and inspiration of his wife, Empress Theodora, recovered many of the western provinces and commissioned the reorganization and codification Roman Law. The Twelfth-Century Renaissance of Roman Law in the West that began in Bologna and Padua relied directly on the *Codex Justinianus* and the *Digest* (see *Philippic* §134 n. 352).

[59]These symbols — *ff*, £, § — were the conventional designators for the headings and subheadings of legal texts.

18 Sed iam ad humanitatis studia, [11v] quae ueluti barbara quaedam apud me lacerantes prae ignoratione et insulsitate habentur, citari me intellego, quippe ubi Ciceronis in primis omnem quae in lucem prodire potuit supellectilem legi. Epistulas quas familiares appellant et eas ad Atticum iterum atque iterum euolui. Vidi eius Officia, Tusculanas, admiranda quae magis praedicauit quam sensit Paradoxa, Senectutem, Amicitiam, atque Orationes illius compositissimas. Saepe numero Philippicas seu Antonianas et quas in Verrem, in Catilinam, in Sallustium aliosque complures non sine uehemen[12r]tia fulminat, cynicas (ut ita dixerim) inuectiuas, in manibus tenui. Vidi Topicorum libellum (et in illum Boethii commentarium), De legibus, De finibus, De mundo, De fato (si suus est). Aperui (neque id raro) Academicam, Diuinationem, Deorumque naturam, ubi qui plures, qui unum, qui nullum deum fateantur disserentes adducit. Vidi Oratorem[21] quem facit ad Brutum; complexus immo exosculatus sum De oratore dialogos, praeter ceteros suos (iudicio meo) et eloquentiae et suauitatis refertissimos. Vidi eiusdem Brutum, qui De claris oratoribus inscribitur.[22] Vidi Scipionem suum somniantem atque Macrobium eo ipso [12v] in somno multa cum Aristotele frustra disceptantem.

19 Post Ciceronem e libris Senecae — in quos Quintilianus et A. Gellius (et eos quidem perlegi) prae uerborum sententiarumque inconexione stomachum nequaquam tenere potuere — quid mortem oppetere, quid uiuere, quid tenuitas, quid frugalitas foret, doctrinam cum sanctissimam tum dei plenissimam exhausi. Et cum ueterum plerique modernorumque earum in[23] prima quas ad Lucilium inscribit epistularum non mediocriter negotiari uideantur, quidue pertritus ille sermo *tota aliud agentibus* [13r] sibi uellet percontentur, ipse uel istac in re quid sentirem quasi sciolus quispiam appingere non dubitaui. Erit tamen semper[24] hac in re *circuli quadraturae*[25] simile quiddam, quae etsi scibilis sit, necdum tamen, inquit Aristoteles, scita est.

[21]Oratorem] *s.l. suppl.* M
[22]Vidi . . . inscribitur] *mg. suppl.* M
[23]in] *s.l. suppl.* M
[24]semper *om. Lomb.*
[25]-rae *coniec. Lomb.* : -ra M

[60]The phrase *studia humanitatis* (cf. *Apology* §33) derived from Cicero's *In Defense of Archia* (2.3), known after 1333, his *In Defense of Murena* (29.61), known only after 1415, and Pliny the Younger's *Panegyricus* (47.3), known after 1433 (Kohl 1992, 188–91; Conte 529). The concept, but not the specific phrase, is discussed by Aulus Gellius (13.17), who was widely read in the Middle Ages and the Renaissance. Salutati recirculated the expression *studia humanitatis* in the latter part of the fourteenth century "to denote both great scholarly and cultural achievement and training proper for the successful orator" (Kohl 1992, 201). Later, Gasparino Barzizza, Vittorino da Feltre, and Guarino Veronese used it to designate "'a well-defined cycle of studies' [Kristeller 1979, 98] . . . grammar, rhetoric, history, poetry, and moral philosophy" (Kohl 1992, 201; see also Black 1987b, esp. 127, and Black 2001, 21, 32, 252, 292, 354, esp. 364–65). The *Declamation against Lucius Sergius Catilina* (29.96), a pseudo-Ciceronian

18 But I now understand that I am summoned to humanistic studies,[60] which through ignorance and stupidity those who attack me regard as barbarities. Here first of all I read all the stuff that Cicero managed to circulate. I repeatedly perused his *Letters* that they call *To his Friends* and even those *To Atticus*. I saw his *On Duties*, *Tusculan Disputations*, and his admirable *Stoic Paradoxes*, which he stated more than understood. I saw his *On Old Age*, *On Friendship*, and his finely ordered *Orations*. I frequently held in my hands his *Philippics* or *Speeches against Mark Antony* and those cynical invectives, so to speak, which he vehemently thundered against Verres, against Catiline, against Sallust, and against many other people.[61] I saw his booklet *Topics* (and Boethius' commentary on it), his *On Laws*, *About the Ends of Goods and Evils*, *On the World*,[62] and *On Fate* (if it is his). I opened (and often) his *Academics*, *On Divination*, and *On the Nature of the Gods*, where he introduced discussants who acknowledged either many gods, one, or none. I saw *The Orator* that he dedicated to Brutus. I embraced, or rather reverently kissed his dialogues *On the Orator*, which is more fully crammed than his other works (in my judgment) with eloquence and charm. I saw his *Brutus*, which is subtitled *On Famous Orators*. I saw his *Scipio's Dream* as well as Macrobius, who while commenting on this dream fruitlessly disputed many things with Aristotle.[63]

19 After Cicero, from Seneca's books — for which Quintilian and Aulus Gellius (yes, even these I have read diligently) could never restrain their distaste on account of the disjointedness[64] of his words and ideas — I extracted how to meet death, how to live, and what poverty and self-restraint were, a teaching both holy and full of God. And although many of the ancients and moderns seem to concern themselves in no small way with the first of those letters that Seneca wrote to Lucilius (that is, they concerned themselves with what that trite phrase "all while doing what is not to the purpose" means),[65] I too, like some dilettante, did not hesitate to scribble my thoughts about it.[66] Yet this question will always be somewhat like "squaring the circle" which even if it is knowable, nonetheless, as Aristotle said, it is not yet known.[67]

---

text from which Rho quoted as early as 1433 (see Introduction 19–20 above), contains an heretofore unrecognized late ancient (?) use of the phrase *studia humanitatis*: ". . . *ferretur amens in omnia, nec ullae rationes consiliorum aut pudoris nec ulla studia humanitatis refrenarent praecipitem atque incitatum cursum vetustae crudelitatis.*" When Rho was laying out the *vocabula invectivarum* (Appendix VIII below) he did not pick up on the phrase *studia humanitatis*, but he may have included it elsewhere in his *Imitations* (which is a large tome).

[61] See Introduction 17–20 above.

[62] Plato's *Timaeus*, translated by Cicero (and surviving only in part), was sometimes known as Cicero's *De essentia mundi* (cf. Pellegrin 1955a, A 604 and A 30).

[63] Cicero's *Scipio's Dream* is a passage from the last book of his *Republic*, which has been preserved only in Macrobius' commentary. Macrobius' dispute with Aristotle can be found in Books 2.14–15 of his commentary (cf. *Apology* §22).

[64] *Inconexio* ordinarily means "asyndeton" or omission of the copula. But in using it to describe Quintilian's (*The Education of the Orator* 10.1.125–31) and Aulus Gellius' (12.2) criticism of Seneca the Younger, Rho has in mind the distance between concept and expression.

[65] Seneca the Younger *Letter* 1.1.

[66] Rho's scholia on this phrase appears at the end of his entry on Seneca (*Imitations* 226r-v).

[67] Aristotle *De decem predicamentis* (trans. Boethius) $7^b.31$–32.

20 Lactantium porro lancea magis — si Hieronymo fidem facimus — quam umbone ualentem, uirum exactissimae eloquentiae atque doctrinae delibans, quam maximam uoluptatem traxi.

21 Quid de utroque Plinio dixerim? Alter mihi rerum historiam texit et uniuersum explicat; alter me dicundi summa leuitate mulcet [13v] et nutrit.

22 Transeo hoc ex loco ad Noctes Atticas atque Saturnalia. Illas mihi A. Gellius rerum uarietate sparsim et inconexe digestas, tanta uerborum elegantia, festiuitate, splendore lectitandas impertit, ut nihil pictius, nihil comptius, nihil uenustius aut concinnius, etsi asello (ut de me aiunt) rudi in cassum lyra sonet, ipse percipiam. Ista uero haec Macrobius, uir non minoris suauitatis dicundi facilitate et iucunditate sermonis, quae gustentur, apponit. Ibi iocos et sales atque cauillos inuenies; ibi loedorias, [14r] decembres, et scommata atque dignissimas risu urbanitates innumeras, ibi iucunda problemata; denique Vergilii, quae apud Graecos latrocinatus est, promisso sermone offendes apertissima furta. Quae, ne repetundarum ab eis ipsis accusaretur, ita perbelle traduxit et in melius accommodauit, ut non tam inde clanculum sublata quam egregie uendicata ac iure possessa uideantur.

23 Inde conclamatus in Philologiae atque Mercurii splendissimas nuptias non sine lyricorum modorum concentu, etsi mihi iam tripudia [14v] obsoleuissent, migro. Ibi uernularum dotalia dona gestantium oratiunculas, quas illarum quaeque pro se coram habuit, uariis umbris intertextas et typis, ex Remigii commentariis perspicuas mihi et illustres, accepi.

24 Quibus habitis, uehor ex hoc symposio in Appuleii libros. Is, cum artis magicae ab nullis non accusaretur, tanta locorum inuentione, tanta dicundi arte se purgat, ut quae illi non perperam sed recte obiecta

---

[68]Lactantius (ca. 250–ca. 325) was a courtier of the Emperor Constantine. Jerome (*Letter* 58.10), speaking of Lactantius' apology for Christianity, *The Divine Institutes*, wrote: "Would that Lactantius, who was very nearly a river of Ciceronian eloquence, had been able to affirm our religion [i.e., Christianity] as easily as he destroyed that of others [i.e., paganism] (*Lactantius quasi quidam fluvius eloquentiae Tullianae, utinam tam nostra affirmare potuisset, quam facile aliena destruxit*)."

[69]Pliny the Elder (23/4–79) was a Roman of equestrian rank, who after a respectable military career went into retirement, perhaps to avoid dealing with Nero. He died in the eruption of Mount Vesuvius in 79, apparently in an attempt (now as commander of the Roman fleet in the Bay of Naples) to rescue victims of the disaster. Although Pliny wrote other works, he was primarily known for his encyclopedic *Natural Histories* (circulated posthumously). These and the material plundered from them by other writers made him an important authority on an enormous array of subjects throughout the Middle Ages and the Renaissance (Conte 497–503).

[70]Pliny the Younger (ca. 61–ca. 112), nephew of Pliny the Elder, is mostly known to us through his ten books of *Letters*, Book X being letters to the Emperor Trajan. His letters were largely ignored in the Middle Ages but in the Renaissance came to rank only behind the letters of Cicero (Conte 525–29).

[71]Aulus Gellius (fl. ca. 170), about whose life little is known, tells us that he wrote his *Attic Nights* in part to educate his children. Although intentionally haphazard in overall arrangement, each short chapter is carefully worked out. In it he quotes and comments on history, law, poetry, philosophy,

20 Next, I took the greatest possible pleasure in plucking the flowers from Lactantius, a man of precise eloquence and learning, who, if we believe Jerome, excels more with the lance than with the shield.[68]

21 What might I say about the Elder and the Younger Pliny? The former elaborated the history of things and explicated the universe for me;[69] the latter charmed and nourished me with the consummate smoothness of his speech.[70]

22 From here I moved on to the *Attic Nights* and *Saturnalia*. The *Attic Nights*, which take up a variety of things having no special order or connection, Aulus Gellius presented to me with such verbal elegance, vivacity, and splendor, that I can perceive nothing more colorful, more refined, more graceful, or more beautiful.[71] I perceive this even if I am (as my adversaries are wont to say about me) like a rude ass for whom the lyre sounds in vain.[72] It is Macrobius, however, a man not inferior in sweet elegance of speech and charm of language, who serves up the *Saturnalia* to be tasted.[73] There you will find jokes and witticisms and railleries. There you will find direct insults, festive pranks, and oblique taunts as well as innumerable urbanities worthy of a laugh. There you will find delightful riddles. And finally, there in a promised discourse,[74] you will encounter Virgil's open plagiarisms, which are texts he stole from Greek authors.[75] Lest these authors accuse him of embezzlement, Virgil beautifully translated and further improved these thefts so that ever since they seem not so much secretly purloined as conspicuously liberated and justly possessed.

23 When summoned thence I moved with a chorus of rhythmic lyres to *The Most Splendid Nuptials of Philology and Mercury*,[76] although for me the dances had now become obsolete. There I accepted the little speeches that each of the servant girls carried in as their dowry gifts. These were interwoven with various images and figures, which the commentaries of Remigius[77] rendered transparent and clear to me.

24 After these were delivered, I was transported from this symposium to the books of Apuleius. When everyone accused him of practicing magic, he exculpated himself with such a vast invention of topics and with such artful speech that

---

grammar, literary criticism, and textual questions, often combining these with anecdotal information. He remained popular with readers (known always as "A. Gellius" or simply "Gellius") right through the Middle Ages and the Renaissance as a guide to various subjects and authors (Greek and Latin), not least on Latinity itself (Conte 583–84; cf. *Philippic* §104).

[72]Cf. Jerome *Letter* 27.1.2.

[73]Ambrosius Theodosius Macrobius, the author of the *Saturnalia*, is variously identified (see *Philippic* §104 n. 262; cf. *Apology* §18).

[74]Macrobius at times promised to take up particular subjects (*Saturnalia* 1.24.19; 5.21.14; and 6.1.1). He seems not, however, to have "promised" the discourse on Virgil's Greek borrowings.

[75]Macrobius *Saturnalia* 5.2–22.

[76]This is a work by Martianus Capella (fl. 410–439), probably originally titled *Philologia*. It had enormous influence throughout the Middle Ages and the Renaissance, not least in designating the "Seven Liberal Arts": Grammar, Dialectic, Rhetoric, Geometry, Arithmetic, Astronomy, and Music (see *Apology* §7).

[77]Remigius of Auxerre (841?–908?) was a Carolingian scholar who, in addition to his *Commentaries on Martianus Capella*, also wrote commentaries on Boethius' *The Consolation of Philosophy* and on Genesis, Psalms, and the Gospel of Matthew.

245 fuerant, nequissime et uehementer illata pro contione atque iudice declararet. Vidi quo pacto ille ipse, [15r] cum in bubonem transire gestisset atque paelex quaepiam — ut aiebat, *mellitula* sua — omne sibi corpus quodam medicamento perduxisset, migrarit in asinum. Tunc primum sub aselli specie (nescio ne Naso simile aut ioco aut serio
250 tradiderit) mirabile dictu mens humana delituit. Impraesentia uerum mirabilius quiddam plane dignoscimus, id est sub seuerissimorum uirorum grauitate et pondere asellos — minimum quidem aureos ast auritos et bipedes — delitescere!

25 Excursis his fabulis, Plutarchum, Traiani praeceptorem,
255 complurium uirorum illustrium ab [15v] incunabulis mores et gesta uidi (ex Leonardo Aretino traducta) depingentem. Qui cum et Parallelas (sic enim liber ille appellari potuit) scriberet atque Vergilio — ut creditur[26] — Homerum, Ciceroni Demosthenem, alios aliis aut pares aut eminentiores afferret, quem e tota Graecia
260 Senecae conferret aut[27] e Latinis Socrati non inuenit.

26 Perlegi porro, quamquam togatus et homo pacis, Vegetium atque Frontinum. Ille disciplinam militarem, hic uero astutias bellicas quas Graeci strategemata nominant, docet. Cupiens exinde priscorum regum spectatissimorumque [16r] uirorum uultus et mores inuisere,
265 aetates illas heroicas rerumque gestarum antecessiones memoratu dignissimas mihi ipsi praesentes efficere, cum uetustissimum non haberem Theopompum, non Aristonem, non Herodotum, non Trogum Pompeium aliosque complures (quos non tam alta uetustas quam damnosa semper incuria aut deleuit aut extinxit), tenui tamen
270 quos legerem et legi quidem Iosephum, Eusebium Caesariensem, compendiarium Trogi Iustinum. Legi Ormestam Orosii, Cornelium Tacitum, Flori Epitomata, quippe [16v] qui cum Titi Liuii res amplissimas illustrissimasque in libelli angustias inculcata eloquentia detrusisset illasque summatim perstrinxisset, et quidem breuis sed
275 opacus euasit. Quo factum ut e uestigio in ipsum Liuium migrare perrexerim; eumque identidem quidem percurri; postque Ciceronis diem non modo gustu meo, at uel eorum qui dicundi in arte dulce quiddam libant, facile principem dixi.

---

[26]ut creditur] *s.l. suppl. M*
[27]aut] *s.l. suppl. M*

[78]That is, in the *Apology* of Apuleius of Madaura (see *Philippic* §144 n. 397).
[79]Apuleius *Metamorphoses* 3.22.
[80]Apuleius' *Metamorphoses* (cf. 3.21–26), or alternatively titled *The Golden Ass*, was a novel telling of his misadventures after a sorceress turned him into an ass.
[81]Ovid (*Metamorphoses* 11.157–93) wrote that Apollo gave King Midas the ears of an ass because Midas preferred the music of Pan to that of Apollo (for Ovid, see *Apology* §30 n. 97 below).
[82]Trajan was the Roman Emperor from 98 to 117 CE. Although Plutarch (50–120 CE) was influential in Trajanic circles, he was not Trajan's teacher. Rho must have in mind John of Salisbury's

he was able to characterize the charges as vilely and viciously brought before the public and the judge, charges that had been not wrongly but rightly preferred against him.[78] I saw, when he longed to change into an owl and some mistress (as he put it, "his little honey")[79] besmeared his whole body with a certain potion, how he turned into an ass.[80] Then for the first time the human mind, amazing to say, hid behind the face of an ass. (Perhaps Ovid related something similar either jokingly or seriously.)[81] At the present, however, we clearly discern something more amazing, namely, that behind the prestige and authority of extremely severe men hide asses — and scarcely golden asses at that, but rather jackasses!

25 Once I had run through these stories, I saw Plutarch, the teacher of Trajan,[82] (as translated by Leonardo Aretino),[83] who depicts the customs and deeds of many illustrious men from their childhood on. When Plutarch wrote his *Parallel Lives* (as we can call that book) and paired Homer with Virgil (as is believed),[84] Demosthenes with Cicero,[85] and other figures with an equal or with someone more eminent, he did not find anyone in all of Greece who could compare to Seneca nor anyone among the Latins who could compare to Socrates.[86]

26 Furthermore, although a civilian and a man of peace, I have read through Vegetius and Frontinus. The former teaches military discipline; the latter the martial cunning that the Greeks call strategy. I then desired to view the faces and customs of ancient kings and preeminent men and to evoke for myself those heroic times and the background of their most venerable exploits. Although I did not have Theopompus of very ancient times, nor Ariston, nor Herodotus, nor Pompeius Trogus, and many others (whom not so much their extreme antiquity as a prolonged ruinous neglect destroyed or annihilated), I took hold of those authors whom I could read. And I did in fact read Josephus, Eusebius of Caesarea, and Justinus, the epitomist of Trogus. I read Orosius' *Ormesta*,[87] Cornelius Tacitus, and Florus' *Epitomata*. Florus, however, by forcing the ample and splendid material of Titus Livy into the confines of a booklet and condensing it to a summary, became because of his pinched eloquence not only brief but also opaque. This immediately led me to move to Livy himself; and I read through him time and again. And I consider him easily the prince of the authors who came after Cicero, not only according to my taste, but also in the judgment of those who are pleased by something sweet in the art of speaking.

---

statement (*Polycraticus* 1): "There exists a letter of Plutarch teaching Trajan. . ." (*Exstat epistola Plutarchi, Traianum instruentis. . .*). John of Salisbury quotes, apparently, the complete letter (see Pade 2000, 63–65; on John of Salisbury, see Southern 1:211, 214–21 and 2:167–77).

[83]Leonardo Bruni da Arezzo (1370–1444); see *Philippic* §34 n. 87 and *Apology* §34 and §37.

[84]Rho's doubt is justified: Plutarch did not write *Lives* of either Homer or Virgil, although a *Life of Homer* circulated under Plutarch's name (see Pade 1998a).

[85]Demosthenes (384–322 BCE) was regarded as the greatest of the Athenian orators; Cicero (106–43 BCE) as the greatest of the Roman orators.

[86]For Seneca the Younger and Socrates, see *Philippic* §75 n. 181.

[87]Orosius' *Memorandum on the Error of the Priscillianists and Origenists* (*Commonitorium de errore Priscillianistarum et Origenistarum*), a work on Spanish heresies written to Augustine after Orosius fled the Vandals in Spain (414), was often known (as here) by the corrupted title *Ormesta* (see Sabbadini 1996, 1:104; Pommerol and Monfrin 1:318n).

27 Vidi, transmissis his, Iulium Celsum Gaii Caesaris quae ferme ubique gentium felicissima bella confecit disserentem. Qui Gaius, [17r] cum ex tempore mediis et in armis commentarios diales belli sui perscriberet, ducens fore tempus quo haud nullus illos exornaret amplificaretque, perpaucos tamen habuit qui rem in tantam manum auderent. Quid si in otio? Audentius inquam etsi non Ciceronem superasset, perfacile tamen illum coaequasset.

28 Legi persaepe Quintum Curtium Suetoniumque Tranquillum: alter Alexandrum, alter Caesares litteris mandat. Et cum his legi Salustium, historias aptius exarantem quam Ciceronem impugnantem. Familiarem mihi porro, post nugas policra[17v]ticas, Valerium feci, qui cum omnium aetatum dicta aut facta paruo libello cudere nequiret, res Romanas tamen et pleras ex exteris perbelle et opportune[28] complexus est.

29 Quid de poetis ausim? Atqui cum hos adduco aut repeto, inflictum ab aduersariis plane uulnus exulcero. Hi sunt qui cum poetas nesciant neque scire agrestes prorsus et inhumani queant, si haud neminem attigisse illos uiderint, mente liuorem atque uehementiam prementes, uerbis tamen censoriis, quasi eos scire sit nefas, mordent lacerantque. Eo fit ut [18r] caliginem mentis quam mihi uolunt ipsi non euadant. Legant ineptissimi atque litteratores Augustinum, Hieronymum, Magnum Basilium, Paulum Apostolum denique Moysen Iuraque canonica. Intellegent plane poetas aliquando didicisse nequaquam sacrilegium, at — si in utramque partem dicundum fuit — eos nosse fuisse quam operae pretium. Verum de his alias.

30 Lasciuos itaque obscenosque uersus Vergilii (quid adulescentes, aiunt, non decet?), ingenium tamen admiratus, paruifeci. Quae tamen seuera et seria illum aequante nemine cecinit, amore, stu[18v]dio, fide prosecutus, complexus, exosculatus sum. Nasonis inde longissimam telam,[29] mira tamen arte perpetuam — non inter (pro pudor!), ut hi femellarii mei, muliercularum textrina, ceterum spectatorum sociorum examina — ductus precibus, saepe totam expleui. Quibus et qua numinis ira correptus, Alcides furore

---

[28]oppor-] -p- *s.l. suppl. M*
[29]telam] *corr. M*

---

[88]Rho here repeats a mistake common at the time that one "Julius Celsus" had written Julius Caesar's *Commentaries on the Civil War* (see Pellegrin 1955a, A 319 and A 320; and Conte 225–33). Walter Burley (*Lives* 104), for instance, wrote: "The historiographer Julius Celsus diligently wrote a work on the war of Caesar, which he divided into five books. . . ." Pier Candido Decembrio in a letter to Bartolomeo Capra (d. 1433) ridicules this mistake, presumably found in Capra's manuscript of Caesar's *Commentaries* (Speyer 47–57; 58–60 for the text of the letter).

[89]Cf. Hirtius *Gallic War* 8.pr.2.

[90]This reflects Cicero's views (*Brutus* 75.261–62) as reported also by Suetonius (*Julius* 55.1–2).

27 Having gone through these authors, I saw Julius Celsus[88] treating the wars that Julius Caesar successfully conducted nearly everywhere in the world. While in the middle of the fighting, Caesar wrote out daily commentaries of his wars on the spot, thinking there would come a time when someone would embellish and amplify them. He knew, however, that few would venture their hand at so great a task.[89] What if he had written in leisure? I would make bold to say that even if he had not surpassed Cicero, nonetheless he would easily have equaled him.[90]

28 I have frequently read Quintus Curtius and Suetonius Tranquillus: the former wrote about Alexander, the latter about the Caesars. And with these I read Sallust, more competent in writing histories than assailing Cicero.[91] Then after the Policratian trifles,[92] I made Valerius[93] my familiar. Although he could not pound the sayings and deeds of all ages into a tiny book, nonetheless he finely and opportunely included in it Roman and much non-Roman material.[94]

29 What dare I say about the poets? But when I cite or repeat them, I obviously aggravate the wound my adversaries have inflicted. These people, although they do not know the poets and as absolute rustics and brutes cannot understand them, nevertheless, crazed by spite and fury, they bite and rend with censorious words anyone who handles them as if to know them were a crime. Consequently, they themselves do not escape the mental darkness that they wish on me. Let these incompetents and pedants read Augustine, Jerome, Basil the Great, the Apostle Paul, and finally Moses and Canon Law.[95] They will clearly perceive that to have once studied the poets is in no way a sacrilege, but — inasmuch as one must speak pro and con — to know them is very worthwhile. But about this another time.

30 I valued little Virgil's lascivious and obscene verse (as they say, "boys will be boys"),[96] while I yet admired his talent. Nevertheless, those severe and serious things that he sang without equal, I pursued, embraced, and reverently kissed with love, zeal, and faith. Next, drawn by entreaties, I have often completed the reading of all of Ovid's tapestry,[97] a huge work but one continuous tale accomplished with

---

[91]Sallust's *Oration against M. T. Cicero* and *Letters to Cicero* were accepted as genuine (their authenticity still subject to debate, the *Oration* usually being rejected) and circulated widely in the Middle Ages and Renaissance (see Osmond and Ulery 187; Osmond 1995, esp. 132–39; Clift 97–121; Conte 242–43; and Schindel).

[92]That is, John of Salisbury's (d. 1180) *Policraticus: Or the Frivolities of Courtiers and the Footprints of Philosophers* (Pellegrin 1955a A 81 and A 503).

[93]Valerius Maximus (fl. ca. 30 CE), whose book *Memorable Deeds and Sayings*, although of modest literary qualities, retained its value right through the Renaissance, that is, as long as history was thought to be "philosophy teaching by example" (Conte 381–82; see also Black 2001, 240–41).

[94]Cf. Valerius Maximus *Praef.*

[95]Rho alludes to a series of patristic and biblical texts found in Canon Law, that is, Gratian's *Decretum* (see Rutherford 1997 and *Philippic* §67 n. 156; cf. *Apology* §17).

[96]This must be an excuse for Virgil's youthful indiscretion. With some inconsistency, Rho could, however, be suggesting a youthful excuse for having himself read the so-called *Appendix Vergiliana*, or Virgil's *Priapeia* (see Introduction n. 127 above)

[97]Publius Ovidius Naso (43 BCE–17 CE) was an Augustan Roman poet and author of, among other things, the racy verse of *The Art of Love*, *Amores*, and *The Remedies of Love*. His *Metamorphoses*, which Rho refers to here, became a fundamental source of mythological knowledge for medieval and Renaissance scholars (Conte 340–64; for his place in the curriculum, see Black 2001, 178–80, 200–08, and esp. 247–52).

debacchatus sit; quo pacto mortem obierit et in deum, ut aiunt, obita morte migrarit aperui. Lucanum inde et Statios, quos in ludo
315 adulescentes passim concinunt, et ipse decantaui.

31 Transeo nunc in aliam turbam ubi Iunium [19r] Iuuenalem, Romanos obscenos mores melius texentem quam castigantem, Persium Flaccumque, multa ex parte lyricum, prae oculis saepenumero conclusi atque reclusi. Comicorum autem primum, quem
320 Coelium dicunt, aut nouissimum, quem Ennium tradunt, nusquam gentium repperi. Hos inter tamen mediantem, Plautum, et familiarem Ciceronis, Terentium, non sine comi uehementia uoluptateque legere potui. Impraesentiarum uero Catullum, Albium Tibullum, Propertium, Martialem obscenum (quem "Cocum" nominant),
325 denique nobis contempora[19v]neum, Panormitam Antonium quempiam, cuius — nisi seria post foedissima (sic enim Vergilius fecit) scripserit — non ingenium sed uita aliquando damnabitur, et huiuscemodi philodoxorum (cum perfunctorie semelque legisse mihi perabundet) frequentissimam turbam missam facio.

330 **32** Atque ad aetatem illam huic nostrae conterminam permixtamque calamum uerto. E Florentina quidem ciuitate clarissima ingenia (nescio ne diuina dixerim) nata sunt. Eiusce namque urbis oriundus, Dantes, Marone praeuio, me per Stiga, per [20r] manes, perque umbras tartareas non Latino (quod eum falso[30] plerique[31]
335 nescisse putant), uerum materno subtegmine pertrahit. Inde in eum locum quo animae corporibus functae at de Christo benemeritae, donec maculis defaecatae euolent, plectuntur sistit. Tandem duce

[30]falso] *s.l. suppl.* M
[31]plerique] -que *suppl.* M

---

[98]Rho's jest (see *Imitations* 132v: *Lupanar*, and 141v–142r: *Meretrix*; Appendix IX below) turns on the *longissima tela* (lengthy yarn, literally the thread which runs lengthways through the loom) and *textrina* (textile shop), which he closely associates with the *gynaeceum* (women's quarters). *Gynaeceum* (Greek: *gunaikeion*) originally simply meant "the women's quarters." In the late Roman Empire it came to refer to the imperial harem. *Gynaeceum* was also used to refer to the textile workshops (*textrina*). Men, however, not women, were forced to labor in these shops (ODB; cf. Jerome *Letter* 53.7 and Wiesen 38).
[99]Ovid *Metamorphoses* 9.135–272.
[100]Marcus Annaeus Lucanus (39–65) was a Roman who wrote an epic poem (*Civil War* or *Pharsalia*) on the conflict between Caesar and Pompey. Widely read in late antiquity and a standard text of the medieval schools, he remained a model through the Renaissance and into the seventeenth century (Conte 440–51). Publius Papinius Statius (ca. 45–96) was a Roman poet whose *Thebais*, *Achilleis*, and *Silvae* competed with the works of Ovid for popularity right through the Middle Ages and into the Renaissance (Conte 481–88; on the place of Lucan and Statius in the educational curriculum, see Black 2001, 200–03, 217–18, and 238–44).
[101]Junius Juvenal (ca. 55–after 127), now commonly called "Juvenal," was the last of the great Roman satiric poets, whose *Satires* span the late first and early second century of the Common Era. He mercilessly lampoons corruption and vice at all levels (Conte 474–79).
[102]Persius Flaccus (34–62), now commonly called "Persius," was a Roman satiric poet holding Stoic views, whose poetry was much read in the Middle Ages and the Renaissance (Conte 468–74).
[103]Read: "Caecilius," that is, Caecilius Statius (d. 168 BCE), a Roman comedic poet from whom we have only fragments (Conte 65–67).

wondrous art — not in the women's quarters[98] (what a disgrace!) as my skirt-chasing adversaries do, but in a throng of distinguished colleagues. I also described to this audience by what divine wrath Hercules was seized when he raged with fury; how he went to his death, and having died became a god, as they say.[99] Next I myself also chanted Lucan and Statius, whom young men in elementary school chant in unison far and wide.[100]

31 Now I pass on to another crowd, where, as I recall, I often having finished and opened up again Junius Juvenal,[101] who is better at elaborating than at censuring obscene Roman customs, and Persius Flaccus,[102] a lyric poet in many passages. But I found absolutely nowhere the first of the comic poets, whom they call Coelius,[103] or the most recent, whom they say is Ennius.[104] I did manage to read — not without warm enthusiasm and pleasure — Plautus,[105] who came between these two,[106] and Cicero's friend Terence.[107] For the moment, however, I omit Catullus, Tibullus, Propertius, the obscene Martial, whom they call "The Cook."[108] And finally I omit our contemporary, a certain Antonio Panormita, whose genius will not be condemned but his life someday will be unless he writes serious verse subsequent to his filthy ones (as Virgil did),[109] and a dense mob of similar glory-seekers (since it more than sufficed me to have read them once, and perfunctorily at that).

32 And now I turn my pen to the age preceding and extending into our own. Indeed, the city of Florence has given birth to famous literary geniuses (perhaps I should say divine). For this city's native son, Dante,[110] with Virgil as his guide,[111] led me through Styx, through abode of the spirits of the dead, and through the Tartarean shadows, not with a Latin (which many falsely think that he did not know) but with a vernacular thread.[112] Next he stopped in the place where souls quit of their bodies but deserving reward from Christ are punished until they fly away cleansed of stains. Finally, with his Beatrice as guide, he traveled through

---

[104]Quintus Ennius (239–169 BCE) was a teacher and playwright, whom the Romans regarded as their most notable archaic poet (Conte 75–83).

[105]Titus Maccius Plautus (ca. 250–184 BCE) was a Roman comedic poet/playwright. Twelve of his plays were only discovered a year or so after Antonio da Rho wrote this *Apology* (see *Philippic* §11 n. 27 and §120).

[106]This particular sequence of "comic poets" — Caecilius, Plautus, Ennius — reflects the ranking of the so-called "Volcacian Canon" as reported by Aulus Gellius (15.24). They all flourished at about the same time.

[107]Rho refers to a statement in Cicero's *On Friendship* (24.89): "which my friend [Terence] said in his *Andria*" (*quod in Andria familiaris meus dicit*). Publius Terentius Afer (ca. 190–159 BCE) was an early Roman comedic poet/playwright (see *Philippic* §21 n. 50).

[108]For Rho's failure to distinguish between the Roman poet Marcus Valerius Martialis (ca. 40–ca. 104) and the expurgated medieval version ascribed to "Martial the Cook," see *Philippic* §22 n. 52.

[109]In the Vatican manuscript, some contemporary has blotted out the lines about Panormita (*Apology* §31: *denique . . . damnabitur*): "and finally I omit . . . (as Virgil did)." Cf. the "corrections" in the same manuscript regarding Candido Decembrio (*Apology* §54 n. 198 below).

[110]Dante Alighieri (1265–1321): *Divine Comedy* — Canticle I: *Inferno*; Canticle II: *Purgatorio*; Canticle III: *Paradisio* (cf. Pellegrin 1955a, A 177, 387, 453, 949, 951, 963; Black 2001, 202, and 303–04; and Witt 2000, 213–24).

[111]Publius Vergilius Maro (70–19 BCE) was the most celebrated of the Roman, Augustan poets and the author of the *Aeneid*, *Eclogues*, and *Georgics* (see *Philippic* §33 n. 77; cf. *Apology* §30 n. 96 above).

[112]See Ronzoni 1–3.

Beatrice illa sua per singulos orbes et planetarum epicyclos, modo hunc caelicolam, modo illum conueniens, ad eum ipsum summum
340 deum et optumum, quem fide credimus et opere fatemur, subuehit.

33 Sed et aliud ingenium ex ea ipsa urbe florentissima exortum est: humanitatis quidem [20v] studia, uerius per id tempus extincta quam sopita, Franciscus Petrarcha e somno uidetur suscitauisse. Cui etsi non eum splendorem suauitatemque dicundi qua
345 multi in praesentia pollent ascribimus, permultam tamen illi gratiarum debitionem non inficiamur. Sat enim fuit, immo bellissimum, immo operae pretium quidem, excitare Tullianum leporem, quem, ipsi iam e latebris eliminatum atque sub diuo conspicuum, per uestigia undequaque uenaremur. Extant enim
350 huiusce Laureati quos ipse conflauit libelli multi: nunc more Vergilii aut eclogas [21r] aut ducum bella uersibus mandat, nunc in utramque fortunam monens, cum magnorum uirorum tum praesertim Senecae atque Ciceronis apertissimae palpantur exuuiae. Dum memorandarum rerum libellum inscribit, quid aliud
355 quam de integro alterum Valerium cudit? Quo fit ut dum multos aemulabundus exprimere certarit, ne unum ex eis priscis quidem reddere potuerit, quippe tamen qui uulgari et quotidiana maternaque Musa omnes excessit.

34 Coluccius Salutatus post hunc uisus est mihi librorum
360 fascibus obsessus, quem, ut huic cata[21v]logo miscerem, Leonardi Aretini auctoritas persuasit. Multus enim fuit in laudibus suis, et epistulae multae ultro citroque commissae, illi — quod alioquin uel esset — illustre nomen perpetuum allaturae.

35 Coluccio inhaerens paene Boccaccium oblitteraram: nunc
365 deorum gentilium originem (immo errorem), nunc montes et flumina tradentem; et inter uaria quae scripsit, "denadecies" quibus

---

[113]The title *Optimus Maximus* was applied to Jupiter "for his beneficence" (cf. Cicero *On his own House* 57.144).

[114]Cf. James 2.14–26.

[115]Rho's play on Florence/flourishing (*urbs florentissima*/*floreo*) is more apparent in Latin than in English. The name of Florence, *Florentia* (The City of Flowers), is a noun form of the verb *floreo* (to bloom, blossom, or flourish).

[116]Francesco Petrarca (1304–74), a poet born in Arezzo to exiled Florentine parents, has long been regarded as "the father of Renaissance humanism" for his efforts to recover, imitate, and celebrate Latin classical literature (see Witt 2000, 230–91).

[117]For the phrase "humanistic studies" (*studia humanitatis*), see *Apology* §18 n. 60.

[118]Rho's hunting metaphor plays on *leporem*, the identical accusative form of *lepor, -oris* (charm) and *lepus, -oris* (a hare).

[119]*Bucolic Poems*, written ca. 1348, is poetry mostly on Cola di Rienzo's revolution in Rome, the corruption of the church, his own love for Laura, his being named Poet Laureate in Rome, and his spiritual struggles (cf. Pellegrin 1955a, A 394 and 395).

[120]That is, *Africa*, an epic poem on Scipio Africanus dedicated (1341) to Robert of Anjou, King of Naples.

the individual orbits and epicycles of the planets, meeting now with this saint now with that, upwards to the supremely beneficent God himself,[113] whom we believe through faith and confess through works.[114]

33 But another great talent also rose from this same flourishing city,[115] Francesco Petrarca,[116] who may be said to have awakened humanistic studies[117] from their slumber, which were more truly extinct than lulled to sleep at the time. Even if we do not ascribe to him that splendor and sweetness of speech in which many presently excel, we nevertheless should not repudiate our great debt of gratitude to him. For it was sufficient, or admirable, nay even worthwhile to awaken the Ciceronian charm,[118] which we were hunting, following its trail everywhere, now that it has been chased from its hiding place and is plainly visible. For many books survive that this Poet Laureate composed: at one time, after the fashion of Virgil, he wrote eclogues[119] or commited to verse the wars of generals;[120] at another, in warning against the variations of Fortune,[121] the most manifest spoils of great men and especially of Seneca and Cicero comforted him.[122] While he wrote his book of things to be remembered,[123] what did he do except mint another Valerius?[124] Hence, while he strove as an imitator to reproduce many of the ancients, he managed to restore not even one of them. Nonetheless, he surpassed all writers in the common, everyday, vernacular Muse.

34 After him I saw Coluccio Salutati[125] surrounded by stacks of books, whom Leonardo Aretino's authority argues that I include in this catalogue.[126] For Aretino was fulsome in his praise, and the extensive correspondence between these two will bring to Salutati for all time an illustrious name that would have been his in any case.

35 In being absorbed with Coluccio, I had almost consigned Boccaccio to oblivion, who relates now the origin (rather the error) of the pagan gods,[127] now

---

[121]That is, *Remedies for Fortune Fair and Foul*, written in late 1350s or early 1360s, which contains two brief dialogues between (Part I) Reason, Joy, and Hope; and (Part II) Reason, Grief, and Fear (cf. Pellegrin 1955a, A 386, 391, 633, 837, 965).

[122]Seneca the Younger (ca. 4 BCE–65 CE) was a Roman, Stoic, moral philosopher (see *Apology* §12 n. 41 above and *Philippic* §75 n. 181). For Marcus Tullius Cicero (106–43 BCE), see Introduction 17–20 above.

[123]Petrarca's *Books of Things Remembered* (ca. 1345) are stories grouped according to some moral or ethical quality that they seek to illustrate (cf. Pellegrin 1955a, A 940). Compare Rho's assessment of Petrarca with that of Professor Ronald G. Witt (2000, 274), who writes: "There can be no question that generally Petrarca sought to capture his personal version of *vetustas* in his writings and that from the standpoint of early fifteenth-century stylists his realizations fell short of the mark. . . . Petrarca's letter [*Letters on Familiar Matters* 1.9] gestured toward the ancient world, but it failed to underwrite his own statement with the signature of the ancient author."

[124]For Valerius Maximus (fl. ca. 30 CE), see n. 93 above.

[125]Salutati (1331–1406) was a humanist Chancellor of Florence, who, besides his many letters, wrote *On the Secular and Religious Life* (1381), *On the Labors of Hercules* (ca. 1391), *On Fate and Fortune* (ca. 1396), and *On Tyranny* (1400). See Witt 1983 and Witt 2000, 292–337.

[126]Leonardo Bruni da Arezzo (1370–1444), a humanist disciple of Salutati, wrote about Salutati this way (*Letter* 1.3 [1:4–6]); cf. *Philippic* §34 n. 87 and *Apology* §25 and §37).

[127]Giovanni Boccaccio (1313–75), in *Genealogies of the Pagan Gods* (ca. 1350–67?), presents the myths about pagan divinities, their allegorical interpretations, and a defense of poetry, all to assist the reading of classical literature, especially poetry (Pellegrin 1955a, A 384).

recrearentur³² animi inuenta uolup iocantem, his tamen superioribus conterraneis suis lingua rituque dicundi consimilem.

36 Et quamquam eiusce urbis sin[22r]gulos praetermitterem, Poggium Florentinum praetermissum iri pro suauitate dicundi, et ea quidem³³ quae totam supellectilem eorum priscorum uirorum redoleat, nequaquam existimaui. Numquam eiusce uiri aut epistulas aut alia quae diuersa confecit opuscula lectito, quin ea ipsa complectar et exosculer. Numquam aut balneas aut thermas inspecto, quin actutum subeat mentem, quin et quantum ab huiuscemodi conciuibus³⁴ in dicundo abhorreat, quantum ipsum Ciceronem referat, quam primum intellegam praedicemque.

37 Ex omni itaque Florentia [22v] hi sunt quos persaepe reuisi, quos aliquando miratus sum. Floruit inde his finitimus et impraesentiarum floret praeter omnes aetatis nostrae constructissimos dicundi uiros eloquentissimus Leonardus Aretinus. Hunc Gasparinus Pergamensis — uir et ipse exactissimae cum eloquentiae tum doctrinae et qui Ciceronem omnino abolitum de integro suscitare potens sit, qui uel in ludis illum summo studio, summa diligentia discipulis singulos dies perbelle tradat et instauret — uirum (sic enim his auribus hausi) [23r] "Atticum"³⁵ nominat, quasi eo uno in nomine eloquentissimorum uirorum laudes, quae uolumen traherentur, in longum complectatur. Ipse uero de hoc uiro recte sentiens, praesertim reuolutis et identidem lectitatis haud nullis Aristotelis libris atque Plutarchi Graecorumque complurium, quos ex integro, cum antehac non plane extarent, a tenebris eduxit in lucem atque Latinos fecit,³⁶ sic mihi persuasi. Si eum³⁷ Cicero contemporaneum tenuisset, per dialogos omnes librorum suorum utpote eloquentiae suae singulare peculium miscuisset.

38 Vidi Antonium Luscum sic soluta orati[23v]one eleganter et egregie perorantem ut quemadmodum Ciceroni non uersus facere ceterum solute dicere singulare et diuinum quiddam uidebatur,

---

³²recrearentur] -creantur *Lomb.*
³³ea quidem] *s.l. suppl. M*
³⁴conciuibus] *s.l. suppl. M*
³⁵Attica eloquentia, *mg. glos.* M¹
³⁶atque . . . fecit] *s.l. suppl. M*
³⁷persuasi <ut>, si eum . . . *coniec. Lomb.*

---

[128]That is, Boccaccio's *On the Names of Mountains, Forests, Fountains, Lakes, Rivers, Lagoons or Swamps and Seas* (1362–66), which was an aid to the reading of classical literature, especially poetry. It may have been an appendix to the *Genealogies of the Pagan Gods* (Pellegrin 1955a, A 382).

[129]Boccaccio's *Decameron* [*The Ten Days*] (1355? or 1365?) was comprised of one hundred stories told as diversions ten each day over a ten day period while the plague of 1348 raged in Florence (cf. Pellegrin 1955a, A 870).

[130]Poggio (1380–1459), known later as Poggio Bracciolini, became famous for important manuscript discoveries in the early 1400s. He later included in his *Facetiae* a story about Rho, who after

[the names of] mountains and rivers.[128] Among the diverse works that he wrote, he also pleasurably recounts in jest the "ten by ten" fictions to restore peoples spirits,[129] yet he is similar in language and style to his aforementioned compatriots.

36 And although I passed over particular individuals of this city, it has never occurred to me to omit Poggio Fiorentino in view of the charm of his speech, which is redolent of the full store of the ancients.[130] Never do I pore over either the letters or the other little works that he wrote for various purposes but that I embrace and reverently kiss them.[131] Never do I observe either baths or warm springs but that he immediately comes to mind,[132] and I also immediately grasp and proclaim how much he distances himself in his speech from his fellow citizens, like those mentioned, and how much he resembles Cicero himself.

37 Accordingly, from all Florence these are the ones whom I read many times over and whom I time and again admired. Furthermore, the extraordinarily eloquent Leonardo Aretino[133] flourished shortly after these men and is flourishing at this very moment beyond all the most skilled literary stylists of our time. Gasparino of Bergamo[134] calls him "Atticus" (I have heard him say this with my own ears), as if to embrace for the ages in that one name the praises of the most eloquent men that would take a volume. Gasparino is himself a man of precise eloquence and learning, being able to revive Cicero, who had been completely forgotten. Every day in his school he skillfully teaches and restores Cicero to his students with the greatest devotion and diligence. I, moreover, share his sentiment and am persuaded Gasparino is right about Aretino, especially after having paged through and read time and again the books of Aristotle, Plutarch, and quite a few Greeks, which before had languished in obscurity and which he brought forth anew from darkness into the light by translating them into Latin.[135] If Cicero had had him as a contemporary, he would have mixed him in as a singular fund of eloquence, so to speak, throughout all his books of dialogues.

38 I saw Antonio Loschi[136] arguing in prose so elegantly and so splendidly that just as Cicero was thought to produce something singular and divine when writing prose but not verse, so too would Antonio be thought innately gifted in

---

reading the confessions of a clumsy author, assigned to the author as penance the reading of his own clumsy book (Poggio 1878, 91–92; 1964, 1:468; 1983, 308–09).

[131]What "little works" Rho could have seen by 1427/28 is unclear. He possibly means Poggio's oration at the Council of Constance or his letters that circulated with titles such as the one on Jerome of Prague. (I thank Arthur Field for this information.)

[132]Poggio's letter on a visit to the baths (*Lettere* 1.46), which circulated widely, may be one of the "little works" that Rho has in mind.

[133]For Leonardo Bruni da Arezzo (1370–1444), see *Philippic* §34 n. 87 and *Apology* §25 and §37.

[134]Gasparino Barzizza (1360–1430) was the most recognized authority on Cicero in the early fifteenth century and someone whom Rho here implies was his teacher. He taught traditional scholastic grammar courses (Universities of Padua, Milan, and Pavia) and also ran a boarding school for boys where he taught humanistic studies (see Mercer 1–6, 112–15; Black 2001, 163–64, and 266–67; and Witt 2000, 462–67).

[135]For the translations of Leonardo Bruni da Arezzo, see *Philippic* §34 n. 87.

[136]Antonio Loschi (ca. 1365–1441) was once Chancellor for the Visconti Dukes of Milan and later Apostolic Secretary (see *Philippic* §47 n. 113, §47–§50, and §63 n. 151).

aeque et huic innatum. Id enimuero dumtaxat putaretur. Contra
uero, sic metra interdum[38] concentu Pierio meditantem, ut quemadmodum Vergilio non solute dicere ceterum uersus Aonios
decantare ex Musis unice datum cernebatur, aeque et huic, quod
Castalium solum esset, crederetur ingenitum.

39 Legi Guarinum Veronensem, qui ornate et facile
loqua[24r]tur, uirum suauissimum eruditissimumque, non minus
quam Latinarum (caelitus credo datum) nouum antistitem litterarum Graecarum. Legi et Cincium[39] Romanum, inter multa quae
terse atque limate conscripsit, bibliothecas priscorum subextinctas
deplorantem. Vidi[40] Rem uxoriam Francisci Barbari, ornatissimi et in
singulis suis eloquentissimi uiri, et cum illo[41] Leonardum Iustinianum
Venetosque complures.

40 Dicerem ab his seorsum longam nunc scribentium plebem,
praesertim qui uariam supellectilem[42] non tam aures [24v] quam
manus docent. At cum paupertati dicatus initiatusque, suburbanum
quo ducam otium rusticationemque nequaquam teneam, eo Polybium
paruifeci. Viturbium[43] uero, architecturae praeceptorem, perlectis
tamen eiusce prologis praefatiunculisque suauissimis, cum aeque *culmo*
atque *auro* iam *tegi*[44] sciam, turbamque[45] consimilem non satis excolui.

41 Quid itaque palabundus plura percurro? Haec ea ipsa sunt
perpauca quae et legi aliquando et intellexi, quorum si nomina
dumtaxat illi ipsi aemuli mei (quid enim non ignorant?) tenerent, si
corticem foris [25r] non medullam dicam delibarent, ignorationis
notam quam mihi uolunt prorsus euaderent. Sed neque mihi ne illis
quidem (uiuunt enim quemadmodum accipiter semper in armis, ita
ipsi semper in maledictis) facere satis existimaui, si solum alienos
codices, si aliena usque dicta reuoluerem, si non, quae mente collo-
caram, foris et coram uerba aliquando facturus exponerem.

---

[38]putaretur . . . interdum] *om. Lomb.*
[39]Cincium] *corr. M*
[40]Vidi] Viri *Lomb.*
[41]cum illo] *corr. M*
[42]supeʎlec-] -l- *s.l. suppl. M*
[43]Viturbium] Veturius *gloss. mg. M*
[44]tegi] *om. Lomb.*
[45]turbamque] -quem *Lomb.*

---

[137]"Pierian," "Aonian," and "Castalian" indicate the excellence of Loschi's Muse. Pierius had nine daughters, who were turned into magpies for competing with the Muses. Aonia is the region of Boeotia containing Mount Helicon, the favorite haunt of the Muses. Castalia was a fountain on Mount Parnassus, sacred to Apollo and the Muses.

[138]Guarino Veronese (1374–1460) learned Greek in Constantinople and trained a generation of humanists in his school, first at Verona and then in Ferrara under the patronage of the Este family (see Black 2001, 15–17, 124–29; Grafton and Jardine 1–28, 33–38; Grendler 1989, 126–29; and Witt 2000, 341–43).

this way. For that at least was the common opinion. Yet, I have also seen Loschi so practicing meters with occasional Pierian harmony that just as it seemed the Muses had granted uniquely to Virgil the gift of singing Aonian verse but not of writing prose, so one would believe too that gift which belongs alone to Castalia was inborn also in Loschi.[137]

39 I have read Guarino Veronese.[138] He is a most suave and erudite man, a new doyen (sent from heaven, I believe) no less of Greek literature than of Latin literature, who speaks ornately and fluently. I have also read Cencio Romano. Among the many things that he has written with elegance and polish, I have read his piece deploring the virtually extinct libraries of the ancients.[139] I saw the *On Wifely Duties* of Francesco Barbaro.[140] He is an ornate and eloquent man in all his writings. And along with him I saw Leonardo Giustiniani and many other Venetians.[141]

40 Apart from this vast crowd of contemporary writers, let me mention especially those who teach various things not so much for the ears as for the hands. But since I am vowed and consecrated to poverty so that I have no means whatsoever to lead a life of leisure and a country life, I have consequently made little of Polybius [sic].[142] Frankly, I have insufficiently cultivated Viturbius [sic],[143] the teacher of architecture, although I have perused his prologues and sweet little prefaces, since I know "men to be covered just as well by thatch as by gold."[144] I have also insufficiently cultivated a group of similar authors.

41 So why do I ramble through more? These are just a few of the things that I have at some time both read and understood. If my rivals themselves could recognize only the names of these works (for of what are they not ignorant?), or if they could sample the outer husk, let alone the kernel of these works, they would completely avoid the stain of ignorance that they wish on me. But I have decided that it is not enough either for me or for them (inasmuch as they live like hawks with talons always out and always screeching) if I constantly resort to the books or statements of others alone, and not explicitly and openly articulate at some time the comments that I have drafted.

---

[139]Cencio dei Rustici's (d. 1445) letter to Francesco da Fiano (written in the summer of 1416) circulated widely. It describes the manuscript discoveries made by Poggio, Bartolomeo da Montepulciano, and Cencio himself (see Bertalot 144–47; and Gordon 187–91).

[140]Francesco Barbaro (1390–1454), a Venetian humanist statesman, dedicated his treatise *On Wifely Duties* (1416) to his close friend, Lorenzo di Giovanni de' Medici, the brother of Cosimo (see Gnesotto 6–105; King 1986, 319–25; and Kohl and Witt 179–228).

[141]Leonardo Giustiniani (ca. 1388–1446), a Venetian statesman and humanist, served as head of the Council of Ten and as Procurator of St. Mark's (see Labalme esp. 8–10, 18–29, 83–86; King 1986, 383–85; for profiles of Venetian humanists, see King 1986, 315–449).

[142]Read: Palladius, Rutilius Taurus Aemilianus (fourth century CE), who wrote fourteen books *On Agriculture* or *On Country Life* (cf. Pellegrin 1955a, A 428 and A 440; and see Conte 637–38). Rho, however, clearly wrote "Polybius" (ca. 200–after 118 BCE), a Greek author of Roman history, whose name and work make no sense in this context.

[143]Read: Vitruvius Pollio (fl. ca. 20 BCE), who wrote ten books *On Architecture* dedicated to Caesar Augustus (Conte 387–88). Rho came by the name "Viturbius" in the Visconti manuscript of Vitruvius (now Paris: Bibl. Nat., MS Lat. 7228, saec. XIV, I + 39 ff.) and in the inventory of the Visconti library, which give *Viturbius De architectis instituendis* (see Pellegrin 1955a, A 254).

[144]Seneca the Younger *Letter* 8.5.

42 Versus itaque calescentibus[46] ingeniis primis et in studiis, nunc hexametros nunc pentametros interdum lyricos ipse conflaui. In hexametris is ordo tenorque suauissimus [25v] uisus est si dactylus feruesceret, si raro in calce metri, saepenumero in medio finem faceret, si non more Persii, Oratii Iuuenalisque in monosyllabam terminaret, si non diu quiesceret, sed more eorum

qui *pedibus plaudunt choreas et carmina dicunt*

non in pauimento dudum sisteret, ast in aere saepius emicaret, si per quosque uersus — quod de industria seruasse Lucanum aiunt — "r" littera quae canina dicitur resonaret. Pentameter autem uisus est uersus pulcherrimus si prosam non oleat, si in primam penthemimerim quod adia[26r]cens rei est, in secunda quod est[47] subsistens locetur, quod apud Nasonem eorum uersuum poetam accuratissimum (eo id sibi Vetula falso ascribitur) factitatum est. Aiebat enim:

Obrutus insanis esset adulter aquis;

item:

Lassaret uiduas pendula tela manus;

et infra:

Ponitur ad patrios barbara praeda deos.

At quid de lyrico dixerim? Eiusce quidem concentus aures, si sine mendicitate atque uiolentia locata in illo sint uerba, admodum mulcet.

43 Habui post haec aetate iam uegetiore orationes complusculas, et eas solutas quidem, nunc in [26v] sanctorum laudibus, nunc in patriciorum uirorum funeribus, atque praesertim aliquot pro clementissimo principe Philippo Maria, Mediolanensium atque Insubrum duce. Quem, assistente saepe corona senatus sui et in consessu primorum omnis huius ciuitatis, laudibus ad caelum tollere nixus sum. Vbi neque tantillam illarum partem prae magnitudine, dignitate, maiestateque

---

[46]cales-] calas- *Lomb.*
[47]quod est] *s.l. suppl. M*

---

[145]Virgil *Aeneid* 6.644.
[146]A group of five-and-one-half feet in classical poetry.
[147]For Ovid, see *Apology* §30 n. 97 above.
[148]A collection of poems written in the twelfth or thirteenth century, now known as Ps.-Ovid's *De vetula* (Klopsch 1967).

42 And so even when I was a student and my talent was first sparked, I composed now hexameters, now pentameters, and occasionally lyric verse. In hexameter the meter and flow seemed most sweet if the dactyl quickened; if the *caesura* occurred frequently in the middle of the line and only rarely at the end; if the line did not end in a monosyllable in the manner of Persius, Horace, and Juvenal; if the line did not remain still for long, but in the style of those who "set the rhythm with dance-steps and chant songs,"[145] it frequently leaped into the air instead of holding constantly to the floor; and if the letter "r" called "canine" resounded through every verse (which they say Lucan deliberately preserved). Pentameter, however, seemed a beautiful verse if it did not savor of prose, if the adjective was located in the first penthemimer,[146] and the noun in the second, which Ovid,[147] the most meticulous poet of this verse, did as a rule (for this reason *The Little Old Woman*[148] is erroneously ascribed to him). For he said:

> **adj.   adj. verb noun noun**
> *Obrutus insanis esset adulter aquis*
> (O would that the adulterer had been sunk in the roiling waters);[149]

likewise:

> **verb   adj.   adj. noun noun**
> *Lassaret viduas pendula tela manus*
> (O would that the hanging loom had exhausted my widowed hands);[150]

and below:

> **verb prep. adj.   adj.   noun noun**
> *Ponitur ad patrios barbara praeda deos*
> (The barbarian spoils are laid before our ancestral gods).[151]

But why should I have spoken about lyric poetry? Mainly because its harmony greatly soothes the ears if the words are placed in it without beggary and force.

43 After these things when I was more mature, I gave several orations — in prose, of course — some in praise of the saints, others at the funeral rites of patricians, but especially several before the most clement prince, Filippo Maria,[152] Duke of Milan and Insubria.[153] I endeavored to extol him to the heavens often when he had assembled his Senate and was surrounded by the leading men of the whole city, but

---

[149]Ovid *Heroides* 1.6.
[150]Ovid *Heroides* 1.10.
[151]Ovid *Heroides* 1.26.
[152]Filippo Maria Visconti (1392–1447) became governor of Pavia in 1402 and Duke of Milan in 1412 (see Cognasso 391–512 and Lucarelli 117–71). Several of Rho's orations for Filippo Maria and others survive (see Rutherford 1990, 95–96).
[153]Insubria is the ancient name of the territory around Milan, nearly synonymous with Lombardy (see *Philippic* §175 n. 507).

rerum suarum (quis enim facibus solem adiuuet?) attingere potui. Partitiones tamen uerborum eis ipsis in orationibus, ritu quorundam nostratum, minutias, et fragmenta, [27r] ne forte Ciceronianas aures fatigarem, usque detrectaui. Cantilenas porro quas rhythmos dicunt, et quae mihi hae per concentum uisae sunt ac si tinnientia[48] puellarum Etruriae cymbala aut quaestuariorum campanulas auribus tenuissem, declinaui. Vbi id plane percepi: hi litteratores, concidentes syllabas[49] non dicam exprimant sed inculcent, minimum alioquin erratum rentur aliis effutire quod neque ipsa Sibylla possit absoluere.

44 His coram oratiunculis habitis, coepi religionum ritu in ecclesiis contionari atque femellas inter uolgusque [27v] promiscuum suggestum conscendens uerba facere. Cuiusuis noxae persuasi paenitudinem, magnifeci uirtutes, quo loco scelera plecterentur et benemeriti sempiterno aeuo fruerentur donarenturque declaraui. Vidi quam facile esset — etsi ludionis aut pantomimi inflexionibus non satis scirem modo Herculis, modo Cybeles et huiuscemodi rerum uarias superinduere personas similitudinesque — hominum genus modo ad lacrimas, modo ad risum incessere. Feci hanc in rem quo gratiam penes audientes mihi ampliorem compararem, insti[28r]tuente me Seneca, *quod munerarii facere solent*. Hi *ad expectationem populi detinendam* uota uaria[50] quae neque confundunt at *per omnes dies pensant*[51] apponunt, *ut sit quod populum et oblectet*[52] *et reuocet. Acrior* enim *est cupiditas ignota* ad quae homines concurrunt *cognoscendi, quam nota* quae iam usu paruifiunt *repetendi*.

45 Voluptas quidem non mediocris fit his qui gymnasiis humanitatis uersantur eloquentissimorum uirorum libellos euoluere, exarata diuini Ciceronis lectitare uolumina. At cum aures coram implentur (*habet* enim, Hieronymus [28v] noster ait, *nescio quid latentis* energiae uiuae uocis actus) prae suauitate dicentis, effunditur audientis animus, exultant uiscera, gestit affectus. Eo fit ut cum antehac eorum uirorum manus eloquentissimas usque miratus sim, in praesentia non modo manus, ceterum uiuae uocis et linguae per aures transfusam magniloquentiam et uehementer et uolupe perceperim. Quos cum frequentes huiuscemodi uerba facientes hactenus[53] hauserim (Vincentium Transalpinum Ordinis Praedicatorum, professionis uero nostrae Iohannem Serauellensem, e Sancta Margarita Anto[29r]nium, Bernardinum

---

[48]tinnien-] tim en- *Lomb.*
[49]syllabas] -bes *Lomb.*
[50]uota uaria] noua paria *Sen. et Lomb.*
[51]pensant] dispen- *Sen. et Lomb.*
[52]oblectet] delec- *Sen. et Lomb.*
[53]hactenus] *s.l. suppl. M*

[154]Rho here criticizes a practice in the *ars dictaminis* in which speeches would end with rhyming verses, often silly, sometimes in the vernacular. (I thank Arthur Field for this information.)

I was unable to attain the least of my purpose on account of the magnitude, dignity, and majesty of his achievements (for who can help the sun with torches?). Nevertheless, in these orations I meticulously avoided the divisions of words, pedantic minutiae, and snippets of quotations customary among some of our countrymen lest perhaps I fatigued his Ciceronian ears. I further shunned the strains that they call prose rhythms, and which to me seemed to sound as if I had the clanging cymbals of Tuscan girls or the bells of alms-collectors ringing in my ears. Here I clearly perceived that those elementary schoolmasters who, I would say, do not weed out but rather cultivate closing sentence rhythms, otherwise imagine it to be a minor error to mislead others in a way that not even the Sibyl herself could unravel.[154]

44 Having publicly delivered these brief orations, I began to preach in the churches as part of the liturgy, even ascending the pulpit to hold forth among women and the lower classes. I urged repentance for every sort of fault, I celebrated virtues, and I made known where sins would be punished and where the deserving would enjoy the reward of eternal life. I saw how easy it was to provoke humankind at one moment to tears, at another to laughter — even though I did not adequately know how to impersonate now Hercules, now Cybele, and the various roles and guises of mythical characters of this sort through the inflections used by an actor or a pantomime. Taking Seneca as my teacher, I turned this fact to my advantage among my listeners, gaining myself the greater favor, "which the producers of gladiatorial shows customarily do." These producers "in order to sustain people's anticipation," add a variety of coming attractions that they do not exhibit all at once but dole out "day by day, so that there is something that might both delight and entice the people. For desire to experience the novelties to which people flock is keener than the desire to rehearse the known" which people slight from familiarity.[155]

45 Indeed, those who frequent humanistic schools derive no small pleasure from perusing the books of the most eloquent men and poring over the transcribed volumes of the divine Cicero. But when the speaker's charm directly fills the ears of the listener, his mind opens, his heart rejoices, and his emotions stir. For as our Jerome says, the live performance "holds some kind of hidden" power.[156] Consequently, although I previously marveled at the eloquent hands of these men, I have now ardently and delightfully perceived the magniloquence not only of the hands but also of the live voice and tongue flooding my ears. Until now I have heard those who regularly make speeches in this manner, that is, the transalpine Vincent of the Order of Preachers;[157] and from our Franciscan Order, Giovanni da Serravalle,[158]

Although the classical meaning of *effutire* is simply "to babble" or "to talk nonsense," I have translated it "mislead" because Rho (*Imitations* 143r: *Mendacium*) says: "*Effutire* is to speak with deception (*cum mendacio dicere*)." For the reference to the Sibyl, cf. Plautus *Pseudolus* 25–26 and Jerome *Against Jovinian* 1.1.

[155] Seneca the Elder *Controversiae* 4.pr.1.

[156] Jerome *Letter* 53.2.

[157] St. Vincent Ferrer (ca. 1350–1419) was a Dominican from Valencia, Spain, who toured Europe preaching penance and performing miracles (see Oakley 261–70).

[158] Giovanni Bertoldi da Serravalle (1355–1445) translated Dante's *Divine Comedy* into Latin and wrote a Latin commentary on it (see Piana 78*; Lombardi 97n).

Senensem et tibi officio comparem Angelum) quid in buccam tamen mortalium ea ipsa eloquentia posset, quid momenti haberet nusquam gentium in quouis te praeter periculum feci. Aiebat enim Cicero habens illam orationem Pro Archia, *Multos homines excellenti animo et uirtute fuisse et sine doctrina naturae ipsius habitu prope diuino per se ipsos et moderatos et graues extitisse*, qui, minimis intincti litteris ingeniis tamen magnis praediti, copiam dicundi amplissimam consecuti sunt. Quibus tamen, si recte intellego, esset doctrina [29v] opus, sine qua — etiam si quid bene dicitur adiuuante natura — tamen id, quia fortuito fit,[54] semper paratum esse non potest. Eo itaque alloquens Brutum Cicero Lucii Appuleii Saturnini eloquentiam probauit minus, qui, etsi promiscuum in uolgus *uisus eloquentissimus est, magis specie tamen et motu atque ipso amictu capiebat homines quam aut dicundi copia aut mediocritate prudentiae*.

46 Tu uero, Reuerendissime Antoni, ab huiuscemodi factionis uiris longe abhorres, qui tuopte ingenio atque natura mirabili (neque me Gnathonicum putes: [30r] *negat quis: nego; ait: aio*) et his certiore semper doctrina et arte contionandi in medium praedicandique tibi praeter omnes aetatis nostrae uiros eminentissimum gradum comparauisti. Non enim quod poetae solent uerba passim fundis, sed quae coram facturus sis, arte et ratione digesta, quam scite et prudenter exponas. Itaque magniloquentiae eo conscendere uisus es, ut iam pro tuo arbitratu possis *dicundo opem ferre supplicibus, excitare afflictos, dare salutem, liberare periculis*, possisque cum uelis *dicundo tenere hominum mentes*, pellicere [30v] affectus, *impellere quo libuerit, unde collibuerit auocare*. Ille ipse es qui *ex infinita multitudine hominum id quod omnibus natura sit datum, uel solus uel cum perpaucis*[55] *facere* possis: tu *populi motus* uehementiasque, tu *iudicum* fora iustitiumque, tu *religiones*, tu *senatus grauitatem* et incessere et absoluere potes.

47 Verum enimuero, dum laudationi tuae inhaereo, uideo quorsum uirulenta[56] aemulorum meorum uerba ruptura sint, et quemadmodum Senecae in theologiam theatralem atque ciuilem (et id Varrone liberius) uehementer inuecto, [31r] eum setius sensisse intus[57] mente foras autem[58] propalamque setius processisse,

---

[54]fit] sit *Lomb.*
[55]cum perpaucis *Cic.* : paucis cum *M*
[56]uirulenta] -tia *Lomb.*
[57]intus] *s.l. suppl. M*
[58]foras autem] *s.l. suppl. M*

---

[159]Rho probably means Antonio di Santa Margherita da Venezia (see Piana 63*; and Lombardi 97n).
[160]For San Bernardino da Siena (1380–1444), see Introduction 10 above.

Antonio di Santa Margherita,[159] Bernardino da Siena,[160] and your associate in office, Angelo.[161] Nonetheless, apart from you, [Antonio da Massa,] I have never experienced anywhere in the world what eloquence itself might do or what power it might hold in the mouth of mortals. For Cicero, when delivering his oration *In Defense of Archia*, said that "many people have existed with excellent mind and virtue, who without instruction were moderate and respected on their own through an almost divine bent of nature itself," who though not steeped in letters nevertheless were endowed with extraordinary talent and achieved the greatest fluency of speech.[162] Yet if I understand correctly, for these people there would still be need of instruction, without which, even if through nature's assistance anything is well said, it cannot always be ready to hand since it happens by chance. Consequently, while speaking to Brutus, Cicero only partially endorsed the eloquence of Lucius Apuleius Saturninus, who, although "he seemed eloquent" in common speech, "nevertheless his appearance, movement, and dress itself captivated people more than did either his fluency of speech or his modest good sense."[163]

46 But, Most Reverend Antonio, you stand at a great distance from men of this faction. For by your own marvelous talent and nature (and please do not think I speak as a disciple of Gnatho: "If anyone says no, I say no; if anyone says yes, I say yes")[164] and by your learning and art (which are always more dependable than talent and nature) in public speaking and preaching, you have attained for yourself preeminent rank beyond all our contemporaries. For you do not pour forth words at random as poets are wont to do, but rather you expound words skillfully and carefully because you have previously organized by art and reason what you were going to deliver in public. Accordingly, you seem to have attained such eloquence that now you can at will "by speaking bring assistance to supplicants, restore the abject, grant safety, and deliver from danger."[165] And now you can at will "by speaking command the attention of people," coax their emotions, persuade them to what you want or dissuade them from what you do not want. For "out of the infinite multitude of men you are the only one or one of very few[166] who can perfect nature's gift to all": you can denounce and dissolve "the people's demonstrations" and outbursts, [and shape] the "judges' courts" and the public's business, "religious ordinances and senatorial authority."[167]

47 But of course while I stick to praising you, I see in what direction my rivals are about to erupt in virulent invective. And just as our Augustine rightly objected that Seneca, when he (even more freely than Varro) forcefully attacked theatrical and civil theology, privately thought one thing but proceeded another

---

[161]Angelo Salvetti da Siena (ca. 1350–1423) was Minister General of the Franciscan Order from 1421–23 (see Piana 58–59; and Lombardi 97n).

[162]Cicero *In Defense of Archia* 7.15.

[163]Cicero *Brutus* 62.224.

[164]Gnatho is a character in Terence's *Eunuch* (252), who became proverbial as the doyen of parasites (cf. Jerome *Letter* 50.4).

[165]Cicero *On the Orator* 1.8.32.

[166]Rho has either clumsily inserted this passage or copied a corrupt manuscript of Cicero, giving *paucis cum* (grammatically nonsensical) instead of *cum perpaucis* (the correct reading).

[167]Cicero (*On the Orator* 1.8.30–31) said that Crassus held these abilities to be the motivation for the pursuit of oratory.

530 Augustinus noster non iniurius obiicit, ita in me (sed utique ius gentium contra) seorsum atque uerba mea sint uitam degere hi balatrones obganniant. Quibus maledicta — quando quidem ob impuritatem uitae faecesque quotidianas omne testimonium eorum putet — facile remitto. Hi sunt qui nebulonum[59] exole-
535 torumque inter examina absentes carpunt: qui inter phialas philosophantes in quosque mortales ferre sententiam uolunt et quasi Catones noui *censoria uir*[31v]*gula* alios *e bibliothecis* eliminare, alios accipere praesumunt.[60] Hi sunt quorum studia noctu plus uini quam olei sapiunt: qui cum post phasides aues et
540 altilia saginata studio, post distentum opiparis dapibus aqualiculum, si combibones ipsi, cum ad secundae mensae bellaria uentum est, Falerno rostra molle fecerint, aut a Musis superati uertuntur in picas, et uino madentes articulata uerba dediscunt; aut a Pallade subacti, cum oestra[61] puellae Arachnes more irretire
545 nequeant, circum incertos [32r] oculos uolitantes mustiones capiunt Domitianique more stilis praeacutis[62] oscitabundi muscas figunt; aut prae temulentia mensae cadentes post cenam dubiam uel statim euomunt uel stertunt et Machometi paradisum somniant.
550 **48** Numquam huiuscemodi uiros, uirorum Optume, in congressu conspicor quin derepente sim tecum teque oculis feram, memor usque fabellae quam te in ecclesia Mantuana superioribus his annis praedicante (consuesti uidelicet inter seria et sancta uerba, uti semisomnes auoces, ad [32v] tempus percomis esse), perdidici.
555 Aiebas enim: "Simia quaepiam libertate manumissa fabri argentarii

---

[59]nebulonum] -lorum *Lomb.*
[60]praesumunt *scripsi* : praesummunt *M*
[61]oestra] ostra *Lomb.*
[62]praeacutis] praecutis *Lomb.*

[168]Cf. Augustine *The City of God* 6.10. Marcus Terentius Varro (116–27 BCE), in his work *On Antiquities*, questioned the gods as represented in myths (mythical theology) and in plays (theatrical theology). Seneca the Younger (ca. 4 BCE–65 CE), a Roman Stoic philosopher, in his lost work *On Superstition*, questioned the gods of the official Roman cults (civil theology) and numinous powers in the earth, rivers, and mountains (natural theology). For Varro, see *Philippic* §27 n. 66; for Seneca the Younger, see *Philippic* §75 n. 181.

[169]Rho elsewhere takes *exoletus* as synonymous with the medieval Latin word "sodomite" (see *Philippic* §22 n. 55 and *Imitations* 133v–135r: *Luxuria*, Appendix IX below). That seems not to be the accusation here, where his other less specific description probably applies (*Imitations* 133v–135r: *Luxuria*, Appendix IX below): *Absoleti* and *exoleti* are impure and foul in lust (*sunt immundi et foetidi in luxuria*).

[170]Cf. Jerome *Against Vigilantius* 1.

[171]That is, Marcus Porcius Cato (234–149 BCE), who was dubbed "Censorius" by his contemporaries for his traditional moral opposition to certain strains of Hellenistic influences coming into Rome.

[172]Jerome *Letter* 61.2.

way outwardly and publicly,[168] so too these buffoons snarl at me (but indeed in violation of the Law of Nations) that I live differently than my speech suggests. I easily overlook their curses — seeing that their whole testimony reeks of the impurity and daily filth of their lives. These are men who in a crowd of freeloaders and lechers[169] tear those not present to pieces, and who, while philosophizing in their cups,[170] want to pass sentence on every possible mortal and presume like new Catos[171] "to blacklist some people from libraries"[172] and to admit others. These are men whose nightly studies smack more of wine than of lamp oil. After pheasants and purposely fattened fowls[173] and after cramming their paunches with sumptuous feasts, when the dessert course arrives,[174] if these drinking companions soak their beaks in Falernian wine, either the Muses overcome them and turn them into magpies (for sodden with wine, they forget how to form distinct words);[175] or overcome by Pallas Athena, since they cannot snare gadflies like the girl Arachne,[176] they either catch gnats buzzing around their blurry eyes and yawning sleepily stab flies with their skewers like Domitian;[177] or falling drunkenly on the table after a dubious dinner,[178] they either promptly vomit or snore and dream of Mohammed's promised Paradise.[179]

48 Never do I spot such men in an assembly, Your Excellency, but that I am suddenly with you and see you before my eyes, continually mindful of the fable that I learned by heart while you were preaching in a Mantuan church years ago.[180] That is to say, you used to be entertaining once in a while during serious and holy speech in order to recapture the attention of the drowsy, for you said:

> A certain monkey, upon being set free, approached the shop of a silversmith, and when he surveyed the house with wrinkled eyes, he observed an image placed on a pedestal (it was a human head made of silver). At first the monkey was dumbstruck, thinking that the image was alive and breathing. It had been fashioned

---

[173]Cf. Jerome *Against Vigilantius* 1.

[174]Cf. Aulus Gellius 13.11.7.

[175]The nine daughters of Pierius were turned into magpies for competing with the Muses.

[176]Pallas Athena, or Minerva, the goddess of arts and crafts as well as wisdom and war, represents artistic ability. The low-born Arachne challenged Athena to a contest in weaving. Arachne was turned into a spider (*arachnes*) after she defeated Athena at the loom (Ovid *Metamorphoses* 6.1–145).

[177]Suetonius (*Domitian* 3.1) relates a story about Domitian, who allegedly spent hours alone and entertained himself by stabbing flies with a skewer. One palace official, when asked if Domitian had any company, remarked: "Not even a fly." For Rho's play on the words *mustiones* and *bibiones* (wine or vinegar gnats), and *combibones* (drinking-buddies/barflies), see *Philippic* §40 n. 102.

[178]For *cena dubia*, see *Philippic* §40 n. 103; cf. also *Philippic* §22 n. 52.

[179]Islam affirms clear moral guidelines while maintaining a positive view of sensual pleasure. This is apparent in its view of Paradise where the faithful will be told to "enter Paradise with your spouses in delight" (Quran 43.70) or they will "recline on couches arranged in rows" and be coupled "with maidens with large, lovely eyes" (Quran 52.18–30). Rho's slur betrays his Christian prejudice, which mandated that the pleasures of Paradise be strictly spiritual.

[180]The General Chapter of the Franciscans met at Mantua in 1418 at the Convent of San Francesco (see Lombardi 103n).

tabernam subiit cumque rugosis oculis domum perlustrasset, simulacrum quoddam scabello positum (erat enim caput hominis argenteum) intuetur. Obstupuit primum, existimans quia uitam et spiritum duceret. Mira nimirum opificis arte fabricatum erat, ut et
560 oculi et supercilia, nares et labra et quaeque lineamenta spirare uiderentur. At illa sculptile aliquandiu contemplata, animaduertens neque frontem rugari [33r] neque supercilia adduci, non palpebras non ipsa labra concurrere, manum attollens colapho percussit atque praecipitem imaginem illam scabello deturbauit. Confestim accurrit
565 quam uacuam et inanem introspectans (erat enim semisupina) subrisit et illudens Graeco sic sermone ait: '*O cephalin acephalon!*'" Tum quidem mihi quem in ludo puellus didiceram uisum est Aesopi uersiculum illum,

    O sine mente caput, O sine uoce genas!

570 ex te de integro insinuari.

49 Dices quorsum iam haec? Plane, praestantissime Pater, hi liuentes mei eam[63] ipsam imaginem exprimunt, [33v] qui, tametsi apparata facie — uerbis enim Flacci utar —

    proiicere[64] *ampullas et sesquipedalia uerba*

575 effutire uideantur ac sine cruore (ut ita dixerim) trucidare Saracenos et Parthos, in ipsis tamen penitissimis uisceribus inanes prorsus sunt atque taeterrimi eorum more qui in fronte tabernae omne splendidum et pretiosum collocant quo praetereuntes alliciant sistantque cum intus sordescant et praeter faecem habeant nihil. Sileant itaque et ommutes-
580 cant qui me aliter uiuere, aliter dicere falso praedicant, quippe [34r] qui semper ne uita aliquando damnaretur flagitiosos quosque perditos et impuros *quorum*, ait Cicero, *magna est natio*, perexhorrui.

50 Integros enimuero ac scientia et moribus praeditos summa obseruantia prosecutus excolui. Habes impraesentiarum te penes
585 socium quempiam (sic enim religio istaec quod tecum perpetuum contubernium trahas[65] appellat), magistrum Scolarium Tuscum, qui cum una adulescentes in[66] philosophia uersaremur atque eiusdem palestrae consocios haberemus, si de moribus illum roges dicet

---

[63]eam *om. Lomb.*
[64]proiicere] *corr. M*
[65]trahas *scripsi* : -hat *M*
[66]in] *s.l. suppl. M*

[181]Cf. Aesop *Fables* (ed. Halm), nn. 47 and 47b; Phaedrus 1.11; Romulus 4.10; Odo de Ceritona 80(68).
[182]Aesop *Fables* 34.4 (*De lupo et capite*).
[183]For Rho's sense of *effutire*, see *Apology* n. 154 above.
[184]Horace *The Art of Poetry* 97.
[185]Cicero *The Response to the Soothsayers* 57.

with such skillful art by the craftsman that even the eyes, nose, lips, and every feature seemed alive. But after the monkey had for a time contemplated the sculpture and noticed that neither the forehead wrinkled nor the brows knit, that neither the eyelids nor lips closed, he raised his hand and landed a blow, which knocked the image headlong from the pedestal. He immediately rushed up, and seeing how empty and useless it was (for it was tipped over), smiled and jokingly said in Greek: *"O kephalen akephalon!"* (O headless head!).[181]

At that moment you introduced me anew, as it were, to that little verse of Aesop which I learned as a boy in elementary school: "O head without a mind, O lips without a voice."[182]

49 You will say: "Where does this lead?" Clearly, most illustrious Father, this statue represents my enviers, who, even if they seem with a straight face (to use Horace's words) "to blurt out bombast" and to mislead[183] with "sesquepedalian words"[184] and seem (as I would say) to slaughter Saracens and Parthians bloodlessly, nevertheless, in their innermost hearts they are absolutely void and hideous. They resemble those who place everything shiny and valuable in front of their shop so that they may allure and stop those passing by, although inside they are filthy and have nothing but trash. And so let those who falsely assert that I live one way and speak another fall silent and remain speechless, since — lest my life at any time be condemned — I have always shunned every indecent, depraved, and foul person, "of whom there is," said Cicero, "a legion."[185]

50 In contrast, I have cultivated upright people who were endowed with both good learning and morals, treating them with the greatest respect. You have with you at present an associate, Master Scolario Tusco[186] (for the Order calls for you to go about with a constant companion). Since as youths he and I were engaged in philosophy together and had classmates in common from the same school, if you ask him about my morals, he will say frankly, when we have both reviewed our past lives (for the memory of our studies has not been forgotten), that we did not graduate from school as thieves, church-robbers, or prowling assassins,[187] but rather he will testify that each of us carried off for himself diplomas and titles in sacred literature. For as the hoary proverb has it, birds of

---

[186]Scolario (or Scolaio) Tusco da Montalcino apparently preceded Rho in entering the Franciscan Order and in receiving his degrees by one year. He would, however, have still been present at Il Santo in Padua when Rho received his degree. Scolario first appears simply by name in the roll call of the Chapter meetings at Il Santo on 8 July 1412. He is listed as a *baccalarius formatus* on 27 November 1421, a *magister sacrae paginae* on 27 January 1422, and again simply by name on 24 March 1423 (see Sartori 991; Rutherford 1990, 83).

[187]Canon Law states that infamous persons (*infames*) cannot be witnesses against others nor aspire to ecclesiastical office (Gratian D.2 C.6.1). Canon Law follows Pope Stephan I, who allegedly identified the "infamous persons" as thieves (*fures*), sacrilegious persons (*sacrilegi*), and other criminals.

590 ingenue, cum recensiti ipsi quique [34v] ab se fuerimus (neque enim studiorum nostrorum memoria oblitterata est), non fures, non sacrilegos, non grassantes sicarios euasisse gymnasiis, ast insignia titulosque sacrarum litterarum pro se quemque reportasse testabitur. Tritum enim prouerbium est similia similibus infici. At ipse Ciceronis sententiam, qua sine labe uersarer, usque complexus sum. Is, cum in
595 Officiis suis declarasset *sanguinis* coniunctionem et beneuolentiam deuincire *homines caritate; magnum* esse *eadem habere monimenta maiorum, eisdem uti sacris, sepulcra habere communia;* ilicet adiecit: [35r] *Sed omnium societatum nulla praestantior est,*[67] *nulla firmior, quam cum uiri boni moribus similes familiaritate coniuncti sunt.*

600 **51** Familiares itaque mei, humanissime Pater, quos intus habeo, libelli mei sunt: illos alloquor, illi me conueniunt, illos amplector, illos exosculor, illi uicem reddunt. Hi sunt qui ne me angoribus dedam iubent, qui me Zenonem profitear persuasum uolunt, id est nullas aegritudines, nullas molestias, nullos maerores admittere. Hi sunt qui
605 a cunabulis mundi ad has aetates nostras, siue diuina illa sint siue humana, foris nullo facto pe[35v]riculo, ut in otiosis tuguriis luculenter ea ipsa uideantur, omnia coram statuunt.

52 A quibus si plerumque diuertere atque animo non quo resoluatur ceterum remittatur interuallum facere collibuerit, dicam
610 nunc tibi e multis qui foris sunt[68] pauculos necessarios meos. Habeo conclaustralem mihi noctu et interdiu quo cum uerser Hippolytum Stupanum, theologiae magistrum, uirum bene moratum quidem atque scientia praeditum, nunc grauem nunc eutrapelum, et qui interloquendum, cum ad te uentum ex spectatissimis mortalibus
615 fuerit, [36r] nullo pacto ab tuis laudibus, quae uel apprime delectant, temperare se possit; qui cum mille laudandi aditus habeat, de te tamen nullum finem[69] attingit ut exeat.

53 Egressus porro claustrum, aut Bartholomaeum Mediolanensem archiepiscopum aut Franciscum Pergamensem antistitem

---

[67]est *Cic.*
[68]sunt] *s.l. suppl. M*
[69]finem *om. Lomb.*

---

[188]Literally, "like is imbued with likes" (Walther 29639d and 29639f).
[189]Cicero *On Duties* 1.17.54–55.
[190]Rho is referring to the books he has been discussing throughout the *Apology*. "Whom I have within me" corroborates the textual evidence that he was discussing many (or most) of these works from memory, not from direct consultation.
[191]That is, Zeno of Citium (335–263 BCE), who founded the Stoic school of philosophy.
[192]Cf. Cicero *On Duties* 1.43.153. For this Stoic notion of wisdom, see *Apology* §6 n. 19.
[193]"In quiet hovels" (*in otiosis tuguriis*) is a metaphor for private reading, *tugurium* resonating among Franciscans as humble retreat from the world. The "Tugurio" is a site near Assisi on the *Rigus*

a feather flock together.[188] But I myself have up to now embraced the following opinion of Cicero and have abided by it without reproach. In his *On Duties*, he declared that the bonds of blood and friendship unite "people with love, and that it is important to have the same monuments as our ancestors, to practice the same religious customs, to share common tombs"; and he immediately added: "but of all social bonds none is more noble, none is more durable than when good men, alike in morals, are bound in intimate friendship."[189]

51 Accordingly, most humane Father, the friends whom I have within me are my books:[190] I speak to them, they come to meet me, I embrace them, I reverently kiss them, and they do the same in turn. These are the friends who bid me not to give in to anguish, who wish to convince me that I should follow Zeno, that is, to admit no anxieties, no annoyances, no sorrows.[191] These are the friends who from the beginning of the world to the present day settle in the open forum all matters yet unproven, be they human or divine,[192] so that one perceives these matter lucidly even in quiet hovels.[193]

52 Inasmuch as it is often enjoyable to take leave[194] of these internal friends and give the mind a break, not in order to be indolent but rather to be refreshed, let me now name for you a few of my many close associates, who are my external friends. I have with me in my convent Ippolito Stupano, Master of Theology, with whom I live night and day.[195] He is a well-mannered man, endowed with knowledge, who can be at one moment grave and at another witty. And when our talk turns to the most highly regarded mortals and you come up, he simply cannot restrain himself from singing your praises, which give him special delight. And although he has a thousand opportunities to laud [other people], he still cannot find a place to stop when praising you.

53 Furthermore, when I emerge from the cloister, I see either Bartolomeo, Archbishop of Milan,[196] or Francesco, Bishop of Bergamo.[197] These are the two lights divinely sent to us mortals for our time. Whatever light shines diffusely among

---

Tortus, i.e., *Rivus Tortus*, celebrated by the early Franciscan writers Thomas of Celano (1.16.45) and Giuliano of Spira (4.24). St. Francis of Assisi lived there in a hovel (*tugurium*) on the advice of Peter Cantor (PL 205, 257) that one could more quickly enter heaven from a hovel than from a palace (*Nam citius de tugurio quam de palatio in caelum ascenditur*). My thanks to John Monfasani and his timely trip to Assisi for this information.

[194]Rho never observes the classical distinction between *divertere* (to separate) and *devertere* (to turn away), the latter being the meaning here.

[195]Rho's statement that "I have [him] with me day and night" indicates that Ippolito was his obligatory Franciscan companion (cf. Celano 1.12.29). The documents of San Francesco Grande consistently identify him as "Ippolito Stupano *da Como*" (Rutherford 1990, 84n and 86n). He should not be confused with "Ippolito *da Milano*" (cf. Monfardini 18n; Lombardi 107n; cf. Piana 1968, 157; Cortese 155 and 159).

[196]Bartolomeo Capra (d. 1433), who, beyond his duties as archbishop, participated in the search for rare works and old manuscripts. In 1423 he wrote to Leonardo Bruni (see *Philippic* §34 n. 87) saying that he had liberated several early manuscripts from their "hideous and foul prison," that is, from some monastery in or near Milan (see Sabbadini 1996, 101–02, 104–05).

[197]Francesco Aregazzi (1375–1437), who like Rho was a Conventual Franciscan, became Bishop of Bergamo in 1403. In 1428 (about the time Rho finishes the *Apology*) the Visconti lost Bergamo to the Venetians (see Raggi). San Francesco Grande, where Rho resided, was the head of the Milanese Franciscan Province. Aregazzi would no doubt have visited there, but Rho says that he saw him outside the cloister.

uiso. Hi sunt hac tempestate nostra mortalibus nobis missa caelitus bina lumina in quibus quicquid sparsim in multos doctos lucis habetur, duobus ipsis profecto congestum est; omnia studia, omnes artes, omnes scientiae in eis ipsis (diuinitus credo) conflatae [36v] sunt. Ponat quae nemo non uelit: aenigmata, captiones, strophas, theoremata, quicquid inextricabile creditur; non abibit scrupulo mentis ambiguus. Hi cum me suaui quadam consuetudine, non dicam necessarium uerum prae humanitate filium propemodum peculiarem, complectantur, utrum tamen[70] eorum fide, amore, et studio mage prosequar nec ipse satis intellego. Id unum certo scio: quandoquidem pro morum sanctimonia et uitae integritate omnis est mea laus inferior, eos utique summe reuereor et obseruo eorumque nominibus semper assurgo.

54 [37r] Ab his auectus, saepenumero Candidum Decembrem papalem ducalemque secretarium ipse conuenio, uirum eloquentissimum deliciarumque Ciceronis refertissimum. Hunc mihi pernecessarium fecit, me uel illi, studiorum similitudo, suauitas consuetudinis, confabulationis societas, interior communicatio. Ex quo si comica, si tragica, si satyrica, si historias quis efflagitet, absentibus libris, ei singula (mirabile dictu) memoriter dicet. Cui narranti dubio procul eam fidem fecero ac si Liuium ac si Herodotum prae oculis in manibus haberem.

55 [37v] Prima tandem nocte transmissa uespera in claustrum reuerto, ubi persaepe Leonardum Cremonensem, professionis nostrae theologum, sidera contemplantem inuenio. Quem si laudare coepero id ausim dicere, post sacrarum litterarum uolumina, quarum peritissimus est, deleantur mathematica, astrorum codices extincti sint, Euclides non ipse Ptolemaeus usquam habeatur,[71] satis ipse superest quo de integro illos suscitet. Plerumque e manibus eius horoscop(i)um tollens, ab se didici, ocello foraminibus e regione[72] concurrentibus admoto, siderum al[38r]titudines, propinquitates, atque recessus. Qui cum me saepe multam in noctem trahat astra suspectanti, cogor ualefaciens aperire cubiculum, impressoque fronti signo crucis, strato non capienti uestigium lassitudinem ponere.

56 Habes ex his, Pater optume, mores meos, quibus rebus institutus, quibus imbutus sim. Exposui quicquid est et id coram. Iam te iudicem habere laetor atque censorem. Prodeant itaque — iam actum

---

[70]tamen *om. Lomb.*
[71]habeatur] -antur *Lomb.*
[72]e regione] *s.l. suppl. M*

---

[198]The "corrections" of the Vatican manuscript read: "I often visit Gluttono Brownnosio, papal and ducal ass-licker, a feeble man, absolutely worn out with Cicero's delightful phrasing. Similar studies, completely vain manners, [etc.] have made him my closest friend. . . . If when books are wanting anyone should demand from him comedies, [etc.], Candido will pitifully recite for that person from memory each of these." (*saepenumero Golididum Decelubrem, papalem ducalemque leccetarium ipse*

the many learned has undoubtedly converged in these two: all studies, all arts, and all sciences have come together in them (through divine providence, I believe). Let anyone pose what he wants: riddles, sophisms, tricks, problems, or anything considered insoluble, he will not leave with doubts and uncertainty. Although these men with a certain pleasant familiarity welcome me into their friendship — not, I would say, just as a close friend but, out of human kindness, virtually as their own son — yet I myself do not adequately understand whether I follow them more for their faith, love, and devotion. This one thing I know for sure: since all my praise falls short of the probity of their morals and the integrity of their life, I in any event revere and honor them supremely and always rise at the mention of their names.

54 When I leave these men, I often visit Candido Decembrio, the papal and ducal secretary, who is an exceptionally eloquent man, absolutely brimming with Cicero's delightful phrasing. Similar studies, pleasant familiarity, companionship in discussion, and inner communication have made him my closest friend or, if you like, have made me his. If when books are wanting anyone should demand from him comedies, tragedies, satires, or histories, Candido will amazingly recite for that person from memory each of these. When he recites, I put complete trust in him. It is as if I held a Livy or Herodotus open in my hand.[198]

55 Finally, right after dark when Vespers are over, I return to the cloister where I often find Leonardo da Cremona,[199] a theologian of our Order, contemplating the stars. How should I begin to praise this man? I dare say, quite apart from the volumes of sacred literature in which he is most skilled, if the books of mathematics were to be wiped out, if the books of astrology were to be destroyed, if neither Euclid nor Ptolemy were to be had anywhere, Leonardo is more than capable of resuscitating them. Often taking the astrolabe[200] from his hands, I have learned for myself the altitudes, approaches, and retreats of the stars by aiming the alidade through directly aligning the apertures. So when he often drags me late at night to gaze at the stars, after saying goodnight, I am reduced to simply opening my cell door and, after having made the sign of the cross on my forehead, to surrendering to exhaustion with the blanket not even covering my feet.

56 From these associates, noblest Father, you will learn my character: how I was educated and what I absorbed. I have revealed everything there is and have done so publicly. Now I am delighted to have you as judge and censor. So let those come forward — and some already have — who do not so much state as

---

convenio, virum ela(n)guentissimum deliciarumque Ciceronis defectissimum. Hunc mihi pernecessarium fecit . . . studiorum similitudo, pervanitas consuetudinis. . . . Ex quo si comica . . . ei singula [miserabile dictu] momoriter dicet.) Cf. the deleted passage of the Vatican manuscript, *Apology* §31 n. 109.

[199]Leonardo di Antonio da Cremona studied in Bologna and wrote notes on Euclid. He is sometimes alleged to have written *Compilation on the Practice of the Metrical Art* (Piana 116*–17*; 62–64). When in 1448 the Repubblica Ambrosiana established a *studium generale* in Milan, the council appointed Leonardo to lecture in mathematics (Maiocchi 2:527–29).

[200]Although Rho clearly writes *horoscopum*, it does not conform to his own definition (*Imitations* 18v): "*Horoscopus* is observing specific times (*inspiciens horas*). *Horoscopium*, however, is the instrument for that purpose (*instrumentum illud*)." For a thirteenth-century manuscript illumination (Paris: Bibliothèque de l'Arsenal, MS 1186, 1v) depicting the use of an astrolabe, see Lindberg 270 and cover; for the history of the astrolabe, see Neugebauer.

est — qui me ignarum omnium rerum[73] non tam dicunt quam cupiunt, perstrepant, garriant, latrent: quod si minus, cum stomachum cohibere neque[38v]ant aut bilem, consulant sibi[74] saltem ne linguam excreent sed de industria mordicus comprimant.

57 *Non est grande*, amplissime Pater (si Hieronymo credimus), *garrire in triuiis, compitis, et plateis, et non crimina sed maledicta congerere, ac de mundo ferre sententiam*: 'hic bene dixit, ille male'; 'iste scripturas nouit, ille delirat'; 'iste loquax, ille infantissimus est.' Vt de omnibus iudicent cuius hoc iudicio* meruere? Loquantur mecum, immo de me tecum, in *scriptis* ut non uolgus, omnia falso iudicans, ceterum tu *de nobis tacitus*[75] lector iudices. Moueant *manum*, fi[39r]gant *stilum, et quicquid* possunt litteris suis et apicibus aperiant. Faciant *occasionem respondendi*, quam tantopere iactant, *disertitudini* eorum. Permittant me non silere, qui aliquando litteras didici et *saepe ferulae* subduxi *manum*. Verum mortuos alloquor, et *foenum in cornu* meo timent. Non erubescant itaque quod Hieronymus non erubuit: qui cum a Blaesilla uirgine — uiso eo libri loco *ubi catalogus omnium mansionum* inscribitur *per quas de Aegypto* uentum est *ad fluenta Iordanis* — rogaretur de dubiis ut *causas* redderet *et rationes singulorum*, [39v] *in quibusdam* ait se haesitauisse, *in aliis inoffenso*[76] *pede* cucurrisse, *in plerisque* illi femellae *simpliciter ignorantiam* fassus est.

58 Quid ergo? Nos omnia cognosse et singulorum habere notitiam praedicabimus? Quid sapiant itaque quid ignorent aemuli mei quid ad me? Ipsi uiderint: id unum ipse Socraticum scio, post tot euoluta et lectitata uolumina, nisi Iesum crucifixum sciuerim, quod nescio.

59 Facturus iam tandem non animo sed uerbis finem, quo abs te comiter abeam, fabellam precor attende.

60 Asellus quispiam [40r] se leoni obuiam dedit, quem leo percipiens, quia sibi — quod moris erat — nullam salutem diceret, non assurgeret, nullum clientelae uestigium faceret, coepit ad aures utrimque cauda repercussa excandescere et suscitare se ira. "Itaque," infit, "uilissima[77] bellua ignauum pecus sic occurris, sic obuius uenis domino et animalium regi neque genuflectis neque adoras?"

---

[73]rerum *om. Lomb.*
[74]sibi] *corr.* M
[75]tacitus] -tur *Lomb.*
[76]inoffenso] *corr.* M
[77]uilis-] *corr.* M

[201]Jerome *Letter* 50.5.
[202]Jerome *Letter* 50.4.
[203]Jerome *Letter* 50.5.
[204]Jerome *Letter* 50.5.

whine, howl, yap, and bark that I am completely ignorant. But failing that, when they cannot restrain either their chagrin or their anger, let them at least take common counsel and consciously bite their tongue before they cough it out.

57 "It is not a great thing" (if we believe Jerome), distinguished Father, "to chatter in the piazzas and at the crossroads and turnouts; to amass not indictments but slanders; to pass judgment on the world: 'this man spoke well, that one poorly'; 'this man knows Scripture, that one raves'; 'this man is long-winded, that one is tongue-tied.' Where did they get the right to judge everyone?"[201] Let them write to me, or rather about me to you, so that not the rabble, who judges everything falsely, but you, "the silent reader, may decide about us."[202] Let them "lift a hand, grip a pen, and disclose whatever they can"[203] with their jots and tittles. Let them "provide an occasion for responding to their eloquence"[204] that they brag about so much. Let them not silence me, who "often rescued his hand from the schoolmaster's cane"[205] when learning his letters. But I address the dead, or rather they fear "the hay on my horns."[206] Well, let them not blush, because Jerome did not blush. When the virgin Blaesilla[207] — whose eye had lit upon a passage of a book where all the campsites[208] that occur "between Egypt and the currents of the Jordan were listed" — asked him to explain "the purpose and reason of each campsite," he said that he had hesitated "on certain ones," had run through "others without a stumble," and had simply confessed to the young woman "his ignorance on most."[209]

58 What happens in such a case? Shall we proclaim that we know everything and have knowledge of every single thing? So what do I care what my rivals know or do not know? Let them observe: after having have perused and pored over an enormous number of volumes, I know this one Socratic fact, apart from knowing Jesus crucified, that I do not know.

59 Now I am finally going to bring this apology to a close — not in spirit but verbally. And so that I may thereby leave you on a cheerful note, please listen to a fable.[210]

60 A certain ass blocked the path of a lion, who noticed that the ass did not give him a greeting, or stand at attention, or make a sign of submission as was the custom. The lion began to burn and stir with anger, flicking his tail from ear to ear. "So," began the lion, "you worthless beast, you barnyard scum, is this the way you greet me? Is this the way you obstruct the path of the Lord and King of Animals? Do you neither bow nor salute?"

---

[205] Jerome *Letter* 50.5; Juvenal 1.15.

[206] Jerome *Letter* 50.5; cf. Horace *Satires* 1.4.34. Romans apparently used hay to blunt or pad the horns of dangerous cattle. Hay on the horns at least signaled danger.

[207] Actually, *Letter* 77 (the one quoted here) eulogizes St. Fabiola (d. 399). Jerome eulogized Blaesilla (d. 389) in *Letter* 39.

[208] That is, the places where the Israelites camped during the Exodus from Egypt and the sojourn in the wilderness.

[209] Jerome *Letter* 77.7.

[210] Cf. Aesop *Fables,* ed. Halm, n. 259; Phaedrus 1.11.

61 Cui asellus subridens et excusso capite auribus longis ludens: "Dic sodes," ait, "qui te nostri regem constituit? Quibus meritis hanc tibi dicionem ascri[40v]bis? Si te recte undique circumscribo (tametsi ceterum animalium uolgus te tanti faciat ut pluris neminem) tantidem inquam 'sum quanti tu et aeque me cuncta timent atque te.'"

62 Itaque multis uerbis ultro citroque habitis, ex composito quo et asellus uerborum suorum periculum faciat, cliuum conscendunt proximum. Quo posteaquam uentum est atque una consedere, confestim asellus ipse oscitare coepit atque horas more suo et sine horologio dicere, quas tam dissono clamore et exasperata uoce cantabat, ut [41r] quae in eo colle constiterant feles, ibices, capellae, ceruorum hinnuli, lepores, et ⟨animalia⟩ huiuscemodi metu in siluam uicinam aufugerent.

63 Quae ipsa intuitus asellus ait: "Cede age, leo, utrum quia princeps et dominus sum ista haec animalia timor incessit."

64 Cui leo: "Egregie quidem rere idque persuadeas[78] tibi uelim, nisi me penes de te extaret certa cognitio (neque enim mente excidere potest quin te semper rudem asinum[79] et imbellem esse dignoscam) utique cum his belluis quae te nesciunt aufugissem."

65 Longa esset fabula, idcirco longiore [41v] circuitu[80] non te traham. Sint haec iam satis multa et plura forsit[81] quam tibi per occupationes tuas necesse esset. Eam tamen fabulam[82] sic intellego. Hi qui me carpunt non homines, ast auriti et bipedes aselli sunt. Quos itaque minimum pertimesco, neque more femellarum laruas et lemures terroresque magicos[83] noctu expauescentium, ipse formidolosus exhorreo. Tu uero (precor, supplico, obsecro) qui asellos professi sunt asellos flocci pendas atque in eorum aures non lyra, ceterum tuba cornea concrepes, filios autem qui ueri filii sunt complec[42r]tare, meque cum illis etsi *abortiuum* suscipe.

66 Vale Francisci compar; uale nostri ordinis speculum; uale huiusce religionis summae meritae princeps. Mei si otium dabitur memor sis, et, Antoni Massa, Raudensem Antonium commendatum habe.

APOLOGIA RAVDENSIS ANTONII EX PROFESSIONE MINORVM ADVERSVS ARCHIDIACONVM QVEMPIAM COMPLICESQVE SYCOPHANTAS TAETERRIMOS SCRIPTA AD ANTONIVM MASSAM MINORVM GENERALEM.
FRATER ANTONIVS RAVDENSIS THEOLOGIAE MAGISTER

---

[78] persuadeas] -des *Lomb.*
[79] asinum *scripsi* : asiinum *M*
[80] circuitu] -to *Lomb.*
[81] forsit *scripsi* : -sis *M*
[82] fabulam] -la *Lomb.*
[83] -que magicos] *s.l. suppl. M*

61 The ass, grinning and flopping his ears about his head, responded: "Tell me, if you don't mind, who made you our king? By what right do you arrogate to yourself this dominion? If I study you from every direction — even though the rest of the animal horde thinks no one is greater than you — I say that I'm just as great as you and that all fear me as much as they fear you."

62 So after many words had been exchanged and they had agreed that the ass should make good his boast, they ascended a nearby hill. When the climb was finished and they stopped together, the ass immediately opened his mouth and began after his fashion to bray the hours without a clock. He chanted them with such a cacophonous racket and raspy voice that the wild cats, mountain goats, nannies, fawns, hares, and other [animals] settled on the hill fled in fear into the nearby forest.

63 After all this had been observed, the ass said: "Come! Tell me, lion, whether fear seized these animals because I'm prince and lord."

64 The lion replied: "You're full of yourself, to be sure, and I would believe your line. And I surely would've fled with these beasts who don't know you, if I didn't have definitive knowledge of you right in front of me. For I can't rid my mind of the fact that you're always a rude and lily-livered ass."

65 It would be a long story, therefore, I shall not drag you on a longer detour. What has already been said is quite a bit and perhaps more than you require since you are so busy. Nevertheless, I understand the fable as follows: those who carp at me are not humans but long-eared, "two-footed asses."[211] And so I do not fear them. Nor frightened, do I tremble like women scared of demons, ghosts, and mysterious sounds in the night. But — I beg, I supplicate, I plead — may you regard as asses those who have revealed themselves to be asses and may you not sound a lyre into their ears but blast a trumpet. May you, however, embrace the sons who are true sons and, although I am "born prematurely,"[212] may you accept me along with them.

66 Farewell, equal of Francis. Farewell, mirror of our order. Farewell, prince of this supremely meritorious religious profession. Remember me if you have the time, and, Antonio da Massa, consider Antonio da Rho worthy of your commendation.

THE APOLOGY OF ANTONIO DA RHO FROM THE ORDER OF FRIARS MINORS AGAINST A CERTAIN ARCHDEACON AND HIS LOATHSOME SYCOPHANT ACCOMPLICES, ADDRESSED TO ANTONIO DA MASSA, GENERAL OF THE FRIARS MINOR. FRIAR ANTONIO DA RHO, MASTER OF THEOLOGY.

---

[211]Cf. Juvenal 9.92; Jerome *Letter* 27.3; and Wiesen 202.

[212]This expression derives from the Apostle Paul (I Corinthians 15:8–9), but is taken here from Jerome (*Letter* 47.3), who described himself this way, adding that he was "the least of all Christians" (see *Apology* §4).

APPENDICES

APPENDIX I

Panormita, *Etsi Facile* (Letter to Rho) Manuscripts

Italics = An unidentified manuscript from which another is said to be copied.
lower case = An uncollated manuscript that derives from a known collated manuscript.

- B^A = Bologna: Biblioteca Universitaria, MS 2948, vol. 28 (*Misc. Tioli*), s. XVIII, pp. 357–61. [Copied from *R*.]
- b^b = Bologna: Biblioteca Universitaria, MS 2948, vol. 28 (*Misc. Tioli*), s. XVIII, pp. 361–62. [Copied from V^L.]
- b^c = Bologna: Biblioteca Universitaria, MS 2948, vol. 36 (*Misc. Tioli*), s. XVIII, f. 36v. [Copied from V^L.]
- F = Florence: Biblioteca Riccardiana, MS 407, s. XV, ff. 219r–220v.
- M = Milan: Biblioteca Ambrosiana, MS M 44 sup., s. XV, f. 195r–195v. [Fragment; text ends at §2: . . . *uoluptate prorsus abhorret*.]
- *R* = Rome: S. Maria del Popolo. [Now lost; exemplar of B^A: *Ex codice cartac. in fol. Bibliot. S. Mariae de Populo Romae pag. 36 tergo et sequen.*]
- *S* = "Soranzi T 59" [Now lost; exemplar of V^M.]
- S^a = Sabbadini and Barozzi 7–9.
- T = Toledo: Biblioteca de Catedral, MS 100.42, s. XV, ff. 97r–100r.
- V^B = Vatican City: Biblioteca Apostolica Vaticana, MS Barb. lat. 42, s. XV (ca. 1466), ff. 256v–259r.
- V^L = Vatican City: Biblioteca Apostolica Vaticana, MS Vat. lat. 2906, s. XV, ff. 39v–40r. [Fragment; text ends at §2: . . . *uoluptate prorsus abhorret*.]
- V^M = Venice: Biblioteca Nazionale Marciana, MS Lat. XIV 221, s. XV, ff. 156r–157v. [Fragment; text ends at §2: . . . *summa et sempiterna*; copied from *S*.]

Stemma

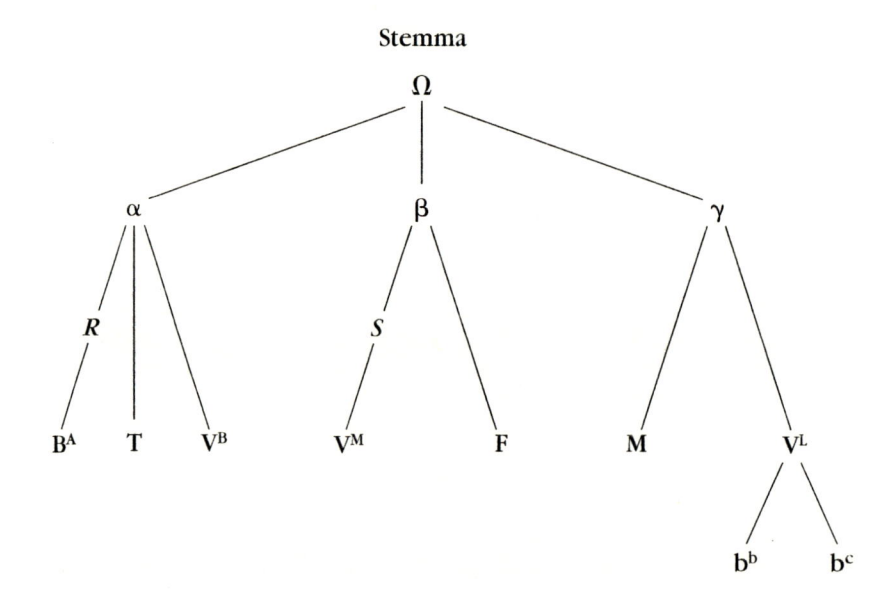

```
                    Ω
         ┌──────────┼──────────┐
         α          β          γ
       / | \       / \        / \
      R  |  \     S   \      M   V^L
     /   |   \   /     \          / \
    B^A  T   V^B V^M    F        b^b  b^c
```

Antonius Panormita ad Antonium Raudensem

⟨1431/32⟩

Antonius Panormita Antonio Raudensi salutem plurimam dicit.

1 Etsi facile multi existimant te quosdam in me uersus edidisse — obscenos quidem illos atque petulantes — ego uel solus adhuc id mihi persuadere non possum. Primum professioni tuae
5 atque religioni minime id congruit hominem exterum, nocentem nemini, honeste agentem, compoetam atque beniuolum tuum maledictis prouocare, cum praesertim cui tantum tribueras, ut alias tuo carmine nihil de me dicere dubitaris —

Antoni mi, nunc decus et lux una latini
10   *eloquii succurre precor —*

et huius generis multa. Deinde non ea rerum ignorantia atque inscitia damnatus es, qui uel meo ingenio uel doctrinae, quae minima est, inuidere debueras, cum praesertim si quid in me sit uel ingenii uel doctrinae, id omne diuo nostro Principi, quem et tu colis, deuo-
15 tum dedicatumque sit, exploratum habeas. Quamquam hi uersus qui nuper in me compositi sunt, rauci, claudi, pingues atque adeo pueriles sunt, ut ex tua uena proficiscantur nequaquam crediderim. Alioquin uana profecto est spes omnis, quam de te maximam Princeps concepit, nam ut poetae cuiusdam uersus est:

20   *Non erit obscuris laudandus uersibus Hector —*

---

1 salutem plurimam dicit *hic* α$V^M S^a$, *post* Panormita V^L : salutem dicit *post* Panormita *FM* ‖ **2** multi] -tum V^L ‖ existimant] -ment *M* ‖ **4** adhuc γ$V^M S^a$: ad hoc *F* : *om.* α ‖ non possum *om.* V^L ‖ tuae *hic* αFMS^a : *post* religioni V^L : *om.* V^M ‖ **5** minime id *tr. F* : *om.* γ ‖ exterum] est enim *M* ‖ **6** nemini] -nem V^M ‖ agentem] degentem *F* ‖ compoetam] -patriotam *F* ‖ atque] : ac *F* : et V^M ‖ **7** maledictis] -dictem V^L ‖ cum *FM* : eum α$V^M S^a$: et V^L ‖ cui] tui *F* ‖ tribueras γV^M : -buas *F* : -bueris $TV^B S^a$: -buis B^A ‖ **8** nihil] nil V^M ‖ **9** Antoni] -nius V^M ‖ mi MS^a : mihi β$B^A TV^B V^L$ ‖ nunc *om.* α ‖ **10** succurre] -currere *T* ‖ **11** huius] -ce *M* ‖ deinde] dein V^M ‖ atque inscitia *bis T* ‖ **12** qui] quod *F* ‖ meo] in eo *F* ‖ doctrinae] -na V^L ‖ **13** debueras] -ris FS^a ‖ **13–14** me sit . . . doctrinae αS^a : uel sit doctrinae *M* : sit *post* ingenii β : uel sit uel docrinae V^L ‖ **14** omne *om. cum lac.* V^L ‖ diuo βS^a : diui γ : di. TV^B : d. B^A ‖ quem et *tr. M* ‖ **15** colis *om.* γ ‖ deuotum *om. cum lac.* V^L ‖ sit] esse S^a ‖ prospectum et *prae* exploratum *F* ‖ **16** hi] duo *M* ‖ rauci *om.* V^L ‖ **16–17** rauci . . . sunt *om. M* ‖ **17** denique *post* adeo β ‖ sunt] sint V^M ‖ **18** profecto *om. F* ‖ profecto est *tr.* V^M ‖ **19** poetae] pote *F* ‖ **20** laudandus α$MV^M S^a$: -dendus *F* : -dis V^L

Antonio Panormita to Antonio da Rho

⟨1431/32⟩

Antonio Panormita sends greetings to Antonio da Rho.

1 Although many readily think that you published some poetry against me — obscene and lewd poetry in fact — I alone cannot yet persuade myself of it. First, it scarcely suits your profession and religion to hurl insults at a foreigner who harms no one, behaves honorably, and is your fellow poet and friend. This is especially true when you valued him so highly that at another time you did not hesitate to say of me in your poetry — "Now, my Antonio, honor and light of the Latin language, pray help me"[1] — and many things like this. Second, you were not condemned for being ignorant and unaware of the facts, as if you should have envied either my genius or learning, which are minimal: for you know for certain that any genius or learning that is in me is entirely devoted and dedicated to our divine prince, whom you too worship. Yet this poetry recently composed against me is raucous, lame, clumsy, and so childish that I never would have believed it mined from your lode. Besides, every great hope that the prince conceived about you is absolutely vain, for as the line of a certain poet goes: "Hector must not be praised with obscure verses"[2] — or "with hackneyed ones" you may add. I could scarcely

---

[1] Antonio da Rho lost poem.
[2] The exact line of Naevius' *Hector proficiens* (cited from Cicero *Tusculan Disputations* 4.31.67 and *Letters to his Friends* 5.12.7 and 15.6.1) is: *Laetus sum laudari me abs te, pater, a laudato viro.*

addas et pertritis. Praeterea ut te auctorem illius maledicentiae non putem, iterum suadet quod is — quicumque fuerit — non quidem poeta sed uersificator, non uersificator sed nequidem syllabicator, non in me solum sed in *Hermaphroditum* meum etiam inuectus est.
25 Et tu pro eruditione tua satis nosti id nobis arte poetica concessum esse, iocos et sales praeludere, *nam*, ut eleganter Catullus ait,

castum decet pium esse poetam
ipsum, uersiculos nihil necesse est.

Et extat in manibus Publii Vergilii Priapeia, opus permaxime lasciuum,
30 ceterum poeta ipse pro morum sobrietate "Parthenias" appellatus est. Plato autem, uir ipse summa doctrina pari sanctimonia praeditus, hisce etiam salibus oblectatus est, cumque interrogaretur quid lasciue ita admodum scriberet respondisse fertur: poetarum est furere. Et generaliter poetam adhuc neminem audiui, neminem legi, quin
35 uerborum aut sententiarum saltem lasciuia non fuerit oblectatus: extat Valerius Martialis; extat Catullus; extat Iuuenalis; extant omnes qui foedioribus uerbis utuntur cum res exigit.

2 Quamquam id nostrum opusculum a tenera usque aetate fuerit compositum, ubi et iocandi et peccandi licentia maior est, nunc
40 autem uerum fateri liceat: alia aetas atque alii mores mihi sunt et studia prorsus diuersa; neque Hermaphroditus cuipiam magis quam mihi ipsi odio est, et editionis simul et lectionis auctorem in primis taedet pigetque non quod illa aetate ludendo deliquerim, sed quod haec mea aetas ab omni lasciuia atque uoluptate prorsus abhorret et
45 seueros mores et seuerum dicendi genus expostulat. Verum enimuero, si uita suppetat, cordi est expurgare nequitiam illam — si modo nequitia est quod poetae omnes factitarunt — seuero ac graui

---

21 addas et pertritis β : addas et perituris TB^A : *om.* $\gamma V^B S^a$ ∥ **22** is] his FT ∥ fuerit] fiunt F ∥ quidem] equidem F ∥ **23** nequidem] neque V^M ∥ **25** et $\alpha FV^L S^a$: ac M : at V^M ∥ tua *om.* V^L ∥ **26** esse *om.* αS^a ∥ **27** pium esse $B^A TS^a$: *tr.* γF : pium *om.* V^B : et pium V^M ∥ **28** uersiculos] -lis γ ∥ nihil] mihi V^L ∥ **29** et] ut V^M ∥ in manibus *om.* α ∥ Priapeia $TV^B V^M S^a$: -peria F : -pea γB^A ∥ **30** pro *om.* F ∥ **31** uir ipse *tr.* γF ∥ **32** hisce] ipse V^M ∥ etiam βM : et $\alpha V^L S^a$ ∥ oblec-] delec- V^B ∥ est *om.* M ∥ quid] quod V^M ∥ **33** lasciue ita *tr.* V^M ∥ lasciue] : -uie F ∥ ita *om.* F ∥ admodum] ad modo F ∥ **34** et . . . poetam *om.* V^L ∥ poetam adhuc *tr.* β ∥ neminem uidi *prae* neminem audiui TV^B ∥ **34–35** quin uerborum . . . fuerit $V^B S^a$: quin in uerborum aut sententiarum saltem lasciuia non fuerit B^A : qui uiorum aut rerum lasciuia saltem fuerit F : quin uerborum aut rerum saltem . . . fuerit γ : qui uerborum saltem aut rerum lasciuia fuerit V^M : qui in uerborum . . . fuerit *s.l. corr.* quin non uerborum . . . furerit T ∥ **35** non *om.* $B^A MS^a T$ ∥ **37** uerbis] uersibus V^L ∥ cum] quom TV^B ∥ **38** quamquam *om. cum lac.* V^L ∥ tenera] te uera F ∥ aetate fuerit *tr.* F ∥ **39** ubi et] et *om.* F ∥ **40** atque alii] aliique V^M ∥ **40–42** mihi sunt . . . et editionis $\alpha\beta S^a$: mihi sunt quam mihi ipsi. Et editionis V^L ∥ **41** Hermaphroditus] -tum M ∥ magis] maiori γ ∥ **41–42** quam mihi ipsi] *post* est M : mihi ipsi *tr.* F ∥ odio est *post* magis V^M ∥ **42** in primis *om.* V^M ∥ **43** non quod] non quia V^M ∥ ludendo] -da M ∥ deliquerim $MTV^B V^M S^a$: -rimus B^A : delin- FV^L ∥ sed quod] quod *om.* V^M ∥ **45** -uero *om.* F ∥ **46** modo *prae* vita $\beta\gamma$ ∥ cordi est $\alpha V^L V^M S^a$: cordiem F ∥ si αV^M ∥ **47** nequitia est $\beta B^A S^a$: est *om.* TV^B ∥ ac αS^a : et F

APPENDIX I
251

think you were the author of this slander, for — whoever he might be — he was definitely not a poet, but a verse writer; and not even a verse writer, but a syllable counter; and he attacked not only me but even my *Hermaphrodite*. And you well know on account of your erudition that the poetic art licenses us to indulge in jokes and witticisms, "for," as Catullus elegantly says, "it is fitting that the poet himself be chaste and pious; his little poems require nothing of the kind."[3] We have in our possession the *Priapeia*, an especially lascivious work, written by Virgil,[4] although the poet himself was called "Parthenias"[5] on account of the sobriety of his character. Now these witticisms even delighted Plato, a man endowed with the highest learning and equal sanctity, and when asked why he wrote so lasciviously, he is said to have responded: "Madness is characteristic of poets."[6] And generally, I have yet to see, hear, or read a poet who did not at least take delight in the wantonness of words or ideas: we have Martial, Catullus, Juvenal, and all who use coarser words when the subject demands it.[7]

2 Although this little work was composed in my tender years, when one jokes and sins with greater license, let me now admit the truth: my age, my character, and my studies are quite different. Nor does anyone hate *The Hermaphrodite* more than I. The author is disgusted and revolted by reading or circulating it, not because I erred in playing at that age, but because my present age instantly recoils from all lewdness and pleasure and demands severe habits and a severe manner of speaking. But of course, if life continues, I would like to purge that sin — if what all poets practice really is sin — by a certain severe

---

[3] Catullus 16.5–6.
[4] See *Philippic* §33 n. 77 and *Apology* §30 n. 96.
[5] The appellation *Parthenias* (meaning "The Maiden" or "The Virgin") comes from Servius *On Virgil's Aeneid* (*Praef.*) but was repeated by Ausonius *Idyllia* (13 finis).
[6] Plato *Phaedrus* 245a.
[7] Cf. Cicero *On Divination* 1.37.80.

quodam orationis stilo, non sine summa et sempiterna fortassis
optimi maximi nostri Principis laude ac gloria, ut si quis deinceps sit
50   qui mihi meisque Musis inuideat, non mihi, quippe qui inuidia
nescio quo pacto carere non possim, sed domino nostro Caesari
inuidisse se intellegat. Mihi quidem sublaudari licet, quod undequaque sim liuore circumuentus. Et profecto res male se habet cum
⟨ali⟩quis sine inuidia poetam euasisse sibi persuadet. Vergilium ipsum
55   nostrorum facile principem ob aemulos atque obtrectatores, genus
hominum perditissimum, urbe Roma semel atque iterum decessisse
et Caietae se continuisse traditum est: *uerum eo magis Maecenati suo
gratus atque iocundus,*

quo poetam sciret liuore non carere.

60   Argumentum quidem praestantiae est inuidia et immortalitatis
coniectura. Omittam hoc loco poetas ceteros, nam Homerum deum
illum poetarum, Terentium, Nasonem atque omnes egregios poetas
quis nescit liuoris dente sepenumero dilaniatos? Sane Musarum
comes inuidia.

65   **3** Sed ad te reuertor, sanctissime sacerdos, qui si ut perhibetur
tute es qui turpes atque obscenos illos in me uersus nuper edideris,
quid est, quaeso, quod a spurcissimis uerbis ne tu quidem absti-
nueris, non quidem adulescens sed grandior natu, non profanus sed
religiosus, non ludendi animo sed iniquitate adductus? Non possum
70   non illud Iuuenalis exclamare:

En animum et mentem cum qua dii nocte loquuntur.

4 Rursum cum a nostro sapientissimo Duce tibi iamdudum
iniunctum esset ut Lucanum in linguam maternam conuerteres, in
quo maiorum suorum industriam, solertiam, fortitudinem legeret,
75   probaret, imitaretur, tu Suetonium Tranquillum traducere maluisti,
ubi adulteria, stupra, incestus, et alia huiusmodi plerumque leguntur, ut si qua insit rosa, sine urtica tum legi non queat: rem profecto

---

48 quodam αS^a : quoddam F ∥ stilo βS^a : filo α ∥ non] sed non V^M ∥ **49** maximi $B^A F S^a$: -mo V^B ∥ ac αS^a : et F ∥ **51** possim $B^A F T S^a$: -sum V^B ∥ domino $F T S^a$: diuo $B^A V^B$ ∥ **52** sublaudari αF : subblandiri S^a ∥ quod $V^B S^a T$: qui $B^A F$ ∥ quod undequaquam] quod in nequaqam *s.l. corr.* T ∥ **53** res male *tr.* F ∥ cum *om.* F ∥ **54** aliquis *scripsi* : quis αS^a : quem F ∥ **56** fuerunt *post* decessisse $\beta\gamma$ ∥ **57** continuisse αS^a : -tulisse F ∥ **59** poetam $F V^B S^a$: poeta $B^A T$ ∥ sciret $V^B S^a$: sciuit F : *om. cum lac.* T : *om. cum. lac. et nota in marg.* "f. 'nouit' seu quidam simile" B^A ∥ **60** quidem αS^a : quid enim F ∥ **61** deum illum αS^a : istum deum F ∥ **63** nescit αS^a : nesciat F ∥ **64** comes $B^A F S^a$: -mis $T V^B$ ∥ **65** perhibetur $F V^B S^a$: -bent $T B^A$ ∥ **66** es qui αS^a : es qua F ∥ illos *om.* αS^a ∥ **67** quidem αS^a : -dam F ∥ abstin- αS^a : obtin- F ∥ **68** non quidem] num *corr.* non T ∥ **69** adductus $B^A T F S^a$: ductus V^B ∥ **70** non *prae* exclamare $\beta\gamma$ ∥ **71** En F : Heus S^a : Heu α ∥ dii nocte αS^a : die noctuque F ∥ loquun- αS^a : loquan- F ∥ **72** nostro sapientissimo *tr.* F ∥ **75** imitaretur] admiraretur, *marg. suppl.* alias 'imitaretur' T ∥ **77** ut $F S^a$: et α ∥ tum $F T V^B S^a$: tamen B^A

and grave style of oration. This can perhaps be done while bringing the highest, eternal praise and glory to our best and greatest of princes, so that if anyone thereafter envies me and my Muse, let him understand that he has envied not me, inasmuch as I could not escape envy anyhow, but our lord Caesar.[8] I may be allowed to receive some slight praise, since I am surrounded on every side by malice. And there is something wrong when a person convinces himself that he can become a poet without incurring envy. We read that Virgil himself, the greatest poet by far, withdrew several times from the city of Rome and confined himself to Gaeta on account of his rivals and detractors, who were a most depraved class of men. "Yet he was made all the more welcome and delightful to his friend Maecenas by the knowledge that the poet could not avoid malice."[9] Indeed, the proof of excellence is envy and the prospect of immortality. Let me omit in this place the other poets, for who does not know that the fangs of malice often tore to shreds Homer, that god among poets, as well as Terence, Ovid, and all the great poets? Envy is clearly a companion of the Muses.

3 But I return to you, most saintly priest. Now if you yourself are, as is said, the one who recently produced that foul and obscene poem against me, why is it, I ask, that not even you have abstained from filthy words? You are no youth but an adult, not a layman but in a religious order, not led by a spirit of play but by hostility. I am obliged to repeat that statement of Juvenal: "Look at the heart and mind the gods talk to at night!"[10]

4 Furthermore, some time ago our most wise Duke[11] bid you translate Lucan into our mother tongue, in whose work the Duke might read, approve, and imitate his ancestors' industry, ingenuity, and strength. But you preferred to translate Suetonius,[12] in whose work one reads about adulteries, illicit sexual acts, incest, and many other such things, so that if there is some rose therein, it cannot be

---

[8] That is, Sigismund, Holy Roman Emperor (see *Philippic* §175 n. 508).

[9] Cf. Panormita (VIII.1429) to Cambio Zambeccari (Sabbadini 1910a, 99–100): *Mihi certe ut debui gratulatus sum et Musis meis, quae non adeo minutae sunt aut obscurae ut invidia omnino careant: invidia argumentum praestantiae est. Virgilius deus ille poetarum urbe Roma non semel Caietam decessit et ad Calabros, fugatus scilicet invidia pessimorum hominum, verum eo magis principibus uiris dilectus et admirabilis, quo minus persecutione et aemulatione careret; Homerum quoque, Nasonem ceterosque poetas egregios quis nesciat plurimum laceratos extitisse?*

[10] Juvenal 6.531.

[11] That is, Filippo Maria Visconti (see Introduction 8–10 and 15–17 above).

[12] See Introduction n. 52 above.

neque diui Francisci professione qua obstringeris neque nostri Principis lectione dignam.

80 **5** Amplius cum haec ad te scripsissem ab Antonio Cremona, uiro officiosissimo, mihi renuntiatum est quosdam nescio quos in te uersus nuperrime descriptos teque me proculdubio auctorem existimare; ea, ut arbitror, ratione quia tua mens in quem deliquerit laboret opus est. Ceterum satis adhuc non gnosti *musas Sicelidas*,
85 quae *paulo maiora* canere solent et aperto quidem, non furtim non clam, more latronum atque proditorum. Si quando autem gratias tibi relaturus ero, nihil me hercle addubitabo tibi bellum indicere atque aliquid aduersum te scribere quod ex officina mea et ex Sicilia illa poetarum matre profectum nemo ambigat, nemo nesciat. Illud
90 mihi satis abunde est maledicentiae causam dedisse. Sed ut epistulae finem faciam, quod clarissima multorum uoce tum uel maxima a consacerdotibus tuis audio, te scilicet illius impudentiae auctorem extitisse; id a te potius accipere concupisco. Tu, fare ingenue. Fare apertius, ut quid ipse facturus sim aliquando deliberem. Ea quidem
95 mihi natura est: neminem offendo *nisi lacessitus iniuria*. Vale.

78 neque α*F* : nec *S*ᵃ ‖ obstrin- α*S*ᵃ : astrin- *F* ‖ **80–81** ab Antonio . . . officiosissimo *om.* α*S*ᵃ ‖ **83** quia α*F* : quod *S*ᵃ ‖ deli- α*S*ᵃ : delin- *F* ‖ **84** satis adhuc *tr.* *F* ‖ **85** solent α*S*ᵃ : consueuerunt *F* ‖ **86** clam more α*S*ᵃ : damnare *F* ‖ **87** hercle *Bᴬ TF* : hercule *V ᴮ S*ᵃ ‖ tibi bellum indicere α*S*ᵃ : te bellum tibi publiciter indicere *F* ‖ **89** nemo ambigat *bis V ᴮ* ‖ **91** maxima *FTV ᴮ S*ᵃ : -me *Bᴬ* ‖ **92** con- *om. F* ‖ scilicet *BᴬFS*ᵃ*T* : si- *V ᴮ* ‖ impudentiae *FS*ᵃ : implicen- α ‖ **94** quid α*S*ᵃ : quod *F*

picked without a thorn. Your decision was unworthy of the profession of St. Francis which binds you and unworthy of our prince's reading.

5 After I had written these things to you more fully, Antonio Cremona, a most responsible man, reported to me that some poetry had been recently written against you and that you doubtlessly thought me the author,[13] for the reason, I suppose, that your mind must struggle against one whom it had maligned. At any rate, you have until now scarcely known "the Sicilian Muses," who are accustomed "to sing somewhat greater things"[14] and indeed publicly, not furtively or secretly like robbers or traitors. So if some day I return your favor, I will not hesitate, by god, to declare war on you and to write something against you that no one could doubt or mistake originated from my workshop and from Sicily, that mother of poets. I am quite content if I gave you cause to slander me. But to close this letter, I hear the clear voice of many people, and the loudest voices are your fellow priests, saying that you were obviously the author of that impudence. But I long to hear this from you instead. Speak candidly, then. Speak openly so that I may plan what I shall do. Indeed, this is my nature: I attack no one "unless provoked by an injury."[15] Farewell.

---

[13]See Introduction 29 above; and Sabbadini 1910a, 90–91, 99–100.
[14]Virgil *Eclogue* 4.1.
[15]Cicero *On Duties* 1.7.20.

APPENDIX II

Antonius Panormita ad Antonium Raudensem

⟨1432⟩

F = Frankfurt am Main, Stadt- und Universitäts-Bibliothek, MS Lat. oct. 136, s. XV (93r)
M = Milan: Biblioteca Ambrosiana, MS H 49 inf., s. XV (140r)
V = Vatican City: Biblioteca Apostolica Vaticana, MS Vat. lat. 3371, s. XV (3v–4r), Autograph: *Liber Bibliothecae Fului Ursini scriptus manu Antoni⟨i⟩ Panormitae.*
B^e = Beccadelli 1746.

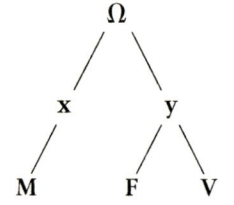

$$\begin{array}{c} \Omega \\ \diagup \quad \diagdown \\ x \qquad y \\ \diagup \quad \diagup \,\diagdown \\ M \quad F \quad V \end{array}$$

Antonius Panormita domino Antonio theologo salutem plurimam dicit.

  Litteras a te proxime accepi quibus ut una conueniamus hortaris gratia beneuolentiae inter nos redintegrandae. Id ego et laudo et
5 iuxta tecum concupisco. Sum profecto qui cuicumque et tibi maxime gratificari uelim. Neque id ipsum quod in praesentia efflagitas per me stetit antehac quo minus fieret, ut tu nosti, nec sane stabit. Rursum petis ut interim ab inuectiuis abstineam. Idque etiam tibi adsentior et calamum frango. Tu modo perstes in proposito. Ego quidem a diis
10 immortalibus nihil uehementius peto quam pacem atque animi tranquillitatem. Ex Ferruffino et Catone iurisconsultis salue et uale.

---

1 Antonius ... dicit *M* : Antonius Panormita salutem plurimam dicit Antonio theologo *F* : Antonius Panormita Antonio theologo salutem dicit *V* || **3** ut] et *F* || **4** redintegrandae *scripsi* : reintegrandae *FMB^e* : reintregan- *V* || **5** iuxta] iusta *F* || **6** non *s.l. suppl. sed in ras. post* me *V* || **7** nec sane stabit *om. yB^e* || **9** in *om. M* || **11** ex] a *B^e*

[256]

Antonio Panormita to Antonio da Rho

⟨1432⟩

Antonio Panormita sends greetings to Antonio da Rho, Theologian.

I just now received a letter from you in which you urge that we get together for the purpose of restoring goodwill between us. I also praise and desire this as much as you do. I am certainly one who wishes to accommodate anyone whatever and particularly you. And I did not prevent this very thing that you now ask from having been done earlier, as you know, nor in fact will I prevent it. You ask in addition that I meanwhile abstain from invectives, and to this even now I agree with you and break my pen. Just remain firm in your intention. I certainly seek nothing more strenuously from the immortal gods than peace and tranquility of mind. Greetings from the jurists Ferruffino and Catone, and goodbye.

APPENDIX III

"Anonymous Invective"
⟨Antonius Raudensis ad Antonium Panormitam⟩
⟨1429/30⟩

A = Milan: Biblioteca Ambrosiana, MS H 49 inf., s. XV, ff. 181r–183v.
S^a = Sabbadini 1910a, 32–34 (selections).

1 [181r] Etsi nonnullos miraturos scio me contra sceleratorum uirorum nequitiam atque singularem pertinatiam pro uero religionis et fidei cultu insultum fecisse, eo tamen sum animo ut breuiorem multo uitam mihi putarim nisi contumeliis et obiurgiis in profligatos
5   ac sceleratos insurrexerim qui longius ac par esset ab hominum conuictu uiuendique norma abierint. Pluris enim existimaui honestissimorum uirorum parti fauere quam perditorum intemperantiae opitulari, sanctiusque esse duxi a claris et spectatis uiris minime aut parum laudari quam a flagitiosis laudem integram consequi.
10   Intelligens profecto uiri boni me potius iusta querella quam dicendi inani gloria esse commotum, ad perditissimorum quippe hominum audacias, paribus studiis animis uoluntatibusque omnes pudici, si qui sunt, qui edepol perpauci sunt, oratione adduci deberent, ut eorum temeritatem opprimerent. Afferrent hercle aetati ac naturae eam
15   castimoniam ut improbi sibi aliquando ab huiuscemodi lenociniis temperarent conseruandaeque uitae et pudicitiae modum stabilirent. Eo essent ingenio infantes ut eorum nata cum moribus uita putaretur, quae tantum grauitatis, ne quidem splendoris dixerim adolescentibus, compararet, ut quodammodo deorum immortalium
20   sibi effigiem accomodauisse crederentur. Laudatur equidem omnium iudicio uerecundia, honestas, ipsa prae ceteris castimonia, quae ab impurissimis et ipsis (ut fortius dixerim) lenonibus corrumpitur, non pueros solum sed adultos ad brutorum officia pelliciunt, putantque sibi maiorem in modum laudi ascribi dum se illius infestae obsceni-
25   tatis artifices egregios praebuerint. Et qui huiuscemodi sunt, degunt sane animantium irrationabilium uitam, nihilque inter asinos et ipsos

18 splen-] l *s.l. suppl.* A

interest. Est enim asinorum uiuere, potare, luxuriari, et quo ferat eos impetus repente accurrere solum quae praesentia sunt; metiuntur non praeterita, non futura, sed quae ante pedes et ob oculos uersan-
30 tur. Sordida sane et foetida eorum natura est, quae minus ad bene beateque uiuendum quam dei immortalis cultus optaret. Prospicit insuper sacrilegiis, fututionibus, et huiusmodi ceteris polluitur.

2 Erit igitur mihi tecum, Antoni Panormita, disciplinarum tuarum atque morum concertatio, qui in tanto uirorum consortio
35 princeps haberis. Temeritatis itaque tuae mendas euoluam. Poetam enim quadam laudationis ambitione per uersus te praedicas, et ea gratia honorem [181v] desideras tamquam Maronis aut Homeri animus corpus tuum subisset, ut Pythagoricorum exigit opinio. Sed quae tua est poesis? quae cithara? quod metrum? Nam quod me
40 maxima animi admiratione mouet non tacebo: opus illud tuum in apertum adducam, quod posteritati mandare uoluisti quasi morum tuorum primitias, ut si omni menda florerent, eos a turpissimis et inhonestis officiis reuocares. In eo tanta est honestas, tantus cultus, tanta grauitas, ut se ceteris antiquorum philosophorum libris longe
45 dissimilem ostendat. Hermaphroditus is inscribitur libellus, qui non in tui mediocrem infamiam aliquando reuertetur. Insunt enim ea morum praecepta ut quemlibet censorium Catonem, sic sermonis gratia dixerim, omni intemperantia, omni libidine, omni denique obscena uolupate ad quoduis maleficium impellant. Et ut aliquando
50 ad tuam impudentiam orationem meam conuertam, ea libello tuo inseruisti, quae Phormionem Terentianum lenociniorum ac scortationum principem obstupescere cogant. Admones imprimis mulieres, ut libidinum suarum intemperantem lasciuiam pruritum non compescant aut arctant, sed omni lasciuia, dedecore, ac turpitu-
55 dine in quouis delectationis genere refocillent, et intensis neruis exacuant. Haec tua est ratio; haec tua sunt uerba:

Cum mea uult futui superincubat Vrsa Priapo.

Et huius generis reliqua, haec ex media philosophia, ex ethicorum uolumine proficiscuntur.

60 **3** Quis enim tam agrestis et incultus? quis tam hebes uino lapideus erit qui se maximum uitae fructum cepisse non putet? Quae uero tam immemor posteritas erit? Quae praeceptis tuis se maxime non efferat? Quae tam ingratae urbes reperientur? Quae te singulari caritatis pietate non prosequantur? Aliud de te referam, quod
65 mecum tacitus non admirari non possum. Cum deuoratis fortunis, dilapidato patrimonio, et uxoris dote absumpta et perdita, Italiam

---

57 Pan. *Herm.* 1.5.1

32 fututi- *scripsi* : futuati- *A* ‖ **56** exacuant *scripsi* : exacruant *A*

tibi ad hospitium paraueris, immo paene exul confugeris, ut inde laudem deportares.

4 Sed quas laudes quaeso? An eas quas uersiculis tuis Raudensem grauiter criminando nactus es, quo famam ac nomen tuum dissipares? Nam si te turpis iactantiae et inanis gloriae uoluptas afficit, non eo pacto id molliri debueras aliorum infamia et scelerato dedecore.

5 Parua quaeror, Antoni, ingrauescit [182r] late hoc tuum uulnus tibi sacrificia tamquam Ioui optimo maximaque decerni uis in tumulo illo ornatissimo. Sacerdotes lautos ac splendidos medius fidius e uia aduocas, claudos scilicet qui ephebos tamquam uictimas ad expianda sacra deducant, quibus ea quae superiore illa tua aetate, cum maxima ignominia perpessus es, ephebis libere educatis et sine malitia afferas.

6 Video pro partis tuae defensione quid mihi obiicias: "Bonum id mihi uisum est (at sum deceptus), falluntur quippe homines humanarum rerum specie. Nonnullis enim subiacent quae forte honestatis specie ipsos inuite detrimenta alliciunt ac incommoda prouehunt." Itaque si hoc rerum intuitu deceptus es, magis uitio quam ueniae dandum puto. Ea quae crassa et supina est excusatio, praesertim apud eum qui in philosophorum grege enumerari uelit. "Non possum ⟨ferre⟩," dicis, "hos mores." O portentum dell⟨. . .⟩! Nullus potest locus his uulneribus reperiri, qui pruritum hunc amoris florentem penitus eradicet. Parendum est uolupati. Nero pueris est abusus; formosum sane tenuit puerum Sporum et pro uxore moechabatur. Fecerat homo sane tui ordinis testiculos abscidi; illum secum uolebat apparatu muliebri ornatum et coma calamistrata, uestibus splendidissimis et gemmis pretiosis. Ea tu forte de re commotus puerum tecum adducis non illepidum, qui si pareret, Venerem ipsam pareret, tantae predicantur formae. Id tu non inficiaris qui illum genere tuo metrico Dianae adaequasti. Notasti oculorum lumina manus et cetera quae ad formae condecentiam spectant. Illum singulari sua uirtute tibi deuinxisti, immo spurcitie inaudita.

7 Sed quid est quod homines de flagitiis tuis dubitent? Cedo. Nonne librorum uolumina ob tanta scelera conflare, si quis omnia quae ab incunabulis per te patrata dicuntur ordine a me exigeret? Quem tandem heus tu, Bauco, his tuis sceleribus usurpabis finem? Quem tandem libidinis tuae modum statues? Verum ad id me referam quod Senis urbe iam effecisti, cum labiis puerilibus morsum dentibus affixeris, tanta erat tua libido, tanta nequitia, tanta erat intemperantia, tantus erat Veneris furor, ut a sordidissima et immunda Venere te non cohiberes. Taceo facta impudica quae sine

---

88–92 cf. Suetonius *Nero* 28

68 deportares] de- *s.l. suppl.* A ‖ **76** ephebos tamquam] ᵇtamquam ᵃephebos *corr.* A ‖ **81** nonnullis : -nullus *corr.* -nullis A ‖ **86** dell . . . *lacuna* A ‖ **105** *prae* intemperantia, nequitia *in ras.* A

nefario scelere explicari non possunt. Praetereo dicta [182v] turpiter, excogitata impudenter.

8 O dii immortales! Quos hic coendi modos litteris spurco et immundo codiculo descripsit? Quam uelem Octauiani temporibus tua te genitrix in lucem produxisset, ut hos tuos mores prestabat dicere amores uersiculis illis depingeres! Nonne tuis laudibus esses ornatus? An ea Octauianum passum tibi persuades cum Publii Nasonis opusculum de amore ornate, dilucide, ac eleganter descriptum in exilium proscripserit, aeque Nasonem auctorem tamen omnia caute, callide, astuteque dicta conspicimus? Itaque non ea putent homines esse uana ad quae te testem aduoco sarmenta. Paleas ignem Vulcanum ipsum tibi parari iussisset, ut benemeritum expurgares supplicium. Non ob hoc excusationem tuam recipio, cum putrida illa tua uox hanc affert rationem. Fecit idem grandis ille Nero, doctus fortasse disciplinis illis Propertii atque Tibulli tui. Idem Achilles in maiorem cineres, ut ais, fecit undique uiros abiectos ad tui laudem explicas.

9 Plura enim scelera mihi pertractanda erunt, si minimam tantum particulam inchoauero. Remoratur me quippe temporis angustia scelera tua haec explicare quae ego sine magno detrimento in medium afferri non possum. Ad tui tamen similitudinem Nasonem, poetam clarissimum, adduxerim, qui ob libellum illum tandem mortem est perpessus. Et si praeclara ediderit opera quae ipsum cuncto terrarum orbi uatem insignem testantur, quis dubitat quin ei uitam propter libelli nonnulla absurde dicta abstulerit Octauianus? Interceptus est in reditu a diis ipsis, ut aiunt, quid hoc est aliud quam quod ille secum Octauiani edicto mortem extulit, sed hunc omitto. Non Cicero idem, non diuini ingenii Aristoteles, non ceteri quos suis bene gestis memoria tenemus haec descripserunt. Fortasse id Virgilium commisisse testaberis; Priapeiam mihi testem adhibebis. Non ex ea re efficies, ut Maronem tantae calumniae auctorem extitisse profitear, quippe qui tanta uixerit pudicitia, ut uirgo a nonnullis publice sit appellatus.

10 Sed sic esto. Nonne ea quae per aetatem fecit a turpi et immunda materia ad illustre et singulare opus reuocauit, seque ab omni turpitudine [183r] expurgatum iri uoluit, quod nec in re quicquam numquam auditum fuit? Aliud magis et magis de te referam eo pacto ut si sibi de te homines persuaserint, id quod de Marone uetustas conceperat, obscenorum et flagitiosorum dictorum materiam nulla inobscurabit obliuio. Longe enim ab his sceleribus fuisse Maronem nemo non dubitabit; de te multo ampliora excogitabunt. Testem habebunt libellum tuum in quo uitam et mores tuos abunde

---

114 ac] *s.l. suppl. A* ‖ 140 nonne ea] *prae* ea, a *in ras. A* ‖ 143 magis et magis *scripsi* : maius et maius *A*

cognoscent. Quis leno tam importunus? quis tam sacrilegus? quis denique tam abiectus? non solum ea dicere uerum excogitare auderet, quae tu, tam laeto animo, tam illari fronte, litteris prodere enixus es, ut tuorum recte factorum monimenta extarent?

11 Horresco ea numerare quae tu de neruorum erectione eloquutus es. An honestum id tibi uisum est, cum haec et alia diceres?

Qui uult posse, suum digitos intrudat in anum;
Sic perhibent Helenae concubuisse Parim?

Sunt et alia saepenumero quae de mentula in medium attulisti.

12 Audi, quaeso, ridiculum et ea maturius euolue, quod si egeris, non dubito quin eo te iure natum memineris, ut tibi ipsi potius displiceas, quam haec quae ipse feceris probari. Natus es equidem omnium iudicio ad perpetuam et sempiternam tui ac tuorum infamiam. Ex qua re non inconuenienter a maioribus nostris hoc natum uidetur esse prouerbium: omnes insulares malos, Siculos uero pessimos — nulla in eis fides, nulla sanctitas, nulla religio, fidifragi, intemperantes, impudici. Quid ad haec mala deterius?

13 Est insuper aliud quod silentio praeterire non possum ac deo immortali accumulatas refero, gratias ob illud beneficium quod multis annis haec nostra Gallia Cisalpina consequuta est. Noluit enim natura optima omnium Italorum parens, Italos uiros sanctissimos iisdem criminibus esse damnatos, quibus et tota Sicilia infecta est. Abdicauit enim illos longe a nobis ne tanti sceleris et tam infesti illorum impudicitia ac intemperantia accusaremur. Interposuit equidem mare, quod cunctam Siciliam ab omni Italia, quae olim illi contines erat, remouet. Gratis igitur naturae ac deo immortali, qui, ut illa menda libidinis expertes essemus, nos seiunctos locorum intercapedine curarunt.

14 Sed uenio ad ephebiam quam te Papie construxisse referunt, in qua omnes scurrae, omnes [183v] libidinosi, omnes denique improbi concurrunt. Magno quidem uiri mali nomine et honore te extollunt et laudant et complexibus tenent, tecum stant ut scelera patrare possint tamquam a magistro disciplinam exposcunt. Nihil eis dulce nisi quam cum Siculo, uerum (ut melius dixerim) Suculo manere.

15 Est aliud, O scelerum sentina, orationis tuae caput, quod me non mediocri dolore cogit, de Guarino uiro praestantissimo cum illum testem ad haec scelera prouocas in illa parte epistolae suae cum diuum Hieronymum tibi utpote exemplum proponit. Sed ut paucis te expediam, aliquis iniusta aliquando iuste operatur, ut

---

155–56 Pan. *Herm.* 1.22.3–4 ‖ **163–65** cf. Petrus Blesensis *Ep.* 46

155 intrudat *Pan.* : intendat *A* ‖ anum *Pan.* : annum *A* ‖ **161** ac] et *in ras.*, ac *s.l. suppl. A* ‖ **185** cogit : coquit *coniec.* S*ᵃ*

diuus Hieronymus correctionis causa saepenumero effecit. Litteras
190 recomendatitias a Gasparino Bergomensi optasti ac non impetrasti. Si qui uero illas tibi obsignarunt, te ex illis extorsisse, et uirtute non habuisse animo tuo concipe. Non Leonardus Aretinus, non Raudensis, non Centius Romanus haec tua laudarunt, immo ut aliquid egregium referam, eorum conspectum fugitas.
195 **16** Omitto conspectum sed patriam tuam, in qua natus es, adire reformidas. Audire quaeso quem sibi errorem falsae opinionis temerarius iste sibi persuadeat. In Siciliam proficisci non uult, propter gigantes montibus oppressos, qui ignem si quando sperauerint pro spiritu euomunt dicit hic adesse barathrum et ne uratur
200 si eo loci accesserit metuit. Audit enim miseros grauiter suppliciis exuri. Quid ergo facies? O minime gentium! Ignorasne illic domi tuae uiros petulantes qui haec nefandissima uitia commisserunt, auditos esse ab aliquibus Siculis, immo uisos in lacu foetidissima puerorum suorum uirilibus pendere, et dum latrinam turbidam ac
205 muscosam exire nituntur? Stercore emisso lenonum ac paediconum suorum faciem polluunt. Tu uero falso terrore moueris nec uitia tua emendas. Quare studii Papiensis te cancellarium dicis, pergratum id omnes habent boni, te poetam contemplantur, ut uirum perniciosum, sceleratum, libidinosum, impium audacem facinorosum,
210 impii uero et sanctum imitantur temperantem, innocentem, et modestum. Quae eius sit dignitas animaduertite: cancellarium se appellat non studii Papiensis sed lupanaris Florentini. Edidit opusculum suum in quo doctores egregie imitatur, quisi. . . .

---

189 causa *mg. suppl. A* || **193** Centius *corr. S^a* : Cientius *A* || **196** audire *coniec. S^a* : audite *A*

APPENDIX IV

Poetic Invectives

⟨1429–33⟩

(1)

B = Brescia: Biblioteca Civica Queriniana, MS A VII 7, s. XV, ff. 159r–160v.
C = Carpentras: Bibliothèque Municipale, MS 361, s. XV, ff. 141v–142r, [*ll*. 1–30].
F^1 = Florence: Biblioteca Laurenziana, MS Plut. 34, cod. 50, s. XV, ff. 108v–109v.
F^2 = Florence: Biblioteca Laurenziana, MS Gad. XCI sup. 43, s. XV, ff. 25r–26r.
F^3 = Florence: Biblioteca Riccardiana, MS 810, s. XV, ff. 13r–14r.
F^4 = Florence: Biblioteca Nazionale Centrale, MS Magl. VIII 1445, s. XV, ff. 287r–288v.
G = Gotha: Forschungsbibliothek, MS Chart. A 717, s. XV, ff. 22r–23v.
M^1 = Munich: Bayerische Staatsbibliothek, MS clm 78, s. XV, ff. 36v–37v.
M^2 = Munich: Bayerische Staatsbibliothek, MS Clm 4393, s. XV, f. 302r, [*ll*. 1–2].
R = Rome: Biblioteca Nazionale, MS Vitt. Eman. 1417 (1866249), s. XV, ff. 203v–205r.
T = Toledo: Biblioteca del Cabildo, MS 100.42, s. XV, ff. 203v–205v.
V^1 = Vatican City: Biblioteca Apostolica Vaticana, MS Vat. lat. 2858, s. XV, ff. 4v–6r.
V^2 = Vatican City: Biblioteca Apostolica Vaticana, MS Vat. lat. 2864, s. XV, ff. 25r–26v.
V^3 = Vatican City: Biblioteca Apostolica Vaticana, MS Barb. lat. 1990, s. XV, ff. 5r–6v.
V^4 = Venice: Biblioteca Nazionale Marciana, MS Lat. XII.179 [4026], s. XV, ff. 1r–2v.
W = Wolfenbüttel: Herzog August-Bibliothek, MS 10.9 Aug. 4to, s. XV, f. 18r, [*ll*. 1–2].

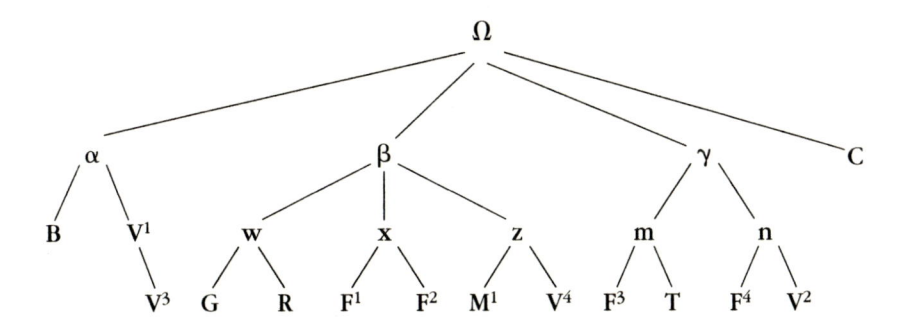

Meretrices Papienses ad Mediolanum
de laudibus Antonii Panormitae

    Plaudite, lenones, meretrices, plaudite: uester
        quam bene membrosus Hermaphroditus adest!
    Vt mulier clunes agitat, superincubat ut uir,
        arrigit et futuit, uult futuique simul.
5 Quam magnos culleos libret si scire cupido est,
        tam paruos dicam, quam gerit ipse caput.
    Et si quam grandem extendit sub pectine penem
        aut muli, aut asini forma uirilis erit,
    nec minor est cunnus quam sit sibi mentula, ut intro
10   late cum culleis ipse Priapus eat.
    Nec solum futuit uuluas, aut accipit inguen
        cunno, ast et teneros irrumat ipse mares.
    Tam bene paedicat puerum quod nulla marisca
        podice succrescit: tam bene trudit opus.

(1) Meretrices ... Panormitae α : Meretrices ... Panormitae poetae Siculi F^3 : Inuectiua in Panormitam Maffei Vegii F^4 : Inuectiua Maphei Vegii in Antonium Panormitam in Hermaphroditum poetam lasciuum V^4 : Inuectiua Maphei Vegii in Antonium Panormitam poetam laureatum Siculum quando intrauit Mediolanum futurus cancellarius. Contra Hermaphroditam [sic] poetam lasciuum inuectiua G : Inuectiua sacrae theologiae doctoris Hermaphroditum poetam lasciuum Antonium Panormitam M^1 : Inuectiua edita a sacrae theologiae doctore magistro Antonio Raudensi in Hermaphroditum poetam lasciuum F^2 : Inuectiua edita a sacrae theologiae doctore magistro Antonio Laudensis [sic] in Hermaphroditum poetam lasciuum R : In Antonium Siculum Panormitam Antonius Raudensis sacrae theologiae doctor inuectiua in poetam Hermaphroditum F^1 : Antonii Raudensis fratris Minorum carmen in Antonii Panormitae detractionem quod libellum Hermaphroditum componuisset. Titulus est Meretrices papienses ad Mediolanum salutem plurimam dicit. T : sine titulo CV^2
1 meretrices] -cum V^2 ‖ **4** arrigit] -gat V^2 : -puit G ‖ uult futuique simul] uultque simul futui n : ut corr. uult G : uultque corr. uult V^4 ‖ **5** quam] corr. V^2V^4 ‖ libret] libeat G : habeat n ‖ **6** tam paruos dicam] dicam tam paruos V^2 ‖ gerit] geris α ‖ **7** grandem]-de GM^1 ‖ extendit $wxnV^4$: extenderit corr. exciderit cum om. suppl. extendit M^1 : extendat αmC : ‖ **8** uirilis] corr. M^1 ‖ erit] corr. B ‖ **9** sibi] tibi G ‖ sit sibi tr. RV^2 ‖ ut intro om. G ‖ **10** late] date G ‖ cum] ad G ‖ ipse] late α ‖ eat] erat G ‖ **11** inguen] ignem z ‖ **12** cunno ... mares] sed teneros et iam irrimat ille mares V^2 ‖ cunno] cum non G ‖ teneros] teretes R ‖ ipse] ille V^2 ‖ **13** paedicat] corr. G ‖ puerum] -ris G : om. C ‖ quod] ut V^2 ‖ nulla] ulla G ‖ **14** succrescit] -cat GV^4

15 Non tamen id peragit faciat quin merda galerum
        cum retrahit penem Siculus iste suum!
    Ipse Panormita est qui se uelit esse poetam,
        qui femora et penes tam bene cantat ouans.
    Currite, lasciui iuuenes, puerique petulci,
20   et quae uis futui, curre puella, cito.
    Tollite! Iam nostras leges uitiauit et artes.
        Quid referam leges? Inficit omne solum.
    Moenia nostra secus serpit: qui uitreus olim
        amnis erat, maculis nunc scatet ipse nouis;
25 nec satis est toti sordes sparsisse Ticino,
        nunc urbem Anguigeram commaculare cupit.
    Tollite! Nec pigeat turba uenit ipsa pudica,
        nam paedicones scortaque sancta trahit;
    dic tales socios, qualem iam diximus illum:
30   sic merda est ano quam bene iuncta suo.
    O felicem urbem tantam, cui fortia facta
        deerat qui caneret! Plaude, poeta uenit.
    Non erat in tota calamum qui uerteret urbe:
        qui exornet proceres Hermaphroditus adest.
35 Tollite in urbe uirum, sed non Quiriti atque Iulitae
        in sacris procul hinc quisque profanus erit.
    Auspiciis mediis monstrum hoc auferte, neque aras
        polluat, et uestri sit mala stella ducis.
    Ipse lupis lenisque simul sua carmina ructet
40   et paediconum facta nefanda probet.

15 quin] *s.u. suppl. M*¹ : quando *G* : quid *F*⁴ ‖ galerum] *corr. F*³ : -rus *C* ‖ **16** cum] quom α ‖ retrahit αγ*R* : retrhait *C* : detrahit *xz* : trahit *G* ‖ Siculus α*mCGF*⁴ : Sicilis *xzRV*² ‖ **17** uelit] uult *V*² ‖ **18** tam] iam *xz* ‖ ouans] omnes *G* ‖ **21** tollite] tolle *F*⁴ ‖ iam] nam *V*² ‖ nostras] uo- *V*¹ : nostrasque *G* ‖ nostras leges *tr. V*² ‖ **22** omne solum] ipse solus *G* ‖ **24** amnis] annis *z* : omnis *x* ‖ maculis αγ*CRF*¹ : masculis *F*² : maribus *GV*⁴ : masculis *mg. corr.* maribus *M*¹ ‖ scatet] stupet *G* : stat aut *V*² ‖ ipse] ille α ‖ nouis] *corr. V*⁴ ‖ **25** toti] toto *C* ‖ sordes] maculas *CTV*² ‖ Ticino *corr. R* ‖ **26** Anguigeram] -rum α*xCF*³ : -rem *G* ‖ **27** pigeat] piget *F*² : pudeat *CF*¹ ‖ pigeat turba *tr. G* ‖ ipsa] ipse *nT* : ille *C* ‖ **28** sancta] multa *n* : pincta *C* ‖ trahit] trhait *C* ‖ **29** dic tales socios] talis turba sua est *V*² ‖ qualem] *mg. corr. M*¹ : quod *F*² ‖ **30** sic] sis *n* ‖ ano *wx* : anno *z* : uano *CF*³ : uanno α*V*² : animo *F*⁴ ‖ iuncta] cuncta *F*³ ‖ suo] sua α*m* ‖ **31** O *om. G* ‖ tantam] -ta α*T* : -tum *G* ‖ **32** deerat] *corr.* defuerat *G* ‖ qui *om. G* ‖ caneret] -rat *G* ‖ plaude] blande *G* ‖ **33** erat in tota] ᵇin tota ᵃerat *M*¹ ‖ uerteret *GF*³ : uolueret *xnCRTV*⁴ : uerteret *mg. corr.* uolueret *M*¹ : uolueret *corr.* uoluerat α ‖ urbe *corr. V*⁴ ‖ **34** qui exornet αγ*F*¹ : qui excitaret *RF*² : quique ornat *G* : quique *ornet V*⁴ : quique ornet *mg. corr. M*¹ ‖ **35** sed non γ*wM*¹ : *om. x* : si non α : sed *V*⁴ ‖ Quiriti αγ*R* : -tae *zF*¹ : -tes *F*² : quaerite *G* ‖ atque Iulitae *om. G* ‖ **35–40** Tollite . . . probet *hic* αγ : *post l. 42* β ‖ **36** in sacris procul hinc] sacris inde procul hinc *V*² : sacris inde procul *F*⁴ ‖ quisque] usque *x* : usque *mg. corr.* quisque *M*¹ ‖ erit] eat *F*⁴*V*⁴ : eat *corr.* erit, *mg. corr.* iterum eat *M*¹ ‖ **37** hi *post* mediis *CF*³ ‖ monstrum] -stri *G* ‖ hoc] *om. F*² : *mg. suppl. M*¹ ‖ auferte] deserte *mg. corr.* auferte *M*¹ : deserte *F*¹ : deferte *F*² : auertite *F*³ ‖ neque γ*BR* : nec β*GV*¹ ‖ aras] auras *V*¹ ‖ **38** polluat] persoluit *F*² ‖ **39** lupis] lupus α ‖ lenis-] leaenis- β ‖ ructet α*nRF*³ : ruptet *T* : uictes *corr.* mittet *M*¹ : mittat *GV*⁴ : uictes *F*¹ : uictet *F*² ‖ **40** nefanda] neganda *V*⁴

APPENDIX IV

        Tollite in urbe uirum qui non spectacula cernat
            principis Anguigeri proelia nonque iocos.
        Sint cunnis sua bella feris; sint bella Priapis
            et cum podicibus certet adusque uelit.
45   Inde locis meritis putridum deferte cadauer,
            membraque iam tumulo condite uiua suo.
        Collum quaeque suum meretrix supponat, et ante
            stent paedicones, lumina quisque ferat.
        Vrsa, Nichina, Helene plorent dulcisque Mathildis
50   defleat et mammis Clodia pulchra suis;
        dilanient crines Zaneta et Galla Pythoque,
            sed scindat uestes ebria semper Io.
        "Te nostrum sepelit," clament, "geniale lupanar;
            quam bene sic moreris, quam bene membra iacent."
55   Scripsimus et titulos sunt sculptaque uerba sepulchro,
            sic quisque ut mores possit habere suos.
        Infamis Siculus iacet hoc Antonius antro
            qui in Venerem et Bacchum spintria totus erat.
        Nunc se Vergilio, nunc sese aequabat Homero,
60   nec lac Pieridum, sed bibit ille merum.
        Hic cecinit cunnos, cecinit cum podice penes,
            paedico exsuperans atque futuator erat.
        Clauditur extrema nostra hac ex urbe cloaca,
            quam bene conueniens moribus ipse locus.

41 qui non spectacula] non qui iam spetacula G : non ut spectacula V^2 : ut spectacula F^4 ‖ cernat] cernet GM^1 : cernit x : cantet n ‖ **42** nonque $\alpha\gamma R$: namque βG ‖ **41–42** Tolite . . . iocos *hic* $\alpha\gamma$: *post l.* 34 β ‖ **43** sint cunnis sua αzmV^2 : sunt . . . sua G : sua . . . sua F^4 : sit . . . sua R : sua . . . sint F^1 : siue . . . sua F^2 ‖ sint bella] sua bella V^2 ‖ **44** podi-] paeli- G ‖ adusque] ubique F^2 ‖ uelit] -lint V^2 ‖ **45** locis] locum F^2 ‖ meritis] *s.u. suppl.* F^3 ‖ deferte] -ris V^2 ‖ **46** membra-] membram- B ‖ **47** collum quaeque suum αV^2 : collum quoque suum RF^4 : collumque suum F^3 : collumque suum *mg. corr.* collum atque suum M^1 : collum atque suum V^4 : atque suum collum G ‖ collum quae suis F^1 : collumque suis F^2 : collum quae meretrix T ‖ meretrix] meritis x ‖ supponat] -nit G ‖ **48** stent] stet R ‖ **49** Nichina] Mina z : Nimas G ‖ Mathildis] Matheldis Gz : Mathaldis V^2 ‖ **50** defleat . . . suis] Annaque Teutonico pictisque et Clodia mammis V^4 ‖ mammis] manibus GM^1 ‖ pulchra $\alpha\gamma R$: picta xGM^1 ‖ **51** Dilanient . . . Pythoque *om.* F^4 ‖ Zaneta] Ganeta B : Ianectaque V^2 : Gianetta *Pan.* ‖ Galla] -lo F^2 ‖ Pytho- $\alpha\gamma V^4$: Pitro- GF^1M^1 : patro- F^2 : picto- R ‖ **52** sed] et V^2 ‖ **53** nostrum $\alpha\gamma R$: monstrum $G\beta$ ‖ sepelit] -dit *corr.* -let M^1 ‖ clament] -mant G : -met V^2 ‖ lupanar *corr.* G ‖ **54** sic $\alpha\gamma RV^4$: sit GM^1 : *om.* x ‖ moreris αmF^1F^4R : morieris F^2 : moriens GV^2z ‖ iacent $\alpha\gamma R$: latent $G\beta$ ‖ **55** sunt] sint n : *om.* G ‖ sculpta- xmF^4 : scripta- αRV^2 : insculpta- GV^4 : inscripta- *corr.* insculpta- M^1 ‖ -que] *om.* RF^2T ‖ sepulchro] -ris G ‖ **56** sic quisque ut mores αm : sic quisque mores $G\beta$: haec ut quisque mores n : sic quisquis ut mores R ‖ **57** infamis] infi- G ‖ hoc] *corr.* M^1 ‖ **58** spintria] spuria R ‖ totus $\alpha\gamma R$: solus $G\beta$ ‖ **59–62** Nunc se . . . futuator erat. *mg. suppl.* T ‖ **59** Nunc] Hunc V^2 ‖ sese] se RV ‖ aequabat γwV^1V^4 : -bit xM^1 : adequabat B ‖ **60** nec] non V^2 ‖ ille] ipse wF^2TV^4 : iste V^2 ‖ **61** penes] penem RV^2 ‖ **62** paedico] -cus G ‖ exsuperans] exuberans V^2 ‖ atque] ac G ‖ futuator mGF^2 : fututor $\alpha znRF^1$ ‖ *prae* erat, id *in ras.* F^3 ‖ **63** ex $\alpha\gamma V^4$: in wx : in *corr.* ex M^1 ‖ cloaca] *corr.* G ‖ **64** *prae* locus, deus *in ras.* B

| 65 | Pro ture hic fumant meretricum stercora, sanguis
menstruus exundat perpetuoque fluit.
Huc coitus tandem manant centone retorto,
faex quoque bracarum contumulata sapit.
Non deerunt bombi ructus uomitusque lutosi,
| 70 | quae cacet aut meiat iam lupa semper erit.
Tolle ergo inferias, quae sint tibi sacra quotannis,
nec nasum obtures, androgynose, tuum.

(2)

M = Venice: Biblioteca Nazionale Marciana, MS Lat. XII 179 [4026], s. XV, f. 3r–v, [*ll*. 1–18].

Q = Brescia: Biblioteca Civica Queriniana, MS A VII 7, s. XV, ff. 160v–161v.

R = Florence: Biblioteca Riccardiana, MS 810, s. XV, ff. 14r–14v.

T = Milan: Biblioteca Trivulziana, MS 793, s. XV, ff. 12r–13r.

V[1] = Vatican City: Biblioteca Apostolica Vaticana, MS Vat. lat. 2858, s. XV, ff. 6r–7r.

V[2] = Vatican City: Biblioteca Apostolica Vaticana, MS Barb. lat. 1990, s. XV, ff. 6v–7v.

C[v] = Cinquini and Valentini 52–53.

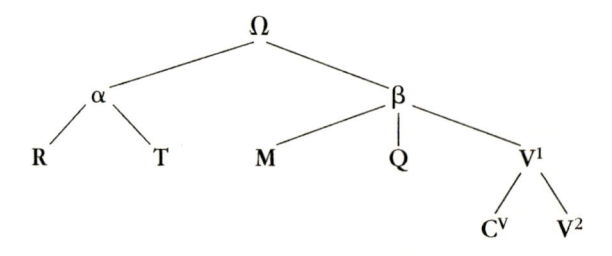

Epitaphium Antonii Panormitae

Insula, Scyllaeis contermina flatibus, undis
    clauditur Ioniis, nomine Trinacria,
terra Syracusis olim regnata tyrannis,
    luxuriae uetitae perfidiaeque ferax;

66 menstruus] *corr.* G || fluit] -at GV[2] || **67** huc] hic R || autem *prae* coitus V[2] || tandem *om.* V[2] || manant αγ : -nent Rβ : -nerent G || tandem manant] *tr.* Gz || **69** non] *corr.* M[1] || deerunt] desunt T : densunt V[2] || bombi *om. cum lac.* T || lutosi] fetentes n || **70** cacet] tacet T : cacat G || meiat] mingat Gz : inerat T || iam] hic n || **71** ergo] igitur T || quae] qui G || sint] sunt αF[1] || sacra] facere T || sacra quotannis] sacraque annis G || **72** obtures] obtines G || androgynose] -nosce F[4] : denrigynose T : cindrogynose V[2] : 'androgynosus' 'hermaphroditus' idem *mg. gl.* R || (2) Epitaphium ... Panormitae QV[1] : Epigramma ... Panormitae M : Vale ossa mea Panormita. Epitaphium impudentissimi et attritae frontis uiri, Antonii Panormitae, poetae Siculi R : Eulogium in sepulchro Antonii Panormitae T || **1** contermina] -nat M || **4** uetitae αβ : uitae *coniec.* C[v]

APPENDIX IV

5   Cyclopes utero saeuosque enixa gigantes
        et quicquid superest corpore feta mali,
    quam mare, ne sanctam posset peruertere terram,
        fluctibus immensis frangit ab Hesperia.
    Haec me foeda tulit tellus. Ego ab urbe Panormi
10   ortus et indignus nominis haud Siculi,
    Italicam colui terram, mensisque superbis
        pontificum assuetus, bracchus erilis eram,
    cumque sacerdotem colerem, mensasque torosque,
        indignos cecini religione sonos.
15 Nam ueterum insanus uatum mirator et ipse
        uates, me summis uatibus esse parem
    rebar. At atra Venus, patriae, moresque sinistri
        mentem traxerunt in scelus omne meam.
    Lemniades Thraciosque optans aequare poetas,
20   sentinam excolui carminibus Latiis.
    Vuluas et coleos, penes, culosque natesque
        stercoraque et merdam turpiter ore canens,
    ne foret intactum quicquam, sum uersibus ausus
        sacrilegis almi rumpere iura thori,
25 et Venerem in sanctam uocem uectare proteruam,
        dissuadere uiris legitimasque faces.
    Quoque fides dictis sceleratis altior esset,
        firmaui exemplo fetida dicta meo.
    Audax et petulans animo, moechusque, gulosus,
30   ipse fui iuuenis, prostibulumque domus
    et foedi comites scelerataque turba clientum,
        fama cuncta mihi cara fuere magis.
    Ah! Quanto melius me si genuisset Orestem
        natura aut asinum uel nihil ipse forem!
35 Humana effigie gestabam corpus, et intus
        humani generis pessimus hostis eram.
    Nomen terra meum nunc execratur, et ibit
        spiritus in Stygias non rediturus aquas,

---

7 mare ne sanctam posset QV^1R : mare nec sanctam posset M : deus ut sanctam nequeat T ‖ terram β : gentem α ‖ 8 frangit β : abscidit R : clausit T ‖ 9 haec αQ : nec MV^1 ‖ 10 nominis] -ne C^v ‖ haud] aut M ‖ 11 Italicam α : -liam β ‖ terram βR : gentem T ‖ 13 sacerdotem β : -tum α ‖ 14 sonos] sonos *alias* 'monos' Q ‖ 15–20 nam . . . Latiis *om.* T ‖ 15 uatum] *s.u. suppl.* R : *corr.* vates V^1 ‖ 17 at *corr.* M ‖ 18 traxerunt] *corr.* R ‖ 19 Lemniades αQ : Lam- V^1 : Sam- C^v ‖ 22 merdam βR : faeces T ‖ *prae* ore, ipse *in ras.* R ‖ 26 uiris] -ros *coniec.* C^v ‖ 27 quoque] cumque C^v ‖ 29 animo βR : iuuenis T ‖ 30 fui αQ : sui V^1 ‖ iuuenis βR : uiuens T ‖ prosti- β : prostri- α ‖ 31 foedi βR : ueri T ‖ turba β : dicta R : uerba T ‖ 32 fama βR : uita T ‖ 33 Ah Q : H^{b}a^a V^1 : Ha α ‖ me si βR : si me T ‖ Orestem β : agrestem α : Orestes C^v ‖ 34 natura *om.* C^v ‖ mater *post* asinum C^v ‖ 35 et β : at α ‖ 37 nomen terra βR : corpus terra *ut uid.* T ‖ nunc execratur et ibit] nuncque execratusque habebit C^v ‖ 38 spiritus] serpens C^v

aeternasque feram poenas pro talibus ausis
40   caelicolis meritum suppliciumque dabo.
Tu modo, posteritas, nostro lege carmina digna
    nomine, et exemplum sit mea uita tuum,
quam paruo aeternum liceat sibi quaerere nomen
    gentibus et taetro quis modus est sceleri.

(3)

B = Milan: Biblioteca Ambrosiana, MS B 124 sup., s. XV, f. 213v.
C = Milan: Biblioteca Ambrosiana, MS C 64 sup., s. XV, f. 159r.
P = Milan: Biblioteca Ambrosiana, MS P 4 sup., s. XV, f. 75v.
V^i = Vismara 1900b, 118.

Iohanna Francigena dei nuntia ad Mediolanenses qui ad eam mittere uolebant magistrum Antonium Raudensem per Antonium Panormitam ut creditur

Dicite io, Patres, quaenam haec sententia uestra est,
ecquis honos in me, turpe ad me mittere monstrum,
Raudensem et uere humana sub imagine monstrum?
An ne sacerdotem incestum me posse putatis
5 cernere, sitque mea dignum pietate loquellas
impuras audire et sceleri responsa referre?
Auertam certe uultum mox, daemone uiso,
daemone, quo nullus toto sceleratior Orco est.
Quo te, spurce, paras? Quo te colis, impie, frustra?
10 Non datur impuris faciem spectare dearum.
Vos tandem moneo, patres, hanc flectite mentem,
quaeque agitis sunto longe prospecta, quod hoc est,
me numquam oratori huic responsa daturam.
Non bene conueniunt pudor et scelus, agnus et hostis.

(4)

C = Milan: Biblioteca Ambrosiana, MS C 64 sup., s. XV, ff. 159r–160r.
B = Milan: Biblioteca Ambrosiana, MS B 124 sup., s. XV, ff. 142r–143r.
D = Naples: Biblioteca Nazionale, MS VI D 7, s. XV, f. 113v.
V^i = Vismara 1900b, 119.

---

40 caelicolis meritum βR : pro meritum superis T ǁ **43** sibi] tibi C^v ǁ nomen βT : regnum R ǁ (3) Iohanna ... creditur CV^i : Iohanna dei nuntia ad patres conscriptos urbis Mediolanensis PB ǁ **1** quaenam] quoniam *coniec.* V^i ǁ **2** ecquis BC : et quis P ǁ honos CP : honor B ǁ **5** mea B : *corr.* CP ǁ **7** uultum *coniec.* V^i : -tus BCP ǁ **8** toto] *marg. suppl.* P ǁ **13** oratori] hortari C ǁ daturam PV^i : -rum BC

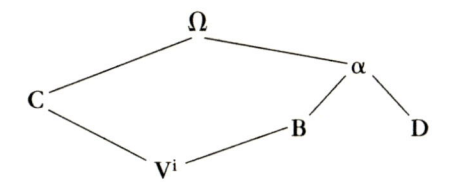

DEFENSIO PRO ⟨ANTONIO⟩ RAUDENSI AD PATRES CONSCRIPTOS CONTRA CALUMNIATOREM INCOGNITUM

Spurce, quid insanis? Quid, sus foedissime, grunnis?
Raudensis famam nomenque celebre putasne
carminibus lacerare tuis? Latratus in auras
non petit astra tuus, non caelum aut aethera tangit.
5   Inuide, Raudensem lanias; non sidera sursum
alta ferit tonitrus, non nimbus, dum cadit, amplos
immergit superos; fragor hic strepitusque per imas
ingreditur terras; sic diuas frangere mentes
uox tua spurca nequit, tumido quae sordet ab ore,
10 quae taetro in sancto garrit uitiata cerebro.
Scipio, si Laelius sapiens, si Cato seuerus
Raudensem insimulent, medicine non locus ullus
iam fuerit: uerbis uiuens morietur in ipsis.
At quis nunc, caput insanum, tua uerba timebit?
15 Cui uitium ridet, uirtus gemit; altius hinc te
nolo, putes, norim nec quo sub sidere natum
aut patria exortum, nec quae incunabula gentis;
ast te hominem nequam declarant uerba tumenti
ore relapsa tuo. Sapiens quis finxerit umquam
20 tot commenta simul? Sapiens uel uera tacebit.
Scis, spurce, officium linguae; per compita garrit,
perstrepit in triuiis, suadet falsissima, fingit
exaudita prius numquam maledicta; Iesum ipsum,
qui caelum terramque regit, dixere uoracem
25 quod biberet uini calices perfusus abunde,
sic meritis obiecta sibi, sic daemone functus.
Dicite io legem, Patres, decreta parate.
In caput hic plectendus erat, qui carmina falso
in populum sparsit. Sed quis iam incognita plectat?
30 Dicite io, Patres, lapides si impinxerit olim,

(4) Defensio . . . incognitum αV^i : Ad eosdem responsio Raudensis C ‖ 3 in αV^i : ad C ‖ 4 tuus corr. D ‖ 8 diuas αV^i : diuis C ‖ 10 sancto α : -tos CV^i ‖ 11 si αV^i : et C ‖ 13 uiuens αV^i : uirens C ‖ 14 caput insanum αV^i : insane caput C ‖ 19 relapsa CDV^i : re- s.u. suppl. B ‖ 23 maledicta αV^i : -dicto C ‖ 25 quod αC : quis V^i ‖ biberet α : -rat CV^i ‖ 26 meritis α : meretrix CV^i ‖ 27 legem patres αV^i : tr. C ‖ 28 carmina DV^i : -ne C : crimina B

non retrahat palmas, monstret digitosque manusque,
se in medium statuat, pugnam committat apertam
et genus et nomen et quae sint munia dicat
sub diuo, coramque aciem descendat in omnem;
35 Raudensem inuadat, uideat quo turbine telum
torqueat et clipeo quantus consurgat in hostem.
Praestiterit reuocare tamen linguamque manumque
quam ferat ipse, altum ueniens pro uulnere uulnus.
Tandem quando sibi facies incognita transit,
40 nec datur in ueras coram dirrumpere uoces,
hos teneat saltem monitus, quos mente reponat:
perlegat atque pedes numeret dum carmina cudit,
nec furor inuoluat metrum; super omnia caute
Vulcanum fugiat, Neptunum semper adoret.

(5)
Milan: Biblioteca Trivulziana, MS 793, s. XV, f. 10v.

IN ANTONIUM PANORMITAM
LAURENTIO VALLAE PETRUS CANDIDUS ⟨DECEMBRIUS⟩

Procerum pectis pueri tingisque capillum,
    uxoris solitus dilaniare comas.
Cur facis hoc, Bechatelle? Quod hic, non illa, sit uxor?
    Paedico speciem non mulieris habet.

(6)
Milan: Biblioteca Trivulziana, MS 793, s. XV, ff. 10v–11r.

IN ANTONIUM PANORMITAM ⟨PETRUS CANDIDUS DECEMBRIUS⟩

Censorem ueritus tonso, Bechatelle, puello,
    (censor enim rex est, tela parata tenens),
corda metu pulsante tamen mulieris amantem
    te facis exclamans: "Depereo pro iam!
5 Depereo pro iam!" Sed abest tibi pusio nusquam,
    pusio qui modo uir, qui modo fit mulier,
pusio, quem puerum dum credimus esse, puella est;
    pusio quem puerum credis puellus erit.
Et quis, io, nequam uel uir uel femina nescit,
10   quas potius partes e muliere petas?
Odit te, odit Hylam illa tuum: nam dispare eam
    femineum inuisum, odit uterque genus.

---

33 munia CDV^i : numina B ∥ **35** telum BCV^i : tellum D ∥ **39** quando] quoniam V^i ∥ **41** teneat BCV^i : tenat D ∥ **(5) 4** mulieris *sic MS, sed lapsu metri notat Fiaschi* ∥ **(6) 8** credis *coniec. Fiaschi* : crede *MS*

Vis non uis fieri haud mirum Bechatetulae adulter.
    Nec mas est tibi mas, nec mulier mulier.
15 Viderit Oedipus quis nescis esse maritus.
    Esse queas moechus an magis esse bechus.
Viderit hoc censor cui uis dare uerba, sed ille
    uerbera post gemina de ratione dabit.

(7)

Milan: Biblioteca Trivulziana, MS 793, s. XV, ff. 11r–12r.

In Antonium Panormitam
Fratri Antonio Raudensi Petrus Candidus ⟨Decembrius⟩

Plaudite! Conueniunt huc omni ex urbe poetae,
quisque cupit nostri scribere gesta ducis.
Vnus adest primum, qui se fert esse poetam.
Nemo, cum id dicat, praedicat ipse tamen
5 quae tua sit grauitas. Dic: qui te laudibus ornas?
De te igitur scribas et sine gesta ducis
iuris consultis te praefers omnibus. Heus tu?
Quam miser expendas quae tua scire putas.
Efferat in medium sua Commentaria, nuper
10 quae facit in Plautum, contribuitque sibi.
Aretine, tuam uenias defendere causam!
Vndique te lacerat perfidus iste quidem,
nec minus iste tuos lacerat, Guarine, labores,
et clamat Plautum nos didicisse male.
15 Non opus esse tuum uersus componere, Lusce,
personat huc illuc et maledicta tibi.
Extollit sese oris: cognoscite, Patres,
quam bene sit demens, ut uideatis eum,
quippe suos calces non est attinguere dignus,
20 neque suum certe soluere sandalium.
Designabit enim subitus uerissima finis.
Haec fore scripta sui cum dabit ad populum
dumque minatur adhuc opus istud nonque moratur,
terra tumens pariet, tu mihi crede, nihil.
25 Alter qui uoluit dignosci, Vergilio par,
hic secum ualeat sitque poeta simul.
Pullulat ecce alius Bibilo puer atque profecto
carminis iste sui dulcia furta timet.
Horum scit nullus quanti fuit esse poetam:
30 quae discunt pueri uir didicere satis.
Sic facilis gressus non est et ad astra uolatus

(7) **11** Aretine *corr.* MS

nondum cognominat clara poesis eos.
Arguit at si quis dictorum errata suorum
respondent: "Virtus non caret inuidia,
35 immo cupit summo nos omnis culmine haberi
si uos, quod nomen uultis habere, decet."
Sed bene cuique uno grauis est iactantia uestra
omnia cum uobis editis esse nota.
Ingenium sublime est et sine sorde patre
40 Aetheia illud nomen plus graue pendus habet.
Nec spectate dies uestros producere terra,
qua non sit qui uos multa docere queat.
Ingenii plures sunt, certe pollicieres,
quam uos et saperent dicere quae superi.
45 At maiora quidem conantur, tam grauiora,
uester quod numquam dicere quit animus.
Carmine quo uostro, id est tanta superbia, uobis
scitis nam modicis tingitis omne solum.
Si quid scriberis laturi iudicium sunt
50 arti uos uobis uomite quae placeant.
Vos alii laudent, se laudans stultus habetur.
Efficite ut uirtus uos ferat ad superos,
non deerunt laudes uirtuti, credite nobis.
Is ueniatus enim qui bene facta colit;
55 amodo si audebit quis se appellare poetam,
is natibus centum uerbera digna ferat.
Pergite uero caculis borea nos esse referri,
atque caput tumidum pascite turibulis.
Gloria uos societ fallax aliquando, ualete,
60 submersi uestris perptuo tenebris.

(8)

Paris: Bibliothèque Nationale, MS Lat. 8580, s. XV, ff. 46r.
Sabbadini and Barozzi 5.

Quos Rhodus ⟨i.e., Antonius Raudensis⟩ cellae frontispicio horum qui nunc extant loco inscriberet Antonius Panormita

Huc, agite, in nostra magna indulgentia cella est.
Soluitur a poena quaeque puella uenit.

(9)

F = Florence: Biblioteca Laurenziana, MS Ashb. 176, s. XV, f. 70v.
V = Vatican City: Biblioteca Apostolica Vaticana, MS Barb. lat. 2069, s. XV, f. 11v.

---

50 quae *corr. MS* ‖ **56** ferat *corr. MS* ‖ **57** uero *s.u. suppl. MS*

W = Wroclaw: Biblioteka Uniwersytecka, MS R 175, s. XV, f. 6v.
G^a = Gaspary 475–76.
N^a = Natale 22–23.
A^r = Arnaldi, Gualdo Rosa, and Monti Sabia 23–23.

In Invidos Antonius Panormita

Quid curem Rhodus quod nostra poemata culpet,
    si mea Maecenas carmina docte probas?
Quid curem quod me cimex Laurentius odit,
    si me Crottiades unus et alter amat?
5 Quid curem carpat uitam Cato Saccus Iacchus,
    si Ferrufino iudice uita proba est?
Quid curem quod me liuor sectetur ubique,
    si semper uirtus inuidiosa fuit?
Curandum placeas tantum doctisque bonisque:
10   summa quidem laus est, displicuisse malis.

(10)

F = Florence: Biblioteca Laurenziana, MS Ashb. 176, s. XV, f. 43r.
V = Vatican City: Biblioteca Apostolica Vaticana, MS Barb. lat. 2069, s. XV, f. 15v.
W = Wroclaw: Biblioteka Uniwersytecka, MS R 175, s. XV, f. 11r.
R^a = Ramorino 1889, 449.
A^r = Arnaldi, Gualdo Rosa, and Monti Sabia 26–27.
N^a = Natale 74.

In ⟨Laurentium⟩ Vallam Antonius Panormita

Carmina componis, Laurenti, stans pede in uno.
    Nil mirum si sic carmina facta cadunt.

(11)

F = Florence: Biblioteca Laurenziana, MS Ashb. 176, s. XV, f. 45v.
V = Vatican City: Biblioteca Apostolica Vaticana, MS Barb. lat. 2069, s. XV, f. 17r–v.
W = Wroclaw: Biblioteka Uniwersytecka, MS R 175, s. XV, f. 12v.
N^a = Natale 22.

Ad Maecenatem Antonius Panormita

Maecenas, quid te superi, quidue, Anguiger heros,
    respiciant? Quid te curia plebsque probent?

---

(9) **1** quod] qui N^a || **2** si mea] sie G^a || docte] docta F || probas] probat N^a || **3** quod] qui N^a || odit] adit N^a || **7** quod] qui N^a || (11) **1** quid FW : quod VN^a || quidue FW : quodue VN^a || **2** quid FW : quod VN^a

Rhodus id in fatis, non in uirtute, reponit.
    Verum id peruerse, ut cetera, Rhodus ait:
5 scilicet insigni carus pietate deis es,
    iustitia plebi, consilioque duci.
Si modo non cesset uirtus, nec numina cessant,
    sed sibi nec uirtus nota, nec ipse deus.

(12)

F = Florence: Biblioteca Laurenziana, MS Ashb. 176, s. XV, f. 54r.
V = Vatican City: Biblioteca Apostolica Vaticana, MS Barb. lat. 2069, s. XV, f. 24v.
W = Wroclaw: Biblioteka Uniwersytecka, MS R 175, s. XV, f. 18r.
N^a = Natale 22.

In Rhodum ⟨i.e., Antonium Raudensem⟩ Antonius Panormita

Thure pio Rhodus dum diuum numina poscit
    quae uis dicendi sorsque futura sibi est,
mira fides, templi uox e testudine missa est:
    non erit orator Rhodus, arator erit!

(13)

V = Vatican City: Biblioteca Apostolica Vaticana, MS Barb. lat. 2069, s. XV, f. 58v.
W = Wroclaw: Biblioteka Uniwersytecka, MS R 175, s. XV, f. 43r.
N^a = Natale 74.

Ad ⟨Laurentium⟩ Vallam Antonius Panormita

Pauca licet scribas, et his dumtaxat in anno:
    si modo non pereunt, carmina multa facis.
At si multa facis, quamuis sint milia centum,
    Valla, nihil scribis si peritura facis.

(14)

V = Vatican City: Biblioteca Apostolica Vaticana, MS Barb. lat. 2069, s. XV, f. 3v.
N^a = Natale 74.

Ad gaudentium ⟨i.e., Laurentium Vallam⟩ Antonius Panormita

Pallatius tibi dat Gaudenti, maxime rhetor,
    dimidium turtae dimidiumque animae.
Deinde petit, quae sint sincera, uocabula turtis.
    Dic "turtae" et mittet dimidium reliquum.

---

(12) **1** thure *VW*: ⟨e⟩nutre *F*: uere *N^a* ‖ pio *WF*: pro *V*: pius *N^a* ‖ **4** arator *FV*: orator *W* ‖ (13) **1** his *W*: bis *VN^a*

APPENDIX V

Petrus Candidus Decembrius ad Antonium Raudensem

⟨1432⟩

B = Bologna: Biblioteca Universitaria, MS 2387, s. XV, f. 132r.
F = Frankfurt am Main: SUB, MS Lat. oct. 136, s. XV, ff. 140v–141v.
M = Milan: Biblioteca Braidense, MS AH.XII.16, s. XV, ff. 91v–92r.
N¹ = Naples: Biblioteca Nazionale, MS V F 18, s. XV, ff. 230v–231r.
N² = Naples: Biblioteca Nazionale, MS VI D 7, s. XV, f. 113v.
V = Vatican City: Biblioteca Apostolica Vaticana, MS Pal. lat. 1592, s. XV, ff. 130v–131r.
F° = Fossati 346–47.

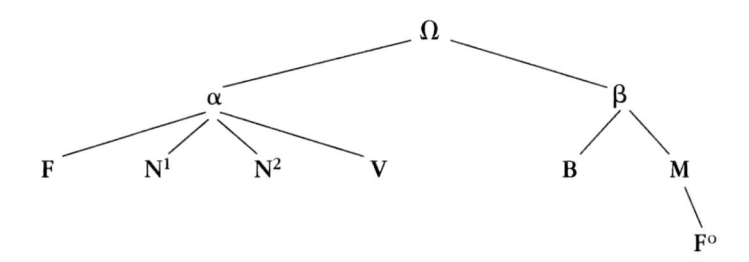

Candidus Decembris, Filippi Ducis secretarius, fratri Antonio Raudensi theologo salutem plurimam dicit.

1 Philippicam tuam, pater et praeceptor colendissime, *lacteo,*
ut Hieronymus tuus inquit, *eloquentiae fonte manantem*, laeto animo
5 suscepi legique, nec me ulla grauitatis tuae et eloquentiae summae
fefellit opinio. Dicam enim liberius quae sentiam: nihil illa ornatius,

---

3–4 Hier. *Ep.* 53.1

1–2 Candidus ... dicit *om. N¹F°* ‖ **2** plurimam dicit *FMV* : *tr. N²* : Ad insignem theologum fratrem Antonium Raudensem Ordinis Minorum laudes Philippicae nuper editae *B* ‖ **4** inquit] ait *N¹* ‖ fonte] fontem *N¹V* ‖ laeto α : lectissimo *M* : laetissimo *B et coniec. F°* ‖ **5** grauitatis ... summae α : amicitiae nostrae β ‖ **6** illa *om. F°*

nihil uberius, nihil splendidius aut elegantius inueniri posse confido; tanta in uerbis dignitas, copia, claritas, tanta uel sententiis etiam uenustas inest, ut nihil supra. Iam itaque tibi, iam tuis studiis,
10 immo Latinis litteris, immo nostrae Italiae congratulor. Tu noster es Cicero. Tu uerius noster Hercules, qui non tantum nos homine importuno illo Panormitano ac furioso, sed etiam immani Caco ac portento quodam liberasti. Tua manu salui sumus. Tibi laudes canimus, spirantem naribus resonat omne nemus. Gaude itaque uirtute
15 tua et fruere. Te maiorum titulis et laudibus adiicimus, quippe Aretino uberior, Barbaro dulcior, Guarino facundior euasisti. Nulla ab his ulterius praesidia, nullas uires petimus. Tu solus monstra uincere et domitare didicisti. Nunc currus tuos, nunc equos, nunc itaque plausus et circumsonantem undique doctorum hominum
20 turbam intueri mihi uideor, ac demum beluam illam Siculam uinclis suis grauem triumphos tuos prosequentem, hinc honestatem, hinc dignitatem quae flagellis illum passim cedant aspicere.

2 Quid hoc triumpho speciosius? quid hac gloria excellentius? quid his meritis tuis pulchrius inueniri posse dicam? Iuuat igitur
25 inter alacres et ouantes de te commilitones tuos sic monstrum affari Siculum: "O impudice nimis et procax, O gomorrhita zelotype, Beccadelle uersificule, O simia demum litteraria, quid tibi cum nostro inuicto Tyrintio? quid tibi cum Ciceroneo praeceptore ac poeta sidereo litis fuerat? Nimium te tibi credidisti qui tam fidenter
30 praeclaros uiros aggredi et insimulare ausus sis. Patere igitur sortem quam quaesisti, et cede loco cum molliculis tironibus tuis, nihil tibi praeter linguam et calamum superest, cum quis bellum geras irritum." Tu uero Raudensis, noster uictor inclite, uale feliciter.

---

8 tanta uel *om.* β ‖ etiam *om.* FN^1V ‖ **9** itaque *om.* β : itque F ‖ **10** immo nostrae α : ac nostrae β ‖ es *om.* β ‖ **11** tu uerius] tuae *corr.* tu V ‖ qui *om.* β ‖ tantum] tamen B ‖ non tantum nos] non tantum non F : nos tantum nos N^1 ‖ **11–12** homine ... Panormitano α : homine illo importuno ac furioso β ‖ **12** etiam *om.* β ‖ **13** quodam *om.* β ‖ facti *prae* sumus N^1 ‖ **14** naribus ... omne α : naribus illum consonat omne β ‖ **15** quippe α : qui profecto β ‖ **16** uberior α : facundior β ‖ dulcior α : subtilior β ‖ facundior α : liberior β ‖ **17** his $βN^1V$: hiis F : iis N^2 ‖ **18** *prae* didicisti, studuisti *in ras.* B ‖ **19** itaque *hic* F : *post* equos N^1N^2V : *post* currus β ‖ hominum *om.* β ‖ **20** Siculam] Siculum B ‖ **21** hinc ... hinc] hincque ... hinc M ‖ honestatem] honestas B ‖ **22** dignitatem] dignitas B ‖ quae] quam B ‖ illum *hic* α : *om.* B : illam *post* quae M ‖ passim] passum FV ‖ cedant] credant N^1 ‖ **23** hoc] haec V ‖ **24** igitur] inquit N^1 ‖ **26** nimis α : nimium β ‖ et *om.* B ‖ procax α : inepte β ‖ **28** quid tibi cum Ciceroneo α : quid cum Ciceroniano β ‖ **29** Raudensi *prae* litis β ‖ litis] lutis F ‖ nimium α : nimirum β ‖ **30** praeclaros] praeclaro M ‖ igitur α : itaque β ‖ **31** loco] locum N^1 ‖ tuis *hic* α : *post* cum β ‖ nihil α : nil β ‖ **32** calamum α : pennem β ‖ **33** uictor inclite *tr.* β ‖ feliciter *om.* N^1

APPENDIX VI

Petrus Candidus ⟨Decembrius⟩ Fratri Antonio Raudensi
⟨postea 5.v.1432⟩

B = Bologna: Biblioteca Universitaria, MS 2387, s. XV, ff. 133v–138v.
M = Milan: Biblioteca Braidense, MS AH.XII.16, s. XV, ff. 92r–95v.

1 [B133v/M92r] Nouum profecto et inauditum hac aetate, pater et praeceptor [M92v] colendissime, oratorum genus poetarumque defluxit, non abiectum usque quaque ac contemptum, sed ut Octauio principi olim exprobatum est cinaedorum, qui *orbem* uel imprimis *digito temperent*. Quorum quidem insolentia quo titulo liberius explicari queat, uehementer addubito, lingulaces an rabulas eos appellauerim. Melius, ut de Regulo scribit Plinius, sic hi non Stoicorum tantum sed omnium plane scriptorum simiae doctissimae ac festiuissimae, diphthongis et alphabetis dumtaxat exornati, cariem priscam et ignotam redolescunt. Prima etenim quaeque epistolarum suarum nota, si modo id nomen [B134r] merae nugae promerentur, ex Ciceronis commentariis, immo ex Duodecim Tabulis eruitur, nonnulla etiam Graece addita, ut quasi in luna maculae sic epistolis interpositae liturae non indeceant. Nec est quod existimes pauculos, hos infinitos propemodum esse scias, quippe qui locustarum more urbem istam potissimum inuecti, priscorum sata laeta, non rodunt solum sed euellant. Iamque (ut mage rideas) eo usque nequitia ipsa processit, ut nouae apud illos scriptorum haereses, noua nomina reperta sint, ut tamquam ex ipsis philosophis uocabula Guariniani itidem et Panormitani uocitentur.

2 O ridiculos homines! O ignauiam singularem! Nihil Ciceroni difficilius uisum est quam oratorem bonum, at his nihil facilius quam malum reperire. Vertenda itaque a nobis denuo Catoniana uetus definitio uidetur, nec inepte dictum puta, orator est uir malus

---

4–5 Suet. *Aug.* 68; cf. John of Salisbury *Policraticus* 1.7 et 3.14 || 7–8 Cf. Plin. *Ep.* 1.5.2

---

2 colendissime *B* : clarissime *M* || 5 temperent] temperet *Suet.* || 23 Catoniana *B* : Catoniniana *M*

25 et dicendi imperitus, nisi forte quod eloquio desit maximarum rerum scientia ac futurorum casuum admirablis quaedam prouidentia suppeditant. In qua re Codrus noster, *bonus augur*, nonnulla ex oraculi fronte decerpta siue ex tripode illa Memphitica iampridem attulit. Comitem Franciscum ⟨Carmagnolam⟩ ex conspiratione
30 elapsum Venetias, id est libertatis domicilium et iustitiae portum se recepisse. [M93r] Recte id arbitror, siquidem carnificinae locus iustitiae [B134v] portus dicitur, ubi cum nonnulli futuras exilii latebras arbitrarentur, breui dignitatis sedem, decoris, honoris, adeptus est, et tandem ornatissimorum patriciorum ordini coaptatus, et quod
35 bonum faustum felixque rei publicae totique Italiae sit, ipsi uero Comiti nequaquam imperium siue necem consecutus.

3 Miror hunc helluonem parasiticum qui alienas mensas his bellariis adornat, quo pinguiora pabula inde referat cum rem publicam senatores, patricios, tribunos maritimae urbi dederit nomine
40 illam pulcherrimo et ornatissimo defraudarit. Siquidem Romae uocabulum adiecisset, quid ulterius ad laudem? Quamquam, si Democrito credimus, multum ad ingenium confert, quo aere, quibus etiam cibis utaris, et propterea Thebis crassum et concretum caelum homines obtusiores, Athenis purum et liquidum. Attici igi-
45 tur auctoris animi gignuntur, peropportune itaque in ipsis paludibus tamquam pinguius euasura Romanae urbis fundamenta iaciantur. Sed nec illa miranda prudentia, qua Romam nouam condere, nouum imperium adoriri nixus est usquam apparuit. O ciues, ubi mens? ubi animus? nimirum casibus uestris fata imminent et cum
50 nihil uiolentiae innixum diutius maneat, tum status iniquitas licet longaeua sit, non potest esse diuturna. Comitem Franciscum, uirum Italicorum pace dixerim ceteris [B135r] ductoribus aetatis nostrae praeponendum, cuius ope tantas uictorias adepti, tot illustres urbes consecuti ex manibus denique potentissimi Principis euasistis, hoc
55 meritorum genere donastis? hac eximia gloria extulistis? his denique laborum praemiis ornauistis? Sunt hi sancti ciuitatis mores? liberalis uita? uirtutis hospitalitas? per hos uiros, per has artes, foris domique conditum, terra marique auctum est imperium? Hos (inquam) uiros, has artes iuuentus Italica contemplabitur? haec primis ab
60 annis mirabitur?

4 Sed ad instituta reuertamur. [M93v] Iamiam minime miror ab his otium nostrum perturbari qui quos modo laudibus ad caelum efferant, eorundem capitibus et titulis insultent. Sed alias Gnathoni

---

24–25 Cf. Quint. *Inst.* 12.1.23–32 ǁ **27** Cic. *Phil.* 2.32.80

26 prouidentia *B* : prudentia *M* ǁ **34** coaptatus *om. M* ǁ quod *B* : quid *M* ǁ **38** bellariis *B* : bellarii *M* ǁ **40** defraudarit *B* : fraudarit *M* ǁ **45** auctoris *B* : acutioris *M*

nostro uberius reponsum dabimus, qui iacto lapide manum tegit,
65 graeculus semibarbatus nihil praeter olera sapit ac legumina.

5 Ad te igitur, uir doctissime, stilum uerto. Quid Siculo nostro festiuius? quid eruditius? Omnis quippe epistola sua sic turgescit et eminet, ut cum incipias maxime addubites utrum annales an poemata mera lecturus sis. Tanta cum dignitate exordia capescit, lit-
70 teras peregrinas aucupatur, cum tamen ea scribat, ut de Antonio dicit Octauius, quae *magis admirentur homines quam intelligant.* Solis, inquit, simulacrum depicturus, [B135v]

Quid dignum tanto feret hic promissor hiatu?

6 Nuper huiusce cohortis omnis ordines inspexi, impetum
75 excepi. Veterani admodum pauci, reliqui tirones hisque lasciui inermesque. Quid uerbis opus? Alexandri phalangem dicito, orbem sibi uendicant, sibi regna et imperia, sibi nationes, urbes asciuere, plurimi tamen ex ipsis medicinae sectatores, nam et ualitudinem diligentissime scrutantur. Si uales, inquiunt, bene est. Si non uales,
80 urina clara non est, et huiusmodi reliqua. Neminem praeterea in salutatum instituto ueteri relinquunt, ut si minimum eloquentiae, plurimum tamen uetustatis adesse appareat.

7 Primus omnium Codrus noster Thrasonis ritu Thaidem suam debellaturus cum uecte procedit, ac schematibus quibusdam et
85 myrobrecis usque quaque Cincinnatus campo sese arduus infert, plurimus apud hunc Aristoteles, plurimus Cicero, multus praeterea Protogenes atque Erymanthus. Omnia denique Latine scripta Graece a nobis interpretanda sunt. Is quippe nonnulla sibi peculiariter attinere profitetur, lingendi magister optimus cum cenam
90 olfecerit. Quid hac uerborum uetustate cariosius? Dein Sallustii sententiis instruc[M94r]tus, *prona et uentri obedientia* dicit animalia, quasi uero supinus ipse tantum meri exhauserit, ut necesse illud fuerit uomere postridie. [B136r] Ciceronem postmodum dormire non sinit, sed ad Graeca usque uocabula prouectus, plurima delet et
95 corrigit, compotationes haud commode ab illo dici, combibia melius explicari, ut bibendi artificem non indocte natum scias, statimque Graece uerbum subdit. Dicam igitur et ipse Graece aliquid ne Latini sermonis penitus ignarus esse uidear. Credas cum hunc audieris barbatum hircum capreis naturam ligurire Socratem
100 postremo et Philodemum suum, cum de parsimonia et sagina disputat in medium adducit, quarum alteram adeo persequitur, ut auro

---

71 Ver. Flac. 18.3 ǁ **73** Hor. *A.P.* 137 ǁ **91** Sall. *Cat.* 1.1

---

64 nostro *B* : uestro *M* ǁ **75** hisque *B* : hique *M* ǁ **87** Protogenes *B* : Prote- *M* ǁ **90** uetustate] *corr. B* ǁ **91** et *BM* : atque *Sall.*

quiduis esuriens ueneat discipulos tenuiores ludibrio sempre habuerit, alteram auaritia potius quam honestate metiatur. Amorem etiam suum cuius ea uis, ut uel obolo facile immutari queat, contu-
105 bernali suo pollicetur, nec iniuria cum his Panormitae poetae celebri, arcta familiaritate deuinctus sit. Iam uero non minor hac tempestate apud nos poetarum prouentus quam *toto mense Aprili* apud Plinium Romae fuit, cum nulla celebret *dies quin recitaret aliquis*.
110 **8** Quid longius rem traho? Hominem in aere suo recipit, laudes proprias libens amplectitur cum se in cutem usque prospexerit. Epistolam denique suam uereor ne orationem non dixisse sacrilegum sit amicitiae testem, posteritati commendat, tamquam cyrographum ad [B136v] tribunal amoris, si operae
115 pretium fuerit necessarium, cum dicam reo impingere libuerit. Quid hac eloquentia disertius? Quid huiusmodi antiquitate uetustius? Quid denique hoc scribendi genere raucidius inueniri potest? Et hic certe ueteranus orator tamquam in mari pina pisciculos cum squilla nanciscitur. Ita is cum suo Siculo adolescentulos incautos nundi-
120 natur. Siquis autem bonis moribus locus adsit, non secus ac ulcera quaedam uirulenta, a corporibus [M94v] resecanda sunt, ne uitam perimant. Sic hi ab omni re publica expellendi, ne iuuentuti malos mores indecoros scribendi ritus inferant. Nullas enim uirtutis umbras, sed solida quaedam uitiorum monumenta ab his infringi,
125 quis non uidet?
 9 Ecce alter ex hac acie tiro, ut inermis ita maxime imperatoris sui uirtutibus innixus, subula potissimum ornatus, pugnam ingreditur. Ita ut unum ex altero natum et conflatum esse putes. Epistolarum statim et tabellariorum ac scabellorum strepitu, totam
130 aciem immiscet, lepore, uenustate, urbanitate, et huiusmodi uocabulis non exundat solum sed scatet et effluit.
 10 Mirum quemadmodum in tanta litterarum inopia, litteratorum tanta copia. Nec enim agricola nisi ab agro, a mari nauita. Hi autem nullum scribendi archetipon, ut ita dixerim, nacti, omnia
135 [B137r] perturbant et miscent. Mea quidem, inquit, sententia Crassum putes uel Antonium non inter priuatos homines sed reges et summae eloquentiae principes Guarinum statuo. Vellem aliquando ut ueterum exempla non semper uerba sectaretur. Quid autem pulchrius quam si Marci Antonii, Luperci more *nudus,*
140 *unctus, ebrius,* diadema regi suo imponeret, ut suae magniloquentiae

---

107–09 Plin. *Ep.* 1.13 ‖ **139–40** Cic. *Phil.* 3.12

102 esuriens *B* : exuriens *M* ‖ **104** facile *B* : facie *M* ‖ **108** celebret *B* : elaberetur *M* ‖ quin *BM* : quo non *Plin.* ‖ **120** prae ulcera, uel *in ras. B* ‖ **128** altero *M* : altera *B* ‖ **133** mari *B* : naui *M*

dicam an maledicentiae fructum uberrimum Musa Attica siue fistula Ionia et ipse uicissim caperet. Doctior profecto Panormita suus, qui coronam iam adeptus regno imminet. Dii immortales, quis horum ineptias aequo animo ferre queat?

145 **11** Quis non huius lauream rideat, etiam si opera admiretur? Ductus est per urbem histrionis ritu inter omnium cachinnos atque ludibria. At his tamquam meritus haec laudi sibi ascribi ab his, quibus ioco esset, existimabat. Quid aliud hoc est, nisi ex stultis insanos facere? Hodie ferie nobis dantur. Quamobrem? Poeta coro-
150 natur. Quis? Nulli proferam.

12 O hominem pistrino dignum! Quis Maronis nostri fastus, quis insolentiam ferre posset, si Maecenatem suum adesse contingisset, cum hic recens tiro, tantopere his rudimentis Ciceroni suo congratulentur? [M95r] Possunt denuo et antiqua Romanae urbis
155 fastigia solo erigi. Iam spes est Ciceronem et Laelium [B137v] reuiuiscere cum nouis Maecenatibus ac Ciceronibus totidem Virgilii tironesque prodierint. Quid plura? Glebarium se constituit. Deinde cum reliqua, diuino oraculo potissimum explicanda uiderentur, epistolam non secus ut auream olim mensam Phoebo sapientes
160 destinarunt, corrigendam illi limandamque promisit. At uero *bonus augur* Laelium crederes ueterum fatorum non ignarus uniuersam supellectilem suam unica litterula euomuit, ut ingenium diligentiam multarum rerum peritiam breui quasi formula depingeret. Litteras, inquit, ad Guarinum emendaui: Varrum poetam de Aeneida ad
165 Augustum scribentem cogita.

13 O elegantem emendatorem! Quid deinde? Eloquentiae, inquit, propheta es. Hem? Laudem Siculam, ut tibi stultio uertas si dum datur, me non uteris et abuteris. *Nonne satius est*, ut Ciceroni placet, *mutum esse quam quod nemo intelligat dicere?* Palatio, inquit,
170 priuatus sum, quia Cambium amisi. Parum affuit quin et mensa diceret. Sed is cum in caelum relatus sit, fortassis effecerit, ut simul liceat diuorum accumbere mensis. Demum addicit: Tu unica nunc superes Panormitae uoluptas ac mel meum, mirum quin fauum uel potius caripassi et albebuth Indorum fercula, quo disertior fieret
175 non [B138r] adiecerit.

14 Vides quanta ab his ludibria, quantae ineptiae aucupari soleant. Quae enim apud alios rara et ferme inopina sunt, apud hos conquisita sine intermissione referuntur. Itaque nullum epistolae exordium placuit, nisi "etsi saepenumero," "saepe et multum," et his

---

160–61 Cic. *Phil.* 2.80 ‖ **168–69** Cic. *Phil.* 3.22

---

141 dicam an maledicentiae *om. M* ‖ **148** existimabat] *corr. M* ‖ **155** Laelium] Tullium *corr.* Laelium *M* ‖ **168** et] *corr. B*

180 similia undique decerpta praemiserint, ut facile appareat, non epistolae principium, sed Titi Liuii aut Plinii eximium quoddam opus incohare. Reliqua uero Xenophonte aut Isocrate aut exoletis ignotisque uocabulis sic intexta et fucata sunt, ut nihil ad rem minimum ad ornamentum conferre uideantur optarem in causis [M95v]
185 publicis, si qua in nos dicenda putarentur, aduersarios huiusmodi eloquentia suffultos adhiberi, qui nec ab ullo intelligi, nec quid ipsi persuaderent, facile inter se dignoscere possent. *Quamobrem ut in senatu semper aliquis est,* ut inquit Cicero, *qui interpretem requirat, sic hi a nobis* sine aedituo aut *interprete* minime *audiendi* uel intelligendi
190 uidentur. Quidam etiam ex his haruspicem desiderant, nam et Graecis multa Hebraice, nonnulla insuper barbara interponere consueuere. Quae tandem nouus tiro ueteres ac confectos rubigine enses exacuens, caligatus inter ceteros (ut uides) exposuit. Cum Euripidem nec minus reliquos Graecorum uates probe nouerit. Multum siquidem apud
195 illum uersiculi non inepti gratiae con[B138v]secuti sunt, qui uel affectione ita diuinctus sit, ut nihil uerum uel ita rudis ut nihil laude dignum inspicere potuerit.

15 Horum igitur nugis saepenumero, pater optime, uexatus diutius tibi me continere non potui, quin et quae rite sentirem, ad
200 te scriberem et plurimorum inscitiam insolentiamque aspernarer.

187–89 Cic.*Fin.* 5.89

180 non *om. M* || **181** quoddam] *mg. suppl. B* || **186** qui *B* : quo *M* || **187** quamobrem ut *BM* : quemadmodum *Cic.* || **188** requirat *BM* : postulet *Cic.* || **189** hi *BM* : isti *Cic.* || a *om. Cic.* || **192** confectos rubigine *B* : *tr. M* || **194** Graecorum] *corr. M* || **196** ut nihil laude *B* : et nihil laude *M*

APPENDIX VII

(1)
Epistola Antonii Panormitae ad Fillipum Mariam Viscontem super Orationem de Effigie Solis

C = Como: Biblioteca Comunale, MS 4.4.6, s. XV, ff. 122r–123r.
T = Tübingen: Universitäts-Bibliothek, MS Mc. 137, s. XV, ff. 273r–273v.

1 [C122r/T273r] Efflagitasti nuper a me, Princeps Illustrissime, tibi Solis effigiem quadrigamque depingi, qua deinceps pro signo non ab re quidem uterere. Nihil enim excogitari potest aptius aut conuenientius uitae tuae quam Solis mira uis et natura. Sol primum,
5 ut ait Cicero, et hinc *dictus* est, *quia cum* exoritur *obscuratis omnibus sideribus solus apparet*. Sic tu, diuine Princeps, ut primum per aetatem licuit, lumine prudentiae et singularis industriae tuae tyrannos, qui plerisque in locis tuis sedes occupant, exegisti, obscurasti, et pacata re solus non sine felicitate quadam subditorum et sempiterna
10 tuae adolescentiae laude et gloria regnare cepisti. [C122v] Deinde, ut astrologorum monimentis traditur, cum Sol aliquo in caeli signo est illud prae ceteris uiuificat illuminatque, ei [T273v] calorem atque uirtutem impartit; cum uero ab signo discedit, illud effectum quodammodo et exanime relinquit. Sic tu cum aliquem fauore ac gratia
15 complecteris, honestas atque magnificas eum quidem quantumque in te est meliorem reddis. Verum si qua eius insolentia aut contumacia deferis infractum, ac prope mortuum non iniuria relinquis. Equidem scio quosdam ex humili loco a te maxime exaltatos atque habitos magnae uirtutis uiros, cum uero propter eorum temeritatem a te
20 tandem destituti sunt, insigne quoddam leuitatis, ingratitudinis, denique proditionis exemplum praestitisse.

5–6 Cic. *N.D.* 2.68 ‖ 11–13 Cf. Censorius *De die natali liber* 8.6

Epistola . . . Solis *scripsi* ‖ **2** quadrigam- *T* : -rigiam- *C* ‖ qua *C* : quia *T* ‖ **5** omnibus *bis C* ‖ **6** ut *C* : et *T* ‖ **7** lumine *C* : numine *T* ‖ **8** tuis *C* : tuas *T* ‖ occupant *C* : -parant *T* ‖ **11** caeli *T* : *om. C* ‖ **12** illuminatque ei *C* : illuminat eique *T* ‖ **13** impartit *C* : -titur *T* ‖ **14** ac *C* : et *T* ‖ **15** -que *om. T* ‖ **17** non *C* : haud quidem *T*

APPENDICES

2 Sed ad Solem redeamus. *Dux et* item *princeps* a Cicerone appellatur, eo quod *omnes luminis maiestate praecedat,* longeque emineat potentia ac magnitudine super alias stellas. Sic et tu cum
25 rerum amplitudine atque armis omnes Italiae principes sine controuersia antecellas, illis et iam quasi ducem te praebes, quem industria armorum, religione, clementia, fortitudine, et pietate imitari ac sequi te queant. Ille insuper *caeli mens appellatur*; at tu nostrum omnium ratio es. Ille *cor caeli*; tu nobilium fere omnium
30 Italicorum uita neque a benefaciendi motu numquam cessas. Haec atque alia quae pleraque Solis sunt praeclaris atque diuinis moribus tuis ita meo iuditio conueniunt, ut nihil quidem ne excogitari possit aptius atque similius. Quare tuum id Solis signum atque propositum laudo proboque, pro quae uirili etiam describere instituo. Non
35 mea quippe quae nulla est, sed maiorum auctoritate ac doctrina fretus, immo plerisque in locis dicam eisdem quibus illi uerbis scripsere: qua in re si cuiquam ex nostratibus, non ego, sed maiores ipsi contradixerint, quaeso id aequo animo ferat patiaturque solum pro laude ac commoditate nostri principis iri superatum. Non
40 enimuero quid nobis sed quid nostro principi ac parenti conducat et faciat satis prospicere debemus, et prae eius laude ac gloria nostramque uel et iam uitam paruifacere.

3 Ego, Filippe princeps et uere Sol, si quid dum maiorum opiniones cogo contrahoque aberrauero, non dico abs te qui astro-
45 rum scientia peritissimus haberis, sed a quouis alio mediocriter erudito emendari et retractari perpetiar. Tuae quidem honestissimae uoluntati [C123r] ac desiderio, ut dixi, satisfacere non meae famae consulere studeo. Ceterum et adsunt tecum clarissimi astrologi, qui dum tu maioribus longeque utilioribus officiis districtus es, poterunt
50 tua uice hoc quicquid est libelli recognoscere, *et male* tornatum, ut ait Horatius, *incudi reddere*, deque se denique iudicium dare. Tu uale Salus et Sol noster.

---

22 Cic. *Rep.* 6.17 ‖ **23** Bocc. *Gen. Deor.* 4.3.15; cf. Cic. *Rep.* 6.17; et Macr. *Somn. Scip.* 1.20.4 ‖ **28–29** Bocc. *Gen. Deor.* 4.3.15; cf. Macr. *Somn. Scip.* 1.20.6 ‖ **50–51** Hor. *Ars* 441

23 eo *C* : pro *T* ‖ maiestate *C* : -tates *T* ‖ **25** omnes *om. T* ‖ **26–27** quasi ducem . . . fortitudine et *om. T* ‖ **28** caeli mens *CT* : mens mundi *Cic., Macr., et Bocc.* ‖ at *C* : ac *T* ‖ **29** es *om. T* ‖ omnium *C* : omni *T* ‖ **31** plera- *C* : plaera- *T* ‖ **34** describere *C* : scribere *T* ‖ **36** dicam *om. T* ‖ **38** contradixerint *C* : -runt *T* ‖ **42** nostramque] -que *om. T* ‖ **44** contrahoque *om. T* ‖ **46** et *C* : atque *T* ‖ tuae *C* : tu *T* ‖ **48** studeo *C* : -dio *T* ‖ **50** quicquid *C* : quidquit *T* ‖ **51** ait Horatius *tr. T* ‖ deque *C* : -que *om. T* ‖ **52** prae salus, salis *in ras. T*

(2)
Antonii Panormitae
Oratio de Effigie Solis

C = Como: Biblioteca Comunale, MS 4.4.6, s. XV, ff. 123r–127r.
T = Tübingen: Universitäts-Bibliothek, MS Mc. 137, s. XV, ff. 237v–276v, [frag.].
V = Vatican City: Biblioteca Apostolica Vaticana, MS Ross. 1024, s. XV, ff. 91r–94r.

1 [C123r/T273v/V91r] Solis effigiem picturus aut celaturus simulacrum primum omnium animaduertat, quam plurimos extitisse Soles uariaque et diuersa mysteria habuisse. Fuit enim Sol primus primi Iouis filius, Sol Vulcani filius, [T274r] Sol Hyperionis
5   filius, Sol Iouis secundi filius, Sol Vulcani Aegyptii filius, Sol Oceani filius. Eos si quis pictor confuderit, utpote tribuens nato Hyperionis citharam aut herbas, aut sagittas, aut reliqua quae non sua sunt, sed aliorum is maxime aberrabit, sua cuique tribui debent. Idque ab illustribus poetis bellissime seruatur. P. Ouidius, poeta celeberrimus,
10 cum persaepe in Hyperionis natum incidisset, non ei accommodat aut uaticinium, aut arcum, aut medicinam, aut quae non sua sunt, contra neque sibi negat quae sua sunt. Legite secundum Metamorphoseos librum in principio ubi de Hyperionis nato habetur fabula, ut liquet in Leucothoe libro quarto neque quicquam
15 confuse dictum comperietis, ut quod alterius esset alteri tribueretur. Sed quae Hyperionis nati sunt ea dumtaxat ascribuntur sibi quod continue id prosequitur, neque mutat institutum. Nam in Leucothoe in haec uerba ait:

   "Ille ego sum," dixit, "qui longum metior annum,
20 *omnia qui uideo, per quem uidet omnia tellus,*
   mundi oculus."

Ex diuerso cum de Sole Iouis filio mentionem habet, non quae Hyperionis, sed quae sua sunt sibi discrete quidem assignat. Ait enim in hunc modum in primo Metamorphoseos libro:

12–13 Cf. Ov. *Met.* 2.1ff. || 14–15 Cf. Ov. *Met.* 4.190 ff. || 19–21 Ov. *Met.* 4.426–28

Antonii . . . Solis *scripsi* || **1** celaturus *CV* : colla- *T* || **2** omnium *om. T* || **5** Sol Oceani filius *om. T* || **8** sua *CV* : sui *T* || tribui *CV* : *corr. T* || **11** arcum *CV* : artium *T* || **12** Contra . . . sunt *om. T* || **14** Leucothoe *scripsi* : Leuchotoe *CV* : Lochotoe *T* || **15** *prae* comperietis, reperietis *in ras. V* || **18** Leucothoe *V* : Leochotoe *C* : Leuchothoe *T* || in *om. V* || **19** annum *TV et Ov.* : ei enim *ut uid. C* || **23** *prae* discrete, districte *in ras. T* || **24** enim *om. C*

>   *mihi Delphica tellus*
> *et Claros et Tenedos Patareaque regia seruit;*
> *Iupiter est genitor, per me, quod eritque fuitque*
> *estque, patet; per me concordant carmina neruis.*
> *Certa quidem nostra est, nostra tamen una sagitta*
> *certior, in uacuo quae uulnera in pectore fecit!*
> *Inuentum medicina meum est, opiferque per orbem*
> *dicor, et herbarum subiecta potentia nobis.*

2 Videtis hic quam prudenter ea quae Iouis [V91v] filii sunt sibi dinumeret, ea, quae Hyperionis sunt, subticeat neque immisceat tametsi totidem, et plura etiam Hyperionis sunt quam Iouis filii, ut statim cum de eo loquemur, liquido apparebit. [C123v] Comperio tamen extitisse nonnullos, qui dum uel Hyperionis, uel Iouis, uel alterius, Solem laudibus ueherent, et sua et quae essent alterius alteri tribuisse. Verum id, ut dixi, laudando non depingendo. Persaepe enim quae proauorum, et aliena sunt, nobis attribuuntur, non recte tamen depinguntur in gestis nostris laudatur plerumque patria nec depingitur. Quam prudenter Horatius in secundo Epodos, cum esset Soles quodammodo confusurus per quae laudes, dico, hoc ipsum ita fecerit, ut secernere potius quam commiscere uideretur. Incipit enim ab Hyperionis Sole:

> *Alme Sol, curru nitido diem qui*
> *promis et celas aliusque et idem*
> *nasceris.*

Postea vero longo et quadringinta fere uersuum interuallo adiungit ea quae Iouis filii sunt:

> *Augur et flagrante decorus arcu*
> *Phoebus acceptusque nouem Camenis,*
> *et salutari leuat arte fessos*
> *corporis artus.*

25–32 Ov. *Met.* 1.515–22 ‖ **46–48** Hor. *Saec.* 9–11 ‖ **51–54** Hor. *Saec.* 61–64

26 Patareaque *C et Ov.* : Patharea- *T* : Panchea- *V* ‖ **29** tamen *TV et Ov.* : tum *C* ‖ sagitta *CT et Ov.* : -gipta *V* ‖ **30** in uacuo *V et Ov.* : est uacuo *CT* ‖ in pectore *V et Ov.* : in om. *CT* ‖ **32** *post* herbarum, est *add. TV* ‖ **34–35** subticeat . . . sunt *om. T* ‖ **36** de eo *CT* : deo *V* ‖ *post* tamen, non *in ras. C* ‖ **41** gestis . . . depingitur *om. C* ‖ **42** in *om. T* ‖ Soles *om. CV* ‖ **43** quae *om. CV* ‖ **44** uide- *CT* : aude- *V* ‖ **48** nasceris *CV* : nostris *T* ‖ **51** flagrante *CTV* : fulgente *Hor.* ‖ **52** Camenis *CV et Hor.* : Camenos *T* ‖ **53** et *CTV* : qui *Hor.* ‖ salutari *CV et Hor.* : salubri *T*

55 **3** Primum id discerni dignoscique uoluit, tam longo carminum interuallo, deinde non ineleganter neque [T274v] ab re. Illum Solem, hunc Phoebum appellat sed laudat Horatius. Ceterum Ouidius qui ad eam rem tamquam pictor accedit tertio libro Metamorphoseos, numquam soles commiscuisse aut conturbasse
60 reperitur. Cicero quoque eo in libro quem De natura deorum scriptum reliquit cum multis in locis tum maxime eo loci definit deos permisceri minime debere, cum ita ait: *Hinc Liber (hunc dico Liberum Semela natum, non eum quem nostri maiores auguste sancteque Liberum cum Cerere consecrauerunt, quod quale sit ex*
65 *mysteriis intelligi potest).* Et reliqua uaria quidem uariis mysteria attributa sunt, quae sub hisdem nominibus permiscere et peruertere ignorantiae erit. Si qui uero difficiles pertinacesque existant [V92r] contendantque deorum nomina, officia, mysteria, res denique eorum omnis confundi uel pingendo posse et debere caueant ne
70 dum unum aliquid ex alio deo alii mutuentur, cetera quasi negligenda abiciant uerbi gratia. Si quis ex Phoebo Iouis filio arcum et sagittas tantum transtulerit ad Hyperionis Solem et reliqua, quae etiam huius sunt, praetermittat: uidelicet citharam, Musas, laurum, tripodas, coruum, diuinationem, medicinam, herbas, et cetera. Is
75 peraeque deridendus est, quasi pictor si quis oculis tantum accurate instuduerit, eosque tandem perfecerit, nasum autem et auris mutilatas emiserit. Quod si quis omnia quae huius sunt, illi etiam accumulare studeat, quis non dico anulus aut sigillum, sed quae demum aula tot tantorumque capax inuenietur. Sed quorsum haec,
80 ut intelligant, ii qui Solis imaginem picturi sunt [C124r] cum multi soles sint, sua cuique tribuere debere, nunc uero omissis aliis solibus.

4 Non enim proposito conducunt ad Hyperionis natum ueniamus. Eum quidem quaerimus qui et Phaëtontis pater est et Solis
85 stella seu planeta Graece appellatur, de quo Ouidius cumulate simul et erudite tractat in secondo Metamorphoseos. Idemque eum Hyperionis filium et eundem Phaëtontis patrem ostendit in

---

62–65 Cic. *N.D.* 2.62

---

59 aut conturbasse *om. T* || **60** quoque *CV* : quo *T* || **60–61** scriptum reliquit *tr. V* || **62** hinc *CV et Cic.* : hunc *T* || **63** Semela *Cic.* : Semele *T* : simile *CV* || eum *V et Cic.* : enim *CT* || nostri maiores *tr. T* || **64** *post* sancteque, censent *add. CV* || Cerere *CV et Cic.* : Ceterere *T* || consecrauerunt *Cic.* : -secrarunt *T* : -seruauerunt *CV* || *post* quod, cum *add. T* || **66** hisdem *CV* : hiscam *T* || **70** mutuentur *CT* : mutentur *V* || **73** huius sunt *tr. V* || **74** prae coruum, quae *in ras. V* || coruum *C* : corum *V* : *om. T* || **75** peraeque *CV* : per ea quae *T* || deridendus *C* : diuiden- *T* || **76** nasum *corr. V* || **77** emiserit *C* : omiserit *TV* || **79** inuenietur *CT* : -tus *V* || **80** ii *om. C* || **80–81** ut intelligant ... debere *om. V* || **81** sint *C* : sunt *T* || **85** planeta *CV* : -tae *T* || **86** eum *om. TV*

Leucothoe sua libro Metamorphoseos quarto. Priusquam ad eius figuram accedamus erit operae pretium paucis absoluere, quis hic quem Solem uocant extiterit, quamue ob rem tam praelustri tamquam principali astro donatus fuerit. Fuit is igitur ut supradictum est Hyperionis filius et Titanis nepos hinc et Titan dictus, uir egregie pietatis et singularis certe uirtutis. Hic cum pater fratresque *aduersum Iouem deosque reliquos bellum* mouissent, obnixique omni ui fuissent et iam *montes montibus* super inicientes diis caelum eripere solus, inquam, hic non modo non iuuit, iam coniuratos caelum rescindere fratres sed ut erat ipse mansuetissimus et religiosus et naturae obediens. Iouis et deorum immortalium partes secutus est. Contra patrum fratrumque superbiam et impietatem [V92v] et stultitiam inauditam ob tam igitur insigne et singulare facinus ab Ioue post uictoriam donatus est, quadriga [T275r] illa mirifica et corona et regia et multis praeterea insignibus. Mox statim haberi cepit et appellari Sol atque ita haberi ut in hunc omne decus ueri Solis delatum sit, ut apud poetas apparet, qui de eo tamquam de uera Solis stella seu planeta locuti sunt. Et sane ut est apud Ciceronem: *Suscepit autem uita hominum consuetudoque communis ut beneficiis excellentes uiros in caelum fama et uoluntate colerent.*

5 His ita breuiter expeditis, ad institutum ueniamus quod est Solis effigiem describere. Igitur a corona eius incipiamus, quo facile appareat Solem, ut ait Cicero, astrorum tenere principatum. Quamquam alii quidam Cicerone omisso tradunt ex eo coronam gestare quod re uera rex fuerit in uita. Alii ideo coronatum dicunt, quod Sol prae ceteris uagis et errantibus stellis regum ac principum signifator existat. Verum hoc postremum sompniantis est primum illud Ciceronis et astrologorum magna quidem et insignis et admirabilis uis Solis est et, ut idem Cicero in sexto De re publica inquit: *Deinde subter fere mediam regionem Sol obtinet, et dux et princeps et moderator luminum reliquorum, mens mundi et temperatio,*

89–90 Cf. Bocc. *Gen. Deor.* 4.1.9 ∥ **94–95** Bocc. *Gen. Deor.* 4.1.2 ∥ **95–101** Cf. Bocc. *Gen. Deor.* 4.3.1 ∥ **106–07** Cic. *N.D.* 2.62 ∥ **110** Cf. Cic. *N.D.* 2.49

88 Leucothoe *scripsi* : Leochotoe *C* : Leochothoe *T* : Leuchotoe *V* ∥ priusquam *CT* : prius quidem *V* ∥ eius *CV* : eum *T* ∥ **89** figuram *om. T* ∥ **91** tamquam *CT* : -que *V* ∥ donatus *corr. V* ∥ **92** Titan *TV* : Titam *C* ∥ **93** pietatis et *CV* : uirtutis ac *T* ∥ singularis *TV* : singulis *C* ∥ pater *V* : patres *CT* ∥ **94** mouissent *CV* : nouissent *T* ∥ **95** et iam *C* : etiam *TV* ∥ super *s.u. suppl. V* ∥ inicientes *corr. V* ∥ **97** mansuetissimus *CT* : -tudinis *V* ∥ **101** quadriga *TV* : -rigia *C* ∥ **103** Sol *om. T* ∥ **104** ueri *corr. V* ∥ **104–05** delatum sit . . . uera Solis *om. T* ∥ **106** uita hominum *bis T* ∥ **107** beneficiis *CT* : -cii *V* ∥ excellentes *CTV* : -tis *Cic.* ∥ et *CTV* : ac *Cic.* ∥ colerent *CTV* : tollerent *Cic.* ∥ **109–10** Igitur . . . appareat *om. V* ∥ **112** coronatum *CT* : -nam *V* ∥ **113** prae *CT* : pro *V* ∥ **115** et insignis *C* : et *om. T* ∥ **117** fere mediam *tr. Cic.* ∥ et dux, et *om. Cic.* ∥ **118** temperatio *CT* : -pora *V*

tanta magnitudine, ut cuncta sua luce lustret et compleat. Id cum ita
120 [C124v] sit an aliunde coronam Soli donemus quam ob omnipotentem, ut ita dixerim, eius potestatem.

6 Deinde iubent coronam esse duodecim radiorum ut si quis pauciores aut plures depinxerit erret et quidem errasse. Martianus de Sole loquens ait:

125 *Radiisque sacratum
bis senis perhibent caput aurea lumina ferre.*

Et adiicit rationem quare duodecim tantum:

Quod totidem menses, totidem quod conficit horas.

Quod si quis Martiano astipulari uoluerit an Vergilio illi magno et
130 uere diuino poterit non assentari. Ait enim in duodecimo [V93r] libro:

*Interea reges ingenti mole Latinus
quadriiugo uehitur curru (cui tempora circum
aurati bis sex radii fulgentia cingunt,
Solis aui specimen).*

135 Vnicuique autem radio suam gemmam inscribunt, ut intelligatur Solem quot annis iter facere per duodecim signa caeli. De his uero gemmis apud Martianum leges prolixius.

7 Sed et quaestionis est an radii solares pingi debeant aequales nec ne. Et diuus Ambrosius in libro Exameron cum illis iuxta
140 uidetur sentire qui aeque pares radios depingunt. Ea gratia quod *Solis radius*, ut idem ait, *nulli proprior nulli longinquior est; neque cum oritur inferior occidentalibus aestimatur, nec uergens in occasum minor orientalibus.* Quamuis enim Indi a Britanis tantum inter se distent quantum oriens ab occasu. *Sol* tamen *a nullo distat, nulli*

117–19 Cic. *Rep.* 6.17 ‖ **125–26** Mart. Cap. 2.188 ‖ **128** Mart. Cap. 2.188 ‖ **131–34** Verg. *Aen.* 12.161–64

119 ut *CV* : et *T* ‖ ita *s.u. suppl. C* ‖ **120** prae coronam, coror *in ras. T* ‖ **122** esse duodecim *om. T* ‖ **123** errasse *scripsi* : erasse *CV* : crasse *T* ‖ **128** quod toti- *CV et Mart. Cap.* : quot toti- *T* ‖ **129** magno *CV* : -na *T* ‖ **130** assentari *CV* : -tiri *T* ‖ enim *om. CV* ‖ in duodecimo libro, *lacuna prae* libro *C* : in duodecimo eius libro *ut uid. TV* ‖ **131** mole *CV* : more *T* ‖ **132** quadriiugo *V* : -riugo *C* : -rigo *corr.* -riugo *T* ‖ cui *CV et Verg.* : ciui *T* ‖ **134** aui *Verg.* : auis *CV* : aeui *T* ‖ **136** solem *CV* : -lum *T* ‖ quot *CV* : quod *T* ‖ signa caeli *tr. TV* ‖ **137** leges prolixius *tr. V* ‖ **139** diuus *CV* : dicit *T* ‖ iuxta *corr. V* ‖ **140** qui *CT* : per *V* ‖ **142** aestimatur *Ambr.* : exti- *CTV* ‖ uergens *CTV* : uergit *Ambr.* ‖ **143** a Bri- *CV* : et Bri- *T* ‖ **144** tamen *CT* : tum *V* ‖ distat *CV* : discat *T*

145 *praesentior, nulli remotior est,* atque *eodem momento* ab utrisque *uidetur cum oritur.* Ambrosius haec fere ad litteram. An autem uera nec ne dicat astronomi uiderint. Iuuit tamen et eius opinionem recensere.

  8 De corona hactenus; nunc ad Solis faciem accedamus.
150 Ea quidem puerilis depingitur capite crinito, quod et Tibullus probat:

   Solis perpetua est Baccho Phoeboque [T275v] *iuuentas,*
   Nam decet intonsus crinis utrumque deum.

  Tum ore uenustissimo, nam deorum, inquit Vergilius, formosis-
155 simus est Apollo omnium. Sed quare puer, cum idem pater dicatur. Eo quod, ut Isidorus ait, *quotidie oriatur et noua luce nascatur,* hinc et *"Phoebum"* dictum, ait, *quasi "ephebum," hoc est "adulescentem."* Quod et Fulgentius probat imberbis ideo et puer Sol pingitur, *quia occidendo et renascendo semper sit iunior. Siue,* ut
160 idem ait, *quod numquam in sua uirtute deficiat ut luna quae crescit et minuitur.*

  9 Sed audio quosdam parum considerate dicentes eo quod influentia sua animantium uigorem augeat et conseruet puerili facie [C125r] depingi quod quale sit dialetici uiderint, qui nisi riserint
165 [V93v] huiusmodi consequens saxei sint opportebit. Illud namque rectius ex hoc antedicto sequeretur. Sol uigorem auget ergo uirilis et robustus inscribitur. Fortis enim et potentis est aliquid tum agere posse, tum auctum seruare, non imbecile non debilis et puerilis aetatis. Crinitus seu comatus non ea ratione depingitur, ut ob id
170 denotet iubaris et radiorum pulchritudinem. Nam Bacchus et multi praeterea intonsi sunt, tamen iubare et radiis caret. Sed cum puerum ueteres illum statuissent, facile eorum ritu puero comam reliquere,

   Nam decet intonsus crinis utrumque deum.

141–46 Ambr. *Hexaëm.* 4.6.25 ‖ **152–53** Tib. 1.4.37–38 ‖ **154–55** Cf. Verg. *Ecl.* 4.57 ‖ **156–58** Isid. *Etym.* 8.11.54 ‖ **159–61** Fulg. *Mit.* 1.17 ‖ **174** Tib. 1.4.38

---

147 uera *C* : uerum *TV* ‖ uiderint *CV* : -rit *T* ‖ **149** *prae* faciem, de solis facie *in ras. C* ‖ **150** ea *T* : eam *C* ‖ Tibullus *corr. C* ‖ **152** solis *V et Tib.* : soli *CT* ‖ perpetua *CTV* : aeterna *Tib.* ‖ Baccho *CT et Tib.* : Bacchi *V* ‖ **155** omnium *om. T* ‖ **156** ut *om. V* ‖ **157** hoc *CT* : id *V* ‖ **158** imberbis *T* : limberbis *CV* ‖ ideo et *CT* : et *om V* ‖ puer *post* pingitur *V* ‖ **159** occidendo *corr. V* ‖ ut *CT* : et *V* ‖ **162** audio *om. T* ‖ **164** qui] *om. T* : *post* nisi *in ras. V* ‖ riserunt *T* : *corr.* -rint *C* : viderint *V* ‖ **165** namque *corr. C* ‖ **166** rectius *TV* : rectimis ‖ **168** seruare *CT* : -rem *V* ‖ **170** et radiorum *CT* : et *bis, semel in ras. V* ‖ **171** caret *C* : *corr. V* : carent *T* ‖ **172** puero *om. T*

175   Tum radii si cui parti interdum accommodantur, non capillis sed oculis, non capiti sed circum omne caput accommodantur. Ouidius in quarto Metamorphoseos:

> *Quid nunc, Hyperione nate,*
> *forma colorque tibi radiataque lumina prosunt?*

180   Et in secundo:

> *at genitor circum caput omne micantes*
> *deposuit radios.*

10 Quod de corona illa duodecim radiorum intelligas. Itidem cum posterius ait: *Imposuitque comis radios*, idest coronam radiatam.
185   Quod si praeter coronae radios de aliis intelligas *circum caput omne emicantibus* nam propterea coma radios signficet, minime hercle. Nam, ut dixi, et Bacchus comatus est, nec radiatus. Sed auratam ideo comam quia et longe pulchrior ea est, et Solis naturae conueniens. Veste autem purpurea induitur eadem et regia ut

190   *purpurea uelatus ueste sedebat*
in solio Phoebus claris lucente smaragdis.

Nam Phoebo Iouis primi filio uestimentum erat aureum. Teste item Ouidio:

Ipse deus uatum palla spectabilis aurea
195   *tractat inauratae consona fila lyrae.*

Quo palam est poetas, ut in principio dicebam, Phoebos non confundisse, sed quod suum esset cuique diuisum tribuisse. Nec obstat quod undecimo Metamorphoseos scribit:

Verrit humum Tyrio saturata murice palla.

178–79 Ov. *Met.* 4.192–93 ǁ **181–82** Ov. *Met.* 2.40–41 ǁ **184** Ov. *Met.* 2.124 ǁ **185** Ov. *Met.* 2.40 ǁ **190–91** Ov. *Met.* 2.23–24 ǁ **194–95** Ov. *Am.* 1.8.59–60 ǁ **199** Ov. *Met.* 11.166

175 *prae* si cui, *uerbum in ras. V* ǁ **184** comis *CTV* : -mae *Ov.* ǁ **185** praeter *CV* : pictor *T* ǁ **186** emicantibus *C* : e- *s.u. suppl. V* : mican- *T* ǁ nam *C* : num *TV* ǁ **187** ut *CT* : et *V* ǁ **191** *prae* in solio, *uerbum in ras. T* ǁ smarag- *TV* : smerag- *C* ǁ **194** *prae* ipse, *uerbum in ras. T* ǁ **195** consona *CV* : sona *T* ǁ **196** poetas *CT* : -ta *V* ǁ Phoebos *CV* : caelos *T* ǁ confundisse *C* : -fudisse *TV* ǁ **197** quod *CT* : communem *V* ǁ diuisum *CV* : -sim *T* ǁ **197–98** obstat quod undecimo *CT* : obstat in primo *V* ǁ **199** Tyrio *TV et Ov.* : Tyro *C*

200 Nam ibi de Iouis secundi et Latone filio loquitur:

Laomedonteis Latonius astitit aruis.

11 Si quidem Phoebus primi Iouis ex qua matre fuerit ortus non inuenitur, [V94r] sed an stantem an sedentem in curru Solem depingemus et rectius est, ut stantem, quales adhuc Romae videmus
205 triumphantium simul et deorum imagines saxis inscriptas. [T276r] Haud enim consentaneum uidetur, eum qui tam arduam rem gereret, tamquam uolucres, flagrantes, contumaces, equos gubernaret, id sedentem, et prope quiescentem acturum.

Nec tibi quadrupedes animosos ignibus illis,
210 *quos in pectore habent, quos ore et naribus afflant*
in promptu regere est, uix me patiuntur, ubi acres
incaluere animi [C125v] *ceruixque repugnat habenis.*

Errant uero si qui eo Ouidii carmine adducti Solem sedentem pingunt,

215 *purpurea uelatus ueste sedebat*
in solio Phoebus.

Nam per id tempus, quod poetae fingunt, ab opere uacabat, nox quidem erat, quod perspicuum et manifestum est, cum statim post subdit:

Dumque ea magnanimus Phaëton miratur opusque
220 *perspicit, ecce uigil nitido patefecit ab ortu*
purpureas aurora fores.

Et item paulo post:

Dum loquor, Hesperio positas in littore metas
umida nox tetigit.

---

201 Ov. *Met.* 11.196 ∥ **209–12** Ov. *Met.* 2.84–87 ∥ **215–16** Ov. *Met.* 2.23–24 ∥ **219–21** Ov. *Met.* 2.11–13 ∥ **223–24** Ov. *Met.* 2.142–43

201 Laome- *scripsi* : Laume- *CTV* ∥ aruis *TV et Ov.* : arens *C* ∥ **206** tam *CV* : per *T* ∥ **209** quadrupedes *CT* : -de- *s.u. suppl.* *V* ∥ **210** prae naribus, s *in. ras.* *V* ∥ afflant *CTV*: efflant *Ov.* ∥ **211** regere *CT* : ricinere *V* ∥ est *om.* *V* ∥ **212** repugnat *CV*: repugnat *T* ∥ **213** eo *CV*: ex *T* ∥ **218** prae et, *uerbum in ras.* *T* ∥ **220–21** patefecit … purpureas *bis* *V* ∥ **221** purpureas *CV* : -rea *T* ∥ **223** littore *CV* : lictore *T*

APPENDIX VII

225 Nos uero non cessantem ab opere non nocturnum Phoebum describimus, sed diurnum et permaxime intentum mysterio suo, praeterea Phaëton *statque super*, non sedet, inquit, in curru. An autem ipse per se currus ducat an per aurigam quaeritur, ueteres aurigam Soli non tribuunt. Ceterum Sol ipse, ut ait Ouidius,
230 *stimuloque et uerbere saeuit*, etiam Phaëtonti inquit *corripe lora manu*. Et paulo post:

>   *manibusque leues contingere habenas*
> *gaudet.*

12 Ea ratione, ut arbitror, quod, ut *dicunt Aratus et Hyginus,*
235 Sol *per se ipsum* mouetur, *non cum mundo* uertitur. Quod Cicero noster, eo in libro qui De natura deorum inscribitur, probat in haec uerba: *Stellae quae inerrantes uocantur* ⟨...⟩ *nec habent aethereos cursus nec caelo inhaerentes, ut plerique dicunt physicae rationis ignari; non est enim aetheris ea natura ut in suas stellas complexa contorqueatur*
240 [V94v] *natura tenuis et perlucens et aequabili calore suffusus aether non satis aptus ad stellas continendas uidetur*. Et adiicit: *Habent igitur suam sphaeram stellae inerrantes ab aetheris coniunctione secretam et liberam*.

13 Cicero haec et recte, mea quidem opinione. Nam, ut
245 astrologi trandunt, *si* quidem Sol *fixus maneret necesse erat* eum semper *eodem loco* atque eadem caeli parte *occidere, qua cum prius fuerat exortus, quemadmodum cetera et sidera et signa oriuntur et occidunt. Praeterea si* cum mundo fixus uerteretur *consequens erat dies ac noctes omnes esse aequales, et quam spatiosus esset dies hodiernus, dies tam*
250 *longus semper esset futurus. Nox quoque simili ratione semper aequalis permaneret, sed quoniam inaequales dies aspicimus, et Solem alio loco*

---

227 Ov. *Met.* 2.150 ‖ **229–30** Ov. *Met.* 2.399 ‖ **230** Ov. *Met.* 2.145 ‖ **232–33** Ov. *Met.* 2.151–52 ‖ **234–35** Isid. *Nat. Rer.* 17.1 ‖ **237–41** Cic. *N.D.* 2.54 ‖ **241–43** Cic. *N.D.* 2.55

---

225 non cessantem *CV*: non *om. T* ‖ **227** *prae* in curru, insedet *V* ‖ **229** Ouidius *s.u. suppl. V* ‖ **230** etiam *C*: et *VT* ‖ **232** habenas *corr. V* ‖ **234** ea *corr. V* ‖ Hyginus *scripsi*: Igi- *CTV* ‖ **235** non ... uertitur *om. V* ‖ noster *TV*: nostrum *C* ‖ **236** eo *C*: *om. V*: et *T* ‖ qui *om. V* ‖ inscribitur *om. V* ‖ **237** inerrantes *CV*: inerretes *T* ‖ **238** inhaerentes *T*: -h- *s.u. suppl. V*: -retes *C* ‖ **239** in suas *CTV*: ui suas *Cic.* ‖ -queatur *CTV*: -queat *Cic.* ‖ **240** natura *CTV*: nam *Cic.* ‖ aequabili *CV*: -bilis *T* ‖ **242** *prae* coniunctione, *uerbum in ras. V* ‖ **243** liberam *CT*: -ralem *V* ‖ **244** haec *CT*: has *V* ‖ et recte *CT*: et *om. V* ‖ **245** erat *CT*: esset *V* ‖ **246** *prae* atque, *uerbum in ras. V* ‖ **248** ac *CV*: et *T* ‖ **249** omnes *om. V* ‖ esset dies hodiernus *CV*: dies *om. T* ‖ tam *CV*: tum *T* ‖ **250** semper *om. V*

occasurum, alio occidisse hesterno uidemus, adeo quia diuersis locis occidit et exoritur, putant ⟨eum⟩ philosophi nequaquam cum mundo fixum uolui, sed ipsum per se moueri.

255 **14** Quapropter et poetae induxerunt Solem per se currus agentem, non [C126r] per aurigam, [T276v] quamquam Dantes, poeta quidam maternus et idiota, in Purgatorio suo horas introducit currus Solis gubernantes, quae a maioribus nostris non ut gubernantes inducuntur sed tamquam inseruientes et administrantes Soli.
260 Iungunt enim equos currum tempori parant, Soli astant spatii aequalibus obsequuntur. At auriga non obsequium sed et magisterium praestat. Neque equos iungit sed etiam illos gubernat, quod ab illustribus poetis, neque horis neque cuipiam aurigae attributum comperio, uerum ipsemet currus agit. Quod itidem uidemus Romae
265 triumphantium atque deorum imagines astentes scilicet et quadrigam per semet ipsas agentes.

15 Restat ut currum Solis depingamus, postremo equos. Sit igitur altus, ut ait Ouidius et uere, *Vulcania munera, currus*. Nec quales inuehuntur Ligna Mediolanum ut quosdam audio nuper pro
270 curru plaustrum lignarium depinxisse, sed quales [V95r] adhuc uidemus in uetustis quibusdam numismatibus aut signis gemmeis inscriptos. Sitque axis aureus,

*temo aureus, aurea summae
curuatura rotae, radiorum argenteus ordo;*
275 *per iuga chrysolithi positaeque ex ordine gemmae.*

16 Nam cum nihil pretiosius sit auro et gemmis, conuenientur igitur ea adaptarunt excelse ac regie Solis maiestati, cumque perlucidae atque igneae praesertim naturae sint rectissime ea quoque Soli accommodarunt, quae maxime Solis saperent naturam.
280 Chrysolithos enim gemma est auro similis cum marini coloris

---

245–54 Isid. *Nat. Rer.* 17.1–2 ∥ **256–61** Dante *Purgatorio* 29.115–54 ∥ **268** Ov. *Met.* 2.106 ∥ **273–75** Ov. *Met.* 2.107–09

---

252 alio occidisse *CT* : alio loco occidisse *V* ∥ hesterno *scripsi* : hexter- *C* : exter- *TV* ∥ diuersis *CV* : -sos *T* ∥ **253** *prae* putant, *uerbum in ras. T* ∥ cum *CT* : eum *V* ∥ **255** currus *CT* : -rum *V* ∥ **256** agentem *CT* : mouentem *V* ∥ **257** idiota *scripsi* : indiota *V* : ideota *CT* ∥ *post* horas, suas *T* ∥ introducit *corr. V* ∥ **258** nostris *om. T* ∥ **260** astant *TV* : adastant *V* ∥ spatii *C* : -tiis *TV* ∥ **261** aequalibus *CT* : inaequa- *V* ∥ at *CV* : ac *T* ∥ **262** sed etiam illos *CV* : sed et illos *T* ∥ **263** cuipiam *CV* : cuiquam *T* ∥ **264** agit *CT* : ait *V* ∥ **265** astentes *C* : astantes *TV* ∥ **269** Mediolanum *CV* : -lanensem *T* ∥ **270** lignarium *om. T* ∥ quales *CT* : aequales *corr. V* ∥ **272** axis *CV* : assis *T* ∥ **274** curuatura *corr. V* ∥ **275** chrysolithi *scripsi* : crhisoliti *C* : troliti *T* ∥ **276** cum *om. V* ∥ pretiosius *corr. V* ∥ **277** ea *post* adaptarunt *V* ∥ adap- *CV* : adop- *T* ∥ **278** naturae *C* : -ra *TV* ∥ **279** quoque *CT* : quae *V* ∥ saperent *CV* : superant *T* ∥ **280** chrysolithos *scripsi* : crhisolitus *C* : crisolitus *TV* ∥ similis *CT* : simul *V*

APPENDIX VII

similitudine. Hunc Aethiopia genuit chrysopis uero aurum tantum uidetur esse. Sunt et eiusdem prope specialis ac nominis gemmae quam multae, uidelicet chrysolithos, chrysolampis, hammochrysos, leucochrysos, melichrysos, chrysocolla, et similia quae quoniam hic
285 non admodum conueniunt in alium suumque reiciamus locum.

17 Quadrigam Soli tribuunt, quamobrem possum respondere cum Martiano quam breuiter,

Quod solus domites, quam dant elementa quadrigam,

ut ratio quadrigae sint quattuor elementa cum quibus Sol omnia et
290 creet et conseruet. At qui eruditi quidam scriptores proinde inquiunt quadrigam habere ut quadrifariam anni distinctionem significet, quam Sol efficiat cursu suo. Quippe, *ut Clemens ait*, Sol *diuersos accipit cursus quibus aeris temperies pro ratione temporum dispensetur, et ordo uicissitudinum permutationumque seruetur.*
295 [C126v] *Nam dum ad altiora conscendit* — quod est quoniam per septentrionem pergreditur — *uer temperat, ubi ad summum caeli uenerit aestiuos accendit calores, decidens* — quod est quoniam per austrum iter facit — *rursum autumni temperiem reddit, ubi uero ad infima redierit frigus hiemaleque producit.* Et sane ut ait Cicero:
300 *Inflectens autem Sol cursum tum ad Septem Triones tum ad Merediem aestates et hiemes efficit et* [V95v] *ea duo tempora quorum alterum hiemi senescenti coniunctum est alterum aestati.*

18 Ego, pace eorum eruditorum, Martiano magis accedo ut sit elementorum ratio potius quam temporum. Nam quid erat opus per
305 quadrigam anni tempora exprimere cum ea iam expressa sint per se ipsa. Nonne circum Solem

Verque nouum stabat cinctum florente corona,
stabat nuda Aestas et spicea serta gerebat,

---

288 Mart. Cap. 2.189 ‖ **292–96** Isid. *Nat. Rer.* 17.3 ‖ **299–302** Cic. *N.D.* 2.49 ‖ **303–05** Cf. Mart. Cap. 7.734

---

281 et *prae* Aethiopia *T* ‖ genuit *V* : ginuit *C* : gignit *T* ‖ chrysopis *scripsi* : crhisopis *CV* : crisopus *T* ‖ uero aurum *tr. T* ‖ tantum *CT* : tamen *V* ‖ **282** specialis *s.u. suppl. C* : speciei *TV* ‖ **283** chrysolithos *scripsi* : crisolectrus *corr.* chriso- *C* : crisolettrus *T* : crhiselectus *V* ‖ chrysolampis *scripsi* : crisolansis *CT* : crhisolansis *V* ‖ hammochrysos *scripsi* : amocrisis *CT* : amochrsis *V* ‖ **284** leucochrysos *scripsi* : leocrhisus *CV* : leocrisis *T* ‖ melichrysos *scripsi* : melectrisis *CV* : meletrisis *T* ‖ chrysocolla *scripsi* : crhisocola *C* : *om. T* : chrisocola *V* ‖ **285** admodum *om. V* ‖ **286** tribuunt *C* : attri- *T* ‖ **294** dispensetur *C* : -citur *T* : -sentur *V* ‖ permutationum- *CT* : -nem- *V* ‖ **295** conscendit *CTV* : -derit *Isid.* ‖ **295–96** quod ... pergreditur *om. CT* ‖ **297–98** quod ... facit *om. CT* ‖ **299** hiemale- *CT* : hiemem- *V* ‖ sane *om. CV* ‖ **300** tum *CV* : cum *T* ‖ **301** et ea *CT* : etiam ea *V* ‖ **302** coniunc- *CTV* : adiunc- *Cic.* ‖ **303** eorum eruditorum *tr. T* ‖ sit *C* : si *V* ‖ **304** potius quam. ... *fine operis T* ‖ **305** quadrigam *s.u. suppl. V* ‖ expressa *V* : -sae *C* ‖ **308** gerebat *V et Ov.* : ferebat *C*

> *stabat et Autumnus calcatis sordibus uuis*
> 310 *et glacialis hiems canos hirsuta capillos.*

Si qui autem dicunt quadrigam Soli attributam ad differentiam lunaris bigae, hinc errant, quod et multis diis quadriga est, nulla tamen lunaris bigae differentia et prospecta. Iterum finge lunam abesse a rerum natura an propterea Sol, Mars, Iupiter, quadrigis eorum 315 priuabuntur.

19 Sed iam Solis equos prosequamur, ut enim illi quattuor rotarum currus adaptatur ut quadripartitas anni uarietates et tempora, aut rectius quattuor elementa significet. Sic eidem *quattuor equi* sunt, *ut per eos* totidem diei *qualitates* et spatia quae diurno ciruitu peragit 320 ostendat. Quod equorum nomine coloresque declarant. *Nam Pyrois, qui primus est, rubens et interpretatur et depingitur*, propterea *quod Sol exoriens* quandam prae se ferat rubedinem. *Eous, qui secundus est*, splendens dicitur *eo quod* illa diei hora, quae tertia est *dissolutis iam uaporibus* a radiis solaribus Sol ipse splendidior candidiorque effulgeat. 325 Idcirco secundus equ⟨u⟩s albus splendidensque depingitur. Aethon, qui tertius est, ardens lucens interpretatur, *nam Sole caeli medium tenente, lux eius corusca est et feruidior* pingitur, itaque Aethon *rubens sed in croceum tendens.*

20 Ita in Deorum genealogiis scriptum leges et Fulgentius 330 haud quaquam dissentit. Phlegon, qui quartus est, dicitur *terram amans*. Quod ab hora nona procliuior uergat ad terram, idest Oceanum, *ultima prona uia est.* Is, ut traditum est, ita pingitur ut *ex croceo colore* tendat *in nigrum* Fulgentius et alii quidam hos equos [V96r] aliter nominant, significatione et re [C127r] tamen eadem 335 puta: Eritheum, Atheona, Lampos et Philegeum. Nos autem Ouidii, poetae celeberrimi, nominibus contenti simus.

> *Interea uolucres Pyrois ⟨et⟩ Eous et Aethon,*
> *Solis equi, quartusque Phlegon hinnitibus auras*
> *flammiferis implent.*

307–10 Ov. *Met.* 2.27–30 ‖ **311–13** Cf. Isid. *Etym.* 36.1–3 ‖ **318–28** Bocc. *Gen. Deor.* 4.3.10 ‖ **329** Bocc. *Gen. Deor.* 4.3.10 ‖ **330–31** Ov. *Met.* 2.67 ‖ **332–33** Bocc. *Gen. Deor.* 4.3.10 ‖ **337–39** Ov. *Met.* 2.153–55: cf. Bocc. *Gen. Deor.* 4.3.5

309 calcatis *V* : calcetis *C* ‖ **312** prae hinc, differentia et prospecta *in ras. V* ‖ et multis *C* : e multis *V* ‖ **313** et *om. C* ‖ **318** eidem *C* : enim *V* ‖ **320** nomine *C* : -na *V* ‖ nam *C* : non *V* ‖ Pyrois *scripsi* : Pyrrhous *CV* ‖ **321** interpretatur *V*: -petratur *C* ‖ depin- *C*: pin- *V* ‖ **322** prae *C* : per *V* ‖ ferat *C* : fert *V* ‖ **323** illa diei *C* : ea dici *V* ‖ candidior- *C* : candior- *V* ‖ **325** albus *V* : album *C* ‖ splendidens- *C* : splendens- *V* ‖ **328** sed *C* : et *V* ‖ **329** genealogiis *C* : -gis *V* ‖ **330** quaquam *C* : quamquam *V* ‖ **332** uia *om. V* ‖ **336** simus *C* : sumus *V* ‖ **337** interea *corr. V* ‖ Pyrois *scripsi* : Pyrrhous *CV*

340 Flammiuomos et Alipides ideo descripserunt poetae, quo partim cursus celeritatem partim calidam lucentemque Solis naturam ostenderent. Hunc igitur tam praeclarum tamque mirificum currum, Sol ille caeli oculus moderatur, quartum id est medium obtinens circulum quo tam superioribus quam inferioribus lucem sideribus
345 praestet. Eum uero circumstant ad extera leuaque dies et mensis et annus, saeculaque et positis spatiis aequalibus horae. Quo deprehendatur, Solem esse et temporum factorem, uerum id quo pacto pingi aut celari possit, Apellis aut Phidiae iudicium fuerit.

21 Hactenus mihi uideor, Gloriosissime Princeps, quicquid
350 ad Solis Hyperionis figuram attineret perstrinxisse. Si quid aut componens festinantia aut in curia praetermissum est, erunt partes eruditissimi uiri Francisci Barbaruariae, clarissimi atque insignis secretarii tui, id ipsum addere, elimare, et supplere. Verum postremo te non fugiat ad scilicet. *Sol ⟨ex⟩oriens cum quadrigis* signum extitisse
355 Amphitryonis, ut a Plauto memoriae proditum est. Vale.

---

354 Plaut. *Am.* 422

---

342 hunc *C* : nunc *V* ‖ praeclarum *C* : praedatum *V* ‖ *prae* tamque, quo tam superioribus tamque inferioribus *in ras. V*

APPENDIX VIII

Invectiva: Ubi "Obloqui"
Excerpta ex libro Imitationum rhetoricarum Antonii Raudensis

MS = Avignon: Bibliothèque Municipale, MS 1054, s. XV.

1 [158r] Obloqui: Si collibuerit lacessitus et inuectiuarum uocabula cognoscere, audi primo Ciceronem In Verrem, In Catilinem, In Antonium, et alios. Ait enim de Verre primo sic: Luxuriet *in flagitiis, crudelitas in suppliciis, auaricia in rapinis, super-*
5   *bia in contumeliis* [Caec. 3]; *homo singulari cupiditate, audacia, scelere praeditus* [Caec. 6]. Item: *Magnum crimen, ingens pecunia, furtum impudens, iniuria non ferenda* [Caec. 30]. Item: *Homo amens ac perditus* [Ver. 1.6.15], libindinosissimus in quo de homine nihil es. *Non ⟨enim⟩ furem,* dicam, *sed ereptorem, non adulterum sed expugna-*
10 *torem pudicitiae, non sacrilegum sed hostem sacrorum religionumque, non sicarium sed* [158v] *crudelissimum carnificem ciuium sociorumque* [Ver. 2.1.3.9]. Item: *Omnium ante damnatorum scelera, furta flagitia, si unum in locum conferantur, uix cum huius parua parte aequari conferrique* possent [Ver. 2.1.8.21]. *Sileatur de nocturnis ⟨eius⟩ baccha-*
15 *tionibus et uigiliis; lenonum, aleatorum, productorum nulla mentio fiat* [Ver. 2.1.12.33]. Item: *Hora nulla uacua a furto, scelere, crudelitate, flagitio reperietur* [Ver. 2.1.12.34]. *O scelus, O portentum in ultimas terras exportandum!* [Ver. 2.1.15.40]. *Si in alium reum diceretur, incredibile uideretur* in te numero [Ver. 2.1.17.44]. *O tempora, O*
20 *mores!* [Catil. 1.2]. *In luto uoluptatum* totus es [cf. Ver. 2.4.24.53].

2 Idem in Verrem: *Tenuerunt ⟨...⟩ locum illum serui, fugitiui, barbari, hostes, sed neque tam serui illi dominorum quam tu libidinum, neque tam fugitiui illi a dominis quam tu ab iure et ab legibus, neque tam barbari lingua aut natione illi quam tu natura et moribus, neque tam*
25 *illi hostes hominibus quam tu — importunum animal* [Ver. 2.1.16.42] et *belua immanis* [cf. Ver. 2.4.43.95] — *dis immortalibus⟨....⟩*

---

6 scelere] et scelere *MS* ‖ 10 sacrorum] sanctorum *MS* ‖ 13 in unum locum *tr. MS* ‖ 15 productorum] proditorum *MS* ‖ 16 nulla hora *tr. MS* ‖ 21 serui] secundum *MS* ‖ 22 barbari] barbara *MS*

APPENDIX VIII   301

Indignitate seruos, temeritate fugitiuos, scelere barbaros, crudelitate hostes uicisti [Ver. 2.4.50.112].

3 Audi nunc illum In Catilinem ⟨immo *Declamatio in Lucium*
30   *Sergium Catilinam*⟩ et complicibus suis sic dicentem: *Nihil modo scio illo uersipellius aut mutabilius hominum memoria, ita ut diuersissimae saepenumero uideantur in eodem ingenio tamquam in scenam quandam taeterrima simul etiam clara redundare* [Decl. 9.32]. *Omitto huius impudicissimas uoces, et omnem mollitiem sceni-*
35   *cam, obtutus impudicos, blanditias muliebres, et omnem denique copiam non mediocrium uitiorum sub illa Phaetontis erudita simul atque insigni pulchritudine delitescentem: mentem plusquam gladiatoriam, sitim incredibilem cruoris humani, uarium inconstantiae genus, uultum nunc demissum, nunc alacrem, nunc scelus anhelantem,*
40   *nunc gratia meretricia florescentem; summum pecuniae desiderium, summum simul prodigalitate contemptum, incredibilem bonorum omnium eximiam cum summis atque ornatissimis ciuibus familiaritatem* [Decl. 9.31]. Item: *Flos pueritiae uenustissimus ad intuentium iocunditatem, cui non libidini potuit flagitiosae iuuentutis? Aut quam*
45   *cupidinis notam non subeundam ultro atque accersendam non cogitauit?* [Decl. 9.29]. Item: *Lux uero illa praeclari atque excellentis ingenii quam omnes diuinique semper et singularem atque inusitatam penitus arbitrentur, nomine inter foedissimas uoluptatum sordes extincta est?* [Decl. 9.30]. *Nihil in eo auiti sanguinis, nihil Romanae*
50   *industriae, nihil splendoris domestici, nihil auitae frugalitatis* [Decl. 28.95]. Item: *Quae nugae, dii immortales! quae portenta scelerum! qui libidinum gurgites!* [Decl. 8.27]. Ibi *coetus infames turpissimorum* hominum [Decl. 7.20] *perditissimorumque adolescentium* [Decl. 5.13]. Ibi *sacrarum libininum* [Decl. 8.26] omnia portenta,
55   omnes pestes aderant, quaecumque *scelerata, crudelia, flagitiosa inaudita* [Decl. 6.18]; quarum pestium quanta in dies redundatio sit ⟨. . .⟩ *immanitate atque furiosissimi hominis*, ⟨. . .⟩ qui *lucem omnis paternae dignitatis, exstinguere moliebatur* [Decl. 3.6–7]; *latro*

30–31 modo scio illo] enim fuit isto monstro *Decl.* ‖ **31** ita ut *Decl.* : ita *om. MS* ‖ **33** scenam quandam] sentina quadam *Decl.* ‖ etiam clara] *om. Decl.* ‖ **34** huius] pestis huius *Decl.* ‖ impudicissimas] impurissimas *Decl.* ‖ et omnem *om. Decl.* ‖ **35** muliebres et] et *om. MS* ‖ **36** Phaetontis] frontis *Decl.* ‖ **37–38** mentem plusquam] praetereo mentem illius plusquam *Decl.* ‖ **38** uarium] mirum *Decl.* ‖ **41–42** summum simul . . . omnium eximiam] summam simul prodigalitatem, contemptum incredibilem omnium bonorum, itemque eximiam *Decl.* ‖ **44** potuit] paruit *Decl.* ‖ **45** cupidinis] turpitudinis *Decl.* ‖ non] esse *Decl.* ‖ **47** diuinique] diuinam esse *Decl.* ‖ **48** arbitrentur] arbitrabantur *Decl.* ‖ nomine] nonne *Decl.* ‖ **49** extincta] restincta *Decl.* ‖ **50** auitae *Decl.* : *om. MS* ‖ **51** quae portenta *Decl.* : quam portenta *MS* ‖ **53** perditissimorum] perditorum *Decl.* ‖ **56** quanta *Decl.* : *om. MS* ‖ **58** paternae] patriciae *Decl.*

perditissimus [Decl. 9.28] *mente sceleratissima* ⟨...⟩ *in omnium*
60 *ciuium stragem perniciemque* [Decl. 3.8]. Item: Rem *barbaram crudelitate, flagitiosissimam perfidia, intolerabilem temeritate inconsideratam, periculo uero et calamitate perniciosissimam rei publicae* [Decl. 4.9]. Item: *Non obdormiscit tamen Catilina, bis destitutus euentu uigiliarum suarum, sed rursum saeuit: et rem publicam*
65 *destrangulandam debellandamque cogitauit* [Decl. 24.81], *caput et fons* [159r] *sceleratae coniurationis* [Decl. 22.74], *fax incendii* ratio [Decl. 24.81]. Item: *Ab hoc execrabili monstro,* ⟨...⟩ *hoste aeque taeterrimo* [Decl. 15.56]; *et taeterrima capita maleficiorum omnium* [Decl. 16.58], *portenta terribilia nostrae ciuitatis ac furiae*
70 *certissimae rei publicae* [Decl. 27.90]. Item: *Perniciosus ciuis acerbissimus hostis, et* ⟨...⟩ *taetram* ⟨...⟩ *horribilem* ⟨...⟩ *infestam rei publicam pestem* [Cic. *Catil.* 1.11]. Item: *Italiam totam ad exitium et uastitatem uocas*⟨....⟩ *Tuorum comitum magna et perniciosa sentina* [Cic. *Catil.* 1.12]. Item: *Incidimus in atrocissimos rei*
75 *publicae fluctus ac miseranam temporum calamitatem* [Decl. 2.3]. De Catilina uide sursum ubi "Laudes."

4 Nunc mei Hieronymi diuersa ac multa ad inuehendum ex epistulis suis accepi quae dicenda sunt et primo sic [Ep. 50.4–5]: *Quotiens iste me in circulis stomachari fecit et adduxit ad choleram,*
80 *quotiens conspuit et consputus abcessit! Sed haec uulgaria sunt et a quolibet de sectatoribus meis fieri possunt: ad libros* ⟨pro⟩*uoco, ad memoriam in posteros transmittendam. Loquamur in scriptis, ut de nobis tacitus lector iudicet, ut, quomodo ego discipulorum gregem ducto, sic ex huius nomine Gnathonici uel Phormionici uocentur. Non est*
85 *grande garrire per angulos et medicorum tabernas ac de mundo ferre sententiam: 'hic bene dixit, ille male; iste scripturas nouit, ille delirat; iste loquax, ille infantissimus est.' Vt de omnibus iudicet cuius hoc iudicio meruit? Contra quemlibet in triuiis strepere et congerere maledicta, non crimina, scurrarum est et parasitarum semper ad lites.*
90 *Moueat manum, figat stilum, commoueat se, et quicquid potest scriptis ostendat. Det nobis occasionem respondendi disertitudini suae*⟨....⟩ *"Etiam nos" didicimus litteras et "saepe manum ferule subduximus"* [Juv. 1.15]. *De nobis quoque dici potest: "Foenum habet in cornu, longe fuge"* [Hor. *Sat.* 1.4.34]. Item: *Voluit* ⟨...⟩ *ut ueteranus miles*
95 *uno rotatu gladii utrumque percutere, et ostendere populis, quod quicquid ipse uellet* ⟨hoc⟩ *scriptura sentiret. Dignetur igitur nobis sermonem suum mittere, et non reprehendendo sed docendo garrulitatem nostram corrigere. Tunc intelleget aliam uim fori esse, aliam triclinii; non aeque*

---

64 saeuit] saeuit immanior *Decl.* ‖ 64–65 et rem publicam . . . cogitauit] et quam rem publicam seruitio non potuerat obruere, destrangulandam penitus ac tollendam cogitauit *Decl.* ‖ 69 ac furiae] furiaeque *Decl.* ‖ 70 rei publicae] populi Romani *Decl.* ‖ 73 comitum] complicium *MS* ‖ 74 incidimus] incidissemus *Decl.* ‖ 93 foenum] ferrum *MS*

inter fusa et calathos puellarum, et inter eruditos uiros de diuinae legis
100 *dogmatibus disputare*⟨. . . .⟩ *Subulci non aderunt, feta scropha non grunniet.* "*Et nos tela, pater, ferrumque haud debile dextra / spargimus, et nostro sequitur de uulnere sanguis*" [Hier. *Ep.* 50.5; Ver. *Aen.* 12.50–51].

5 Idem Hieronymus Aduersus Vigilantium sic ait: *Exortus est*
105 (post multa monstra) *subito Vigilantius, qui immundo spiritu pugnet contra Christi spriritum, et martyrum neget sepulchra ueneranda; damnandas esse uigilias. Numquam nisi in Pascha Alleluia cantandum: continentiam, heresim; pudicitiam, libidinis seminarium. Et quomodo Euphorbus in Pythagora renatus esse perhi-*
110 *betur, sic in Iouiniani mens praua surrexit: ille Romanae ecclesiae damnatus, inter phasides aues et carnes suillas non tam emisit spiritum quam eructauit. Iste caupo Galogeritanus, et in peruersum propter nomen uiculi mutus Quintilianus miscet aquam uino: et artificio pristino, suae uenena perfidiae catholicae fidei sociare conatur,*
115 *impugnare uirginitatem, odisse pudicitiam, in conuiuio* ⟨. . .⟩ *contra sanctorum ieiunia declamare: dum inter phialas philosophatur, et ad placentas liguriens, psalmorum modulatione mulcetur: ut tantum epulas Dauid et Idithum* [159v] *cantores, et Asaph et filiorum Chore cantica audire dignetur* [Ad. Vigil. 1].

120 **6** Item ipse Hieronymus ad Rusticum: *Testudineo* ⟨*Grunnius*⟩ *incedebat ad loquendum gradu, et* ⟨*per*⟩ *intervalla quaedam, uix pauca uerba capiebat, ut eum putares singultire, non proloqui. Et tamen cum mensa posita, librorum exposuisset struem, adducto supercilio, contractisque narribus, ac fronte rugata, duobus digitulis concrepabat, hoc*
125 *signum ad audiendum discipulos prouocans. Tunc meras nugas fundere, et aduersum singulos declamare: criticum diceres esse Longinum, censorem* ⟨*que*⟩ *Romanae facundiae, notare quem uellet, et de senatu doctorum excludere. Hic bene numatus, plus placebat in prandiis. Nec mirum,* ⟨*si qui*⟩ *multos increpare solitus multum in escam resolutus*
130 *erat, facto cuneo circumstrepentium garrulorum, procedebat in publicum: intus Nero, foris Cato. Totus ambiguus, ut ex contrariis diuersisque naturis, unum monstrum nouamque bestiam diceres esse compactam, iuxta illud poeticum:* "*prima leo, postrema draco, media ipsa chimera*" [Ep. 125.18; Lucr. 5.905].

135 **7** Item ad Eustochium de uirginitate seruanda ait: *Sed ne tantum uidear disputare de feminis, uiros* ⟨*quo*⟩*que fuge, quos uideris catenatos, quibus feminei contra apostolum crines, hircorum barba, nigrum pallium et nudi in patientia frigoris pedes. Haec omnia argumenta sunt diaboli. Talem olim Antonium, talem nuper*
140 *Sophronium Roma congemuit. Qui postquam nobilium introierint domos et* ⟨*deceperint*⟩ *mulierculas* "*oneratas peccatis, semper dicentes*

---

130 cuneo] cuncto *MS* ‖ -strepentium] -stare pennum *MS* ‖ 131 Nero] uero *MS*

et numquam ad scientiam ueritatis peruenientes," tristitiam simulant et quasi longa ieiunia furtiuis noctium cibis protrahunt; pudet dicere reliqua, ne uidear inuehi potius quam monere. Sunt alii (de mei ordinibus loquor) qui ideo presbyterium et diaconatum ambiunt, ut mulieres licentius uideant. Omnis his cura de uestibus, si bene oleant, si pes laxa pelle non folleat. Crines calamistri uestigio rotantur, anuli de digitis radiant et, ne plantas umidior uia aspergat, uix imprimunt summa uestigia. Tales cum uideris, sponsos magis aestimato quam clericos. Quidam in hoc esse studium uitamque posuerunt ut matronarum ⟨nomina⟩, domos moresque cognoscant. E quibus unum qui huius artis est princeps breuiter strictumque describam, quo facilius magistro cognito discipulos ⟨re⟩cognoscas. Cum sole festinus exurgit; salutandi ei ordo disponitur; uiarum compendia requiruntur, et paene usque ad cubicula dormientium senex importunus ingreditur. Si puluillum uiderit, si mantele elegans, si aliquid domesticae supellectilis, laudat, miratur, attrectat, et se his indigere conquerens non tam impetrat quam extorquet, quia singulae metuunt ueredarium urbis offendere. Huic inimica castitas, inimica ieiunia; prandium nidoribus probat et 'altilis'⟨. . . .⟩ Os barbarum et procax et in conuicia semper armatum. Quocumque te ueteris, primus in facie est. Quicquid nouum insonuerit, aut auctor aut exaggerator est fama. Equi per horarum momenta ⟨mutantur⟩ tam nitidi quam feroces, ut illum Thracii regis putes esse germanum [Ep. 22.28].

8 Item ex diuersis eius inuectiuis haec pauca notarii: *Tacui, numquid semper tacebo? dicit Dominus* [cf. Isai. 42.14]⟨. . . .⟩ *Quotidie exposcor fidem, quasi sine fide renatus sim. Confiteor, ut uolunt, non credunt*⟨. . . .⟩ *Vnum tantum placet, ut hinc recedam* [Ep. 17.3]. Item [Ep. 109.2]: *Ego, ego ⟨uidi⟩ hoc aliquando portentum, et testimoniis scripturarum, quasi uinculis Hippocratis uolui ligare furiosum: sed abiit, excessit, euasit, erupit. Et alibi sic: Inter* [160r] *mulierum textrinas cantato, immo legendas propone in tabernis tuis: ut facilius per has naenias uulgus indoctum prouoces ad bibendum* [Ad. Vigil. 1.6]. Dic⟨it⟩ quoque: *O insanum caput* [Ad. Vigil. 1.5]. *O portentum in terras ultimas deportandum* [Ad. Vigil. 1.10] *O infelicissime mortalium* [Ad. Vigil. 1.10]. Et: *Cerebrum omni crimine obsessum* [Ep. 2]. *De barathro pectoris sui coenosam spurcitiam* euomisti [Ad. Vigil. 1.8]. *Spiritus iste immundus est qui haec te cogit scribere* [Ad. Vigil. 1.10]. *Ad intimum cerebrum sentinae putredo peruenit* [Ep. 61.3], qui *quasi Orcus in tartaro, non tricipitem, sed multorum ⟨capitum⟩ habuit cerebrum qui cuncta traheret laceraretque* [Ep. 130.7].

174 per] pro MS

APPENDIX VIII

9 Item: *Iuxta errorem Origenis tunc ueniam consequaris,*
185 *quando diabolus consecuturus est, qui numquam plus quam per os tuum comprehenditur blasphemasse* [Ep. 61.4]. Et alibi: *Eructauit immundissmam crapulam, cui praecidenda est a medicis lingua, immo insanum curandum caput, ut qui loqui nescit, discat aliquando reticere* [Ep. 109.2]. Item: *Iunguntur nostri ordinis, qui et roduntur*
190 *et rodunt, aduersus nos loquaces per se muti* [Ep. 54.5]. Et alio loco: *Homo ⟨. . .⟩ et solus in universo mundo sibi et laicus et sacerdos, qui, ut ait ille, loquacitatem facundiam existimat, et maledicere omnibus, signum bonae conscientiae arbitratur* [Ad. Helu. 1.1]. *Homo rusticanus et uix primis quoque imbutus litteris* [Ad. Helu., lib. subs.].
195 Item: *Imperitissime hominum, ista non legeras, et toto scripturarum pelago derelicto, ad iniuriam Virginis tuam rabiem contulisti* [Ad. Helu. 1.16]. Dicit etiam: *Praetermitto uitia sermonis, quibus omnis liber tuus scatet. Taceo ridiculum exordium. O tempora! O mores!* [Ad. Helu. 1.16]. Item: *Os fetidum, rursum os aperit et putorem spurcissi-*
200 *mum ⟨. . .⟩ profert* [Ep. 109.1]. Et alio loco: *Plus aliquid dixerim, quod redundet in auctoris caput et insanum cerebrum, uel sanet aliquando uel deleat, ne tantis sacrilegiis ⟨simplicium⟩ animae subuertantur* [Ep. 109.1]. *O infelicem hominem et omni lacrimarum fronte plangendum* [Ep. 109.1]. *O praecidendam linguam, ac per partes et*
205 *frustra lacerandam ⟨. . .⟩ non tam somno stertis, quam lethargo* [Ep. 61.4]. Item: *Quicquid enim amans loquitur, uociferatio et clamor est appellandus* [Ep. 109.2]. Dicit etiam: *Mitte nenias illius et ineptias, ut Iohannem Baptistem audiat praedicantem: "Iam securis ad radicem arboris posita est"* [Ep. 109.4; Matt. 3.10]. Item: *Desine me*
210 *lacessere et obruere uoluminibus tuis. Parce saltem nummis tuis, quibus notarios librariosque conducens, eisdem et scriptoribus uteris et fautoribus: qui te ideo forsitan laudant, ut lucrum in scribendo faciant. Si libet exercere ingenium, trade te grammaticis atque rhetoribus, disce dialectiam, sectis instruere philosophorum, ut cum*
215 *omnia didiceris, saltem tunc tacere incipias* [Ep. 61.4]. Item: *Age poenitentium, et in sacco uersare et cinere et tantum scelus iugibus absterge lacrimis* [Ep. 61.4]. Dicit quoque: *Tribuat tibi Christus, ut audias et tacias, ut intelligas et sic loquaris* [Ep. 61.4]. Item: *Hoc plango quod te ipsi non plangis, quod te non sentis mortuum, quod*
220 *quasi gladiotor paratus Libitinae in proprium funus ornaris ⟨. . .⟩ dentes puluere teris* [Ep. 147.8]. Item: *Vos ⟨. . .⟩ talpae caprearum in me oculos possidetis* [Ep. 84.7]. Ait etiam: *Sciens et uidens in*

---

184 consequaris] consecuturus es *MS* ‖ 185 consecuturus est] consequetur *MS* ‖ 189 -guntur] -gantur *MS* ‖ 203 omni] omnium *MS* ‖ fronte] fonte *MS* ‖ 204 et] in *MS* ‖ 206 amans] amens *MS* ‖ 210 lacessere] lacerare *MS* ‖ nummis] minis *MS* ‖ 213 trade] tande *MS* ‖ te] et *MS* ‖ 214 -toribus] -toricis *MS* ‖ 219 te non] tu non *MS* ‖ 220 Libitinae] libidini *MS*

flamma mitto manum, abducentur supercilia, extendatur brachium. "Iratusque Chremes tumido desaeuiet ore" [Hor. A.P. 94]. *Consurgent procere aduersus epistolam meam turba patricia detonabit me - magnum me seductorem clamitans et in terras ultimas exportandum. Addant si uolunt et Samaritem ut domini mei titulum recognoscam* [Ep. 54.2].

10 Si amplius in hac materia de Hieronymo expectas, ego non ille fuerim, sed tute Aduersus Iouinianum, Vigilantium, Rufinum epistolas legito. [160v] Ibi huiusce materiae supellectilem magnam inuenies. Plinius inquit sic: *In summa auaritia sumptuosus, in summa infamia gloriosus* [Ep. 4.2.5]. Item: *Vnde ⟨hoc⟩ augurer quaeris? Non quia affirmat ipse, quo mendacius nihil est, sed quia certum est Regulum esse facturum, quicquid fieri non oportet* [Ep. 4.2.8]. Item de ipso Regulo: *Imbecillum latus, os confusum, hesitans lingua, tardissima inuentio, memoria nulla, nihil denique praeter ingenium insanum, et tamen eo impudentia ipsoque illo furore peruenit ut* plurimus *orator uideatur* [Ep. 4.7.4]. Item: *Regulus omnium bipedum nequissimus* [Ep. 1.5.14]. *Cui non est cum Cicerone aemulatio* sed *est contentus eloquentia saeculi nostri* [Ep. 1.5.11]. Item: *Insectatur* illum *et simiam Stoicorum appellat* [Ep. 1.5.2]. Et alibi: *Expalluit notabiliter, quamuis placeat semper* [Ep. 1.5.13]. Item alio loco sic ait: *Quid hunc putamus domi facere, qui in tanta re tam serio tempore tam scurriliter laudat?* [Ep. 4.25.3].

11 Sed si uis legere responsionem Plinii contra de se obloquentes, uide super ubi "Luxuria." Macrobius ait: *Erat enim homo amarulenta dicacitate et lingua proterue mordaci procax ac securus offensarum, quas sine delectu cari uel non amici in se passim uerbis odia serentibus prouocabat* [Sat. 1.7.2].

12 Sed redeamus iterum ad Ciceronem. Ait enim contra Pisonem: *Iamne uides, belua, iamne sentis quae sit hominum querella frontis tuae? Nemo queritur Syrum nescio quem de grege nouiciorum factum esse consulem; non enim nos color iste seruilis, non pilosae genae, non dentes putridi deceperunt: oculi, supercilia, frons, uoltus denique totus, qui sermo quidam tacitus mentis est, hic in fraudem homines impulit; hic eos, quibus erat ignotus, decepit, fefellit, induxit. Pauci ista tua amarulenta uitia noramus; pauci tarditatem ingeni, stuporem debilitatemque linguae* [Pis. 1]. Item: *Obrepsisti ad honores errore hominum, commendatione fumosarum imaginum, quarum simile habes nihil praeter colorem* [Pis. 1]. Et infra uocat

---

224 iratus-] natus- *MS* ‖ desaeuiet] desinit *MS* ‖ **225** aduersus epistolam meam] et in epistola mea *MS* ‖ **238** eo] ea *MS* ‖ ipsoque illo] eoque ipso uel *MS* ‖ furore] fauore *MS* ‖ **240** cui non est] non est illi *MS* ‖ **252** sit] fuit *MS* ‖ **253** nemo] nemo non *MS* ‖ **256** denique] deinde *MS* ‖ hic] his *MS* ‖ **257** hic eos] hac hos *MS* ‖ **258** induxit] illusit *MS* ‖ amarulenta *MS* : lutulenta *Cic.* ‖ noramus] notamus *MS* ‖ **259** ingeni] ingenii *MS*

eum beluam importunam, fatale portentum, prodigiumque rei publicae [Pis. 8–9]. Dicit de eodem sic: *Ab eodem homine in stupris inauditis nefariisque uersato uetus illa magistra pudoris et modestiae,*
265 *censura, sublata est* [Pis. 9]. Vocat etiam illum: *bustum rei publicae* [Pis. 9], et proditorem *templorum, arcem ciuium perditorum, receptaculum ueterum Catilinae militum, castellum forensis latrocini, bustum legum omnium ac religionum* [Pis. 11]. Vocat eum carnificum [Pis. 11]. Item: *Insignem nequitiam frontis inuolutam integumentis*
270 [Pis. 12]. Item de eodem Pisone sic: *Memnistine, caenum, cum ad te quinta fere hora cum Pisone uenissem, nescio quo e gurgustio te prodire, inuoluto capite, soleatum? et cum isto ore foetido taeterrimam nobis popinam inhalasses, excusatione te uti ualetudinis, quod diceres uinolentis te quibusdam medicaminibus solere curari? quam nos*
275 *causam cum accepissemus — quid enim facere poteramus? — paulisper stetimus in illo ganearum tuarum nidore atque fumo; unde tu nos cum improbissime respondendo, tum turpissime ructando eiecisti* [Pis. 13]. Et infra: *Respondes altero ad frontem sublato, altero ad mentum depresso supercilio* [Pis. 14]. Et post pauca ait: *Tu, fur-*
280 *cifer, senatum consul in contione condemnas?* [Pis. 14]. Item: *Facis quod nulla in barbaria quisquam tyrranus?* [Pis. 17]. Et: *Quis hoc fecit ulla in Scythia tyrannus, ut eos, quos luctu afficeret, lugere non sineret?* [Pis. 18]. Et in eodem: *Tu, ex tenebricosa popina consul extractus* [Pis. 18]. Et subdit infra: *Ego istius* [161r] *pecudis ac*
285 *putridae carnis consilio scilicet aut praesidio niti uolebam? Ab hoc eiecto cadauere quicquam mihi aut opis aut ornamenti expectabam?* [Pis. 19]. Item: *Frontis tuae nubeculam aut collegae tui contaminatum spiritum* [Pis. 20]. Item de illo sic: *Cum quidem tu, O uaecors et amens, cum omnes boni abditi inclusique maererent, templa geme-*
290 *rent, tecta ipsa urbis lugerent, complexus es illud funestum animal ex nefariis stupris, ex ciuili cruore, ex omni scelerum importunitate et flagitiorum impunitate conceptum* [Pis. 21]. Et infra: *Quid cum tuis sordidissimis gregibus intemperantissimas perpotationes praedicem? Quis te illis diebus sobrium, quis agentem aliquid quod esset libero*
295 *homine dignum, quis denique in publico uidit? Cum collegae tui domus cantu et cymbalis personaret cumque ipse nudus conuiuio saltaret* [Pis. 22]. Et infra: *Aliquod Lapitharum aut Centaurorum conuiuium ferebatur; in quo nemo potest dicere utrum iste plus biberit an uomuerit an effuderit* [Pis. 22]. Item: *Geminae uoragines scopu-*
300 *lique rei publicae* [Pis. 41]; *hae sunt impiorum furiae, hae flammae,*

---

265 censura] seueritas *MS* ‖ 268 ac] et *MS* ‖ 274 medicaminibus] medicationibus *MS* ‖ 275 quid] quicquid *MS* ‖ 277 ructando] eructando *MS* ‖ 283 tenebricosa] tenebrosa *MS* ‖ 285 niti] uti *MS* ‖ 286 aut] et *MS* ‖ 289 cum omnes] tum omnes *MS* ‖ 290 ipsa urbis] urbis ipsa *MS* ‖ 291 stupris] strupris *MS* ‖ 292 conceptum] concretum *MS* ‖ cum] enim *MS* ‖ 299 an . . . an] aut . . . aut *MS*

hae faces [Pis. 46]. Dicit etiam: *Ego te non uaecordem, non furiosum, non mente captum, non tragico illo Oreste aut Athamante dementiorem putem* [Pis. 47]. Et infra: *Quid est aliud furere, quam non cognocere homines, non cognoscere leges, non senatum, non ciuitatem?*
305 [Pis. 47]. Item: *Quos tu Maeandros ⟨. . .⟩ quae deuerticula flexionesque quaesisti? Quod te municipium uidit? Quis amicus inuitauit? Quis hospes aspexit? Nonne tibi nox erat pro die, solitudo pro frequentia, caupona pro oppido?* [Pis. 53]. *O scelus! O pestis! O labes!* [Pis. 56]. *O tenebrae! O lutum! O sordes! O paterni generis oblite, materni
310 uix memor!* [Pis. 62]. It infra: *Quid nunc te, asine, litteras doceam? Non opus est uerbis, sed fustibus* [Pis. 73]. Haec et multa alia Cicero in hunc uirum dixit quae gratia breuitatis omitto.

13 Vnum cum multa de Marco Antonio dicat Cicero refferam, et est Quintiliani immo *Caeli in* ipsum *Antonium* sic:
315 *Namque ipsum offendunt temulento sopore profligatum, totis praecordiis stertentem ructuosos spiritus geminare, praeclarasque contubernales ab omnibus spondis transuersas incubare et reliquas circum iacere passim: quae tamen exanimatae terrore, hostum aduentu percepto, excitare Antonium conabantur, nomen inclamabant, frustra
320 a ceruicibus tollebant, blandius alia ad aurem inuocabat, uehementius etiam nonnulla feriebat: quarum cum omnium uocem tactumque noscitaret, proximae cuiusque collum amplexu petebat: neque dormire excitatus neque uigilare ebrius poterat, sed semisomno sopore inter manus centurionum concubinarumque iactabatur* [Quint. Inst.
325 4.2.124].

14 Dicam iamtandem quibus uerbis et ego Raudensis in quempiam Sycophantem usus sim: *Nouum ⟨. . .⟩ monstrum, nouumque portentum quoddam, istac aetate nostra exortum est, magnum, ut aiunt, 'horrendum ingens,' cui ⟨. . .⟩ non torui, non truces
330 desint oculi; non rabies, non pestis absit* [Raud. Phil. 1]. *Spumat enim, stridet, bacchatur, insanit⟨. . . .⟩ Crederes illum inhumanum alterum Cacum aut Geryonem esse, seu ⟨. . .⟩ Nemeum prae ferocia leonem* seu *aprum illum Erymanthium urbes, nationes, prouincias dentibus depopulaturum* [Raud. Phil. 2]. Item dixi ipsum habere
335 non Socraticam [Raud. Phil. 4] sed *lubricam* atque *procacem linguam* [Raud. Phil. 5]. Dixi *me faecibus sordibusque suis* non [161v] *diutius immoraturum* [Raud. Phil. 6]. Dixi in capite: *Natura ab huiuscemodi corruptissimo inquinatissimoque hominum genere longe* abhorrere, sed *et a commilitionibus suis quanto absen-
340 tior atque distractior eo amplius frugi et incolumis iudicari* [Raud. Phil. 6]. Dixi ipsum habere turpia et petulantia uerba, *exquisita*

---

302 aut] et *MS* || 307 solitudo] num solitudo *MS* || frequentia] infrequentia *MS* || 314 Caeli] Caelii *MS*

APPENDIX VIII

et *elaborata flagitia* [Raud. *Phil.* 6] — *horrida, taeterrima, perobscena* — *quibus ita immiscetur, confunditur, illabitur, ut ambiguum nouumque animal quoddam, cui multum bestiae,* ⟨. . .⟩
345 *nihil hominis* ⟨*in*⟩*esse, uideatur* [Raud. *Phil.* 8]. Plenum hunc uirum *undique rimarum esse e quibus sanctissimi illi mores sui* ⟨. . .⟩ *clare quidem et lucelente introspicerentur* [Raud. *Phil.* 9]. Vocaui ipsum gymnosophistam philosophum quendam, qui *deuorato pudore* mihi si *nudus* occurret [Raud. *Phil.* 9]. Dixi me timere
350 *prouinciam tam grandem et inextricabilem ne forte introgressus scaenam illam uirtutum suarum, immo petulantiarum labyrinthum, inde me expedire aut eliminare sine subtegmine more Thesei et globo possem* [Raud. *Phil.* 9]. Despexi illum tamquam nouum Pyrrhiam aut Getam aut Tersitem, quem *Hector ex equo* non dicam lancea
355 sed festuca perfacile deturbare posset. Despexi illum tamquam lepusculum quem *canes Alexandri* non inuadebant nec aliud *animal praeter leones* tanta erat illorum generositas [Raud. *Phil.* 10]. Dixi quod *linguae suae* sicut nec *uitae alieni parcere* didicerat, quod *rabula* ⟨. . .⟩ *circumforaneus, et saeuiens fera canisque alter ille*
360 *Cerberus, honestissimis quibusque* ⟨*uiris*⟩ *semper* illatraret [Raud. *Phil.* 11]. Appellaui ipsum "subulcum" [Raud. *Phil.* 11]. Item: *Ipsum* totum in seipsum *reiicio, ut qui uir corruptissimus uulgo* praecognitus est, *tandem sese introspiciat scruteturque;* ⟨*et*⟩ *qualis pro studiorum suorum exercitatione Cato aut Laelius hactenus*
365 *euaserit intelligat* [Raud. *Phil.* 13]. Dixi quoque: *Dum probe loqui, unus e numero brutorum nescit, uel obmutescat omnino uel* saltem *conticescat. Quod si secus, ut insolentissimus est, urgebit ac perget.* Videat *quando* ⟨. . .⟩ *promiscue singulos carpere dilacerareque semper accinctus est, ne amens inopsque consilii sibi ipsi manum inferat*
370 *nomenque suum sanctum exulceret atque* antiquis notis *notas recentes* maculis *quoque* senescentibus *nouas* quasdam *macules insuat,* ⟨. . .⟩ ⟨*quasdam*⟩ *nulla tempestate, nulla aetate hominum dissuendas* [Raud. *Phil.* 13]. Item: *Video* illum *furore illo poetico iuxta Democriti Platonisque sententiam iam exalbescere, immo excandescere*
375 [Raud. *Phil.* 14].

15 Notaui etiam derisoria uerba sic: *Hei paene occidi! Nam siquidem peracutum hunc hominem cernimus et argutum. Attende, rogo, quam instructus nouus hic Achilles descendat in aciem. Quid Achilles? Verius illum simiam quandam litterariam dixerim. Putatne igitur*
380 *sapiens simia haec? Putatne rugatis labiis* curuatisque *naribus persuadere posse, ut uirtutes uitia ita confundi commiscerique, ut seorsum* ea *illa Princeps noster minime percipiat?* [Raud. *Phil.* 16–17] Item: *Videsne hunc primum impetum? Haec sunt profecto uerba* — *quid*

---

342 perobscena] *bis, semel in rasura* MS ǁ **366** unus] *om. cum lacuna* MS

rides, Candide? — *quae interloquendum* ⟨*me*⟩, ⟨. . .⟩ *ut paene* com-
385 mutescam *terrent, perinde quidem atque elephantos porcina uoce deterreri testemur. O ineruditum hominem uixdum primis elementis imbutum!* [Raud. *Phil.* 18]. Item: *Excrea pulmonem,* ⟨. . .⟩ *quod si minus, saltem caenosam illam aestuantemque linguam mordicus* comprimas [Raud. *Phil.* 18]. Item: *Excors et* [162r] ⟨. . .⟩ *gladiator inermis*
390 *me uulnerare satagit* [Raud. *Phil.* 19].

16 Impetit quidem aut saltem delirat Sycophanta noster, immo Pantomimus, *qui comediarum lectionibus dumtaxat quotidie* ⟨. . .⟩ *sudat atque uersatur* — *haec est enim sua sancta et sola religio, neque philosophiae aut alteri doctrinae afficitur* [Raud. *Phil.* 21]. *Cum*
395 *Syro illo Epicuro 'popinali, scortis,' exoletisque deditus* est, *uel utique caupo quispiam temulentus glutones, helluones, ambrones, gurdos, lurcones, decoctores, nepotes, popinones, parasitos amplectitur; et 'in pridiana semesaque obsonia' atque fragmenta pingui iure natantia secum transit; ipsique Siro, quasi nactus nouam academiam usque adeo*
400 *se totum dedicauit, ut recte Zethus alter Pacuuianus optimis sanctisque moribus immo philosophiae bellum indixerit, flagitia uel simul* ⟨. . .⟩ *perhorrenda non re minus quam sermone ligurire uideatur* [Raud. *Phil.* 22]. *Pro sceleratum!*⟨. . .⟩ *Absolutior enim atque liberior, quantum ad me attinet, uir iste redditur quod ea flagitia factitarit quae a uerecundo*
405 *et modesto uiro audiri non possunt* [Raud. *Phil.* 23]. Item: *Tunc turpius id quidem et inconsultius, dum* ⟨. . .⟩ *conscius et ultroneus in uoluptatum officinam quandam, immo extremam latrinam se* diluere et *dealbare contendit* [Raud. *Phil.* 25]. Item: *Cernimus hunc grammaticulum* ⟨*ita*⟩*que purum, ut ita dixerim, onagrum,* nudum *ludi*
410 *puerilis subsellia aut pedagogium exuisse*⟨. . . .⟩ *Sonos* historiarum *et antiquas tubas* — *ut auritus est* — *exaudit quidem; quid sibi uelint nihil exaudit. Fabulas* dumtaxat *femineas* noctu *inter* textrina *colos et fusos aut Karoli Regis et Arturi cantilenas compitis et plateis* ⟨. . .⟩ *decantatas* rectius *intelligit* [Raud. *Phil.* 27]. *Pro ridiculum caput!*
415 [Raud. *Phil.* 28]. *Ferreus ut assolet, riget, obstupescit, et indomitus calcitrat* [Raud. *Phil.* 28]. Item: *Quo abis,* ⟨*inuicte*⟩? *Quid tergiuersaris, grauissime censor?* [Raud. *Phil.* 29]. *Bacchatur exinde et quasi cynocephaleus Mercurius uidetur obliterare* [Raud. *Phil.* 30]. *Nunc iam urinam huius quam honestissimi uiri speculemur. Quid sabulosa*
420 *est? Codrus hic profecto torsionem iliacam patitur. Procuret itaque se ne crepuerit*⟨. . . .⟩ *Ex liuore magis quam ualitudine illa crepuisse uidebitur* [Raud. *Phil.* 32]. Item: *Sunt istaec poemata illa sua insignia Vergilium, ut ait, obscruatura?*⟨. . .⟩ *Nulla tamen ad aures suas quae loquerentur in hunc diem uisa Caliope*⟨. . . .⟩ *Logi sunt et nugae.*
425 *Quorsum igitur tam insolens sui aestimatio? Quid de se sibi tam*

---

400 Zethus] Getus *MS* ‖ **415** ferreus] ferrens *MS* ‖ **416** inuicte] om. cum lacuna *MS* ‖ **418** -phaleus] -phalus *MS* *magnifice persuadet ut "caprearum oculos" ipse "talpa" glebosa contemnat? Non tibi inter sanos furere* ⟨...⟩ *inter sobios bacchari istic uinolentus insularis uidetur?* [Raud. *Phil.* 33]. *Quid uenenum inglutit? Quid non euomit? Quid singulos clanculum et in angulis mordet, me uero palam? Extingueturne umquam haec febris? Vmquamne cerebri uitio sanus emerserit?* [Raud. *Phil.* 34]. Item: *Permoleste ferre uidetur Orpheus hic noster, uersiculos quosdam aduersus nomen suum celebre famamque eius sanctam et celibem editos esse* [Raud. *Phil.* 36]. *Sed hic circulator facile blaterat* [Raud. *Phil.* 37].

17 Multa huiusce generis uerba et plura immo et mordaciora quam hucusque scripserim, respondendo litteris suis annotaui quae narratui nimis prolixa fierent. Singula quae in me hominum scelestissimus oblatrauerat, in fronem suam omnino reieci. Et qui me suis maledictis uulnerare conatus est, ipse non rediturus uulneratus abscessit. Audias tamen uelim quaeque quasi in calce [162v] ipsius responsionis apposui: *Vt quanti te habeam quotidianasque tragoedias et uociferationes illas tuas quantopere perhorrescam aliquotiens intelligas, nolo equidem ex me audias, sed ab Demetrio, uiro ornatissimo, id eleganter ab eo diei solitum accipies. Eo loco aiebat: Mihi sunt "uoces imperitorum, quo crepitus uentre" redoliti. Quid enim mea refert sursum isti an deorsum sonent? Ita aeque: Quanta dementia* ⟨est⟩ *uereri ne infamer ab infamibus* [Raud. *Phil.* 183]. *Fatebor enimuero, si me exornasses, Sycophanta sanctissime, laudibusque tuis cumulatius expolisses, tuae palestrae, tuae factionis et scholae, immo tuae ephebiae dicerer; ex tuis cinaedus unus et tecum infamis sine controuersia ab omnibus quibusque digito* ⟨...⟩ *designarer. Nunc quando me carpis dilacerasque inauditaque flagitia de me* ⟨pro⟩ *more tuo libellis infamibus et uersibus mandas, signum hoc unum est et tuba quaedam clamitans: me tibi moribusque tuis omnino dissentire, in quem desaeuisti dum corrigi noluisti* [Raud. *Phil.* 184]. *Quid amplius? Ego tandem, mi Sycophanta, satis mihi fecisse morem uel mihi gessisse et his quoque qui mecum recte, modeste, honeste sentiunt teque quam notissimum habent arbitrabor, si tibi olim nullum responsum dedam, qui mentiri semper didicisti fingere nequaquam. Te tamen obtestor per crucem domini et passionem eius, per fidei nostrae uinculum ac necessitudinem* in Christo *intimam, ne animam tuam, pro qua Christus* ipse *in cruce ut illam redimeret mortem obiuit, negligas floci pendasque. Ceterum illam sacerdotibus — leprosa enim est — aperias et ostendas, atque in partes honesti uiri aetate iam fracta te recipias et oro et obsecro. Cuius est — ut Pericles aiebat — et oculos et manus et linguam castigatam* habere, *neque posthac tela in lapidem intorqueas, quae retrouersa plerumque uulnerant uulnerantem* [Raud. *Phil.* 185]. *Dices iam, si recte coniicio, hos monitus uacuos et inanes esse quandoquidem iam ad aerarium res tua deuoluta sit. Sed non sic, mi Sycophanta, non sic derepente a bona mente occidendum*

est. *Etenim si de te excursis superioribus annis fama oblocuta est, medicamentum habes: cesset uitium cessabit et rumor. Proiice abs te, rogo, Catullum, Propertium, Tibullum, et huiusce latrinae insequentem foedissimam turbam apud gentiles qui deum ignorabant concelebratam.*
475 *Et nunc litteras sacras, nunc Hieronymum, nunc Augustinum ceterosque ad bene beateque uiuendum caelitus datos antistites, si potes — poteris enim si uolueris — quam tibi familiares efficias. Plura monerem quidem at quoniam te surdum et oculis omnino captum percipio, fit quod neque monitus diuinos exaudis neque de caeli*
480 *pulchritudine aut stellarum mira uarietate his obuolutus in tenebris iudicium ullum* facere *potes* [Raud. *Phil.* 186]. *Adeas igitur eam lucem, consulo, quae sanat et "illuminat omnem hominem uenientem in hunc mundum." Nam quandoquidem ad haec uulnera quae infliguntur ex lingua illa tua paene medicus est nullus, lingua uel ipsa*
485 *atque oculis abutuntur ceterisque sensibus, dum deum ipsum non laudare, non audire, non intueri uolumus. Absterget dominus et deus meus linguam ipsam ponetque "digitos in auriculas" tuas, et conualesces. "Lutum" quoque "ex sputo" pius et misericors ipse conficiet linietque oculos tuos* [163r] *quos cum ad fontem Siloe laueris uisum actutum*
490 *accipies. Neque ex oraculo illo Delphico ceterum ex Christo eo ipso audies "cognosce te ipsum," euadesque iam tui censor ac iudex, qui mei et aliorum in hunc diem caecus insimulator accessisti* [Raud. *Phil.* 187]. *Vale,* Sycophanta *sanctissime, et si potes, me ama; si minus, saltem dilige; si minus, uel ipsum fac ut lubet. Ego uero diuina ex lege*
495 *te diligere uel persequentem compellor, nam et "qui proximum diligit, legem impleuit"* [Raud. *Phil.* 188]. *At quoniam loco cedit* ipse Sycophanta noster *in mores suos utpote "canis ad uomitum" quemadmodum et prius abit, ego iam sermonis in calce, quasi postliminii iure ad te, Candide optime, me recipio* [Raud. *Phil.* 189]. Et infra: *Etenim*
500 *uti apud familiarem mihi philosophum repperi: "Cum inquinatissimis hominibus non" est "conuicio decertandum neque maledictis apud impudentes et improbos uelitandum, ne tantisper similis et compar eorum fias, dum paria et consimilia dicas atque audias." Cum enim Metellus Numidicus, uir utique sapientissimus, a C. Manlio, tribuno*
505 *plebis, "apud populum in contione" lacesseretur "dictis petulantibus" iactareturque, ait: "Nunc quod ad illum attinet, Quirites, quoniam se ampliorem putat esse, si se inimicum mihi" dictitauerit, "quem ego mihi neque amicum neque inimicum recipio," de eo "non sum ego plura dicturus. Nam cum indignissimum arbitror cui a uiris bonis*
510 *benedicatur, tum ne idoneum quidem cui a probis maledicatur. Nunc si in eo tempore huiuscemodi homunculum" nominem, "in quo punire non" possim, "maiore honore quam contumelia" afficiam* [Raud. *Phil.* 191]. *Quid ergo, mi Candide, optimi ac sancti cuiusque uiri id esse imprimis unum arbitror? Errata castigare debeat; litigare*
515 *non debeat. Tu uero uale.* Sycophantem *quoque — ut amplius*

ualeas — similemque palaestram — quod et facis — fuge. Deum cole et time. Te uel aeque mihi atque te tibi omnino crede [Raud. *Phil.* 192].

18 Et de his iam satis, nam ex oppositis opposita saepe cognoscuntur. Ibi enim Philippi regis et Alexandri, ibi Hannibalis, ibi Catiline uirtutes et uitia immixta percipies. In hac materia uti poteris coloribus Ciceronis, scilicet "contrario," "articulo," "conduplicatione," "pronominatione," et "nominatione." Et si plures colores habere uolueris, accipe in littera "L" ubi "Laudes," nam ibi multi numerantur colores qui pertinent ad "laudem" et "vituperationem," et ubi "odium."

---

525 vituperationem] vituperium *MS*

APPENDIX IX

"Words We Ought to Use only to Execrate Vice."

Excerpta ex libro *Imitationum rhetoricarum* Antonii Raudensis

MS = Avignon: Bibliothèque Municipale, MS 1054, s. XV.

Anus [12v]: **podex, culus, extalis, clunis, nates** omnia circa impudicas partes sunt. Vnde Iuvenalis ait: *Promittunt atrocem animum, sed podice leui / caeduntur tumidae medico ridente mariscae* [2.12–13]. Et loquitur de quibusdam flagitiosis hominibus litterae
5 autem sacrae dicunt: *Computrescentur extales eorum* Philistinorum [I Sam. 5.9]. Sunt enim carnes prope podicem. Idem quoque Iuuenalis inquit: *Laudare paratus, / si bene ructauit, si rectum minxit amicus, / si trulla inuerso crepitum dedit aurea fundo* [3.106–08], (idest "ano"). Alter templi Dianae incensor ait: *Vt dubius prostes*
10 *culus anos loquitur.*
    Femina [82v]: **femella.** Virgilius dicit sic: *Tanti dux femina facti* [*Aen.* 1.364]. Inde **effemino, -as** et **effeminatus** quasi femina factus, scilicet mollis et eneruis. Dicimus etiam "Fractum in femina uirum," et "puellascere," idest "effeminari" uel "reuirescere"
15 exponit Nonius [M 154]. **Cinaedus** dicitur homo mollis, effeminatus, immundus, ut canis. Iuuenalis ait: *Inter Socraticos notissima fossa cinaedos* [2.10]. Dicimus etiam "Feminam esse indomitum animal, impotens natura." Item appellamus quandoque patronam et matronam. Nonius dicit quod *matrona est quae pepercit semel, sed*
20 *materfamilias quae saepius* [M 442]. Quidam autem "matronam locupletiorem" dicunt [Non. M 442].
    Gulosus [99r–v]: **helluo, gluto, ambro, uorax, popina, parasitus, scurra, gurdus, ganeo, lurcho, comedo, -onis, nepos** in idem redeunt. Vide imitationes. Cicero De lege agraria: *Vid⟨et⟩e nunc ⟨. . .⟩*
25 *ut impurus helluo turbet rem publicam, ut a maioribus nostris possessiones relictas disperdat ac dissipet, ut sit non minus in popoli Romani patrimonio nepos quam in suo* [1.1.2]. **Nepos** dictus est a genere quaedam scorpionum, qui natos suos consumunt, excepto eo, qui dorsum eius

26 patrimonio] patrocinio *MS*

insederit. Inde homines qui bona parentum pro luxuria consumunt
30 **nepotes** dicuntur. Cicero ibidem ait: *Vt in suis rebus, ita in re publica luxuriosus nepos* [Agr. 2.18.48]. In oratione uero ad pontifices Pro domo sua inquit: *Porticum* ⟨. . .⟩ *pauimentam trecentum pedum concupierat, amplissimum peristylum* [44.116] (appositio est), idest, locus ubi pulmenta tunduntur, quia domus Clodii erat uoluptatum officina.
35 Apuleius inquit: *Sic praeco lurchonem alloquebatur dicacule* [Met. 8.25]. **Lurchones** sunt ⟨. . .⟩ *cum auiditate cibum sumentes* [Non. M 10]. Inde **lurchare** quidam ait: *Viuite lurchones, comedones* ⟨. . .⟩ *lurchate lardum* [Lucil. Sat. 2.frag.67; Non. M 11]. Iuuenalis ait: *Radere tubera terrae, / boletum condire et eodem iure natantis / mergere ficedulas*
40 *didicit nebulone parente / et cana monstrante gula* [14.7–10]. Terentius ait: *Patria abligurierat bona* [Eun. 235]. Cicero in oratione Pro Sestio inquit: *Tu gurges et uorago patrimoni helluabare* [52.111]. A. Gellius ait: *Cum* ⟨. . .⟩ *in patrimoniis amplis helluarentur et familiam atque pecuniam prandiorum gurgitibus proluissent* [2.24.11]. Et alibi ait: *Hanc*
45 *peragrantis gulae* ⟨. . .⟩ *industriam* [6.16.6]. **Castrimargia:** gulae concupiscentia; **ambro:** consumptor patrimonii. **Comeso, -as:** per unum "m" et unum "s" unde dicitur: "Patrimonio non comeso, sed deuorato"; et "Comensabantur in conuiuiis," idest, superfluae et gulosae comedebant. Dicimus etiam: "Luxuria popinali, scortis, et potationibus
50 deditus." [Apul. Met. 8.1] **Gluto:** prodigus in gula. **Parasitus:** quasi in parapside situs, adulator, et patiens omnia prope gulam. Inde **parasitaster** diminutiuum; **scurra:** qui adulatur et sequitur aliquem, cibi gratia, quasi histrio. **Ligurire, abligurire, digustare, glutire, sorbere, deuorare, ganeo:** gulosus in tabernis. Hieronymus ait:
55 *Quaerit quemadmodum post saturitatem quoque esuriat* [Ep. 125.9]. Et alibi: *Quaerit quemadmodum non impleat uentrem, sed farciat* [Comm. in Luc. 15.186.2]. **Farctores** sunt qui uiscera uisceribus implent. Horatius ait: *Offas in iure natantes*. Terentius dicit: *Ex iure hesterno* [Eun. 939], idest aqua pingui cocta seu brodis. Hieronymus ad
60 Nepotianum dicit: *Quid prodest oleo non uesci, et molestias quasdam difficilitatesque ciborum quaerere: caricas, piper, nuces, palmarum fructus, similam, mel, pistacia? Tot*⟨a⟩ *ortorum cultura uexatur, ut cibario non uescamur pane?* [Ep. 52.12] Et ibi infra: *Audio praeterea quosdam contra rerum hominumque naturam, aquam non bibere, nec uesci pane; sed*
65 *sorbitiunculas delicatas et contrita olera, betarumque succum, non calice sorbere, sed concha* [Ep. 52.12].
LASCIVIUS [115v]: **mollis, catamitus, cinaedus, petulans,** familiares sunt. *Petulantia*, ut ait Cicero De re publica, *a petendo* dicitur *a procando et poscendo procacitas* dicitur [Cic. Rep. 4.6;

---

33 peristylum] pistillum *MS* ‖ 69 procando] prae- *MS*

70   *Frag.* Non. M 23]. Item **lasciuia, libido,** et **importunitas** est petulantia. Iuuenalis inquit: *Inter Socraticos notissima fossa cinaedos* [2.10]. Et Apuleius ait: *Scitote / qualem: cinaedum et senem ⟨cinaedum⟩ caluum* [Met. 8.24]. **Catamitus** quidam puer fuit, scilicet **Ganymedes;** unde Catamiti, idest "molles." Plautus dicit: *Vbi*
75   *aquila Catamitum raperet, aut ⟨ubi⟩ Venus Adonem?* [Men. 144]. Item Apuleius ait: *Vidi ⟨. . .⟩ simiam pileo textili crocotisque Phrygiis catamiti* [Met. 11.8].

     Leno et **Lena** [127r]: **agapeta** est conciliator libidinum. Vnde dictum est: Dimitte consortium agapetarum [Hier. *Ep.* 42.4].
80   Dicitur de Heliogabale quod habebat *emissarios qui ei bene uasatos perquirerent eosque ad aulam perducerent, ut eorum conditionibus frui posset* [Lamp. 5.4.1]. *Sagae mulieres dicuntur indagatrices ad libidinam uirorum* [Non. M 22–23]. Spero quod **sphintria** sit inuentor nouarum libidinum. **Leno** est conciliator strupri, eo quod mentes
85   miserorum blandiendo et deliniendo seducat. **Lenocinium:** uxoris meretricio, mariti consensu. Vnde Suetonius ait: *Matronas prostrate pudicitia, quibus accusator publicus deesset, ut propinqui more maiorum de communi sentitiam coercerent* Tiberius auctor fuit [Tib. 35.1]. Vnde et *feminae famosae, ut ad euitandas legum poenas iure ac digni-*
90   *tate matronali exoluerentur, lenocinium profiteri coeperunt* [Tib. 35.2]. Iuuenalis inquit: *Expectas ut non sit adultera Large / filia, quae numquam maternos dicere moechos / tam cito nec tanto poterit contexere cursu, / ut non terdecies respiret? conscia matri / uirgo fuit, ceras nunc hac dictante pusillas / implet et ad moechum dat eisdem ferre*
95   *cinaedis* (idest "conciliatoribus stupri") [14.25–30].

     Lupanar [132v]: **lustrum, fornix, prostibulum.** Terentius dicit: Stabat *in ganeum* [Ad. 359] (idest "prostibulum"), et *In gynaeceo* (idest "prostibulo") [Phor. 862]. Vide infra ne moram tibi trahas, ubi "meretrix." Apuleius adiectiue sic dicit cum se *lupanari maculasset infamia*
100   [Met. 9.26]. Item **Ephebia** est prostitutionis locus epheborum. Vnde in Sacris Litteris: *Gymnasium et ephebiam constituere* petebat [II Macc. 4.9]. Cicero in oratione Pro Sestio inquit: *Hominem emersum subito ex diuturnis tenebris lustrorum et stuprorum, ⟨uino⟩, ganeis et lenociniis adulteriisque confectum?* [9.20].
105   **Luxuria** [133v–135r]: **libido, libidinitas, pro libidine. Simplex fornicatio** est carnale commercium praeter legitimum coitum, citra adulterium. **Adulterium** est uiolatio alterius tori. **Incestus** est cognoscere monialem uel copula carnali adiunctam, uel aliqua affinitate propinquam. **Contra naturam** est cum homo
110   effundit semen extra locum ad hoc deputatum. **Fornicatio** est actus

---

76 simiam] summa *MS* ‖ crocotis-] crociis- *MS* ‖ 80 uasatos] natos *MS* ‖ 97 gynaeceo] genetheo *MS*

APPENDIX IX 317

omnis illiciti coitus qui fit extra uxorem. Intellegitur autem specialiter in usu uiduarum, concubinarum, et meretricum. **Stuprum:** illicita uirginum defloratio. **Raptus:** cum puella uiolenter a domo patris educitur, ut in uxorem habeatur. **Futuo, -is; coeo, -is; sub-**
115 **igito.** Terentius: *Amicam eius subigitant* [Hau. 566]; et *Vitiauit Glycerium* [Eun. 654 & 953; Ad. 467]. Hieronymus ait: *Nihil sic inflammat corpora et titillat membra gentalia sicut indigestus cibus* [Ep. 54.10]. Dicit etiam: *Bonum est uinum non bibere et carnes non manducare* [Ep. 54.10]. Audient haec mulieres, *qui carnes*
120 *comedentes, ⟨quae⟩ carnibus seruiunt, quarum feruor despumat in coitum* [Ep. 77.7]. Dicit quoque: *Nocte et die patitur priapismum.* **Poppysma** est extrema pars coitus. Iuuenalis inquit: *Talia uerbis / Herculeis inuadunt et de uirtute locuti / clunem agitant. "Ego te ceuentem, Sexte uerebor?"* [2.19–21]. **Ceuere** et **Crissari** sunt actus
125 oppositi. Et alibi de uxore Claudii: *Tristis abit* (scilicet, de lupanari insatiata), *sed quod potuit tamen ultima cellam clausit, adhuc ardens rigidae tentigine uoluae* [Juv. 6.128–29]. Alii Cadurcum tentiginem uocant, sicut praeputium uiri. Item de eadem uxore sic: *Tunc nuda papillis / prostitit auratis titulum mentita Lyciscae* (scilicet, "meretri-
130 cis") *ostenditque tuum, generose Britannice, uentrem* [Juv. 6.122–24]. Et alibi inquit: *Hispada membra quidem et durae per bracchia saetae / promittunt atrocem animum, sed podice leui / caeduntur tumidae medico ridente mariscae* [Juv. 2.11–13]. **Eugium** est *media pars inter naturalia membra muliebria* exponit Nonius [M 107]. Macrobius
135 ait: Tunc et pubes et genae et aliae partes corporis, pilis uestiuntur [Sat. 7.7.3]. Hieronymus dicit: *Quasi oestro libidinis* (idest "irritamenta") [Ep. 79.11]; et *Carnis titillationes* [Ep. 52.3]; ⟨et⟩ *Emissarii facti sunt,* quasi equi a equas [Comm. in Ier. 1.7]. Cicero De fato ait: *Stilponem Megaricum philosophum acutum sanum hominem et*
140 *probatum temporis illius accepiums, hunc scribunt ipsius familiares et ebriosum et mulierosum fuisse* [5.10]. Idem In Pisonem sic ait: *Itaque admissarius iste, simulatque audiuit uoluptatem a philosopho tantopere laudari, nihil expiscatus est: nisi sic sensus suos omnes uoluptarios incitauit, sic ad illius hanc orationem adhinniuit* (idest uersum equi
145 fecit ubi luxuriam notat), *ut non magistrum uirtutis, sed auctorem libidinis a se illum inuentum arbitraretur* [28.69]. Nonius dicit quod *uirosae mulieres dicuntur, uirorum appetentes, uel luxuriosae* [M 21]. Vnde quidam dicit: *Habeo uetulam et uirosam uxorem* [Lucil. *Sat.* 7.frag.287–88; Non. M 21]. *Sollicitatores aliarum nuptiarum*
150 *utrumque matrimoniorum interpellatores, etsi effeto sceleris potiri non possunt proper uoluntatem perniciosae libidinis extra ordinem puniuntur Pandectae de extraordinariis criminibus* [Dig. 47.11.1/11.3.14].

---

129 mentita] mere ita *MS* || **139** Stilponem *Cic.* : Sthilipphonem *MS*

Suetonius de Nerone sic ait: *Super ingeniorum paedagogia et nupta concubinatus uestali uirgini Rubrice uim intulit* (idest "puerorum scholam") [Ner. 28.1]. Idem de eodem: *Puerum Sporum exceptis testibus et in mulierbrem naturam transferre conatus, cum dote et flammeo persolemnia nupiarum celeberrimo officio deductum ad se pro uxore habuit; extatque cuiusquam non inscitus iocus bene agi potuisse cum rebus humanis, si Domitius Neronis pater talem habuisset uxorem* [Ner. 28.1]. De Alexandro Lampridius rem oppostiam dicit: *Exoletorum itaque expers fuit, ut,* ⟨. . .⟩ *legem de his auferendis ferre uoluerit* (scilicet "sodomitis") [Lampr. *Alex. Sev.* 39.2]. De ipso Nerone dicitur: *Suam pudicitiam usque adeo prostituit, ut* omnia membra sua contaminaret [Suet. *Ner.* 29.1]. Item: "Homo uenereus ueneripeta"; et "Mulieribus admiscetur"; et "Mulieribus operam dat"; et "Homo femellarius." **Absoleti** et **exoleti** sunt immundi et foetidi in luxuria. **Agapeta** qui cum mulieribus illicite conuersatur. **Paedico, -as; irrumo, -as; paedico, -onis** sodomita est. **Priapus, penis, inguen, mentula, genitalia, calci, testes, testiculi** uirorum sunt. **Volua, cunnus, femur** sunt mulierum. Huiuscemodi uocabulis nullo pacto uti debemus nisi ad detestanda uitia. Sunt tamen haudnulli hac nostra tempestate homines impudentissimi, qui his uocabulis non solum iocantur, non solum uersus instruunt, sed quod flagitiosissimum est, utriusque sexus concubitus detestandos et promiscuas obscenitates, non tam litteris mandant, quam docent glorianturque: quandoquidem uirtute innotescere nequeunt, horrendis saltem et igne dignis praeceptionibus illustres, uerius dixerim insanes euadere, qui tamen cum ab honestissimis uiris redarguantur, *ad excusandas excusationes in peccatis* [Ps. 140.4], statim se muniunt uerbo et exempla. Nam Catullum euestigio adducunt in medium dicentum: *Castum decet esse*⟨. . .⟩ [16.5].

MERETRIX [141v-142r]: **lupa, scorta, ganea, paelex** in idem quasi redeunt. Vide imitationes. A. Gellius dicit quendam *esse incolam sordentium ganearum* [9.2.6]. Est enim **ganea, meretrix, locatrix** quae moratur in occultis et subterraneis locis. Terentius dicit: Stabat *in ganeum* (idest "lupanar") [Ad. 359], et *in gynaeceum* (idest "prostibulo") [Phor. 862]. **Meretrix** procax est quae semper petit. Macrobius dicit quod mulier quaedam erat pulcherrimum scortum [Sat. 1.10.13]. Item: *Exigue nocte in complexu scortorum* et cum seminis [Sen. *Dial.* 10.16.5.1]. Suetonius dicit: *Scorta meritoria* [Cl. 15.4.6]. Et Hieronymus ait: *In morem scortorum prostituere castitatem* [Ep. 54.15]. Quidam dicit quod scortari in iuuene non est uitium. Dicimus etiam "hominem scortatorem." Et de Nerone dicit Suetonius: *Cenitabat* ⟨. . .⟩ *inter scortorum totius urbis et ambubaiarum*

---

169 penis] pennes *MS* ǁ **186** gynaeceum] genetheo *MS*

APPENDIX IX 319

195   *ministeria* [27.2]. Dicimus etiam: *'Ex uulgato corpore' eam lupam dixerunt* [Lact. *Inst.* 1.20.2]. Item: Ducebat secum exoletos et lupanas [Cic. *Mil.* 21.55]. Seneca dicit: *Paellices caelum tenent* [*H.F.* 5]. **Pellicatus** locus concubine. Et propter *pelicatus suspiciones* (idest "concubinatus") [Ambr. *Abrah.* 1.4.24; Cic. *Off.* 2.7.25]. **Meretrix** hones-
200   tioris locis est et quaestus, nam a merendo dictae sunt [Isid. *Diff.* 1.263]. **Prostibula** *quod ante stabulum stet quaestus diurni et nocturni cause. Sed primae tantummodo noctu faciunt* declarat Nonius [M 423]. A Gellius ait: *Ob elegantiam* ⟨. . .⟩ *formae grandem pecuniam demerebat* [1.8.3]. Et alibi sic ait: *A lenone domino puer ad merendum*
205   *artabatur* [Gell. 2.18.3]. Suetonius ait matronas Romanas crebro ad meretriciam professae sunt [*Tib.* 35]. Quintilianus ait: *Ex meretrice natus ne concionetur: quae filium habebat, prostare cepit prohibetur adolescens concione* [Inst. 7.6.3]. Suetonius item inquit: Tributo publicio tenri uoluit Gallicula, *et quae meretricium et quiue lenocinium fecissent*
210   [*Cal.* 40.1].

        Mimus [144v-145r]: ⟨. . .⟩ Hieronymus dicit: *Comedi⟨ae⟩ et Mimographi,* ⟨. . .⟩ *te nouercam declamabunt* [Ep. 54.15]; et alio loco: Ibi saltanti *histriones et mimi* [Isid. *Orig.* 18.43.1]. *Cinaedi dicti sunt apud ueteres saltatores*, sicut exponit Nonius [M 5] in Plauto
215   [*Aul.* 422].

        Scelus [221v]: **flagitium** in anima; **facinus** extra tamen ipsa aliquando confundimus. **Sacrilegium** licet suam propriam signationem habeat, tamen saepe illo abutimus et pro omni scelera flagitio, facinore, uitio, et turpitudine ponimus. Verbi causa: *Ne*
220   *tantis sacrilegiis, simplicium animae subuertantur* [Hier. *Ep.* 10.1]; et *Sacrilegia minuta puniuntur, magna in triumpho feruntur* [Sen. *Ep.* 87.23]. Item: *Sacrilegium tantum audire non possum patienter* [Hier. *Ep.* 109.3]. Sic et aliquando accipitur flagitium, ut cum dicimus: "Inter cetera notata lasciua flagitia"; et "Super adulteria, facinora,
225   scelera"; et "Omne tale flagitium." Terentius dicit: *Ah minime gentium* (idest "nequissime") [Ad. 342]. Et ibi "carnufex," hominum impudentissime [Cf. Ter. *And.* 651]. Item: *Ducebantur duo nequam cum illo, caenosam spurcitiam euomentes. Et prope turpitudinem uitae sordesque domesticas, testimonium tuum feret, 'ut paene cum lacte nutri-*
230   *cis, errores suxisse uideatur'* [Cic. *Tusc.* 3.1.2]. Suetonius dicit ibi: *Quisque profligatissimus* [Tib. 35.2]. Terentius saepe dicit: *Farcifer.* Dicimus etiam "Perditissimos uiros"; et "Quid perditius?"; et "Pro scelus." Item: "Conteram scelestos et pecatores"; et "Nihil scelestius"; et "Sceleratissimus"; et "Sceleratius." *Parce pias scelerare manus* [Verg.
235   *Aen.* 3.42]; *Nefarii a farre* (idest *sine farre*) [Hor. *Sat.* 2.8.87], quod in sacrificiis consecratur purissimum.

209 quiue] quae *MS*

TABERNA [235r]: **ganea taberna, ganeo tabernarius.** A. Gellius dicit: *In caupona* seu *cauponula* latebat [6.11.4–6]. Iuuenalis dicit pauperes in Roma non posse dormire, sed diuites sic: *Nam quae meritoria somnum admittunt?* [3.234–235], idest tabernae uel apothecae, magnis apibus dormietur in urbe, idest a diuitibus solum. **Popinae, nundinae, argisteria, stationes** idem significare uidentur; sed **popina** proprie est locus iuxta balnea publica ubi post lauacritum, a fame et siti, homines reficiuntur.

TEXO [241v]: Hieronymus ait: *Inter mulierum radios et textrina* ⟨di⟩*lanior* [Ep. 57.13]; et Mulier *ibat ad textrinum opus quotidie* [Job. 2.19]. **Textor** et **textrix:** Terentius dicit *in gynaeceo* [Phor. 862], (idest "textrino," uel est locus ubi mulieris congregantur ad filandum tempore hiemali).

VITIOSUS [257v]: **uitia** flagitiis laeuiora sunt. **Exoleti,** idest foetidi praesertim in luxuriae uitio. A. Gellius dicit: *In uitiis morum obiurgantis* [12.2.1]. Et alibi ait: *Nemo quisquam tam effetis est moribus* (idest tam uitiosus) [2.6.9]. *Impurissimus* saepe a Terentio dicitur.

---

247 gynaeceo] genetheo *MS* ‖ 252 effetis] efflictis *Gel.*

BIBLIOGRAPHY

Adam, Rudolf Georg, 1974. "Francesco Filelfo at the Court of Milan (1439–1481): A Contribution to the Study of Humanism in Northern Italy." Diss., Oxford University.

Adams, J. N., 1982. *The Latin Sexual Vocabulary.* Baltimore: Johns Hopkins University Press.

Adorno, Francesco, 1955. "Quattro lettere e un carme di Lorenzo Valla." *Rinascimento* 6:117–24.

Aesop, 1868. Αἰσωπείων μύθων συναγωγή; *Fabulae aesopicae collectae.* Ed. Karl Halm. Leipzig: Teubner.

Aguzzi-Barbagli, Danilo, 1988. "Humanism and Poetics." In Albert Rabil, Jr., ed., *Renaissance Humanism: Foundations, Forms, and Legacy.* Philadelphia: University of Pennsylvania Press. 3:85–169.

Altamura, Antonio, 1941. "Per una edizione critica dell'*Hermaphroditus.*" *La Rinascita* 4:271–75.

Ambrosioni, Annamaria, 1980. "S. Ambrogio di Milano." In Giorgio Picasso, ed., with preface by Angelo Paredi, *Monasteri benedettini in Lombardia.* 25–37. Fontes Ambrosiana 65. Milan: Silvana Editoriale.

Ames-Lewis, Francis, 1984. *The Library and Manuscripts of Piero di Cosimo de' Medici.* New York-London: Garland Publishing.

Arbesmann, Rudolph, O. S. A., 1965. "Andrea Biglia: Augustinian Friar and Humanist." *Analecta augustiniana* 28:154–218.

Argelati, Filippo, 1965. *Bibliotheca scriptorum mediolanensium, seu acta et elogia virorum omnigena eruditione illustrium qui in metropoli Insubriae oppidisque circumiacentibus orti sunt.* 1745. Ridgewood, NJ: The Gregg Press.

Aristoteles. 1972. *Ethica Nicomachea.* Trans. by Robert Grosseteste. Aristoteles Latinus 26.1–3. Leiden: Brill / Brussels: Desclée de Brouwer.

Arnaldi, F., L. Gualdo Rosa, and L. Monti Sabia, eds., 1964. *Poeti latini del Quattrocento.* Milan-Naples: Ricordo Ricciardi.

Backus, Irena, ed., 1997. *The Reception of the Church Fathers in the West: From the Carolingians to the Maurists.* 2 vols. Leiden-New York-Cologne: Brill.

Bailey, Derrick Sherwin, 1975. *Homosexuality and the Western Christian Tradition.* London: Longmans, Green, and Company.

Baron, Hans, 1966. *The Crisis of the Early Italian Renaissance: Civic Humanism and Republican Liberty in an Age of Classicism and Tyranny.* Rev. ed. Princeton: Princeton University Press.

Battistella, Antonio, 1889. *Il Conte Carmagnola: Studio storico con documenti inediti.* Genoa: Annuario Generale d'Italia.

Beaumatin, E., and M. Garcia, eds., 1995. *L'invective au Moyen Âge: France, Espagne, Italie.* Actes du Colloque "L'invective au Moyen Âge," Paris, 4–6 février 1993." In *Atalaya: Revue Française d'Études Médiévales Hispaniques* 5, 1994. Toulouse: La Sorbonne Nouvelle.

Beccadelli, Antonio (il Panormita), 1746. *Epistolarum gallicarum libri IV.* Per N.N. Clericum Regularem Teatinum. Naples: Iohannis de Simone.

———, 1824. *Hermaphroditus.* Ed. with additional epigrams F. C. Forberg. Koburg: Meusel.

———, 1908. *Hermaphroditus.* Ed. Frederick Wolff-Untereichen. Trans. and comm. by A. Kind. Leipzig: A. Weigel.

———, 1990a. *Hermaphroditus.* Ed. Donatella Coppini. Humanistica 10. Florence: Bulzoni.

———, 1990b. *Epistolae tuae.* . . . "Epistola ad Poggium Florentinum." Ed. Donatella Coppini. Appendix III, 151–59. In Antonii Panhormitae. *Hermaphroditus.* Ed. Donatella Coppini. Humanistica 10. Florence: Bulzoni.

———, 2001. *Hermaphroditus.* Trans., intro., and notes by Eugene O'Connor. Lanham-New York-London: Lexington Books.

Beck, G. F. H., 1832. *Dissertatio inauguralis de Orosii historici fontibus et auctoritate, et altera de Antonii Raudensis aliquo opere ineditio, cum Hilarii carmine in natalem Machabaeorum Matris.* Marburg.

Bernardino da Siena, St., 1957. *Le prediche volgari.* Ed. Ciro Cannorozzi. 2 vols. Florence: Typografia E. Rinaldi.

———, 1986. "Sermons." In Eric Cochrane and Julius Kirshner, eds., *University of Chicago Readings in Western Civilization*, vol. 5. Trans. by Lydia G. Cochrane. 117–38. Chicago: University of Chicago Press.

Bertalot, Ludwig, 1929–30. "Cincius Romanus und seine Briefe." In *Studien zum italienischen und deutschen Humanismus.* Ed. P. O. Kristeller. 2 vols. Storia e Letteratura: Raccolta di Studi e Testi 129–130. Rome: Edizione di Storia e Letteratura, 1975. 2:131–80. Reprint from *Quellen und Forschungen aus italienischen Archiven und Bibliotheken* 21 (1929–30) 209–55.

Besomi, Ottavio, and Mariangela Regoliosi, eds., 1984. Laurentii Valle, *Epistole.* Thesaurus Mundi 24. Padua: Antenore.

Bignami Odier, Jeanne, 1979. *La Bibliothèque vaticane de Sixte IV à Pie XI. Recherches sur l'histoire des collections de manuscrits.* Studi e testi 272. Vatican City: Biblioteca Apostolica Vaticana.

Bihl, M., 1924. "Antoine de Ro (Rodo, Raudo, Raudensis, Ravidensis, Rachidensis)." *Dictionaire d'Histoire et de Géographie Ecclésiastiques.* Paris: Latouzey & Ané. 3:807–08.

Billanovich, Giuseppe, 1963. "Giovanni del Vergilio, Pietro da Moglio, Francesco da Fiano." *Italia medioevale e umanistica* 6:203–34.

———, 1965. "Auctorista, umanista, orator." *Rivista di cultura classica e medioevale* 7:143–63.

Black, Robert, 1985. *Benedetto Accolti and the Florentine Renaissance.* Cambridge: Cambridge University Press.

———, 1987a. "Humanism and Education in Renaissance Arezzo." *I Tatti Studies: Essays in the Renaissance* 2:171–237.

———, 1987b. "The New Laws of History." *Renaissance Studies* 1:126–56.

———, 1992a. "Cosimo de' Medici and Arezzo." In Francis Ames-Lewis, ed., with intro. by E. H. Gombrich. *Cosimo "il Vecchio" de' Medici, 1389–1464.* 33–47. Oxford: Clarendon Press.

———, 1992b. "Politica e cultura nell'Arezzo Rinascimentale." In *Arezzo al tempo dei Medici: Politica, cultura, arte in una città dominata.* 16–31. Arezzo: Studio La Piramide.

———, 1996. "Cicero in the Curriculum of Italian Renaissance Grammar Schools." *Ciceroniana*, n.s., 9:105–20.

———, 2001. *Humanism and Education in Medieval and Renaissance Italy: Tradition and Innovation in Latin Schools from the Twelfth to the Fifteenth Century.* Cambridge: Cambridge University Press.

Boccaccio, Giovanni, 1951. *Genealogie deorum gentilium libri.* Ed. Vincenzo Romano. 2 vols. Scrittori d'Italia 200–01. Bari: Giuseppe Laterza & Figli.

Bolgar, R. R., 1954. *The Classical Heritage and Its Beneficiaries.* Cambridge: Cambridge University Press.

Bonacursius de Monte Magno, 2002. "Oratio L. Catilinae in M. Ciceronem." Ed. R. F. Glei and M. Köhler. *Neulateinisches Jahrbuch* 4:173–96.

Boralevi, Bice, 1911. "Di alcuni scritti inediti di Tommaso Morroni da Rieti." *Bollettino della R. Deputazione di storia patria per l'Umbria* 17:535–614.

Bordin, Bernardino, 1976. "Profilo storico-spirituale della Comunità del Santo." In Antonio Poppi, ed., *Storia e cultura al Santo: Fonti e studi per la storia del Santo a Padova.* 3 vols. Padua: Neri Pozza. 3/1:15–115.

Borsa, Mario, 1893. "Pier Candido Decembrio e l'Umanesimo in Lombardia." *Archivio storico lombardo* 20:5–75, 358–441.

Bosco, Umberto, 1948. "Precisazioni sulle *Invective contra medicum.*" *Studi petrarcheschi* 1:97–109.

Boswell, John, 1980. *Christianity, Social Tolerance, and Homosexuality: Gay People in Western Europe from the Beginning of the Christian Era to the Fourteenth Century.* Chicago-London: University of Chicago Press.

———, 1994. *Same-Sex Unions in Premodern Europe.* New York: Villard Books.

Bottini, Diego, 1984. "Il Decembrio e la traduzione della *Repubblica* di Platone: Dalle correzioni dell'autografo di Uberto alle integrazioni greche di Pier Candido." In Rino Avesani et al., eds., *Vestigia: studi in onore di Giuseppe Billanovich*. 2 vols. Storia e Letteratura: Raccolta di Studi e Testi 162–163. Rome: Edizioni di Storia e Letteratura. 1:75–91.

Bouwsma, William J., 1975. "The Two Faces of Humanism: Stoicism and Augustinianism in Renaissance Thought." In Heiko Oberman et al., eds., *Itinerarium Italicum: The Profile of the Italian Renaissance in the Mirror of Its European Transformations*. 34–60. Studies in Medieval and Reformation Thought 14. Leiden: Brill.

Boyle, Leonard E., O. P., 1993. "The Vatican Library." In *Rome Reborn: The Vatican Library and Renaissance Culture*. Ed. Anthony Grafton. xi–xx. Washington-Vatican City: Library of Congress / Biblioteca Apostolica Vaticana.

Brackett, John K., 1993. "The Florentine Onestà and the Control of Prostitution, 1403–1680." *The Sixteenth Century Journal* 24:273–300.

Brotto, Giovanni, and Gasparo Zonta, 1922. *La facoltà teologica dell'Unversità di Padova: Parte I (Secoli XIV e XV)*. Padua: Tipografia del Seminario.

Bueno de Mesquita, Daniel M., 1989. "L'onore dell'officiale." In Craig Hugh Smyth and Gian Carlo Garfagnini, eds., *Florence and Milan: Comparisons and Relations*. 135–56. I Tatti Studies 11. Florence: La Nuova Italia Editrice.

Burgess, Theodore C., 1902. "Epideictic Literature." *Studies in Classical Philology* 3:89–261.

Burley, Walter, 1472. *De uita et moribus philosophorum et poetarum*. Nuremberg: A. Koberger.

Butler, Shane, 2002. *The Hand of Cicero*. London-New York: Routledge.

Calderini, Aristide, 1939–40. "Indagini intorno alla Chiesa di S. Francesco Grande in Milano." *Rendiconti del Reale Istituto Lombardo di Scienze e Lettere* 73:97–132.

———, 1940. "Documenti inediti per la storia della Chiesa di S. Francesco Grande in Milano." *Aevum* 14:197–230.

Camporeale, Salvatore I., O. P., 1972. *Lorenzo Valla: umanesimo e teologia*. Florence: Istituto Nazionale di Studi sul Rinascimento.

———, 1976. "Lorenzo Valla tra Medioevo e Rinascimento: 'Encomion S. Thomae' — 1457." *Memorie Domenicane*, n.s. 7:11–194.

Caplan, Harry, 1970. *Of Eloquence: Studies in Ancient and Medieval Rhetoric*. Ed. A. King and H. North. Ithaca: Cornell University Press.

Casson, Lionel, 2001. *Libraries of the Ancient World*. New Haven: Yale University Press.

Casta, Mario, 1984. *Letteratura italiana*. Vol. I. Dalle origini al Quattrocento. Milan: Mursia.

Castiglioni, Carlo, 1954. "Gli ordinari della metropolitana attraverso i secoli." *Memorie storiche della Diocesi di Milano* 1:11–56.

Castiglioni, Luigi, 1929. "Review of H. Kristoferson, *Declamatio in L. Sergium Catilinam* (Göteborg: Eranos Verlag, 1928)." *Bollettino di filologia classica* 35:268.

Catalano, Aldo, 1960–61. "Cosma Raimondi: la vita e le opere." Tesi di laurea. Milan: Università Cattolica del S. Cuore.

Catalano-Tirrito, Michele, 1910. *Nuovi documenti sul Panormita tratti dagli archivi palermitani*. Biblioteca della Società di Storia Patria per La Sicilia Orientale 1. Catania: Niccolò Giannotta.

Cattaneo, Enrico, 1954. "Istituzioni ecclesiastiche milanesi." In *Storia di Milano*. 16 vols. Milan: Fondazione Treccani degli Alfieri. 4:614–721.

Celano, Thomas de. 1228. *Vita prima S. Franciisci*. In *Analecta Franciscana*, Vol. 10: *Legendae S. Francisci Assisiensis Saeculis XIII et XIV Conscriptae*. Ad Claras Aquas, Coll. S. Bonaventurae, 1927.

Cenci, Cesare, 1971. *Manoscritti francescani della Biblioteca Nazionale di Napoli*. Spicilegium Bonaventurianum 7. Quaracchi: Typographia Collegii S. Bonaventurae.

———, 1976. "Ludovico da Pirano e la sua attività letteraria." In Antonio Poppi, ed., *Storia e cultura al Santo: Fonti e studi per la storia del Santo a Padova*. 3 vols. Padua: Neri Pozza. 3/1:265–78.

Cerulli, Enrico, 1966. "Berdini, Alberto (in religione Alberto Sarteano)." In *Dizionario biografico degli Italiani*. Rome: Istituto della Enciclopedia Italiana. 8:800–04.

Chamberlin, E. R., 1965. *The Count of Virtue: Giangaleazzo Visconti, Duke of Milan.* New York: Charles Scribner's Sons.
Chittolini, Giorgio, 1989. "L'onore dell'officiale." In Craig Hugh Smyth and Gian Carlo Garfagnini, eds., *Florence and Milan: Comparisons and Relations.* 101–33. I Tatti Studies 11. Florence: La Nuova Italia Editrice.
[Cicero, M. Tullius], Pseudo-, 1991. *Orationes spuriae, pars prior: Oratio pridie quam in exilium iret; Quinta Catilinaria; Responsio Catiline.* Ed. Maria de Marco. Rome: Mondadori.
Cinquini, Adolfo, 1902. *Lettere inedite di Pier Candido Decembrio (a. 1399–1477).* Rome: Tipografia della R. Accademia dei Lincei.
Cinquini, Adolfo, and Roberto Valentini, 1907. *Poesie latine inedite di A. Beccadelli detto il Panormita.* Aosta: Giuseppe Allasia.
Clift, Evelyn Holst, 1945. *Latin* Pseudepigrapha: *A Study in Literary Attributions.* Baltimore: J. H. Furst.
Cochrane, Eric, 1989. "Comment: A Historiographical Paradigm." In Craig Hugh Smyth and Gian Carlo Garfagnini, eds., *Florence and Milan: Comparisons and Relations.* 57–60. I Tatti Studies 11. Florence: La Nuova Italia Editrice.
Coffey, Michael, 1976. *Roman Satire.* London: Methuen and Co. Ltd. / New York: Barnes and Noble.
Cognasso, Francesco, 1955. "Il ducato visconteo da Gian Galeazzo a Filippo Maria." In *Storia di Milano.* 16 vols. Milan: Fondazione Treccani degli Alfieri. 6:3–383.
———, 1966. *I Visconti.* Varese: La Tipografica Varese.
Colangelo, Francesco, 1820. *Vita di Antonio Beccadelli soprannominato il Panormita.* Naples: Tipografia di Angelo Trani.
Colombo, Cesare, 1965. "Quattro lettere inedite di Guarino." *Italia medioevale e umanistica* 8:223–24.
Conte, Gian Biagio, 1994. *Latin Literature: A History.* Trans. by J. B. Solodow. Revised D. Fowler and G. W. Most. Baltimore-London: Johns Hopkins University Press.
Copenhaver, Brian, 1992. *The Greek Corpus Hermeticum and the Latin Asclepius in a New English Translation, with Notes and Introduction.* Cambridge-New York: Cambridge University Press.
Copenhaver, Brian P., and Charles B. Schmitt, 1992. *Renaissance Philosophy.* A History of Western Philosophy 3. Oxford-New York: Oxford University Press.
Coppini, Donatella, ed. and intro., 1990. Antonii Panhormitae, *Hermphroditus.* Rome: Bulzoni.
———, 1997. "'*Dummodo non castum*': Appunti su trasgressioni, ambiguità, fonti e cure strutturali nell'*Hermaphroditus* del Panormita." In *Filologia umanistica per Gianvito Resta.* Ed. V. Fera and G. Ferraú. Medioevo e Umanesimo 94. Padua: Editrice Antenore. 1:407–27.
Corbellini, Alberto, 1915/16/17. "Apunti sull'Umanesimo in Lombardia." *Bollettino della Società Pavese di Storia Patria* 15:327–62, 16:109–73, 17:5–51.
———, 1930. "Note di vita cittadina e universitaria pavese nel Quattrocento." *Bollettino della Società Pavese di storia patria* 30:1–291.
Corio, Bernardino, 1978. *Storia di Milano.* 2 vols. [Turin]: Editrice Torinese.
Cornelli, Vicenzio, 1716. *Effigies et series chronologica ministrorum generalium totius ordinis S. Francisci Minorum Conventualium concinnatae.* Venice.
Corradi, Augusto, 1878. *Memorie e documenti per la storia dell'Università di Pavia e degli uomini più illustri che v'insegnarono.* Part I^a: Serie dei Rettori e Professori con annotazioni. Pavia: Successori Bizzoni.
Cortese, Dino, 1976. "I teologi del Santo nel secolo XV." In Antonio Poppi, ed., *Storia e cultura al Santo: Fonti e studi per la storia del Santo a Padova.* 3 vols. Padua: Neri Pozza. 3/1:153–67.
Cosenza, Mario E., 1962–67. *Biographical and Bibliographical Dictionary of the Italian Humanists.* 6 vols. Boston: G.K. Hall.
Cossart, Michael de, 1984. *Antonio Beccadelli and the Hermaphrodite.* Liverpool: The Janus Press.
Crook, J.A., 1995. *Legal Advocacy in the Roman World.* Ithaca, NY: Cornell University Press.
Curtis, Stanley J., 1950. *A Short History of Western Philosophy in the Middles Ages.* Westminster, MD: Newman Press.

Curtius, Ernst Robert, 1973. *European Literature and the Latin Middle Ages.* Trans. by Willard R. Trask. Bollingen Series 36. 1953. Princeton: Princeton University Press.

Dalfen, Joachim. 1974. *Polis und Poiesis.* Munich: Wilhelm Fink Verlag.
Dalla, Danilo, 1987. *"Ubi Venus mutatur": Omosessualità diritto nel mondo romano.* Seminario Giuridico della Università di Bologna 119. Milan: A. Giuffrè.
D'Amico, John F., 1983. *Renaissance Humanism in Papal Rome: Humanists and Churchmen on the Eve of the Reformation.* Baltmore-London: Johns Hopkins University Press.
Da Schio, Giovanni, 1858. *Sulla vita e sugli scritti di Antonio Loschi Vicentino, uomo di lettere e di stato.* Padua: Coi Tipi del Seminario.
Davies, Percival Vaughan, ed. and trans., 1969. Macrobius. *The Saturnalia.* New York-London: Columbia University Press.
Dazzi, Manlio, 1964. *Il Mussato preumanista (1261–1329): l'ambiente e l'opera.* Collana di Varia Critica 22. Vicenza: Neri Pozza.
Debby, Nirit Ben-Aryeh, 2001. *Renaissance Florence in the Rhetoric of Two Popular Preachers: Giovanni Dominici (1356–1419) and Bernardino da Siena (1380–1444).* Late Medieval and Early Modern Studies 4. Turnhout: Brepols.
Decembrio, Pier Candido, 1432. "In Antonium Siculum Panhormitam et Guarinum eius praeceptorem invectivae prima pars." *[Novis adhuc monstris // proprius assignetur locus.].* Milan: Biblioteca Braidense, MS AH XII 16, ff. 77r–88v. [Also Bologna: Biblioteca Universitaria: MS 2387, ff. 112r–128r; and selections in Sabbadini 1891, 16, 33–34, 39; and Gabotto 192–95].
De la Mare, Albina, 1973. *The Handwriting of the Italian Humanists.* Oxford: Oxford University Press.
———, 1992. "Cosimo and His Books." In *Cosimo il Vecchio de' Medici, 1389–1464.* Ed. F. Ames-Lewis. 115–56. Oxford: Clarendon Press.
De Marco, Maria, 1960a. "Note sul testo della 'Quinta Catilinaria' e della 'Responsio Catilinae.'" *Aevum* 34:281–97.
———, 1960b. "La doppia redazione della 'Quinta Catilinaria' e della 'Responsio Catilinae.'" *Ciceroniana* 2:125–45.
———, 1961–64. "La redazione Γ della 'Quinta Catilinaria' e della 'Responsio Catilinae.'" *Ciceroniana* 3–4:185–91.
———, ed., 1991a. *Declamatio in Lucium Sergium Catilinam.* Latin text with Italian translation and notes. In [Cicero]. *Opere spurie e dubbie. Orationes.* 89–154. Milan: Mondadori.
———, ed., 1991b. [Cicero]. *Opere spurie e dubbie. Orationes.* Milan: Mondadori.
D'Episcopo, Francesco, ed., 1985. *San Bernardino da Siena, predicatore e pelligrino.* Gallatina (Lecce): Congedo.
De Rijk, L. M. 1970. "On the Life of Peter of Spain, the Author of the Tractatus called afterwards Summulae logicales." *Vivarium* 8:123–54.
———, ed., 1972. *Peter of Spain (Petrus Hispanus Portugalensis), Tractutus called afterwards Summulae logicales. First Critical Edition from the Manuscripts with an Introduction.* Philosophical Texts and Studies 22. Assen: Van Gorcum.
De Segovia, Juan, O. P., 1873. *Monumenta conciliorum generalium saeculi XV.* Vol. 2. Vienna: Typis C.R. Officina Typographicae Aulae et Status.
De Sessevalle, François, 1935–37. *Histoire générale de l'Ordre de Saint François. Première partie: Le Moyen-Âge (1209–1517).* 2 vols. Paris: Revue d'Histoire Franciscaine.
Di Camillo, Ottavio, 1976. *El humanismo castellano del siglo XV.* Trans. by Mauel Lloris. Valencia: F. Torres.
Di Napoli, Giovanni, 1971. *Lorenzo Valla: Filosofia e religione nell'umanesimo italiano.* Uomini e Dottrine 17. Rome: Edizioni di Storia e Letteratura.
———, 1973. *Studi sul Rinascimento.* Il Pensiero Europa 2. Naples: Giannini.
Dionisotti, Carlo, 1937. "Miscellanea umanistica transalpina. Nota aggiunta: il Panormita e la polemica col Raudense." *Giornale storico della letteratura italiana* 110:297–300.

Ditt, Ernst, 1931. "Pier Candido Decembrio: contributo alla storia dell'Umanesimo italiano." *Memorie del Reale Istituto Lombardo de scienze e lettere: Classe di lettere scienze morali e storiche* 24:21–108.

Dizionario Garzanti della lingua italiana. 1981. Milan: Garzanti Editore.

Eisenstein, Elizabeth L., 1979. *The Printing Revolution in Early Modern Europe.* 2 vols. Cambridge: Cambridge University Press.

Esposito Frank, Maria, 1999. *Le insidie dell'allegoria: Ermolao Barbaro il vecchio e la lezione degli antichi.* Venice: Istituto Veneto di Scienze Lettere ed Arti.

Fabiano, Carolina, 1949. "Pier Candido Decembrio traduttore d'Omero." *Aevum* 23:36–51.

Facio, Bartolomeo, 1978. *Invective in Laurentium Vallam.* Critical edition and intro. Ennio I. Rao. Studi e Testi di Letteratura Italiana 15. Naples: Società Editrice Napoletana.

Febvre, Lucien, and Henri-Jean Martin, 1976. *The Coming of the Book: The Impact of Printing, 1450–1800.* Trans. by D. Gerard. London-New York: Verso.

Ferrari, Mirella, 1979. "Per una storia delle biblioteche francescane a Milano nel Medioevo e nell'Umanesimo." *Archivum franciscanum historicum* 72:429–64.

———, 1984. "Fra i *Latini scriptores* di Pier Candido Decembrio e biblioteche umanistiche milanesi: codici di Vitruvio e Quintiliano." In Rino Avesani et al., eds., *Vestigia: Studi in onore di Giuseppe Billanovich.* 2 vols. 247–96. Storia e letteratura: Raccolta di Studi e Testi 162–163. Rome: Edizioni di Storia e Letteratura.

———, 1988. "La 'littera antiqua' a Milan, 1417–1439." In Johanne Autenrieth and Ulrich Eigler, eds., *Renaissance- und Humanistenhandschriften.* 13–29. Munich: R. Oldenbourg Verlag.

Field, Arthur, 1986. "Cristoforo Landino's First Lectures on Dante." *Renaissance Quarterly* 39:16–48.

———, 1988. *The Origins of the Platonic Academy of Florence.* Princeton: Princeton University Press.

———, 1996. "Lorenzo Buonincontri and the First Public Lectures on Manilius (Florence, ca. 1475–78)." *Rinascimento* 36:207–25.

———, 1998. "Leonardo Bruni, Florentine Traitor? Bruni, the Medici, and an Aretine Conspiracy of 1437." *Renaissance Quarterly* 51:1109–50.

Filelfo, Francesco, 2005. *Satyrae I (Decadi I–V).* Critical edition by Silvia Fiaschi. Rome: Edizioni di Storia e Letteratura.

Fois, Mario, 1969. *Il pensiero cristiano di Lorenzo Valla nel quadro storico-culturale del suo ambiente.* Analecta Gregoriana 174. Rome: Editrice dell'Università Gregoriana.

Forcellini, Egidio, 1858–60. *Totius latinitatis lexicon opera et studio Aegidii Forcellini lucubratum.* Prato: Typis Aldinianis.

Fossati, F., 1926. "Note on Antonio da Rho." In P. C. Decembrio, *Vita Philippi Mariae tertii Ligurum ducis.* Eds. A. Butti, F. Fossati, and G. Petraglione. Rerum Italicarum Scriptores, 2nd ed., 20/1:346–57.

Fredborg, Karin Margareta, 1987. "The Scholastic Teaching of Rhetoric in the Middle Ages." *Cahiers de l'Institut de Moyen-Âge Grec et Latin* 55:85–105.

Fubini, Riccardo, 1961. "Antonio da Rho." In *Dizionario biografico degli Italiani.* Rome: Istituto della Enciclopedia Italiana. 3:574–77.

———, 1966. "Tra umanesimo e concili: note e giunte a una publicazione recente su Francesco Pizolpasso (1370c.–1443)." *Studi medievali*, 3rd ser., 7:323–70.

———, 1974. "Intendimenti umanistici e riferimenti patristici dal Petrarca al Valla: note sugli sviluppi della saggistica morale nell'umanesimo." *Giornale storico della letteratura italiana* 91:520–78.

———, 2003a. *Humanism and Secularization from Petrarch to Valla.* Durham: Duke University Press.

———, 2003b. *Storiografia dell' umanesimo in Italia da Leonardo Bruni ad Annio di Viterbo.* Rome: Edizioni di Storia e Letteratura.

Fumagalli, Giuseppe, 1934–81. *L'ape latina.* Milan: Hoepli.

Gabel, Leona C., 1964. "The First Revival of Rome, 1420–1428." In Leona Gabel et al., eds., *The Renaissance Reconsidered: A Symposium.* 13–25. Smith College Studies in History 44. Northhampton: Smith College.

Gabotto, Ferdinando, 1893. "L'attività politica di Pier Candido Decembrio." *Giornale ligustico di archeologia, storia e letteratura* 20:161–98, 241–70.
Gaisser, Julia Haig, 1993. *Catullus and his Renaissance Readers*. Oxford: Clarendon Press.
Gamberini, Andrea, and Francesco Somaini, 2001. *L'età dei Visconti e degli Sforza, 1277–1535*. Milan: Skira.
Garin, Eugenio, 1955. "La cultura milanese nella prima metà del XV secolo." In *Storia di Milano*. 16 vols. Milan: Fondazione Treccani degli Alfieri. 6:546–608.
———, 1965. *Italian Humanism: Philosophy and Civic Life in the Renaissance*. Trans. by Peter Munz. New York: Harper & Row.
———, 1989. "Umanisti e filosofi nel Quattrocento a Firenze e a Milano: Convergenze e Contrasti." In Craig Hugh Smyth and Gian Carlo Garfagnini, eds., *Florence and Milan: Comparisons and Relations*. I Tatti Studies 11. 3–15. Florence: La Nuova Italia Editrice.
Garnsey, Peter, 2002. "Lactantius and Augustine." In A. K. Bowman, H. M. Cotton, M. Goodman and S. Price, eds., *Representations of Empire: Rome and the Mediterranean World*. 153–79. Oxford: Oxford University Press.
Garzia, Raffa, 1924. "L'*Hermaphroditus* del Panormita." In *Consensi e dissensi*. 5–82. Bologna: Stabilimenti Poligrafici Riuniti.
Gaspary, A., 1886. "Einige ungedruckte Briefe und Verse von Antonio Panromita." *Vierteljahrsschrift für Kultur und Litteratur der Renaissance* 1:474–84.
Gill, Joseph, S. J., 1959. *The Council of Florence*. Cambridge: University of Cambridge Press.
———, 1961. *Eugenius IV: Pope of Christian Union*. The Popes through History 1. London: Burns & Oats.
Glei, Reinhold F., 2002. "Catilinas Rede gegen Cicero: literarische Fälschung, rhetorische Übung oder politisches Pamphlet?" *Neulateiniches Jahrbuch* 4:155–72.
Gnesotto, Attilio, ed., 1915–16. "Francesco Barbaro, *De re uxoria*, e la lettera prefatoria ad Lorenzo di Giovanni de' Medici (1395–1440)." *Atti e memorie della R. Accademia di scienze, lettere ed arti in Padova* 32:6–105.
Goodman, Howard L., 1993. "Paper Obelisks: East Asia in the Vatican Vaults." In Anthony Grafton, ed., *Rome Reborn: The Vatican Library and Renaissance Culture*. 251–92. Washington: Library of Congress / Vatican City: Biblioteca Apostolica Vaticana.
Gordon, Phyllis, trans. and annot., 1974. *Two Renaissance Book Hunters: The Letters of Poggius Bracciolini to Nicolaus de Niccolis*. New York: Columbia University Press.
Grafton, Anthony, 1988. "Quattrocento Humanism and Classical Scholarship." In Albert Rabil, ed., *Renaissance Humanism: Foundations, Forms, and Legacy*. Philadelphia: University of Pennsylvania Press. 3:23–66.
———, 1991. *Defenders of the Text: The Traditions of Scholarship in an Age of Science, 1450–1800*. Cambridge, MA: Harvard University Press.
———, ed., 1993. *Rome Reborn: The Vatican Library and Renaissance Culture*. Washington: Library of Congress / Vatican City: Biblioteca Apostolica Vaticana.
Grafton, Anthony, and Lisa Jardine, 1986. *From Humanism to the Humanities: Education and the Liberal Arts in Fifteenth- and Sixteenth-Century Europe*. Cambridge, MA: Harvard University Press.
Gray, Hanna H., 1963. "Renaissance Humanism: The Pursuit of Eloquence." *Journal of the History of Ideas* 24:497–514.
Greenfield, Concetta Carestia, 1981. *Humanist and Scholastic Poetics, 1250–1500*. Lewisburg: Bucknell University Press / London-Torono: Associated University Press.
Grendler, Paul F., 1988. "Chivalric Romances in the Italian Renaissance." *Studies in Medieval and Renaissance History* 10:57–102.
———, 1989. *Schooling in Renaissance Italy: Literacy and Learning, 1300–1600*. Baltimore-London: Johns Hopkins University Press.
Griffiths, Gordon, James Hankins, and David Thompson, trans. and intro., 1987. *The Humanism of Leonardo Bruni: Selected Texts*. Binghamton: Medieval & Renaissance Texts & Studies.
Griggio, Claudio, 1996. "Note sulla tradizione dell'invettiva dal Petrarca al Poliziano." In *Bufere e molli aurette: polemiche letterarie dallo Stilnovo alla "Voce."* Ed. Maria Grazia Pensa and Silvio Ramat. 37–51. Milan: Angelo Guerini e Associati.

Gualdo, Germano, 1989. "Antonio Loschi, segretario apostolico (1406–1436)." *Archivio storico italiano* 147:749–69.
Gualdo Rosa, Lucia, 1984. *La fede nella "paideia": Aspetti della fortuna europea di Isocrate nei secoli XV e XVI.* Studi storici 140–142. Rome: Istituto Storico Italiano per il Medio Evo.
———, 1992. "Un nuovo testimone della 'Posteritati' ed altri nuovi codici petracheschi." *Studi Petrarcheschi* 9:221–42.
———, 1994. "Due nuove lettere del Bruni e il ritrovamento del 'Materiale Bertalot.'" *Rinascimento,* n.s. 34:115–41.
Gualdo Rosa, Lucia, Sergio Ingegno, and Anna Nunziata, 1996. *"Molto più preziosi del' oro": codici di casa Barzizza alla Biblioteca Nazionale di Napoli.* Intro. by Lucia Gualdo Rosa. Annali dell'Istituto Universitario Orientale di Napoli, Dipartimento di studi del mondo classico ed del Mediterraneo antico, Quaderni II. Naples: Luciano Editore.
Gundersheimer, Werner L., 1973. *Ferrara: The Style of a Renaissance Despotism.* Princeton: Princeton University Press.

Hamilton, Alastair, 1993. "Eastern Churches and Western Scholarship." In Anthony Grafton, ed., *Rome Reborn: The Vatican Library and Renaissance Culture.* 225–49. Washington: Library of Congress / Vatican City: Biblioteca Apostolica Vaticana.
Hankins, James, 1990. *Plato in the Renaissance.* 2 vols. Columbia Studies in the Classical Tradition 17. Leiden: Brill.
———, 1993. "The Popes and Humanism." In Anthony Grafton, ed., *Rome Reborn: The Vatican Library and Renaissance Culture.* 47–85. Washington: Library of Congress / Vatican City: Biblioteca Apostolica Vaticana.
———, 1997. *Repertorium Brunianum: A Critical Guide to the Writings of Leonardo Bruni.* Vol. I: Handlist of Manuscripts. Istituto Storico Italiano per il Medio Evo: Fonti per la storia dell'Italia medievale, Subsidia 5. Rome: Palazzo Borromini.
Hay, Denys, 1977. *The Church in Italy in the Fifteenth Century: The Birkbeck Lectures, 1971.* Cambridge: Cambridge University Press.
Henderson, Jeffrey, 1991. *The Maculate Muse.* Oxford-New York: Oxford University Press.
Hergemöller, Bernd-Ulrich, 2001. *Sodom and Gomorrah: On the Everyday Reality and Persecution of Homosexuals in the Middle Ages.* Trans. by John Phillips. London-New York: Free Association Books.
Hinks, Roger, 1976. *Myth and Allegory in Ancient Art.* 1939, London, The Warburg Institute. Nendeln-Liechtenstein: Kraus Reprint.
Hollar, John A., 1972. "The Traditions of Satire and Invective in Catullus." Diss. Saint Louis: Washington University.
Hyginus, 1960. *The Myths of Hyginus.* Trans. and ed. Mary Grant. Lawrence: University of Kansas Press.
———, 1993. *Fabulae.* Ed. Peter K. Marshall. Bibliotheca Scriptorum Graecorum et Romanorum Teubneriana. Stuttgart: Teubner.

Ianziti, Gary, 1980. "From Flavio Biondo to Lodrisio Crivelli: The Beginnings of Humanistic Historiography in Sforza Milan." *Rinascimento* 20:3–39.
———, 1988. *Humanistic Historiography under the Sforzas: Politics and Propaganda in Fifteenth-Century Milan.* Oxford: Clarendon Press.
———, 1989. "The Rise of Sforza Historiography." In Craig Hugh Smyth and Gian Carlo Garfagnini, eds., *Florence and Milan: Comparisons and Relations.* 79–94. I Tatti Studies 11. Florence: La Nuova Italia Editrice.
Ijsewijn, Jozef, 1990. *Companion to Neo-Latin Studies: Part I: History and Diffusion of Neo-Latin Literature.* 2nd ed. Supplementa Humanistica Lovaniensia 5. Louvain: Peeters Press / Leuven University Press.
Ijsewijn, Josef, with Dirk Sacré, 1998. *Companion to Neo-Latin Studies: Part II: Literary, Linguistic, Philological, and Editorial Questions.* 2nd ed. Supplementa Humanistica Lovaniensia 14. Louvain: Leuven University Press.

Iriarte, Lázaro, O. F. M. Cap., 1982. *Franciscan History: The Three Orders of St. Francis of Assisi.* Trans. by Patricia Ross. Chicago: Franciscan Herald Press.

Jansen, Katherine Ludwig, 1995. "Mary Magdalen and the Mendicants: The Preaching of Penance in the Late Middle Ages." *Journal of Medieval History* 21:1–25.

———, 2000. *The Making of the Magdalen: Preaching and Popular Devotion in the Later Middle Ages.* Princeton: Princeton University Press.

Jordan, Louis, and Susan Wool, 1984/86/89. *The Inventory of Western Manuscripts in the Biblioteca Ambrosiana.* 3 vols. Notre Dame: University of Notre Dame Press.

Jordan, Mark D., 1997. *The Invention of Sodomy in Christian Theology.* Chicago: University of Chicago Press.

Kallendorf, Craig W., ed. and trans., 2002. *Humanist Educational Treatises.* The I Tatti Renaissance Library. Cambridge, MA: Harvard University Press.

Kelly, J. N. D., 1975. *Jerome: His Life, Writings, and Controversies.* London: Duckworth.

Kempter, Gerda, 1980. *Ganymed: Studien zur Typologie, Ikonographie un Ikonologie.* Cologne: Böhlau Verlag.

Kennedy, George A., 1972. *The Art of Rhetoric in the Roman World, 300 B.C.–A.D. 300.* Princeton: Princeton University Press.

———, 1980. *Classical Rhetoric and Its Christian and Secular Tradition from Ancient to Modern Times.* Chapel Hill: University of North Carolina Press.

Kennedy, Ruth W., 1964. "The Contribution of Martin V to the Rebuilding of Rome, 1420–1431." In Leona Gabel et al., eds., *The Renaissance Reconsidered: A Symposium.* 27–39. Smith College Studies in History 44. Northhampton: Smith College.

Kessler, Eckhard, 1989. "Die Pädagogik der italienischen Humanisten im Kontext des späten Mittelalters." In H. Boockmann, B. Moeller, and K. Stackmann, eds., *Lebenslehren und Weltentwürfe im Übergang vom Mittelalter zur Neuzeit.* 160–80. Göttingen: Vandenhoeck & Ruprecht.

King, Margaret L., 1986. *Venetian Humanism in an Age of Patrician Dominance.* Princeton: Princeton University Press.

———, 1988a. "Book-Lined Cells: Women and Humanism in the Early Italian Renaissance." In Albert Rabil, ed., *Renaissance Humanism: Foundations, Forms, and Legacy.* Philadelphia: University of Pennsylvania Press. 1:434–53.

———, 1988b. "Humanism in Venice." In Albert Rabil, ed., *Renaissance Humanism: Foundations, Forms, and Legacy.* Philadelphia: University of Pennsylvania Press. 1:209-34.

Klopsch, Paul, ed., 1967. Pseudo-Ovidius, *De uetula: Untersuchungen und Text.* Mittellateinische Studien und Texte 2. Ed. K. Langosch. Leiden-Cologne: Brill.

Kohl, Benjamin G., 1992. "The Changing Concept of the *studia humanitatis* in the Early Renaissance." *Renaissance Studies* 6:185–209.

Kohl, Benjamin G., and Ronald G. Witt, eds. and trans., 1978. *The Earthly Republic: Italian Humanists on Government and Society.* With Elizabeth B. Wells. Philadelphia: University of Pennsylvania Press.

Kolve, V. A., 1998. "Ganymede / *Son of Getron:* Medieval Monasticism and the Drama of Same-Sex Desire." *Speculum* 73:1014–67.

Koster, Severin, 1980. *Die Invektive in der griechischen und römischen Literatur.* Meisenheim am Glan: Verlag Anton Hain.

Kraye, Jill, and M. W. F. Stone, eds., 2000. *Humanism and early Modern Philosophy.* London-New York: Routledge.

Kristeller, Paul O., 1977–97. *Iter Italicum.* 6 vols. and index. Leiden: Brill.

———, 1979. *Renaissance Thought and Its Sources.* Ed. M. Mooney. New York: Columbia University Press.

———, 1984/85. *Studies in Renaissance Thought and Letters.* 2 vols. Storia e Letteratura: Raccolta di Studi e Testi 54 & 166. Rome: Edizioni di Storia e Letteratura.

———, 1988a. "Renaissance Humanism and Classical Antiquity." In Albert Rabil, ed., *Renaissance Humanism: Foundations, Forms, and Legacy.* Philadelphia: University of Pennsylvania Press. 1:5–28.

———, 1988b. "Humanism and Moral Philosophy." In Albert Rabil, ed., *Renaissance Humanism: Foundations, Forms, and Legacy.* Philadelphia: University of Pennsylvania Press. 3:271–309.

Kristoferson, Hans, ed., 1928. *Declamatio in Lucium Sergium Catilinam.* Text och Tradition. Göteborg: Elanders Boktryckeri Aktiebolag.

Labalme, Patricia H., 1969. *Bernardo Giustiniani: A Venetian of the Quattrocento.* Uomini e Dottrini 13. Rome: Edizioni di Storia e Letteratura.

Lactantius, L. Caecilius Firmianus, 2003. *Divine Institutes.* Trans. with intro. and notes by Anthony Bowen and Peter Garnsey. Liverpool: Liverpool University Press.

Lamy, Marielle, 2000. *L'Immaculée Conception étapes et enjeux d'une controverse au Moyen Âge (XIIe–XVe siècles).* Collection des Études Augustiniennes: Série Moyen Âge et Temps Modernes 35. Paris: Institut d'Études Augustiniennes.

Laureys, Marc, 2003. "Per una storia dell' invettiva umanistica." *Studi umanistici piceni* 23:9–30.

Lee, Egmont, 1978. *Sixtus IV and Men of Letters.* Temi e Testi 26. Rome: Edizioni di Storia e Letteratura.

Liebermann, Wolf-Lüder, 1998. "Invektive." In *Der neue Pauly, Enzyklopädie der Antike.* Ed. H. Cancik and H. Schneider. Stuttgart-Weimar: J.B Metzler. 5:1049–51.

Li Gotti, Ettore, 1940. "Il Beccadelli e l'*Hermaphroditus.*" *Archivio storico per la Sicilia* 6:261–64.

Lindberg, David C., 1992. *The Beginnings of Western Science: The European Scientific Tradition in Philosophical, Religious, and Institutional Context, 600 B.C. to A.D. 1450.* Chicago-London: University of Chicago Press.

Locatelli, S., 1931. "Bartolomeo Bayguera ed il suo *Itinerarium* (1425)." *Commenari dell'Ateneo di Brescia per l'anno 1931.* Brescia: Ateneo di Brescia.

Lombardi, Giuseppe, ed., trans., and intro., 1982. Antonio da Rho, *Apologia - Orazioni.* Edizione Nazionale dei Classici del Pensiero Italiano, 2nd ser. 36. Rome: Centro Internazionale di Studi Umanistici.

———, 2003. *Saggi.* Preface by Massimo Miglio. Rome: Roma nel Rinascimento.

Lorch, Maristella, 1988. "Petrarch, Cicero, and the Classical Pagan Tradition." In Albert Rabil, ed., *Renaissance Humanism: Foundations, Forms, and Legacy.* Philadelphia: University of Pennsylvania Press. 1:71–94.

Lucarelli, Giuliano, 1984. *I Visconti di Milano e Lucca risorta a stato autonomo.* Lucca: Maria Pacini Fazzi Editore.

Ludwig, Walther, 1990. "The Origin and Development of the Catullan Style in Neo-Latin Poetry." In Peter Godman and Oswyn Murray, eds., *Latin Poetry and the Classical Tradition: Essays in Medieval and Renaissance Literature.* 181–97. Oxford: Clarendon Press.

———, 2001. "Der Ritter und der Tyrann: Die humanistischen Invektiven des Ulrich von Hutten gegen Herzog Ulrich von Württemberg." *Neulateinisches Jahrbuch* 3:3–16.

Lutz, Cora E., ed. and intro., 1962. *Remigii Autissiodorensis Commentum in Martianum Capellam, Libri I–II.* Leiden: Brill.

Maffei, Timoteo, 2000. *In sanctem rusticitatem litteras impugnantem.* Intro., critical ed., and comm. by Patrizia Sonia De Corso. Pref. by Agostino Sottili. Verona: Archivio Storico Curia Diocesana.

Magenta, Carlo, 1883. *I Visconti e gli Sforza nel Castello di Pavia.* 2 vols. Milan: Hoepli.

Magni, Domenico, 1937. "Gasparino Barzizza, una figura del primo Umanesimo." *Bergomum* 31:104–18, 143–70, 205–22.

Maiocchi, Rodolfo, ed., 1905/13/15. *Codici diplomatico della Università di Pavia.* 2 vols. in 3 pts. Pavia: Successori Fratelli Fusi.

———, 1907. "Il Concilio Generale di Pavia del 1423." *Rivista di scienze storiche* 4:401–17.
Mancini, Girolamo, 1891. *Vita di Lorenzo Valla*. Florence: Sansoni.
Marrou, Henri I., 1956. *A History of Education in Antiquity*. Trans. by George Lamb. New York: Sheed & Ward.
———, 1957. *St. Augustine and His Influence through the Ages*. Trans. by P. Hepburne-Scott. New York: Harper Torchbooks.
Marsh, David, 1979. "Grammar, Method, and Polemic in Lorenzo Valla's *Elegantiae*." *Rinascimento*. Ser. 2. 19:91–116.
———, 1980. *The Quattrocento Dialogue: Classical Tradition and Humanist Innovation*. Cambridge, MA: Harvard University Press.
———, 1992. "Xenophon." In *Catalogus translationum et commentariorum: Mediaeval and Renaissance Latin Translations and Commentaries*. Vol. 7. 75–196. Washington, DC: The Catholic University of America Press.
———, 1998a. *Lucian and the Latins: Humor and Humanism in the Early Renaissance*. Ann Arbor: University of Michigan Press.
———, 1998b. "Lucian and Paradox in the Early Quattrocento." In *Acta Conventus Neo-Latini: Proceedings of the Ninth International Congress of Neo-Latin Studies, Bari, 29 August to 3 September 1994*. Medieval and Renaissance Texts and Studies 184. 395–400. Tempe, AZ: Medieval & Renaissance Texts & Studies.
———, 1999. "Dialogue and Discussion in the Renaissance." In *The Cambridge History of Literary Criticism*. Vol. 3. *The Renaissance*. 265–70. Cambridge: Cambridge University Press.
———, 2000a. "Alberti, Scala, and Ficino: Aesop in Quattrocento Florence." *Albertiana* 3:105–18.
———, 2000b. "Lucian's *Slander* in the Early Renaissance: The Court as *Locus invidiae*." *Allegorica* 21:62–70.
———, ed. and trans., 2003. Francesco Petrarca. *Invectives*. The I Tatti Renaissance Library 11. Cambridge, MA-London: Harvard University Press.
Martin, Henri-Jean, 1994. *The History and Power of Writing*. Trans. by Lydia G. Cochrane. Chicago-London: University of Chicago Press.
Mattei, Felice Antonio, O. F. M., 1760. *De vita et scriptis Antonii Rhaudensis Minoritae Conventualis epistola (ad Larentium Ganganellium)*. 1–46. Ferrara.
McKibben, William T., 1951. *"In bovem mugire."* *Classical Philology* 46:165–72.
McManamon, John M., S. J., 1979. "Renaissance Preaching: Theory and Practice." *Viator* 10:356–73.
———, 1982. "Innovation in Early Humanist Rhetoric: The Oratory of Pier Paolo Vergerio the Elder." *Rinascimento*, n.s., 22:3–32.
———, 1985. "Pier Paolo Vergerio (the Elder) and the Beginnings of the Humanist Cult of Jerome." *The Catholic Historical Review* 71:353–71.
———, 1989a. *Funeral Oratory and the Cultural Ideals of Italian Humanism*. Chapel Hill: University of North Carolina Press.
———, 1989b. "Continuity and Change in the Ideals of Humanism: The Evidence from Florentine Funeral Oratory." In Marcel Tetel, Ronald G. Witt, and Rona Goffin, eds. *Life and Death in Fifteenth-Century Florence*. 68–87. Durham, NC: Duke University Press.
———, 1996. *Pierpaolo Vergerio the Elder: The Humanist as Orator*. Medieval & Renaissance Texts & Studies 163. Tempe, AZ: Medieval & Renaissance Texts & Studies.
McNeill, John T., and Helena M. Gamer, ed. and trans., 1938/90. *Medieval Handbooks of Penance: A Translation of the Principal Libri Poenitentiales*. Records of Western Civilization. New York: Columbia University Press.
Medici, Gabriele Cornaggia, 1936. "Il vicariato visconteo sui concilii generali riformatori." In *Studi in onore di Francesco Scaduto*. 2 vols. Florence: Casa Editrice Poligrafia Universitaria. 1:89–128.
Mercati, Giovanni, 1937. "Miscellanea di note storico-critiche." In *Opere minori raccolte in occasione del settantesimo natalizio sotto gli auspicii di S. S. Pio XI*. 108–17. Studi e testi 76. Vatican City: Biblioteca Apostolica Vaticana; Reprint from *Studi e documenti di storia e diritto* 15 (1894): 303–47.

Mercer, R. G. G., 1979. *The Teaching of Gasparino Barzizza with Special Reference to his Place in Paduan Humanism.* MHRA Texts and Dissertations 10. London: The Modern Humanities Research Association.

Merrill, Norman W., 1975. "Cicero and Early Roman Invective." Diss. Cincinnati: University of Cincinnati.

Mésoniat, Claudio, 1984. *Poetica Theologia: la "Lucula Noctis" di Giovanni Dominici e le dispute letterarie tra '300 e '400.* Uomini e Dottrine 27. Rome: Edizioni di Storia e Letteratura.

Monfardini, Bruno, 1970/71. "Antonio da Rho e le *Imitationes rhetoricae*." Tesi di laurea. Milan: Università Cattolica del S. Cuore.

Monfasani, John, 1976. *George of Trebizond: A Biography and a Study of his Rhetoric and Logic.* Leiden: Brill.

———, 1983. "The Byzantine Rhetorical Tradition and the Renaissance." In *Renaissance Eloquence: Studies in the Theory and Practice of Renaissance Rhetoric.* Ed. James J. Murphy. 174–87. Berkeley-Los Angeles-London: University of California Press.

———, ed., 1984. *Collectanea Trapezuntiana: Texts, Documents, and Bibliographies of George of Trebizond.* Medieval & Renaissance Texts & Studies 25. Binghamton, NY: MRTS in conjuction with The Renaissance Society of America.

———, 1988. "Humanism and Rhetoric." In Albert Rabil, ed., *Renaissance Humanism: Foundations, Forms, and Legacy.* Philadelphia: University of Pennsylvania Press. 3:171–235. And in *Language and Learning in Renaissance Italy: Selected Articles.* Brookfield: Variorum, 1:171–235.

———, 1990. "In Praise of Ognibene and Blame of Guarino: Andronicus Contoblancas's Invective against Niccolò Botano and the Citizens of Brescia." *Bibliothèque d'Humanisme et Renaissance* 52:309–22.

———, 1991. "The Fraticelli and Clerical Wealth in Quattrocento Rome." In John Monfasani and Ronald G. Musto, eds., *Renaissance Society and Culture: Essays in Honor of Eugene F. Rice, Jr.* 177–95. New York: Italica Press.

———, 1992. "Episodes of Anti-Quintilianism in the Italian Renaissance: Quarrels on the Orator as a *Vir Bonus* and Rhetoric as the *Scientia Bene Dicendi*." *Rhetorica* 10:119–38.

———, 1994. *Language and Learning in Renaissance Italy: Selected Articles.* Brookfield: Variorum.

———, 1995. *Byzantine Scholars in Renaissance Italy: Cardinal Bessarion and Other Emigrés: Selected Essays.* Brookfield: Variorum.

———, 2004a. *Greeks and Latins in Renaissance Italy: Studies on Humanism and Philosophy in the 15th Century.* Aldershot, GB-Burlington, VT: Ashgate Variorum.

———, 2004b. "Renaissance Ciceronianism and Christianity." In Patrick Gilli, ed., *Humanisme et Église en Italie et en France méridionale (XVe siècle–milieu du XVIe siècle).* Collection de L'École Française de Rome 330. Rome: École Française de Rome.

Monfasani, John, and Ronald G. Musto, eds., 1991. *Renaissance Society and Culture: Essays in Honor of Eugene F. Rice, Jr.* New York: Italica Press.

Moorman, John, 1968. *A History of the Franciscan Order from Its Origins to the Year 1517.* Oxford: Clarendon Press.

Morigia, Paolo, 1592. *Historia dell'antichità di Milano.* Venice: Appresso i Guerra.

Mormando, Franco, 1999. *The Preacher's Demons: Bernardino da Siena and the Social Underworld of Early Renaissance Italy.* Chicago-London: University of Chicago Press.

Motta, Emilio, 1906. "Il necrologio del Convento di S. Francesco di Milano." *Archivio storico lombardo* 33:171–73.

Müllner, Karl, ed., 1902. "Drei Briefe Antons von Rho." *Wiener Studien: Zeitschrift für classische Philologie* 23:143–57.

———, ed., 1970. *Reden und Briefe italienischer Humanisten.* Intro., bibl., and indices by Barbara Gerl. 1899. Munich: Wilhelm Fink.

Müntz, Eugène, 1882. *Les Arts à la cour des papes.* 3 vols. Paris: Ernest Thorin.

Müntz, Eugène, and Paul Fabre, 1887. *La bibliothèque du Vatican au XVième siècle.* Paris: Ernest Thorin.

Muir, Dorothy, 1924. *A History of Milan under the Visconti.* London: Methuen.

Natale, Michele, 1902. *Antonio Beccadelli, detto il Panormita*. Caltanissetta: Tipografia dell' Omnibus.
Nauta, Lodi, 2003. "William of Ockham and Lorenzo Valla: False Friends. Semantics and Ontological Reduction." *Renaissance Quarterly* 56:613–51.
Neugebauer, O., 1949. "The Early History of the Astrolabe. Studies in Ancient Astronomy IX." *Isis* 40:240–56.
Nisard, Charles, 1860. *Les gladiateurs de la république des lettres aux XVe, XVIe et XVIIe siècles*. 2 vols. Paris: Michel Levy Fratres.
Nisbet, R. G. M., ed. and intro., 1961. Cicero. *In L. Calpurnium Pisonem Oratio*. Oxford: Clarendon Press.
Noonan, J. T., 1979. "Gratian Slept Here: The Changing Identity of the Father of the Systematic Study of Canon Law." *Traditio* 35:145–72.

Oakley, Francis, 1979. *The Western Church in the Later Middle Ages*. Ithaca: Cornell University Press.
O'Connor, Eugene, 1997. "Panormita's Reply to his Critics: The *Hermaphroditus* and the Literary Defense." *Renaissance Quarterly* 50:220–33.
O'Daly, Gerard J. P., 1999. *Augustine's City of God: A Reader's Guide*. Oxford: Clarendon Press.
Odo de Ceritona, 1884. *Fabulae*. In *Les Fabulistes Latins depuis le siècle d'Auguste jusqu'à la fin du Moyen Âge*. Ed. Léopold Hervieux. Paris. 2:587–713.
L'Oeuvre Priapique des Anciens et des Modernes. 1914. Paris: Bibliothèque des Curieux.
O'Malley, John W., S. J., 1969. "Recent Studies in Church History, 1300–1600." *The Catholic Historical Review* 55:394–437.
———, 1979. *Praise and Blame in Renaissance Rome: Rhetoric, Doctrine, and Reform in the Sacred Orators of the Papal Court, c. 1450–1521*. Durham, NC: Duke University Press.
———, 1981. *Rome and the Renaissance: Studies in Culture and Religion*. London. Variorum Reprints.
———, 1983. "Content and Rhetorical Form in Sixteenth-Century Treatises on Preaching." In *Renaissance Eloquence: Studies in the Theory and Practice of Renaissance Rhetoric*. Ed. James J. Murphy. 238–52. Berkeley-Los Angeles-London: University of California Press.
———, 1986. "Form, Content, and Influence of Works about Preaching before Trent: The Franciscan Contribution." In *I Frati Minori tra '400 e '500: Atti del XII Convegno Internazionale* (Assisi, 18–20 October 1984). 25–50. Assisi: Università di Perugia, Centro di Studi Francescani.
———, 2004. *Four Cultures of the West*. Cambridge, MA: Belknap Press of Harvard University Press.
Osmond, Patricia J., 1995. "*Princeps Historiae Romanae:* Sallust in Renaissance Political Thought." *Memoirs of the American Academy in Rome* 40:101–43.
———, 2000. "Catiline in Fiesole and Florence: The After-life of a Roman Conspirator." *International Journal of the Classical Tradition* 7:3–38.
Osmond, Patricia J., and Robert W. Ulery, 2003. "Sallustius." In *Catologus translationum et commentariorum: Mediaeval and Renaissance Latin Translations and Commentaries, Annotated Lists and Guides*. Vol. 3. Virginia Brown, ed. in chief, James Hankins, and Robert A. Kaster, assoc. eds. 183–326. Washington, DC: Catholic University of America Press.

Pabel, Hilmar M., 2002. "Reading Jerome in the Renaissance: Erasmus' Reception of the *Adversus Jovinianum*." *Renaissance Quarterly* 55:470–97.
Pade, Marianne, 1988–89. "Guarino, his Princely Patron, and Plutarch's *Vita Alexandri ac Caesaris:* An *ineditum* in Archivio di S. Pietro H 31." *Analecta Romana, Instituti Danici, Separatum* 17–18:133–47.
———, 1998a. "Sulla fortuna delle *Vite* di Plutarco nell'Umanesimo Italiano del Quattrocento." *Rivista di filologia, iconografia, e storia della tradizione classica: Fontes* 1:101–16.
———, 1998b. "Curzio Rufo e Plutarco nell'*Istoria d'Alexandro Magno:* volgarizzamento e compilazione in un testo di Pier Candido Decembrio." *Studi umanistici piceni* 18:101–13.

———, 1999. "Zur Rezeption der griechischen Historiker im italienischen Humanismus des fünfzehnten Jahrhunderts." *Neulateinisches Jahrbuch* 1:151–69.

———, 2000. "Plutarch, Gellius, and John of Salisbury in Humanist Anthologies." In *Ab Aquilone: Nordic Studies in Honour and Memory of Leonard E. Boyle, O. P.*, ed. Marie-Louise Rodén. 57–70. Rome: Svenska Institutet i Rom.

———, 2003. "Thucydides." In *Catalogus translationum et commentariorum: Mediaeval and Renaissance Latin Translations and Commentaries, Annotated Lists and Guides*. Vol. 3. Virginia Brown, ed. in chief, James Hankins and Robert A. Kaster, assoc. eds. 103–81. Washington, DC: Catholic University of America Press.

Panizza, Letizia A., 1978. "Lorenzo Valla's *De vero falsoque bono*: Lactantius and Oratorical Scepticism." *Journal of the Warburg and Courtauld Institutes* 41:76–107.

Paredi, Angelo, 1961. *La biblioteca del Pizolpasso*. Milan: Ulrico Hoepli.

Parker, Holt N., 1997. "The Teratogenic Grid." In *Roman Sexualities*. Ed. J. P. Hallet and M. Skinner. 47–65. Princeton: Princeton University Press.

Parker, W. H., ed., trans., and comm., 1988. *Priapea: Poems for a Phallic God*. London-Sydney: Croom Helm.

Pasoli, Elio, ed. and intro., 1989. *Appendix Sallustiana: Invectiva in M. Tullium Ciceronem*. Bologna: Pàtron Editore.

Pastor, Ludwig, 1891. *The History of the Popes: From the Close of the Middle Ages*. Ed. F. I. Antrobus. The Catholic Standard Library 1. London: J. Hodges.

Patrucco, Ursala, 2001. *Die Geschichte der Visconti: Von den Seeschlachten um die Vorherrschaft über de Lago Maggiore bis zum Hergogtum von Mailand und Norditalien*. Verbania: Alberti Libraio Editore.

Pellegrin, Elisabeth, 1955a. *La bibliothèque des Visconti et des Sforza ducs de Milan, au XVe siècle*. Publications de l'Institut de Recherche et d'Histoire des Textes 5. Paris: CNRS.

———, 1955b. "Bibliothèques d'humanistes Lombards de la cour des Visconti Sforza." *Bibliothèque d'Humanisme et Renaissance* 17:218–45.

Percival, W. Keith, 1988. "Renaissance Grammar." In Albert Rabil, ed., *Renaissance Humanism: Foundations, Forms, and Legacy*. Philadelphia: University of Pennsylvania Press. 3:67–83.

Percy, William Armstrong, III, 1996. *Pederasty and Pedagogy in Archaic Greece*. Urbana-Chicago: University of Illinois Press.

Peters, F. E., 1967. *Greek Philosophical Terms: A Historical Lexicon*. New York: New York University Press / London: Univesity of London Press Limited.

Petrarca, Francesco, *Opere latine*, 1975. Ed. Antonietta Bufano. With Italian translation. 2 vols. Turin: U.T.E.T.

———, 2003. *Invectives*. Ed. and trans. David Marsh. I Tatti Renaissance Library. Cambridge, MA / London: Harvard University Press.

Petrucci, Armando, 1995. *Writers and Readers in Medieval Italy: Studies in the History of Culture*. Ed. and trans. by Charles M. Radding. New Haven-London: Yale University Press.

Phaedrus. 1884. *Fabularum libri V*. In *Les Fabulistes Latins depuis le siècle d'Auguste jusqu'à la fin du Moyen Âge*. Ed. Léopold Hervieux. Paris: Firmin-Didot & cie. 2:3–74.

Piana, Celestino, O. F. M., 1970. *Chartularium Studii Bononiensis S. Francisci (Saec. XIII–XVI)*. Analecta Franciscana 11. Claras Aquas: Collegii S. Bonaventurae.

Picinelli, Filippo, 1652. *Ateneo dei letterati milanesi*. Milano: F. Vigone.

Pierrugues, Pierre, 1826. *Glossarium eroticum linguae Latinae, siue Theogoniae, legum et morum nuptialium apud Romanos explanatio nova*. Paris: Dondey-Dupré.

Pitcher, Roger, 1993. "The *molis vir* in Martial." In K. Lee, C. Mackie, and H. Tarrant, eds., *Multarum artium scientia: A "chose" for R. Godfrey Tanner*. 59–67. *Prudentia* Suppl. Number.

Pizzagalli, Daniela, 1994. *Bernabò Visconti*. Milan: Rusconi.

Plato. 1960. *Phaedrus*. Translated by Harold North Fowler. Loeb Classical Library. London-Cambridge, MA: Harvard University Press.

Pratesi, Riccardo, O. F. M., 1957. "Antonio Rusconi, Ministro Generale O.F.M., conferma Giacomo Primadizzi Vicario degli Osservanti Cismontani (14 Novembre 1446)." *Archivum franciscanum historicum* 50:225–31.

———, 1961. "Antonio da Massa Marittima." In *Dizionario biografico degli Italiani*. Rome: Istituto della Enciclopedia Italiana. 3:555–56.

Predari, Francesco, 1857. *Bibliografia enciclopedia milanese*. Milano: M. Carrara.

Poggio Fiorentino (Bracciolini), 1878. *Les Facéties de Pogge: Traduites en Français avec le Text Latine, Édition complète*. 2 vols. Paris: Isidore Liseux.

———, 1964. *Opera omnia*. Intro. Riccardo Fubini. Turin: Bottega d'Erasmo.

———, 1983. *Facezie*. Latin text and Italian trans. and notes by M. Ciccuto. I Classici della Biblioteca Universale Rizzoli, L 418. Milan: Rizzoli.

———, 1984. *Lettere*. Ed. Helene Harth. 3 vols. Florence: Olschki.

Pommerol, Marie-Henriette Jullien de, and Jacques Monfrin, 1991. *La Bibliothèque Pontificale à Avignon et à Peñiscola pendant le Grand Schisme d'Occident et sa dispersion: Inventaires et Concordances*. Collection de l'École Française de Rome 141. Rome: École Française de Rome, Palaise Farnèse.

Pontarin, Francesco, and Chiara Andreucci, 1972. "La tradizione del carteggio di Lorenzo Valla." *Italia medioevale e umanistica* 15:171–213.

Puccinelli, Placido, 1655. *Chronicon insignis Monasterii DD. Petri et Pauli de Glaxiate Mediolani*. Milan: Giulio Cesare Malatesta.

Rabil, Albert, Jr., ed., 1988a. *Renaissance Humanism: Foundations, Forms, and Legacy*. 3 vols. Philadelphia: University of Pennsylvania Press.

———, 1988b. "Petrarch, Augustine, and the Classical Christian Tradition." In Albert Rabil, ed., *Renaissance Humanism: Foundations, Forms, and Legacy*. Philadelphia: University of Pennsylvania Press. 1:95–114.

———, 1988c. "Humanism in Milan." In Albert Rabil, ed., *Renaissance Humanism: Foundations, Forms, and Legacy*. Philadelphia: University of Pennsylvania Press. 1:235–63.

Raggi, Angelo Maria, 1962. "Aregazzi (Regazzi; lat. *Aregatius, de Agregaciis, de Regatiis*), Francesco, vescovo di Bergamo, beato." In *Bibliotheca Sanctorum*. 13 vols. Rome: Istituto Giovanni XXIII. 2:396–99.

Ramorino, Felice, 1880. *Contributi alla storia biografica e critica di Antonio Beccadelli*. Palermo.

———, 1889. "Notizia di alcune epistole e carmini inediti di Antonio il Panormita." *Archivio storico italiano*, 5th ser., 3:447–50.

Rao, Ennio I., ed. and intro., 1978. Bartolomeo Facio. *Invective in Laurentium Vallam*. Critical edtion. Studi e Testi di Letteratura Italiana 15. Naples: Società Editrice Napoletana.

———, 1988–90. "The Humanist Invective as a Literary Genre." In *Selected Proceedings of the Pennsylvania Foreign Language Conference*. Ed. G. Martin. 261–67. Pittsburg: Duquesne University Department of Modern Languages Publications.

Rashdall, Hastings, 1936. *The Universities of Europe in the Middle Ages*. Ed. F. M. Powicke and A. B. Emden. 3 vols. Oxford: Clarendon Press.

Regoliosi, Mariangela, 1969. "Nuove ricerche intorno a Giovanni Tortelli." *Italia medioevale e umanistica* 12:129–96.

———, 1980. "Per la tradizione delle 'Invective in L. Vallam' di Bartolomeo Facio." *Italia medioevale e umanistica* 23:389–97.

———, ed. and intro., 1981. Lorenzo Valla, *Antidotum in Facium*. Padua: Editrice Antenore.

———, 1983. "Umanesimo lombardo: la polemica tra Lorenzo Valla e Antonio da Rho." In *Studi di lingua e letteratura lomarda offerti a Maurizio Vitale*. 2 vols. Pisa: Giardini. 1:170–79.

———, 1984. "Le due redazione delle *Raudense note* e le *Elegantiae* del Valla." In *Vestigia: Studi in onore di Giuseppe Billanovich*. 2 vols. Ed. Rino Avesani et al. Storia e Letteratura: Raccolta di Studi e Testi 162–163. Rome: Edizioni di Storia e Letteratura. 2:559–73.

Resta, Gianvito, 1954. *L'epistolario del Panormita: studi per una edizione critica*. Università degli studi di Messina, Facoltà di Lettere e Filosofia: Studi e Testi diretti da Michele Catalano 3. Messina: Università degli Studi.

———, 1962. *Le epitomi di Plutarco nel Quattrocento*. Miscellanea Erudita 5. Padua: Editrice Antenore.

———, 1964. *Giorgio Valagussa: umanista del Quattrocento*. Miscellanea Erudita 13. Padua: Editrice Antenore.

———, 1965. "Antonio Beccadelli." In *Dizionario biografico degli Italiani*. Rome: Istituto della Enciclopedia Italiana. 7:400–06.

Rho, Antonio da (Antonius Raudensis), 1433/43. *Imitationes rhetoricae*. Avignon: Bibliothèque Municipale, MS 1054 (selections in Appendices VIII and IX above).

Rho, Paolo da, saec. XVII. *Dell'origine et progressi della famiglia da Rho milanese*. Milan: Biblioteca Ambrosiana, MS D 103 inf., ff. 1r–52r.

Ricci, Pier Giorgio, 1974. "La tradizione dell'invettiva tra il Medioevo e l'Umanesimo." *Lettere italiane* 26:405–14.

Rice, Eugene F., Jr., 1973. *The Renaissance Idea of Wisdom*. 1958. Westport, CT: Greenwood Press.

———, 1985. *Saint Jerome in the Renaissance*. Baltimore-London: Johns Hopkins University Press.

———, 1988. "The Renaissance Idea of Christian Antiquity: Humanist Patristic Scholarship." In Albert Rabil, ed., *Renaissance Humanism: Foundations, Forms, and Legacy*. Philadelphia: University of Pennsylvania Press. 1:17–28.

Richlin, Amy, 1983. *The Garden of Priapus: Sexuality and Aggression in Roman Humor*. New Haven-London: Yale University Press.

———, 1999. "Cicero's Head." In James I. Porter, ed., *Constructions of the Classical Body*. 190–211. Ann Arbor: University of Michigan Press.

Rizzo, Silvia, 1973. *Il lessico filologico degli umanisti*. Rome: Edizioni di Storia e Letteratura.

Rocke, Michael, 1996. *Forbidden Friendships: Homosexuality and Male Culture in Renaissance Florence*. New York-Oxford: Oxford University Press.

Roeder, Günther, 1916–24. "Thoth, ägyptischer Gott." In *Ausführliches Lexikon der griechischen und römischen Mythologie*. 6 vols. Leipzig: Teubner. 5:825–63.

Rolfi, Gianfranco, 1994. "Giovanni Vitelleschi, Archivescovo di Firenze: La sua azione militare all'epoca del Concilio." In Paolo Viti, ed., *Firenze e il Concilia del 1439*. 2 vols. Florence: Olschki. 1:121–46.

Romm, James S., 1992. *The Edges of the Earth in Ancient Thought*. Princeton: Princeton University Press.

Romulus. 1884. *Fabularum libri IV*. In *Les Fabulistes Latins depuis le siècle d'Auguste jusqu'à la fin du Moyen Âge*. Ed. Léopold Hervieux. Paris: Firmin-Didot & cie. 2:176–230.

Ronconi, Giorgio, ed., 1972. Ermolao Barbaro il Vecchio. *Orationes contra poetas epistolae*. Florence: Sansoni.

———, 1976. *Le origini delle dispute umanistiche sulla poesia (Mussato e Petrarca)*. Rome: Bulzoni.

Ronzoni, D., 1902. "L'*Apologia* di Antonio Raudense e la fortuna di Dante nel Quattrocento." *Giornale Dantesco* 10:1–3.

Rosso, Paolo, 2001. *Il* Semideus *di Catone Sacco*. Milan: A. Giuffrè.

Rüben, Heinrich, 1975. *Der Humanist und Regularkanoniker Timoteo Maffei aus Verona (ca. 1415–1470): Eine Biographie zum Problem des christlichen Humanismus in der italienischen Renaissance*. Aachen: Druckerei Hunko.

Rutherford, David, 1990. "A Finding List of Antonio da Rho's Works and Related Primary Sources." *Italia medioevale e umanistica* 30:75–108.

———, 1993. "Timoteo Maffei's Attack on Holy Simplicity: Educational Thought in Gratian's *Decretum* and Jerome's *Letters*." In L. Grane, A. Schindler, and M. Wriedt, eds., *Auctoritas Patrum: Contributions on the Reception of the Church Fathers in the 15th and 16th Centuries*. 159–73. Veröffentlichungen des Instituts für Europäische Geschichte Mainz, Beiheft 37. Mainz: Philipp von Zabern.

———, 1997. "Gratian's *Decretum* as a Source of Patristic Knowledge in the Italian Renaissance: The Example of Timoteo Maffei's *In sanctam rusticitatem* (1454)." In Irena Backus, ed., *The Reception of the Church Fathers in the West: From the Carolingians to the Maurists*. 2 vols. Leiden-New York-Cologne: Brill. 2:511–35.

———, 1998. "Antonio da Rho on Patristic Authority: The Status of Lactantius." In L. Grane, A. Schindler, and M. Wriedt, eds., *Auctoritas Patrum II: New Contributions on the Reception of the Church Fathers in the 15th and 16th Centuries.* 171–86. Veröffentlichungen des Instituts für Europäische Geschichte Mainz, Beiheft 44. Mainz: Philipp von Zabern.

Sabbadini, Remigio, 1885a. *Storia del ciceronianismo e di altre questioni letterarie nell'età della Rinascenza.* Turin: Ermanno Loescher.

———, 1885b. "Notizie sulla vita e gli scritti di alcuni dotti umanisti del secolo XV raccolte da codici italiani." *Giornale storico della letteratura italiana* 5:148–79; 6:163–76.

———, 1890. *Biografia documentata di Giovanni Aurispa.* Noto: Fr. Zammit.

———, 1896a. *La scuola e gli studi di Guarino Guarini Veronese (Con 44 documenti).* Catania: Francesco Galati.

———, 1896b. "Guarino Veronese e la polemica sul Carmagnola." *Nuovo archivio veneto* 11:7–8.

———, 1910a. *Ottanta lettere inedite del Panormita tratte dai codici Milanesi.* Biblioteca della Società di Storia Patria per La Sicilia Orientale 1. Catania: Niccolò Giannota.

———, 1910b. "Henricus Hyla Pratensis." *Rendiconti del Reale Istituto Lombardo di scienze e letteratura* 43:260–62.

———, 1911. "Niccolò Cusa e i conciliari di Basilea alla scoperta dei codici." *Rendiconti della Reale Accademia de Lincei, classe de scienze morali, storiche e filologiche,* 5th ser., 20:3–40.

———, 1914. *Storia e critica di testi latini.* Catania: F. Battiato. (Second edition. Medievo e Umanesimo 11. Giuseppe Billanovich e Giovanni Pozzi, eds. Padua: Antenore, 1971).

———, 1916. "Come il Panormita diventò poeta aulico." *Archivio storico lombardo* 43:5–28.

———, 1922. *Il metodo degli umanisti.* Florence: Felice le Monnier.

———, ed., 1931. *Carteggio di Giovanni Aurispa.* Rome: Tipografia del Senato.

———, 1996. *Le scoperte dei codici latini e greci ne'secoli XIV e XV.* 2 vols. 1905/14. Florence: Le Lettere.

Sabbadini, Remigio, and Luciano Barozzi, 1891. *Studi sul Panormita e sul Valla.* Florence: Successori Le Monnier.

San Antonio, Juan de, O. F. M., 1966. *Bibliotheca universa francescana.* 1732. Farnborough: Gregg Press.

Sarteano, Alberto, O. F. M. Obser., 1688. *Opera omnia in ordinem redacta ac argumentis et adnotationbus illustrata a Francisco Haroldo.* Rome: Joannis Baptista Bussottus.

Sartori, Antonio, O. F. M. Conv., 1958. *La Provincia del Santo dei Frati Minori Conventuali.* Padua: Messaggero.

———, 1983. *Archivio Sartori: Documenti di storia e arte francescana.* Vol. 1: Basilica e Convento del Santo. Ed. G. Luisetto, O. F. M. Conv. Padua: Biblioteca Antoniana.

Saslow, James, 1986. *Ganymede in the Renaissance: Homosexuality in Art and Society.* New Haven: Yale University Press.

Sassio, Giuseppe Antonio, 1729. *De studiis litterariis mediolanensium.* Milan: Malatesta.

Schanz, Martin, 1922. *Geschichte der römischen Literatur bis zum Gesetzgebungswerk des Kaisers Justinian.* 3rd ed. by Hosius and Krüger. Munich: C.H. Beck'sche.

Schindel, Ulrich, 1980. "Die Invektive gegen Cicero und die Theorie der Tadelrede." *Nachrichten der Akademie der Wissenschaften, Göttingen: Philosophisch-Historische Klasse* 5: 1–16.

Seel, Otto, 1966a. *Die Invektive gegen Cicero.* Wiesbaden: Scientia Verlag Aalen.

———, 1966b. *Sallusts Briefe und die pseudosallustische Invektive.* Nuremberg: Verlag Hans Carl.

Sherr, Richard, 1993. "Music and the Renaissance Papacy: The Papal Choir and the Fondo Cappella Sistina." In Anthony Grafton, ed., *Rome Reborn: The Vatican Library and Renaissance Culture.* 199–223. Washington: Library of Congress / Vatican City: Biblioteca Apostolica Vaticana.

Siegel, Jerrold E. 1968. *Rhetoric and Philosophy in Renaissance Humanism: The Union of Eloquence and Wisdom, Petrarch to Valla.* Princeton: Princeton University Press.

Simonetta, Marcello, 2004. *Rinascimento segreto: il mondo del segretario da Petrarca a Machiavelli.* Milan: Franco Angeli.

Sinistrari d'Ameno, R.-P., 1921. *De sodomia tractatus in quo exponitur doctrina nova de Sodomia foeminarum a Tribadismo distincta.* Texte Latin et Traduction Française. Paris: Bibliothèque des Curieux.

Siraisi, Nancy G., 1990. *Medieval and Early Renaissance Medicine: An Introduction to Knowledge and Practice.* Chicago-London: University of Chicago Press.

———, 1993. "Life Sciences and Medicine in the Renaissance World." In Anthony Grafton, ed., *Rome Reborn: The Vatican Library and Renaissance Culture.* 169–98. Washington: Library of Congress / Vatican City: Biblioteca Apostolica Vaticana.

Southern, R. W., 1995. *Scholastic Humanism and the Unification of Europe.* 2 vols. Oxford: Blackwell.

Sparacio, Domenico, 1924. "Il primo convento di S. Francesco in Milano ed i suoi abitatori." *Miscellanea francescana* 24:150–54.

Speyer, Wolfgang, 1993. *Italienische Humanisten als Kritiker der Echtheit antiker und christlicher Literatur.* Abhandlungen der Geistes- und Sozialwissenschaftlichen Klasse, Jahrgang 1993, Nr. 3. Mainz-Stuttgart: Akademie der Wissenschaften und der Literatur.

Spira, Julianus de. ca. 1235. *Vita S. Francisci.* In *Analecta Franciscana,* Vol. 10: *Legendae S. Francisci Assisiensis Saeculis XIII et XIV Conscriptae.* Florence, Ad Claras Aquas: Typographia Collegii S. Bonaventurae, 1936.

Stahl, William H., 1959. "Dominant Traditions in Early Medieval Latin Science." *Isis* 50:95–124.

Stieber, Joachim W., 1978. *Pope Eugenius IV, the Council of Basel, and the Secular and Ecclesiastical Authorities in the Empire: The Conflict over Supreme Authority and Power in the Church.* Studies in the History of Christian Thought 13. Leiden: Brill.

Stinger, Charles L., 1977. *Humanism and the Church Fathers: Ambrogio Traversari (1386–1439) and Christian Antiquity in the Italian Renaissance.* Albany: SUNY.

———, 1985. *The Renaissance in Rome.* Bloomington: Indiana University Press.

———, 1988. "Humanism in Florence." In Albert Rabil, ed., *Renaissance Humanism: Foundations, Forms, and Legacy.* Philadelphia: University of Pennsylvania Press. 1:175–208.

Swerdlow, N. M., 1993. "The Recovery of the Exact Sciences of Antiquity: Mathematics, Astronomy, Geography." In Anthony Grafton, ed., *Rome Reborn: The Vatican Library and Renaissance Culture.* 125–68. Washington: Library of Congress / Vatican City: Biblioteca Apostolica Vaticana.

Syme, Ronald, 1964. "The False Sallust." Appendix II in Ronald Syme, *Sallust.* Berkeley-Los Angeles: University of California Press.

Tentler, Thomas N., 1977. *Sin and Confession on the Eve of the Reformation.* Princeton: Princeton University Press.

Tierney, Brian, 1955. *Foundations of the Conciliar Theory: The Contributions of the Medieval Canonists from Gratian to the Great Schism.* Cambridge: University Press.

Tirrito, M. Catalano, 1910. *Nuovi documenti sul Panormita tratti dagli archivi palermitani.* Biblioteca della Società di Storia Patria per La Sicilia Orientale 1. Catania: Niccolò Giannota.

Trinkaus, Charles, 1970. *In Our Image and Likeness: Humanity and Divinity in Italian Humanist Thought.* 2 vols. Chicago: University of Chicago Press.

———, 1978. "*Antiquitas* versus *Modernitas*: An Italian Humanist Polemic and Its Resonance." *Journal of the History of Ideas* 48:11–21.

———, 1979. *The Poet as Philosopher: Petrarch and the Formation of Renaissance Consciousness.* New Haven: Yale University Press.

———, 1983a *The Scope of Renaissance Humanism.* Ann Arbor: University of Michigan Press.

———, 1983b. "Humanism and Poetry: The Quattrocento Poetics of Bartolomeo della Fonte." In Charles Trinkaus, *The Scope of Renaissance Humanism.* 88–139. Ann Arbor: University of Michigan Press.

———, 1989. "Humanistic Dissidence: Florence versus Milan, or Poggio versus Valla." In Craig Hugh Smyth and Gian Carlo Garfagnini, eds., *Florence and Milan: Comparisons and Relations.* 17-40. I Tatti Studies 11. Florence: La Nuova Italia Editrice.

Ughello, Ferdinando, 1717–22. *Italia sacra, sive de episcopis Italiae.* 10 vols. Venice: Sebastiano Coleti.

Ullman, Berthold L., 1917. "Horace on the Nature of Satire." *Transactions and Proceedings of the American Philological Association* 48:111–32.

———, 1923. "Petrarch's Favorite Books." *Transactions of the American Philosophical Society* 54: 21–38. Reprinted in B. L. Ullman, 1973. *Studies in the Italian Renaissance.* 2nd edition. Storia e Letteratura: Raccolta di Studi e Testi 51. Rome: Edizioni di Storia e Letteratura.

———, 1960. *The Origin and Development of Humanistic Script.* Rome: Edizioni di Storia e Letteratura.

———, 1973. *Studies in the Italian Renaissance.* 2nd edition. Storia e Letteratura: Raccolta di Studi e Testi 51. Rome: Edizioni di Storia e Letteratura.

Ullman, Berthold L., and Philip A. Stadter, 1972. *The Public Library of Renaissance Florence: Niccolò Niccoli, Cosimo de' Medici, and the Library of San Marco.* Medioevo e Umanesimo 10. Padua: Editrice Antenore.

Valla, Lorenzo, 1962. *Opera omnia.* Ed. Eugenio Garin. 2 vols. Monumenta Politica et Philosophica Rariora 5 and 6. Turin: Botega d'Erasmo.

———, 1970. *De vero falsoque bono.* Ed. Maristella de Panizza Lorch. Bari: Adriatica.

———, 1977. *On Pleasure / De voluptate.* Trans. by A. Kent Hieatt and Maristella Lorch. Intro. Maristella de Panizza Lorch. New York: Abaris Books.

———, 1981. *Antidotum in Facium.* Ed. and intro. Mariangela Regoliosi. Padua: Editrice Antenore.

Van Steenberghen, Fernand, 1991. *La Philosophie au XIIIe Siècle.* Louvain: Peeters.

Vasoli, Cesare, 1968. *La dialettica e la retorica dell'Umanesimo: "Invenzione" e "Metodo" nella cultura del XV e XVI secolo.* Milan: Feltrinelli.

———, 1989. "La trattativa politica a Firenze e a Milano." In Craig Hugh Smyth and Gian Carlo Garfagnini, eds., *Florence and Milan: Comparisons and Relations.* 67–78. I Tatti Studies 11. Florence: La Nuova Italia Editrice.

Verga, Ettore, 1901. "Le sentenze criminali dei Podestà milanesi, 1385–1429." *Archivio storico lombardo*, ser. 3, 16:96–142.

———, 1918. "Un caso di coscienza di Filippo Maria Visconti, Duca di Milano (1446)." *Archivio storico lombardo* 45:427–87.

Veronese, Guarino, 1990. Epistola Iohanni Lamolae. "Guarini in *Hermophroditon* iudicium." Appendix I, pp. 145–47. In Antonii Panhormitae. *Hermaphroditus.* Ed. Donatella Coppini. Humanistica 10. Florence: Bulzoni. [Expurgated version that Panormita circulated with his *Hermaphroditus.*]

Vickers, Brian, 1986. "Valla's Ambivalent Praise of Pleasure: Rhetoric in the Service of Christianity." *Viator* 17:271–319.

Vircillo Franklin, Carmela, 2002. "*Pro comuni doctorum virorum comodo:* The Vatican Library and Its Service to Scholarship." *Proceedings of the American Philosophical Association* 146:363–84.

Vismara, Felice, 1900a. *L'invettiva, arma preferita dagli Umanisti nelle lotte private, nelle polemiche letterarie, politiche e religiose.* Milan: Uberto Allegretti.

———, 1900b. "I pretesi rapporti dei Milanesi con Giovanna d'Arco." *Archivio storico lombardo* 27:117–25.

Viti, Paolo, 1987. "Decembrio, Pier Candido." In *Dizionario biografico degli Italiani.* Rome: Istituto della Enciclopedia Italiana. 33:488–98.

———, ed., 1994a. *Firenze e il Concilio del 1439.* 2 Vols. Florence: Olschki.

———, 1994b. "Leonardo Bruni e il Concilio del 1439." In Paolo Viti, ed., *Firenze e il Concilia del 1439.* 2 vols. Florence: Olschki. 2:509–75.

Voigt, Georg, 1880. *Die Wiederbelebung des klassischen Altertums oder das erste Jahrhundert des Humanismus.* 2 vols. Berlin: Georg Reimer.

———, 1888–97. *Il Risorgimento dell'antichità classica ovvero il Primo secolo dell'Umanesimo.* 2 Vols. Trans., pref., and notes by Diego Valbusa. Vol. 3: Additions and corrections with bibliographic and analytic index by Giuseppe Zippel. Florence: Sansoni.

Wadding, Luke, O. F. M., 1906. *Scriptores Ordinis Minorum quibus accessit syllabus illorum qui ex eodem ordine pro fide Christi fortiter occubuerunt.* 1625–54. Rome: Attilio Nardecchia.

Walters, Jonathan, 1998. "Making a Spectacle: Deviant Men, Invective, and Pleasure." *Arethusa* 31:355–67.

Walther, Hans. 1963–69. *Lateinische Sprichworter und Sentenzen des Mittelalters in alphabetischen Anordnung.* 6 vols. Göttingen, Vandenhoeck & Ruprecht.

Ward, John O., 1983. "Renaissance Commentators on Ciceronian Rhetoric." In *Renaissance Eloquence: Studies in the Theory and Practice of Renaissance Rhetoric.* Ed. James J. Murphy. 126–73. Berkeley-Los Angeles-London: University of California Press.

Watson, Alan, 1987. *Roman Slave Law.* Baltimore-London: Johns Hopkins University Press.

Weiss, Roberto, 1988. *The Renaissance Discovery of Classical Antiquity.* 2nd ed. Oxford: Basil Blackwell.

Wiesen, David S., 1964. *St. Jerome as a Satirist: A Study in Christian Latin Thought and Letters.* Ithaca: Cornell University Press.

Wilcox. Donald J., 1969. *The Development of Florentine Humanist Historiography in the Fifteenth Century.* Cambridge, MA: Harvard University Press.

Witke, Charles, 1970. *Latin Satire: The Structure of Persuasion.* Leiden: Brill.

Witt, Ronald G., 1976. *Coluccio Salutati and his Public Letters.* Travaux d'Humanisme et Renaissance 151. Geneva: Librairie Droz.

———, 1977. "Coluccio Salutati and the Conception of the *Poeta Theologus* in the Fourteenth Century." *Renaissance Quarterly* 30:538–63.

———, 1983. *Hercules at the Crossroads: The Life, Works, and Thought of Coluccio Salutati.* Duke Monographs in Medieval and Renaisance Studies 6. Durham, NC: Duke University Press.

———, 1988. "Medieval Italian Culture and the Origins of Humanism as a Stylistic Ideal." In Albert Rabil, ed., *Renaissance Humanism: Foundations, Forms, and Legacy.* Philadelphia: University of Pennsylvania Press. 1:29–70.

———, 1990. "Civic Humanism and the Rebirth of the Ciceronian Oration." *Modern Language Quarterly* 51:167–84.

———, 2000. *"In the Footsteps of the Ancients": The Origins of Humanism from Lovato to Bruni.* Studies in Medieval and Reformation Thought 74. Leiden-Boston-Cologne: Brill.

———, 2001. *Italian Humanism and Medieval Rhetoric.* Aldershot-Burlington-Singapore-Sydney: Ashgate Variorum.

Wolff, Max von, 1894. *Leben und Werke des Antonio Beccadelli genannt Panormita.* Leipzig: E.A. Seemann.

Wray, David L., 1996. "Catullus: Sexual Personae and Invective Tradition." Diss. Cambridge: Harvard University.

Zaccaria, Vittorio, 1952. "L'epistolario di Pier Candido Decembrio." *Rinascimento,* 2nd ser., 3:85–118.

———, 1956. "Sulle opere di Pier Candido Decembrio." *Rinascimento,* 2nd ser., 7:13–74.

———, 1959. "Pier Candido Decembrio traduttore della 'Reppublica' di Platone: Notizie dall'epistolario del Decembrio." *Italia medioevale e umanistica* 2:179–206.

———, 1975. "Pier Candido Decembrio, Michele Pizolpasso e Ugolino Pisani: Nuove notizie dall'epistolario di P. C. De cembrio, con appendice di lettere e testi inediti." *Atti dell'Istitutio Veneto di Scienze, Lettere ed Arti: classe di scienze morali, lettere ed arti* 137:187–212.

Ziliotto, Baccio, 1937. "Frate Lodovico da Pirano (1390?–1450) e le sue *Regulae memoriae artificialis.*" *Atti e memorie della Società Istriana di Archeologia e Storia Patria* 49:187–226.

Zimmerer, Heinrich, ed., 1888. *Declamatio in Lucium Sergium Catilinam: Eine Schuldeklamation aus der römischen Kaiserzeit.* Inaugural-Dissertation zur Erlangung der philosophischen Doctorwürde. Munich: Akademische Buchdruckerei von F. Straub.

INDEX OF NAMES AND TOPICS

abacus 203
Academy (Platonic) 56, 74, 123
Achelous 107
Achilles 63, 87, 159, 181, 205, 309
Adonis (god) 111, 123
Adonis (Panormita's lover) 34, 111, 115–19, 123, 131
Aemilius Paulus 75
Aeneas 155, 157, 159, 283
Aeschines 1
Aesop 233, 239
Aestas 297
Aetheia 274
Aethon 298
Agesilaus 159
Aguzzi-Barbagli, Danilo 37
Alain of Lille 201
Alanus 201
Albericus (mythographer) 91
Alcestis 165, 167
Alceus (see also Hercules) 173
Alex 119
Alexander the Great 17, 59, 159, 215, 281, 309, 313
Alexander Severus 67, 318
Alexandria 201
Alfonso V of Aragon 3, 36
Alfonso X of Castile 137, 203; *Alfonso's Tables* 203
Alzate, Pietro, O.P. 23, 24
Alzina, Giovanni 13
Amata 160, 161
Ambrose 121, 291–92
Amphion 67
Anacreon 167
Angelo Salvetti da Siena 229
Anguiger 266–67, 275
Antipater of Sidon 99
Antisthenes 79
Antonio da Cremona 28–29, 36, 255
Antonio da Massa Marittima 22–23, 25–26, 197, 229, 231, 241
Antonio da Novi 135
Antonio di Santa Margherita da Venezia 228–29

Antonio Roselli da Pratovecchio 141
Antonius 111, 181, 282
Aonia/Aonian 222–23
Apelles 77, 161, 299
Aphrodite 91
Apollo (Phoebus) 103, 125, 135, 139, 151, 165, 212, 222, 283, 288–89, 292–95; of Delphi 125; of Palermo 123; of Sicily 123, 125
Apollonius 199
apostle(s) 26, 97, 103–05, 161, 199, 215, 241, 303
Appendix Vergiliana 29, 33, 180, 215, 251
Apuleius of Madaura 153, 211–12, 315–16
Aquarius (constellation) 113
Arachne 231
Aratus 137, 295
Arcadia 51
Archilochus of Paros 93
Areopagus 123
Arezzo 218
Ariadne 57
Aries (constellation) 139
Aristides 74–75, 153
Ariston of Ceos 63, 213
Ariston of Chios 63
Aristophanes 157, 173
Aristotelian/Peripatetic 79, 99, 132
Aristotle 4, 24, 38, 75, 79, 97, 99, 123, 132, 137, 167, 200–01, 203, 205, 209, 221, 281; pseudo- 75
arithmetic 211
Arnobius of Sicca 21
ars dictaminis 226
Arthur, King 69, 310
Asaph 303
Asclepiades 149
Asculum 53
ass(es) 65, 67, 69, 107, 109, 111, 145, 153–55, 179, 201, 211–13, 239–41
Assisi 234
Assur-danin-pal 100
Assyria 100

[341]

Assyrians 139
Astrea (goddess) 113
astrolabe 237
astronomer/astrologer 135, 137, 201, 285–99,
astronomy/astrology 113, 135–41, 155, 202–03, 211, 237
Atella (Oscan town) 147
Atellan farce 147
Athamantes 308
Athena (Pallas) 231
Athens/Athenians 60, 127, 151, 153, 157, 280, 283
Atticus 75, 221
Augustine, Saint 15, 18, 26, 71, 76, 96–97, 111, 117, 123, 132, 185, 200, 206, 213, 215, 229, 312
Augustus (see Octavius)
Aulus Gellius 121, 209–11, 315, 318–20
Aurispa, Giovanni 33–34, 115–19, 133, 141
Authenticae Justiniani (Authentics of Justinian) 144–45
Aventine Hill 134
Averroës 132–33

Bacchus 153, 165, 267, 292–93
Balaam 109, 111
Balbo, Sancio 30, 117
Bandello, Stefano, da Tortona 23
Barbaro, Francesco 278
Barbavara, Francesco 11–12, 33, 36, 88, 129, 223, 299
Barozzi, Luciano 30, 34, 83, 93, 95, 133
Bartolomeo da Montepulciano 223
Barzizza, Gasparino 2, 25, 28, 208, 221, 263
Basil the Great 26, 75, 215
Bathyllus 163
Baucus 260
Beatrice 219
Beccadelli family 142; "Beccadelli" (name; see also Panormita) 27, 64–65, 103, 141, 144–45, 175, 272–73, 278
Beelphegor 77
Beelzebub 179
Behemoth 179
Belial 125
Bergamo 25, 235
Bernardino da Siena 10, 27, 228–29
Bertalot, Ludwig 223
Besomi, Ottavio 102
Besozzi, Paganino 23

Bessarion 20
Bethlehem 115
Big Dipper (constellation) 139
Bignami Odier, Jean 16
Black, Robert 17, 64–65, 69, 74, 141, 201, 208, 215–17, 221–22
Blaesilla 239
Boccaccio, Giovanni 63, 91, 219–21
Boeotia 222
Boethius 202, 209, 211; *Fundamentals of Music* 202
Bologna 32, 34, 57, 64, 95, 113, 142–43, 200, 207, 237
book(s) 12–14, 17–18, 22, 26–27, 30, 34, 39, 65, 71, 73, 75, 77, 82, 91–95, 101, 111, 113, 117, 125, 138–39, 141, 147, 179, 181, 183, 199, 201, 207, 209, 211, 213, 215, 219, 221, 223, 227, 234–37, 239, 259
Boötes (constellation) 139
Borsa, Mario 51
Bossi, Ambrogio 23
Boswell, John 145
Bowen, Anthony 38
Boyle, Leonard E. 101
Brecia 11
Britain/Britains 182, 291, 317
Brivio, Dionigi 23
Brivio, Maffiolo 23
Bronze Bull (see Sicilian Bull)
brothel(s) 77–78, 99, 101, 107, 183, 260, 263, 267, 311, 316, 319
Bruni, Leonardo 2, 74–75, 143, 213, 219, 221, 235, 263, 273, 278
Brutus 209, 229
Bussi, Giovanni Andrea 20
Bussone, Francesco, "il Carmagnola" 35, 280
Butler, Shane 4, 17, 19
Bythinia 149

C. Manlius 312
Cacus 51, 278, 308
Cadurcus 317
Caecilius 27, 216
Caligula (Emperor) 69, 183, 319
Calliope 73, 310
Camenae 288
Campanus de Novara 201
Camporeale, Salvatore, O.P. 37
Canon Law 26, 96, 141, 207, 215, 233
Capra, Bartolomeo 19, 22–23, 27, 82–83, 88, 94, 213, 235–37

INDEX OF NAMES AND TOPICS

Carmagnola (see Bussone, Francesco)
Carneades 74–75
Carthage/Carthaginians 99, 153
Casson, Lionel 100
Castalia/Castalian 222–23
Castiglioni, Carlo 23
Castiglioni, Luigi 20
Catalano-Tirrito, Michele 141
Catamite (see Ganymede)
Catiline 19–20, 107, 119, 159, 209, 301–02, 307
Cato, Marcus Porcius "Censorius" (234–149 BCE) 60–61, 74–75, 82–83, 107, 153, 230–31, 259, 271, 279, 303, 309
Cato Uticensis, Marcus Porcius (95–46 BCE) 107
Cato III 107
Cattaneo, Enrico 25
Catullus 27, 37–38, 95–97, 185, 217, 249, 312, 318
Cenci, Cesare 200
Cencio dei Rustici 223, 263
Centaur(s) 179, 307
Cerberus 59, 179, 309
Ceres 289
Certosa of Pavia 8
Chaldean 119
Charlemagne 69, 310
Charmander 137
Charybdis 51, 171
Chastity (personification) 113
Chimera 107, 171
Chora 303
Chremes 175, 396
Christ 38, 77, 97, 103, 115, 125, 149, 161, 179, 183, 185, 187, 217, 303, 305, 311, 311–12
Christian 55, 59, 82, 102, 105, 111, 143, 199–200, 205, 210, 231, 241
Chrysippus of Soli 56–57, 91
Churches: San Francesco (Mantua) 231; San Francesco Grande (Milan) 10–11, 15, 22, 24, 85, 177, 235; San Marco (Florence) 101; San Marco (Venice) 223; Santa Maria Nascente, Il Duomo (Milan) 8, 9, 11, 23–25, 135; Sant' Ambrogio (Milan) 88, 177; Sant' Angelo (Milan) 10; Sant' Antonio, Il Santo (Padua) 233
Cicero 1–2, 4–5, 15, 17–20, 22, 55, 60–61, 65, 67, 71, 75, 107, 111, 115, 119, 123, 125, 129, 130–31, 137, 151, 157, 159, 163, 171–73, 175, 181, 199–201, 206, 209–10, 213–15, 217, 219, 221, 227, 229, 233, 235, 237, 278–79, 281, 283–86, 289–90, 295, 297, 300–02, 306, 308, 313, 315–16; pseudo- 2, 4, 5, 19–20, 200–01, 208
Ciceronian 7, 18, 219, 227, 278
Cincinnatus 281
Cinna 79
Cinquini, Adolfo 27, 34, 116
Cirrha 165
Cisalpine Gaul 129, 262
Claros 288
Claudian 3, 21
Claudius 317
Cleanthes 91
Clement 297
Cleon 157
Cleophon 157
Clift, Evelyn Holst 215
Clodia 267
Clodius 315
Clodius Pulcher 107
Codex Justiniani (The Code of Justinian) 144–45, 207
Codrus 73, 280–81, 310
Coffey, Michael 6, 7, 18, 22
Cognasso, Francesco 225
Cola di Rienzo 218
Colangelo, Francesco 142
Constans I (Emperor) 145
Constantine I (Emperor) 14, 115, 145, 210
Constantinople 222
Constantius II (Emperor) 21, 145
Conte, Gian Biagio 17, 29, 59, 63, 65, 69, 73, 121, 153, 208, 210–11, 214–16, 223
Copenhaver, Brian P. 151
Coppini, Donatella 27, 91, 95, 97, 141
Corbellini, Alberto 27, 66
Cordoba 132
Corpus Iuris Civilis (Body of Civil Law) 144–45
Corradi, Augusto 23, 135
Cortese, Dino 235
Corydon 119
Cossart, Michael de 27
Cotta, Pietro 23
Council of Basel 9, 11, 15–16, 200
Council of Constance 9, 141, 221
Council of Ferrara-Florence 200
Council of Nicaea 205

courtesan(s)/prostitute(s)/whore(s) 5, 10, 28, 31–33, 67, 76, 97, 99, 101–02, 105, 123, 143, 147, 181, 265–68, 310, 316, 318–19
Crassus 55, 91, 111, 181, 229, 282
Crook, J. A. 4
Crotto, Luigi 88, 275
Curtis, Stanley J. 132
Cybele 227
Cyclops 51, 170–71, 269

Dalfen, Joachim 61
Dalla, Danilo 145
Danae 173
Dante 217, 227, 296
David, King 59, 115, 121, 175, 303
Debby, Nirit Ben-Aryeh 10
Decembrio, Angelo 11
Decembrio, Pier Candido 11–12, 15, 28, 35–36, 40–02, 51, 53, 55, 57, 60, 63–64, 69, 73, 81, 83, 87, 91, 102, 113, 115, 117, 119, 121, 127, 131, 135–39, 142–43, 147, 187, 272–73, 277, 279, 310, 312; *Dialogue on the Palermian Sun* [lost] 138–39, 214, 217, 235, 237
Decemviri (The Ten Men) 149
Decency (personification) 73
Declamation against Lucius Sergius Catilina 19–20, 301
Decretals 206
De la Mare, Albina 128
Delphi/Delphic 103, 165, 185, 288, 312
De Marco, Maria 19–20
Demea 65, 67, 69
de'Medici family 101; Cosimo, "il Vecchio," 27, 32, 91, 141, 223; Lorenzo di Giovanni 223
Demetrius of Sunion 183, 311
Democritus 61, 280, 309
Demosthenes 1, 17, 75, 213
De Rijk, L. M. 83
d'Este family 222; Niccolò, III 133
Deucalion 149
Devil 105, 111, 171
Diana 260, 314
Digesta Justiniani (Digests of Justinian) 144–45, 207
Diogenes the Stoic 60
Dionysius II of Syracuse 169
Ditt, Ernst 51
Dives 161
Dominican Order 227
Domitian (Emperor) 62, 231
Duns Scotus 16, 205

Egypt/Egyptians 57, 151, 239, 287
Elena (prostitute) 102
eloquence/eloquent 55, 71, 75, 83, 103, 111, 115, 129, 133, 159, 163, 175, 181, 201, 207, 209, 210–11, 213, 221, 229, 239, 277, 283
Eloquence (personification) 201
Ennius 27, 136, 217
Enrico da Napoli (see also Hylas) 34, 112
Enrico Hylas da Prato 34
envy/jealousy (see also rivals) 29, 73, 111, 125–61, 167, 173, 197, 205, 233, 249–53
Eous 298
Ephesus 81, 99
Epicurean 67, 79, 123, 143, 310
Epigenes of Byzantium 137
Ergoteles 34, 88, 111–13, 119, 142
Erymanthian boar 51, 308
Erymanthus 281
Esposito Frank, Maria 37
Ethiopia 297
Euathlius (see also Hippias of Elis) 127
Euclid 201, 237
Euphorbus 125, 303
Euripedes 67, 165, 284
Euryale 173
Eusebius of Caesarea 63, 71, 213
Eustathius (of Cappadocia?) 155, 157
Eustochium 303
Evander 69
Evrard de Béthune 73

Fabiola, Saint 239
Fabius Pictor 128–29
Fabre, Paul 101
Facio, Bartolomeo 2, 14
Fantazzi, Charles 78
Ferrara 133, 222
Ferrari, Mirella 10, 51, 128
Feruffino, Domenico 36
Feruffino, Giovanni 28, 102, 257, 275
Fiaschi, Silvia 2
Field, Arthur 2, 75, 226
Filelfo, Francesco 2
Filippa (wife of Panormita) 102
Flavianus, Virius Nicomachus 155
Florence 8, 33, 75, 101, 141, 217–19, 221, 263
Florus 63, 213
Forlì 200
Fossati, F. 25–26
Francesco Aregazzi 235–37
Francesco Crivelli, O. F. M. 23
Francesco da Fiano 223

INDEX OF NAMES AND TOPICS

Francis of Meyronnes 205
Francis of Assisi 9, 22, 125, 161, 235, 255
Franciscan Order 9–11, 15–16, 22, 24–27,
    83–84, 161, 197, 199, 229, 231,
    233–35, 237, 255
Frontinus 213
Fronto 157
Fulgentius 292, 298
Fumagalli, Giuseppe 69
Futuarian Laws (Fuckers' Laws) 33, 147,
    149, 151

Gabii/Gabine 131
Gabotto, Ferdinando 51
Gaeta 253
Gaisser, Julia Haig 95, 120–21
Galla (prostitute) 102, 267
Galogeritanus 303
Gambaloita, Manfredo 23
Ganymede(s)/Catamite(s) 33, 65, 89, 101,
    111–13, 123, 131, 147, 316
Garnsey, Peter 38, 206
Gemonian Steps 134–35
Genoa 23, 88
geographer 201
geometry 201, 203, 211
Gerardo da Cremona 201
Germans 99
Gervaso da Piacenza 135, 138
Geryon 51, 308
Geta 58–59, 309
Giacomo della Torre da Forlì 11, 83
Giacomo (monk) 142
Gianetta (prostitute; see also Zaneta) 102
Giants 170–71, 263, 269
Giles of Rome 201
Gill, Joseph 9
Giovanni Bertoldi da Serravalle 227
Giovanni d'Andrea 207
Giovanni di Grado 51
Giuliano of Spira 235
Giustiniani, Leonardo 223
glutton(s) 66–67, 78–79, 144, 179, 236,
    269, 310, 314
Gnatho 109, 229, 280, 302
Gnesotto, Attilio 223
Gomorita 278
Gomorrah 187
Gonzaga, Gian Francesco 27
Gordon, Phyllis 223
Gorgias of Leontini 127
Gorgo 173
Gorgons 173
Gracchi 75
Graecismus 73

Grafton, Anthony 133, 222
Granius 109
Grassi, Giovanni 23
Gratian *Decretum* 96, 206
Great Western Schism 9, 207
Greece 53, 125, 183, 213, 281
Greek (language) 115, 121, 128, 144, 155,
    161, 205–06, 216, 221–23, 233,
    279, 281, 289
Greeks 55, 99–100, 149, 199, 204, 211,
    213, 221, 284
Greenfield, Concetta Carestia 37
Gregory the Great 171
Grendler, Paul F. 69, 133, 146, 222
Guarino Veronese 27, 32, 35, 95–97,
    130–31, 208, 222–23, 262, 273,
    278–79, 282
Guglielmo da Casale Monferrato 25
Gundersheimer, Werner L. 133
Gymnosophist(s) 57, 309

Hadrian 72, 115
Hankins, James 75
Hannibal 99, 313
Hebrew (language) 206, 284
Hebrews (see also Israelites and Jews)
    149, 205
Hector 58–59, 159, 249, 309
Hecuba 58
Helen of Troy 262
Helena (prostitute) 267
Heliogabalus 100–01, 316
Hell 135
Helvidius 3, 18, 22, 36, 117, 175
Henderson, Jeffrey 93
Hera 149
Hercules 17, 34, 51, 53, 107, 119, 125,
    170, 181, 217, 227, 278, 317
Hergemöller, Bernd-Ulrich 67, 89, 92,
    103, 145, 187
Hermaphrodite 31, 265–66
Hermaphrodite (offspring of Hermes
    and Aphrodite) 91
hermaphroditic 149
Hermes 71, 91
Hermes Trismegistus 151
Hermetica 151
Herodotus 63, 159, 213, 237
Herostratus 80
Hesiod 137
Hespera 269
Hesperius 294
Hippias of Elis (see also Euathlius) 125, 127
Hippocrates 132–33, 149, 304
Hippolyte (Queen of the Amazons) 127

Hippolytus 127
history 61–77, 121, 128, 137, 159, 203, 208, 210–11, 213–15, 223, 237, 310
Hollar, John A. 6
Homer/Homeric 38, 51, 59, 75, 103, 136, 155, 159, 173, 213, 253, 259, 267
Horace 21, 27, 99, 125, 173, 225, 233, 286, 288–89, 315
Hortensius Corbio 107
humanistic studies (see *studia humanitatis*)
Humiliati 16
Hydra (constellation) 139
Hydra (monster) 173, 179
Hyginus (mythographer) 113, 295
Hylas (Roman pantomime) 153
Hylas 34, 112, 119, 142, 272
Hyperbolus 157
Hyperion 287–90, 293, 299
Hypocras (see Hippocrates)

Ianziti, Gary 64
Ibn Rushd (see Averroës)
Iceland 182
Idithum 303
Immaculate Conception 16
Imprecatory Psalms 21
India/Indian 57, 165, 283
Inquisition 22, 35, 59–61, 67, 145
Insubria/Insubrians 177, 225
invective 1–7, 17–22, 26, 28, 32, 35–36, 123, 206, 209, 229, 257, 300
Ionia 283
Ippolito da Milano 235
Ippolito Stupano da Como 235
Islam/Islamic 132, 231
Isocrates 132–33, 284
Israelites (see also Jews) 109, 239
Italy/Italians 119, 121, 133, 135, 145, 171, 181, 259, 262, 269, 278, 280, 286
Itys 34
Ius gentium (Law of Nations) 231; *Ius postliminii* (Law of the Returning Exile) 187

Jansen, Katherine Ludwig 105
Jardine, Lisa 133, 222
Jehoakim 65
Jerome of Prague 221
Jerome, Saint 1, 3, 15, 17–18, 20–22, 26, 37, 39, 71, 75, 77, 96–97, 111, 115, 117, 123, 125, 129, 169, 173, 175, 179, 185, 199, 206, 210–11, 215, 227, 239, 262–63, 277, 302–06, 312, 315, 317, 319–20

Jesus of Nazareth 97, 105, 117, 160–61, 163, 179, 183, 187, 205, 239
Jews/Jewish 21, 97, 105, 143
Joan of Arc, pseudo- 31, 181, 270
Job 179
Johannes de Ianua 81
John, Saint 97
John the Baptist 163, 305
John of Jerusalem 22
John of Salisbury 66, 212, 215
Jordan, Mark D. 66–67, 187
Joseph, Saint 117
Josephus 63, 213
Jove 115, 123, 287–88, 290, 294
Jovinian 18, 22, 206, 306
Judas Iscariot 160–61
Julian the Apostate 21
Julio-Claudians 215
Julius Caesar 17, 107, 109, 159, 214–16
Julius Celsus 214–15
Jupiter (god) 103, 113, 218, 288
Jupiter (planet) 298
Justice (goddess) 113
Justinian (Emperor) 144, 207
Justinian Plague 145
Justinus 63, 213
Juvenal 21–22, 27, 93, 95, 119, 197, 216–17, 225, 251, 253, 314–17, 320

Kelly, J. N. D. 18, 75
Kempter, Gerda 113
Kennedy, George A. 4
King, Margaret L. 223
Kohl, Benjamin G. 208, 223
Koster, Severin 6
Kristeller, Paul O. 208
Kristoferson, Hans 19–20
Kublai Kahn 204

Labyrinth 57
Lactantius 14–15, 16, 38, 85, 206–07, 210–11
Laelius 271, 283, 309
Laelius, C. 60–61
Lamola, Giovanni 93, 95, 97, 117
Lampos 298
Lampridius 63, 318
Lamy, Marielle 16
Laomedon 294
Latin (language) 115, 121, 132, 157, 169, 197, 199, 205, 211, 217–18, 221, 223, 227, 278, 281
Latins 99, 211
Latinus 160–61, 291

INDEX OF NAMES AND TOPICS 347

Latium 131
Latona 294
Laura 218
Lazarus 161
Lee, Egmont 101
Lemniades 269
Leonardo di Antonio da Cremona 237
Leucothoe 287, 290
Leviathan 179
Lex Julia (Julian Law) 89, 92, 145, 147; *Lex Licinia* (Licinian Law) 147; *Lex Romana Visigothorum* (Roman Law of the Visigoths) 92; *Lex Scantinia* (Scantinian Law) 89, 147; *Lex Voconia* (Voconian Law) 147
Liber 289
liberal arts 203, 211
Libitina 305
Libra (constellation) 139
libraries (see also Visconti Library) 15, 71–72, 100–01, 231
Lilybaeum 171
Lindberg, David C. 203, 237
Lippincott, Kristen 119, 139
littera antiqua 127–29, 157, 279
Little Dipper (constellation) 139
Livy 15, 63, 137, 149, 159, 213, 237, 284
Lodovico da Pirano 11, 200–01
Lombardi, Giuseppe 11, 22–23, 25, 83, 200–01, 227–29, 231, 235
Lombardy 8, 34, 36, 129, 176–77, 225
Longinus 303
Loschi, Antonio 26, 83, 85, 87, 95, 221–23, 273
Lucan 27, 159, 216–17, 225
Lucano Miniato 142
Lucarelli, Giuliano 225
Lucceius, Lucius 159
Lucian 115, 173
Luciferians 22
Lucilius, Gaius 129, 159, 209
Lucius Apuleius Saturninus 229
Ludwig, Walther 1, 4, 95
Luigi La Strata 23
Lycurgus 71, 151
Lygdamus 170–71
Lysias of Syracuse 132–33
Lysippus 161

M. Porcius Latro, pseudo- 19–20
Macrobius, Ambrosius Theodosius 13, 121, 155, 209, 211, 306, 317–18
Madaura (North Africa) 153
Maecenas 73, 253, 283

Maecenas(es) 88–89, 107, 132–33, 141, 153, 173, 177, 179, 275, 283
magpies (see also Muses) 125, 169, 222, 231
Maiocchi, Rodolfo 23–24, 135, 237
Malta 204
Mantua 231
manuscripts (see also books) 15–16, 19–20, 25–26, 32, 36, 41–42, 101, 127, 149, 170, 214, 217, 220, 223, 229, 235–37
Marco da Vimercato 23–24
Marco de' Benvenuti, Lorenzo 2
Mark Antony 17, 19, 61, 67, 119, 173, 209, 281–82, 303
Mars (god) 111, 119, 173
Mars (planet) 298
Mars Hill (see Areopagus)
Marsh, David 1, 115
Martial 27–28, 38, 66, 79, 111, 217, 251
Martial the Cook 66, 79, 217
Martianus Capella 200–01, 211, 291, 297
Martin, Henri-Jean 3
Mary Magdalen 104–05
mathematics 203, 237
Matilda (prostitute) 102, 267
Matteo Pritelli da Cremona 11, 200–01
McKibben, William T. 145
McManamon, John 18
Memphis 289
Mercer, R. G. G. 221
Mercury (god) 71, 91, 113, 299, 310
Mercury (planet) 203
Mercury Trismegistus (see also Thoth) 149
Merrill, Norman 4–5, 21
Messiah 163
Metellus Numidicus 312
Midas, King 212
Milan/Milanese 8–12, 16, 23–25, 28, 31, 83, 88, 95, 121, 177, 225, 235, 237, 265, 270, 296; *studium* 221, 237
Minerva (see also Athena) 131, 153, 155, 157, 163, 231
Minotaur 57
Mithridates 79
Mnesarchus 74–75
Moabite(s) 77, 109
Mohammed, The Prophet 231
Monfardini, Bruno 12, 14, 24, 83, 235
Monfasani, John 68, 163, 201, 235
Monfrin, Jacques 213
monster(s)/portent(s) 31, 51–53, 55, 59, 69, 91, 103, 107, 125, 147, 169–71, 173, 179, 187, 266, 278, 301, 303, 308

Moon 135, 139, 141, 203, 279
Moorman, John 10
Mormando, Franco 10
Moses 26, 149, 175, 215
Mount(s): Caucasus 143; Etna 60, 171; Helicon 117, 125, 165, 222; Nysa 165; Olympus 143; Parnasus 136–37, 222; Vesuvius 210
Müntz, Eugène 101
Muse(s) 29, 73, 85, 87, 117, 123, 125, 136, 151, 165, 167, 169, 219, 222–23, 231, 253, 255, 283, 289
music 202–03, 211
Muzano, Maffeo 31

Naevius, Gnaeus 159, 162–63
Naples 147, 218
Nearchus 169
Nemean lion 51–53, 308
Neoptolemus 137
Nepotian 315
Neptune 272
Nero (Emperor) 69, 100–01, 183, 210, 260, 303, 318
Nerva (Emperor) 73
Neugebauer, O. 237
Nicander of Colophon 137
Niccoli, Niccolò 2
Nichina (prostitute) 267
Nicolas Bonet 204–05
Nisbet, R. G. M. 5
Nonius 317, 319
Novellae Justiniani (Novels of Justinian) 144–45
Numa Pompilius 71, 151
Nymphs 119

Oakley, Francis 227
Ocean 287, 298
Octavius Caesar (Augustus) 17, 73, 153, 157, 223, 283
Octavius 279, 281
O'Daly, Gerard J. P. 206
Oddo Colonna (see Pope Martin V)
Odysseus 59, 143, 170
Oenipion 113
O'Malley, John W. 4, 26
oracle(s)/prophet(s) 65, 96–97, 103, 121, 127, 175, 185, 280, 283, 312
orator/rhetorician 2, 4, 82–83, 87, 123, 127, 132, 137, 163, 169, 181, 197, 200–01, 208–09, 213, 276, 279, 305

oratory/rhetoric 1–7, 11, 17–22, 26, 28, 32, 35–36, 127, 132–33, 163, 201, 208, 211, 225–27, 229, 253
Orcus 270, 304
Orestes 269, 308
Origen 39, 75, 77, 206, 305
Orion (constellation) 112–13
Orosius 21, 63, 71, 213
Orpheus 76–77, 173, 311
Osmond, Patricia J. 19–20, 215
Ovid 3, 19, 27, 103, 212–13, 215–16, 224–25, 253, 287, 289, 293–96, 298; pseudo- 224–25

Pachynum 171
Pacuvius 67, 310
Pade, Marianne 213
Padua 8, 10–11, 24, 207
Palermo/Palermitan 27, 64, 85, 99, 169, 177, 187, 269
Palladius, Rutilius Taurus Aemilianus 223
Pan 212
Pandectae Justiniani (Pandects of Justinian) 144–45, 317
Pannonians 99
Panormita, Antonio 7, 12, 17, 19, 21–22, 27–37, 39, 41–42, 51–189, 217, 245–60, 265–68, 270, 272–76, 278–79, 282–83, 285, 287; "Publio" 118–19; *Commentary on Plautus* 59, 131, 273; *Etsi facile* 31–32, 36, 38, 53, 63, 73, 74, 76–78, 83, 94–95, 105, 187, 245–55; *Hermaphrodite* 22, 27–28, 30, 33–34, 36, 91, 93–95, 97, 101, 103, 111, 113, 117, 123, 125, 131, 141, 147, 151, 153, 181, 183, 251, 259; *Oration on the Sun* 35, 135, 177; *Priapeia* 74, 77, 95, 180–81
Parma 27
Parthenias 251
Parthians 139, 233
Paul, Saint (see also Saul of Tarsus) 21, 26, 64, 103, 105, 199, 215
Paul of Milan 121
Paulinus of Nola 115
Pavia 11–12, 23–24, 27–28, 31, 53, 135, 177, 225, 262, 265
Peking 204
Pelagians 22
Pellegrin, Elisabeth 11, 20, 25, 113, 200–02, 209, 214, 217–20, 223
Pelorus 171

INDEX OF NAMES AND TOPICS

Penates 155
Penelope (wife of Odysseus) 143
Penelope (Panormita's alleged first wife) 143
Percy, William Armstrong, III 76
Pericles 132, 157, 185, 311
Perillus 161
Perseus (hero) 17, 27, 136, 173
Perseus (constellation) 112–13
Persius 199, 216, 225
Peter, Saint 97
Peter of Blois 201
Peter Cantor 235
Peter Lombard 1, 205
Peter of Spain 83
Petrarca, Francesco 1, 7–8, 19, 21, 38, 63, 218–19
Petronius 22
Phaëton 289, 294–95, 301
Phalaris of Acragas (Agrigento) 161, 169–70
Pharisee 105
Phidias 299
Philip 91
Philipp II of Macedonia 17, 313
Philistines 314
Philoctetes 91
Philodemus 281
philosopher(s) 17, 38, 56–57, 63, 65, 71, 73–75, 82–83, 87, 89, 91, 97, 99, 101–03, 121, 123, 129, 135, 155, 169, 171, 183, 189, 199, 203, 205, 215, 219, 230, 259, 279, 281, 296, 303, 305, 309–10, 312, 317
philosophy 3, 16, 26, 37, 39, 65, 67, 83, 85, 121, 135, 137, 155, 167, 203, 208, 210, 215, 231, 233–34, 259
Phlegon 298
Phoebus (see Apollo)
Phoenicians (see Punics)
Phoenix 85
Phormio 99, 101
Phormio (Terence) 259, 302
Phoroneus, King 149
Phrygians 316
Piana, Celestino 200, 227–29, 235, 237
Piccinino, Francesco 135
Piccinino, Niccolò 26, 28
Pierius/Pierian 169, 222–23, 231, 267
Pillars of Hercules 73
pimp(s) 5, 31, 99, 101, 147, 262, 265, 300, 316, 319
Pindar 34
Piso 19, 123, 307

Pitonessa (prostitute) 102, 267
Plato 15, 61, 75, 93, 103, 121, 123, 125, 167, 171, 203, 205, 209; pseudo- 120–21, 251, 309
Platonic 56
Plautus 27, 32, 59, 69, 109, 123, 130–31, 145, 154, 163, 175, 197, 217, 273, 299, 316, 319
Pliny the Elder 210–11
Pliny the Younger 72, 145, 157, 210–11, 279, 282, 284, 306
Plutarch 17, 74–75, 159, 206, 212–13, 221
poet/poetry 2–3, 6–7, 21, 24, 26–38, 57, 59, 61, 65–66, 73, 76–105, 107, 109, 111–13, 115, 117, 120–21, 123, 125, 127, 129, 131, 136–37, 139, 142, 151, 153–55, 157, 159, 161, 163, 165, 167, 169, 171, 173, 175, 177–81, 183, 199, 203, 208, 210, 215–21, 225, 229, 249, 251, 255, 259, 266, 269–70, 273–76, 279, 282–83, 293, 296, 298
Poggio Fiorentino (Bracciolini) 2, 20, 27, 32–33, 38, 95, 103, 120, 220–21, 223
Polybius [sic] 223
Polyphemus 51, 170
Pommerol, Marie-Henriette Jullien de 213
Pompey 216
Pomponius Laetus 20
Pontano, Francesco 116–17
Pontano, Lodovico 116
Pontifex Maximus 155
Popes: Boniface VIII 207; Clement V 207; Eugenius IV 14–16, 141; Gregory IX 207; Martin V 9, 25, 135, 141; Stephan I 233
portent (see monster)
Poseidon 149
preaching 227, 229
Priam 58, 262
Priapeia 29–30, 73, 180, 215, 251
Priapus 77, 173, 259, 265, 267
Prodicus of Ceos 127
Propertius 27, 79, 111, 136, 185, 217, 312
prophet (see oracle)
prostitute (see courtesan)
Prostitutes of Pavia 28–29, 31–32, 181
Protagoras of Abdera 127
Protogenes 281
Psalms 59, 107
Ptolemy (Claudius Ptolemaeus) 137, 201, 237
Publican(s) 105, 180–81

Puccinelli, Placido 16
Punics 53, 99
Pylades 153, 163
Pyrois 298
Pyrrhia 58–59
Pyrrhus 53, 75
Pythagoras 125, 202–03, 303
Pythagorean 85, 259
Pytho (see Pitonessa)

Quintillian 2, 4, 6, 19, 125, 209, 303, 308, 319
Quintus Curtius 63, 159, 215
Quintus Mucius Scaevola 130–31
Quirites 312

Ramorino, Felice 30
Rao, Ennio I. 2–3, 21
Regoliosi, Mariangela 17, 34, 102, 142
Regulus 279, 306
Remigius of Auxerre 211
Repubblica Ambrosiana 237
Resta, Gianvito 27
rhetoric (see oratory)
rhetorician (see orator)
Rho, Agata da 11
Rho, Antonio da 1–3, 7–18, 22–40, 51–241, 260, 263, 270–73, 278–79, 308; "Anonymous Invective" 30, 96, 102, 142, 143, 187; *Genealogy of the Scipios and Catos* 12; lost poem 249; *Metrica commendatio Martini V* 9; *Rhetorical Imitations* 12, 19, 40; *Three Dialogues against Lactantius* 14–16, 38, 40
Rho (village) 10, 117
Rhodes (Panormita's sobriquet for Rho) 154–55, 179, 274–76
Ricci, Antonio (Abbot of Sant' Ambrogio) 177
Ricci, Pier Giorgio 2
Ricci, Zanino 177
Rice, Eugene F., Jr. 18, 200
Richlin, Amy 17, 77, 87, 123, 145, 173
rival(s) 6, 8, 10, 28, 67, 167, 199, 203, 207, 223, 229, 239, 253
River(s): Jordan 239; Meander 101, 173, 308; Tiber 134; Ticino 177, 266
Robert of Anjou, King 218
Roberto da Lecce 27
Rocke, Michael 66, 79, 145
Roeder, Günther 71
Roland (Orlando) 69
Rolandus Scibbeke de Alamania 137, 188

Roman Law (see also *Ius*, *Lex*, and *Twelve Tables*) 144–45, 207
Romans 53, 93, 100, 103, 105–06, 131, 136, 149, 151, 217, 239, 314
Rome 14, 16–17, 34, 78, 95, 97, 103, 131, 134, 141–42, 149, 153, 155, 163, 183, 199, 218, 230, 253, 280, 282, 296, 301, 303, 320
Romm, James S. 182
Roncesvalles 69
Ronzoni, D. 217
Roscius (Roman actor) 153
Rufinus of Aquileia 1, 22, 75, 306
Rusconi, Antonio 10

Sabbadini, Remigio 14, 16, 20, 27, 29–31, 34–35, 37, 59, 77, 83, 88, 93, 95, 102, 115–16, 129, 132–33, 141–42, 154, 235
Sacco, Catone 28, 36–37, 143, 257, 275
sacred literature/sacred page (see also theology) 11, 24, 37, 83, 85, 185, 205, 233, 237, 314, 316
Sacred Scripture / Holy Writ 17–18, 55, 107, 109, 132, 211, 239
Sacred Themis 103
Sallust 1, 19–20, 63, 157, 209, 215, 281; pseudo- 215
Salutati, Coluccio 74, 208, 219
Sanhedrin 97
Saracens 233
Sardanapalus 100–01
Sarteano, Alberto 10, 15, 27
Sartori, Antonio 233
Saslow, James 113
Satan 125
Saturn (planet) 139, 203
Saul, King 59
Saul of Tarsus (see also Paul, Saint) 105
Schanz, Martin 20
Schindel, Ulrich 19, 215
Schmitt, Charles B. 151
Schurgacz, Katrin 19
Scibbeke, Rolandus 41
Scipio 15, 271
Scipio Africanus 163, 218
Scolario Tusco da Montalcino 233
Scriptores historiae augustae 11
Scylla 51, 171
Scythia/Scythians 268, 307
Seel, Otto 19
Segovia 16
Semele 289

INDEX OF NAMES AND TOPICS

Seneca the Younger 15, 102–03, 167, 203, 205, 209, 213, 219, 227, 229–30
Septicius Clarus 72
Sertorius 75
Servius Sulpicius Galba 130–31
Sforza, Francesco 10
Sibyl(s) 103, 149, 227
Sicily/Sicilian 29, 32, 36, 51, 59–61, 63, 68–69, 73, 84–85, 93, 102, 115, 117, 123, 127, 139, 141, 143, 151, 161, 167, 169, 171, 175, 255, 262–63, 266–67, 269, 278, 281–83; Sicilian (Bronze) Bull 161, 170–71; Sicilian Muses 29, 123–25, 255
Siena 16, 32, 113, 141–43, 260
Sigismund (Holy Roman Emperor) 27, 176–77, 253
Siloam 185, 312
Simonetta, Marcello 51
Siraisi, Nancy G. 132–33
Siren 179
Sironi, Grazioso 23
Socrates/Socratic 15, 61, 69, 103, 183, 213, 239, 281, 308, 314, 316
Sodom 187
sodomite(s)/sodomy 10, 32–33, 35, 65–67, 78–79, 99, 101, 143, 147, 165, 183, 187, 311, 314, 316, 319
Solomon 55, 60, 230
Solon 71, 151
Sophist(s) 125, 127
Sophocles 161
Sophronius 303
Southern, R. W. 213
Spain 121, 213
Spartans 93, 151
Speyer, Wolfgang 214
Sphinx 109
Spilimbergo, Giovanni 130
Sporus 100–01, 260, 318
Stadter, Philip A. 101
Statius 27, 216–17
Sthenno 173
Stilpo of Megara 317
Stoic(s) 56, 63, 74, 79, 89, 102, 125, 143, 183, 200, 216, 219, 230, 234, 279, 306
Straits: of Gibraltar 73; of Messina 171
Strassoldo, Lodovico 16
studia humanitatis (humanistic studies) 7, 15, 208–09, 218–19
Stymphalians 179
Styx 217, 269
Subiaco 16

Suetonius 11, 62–63, 69, 71–73, 159, 199, 206, 214–15, 253, 316, 318–19
Sun 135, 137, 139, 203, 227, 281, 285–99
Syracuse/Syracusans 99, 151, 268
Syrus 67, 69, 306, 310

Tacitus 63, 213
Tebaldi, Tomaso, da Bologna (see also Adonis and Ergoteles) 34, 88, 111–12, 119
Temple of Diana 80–81
Tenedos 288
Tentler, Thomas N. 145
Terence 27, 58–59, 65, 109, 175, 217, 253, 315–17, 319–20
Tertullian 21
Thais (prostitute) 102, 281
Thasymachus of Chalcedon 127
Thebes 280
Themistocles 159
Theocritus 151, 167
Theodora (Empress) 207
Theodosius (Emperor) 121
theology/theologian (see also sacred literature) 7, 9, 11, 14, 16, 23–26, 30, 37, 39, 67, 76, 117, 200–01, 204–05, 229–30, 235, 237, 241, 257
Theophrastus 79
Theopompus 63, 213
Thersites 59, 204–05, 309
Theseus 57, 127, 309
Thessaly/Thessalians 173, 204, 307
Thomas of Celano 235
Thoth 71, 151
Thrace/Thracians 76, 269, 281, 304
Thucydides 63
Tiberius (Emperor) 316
Tibullus 27, 79, 111, 185, 217, 292, 312
Tierney, Brian 207
Titan 290
Titinius 58
Tityrus 173
Torah 149, 183
Trajan (Emperor) 72, 75, 210, 212–13
Transalpine Gaul 205
Trebizond, George of 2
Trinkaus, Charles 37
Trogus 63, 213
Troy/Trojans 58, 155, 204
Tuscan 227
Twelve Tables 89, 93, 149, 279
Twin Carts (constellations) 139
Typhon 171

Ulery, Robert W. 19–20, 215
Ullman, Berthold L. 6–7, 101, 128, 203
Ultima Thule 182–83
Universities: Bologna 207; Oxford 205; Padua 141, 207, 221; Paris 204–05; Pavia 135, 177, 221, 262
Ursa (prostitute) 102, 259, 267
Ursa Maior (constellation) 139
Ursa Minor (constellation) 139

Valencia (Spain) 227
Valentini, Roberto 27, 34, 116
Valentinian III (Emperor) 11
Valerius Maximus 165, 215, 219
Valla, Lorenzo 2–3, 10–15, 28, 34, 36–37, 39, 113, 117, 142–43, 272, 275–76
Van Steenberghen, Fernand 83
Vandals 213
Vargula 109
Varro 6, 69, 229, 230
Vegetius 213
Vegio, Maffeo 14, 28, 31–32, 143
Venice/Venetians 223, 235, 280
Venus 91, 94–95, 111, 115, 119, 123, 145, 153, 260, 267, 269, 316
Verona 95, 222
Verres 4, 19, 209
Vespasian (Emperor) 183
Victorinus, Gaius Marius 201
Victorinus of Pettau 132–33
Vigilantius 22, 303, 306
Vincent of Beauvais 66
Vincent, Ferrer 227
Virbius 127
Virgil 26–27, 29–30, 38, 73, 103, 118, 125, 129, 151, 155, 157, 159, 161, 163, 165, 169, 173, 211, 213, 215, 217, 219, 223, 253, 259, 267, 283, 291–92, 310; pseudo- (see *Appendix Vergiliana*)
Virgin Mary 103, 117, 305
Virgo (constellation) 113
Virtue (personification) 159
Visconti family 8, 12, 83, 221, 235; Bertola 25; Filippo Maria 8–9, 11, 15–16, 27, 34–35, 63, 73, 88, 135, 225, 253, 277, 285–86, 299, 309; Gian Galeazzo 8; Giovanni Maria 8
Visconti Library (see also Pellegrin) 11, 20, 25–26, 113, 201, 223
Vismara, Felice 2, 23
Viti, Paolo 9, 51
Vitruvius 223
Vittorino da Feltre 208
Viturbius (see Vitruvius)
Voigt, Georg 2
Volcacian Canon 217
Vulcan 51, 60–61, 94, 272, 287, 296

Walter Map 66
Walther, Hans 234
Watson, Alan 187
Wenceslaus (Holy Roman Emperor) 8
Wiesen, David S. 7, 21, 51, 66, 75, 79, 91, 99, 107, 111, 123, 147–48, 152–53, 177, 186, 216, 241
Windelin of Speyer 20
Witke, Charles 7, 136, 151
Witt, Ronald G. 17, 75, 146, 217, 219, 221–23

Xenophon 75, 159, 284

Zambeccari, Cambio, da Bologna 28–30, 33, 179, 283
Zaneta (prostitute; see also Gianetta) 267
Zeno of Citium 79, 89, 169, 234–35
Zeno of Eleas 169
Zethus 67, 310
Zeus 113, 171, 173
Zimmerer, Heinrich 19
Zodiac 113

INDEX OF TEXTS CITED

Ancient Texts

Aesop *Fables* 34.4 **232**
Ambrose *Abraham* 1.4.24 **319**
  Apology for the Prophet David
    1.4.15 **121**
  Education of a Virgin 4.31 **121**
  Expositions on the Psalms 19.2 **185**
  Hexameron 4.6.25 **292**; 6.6.39 **185**
  Letter 51 **121**
Apuleius *Metamorphoses* (*The Golden Ass*)
    3.14 **153**; 3.21–26 **212**; 3.22
    212; 4.10 **149**; 8.1 **67**, **315**;
    8.24 **316**; 8.25 **315**; 9.26 **316**;
    11.8 **316**
Aristotle *De decem predicamentis*
    7^b.31–32 **209**
  Eudemian Ethics 1220^b **99**
  Nicomachean Ethics (trans. Lincolniensis)
    54^{b}20 **97**; (trans. Grosseteste)
    95^{b}5–95^{b}10 **136–37**
  On Interpretation (trans. Boethius)
    16^{a}3–4 **97**
  Praedicamenta 2.4.2 **99**
  Problemata 30.1 **167**
  Rhetoric 1358^b **4**; 1366^a–1367^b **4**
Augustine *Against the Letter of Parmenianus*
    2.29 **159**
  City of God 2.9 **89**, **93**, **157**; 2.14 **93**;
    6.10 **230**; 14.17 **57**; 16.8 **71**;
    18.14 **76**
  Letter 153.6.16 **151**
  On Heretics 84 **117**
  On the Sermon on the Mount 2.5.24 **167**
  On Acts with Felix the Manichaean
    1.4 **160**
  Questions on the Heptateuch 1.127 **66**;
    1.136 **66**
Aulus Gellius 1.8.3 **319**; 1.15.1 **154**; 2.6.9
    320; 2.6.18 **80**; 2.18.3 **142**, **319**;
    2.24.11 **315**; 3.3.14 **162**; 3.3.15
    162; 6.11.4–6 **320**; 6.16.6 **315**;
    7.11.1 **189**; 7.11.1–3 **189**; 9.2.6
    318; 9.9.4–11 **151**; 11.7.3 **69**; 12.2
    209; 12.2.1 **320**; 13.11.7 **231**; 13.17
    208; 15.24 **217**; 19.11 **120**

Boethius *Fundamentals of Arithmetic*
    2.4 **202**
  Geometric Art 1 **202**

Censorinus *The Birthday Book* 8.6 **285**
Catullus 16.5 **99**, **318**; 16.5–6 **83**, **95**,
    251; 16.5–9 **97**; 95.6–7 **167**
Cicero *About the Ends of Good and Evil*
    2.8.24 **60**; 3.12.41 **200**; 5.89 **284**
  Against Caecilius Niger 3 **300**; 6 **300**;
    30 **300**
  Against Catiline 1.2 **300**; 1.11 **302**;
    1.12 **302**
  Against Piso 1 **306**; 8–9 **306–07**; 9 **307**;
    11 **307**; 12 **307**; 13 **307**; 14 **307**;
    17 **307**; 18 **307**; 19 **307**; 20 **307**;
    21 **307**; 22 **307**; 41 **307**; 46
    307–08; 47 **308**; 53 **308**; 56 **308**;
    62 **308**; 69 **123**, **317**; 73 **308**
  Brutus 8.30 **127**; 62.224 **229**;
    75.261–62 **214**
  In Defense of Archia 2.3 **208**; 7.15 **229**;
    11.26 **198**
  In Defense of Caelius 5.12 **107**; 6.13
    107; 15.36 **119**
  In Defense of Cluentius 84 **137**
  In Defense of Marcellus 22 **144**
  In Defense of Milo 21.55 **319**
  In Defense of Murena 29.61 **208**
  In Defense of Sestio 9.20 **316**; 52.111
    315; 57.121 **198**
  Laws 3.1.3 **151**; 3.3.6 **149**
  Letters to Friends 20.19 (1.9.19) **91**;
    22.1 (5.12.1) **159**; 22.1–2
    (5.12.1–2) **158**; 22.3 (5.12.3)
    159; 22.7 (5.12.7) **160**, **249**;
    22.7–8 (5.12.7–8) **159**; 112.1
    (15.6.1) **249**
  On Agrarian Law 1.1.2 **314**;
    2.18.48 **315**
  On Divination 1.37.80 **61**, **251**

[353]

354 INDEX

Cicero (*Continued*)
  On Duties 1.7.20 **255**; 1.17.54–55 **234**; 1.31.110 **153**; 1.40.144 **185**; 1.43.153 **200**, **234**; 2.7.25 **319**
  On Fate 5.10 **317**
  On Friendship 24.89 **217**
  On His Own House 44.116 **315**; 57.144 **218**
  On Invention 1.34–36 **5**; 2.177–78 **5**
  On the Nature of the Gods 1.54 **206**; 1.79 **153**; 2.49 **290**, **297**; 2.54 **295**; 2.55 **295**; 2.62 **289–90**; 2.68 **285**
  On the Orator 1.8.30–31 **229**; 1.8.32 **229**; 1.16.69–70 **137**; 2.6.25 **129**; 2.9.36 **71**; 2.11.45 **55**; 2.18.75 **99**; 2.37.155 **67**; 2.46.194 **61**; 2.60.244 **109**; 2.85.349 **4**; 3.1.4 **91**; 3.32.127 **125**; 3.35.141 **91**; 3.50.194 **99**
  Philippics 2.4.7 **61**; 2.32.80 **280**; 3.9.22 **163**; 5.7.20 **99**
  Republic 4.6 **315**; 4.10.11 **157**; 4.10.12 **89**, **93**; 6.17 **286**, **291**
  Response to the Soothsayers 57 **232**
  The Orator 2.7 **163**; 22.73 **77**; 42.145 **99**
  Tusculan Disputations 1.1.1–3 **198**; 2.1.1 **137**; 2.11.27 **93**; 3.1.2 **319**; 4.14.33 **61**; 4.31.67 **159**, **249**; 4.35.74 **87**
  Verrine Orations 1.6.15 **300**; 2.1.3.9 **300**; 2.1.8.21 **300**; 2.1.12.33 **300**; 2.1.12.34 **300**; 2.1.15.40 **300**; 2.1.16.42 **300**; 2.1.17.44 **300**; 2.4.24.53 **300**; 2.4.43.95 **300**; 2.4.50.112 **301**
Curtius 9.1.31–33 **59**

Declamation against L. Sergius Catiline 2.3 **302**; 3.6–7 **301**; 3.8 **302**; 4.9 **302**; 5.13 **301**; 6.18 **301**; 7.20 **301**; 8.26 **301**; 8.27 **301**; 9.28 **302**; 9.29 **301**; 9.30 **301**; 9.31 **301**; 9.32 **301**; 16.58 **302**; 22.74 **302**; 24.81 **302**; 27.90 **302**; 28.95 **301**; 29.96 **208**

Elegy on Maecenas 83 (*Appendix Vergiliana*) **173**

Fulgentius *Mythologies* 1.17 **292**

Giaus *Institutiones* 1.129 **187**

Hesiod *Works and Days* 293 **136–37**
Hirtius *Gallic War* 8. praef. 2 **214**
Homer *Iliad* 2.211–77 **59**
  Odyssey 9.152–566 **170**; 12.234–59 **171**
Horace *Art of Poetry* 21–22 **132**; 94 **175**, **306**; 97 **152–53**, **176**, **232**; 137 **281**; 139 **143**; 372–73 **171**; 385 **153**; 441 **286**
  Carmen Saeculare 9–11 **288**; 61–64 **288**
  Epistles 1.13.14 **58**; 2.1.115–16 **99**; 2.1.152–55 **93**; 2.1.210–11 **127**; 2.1.229–31 **159**; 2.1.269–70 **125**, **167**; 2.2.208–09 **173**
  Satires 1.4.10 **167**; 1.4.34 **239**, **302**; 2.8.87 **319**
Hyginus *Poetic Astronomy* 2.12 **113**; 2.34 **113**

Iamblichus *Life of Pythagoras* 9.4 **202**; 14.63 **85**, **125**; 64.114 **202**
Isidore of Seville *Differences* 1.263 **319**
  Etymologies 5.20.1 **151**; 8.11.54 **292**; 12.8.16 **79**; 18.43.1 **319**; 19.24.7 **131**; 36.1–3 **298**
  On the Nature of Things 17.1 **295**; 17.1–2 **296**; 17.3 **297**
Iulius Paulus *Digesta* 49.15.19 **187**

Jerome *Against Helvidius* 1 **175**; 1.1 **305**; 1.16 **305**; 1.17 **111**; lib. subs. **305**
  Against Jovinian 1.1 **227**; 1.34 **153**; 1.40 **186**
  Against Rufinus 1.6 **75**; 1.31 **180**
  Against Vigilantius 1 **52**, **125**, **179**, **230**, **231**, **303**; 1.2 **53**, **144**; 1.5 **304**; 1.6 **304**; 1.8 **147**, **304**; 1.10 **304**; 1.15 **125**
  Commentary on Amos 2.5 **139**
  Commentary on Ezekiel prol. **81**; 2.12 **111**; 3.7–9 **123**
  Commentary on Isaiah 8.25.9 **77**
  Commentary on Jeremiah 1.7 **317**
  Commentary on Luke 15.186.2 **315**
  Commentary on Titus 1.7 **79**
  Commentary on Zacharia 3 **123**
  Hebraic Questions praef. **76**, **140**, **165**; Genesis 37.36 **66**
  Letters 2 **304**; 7.5 **91**; 10.1 **319**; 17.3 **304**; 21.13 **37**, **169**; 22 **18**, **75**, **206**; 22.28 **303–04**; 22.29 **125**; 27.1.2 **111**, **211**; 27.2 **177**; 27.3 **241**; 39 **239**; 42.4 **316**; 47.3 **199**, **241**; 50.4 **229**, **238**; 50.4–5 **302**;

INDEX OF TEXTS CITED

50.5 **238–39, 302–03**; 50.22 **111**; 52.3 **111, 317**; 52.12 **315**; 52.14 **185**; 53.1 **277**; 53.2 **227**; 53.7 **99, 153, 216**; 54.2 **305–06**; 54.5 **305**; 54.10 **66, 317**; 54.15 **318–19**; 57.13 **69, 320**; 58.3 **115**; 58.10 **210**; 61.2 **71, 230**; 61.3 **149, 304**; 61.4 **148, 305**; 66.9 **128**; 70.6 **74**; 75.3 **103, 125**; 77.7 **239, 317**; 79.11 **317**; 84.7 **64, 305**; 106.57 **51**; 107.4 **130**; 109.1 **123, 149, 305**; 109.2 **304, 305**; 109.3 **148, 319**; 109.4 **305**; 125 **75, 206**; 125.16 **152**; 125.18 **107, 152–53, 303**; 130.5 **79**; 130.7 **304**; 147.8 **305**
Life of St. Paul, the First Hermit 3 **97**
On Illustrious Men 135 **199**
Justinian *Codex* 9.9.31 **145**
  Digesta 1.2.2.45 **130**; 47.11.1/11.3.14 **317**
  Novella 77.1 **145**
Juvenal 1.1–2 **55, 197**; 1.15 **169, 239, 302**; 2.10 **314, 316**; 2.11–13 **317**; 2.12–13 **314**; 2.19–21 **317**; 2.36–50 **89**; 2.40 **107**; 3.76–77 **127**; 3.78 **127**; 3.106–108 **314**; 3.234–35 **320**; 6.34 **119**; 6.122–24 **317**; 6.128–29 **317**; 6.531 **109, 112, 113, 125, 253**; 7.24–25 **94**; 7.237–40 **92**; 9.92 **241**; 10.122 **163, 198**; 14.25–30 **316**

Lactantius *Divine Institutes* 1.6.2–5 **71**; 1.11.24–25 **38**; 1.20.2 **319**; 3.20.11–12 **140**
  On the Wrath of God 20.10–11 **140**
Lampridius *Alexander Severus* 39.2 **67, 318**
  Heliogabalus 5.4.1 **316**
Livy 3.33.3 **149**; 5.34 **177**; 8.8.11 **95**; 21.4.9–10 **53**; 22.29.8 **137**; 29.19.11–12 **57**
Lucilius 2.frag.67 **315**; 7.frag.287–88 **317**
Lucretius 5.905 **107, 303**

Macrobius *Saturnalia* praef. 11 **85**; 1.7.2 **306**; 1.10.13 **318**; 1.24.11 **157**; 1.24.16 **155**; 1.24.17 **155**; 1.24.18 **157**; 1.24.19 **211**; 2.2.15 **120**; 3.17.10 **151**; 5.1.7 **157**; 5.2–22 **211**; 5.21.14 **211**; 6.1.1 **211**; 7.7.3 **317**
  Scipio's Dream 1.20.4 **286**; 1.20.6 **286**; 2.14–15 **209**

Martial 5.76 **79**; 9.70.1 **119**; 9.70.5 **119**; 12.77 **73**
Martianus Capella 2.188 **291**; 2.189 **297**; 5.425–38 **201**; 7.734 **297**

Nonius M 5 **319**; M 10 **315**; M 11 **315**; M 21 **317**; M 22–23 **316**; M 23 **315–16**; M 107 **317**; M 154 **314**; M 423 **319**; M 442 **314**

Origen *Commentary on the Song of Songs* 2 **185**
  Homilies on Numbers 20.1 **77**
Orosius *Histories against the Pagans* 1.21 **157**
Ovid *Amores* 1.8.59–60 **293**
  Fasti 1.400 **173**; 1.543–74 **52**
  Heroides 1.6 **225**; 1.10 **225**; 1.26 **225**
  Metamorphoses 1.150 **113**; 1.169 **101**; 1.463–64 **169**; 1.515–22 **288**; 2.1 ff. **287**; 2.11–13 **294**; 2.23–24 **293, 294**; 2.27–30 **298**; 2.40 **293**; 2.40–41 **293**; 2.67 **298**; 2.84–87 **294**; 2.106 **296**; 2.107–09 **296**; 2.124 **293**; 2.142–43 **294**; 2.145 **295**; 2.150 **295**; 2.151–52 **295**; 2.153–55 **298**; 2.399 **295**; 4.190 ff. **287**; 4.192–93 **293**; 4.426–28 **287**; 5.349–52 **171**; 6.1–145 **231**; 9.1–88 **107**; 9.135–272 **216**; 10.79–85 **76**; 10.152–54 **76**; 11.157–93 **212**; 11.166 **293**; 11.196 **294**; 15.544 ff. **127**

Paul of Milan *Life of St. Ambrose* 14.24 **121**
Persius praef. 2 **136**; 1.27–28 **198**; 1.43 **167**
Plato *Letter* 7 **169**
  Phaedrus 245a **61, 251**
  Republic 10.607a-d **93**
  Timaeus 36–37 **202**
Plautus *Amphitryon* 422 **299**
  Asinaria 751–54 **171**
  Aulularia 325–26 **88**; 422 **319**
  Bacchides 651–60 **87**
  Captivi 583 **197**
  Curculio 54 **145**; 197 **175**
  Epidicus 60a **59**; 166a–166b **123**
  Menaechmi 144 **316**
  Pseudolus 25–26 **227**
Pliny the Elder *Natural Histories* 6.220 **182**; 7.73 **170**; 7.160 **137**; 7.193 **137**; 9.69 **81**; 9.121–22 **131**; 34.19.89 **161**

Pliny the Younger *Letters* 1.5.2 **279**, **306**; 1.5.11 **306**; 1.5.14 **149**, **306**; 2.11.9 **151**; 3.3.6 **144**; 4.2.5 **306**; 4.2.8 **306**; 4.7.4 **306**; 4.25.3 **306**; 5.10 **72**
Panegyricus 47.3 **208**
Plutarch *Cicero* 48–49 **17**
Moralia 810.E-F **185**
Porphyry *On Pythagoras* 26 **85**, **125**; 27 **85**, **125**; 45 **85**, **125**
Propertius 3.3 **136**
Prudentius *Crowns of Martyrdom* 10.233–34 **113**

Quintilian *Education of the Orator* 3.4.4 **4**; 3.4.11 **4**; 4.2.124 **308**; 6.3.47 **147**; 7.6.3 **319**; 9.4.41 **163**, **198**; 10.1.55 **151**; 10.1.93 **6**; 10.1.125–31 **209**; 11.1.24 **163**, **198**; 11.3.114 **152**; 12.1.23–32 **163**, **280**

Rhetoric to Herennius 3.13–15 **5**

Sallust *Catilina* 1.1 **281**
Seneca the Elder *Controversiae* 3.pr.8 **163**; 3.pr.10 **163**; 4.pr.1 **227**
Suasoriae 2.17 **152**
Seneca the Younger *Dialogues* 5.9.2 **202**; 9.17.10 **167**; 10.16.5.1 **318**
Hercules furiens 5 **319**
Letters 1.1 **209**; 2.5 **203**; 8.5 **223**; 20.9 **183**; 36.4 **146**; 87.23 **319**; 62.3 **183**; 65.1 **204**; 67.7 **204**; 88.3 **199**; 88.10 **201**; 88.14 **203**; 91.19 **183**
Natural Questions 7.4.1 **137**; 7.5.2 **137**; 7.6.1 **137**
Servius *On Virgil's Aeneid* praef. **251**
Solinus 1.74 **170**
Strabo 5.213 **177**
Suetonius *Augustus* 45.4 **153**; 87.1 **55**
Caligula 22.1 **69**; 40.1 **319**
Claudius 35.2 **169**
Domitian 3.1 **231**
Julius 55.1–2 **214**
Nero 27.2 **318–19**; 28 **100**, **260**; 28.1 **318**; 29.1 **318**
Tiberius 34 **67**; 35 **319**; 35.1 **316**; 35.2 **316**, **319**; 53.2 **134**

Terence *The Brothers* 342 **319**; 359 **316**, **318**; 415–18 **65**; 420–29 **67**; 467 **317**
The Eunuch 235 **315**; 252 **229**; 445 **91**; 654 **317**; 939 **315**; 953 **317**

The Lady of Andros 651 **319**
Phormio 343 **79**; 862 **316**, **318**, **320**; 867 **152**
The Self-Tormentor 566 **317**
Tibullus 1.4.37–38 **292**; 1.4.38 **292**

Ulpian *Digesta* 49.15.21.1 **187**

Valerius Maximus *praef.* **215**; 3.2.ext.2 **169**; 3.2.ext.3 **169**; 3.5.4–5 **106**; 3.7.11.ext.1 **165**; 6.12.ext.1 **93**; 8.14.ext.5 **80**
Varro *On Agriculture* 2.2.11 **61**
Verrius Flaccus 18.3 **281**
Virgil *Aeneid* 1.68 **155**; 1.79 **112**; 1.216 **171**; 1.364 **314**; 1.600 **175**; 3.42 **319**; 3.48 **110**, **175**; 3.516 **139**; 4.181 **51**; 5.830 **197**; 6.19 **143**; 6.129 **144**; 6.417–23 **59**; 6.563 **165**; 6.644 **224**; 7.312 **134**; 7.765ff. **127**; 8.224 **142**; 12.50–51 **303**; 12.161–64 **291**; 12.593–611 **160**; 12.603 **160**
Eclogues 2.1 **119**; 4.1 **255**; 4.1–2 **167**; 4.57 **292**; 7.21–28 **73**; 8.55 **172**
Georgics 1.30 **182**; 1.336–37 **203**; 3.9 **101**

Neo-Latin Texts

Anonymous (Rho?) *Invective* **96–97**, **102**, **142**, **143**, **187**
Anonymous *Prostitutes of Pavia* 49–51 **102**, **181**
Anonymous *Rhymed Life of the Blessed Virgin and Savior* **103**
Aurispa, Giovanni, *Letters* [lost] **115–17**

Boccaccio, Giovanni *Genealogies of the Gods* 3.21 **91**; 4.1.2 **290**; 4.1.9 **290**; 4.3.1 **290**; 4.3.5 **298**; 4.3.10 **298**; 4.3.15 **286**
Bruni, Leonardo *Letter* 1.3 (1.4–6) **219**

Cencio dei Rustici *Letter to Francesco da Fiano* (1416) **223**

Dante *Purgatorio* 29.115–54 **296**
Decembrio, Pier Candido *Against Panormita and Guarino* 1432 (Novis adhuc) **57**, **64**, **102**, **142–43**

INDEX OF TEXTS CITED

Dialogue on the Panormitan Sun [lost] 138–39
Letter to Rho (Novum profecto) 35
Letter to Rho (Philippicam tuam) 39

Erasmus, Desiderius *Adagia* I.i.84 **87**

Filelfo, Francesco *Satyrae* 3.6 **2**

Giuliano of Spira *Life of St. Francis* 4.24 **235**
Gratian *Decretum* D.2 C.6.1 **233**; D.36–38 **96, 215**
Guarino Veronese *Letter to Panormita* (2.II.1426) **95, 151**
Letter to Spilimbergo (mid-1432) **130**

Jacobus de Voragine *Golden Legend* (Nativity) **103**
Joan of Arc, Pseudo- *Against Antonio da Rho* **181**
John of Salisbury *Policraticus* 1 **213**; 1.7 **279**; 3.13 **145**; 3.14 **279**

Odo de Ceritona *Life of St. Francis* 80(68) **232**

Panormita *Against Valla* 1 **167**
Hermaphrodite 1.3.1–4 **91, 100**; 1.4.4 **153**; 1.5.1 **259**; 1.13 **91**; 1.22.3–4 **262**; 1.42.3–4 **91**; 2.20 **91**; 2.37 **33, 101–02**
Letter to Antonio Cremona (IX.1429) **29**
Letter to Antonio da Rho (Etsi facile) **38, 53, 63, 73–74, 76–78, 83, 93–95, 109, 117, 120, 125, 151–52, 161, 181, 187, 245–55**
Letter to Bartolomeo Capra (1.XII.1426) **82, 94**
Letter to Cambio Zambeccari (VIII.1429) **29, 253**
Letter to Cambio Zambeccari (1429/30) **30, 178**
Letter to Filippo Maria Visconti (On the Sun) **135, 285–86**
Letter to Francesco Barbavara (mid-1432) **129**
Letter to Giovanni Aurispa [lost] **119, 134**
Letter to Giovanni Lamola (20.IX.1427) **93**
Letter to Marcettus (1429) **112**
Letter to Maffeo Muzano (early 1432) **31**
Letter to Poggio Bracciolini (Epistolae tuae) **120**

Letter to Sancio Balbo (III/IV.1430) **30, 117**
Oration on the Imagery of the Sun **18, 135, 287–99**
Poem to Ergoteles 1–10 **34**
Peter of Blois *Letter* 46 **171, 262**
Peter Cantor *PL* 205, 257 **235**
Peter Lombard *Sentences* 4.1.4 **205**; 4.43 **1**
Peter Abelard *Sic et Non* Quaest. 156 **151**
Petrarca, Francesco *Against a Physician* 4.203 **1**
Letters on Familiar Matters 1.9 **219**; 6.3.42 **60**
Phaedrus 1.11 **232, 239**
Poggio *Letter on the Baths* 1.46 **221**
Letter to Panormita 2.5 (3.IV.1426) **95, 103**
Letter 3.10 (31.XI.1451) **20**

Rho, Antonio da "Anonymous Invective" **96–97, 102, 142–43, 187**
Funeral Oration for Niccolò Piccinino (1444) **26**
Letter to Gervaso da Piacenza (1431) **135, 138–39**
Metrica commendatio Martini V **9**
Philippic 2 **308**; 4 **308**; 5 **308**; 6 **308–09**; 8 **309**; 9 **309**; 10 **309**; 11 **309**; 13 **309**; 14 **309**; 16–17 **309**; 18 **309–10**; 19 **310**; 21 **310**; 22 **310**; 23 **310**; 25 **310**; 27 **310**; 28 **310**; 29 **310**; 30 **310**; 32 **310**; 33 **310–11**; 34 **311**; 36 **311**; 37 **311**; 183 **311**; 184 **311**; 185 **311**; 186 **311–12**; 187 **312**; 188 **312**; 189 **312**; 191 **312**; 192 **312–13**
Poem to Antonio Loschi [lost] **249**
Rhetorical Imitations **10, 13–14, 18, 24, 32, 37, 57, 65, 67, 76, 78–79, 81, 88, 101, 111, 197, 203, 209, 216, 227, 237, 300–13, 314–20**
Romulus 4.10 **232**

Thomas of Celano *Life of St. Francis* 1.12.29 **235**; 1.16.45 **235**

Valla, Lorenzo *Antidote against Facio* 4.14.2 **113**
Elegances of the Latin Language 2.praef. **13, 14**
In Facium 3.8.34 **142**
Notations on the Errors of Antonio da Rho praef. **13, 15, 39**
On Pleasure 1.24.3–4 **143**; 1.43.2 **143**; 3.25.17 **11**

Vegio, Maffeo *Letter to Valla* (1442?) **14**
Visconti, Bertola *Letter* (7.VIII.1432) **25**

Walter Burley *Lives and Customs of the Philosophers* 21 **93**; 104 **214**

Sacred Texts

Genesis 18.1–19.29 **187**
Exodus 32.15–16 **149**
Leviticus 14.2–4 **183**
Numbers 22.21–31 **109**; 25.1–3 **77**
Deuteronomy 13.13 **125**; 21.11–13 **37**; 32.35 **175**
I Samuel 5.9 **314**; 24.1–23 **59**
Job 2.19 **320**; 15.15 **106**; 40.15–24 **179**; 41.1–34 **179**
Psalms 5.10 **21**; 9(A).5 **176**; 9(B)/10.15 **21**; 17/18.3 **176**; 26/27.1 **175**; 26/27.3 **176**; 27/28.4 **21**; 30/31.9 **144**; 30/31.17–18 **21**; 34/35 **21**; 39/40.14–15 **21**; 49/50.20–21 **175**; 51/52.6–7 **176**; 52/53.4 **106**; 57/58 **21**; 58/59 **21**; 68/69 **21**; 82/83 **21**; 84/85.12 **115**; 93/94 **21**; 108/109 **21**; 136/137 **21**; 139/140 **21**; 140/141.3 **175**; 140/141.4 **95**, **318**
Proverbs 26.5 **55**; 26.11 **76**, **140**, **165**, **186**
Isaiah 42.14 **304**
Jeremiah 22.19 **65**
Ezechiel 3.7–9 **123**

II Maccabees 4.9 **316**

Matthew 3.10 **172**, **305**; 5.8 **104**; 5.11–12 **110**; 5.15 **197**; 5.43–44 **185**; 5.44 **60**; 7.4–5 **187**; 8.1–4 **183**; 10.24–25 **179**; 11.3 **163**; 11.19 **180**; 18.6 **148**; 25.41 **110**; 26.73 **97**; 27.5 **160**
Mark 1.40–44 **183**; 4.21 **197**; 7.33 **185**; 15.40 **105**; 16.1 **105**; 16.9 **105**
Luke 3.9 **172**; 5.12–14 **183**; 6.41–42 **187**; 6.44–45 **97**; 7.19–21 **163**; 7.36–50 **104–05**; 11.33 **197**; 16.19–31 **161**; 18.10–14 **105**; 18.13 **105**; 23.39–43 **104**
John 1.9 **185**; 3.31 **97**; 9.6–7 **185**
Acts 1.18–19 **160**; 7.57–8.3 **105**; 9.1–2 **105**
Romans 5.20 **105**; 9.3 **21**; 12.3 **159**; 12.19 **175**; 13.8 **185**
I Corinthians 5.5 **21**; 15.8–9 **199**, **241**; 15.9 **105**; 15.33 **104**; 16.22 **21**
II Corinthians 6.14–15 **125**; 12.6 **199**
Galatians 1.9 **21**
I Thessalonians 5.21 **64**
I Timothy 1.20 **21**
II Timothy 4.3 **111**
James 2.14–26 **218**
II Peter 2.22 **76**, **140**, **165**, **186**
I John 1.8 **106**
Jude 12 **172**

Quran 43.70 **231**; 52.18–30 **231**

INDEX OF MANUSCRIPTS

Avignon: Bibliothèque Municipale
   MS 1054   **40, 300, 314**
Bologna: Biblioteca Universitaria
   MS 2387   **277, 279, 325**
   MS 2948, vol. 28   **245**
   MS 2948, vol. 36   **245**
Brescia: Biblioteca Civica Queriniana
   MS A VII 7   **264, 268**
Carpentras: Bibliothèque Municipale
   MS 361   **264**
Como: Biblioteca Comunale
   MS 4.4.6   **285, 287**
Florence: Biblioteca Laurenziana
   MS Plut. 34, cod. 54   **141, 264**
   MS Ashb. 176   **274–76**
   MS Gad. XCI sup. 43   **264**
Florence: Biblioteca Nazionale Centrale
   MS Magl. VIII 1445   **264**
Florence: Biblioteca Riccardiana
   MS 407   **245**
   MS 810   **264, 268**
   MS 827   **51**
Frankfurt am Main: Stadt- und Universitäts-Bibliothek
   MS Lat. oct. 136   **256, 277**
Gotha: Forschungsbibliothek
   MS Chart. A 717   **264**
Milan: Archivio di Stato
   fondo Notai, R.C., busta 202   **23**
Milan: Biblioteca Ambrosiana,
   MS D 103 inf.   **335**
   MS H 48 inf.   **25**
   MS H 49 inf.   **256, 258**
   MS B 116 sup.   **9**
   MS B 124 sup.   **26, 41, 47–48, 85, 123, 133, 141, 270**
   MS C 64 sup.   **270**
   MS M 44 sup.   **245**
   MS M 49 sup.   **42, 193, 195**
   MS P 4 sup.   **270**
Milan: Biblioteca Nazionale Braidense
   MS AH.XII.16   **39, 277, 279, 325**
Milan: Biblioteca Trivulziana
   MS 793   **268, 272–73**

Munich: Bayerische Staatsbibliothek
   MS clm 78   **264**
   MS clm 4393   **264**
Naples: Biblioteca Nazionale
   MS V F 18   **277**
   MS VI D 7   **41, 47, 49, 85, 101, 123, 133, 137, 141, 277**
Padua: Biblioteca Capitolare
   MS C 72   **14, 40**
Paris: Bibliothèque de l'Arsenal
   MS 1186   **237**
Paris: Bibliothèque Nationale
   MS Lat. 7228   **223**
   MS Lat. 8580   **274**
Rome: Biblioteca Nazionale
   MS Vitt. Eman. 1417 (1866249)   **264**
Toledo: Biblioteca del Cabildo
   MS 100.42   **245, 264**
Tübingen: Universitäts-Bibliothek
   MS Mc. 137   **285, 287**
Vatican City: Biblioteca Apostolica Vaticana
   MS Barb. lat. 42   **245**
   MS Barb. lat. 1990   **264, 268**
   MS Barb. lat. 2069   **274–76**
   MS Ottob. lat. 1321   **12, 42, 193, 217, 236–37**
   MS Ottob. lat. 1903   **15**
   MS Pal. lat. 1592   **135, 277**
   MS Ross. 1024   **287**
   MS Urb. lat. 437   **11**
   MS Vat. lat. 227   **iv, 15**
   MS Vat. lat. 2858   **264, 268**
   MS Vat. lat. 2864   **264**
   MS Vat. lat. 2906   **245**
   MS Vat. lat. 3371   **33, 256**
Venice: Biblioteca Nazionale Marciana
   MS. Lat. XII 179   **264, 268**
   MS Lat. XIV 221   **245**
   MS Marc. lat. Z 427   **20**
Wolfenbüttel: Herzog August-Bibliothek
   MS 10.9 Aug. 4to   **264**
Wroclaw: Biblioteka Uniwersytecka
   MS R 175   **275–76**